LEITHS
VEGETARIAN
BIBLE

LEITHS VEGETARIAN BIBLE

POLLY TYRER

with contributions by

Fiona Burrell, Alison Cavaliero, Max Clark, Debbie Major

Photography by Graham Kirk

BLOOMSBURY

First published in Great Britain in 2002
Bloomsbury Publishing Plc, 38 Soho Square, London W1D 3HB

Text copyright © 2002 by Leiths School of Food and Wine
Photography © Graham Kirk
Prop Stylist: Claire Hunt
Food Stylist: Polly Tyrer

A CIP catalogue record for this book is available from the British Library

ISBN 0 7475 5716 0

10 9 8 7 6 5 4

Typeset by Hewer Text Limited, Edinburgh
Printed in Great Britain by Butler & Tanner Ltd, Frome and London

For Charlotte, a natural-born vegetarian

CONTENTS

ACKNOWLEDGEMENTS

Leiths *Vegetarian Bible* has been a marathon of writing that I have worked on for a period of two years. When exploring the infinite world of vegetables, I quickly realized that the difficulty was not going to be discovering material but where to stop.

This project has been a combined effort and I would especially like to thank the other contributors, Fiona Burrell, Alison Cavaliero, Max Clark and Debbie Major, who have been inspired, efficient and great fun to work with.

An extra special thanks to Jenny Kieldsen who has not only been my mentor throughout but has also tested and eaten her way through at least 300 recipes.

The creative eye of Graham Kirk has resulted in beautiful photographs for which I thank him. The photographs have also benefited from the expert advice of Andrew Thorogood and Claudia Frewin at Classic Fresh Foods of Covent Garden who supplied the vegetables for photography.

Leiths School of Food and Wine has, as always, provided great support, especially Caroline Waldegrave and Max Clark. The reassurance and expertise of Marian McCarthy at Bloomsbury and editor Helen Campbell have been much appreciated. A huge thank-you to friends and family for their tolerance and understanding. Finally, a word in memory of Graham Fell and thanks to his company WG software for printing my manuscript.

FOREWORD

by Caroline Waldegrave

This book is primarily by Polly Tyrer, who wrote the majority of the recipes as well as the introductions to the different sections. She has been brilliantly helped by Fiona Burrell, Alison Cavaliero, Max Clark and Debbie Major who have between them written 950 recipes. I think it is the collaboration between them that makes the book so special. Each writer has contributed her own particular skill and her own particular style of cooking, making for a satisfyingly eclectic mix of recipes. Alison (Vice-Principal of Leiths) is the only vegetarian. Max (buyer at Leiths),

Debbie and Fiona (ex co-Principal at Leiths) are all non-vegetarians who have loved inventing vegetarian dishes that they as meat-eaters enjoy.

I have been an enthusiastic taster of all the recipes tested at the School. I am not vegetarian, but of my four children two are semi-vegetarian, so that I know from experience that this book will fill a need – offering vegetarian dishes that non-vegetarians will relish rather than disdain.

I do hope you enjoy cooking from our *Vegetarian Bible*.

INTRODUCTION

INTRODUCTION

A marketful of fresh vegetables is an inspirational sight. Such a visual feast is hard to resist. The project of compiling the *Vegetarian Bible* has been an exciting one. We have felt like artists blending the colours, textures and flavours of fresh produce, grains, pasta and pulses into this collection of new recipes. Our ideas range from snacks to main meals, comforting dishes to cook in a big pot, glamorous recipes for special occasions, delicious homemade breads and cakes, and a few desserts to finish off.

The way we cook and eat has an impact on who we are and how we feel about ourselves. A vegetarian diet is wholesome all the way through and no longer means a lifetime of lentils! Travel and availability of ingredients have had a great influence on the dishes that we cook. Cooking can be briefer and lighter. We stir-fry, griddle and steam, whipping up meals in minutes. Careful use of seasonings and skilful reduction of stocks and sauces bring a depth of flavour to vegetarian cookery that some complain is lacking.

There is a heavy cultural influence in many vegetarian recipes. Vegetables, pulses and grains are good vehicles for exotic herbs and spiced sauces laced with yoghurt or oils. This is hardly surprising as the Middle East, the Far East, India and China are large-scale vegetable growers with cuisines that have developed accordingly. The cultures and religious beliefs of these regions have also provided a basis for many vegetarian dishes.

Vegetables are vital to our well-being. Research reveals the link between good health and a diet high in fruit, vegetables and fibre. Vegetarianism can reduce the risk of heart disease, cancer, gastric ailments and diabetes. This is borne out by the lower incidence of these diseases in areas such as the Mediterranean where the diet includes plenty of vegetables, olive oil and red wine. Historically food was used to treat illness. We are now rethinking links between health and diet and rediscovering the benefits of complementary treatments using plant-based remedies.

Many people moved to be vegetarian will grow their own produce; there is little better in flavour and tenderness than vegetables freshly plucked from the garden. Organic produce is guaranteed to be free from anything of genetically modified origins, and is grown without the use of artificial pesticides, chemicals and fertilizers. It is reputed to contain more nutrients and certainly has good, fresh flavour.

Fresh local produce can be bought from farm shops, farmers' markets and small local suppliers – look out for these. Box schemes mostly supplying organic produce provide a selection of whatever is currently in season delivered to your door. Whether you buy organic or not, it is generally best to follow the seasons. There are also many interesting shops supplying pulses, grains, spices, yoghurts and cheeses which are often sourced from specialist, local manufacturers.

The *Vegetarian Bible* has been arranged according to vegetable types so that you can look up recipes that use your favourite vegetable or whatever is to hand in the refrigerator or store cupboard. Remember that the recipes are a guide, a basis for improvisation to be fine-tuned to individual tastes. Vegetarian recipes are very versatile: first courses can easily be turned into a main course by increasing the quantities and some main courses may be adjusted to make a snack. Try serving vegetarian food 'mezze style'. Several side dishes served with bread are substantial enough for a main meal and make interesting eating with a variety of flavours and textures.

The fashion for being vegetarian waxes and wanes. We are now very conscious of lifestyle, health and fitness, while increasingly people choose not to eat meat as a matter of principle. The choice is a serious one. Increasing numbers of young people are opting to become vegetarian, making it all the more important to ensure that their diet meets all the requirements for variety and good health.

Whether you are a full or part-time vegetarian, about to become a convert or simply love vegetables, all the information is here for understanding and managing a vegetarian diet. The book is a true celebration of vegetables in all their glory.

All recipes serve 4 unless otherwise stated.

CONVERSION TABLES

The tables below are approximate, and do not conform in all respects to the conventional conversions, but we have found them convenient for cooking. Use either metric or imperial measurements: do not mix the two.

Weight

Imperial	Metric	Imperial	Metric
¼oz	7–8g	½oz	15g
¾oz	20g	1oz	30g
2oz	55g	3oz	85g
4oz (¼lb)	110g	5oz	140g
6oz	170g	7oz	200g
8oz (½lb)	225g	9oz	255g
10oz	285g	11oz	310g
12oz (¾lb)	340g	13oz	370g
14oz	400g	15oz	425g
16oz (1lb)	450g	1¼lb	560g
1½lb	675g	2lb	900g
3lb	1.35kg	4lb	1.8kg
5lb	2.3kg	6lb	2.7kg
7lb	3.2kg	8lb	3.6kg
9lb	4.0kg	10lb	4.5kg

Australian cup measures

	Metric	Imperial
1 cup flour	140g	5oz
1 cup sugar (crystal or caster)	225g	8oz
1 cup brown sugar, firmly packed	170g	6oz
1 cup icing sugar, sifted	170g	6oz
1 cup butter	225g	8oz
1 cup honey, golden syrup, treacle	370g	12oz
1 cup fresh breadcrumbs	55g	2oz
1 cup packaged dry breadcrumbs	140g	5oz
1 cup crushed biscuit crumbs	110g	4oz
1 cup rice, uncooked	200g	7oz
1 cup mixed fruit or individual fruit, such as sultanas	170g	6oz
1 cup nuts, chopped	110g	4oz
1 cup coconut, desiccated	85g	3oz

Approximate American/European conversions

Commodity	USA	Metric	Imperial
Flour	1 cup	140g	5oz
Caster and granulated sugar	1 cup	225g	8oz
Caster and granulated sugar	2 level tablespoons	30g	1oz
Brown sugar	1 cup	170g	6oz
Butter/margarine/lard	1 cup	225g	8oz
Sultanas/raisins	1 cup	200g	7oz
Currants	1 cup	140g	5oz
Ground almonds	1 cup	110g	4oz
Golden syrup	1 cup	340g	12oz
Uncooked rice	1 cup	200g	7oz
Grated cheese	1 cup	110g	4oz
Butter	1 stick	110g	4oz

Liquid measures

Imperial	ml	fl oz
1 teaspoon	5	
2 scant tablespoons	28	1
4 scant tablespoons	56	2
¼ pint (1 gill)	150	5
⅓ pint	190	6.6
½ pint	290	10
¾ pint	425	15
1 pint	570	20
1¾ pints	1000 (1 litre)	35

Australian

250ml	1 cup
20ml	1 tablespoon
5ml	1 teaspoon

Approximate American/European conversions

American	European
1 teaspoon	1 teaspoon/5ml
½fl oz	1 tablespoon/½fl oz/15ml
¼ cup	4 tablespoons/2fl oz/56ml
½ cup plus 2 tablespoons	¼ pint/5fl oz/150ml
1¼ cups	½ pint/10fl oz/290ml
1 pint/16fl oz	1 pint/20fl oz/570ml
2½ pints (5 cups)	1.1 litres/2 pints
10 pints	4.5 litres/8 pints

Useful measurements

Measurement	Metric	Imperial
1 American cup	225ml	8fl oz
1 egg, medium	56ml	2fl oz
1 egg white	28ml	1fl oz
1 rounded tablespoon flour	30g	1oz
1 rounded tablespoon cornflour	30g	1oz
1 rounded tablespoon caster sugar	30g	1oz
2 rounded tablespoons fresh breadcrumbs	30g	1oz
2 level teaspoons gelatine	8g	¼oz

30g/1oz granular (packet) aspic sets
570ml/1 pint liquid.

15g/½ oz powdered gelatine, or 4 leaves, will set 570ml/1 pint liquid. (However, in hot weather, or if the liquid is very acid, like lemon juice, or if the jelly contains solid pieces of food and is to be turned out of the dish or mould, 20g/¾oz should be used.)

Wine quantities

Imperial	ml	fl oz
Average wine bottle	750	25
1 glass wine	100	3½
1 glass port or sherry	70	2
1 glass liqueur	45	1

Lengths

Imperial	Metric
½in	1cm
1in	2.5cm
2in	5cm
6in	15cm
12in	30cm

Oven temperatures

°C	°F	Gas mark	AMERICAN	AUSTRALIAN
70	150	¼	COOL	VERY SLOW
80	175	¼	COOL	VERY SLOW
100	200	½	COOL	VERY SLOW
110	225	½	COOL	VERY SLOW
130	250	1	VERY SLOW	VERY SLOW
140	275	1	VERY SLOW	SLOW
150	300	2	SLOW	SLOW
170	325	3	MODERATE	MODERATELY SLOW
180	350	4	MODERATE	MODERATELY SLOW
190	375	5	MODERATELY HOT	MODERATE
200	400	6	FAIRLY HOT	MODERATE
220	425	7	HOT	MODERATELY HOT
230	450	8	VERY HOT	MODERATELY HOT
240	475	8	VERY HOT	HOT
250	500	9	EXTREMELY HOT	HOT
270	525	9	EXTREMELY HOT	VERY HOT
290	550	9	EXTREMELY HOT	VERY HOT

NUTRITION

by Karen Sorensen S.R.D., Guy's and St Thomas' Hospital, N.H.S. Trust

INTRODUCTION

Food plays a vital role in our lives. At its most basic, it provides us with the nutrients essential to our existence and general health. A regular intake of food is required by the body to work, grow and repair itself.

Food also influences physical and mental well-being, and plays an important part in our social activities. It is used to celebrate and commiserate, to reward and to give pleasure, and as a sign of affection and caring.

A balanced variety of foods needs to be eaten for the body to function efficiently, as well as fulfilling these wider functions. A vegetarian diet can provide all the nutrients required and, properly planned, can be a healthier option than many traditional diets.

All foods are made up of the same main constituents: protein, fat, carbohydrate, vitamins and minerals, in differing amounts. All these elements (known as nutrients) must be included in the diet, although specific requirements for each vary according to individual needs, circumstances and activity.

The Vegetarian Diet

Some vegetarians who do not include meat, poultry or fish in their diet will eat eggs, milk, cheese and other dairy products. Vegans eat none of these, relying instead on vegetables, fruit, nuts, seeds and vegetarian alternatives to dairy produce. This book has been written for lacto-ovo-vegetarians but information on vegetarian alternatives to dairy products can also be found on page 21.

ENERGY REQUIREMENTS

Energy provides fuel for the body, and is often referred to by one of its measurements –
calories. The energy requirement for each individual is to balance *the amount of energy taken in from food* with *the amount of energy used by the body* to maintain its normal processes. This amount differs from person to person and is affected by a variety of factors, such as age, gender and level of physical activity. Almost three-quarters of the energy utilized by the body is used in basic involuntary activities such as breathing, keeping the heart beating and maintaining body temperature. This is often referred to as the Basal Metabolic Rate (BMR). Additional energy is used during processes such as digestion of food and physical activity. It is the latter which can affect weight loss or weight gain.

Periods of intense growth, such as childhood, adolescence and pregnancy, significantly increase energy needs. For example, a one-year-old child needs about 1,200 kcalories per day, an adolescent boy about 2,700 kcalories per day, and an adult male about 2,500 kcalories per day. Women have slightly lower requirements on average than men.

Fat and Carbohydrate as Energy Sources

The main energy sources in the diet are fat and carbohydrate. Protein can be used as an energy source, but this is a complex process, and protein is needed by the body primarily for its growth and repair functions.

Carbohydrate foods such as bread, potatoes, rice, pasta and cereals are the main sources of energy in the British diet, along with spreading fats and fat in food. A healthy diet contains a higher proportion of energy from starchy foods, especially those high in fibre.

Weight for weight, fat has more than twice the calories of carbohydrate or protein. This makes it an excellent energy source where requirements are particularly high, but it needs to be taken in moderation in a normal diet.

PROTEIN

Structure and Function

Protein foods are made up of amino acids, which are small organic compounds. When food containing protein is digested, it is broken down into its constituent amino acids. Amino acids are usually classified into those which the body can synthesize or make itself, and are therefore non-essential, and those which have to be obtained from the diet, and are therefore known as indispensable or essential amino acids. There are nine essential amino acids.

Protein is essential to life. The body needs it in a variety of foods to ensure repair and growth of tissues and to provide vital supplies of nitrogen and other chemicals.

Different tissues in the body are composed of different types and combinations of amino acids. Some protein foods (generally those from animal sources) contain all the essential amino acids, and these are known as high biological value (HBV) protein. Foods which have small amounts of some essential amino acids are known as low biological value (LBV) protein, and these are usually proteins from vegetable sources. Due to the way that the various amino acids are distributed in nature, it is important when following a vegetarian diet to choose a wide range of protein sources when planning meals. Protein foods need to be combined to provide all the essential amino acids. For example, a combination of plant protein foods, such as beans and bread, can provide a meal which in total has a high biological value. This principle is essential in planning a well-balanced vegetarian diet.

Normal Requirements

Individual requirements for protein vary from person to person, although requirements are usually expressed as figures for population groups. Protein in the body is constantly being broken down and resynthesized, especially during periods of growth such as childhood, adolescence and pregnancy. Unlike fat and carbohydrate, protein in excess of immediate requirements cannot be stored by the body. This means that protein foods need to be eaten daily to fulfil the body's requirements.

The current Dietary Reference Values for Protein, as published by the Department of Health, suggest protein intakes of 45g (women) and 55.5g (men) of protein per day for an adult aged between nineteen and fifty. Older adults and pregnant and lactating women have slightly higher requirements. There are separate figures for children, who have proportionally higher needs because of their increased rate of growth.

The average protein intake in the UK is significantly higher than this, even for those on a vegetarian diet. A person consuming cereal and milk for breakfast, a cheese sandwich for lunch, and a bean and vegetable hotpot for dinner is already consuming about 40g of protein before the contribution from other foods is taken into account.

Sources of Protein in Vegetarian Foods

These days there are a wide range of foods, both natural and ready-made, which can provide protein in a vegetarian diet. Natural sources include:

- Eggs, cheese, milk, yoghurt
- Beans, peas, lentils, nuts, seeds
- Bread, flour cereals, pasta, rice

In addition it is now possible to buy a wide range of meat-free products and ready meals. These can be very useful when time is short, or when the non-meat eater is a member of a meat-eating family. Personally, I cannot see the attraction of products which pretend to be meat, such as vegetarian sausages and burgers, but this is only a personal view, and many people find these useful, particularly for barbecues, etc.

Several examples of how vegetarian protein foods can be combined to give good protein intake are shown below:

EXAMPLE 1	GMS PROTEIN	EXAMPLE 2	GMS PROTEIN
Bran flakes (medium portion)	5	2 slices of wholegrain toast	7
150ml (¼ pint) milk	5	1 boiled egg	7.5
	<u>10</u>		<u>14.5</u>

EXAMPLE 3	GMS PROTEIN	EXAMPLE 4	GMS PROTEIN
200g/7oz baked beans	10	Lentil dhal (medium portion)	8
2 slices of wholegrain toast	7	Boiled rice	4
	<u>17</u>		<u>12</u>

EXAMPLE 5	GMS PROTEIN	EXAMPLE 6	GMS PROTEIN
Chickpea hotpot (medium portion)	10	Jacket potato	4
Pasta (medium portion)	5	Cheese	10
		and sweetcorn	2
	<u>15</u>		<u>16</u>

CARBOHYDRATE

Structure and Function

Dietary carbohydrate is made up of sugars and starches. Carbohydrates contribute to the taste and texture of food and provide essential supplies of dietary fibre. Sugars and starches are made of chemical units called saccharides. Sugars are either made of one unit (monosaccharides or simple sugars, e.g. glucose, fructose) or two units (disaccharides, e.g. sucrose, lactose). Starches contain many saccharide units (polysaccharides). Some foods contain non-starch polysaccharides which cannot be digested, and it is these which constitute 'dietary fibre'.

The main role of carbohydrate in the diet is as an energy source. Carbohydrates are digested by the body and broken down into glucose, which is absorbed into the bloodstream. It is this glucose which acts as the 'fuel' for the body, in the same way that petrol is the fuel for a car.

Sugar in the diet provides an easily and quickly absorbed form of energy. Much has been made of the well-documented adverse effects of sugar, such as dental caries. It is more useful to look at sugars as part of the overall diet. Sugars can be divided into those which are naturally present in food as part of cells (intrinsic sugars), such as the sugar in fruit, and those which are not (extrinsic sugars). Milk is the exception, as it contains an extrinsic sugar (lactose). This knowledge allows us to look at the overall quality of a diet. Naturally occurring sugars (intrinsic and milk sugars) should form a higher proportion of the sugar in the diet than non-milk extrinsic sugars, such as sucrose (table sugar). A diet high in added sugar is likely to be poor in other nutrients, and the small volume and attractive taste of sugar make it easy to eat too much, which may lead to obesity.

Sugars have important properties in cooking. They keep gluten soft in cakes, provide a medium for yeast in baking and strengthen the structure of egg white.

Starch is the main carbohydrate present in all foods and forms a major part of our diet. It is composed of complex links of glucose units, and these are broken down to provide energy. In cooking, starch swells and the starch cells burst and gelatinize, improving digestibility, palatability and texture.

Non-starch polysaccharides are more commonly (and less accurately) known as dietary fibre. They are a form of carbohydrate which cannot be digested by the body. From this characteristic come the beneficial effects of fibre in improving bowel function, reducing constipation and reducing the risk of bowel diseases. Some foods, particularly oats and pulses, contain soluble forms of fibre, such as pectin, and these have been shown to be effective in controlling glucose and cholesterol levels in the blood.

Foods high in fibre are filling and add bulk to the diet, which is particularly helpful for those trying to cut down on fat or lose weight.

Normal Requirements
Starch (complex carbohydrates) should provide the main source of energy in the diet. Individual requirements vary, depending on, for example, levels of activity. However, general health recommendations suggest that an overall increase in carbohydrate intake, particularly from cereals, fruit and vegetables, is beneficial. At least half our energy requirements should come from starchy foods. Meals should contain plenty of potato, rice, pasta, bread or cereals.

As an example, an average woman requiring 2,000 kcalories per day, obtaining half her energy intake from carbohydrate, would be eating: 5 tablespoons breakfast cereal, 4 slices of bread, a large portion of spaghetti, 3 portions of fresh fruit, 2 portions of vegetables (one of which should be beans or peas), 285ml/ ½ pint semi-skimmed milk, as well as other foods to make up a normal diet.

Sources of Carbohydrate in Food
- Bread, breakfast cereals, rice, pasta, potatoes (wholegrain varieties are the best sources of fibre)
- Fruit, vegetables, milk
- Sugar, confectionery, cakes and biscuits, preserves

FATS

Structure and Function
Fat acts as an energy source and forms the major part of adipose tissue, the fatty layer beneath the skin which protects body tissue and organs and helps to maintain body temperature. Fat in the diet consists of triglycerides (which are composed of fatty acids), cholesterol and phospholipids. Some fatty acids are essential to the body, and fat also acts as a carrier for fat-soluble vitamins.

Triglycerides form the largest component of dietary fat and are made up of three (hence tri-) fatty acids and glycerol. It is the different types of fatty acid, whether they are liquid or solid at room temperature, and their chemical make-up, which determine their nutritional properties. The essential fatty acids (linoleic and linolenic acids) are those which the body cannot make itself. All fatty acids are used in the body for a variety of important processes such as immune function.

Fatty acids are distinguished chemically into **saturated**, **mono-unsaturated** and **poly-unsaturated** fatty acids.

Fats containing saturated fatty acids are solid at room temperature and are usually found in foods from animal sources, such as cheese or butter.

Unsaturated fats are generally found in foods of vegetable origin and are naturally liquid at room temperature. Mono-unsaturated fatty acids are found primarily in olive oil. Nowadays sophisticated technology allows the use of both of these as spreads.

Cholesterol is a complex steroid compound which is not only essential but is synthesized by the body itself. Plasma cholesterol is not affected by cholesterol in the diet, but by the total fat in the diet.

Fat in food provides flavour, smooth texture and fullness.

Normal Requirements
Some fat is necessary in the diet, to provide the essential fatty acids, but this can easily be obtained from foods which contain fat naturally,

such as milk. It is not necessary to add fat to foods for spreading and cooking, but fat does make food more palatable, and small amounts of fat can be used in a healthy diet. Too much fat in the diet, however, especially fat with a high proportion of saturated fatty acids, is linked to a high incidence of coronary heart disease.

Choosing more food from vegetable sources can reduce the overall fat intake. It is important that a wide variety of foods is chosen in a vegetarian diet. An over-reliance on dairy foods, such as cheese and eggs, as protein sources can lead to a high fat intake. This can often be a problem when only one member of the family is vegetarian. However, a wide variety of options is available, as illustrated by the recipes in this book. Using suitable ready meals can also be useful in these circumstances.

Sources of Fat in Food
- Butter, margarine, oil
- Nuts, seeds, milk, cheese, cream, eggs
- Pastry, cakes, biscuits, crisps, fried foods

VITAMINS

Vitamins are a group of organic compounds, so called because they are vital to life, essential in the body in small amounts. They perform specific roles in the metabolic process, such as in energy metabolism, blood-clotting and absorption of other nutrients.

Vitamins are divided into two groups: those which are fat-soluble, and are found in association with fat, and those which are water-soluble. Water-soluble vitamins, as the name suggests, are soluble in water, and care must be taken in preparation and cooking to preserve the vitamins.

Normal Requirements
Vitamin requirements for groups of the population are defined in tables provided by the Department of Health. Vitamins are found in a wide range of food sources, and a well-balanced diet, based on a wide variety of foods including plenty of fresh fruit and vegetables, should provide adequate vitamin intakes for most people.

Supplementary vitamins are not usually necessary, although those following a very strict vegetarian diet which excludes milk and dairy foods will need vitamin B_{12} supplements.

Antioxidants
A number of vitamins have now been recognized as having strong antioxidant properties. These are vitamin C, vitamin E and beta-carotene. Antioxidants neutralize the effect in the body of free radicals, substances produced during the body's normal processes, but potentially harmful if not mopped up. Free radicals are believed to play a role in cardiovascular disease, ageing and cancer.

The growing importance attached to the role of antioxidant vitamins, particularly those in fresh fruit and vegetables, has led to the 'Take Five' initiative internationally, encouraging intake of at least 5 portions of fruit and vegetables daily.

Water-soluble Vitamins

VITAMIN	FUNCTIONS	VEGETARIAN FOOD SOURCES
Vitamin C	Maintains connective tissue, e.g. skin, gums. Important role in wound healing. Antioxidant	Potatoes, green vegetables, fruits, especially citrus
Vitamin B_1 (Thiamine)	Release of energy from carbohydrate	Milk, wholemeal bread, potatoes, fortified bread and cereals
Vitamin B_2 (Riboflavin)	Utilization of energy from food	Milk, eggs, dairy produce, yeast extracts

Water-soluble Vitamins—contd

VITAMIN	FUNCTIONS	VEGETARIAN FOOD SOURCES
Vitamin B_3 (Niacin)	Utilization of energy from food	Bread and flour, fortified cereals, vegetables, milk
Vitamin B_6 (Pyridoxine)	Metabolism of amino acids and formation of haemoglobin	A wide range of foods, including milk, eggs, wholegrain cereals
Vitamin B_{12}	Growth and metabolism. Red blood cells	Occurs only in animal products. Eggs, milk and dairy foods. Useful to include items fortified with vitamin B_{12} such as vegetarian yeast extracts
Folic Acid	Many functions in body. Important for reduction of risk of neural tube defects. Women planning a pregnancy and in the early stages of pregnancy should have folic acid supplements	Green leafy vegetables, fortified bread and cereals

Fat-soluble Vitamins

VITAMIN	FUNCTIONS	VEGETARIAN FOOD SOURCES
Vitamin A (Retinol) Only in animal products, but body can convert beta-carotene in fruit and vegetables into Retinol	Essential for healthy skin and tissues. Resistance to disease, light perception	Eggs, carrots, green and yellow vegetables, margarine (fortified by law)
Vitamin D Produced by action of sunlight on skin, in addition to dietary sources	Controls and maintains absorption of calcium, essential for healthy bones and teeth	Margarine (fortified by law), eggs, fortified cereals, butter
Vitamin E	Antioxidant, protects cell membranes	Plant sources, especially wheatgerm and green vegetables
Vitamin K	Blood-clotting	Green vegetables, egg yolk

Minerals and Trace Elements

Minerals are naturally occurring chemicals which are essential in small quantities for the body to carry out its normal functions. Trace elements are needed in even smaller quantities and usually act in enzyme systems.

Like vitamins, minerals and trace elements occur widely in a varied diet, and normal requirements should be obtained from a balanced, varied diet which provides adequate energy.

Pregnant women and those with heavy periods may need to take an iron supplement, and a family doctor or dietitian can advise.

MINERAL	FUNCTIONS	VEGETARIAN FOOD SOURCES
Iron	Formation of haemoglobin which transports oxygen around the body. Deficiency can lead to anaemia	Cereal products, egg yolk and green leafy vegetables. Absorption improved by combining foods containing Vitamin C
Calcium	Gives strength to teeth and bones, in combination with phosphorus. Required for muscle contraction, nerve activity, normal blood-clotting	Milk and dairy produce, green leafy vegetables, flour, bread
Sodium	Essential for muscle and nerve activity. High intakes related to increased blood pressure	Table salt, bread, cereals, processed foods
Potassium	Complements sodium in function of cells, and fluid balance	Fruit, fruit juices, vegetables, milk
Magnesium	Enzyme function and energy utilization	Wide range of foods, especially those of vegetable origin
Zinc	Wound healing. Component of many enzymes	Dairy produce and eggs

WATER

Water is an essential component of all the cells and tissues in the body. An adult body contains about 60% water. Water is the main constituent of the body fluids, such as blood and urine, and acts as a solvent for minerals and vitamins. Lack of fluid, especially in the elderly, can be a major cause of constipation. Fluid is therefore an essential part of any diet. It can be taken in plain water, or in drinks, sauces, etc. Normal fluid intake should be not less than 1.5 litres per day, which is about 6–8 cups.

Special Requirements in the Vegetarian Diet

A vegetarian diet, as highlighted above, can be a healthy and satisfying one which provides all the nutrients needed by the body. However, special attention may be required at certain times of life to ensure that all nutrients are provided.

Pregnancy has been mentioned several times above, and the main points to note are that folic acid supplements will be advised and it may be necessary to take an iron supplement. Calcium requirements are increased during pregnancy and a good intake of milk and dairy products will supply this, as well as a small increase in energy to provide for the needs of both mother and baby.

Older people, particularly women, should ensure their intake of calcium is adequate. It is not possible to prevent the onset of osteoporosis after the menopause, but continuing to take regular exercise and maintain activity and a diet which contains milk and dairy foods may contribute to controlling it.

Children of various ages may have special requirements. In a vegetarian family, there is no reason why a child should not follow a vegetarian diet. However, babies and small children have proportionally higher requirements for their size than adults, and it is important that their diet is not too bulky, to allow them to eat enough of the right foods. A wide range of food should be introduced at weaning and during early years, to ensure good eating habits and an adequate mix of vitamins and minerals.

Adolescents have increased requirements during periods of growth. If they also choose this time to become vegetarian, particularly if still living at home, it is important that they learn how to follow a vegetarian diet sensibly, in order to maintain adequate intakes. Alternative protein sources to meat and fish, such as those featuring in this book, are essential to growth. These can often be eaten with the other components of the family's non-vegetarian meals, such as the starch and vegetable choices.

Summary
For all its life-giving and therapeutic properties, food is to be enjoyed. If a variety of food is eaten, chosen from a range of food groups, in appropriate proportions, anyone's diet can

provide for both the body's fundamental physical requirements and the enjoyment of food, with its important psychological aspects. The recipes in this book are designed to provide a happy balance of these two interlinked roles of food in our lives. Don't let anyone tell you that a vegetarian diet cannot be healthy and enjoyable.

SPECIAL DIETS

All special diets require modification of one or more components of the diet. It is essential that professional help and advice are sought when preparing special diets for medical conditions. Changes in the diet need expert supervision to ensure that all nutrients are still provided.

A few of the more common diets are outlined below. The Dietetic Department at your local hospital can give further advice on the cooking modifications needed for these and other therapeutic diets.

Weight-reducing, Diabetic and Lipid-lowering Diets
All medical conditions which need these diets require a change to a healthy lifestyle, including a diet which is based on fresh foods and is high in fibre and low in fat. The emphasis should be on wholegrain bread and cereals and fresh fruit and vegetables, with moderate portions of vegetarian protein sources. These dietary modifications are all based on healthy eating principles and as such can easily be followed by partners and the rest of the family. Drastic changes should be avoided, as this generally means the diet is difficult to keep to. The appropriate changes made to diet and lifestyle can be incorporated into the normal diet permanently.

Gluten-free Diet
This diet is specifically for the treatment of coeliac disease. It requires complete avoidance of gluten, a protein found in wheat, rye, barley and oats. All foods containing these, even in small amounts, must be avoided. Gluten-free flour, bread, pasta and biscuits are available on prescription and from chemists, and can be used to make gluten-free versions of many

foods. Rice, soya, corn and potato flour are naturally gluten-free, and can also be used. As gluten is the component of flour which gives it stretchiness and air-holding qualities, it takes time to adapt to gluten-free flours.

Many manufactured products contain gluten and labels must be checked carefully.

Dietary Change on Religious and Moral Grounds

Many people choose to follow a specific set of dietary rules for ethnic, cultural, moral and religious reasons. These may be dictated by religious texts, such as the Koran for Muslims. They may involve special methods of preparation and/or slaughter of foods, or the avoidance of certain foods together at the same meal. A number of religious festivals may provide the opportunity for special foods, or fasting for periods of time. It is very important when cooking for other people to find out if they have any such dietary restrictions, and adhere strictly to them.

The information given below outlines the generally accepted guidelines for the most widely followed of these diets.

Hindu

Orthodox or strict Hindus are vegetarian. Many do not eat eggs and will only eat vegetarian cheese (which does not contain animal rennet). Hindus never eat beef, as the cow is considered a sacred animal. Some non-Orthodox Hindus may eat chicken, mutton and, occasionally, fish. Milk, yoghurt and butter are permitted.

Muslim

Muslims can only eat meat which is *halal* and has been killed according to Islamic law. This can be obtained from a *halal* butcher. Pork is strictly forbidden, as are all of its products. Care must be taken with cooking fats, which must be of vegetable origin or from *halal* sources. Fish, eggs, milk and dairy products are allowed. Alcohol is strictly avoided by most Muslims, and should not be used in cooking.

At certain times of the Islamic calendar, in particular Ramadan, Muslims will fast during the hours of daylight and eat late at night and early in the morning. There are a number of important festivals which are celebrated by special food customs.

Jewish

Jews can only eat meat from animals which have been ritually slaughtered and prepared to render them 'kosher'. Pork is forbidden, but lamb, beef and goat are acceptable if 'kosher'. Fish which have fins and scales are allowed, but shellfish are not. Chicken, turkey, duck, goose, and among the game birds only partridge and pheasant are permitted.

The other important aspect of the Jewish diet is that meat and dairy foods must be kept apart in cooking, and must not be eaten at the same meal.

FOOD SAFETY

by Karen Sorensen

Food safety and hygiene are essential in every kitchen, from the domestic to the professional. Cooks need to be aware of the harmful organisms which can be present in foods, and how to minimize risks by careful shopping, food-handling and cooking.

Shopping for Food

All packaged perishable foods should be labelled with a 'use-by' date. This is the date within which the food will be safe to eat if stored correctly. It is illegal for shops to sell foods which are past their use-by date. Where foods are purchased unpackaged, be aware of the date of purchase, and use within a short time. Be aware of shop hygiene, and avoid buying fresh, chilled or frozen food in shops where chilled or frozen cabinets are not well maintained.

Try to buy small quantities of fresh food as you need them – this will also ensure good nutritional content. When shopping for dry goods, avoid damaged packets, dented cans or any poorly stored foods. Remember that chilled and frozen foods need to be kept at an appropriate temperature. Keep them in a cool-bag and put them into a refrigerator or freezer as soon as possible.

Storing and Refrigerating Food

Raw and cooked foods must always be kept separate. Raw ingredients should be kept at the bottom of the refrigerator, with cooked products above them. Make sure that raw foods do not drip on to fresh vegetables or salad if these are kept at the bottom of the refrigerator.

All eggs and dairy products should be stored in the refrigerator. Bacterial growth is very restricted at low temperatures, and the coldest part of the fridge should be kept at 5°C or lower.

Do not put hot food in the refrigerator, as this will increase the internal temperature. Instead, partially cover hot food and keep it in the coolest part of your kitchen. Refrigerate or freeze as soon as it reaches room temperature.

Kitchen Hygiene

Good basic kitchen hygiene avoids the risk of bacterial contamination of food from the atmosphere or from insects, etc. and reduces cross-contamination between raw and cooked foods.

It is essential to wash hands thoroughly before handling any food and after any potential contact with bacteria, such as going to the lavatory or handling refuse.

Wash all food which is to be eaten raw thoroughly in fresh water.

Never use the same knife or chopping board for preparing raw and cooked foods. It is a good idea to keep separate sets of boards and utensils for raw and cooked foods. These can be obtained colour coded, to avoid confusion.

Always keep raw and cooked food separate until serving.

Do not leave food uncovered or unwrapped around the kitchen. Cover food when not in use. Keep food refrigerated as much as possible.

Cooking Food

Food must be cooked sufficiently to kill any bacteria which may be present. This means cooking food so that the temperature at the centre reaches 70°C for at least 2 minutes. This will kill most bacteria which could cause food poisoning.

Eggs may be a source of salmonella, and should be cooked thoroughly, especially for the very young or very old.

Frozen food must be defrosted completely before cooking, to allow the food to cook right through when it is heated.

Reheating Food

Cooked food should never be reheated more than once. It should have been stored in a refrigerator and must be reheated until really hot all the way through.

Do not mix hot and cold foods together unless both are to be immediately reheated thoroughly. The cool food may contain some bacteria which will contaminate the whole dish.

Food Poisoning

Food is one of the ideal mediums in which bacteria can grow. Bacteria multiply rapidly to levels at which they can cause food poisoning, given warmth, time and moisture. This makes the conditions in food left out in a kitchen for any length of time an ideal breeding ground for bacteria. All the precautions outlined above are essential to prevent the multiplication of the bacteria which can cause food poisoning.

Food poisoning is at least unpleasant, and at worst, in vulnerable groups like the elderly, babies and those in hospital, life-threatening. Precautions to prevent it must be taken during all preparation and cooking of food. Never prepare food for other people if you are suffering from the symptoms of food poisoning.

Listeriosis

Listeriosis is a rare but dangerous form of food poisoning which can cause serious problems during pregnancy. Special dietary advice to avoid infection with the listeria bacteria is important for vulnerable groups, and especially during pregnancy. Ripened soft cheeses such as Camembert, Brie and blue-veined varieties should be avoided. Ready-to-eat or cooked chilled meals must be reheated thoroughly until piping hot.

Food Additives

Many people express concern about additives in our food. Certainly, a diet which is based mainly on a variety of fresh ingredients, well prepared and freshly cooked, is ideal. However, many food products rely on some form of additives, like preservatives, to ensure that they are safe for us to eat. The range of foods available to us would be severely restricted if these were not used in moderation. Similarly, many foods would look unpalatable after processing if some colouring were not added to them.

The legislation governing additives in the United Kingdom is extensive, and all foods containing additives are labelled as such. 'E' numbers show that an additive is accepted as safe throughout the European Community. Many of these are derivatives of natural products, like red colouring derived from beetroot (E162).

The key to all of this is to base the diet on fresh foods, using processed foods in moderation.

SPECIAL INGREDIENTS

Oils: A bottle of sunflower or vegetable oil and a bottle of good-quality extra virgin olive oil are essential for the store cupboard. In addition, consider supplementing these with some flavoured oils. Walnut and hazelnut have a luxurious flavour. Use to drizzle on salads or on top of hot dishes or to fry croûtons or nuts for warm salads. Sesame oil can be heated to high temperatures so is particularly good for stir-frying. The oriental variety is made from toasted sesame seeds and so is darker in colour. Choose a medium-coloured oil for a good nutty flavour. Groundnut oil is made from peanuts and is a good-quality all-purpose oil with almost no flavour at all. Peanut oil bought in oriental supermarkets has a deliciously nutty flavour and is used as a condiment in a similar way to walnut or hazelnut oil.

Balsamic vinegar is made from grape juice that has undergone a lengthy fermentation and ageing process, hence its rich, sweet flavour. It can be added to sauces or marinades and it is delicious enough to be used alone as a dressing. It is worth investing in a mid-priced bottle as cheaper vinegars are harsh.

Rice wine vinegar is pale yellow and has a clear, sweet flavour. It is classically used to flavour sushi rice but is also useful for dressings, marinades and dipping sauces where a more delicate flavour is desired.

Soy sauce: There are several varieties. Light soy sauce is pale in colour, thin and very salty. Shoyu is a Japanese light soy sauce that is less salty and slightly sweeter. Dark soy sauce is heavier and sweeter. Indonesian sweet soy sauce is thick and syrupy. It is richly flavoured and excellent in marinades or served as a dipping sauce.

Pomegranate syrup is made from pomegranate juice that has been boiled down to a thick, dark red/brown sauce. The syrup is used in Middle Eastern dishes. It has a fresh, fruity tartness which can be used to spike a salad dressing or casserole.

Creamed coconut is bought in a hard block and needs to be chopped or dissolved in boiling water before use. It works well as a thickening agent if added directly to sauces at the end of cooking.

Coconut milk is not the liquid inside the coconut but is extracted by soaking grated coconut in boiling water. It can be bought in cans or small cartons. Coconut milk is less intense than creamed coconut and one is not necessarily a substitute for the other. Home-made coconut milk can be extracted by covering the grated flesh of half a coconut or 225g/8oz desiccated coconut with 290ml/½ pint boiling water. Allow to cool, then pour through a sieve, squeezing out as much liquid as possible.

Lemongrass is the essence of Southeast Asian cooking. It is sold in stalks and can be found in oriental food stores or in the herb section of major supermarkets. To prepare: remove the outer layer and crush the stem with the flat side of a knife. Chop the lower part but use the tougher top part whole, for flavouring soups, stocks or rice. Remove at the end of cooking.

Galengal is similar to root ginger, with an ivory-coloured skin mottled with brown. It tastes like freshly flavoured ginger with a strong dash of lemon. Use it in the same way as ginger in soups, stir-fries and mild curries.

Curry leaves are the bay leaves of India. With their mild curry flavour they are used to enhance subtly spiced curries, side dishes or marinades. They can be bought fresh in Asian stores or dried in major supermarkets.

Kaffir lime leaves are used in a similar way to curry leaves but give a strong citrus flavour. The fresh leaves have a strong aromatic flavour but are hard to come by in this country. Dried leaves are available from both specialist stores and supermarkets.

Olives: Green olives ripen through the colour spectrum to muddy brown, purple, dark brown and black. The change in flavour is as subtle and complex as that of ageing wine. It is well worth seeking out some favourite olives as they make a quick snack on their own and add depth of flavour to many salads or casseroles. The quality of pre-packed olives can vary a great deal. To be on the safe side, purchase olives from a delicatessen and try one first. As green olives are the least ripe they should never be soft or wrinkled. 'Cracked' green olives are smashed with a mallet, breaking the flesh but not the stone. They are soaked in brine which can penetrate easily because of the cracking. This produces a crunchy olive with a powerful flavour. Black olives may be smooth and shiny, or the very ripe wrinkled variety which have a deep oily flavour.

Kumquats are about the size of a fresh date but bright orange in colour. They are used in cooking in the Middle East. When ripe, the flesh is sweet with a sharp flavour. Beware of under-ripe fruit as it is bitter and unpalatable. Kumquats can be added to a fruit bowl, served with cheese and make a good accompaniment to bitter salads or spiced dishes.

Mustards: At least two sorts need to be kept in store – English mustard, either in powder or paste form, and a milder aromatic mustard such as Dijon or a French wholegrain.

Seeds may look small and insignificant but they are packed with vitamins, minerals, oils and proteins. They are a very versatile addition to the vegetarian diet. Scatter them over breakfast cereal or salads or stir into rice, pasta, stir-fries or soups. All seeds are delicious toasted in a dry frying pan for a few minutes (see instructions on page 22). Buy them in small quantities and store in an airtight jar. Tahina is made from ground sesame seeds.

Yeast: Fresh yeast gives a particularly good result and that fantastic aroma of freshly baked bread. It should be pale beige and crumbly. Fresh yeast can be bought from health food shops, supermarkets or local bakers but is becoming increasingly difficult to find. Fast-action easy-blend yeast is made in fine granules so that it can be mixed directly into the flour. This yeast is easy to use and only one rising is needed.

Stock: Use home-made stock wherever possible (see pages 529–31). The next best thing is chilled stock, which can be stored in the freezer, or powdered Swiss bouillon.

Dairy products: Some vegetarians may question the use of dairy products on moral or health grounds. However, small amounts provide valuable protein, vitamins and minerals and are useful in cooking for thickening and enriching dishes. The recipes in this book contain liberal use of dairy products.

Cow's milk is still the most widely used milk. Skimmed or semi-skimmed milk retains the nutritional value while containing only a fraction of the fat or calories of whole milk. Organic milk comes from herds that eat pesticide-free feed and are not routinely treated with hormones or antibiotics. **Goat's milk** has a strong, musty flavour. There is a variety of goat's milk products available, such as cheese, yoghurt and ice cream. Ewe's milk is sweet and less assertive-tasting than goat's. It is traditionally used to make Greek yoghurt.

Cream: The fat content of cream varies a great deal. **Clotted cream** is 55% fat, **double cream**

48% and **single cream** 18%. **Soured cream** is treated with lactic acid and is 20% fat. **Crème fraîche** is a cultured cream rather like soured cream but with 35% fat. Whether cream is suitable or not for boiling will depend on the fat content. With **crème fraîche** there is no fear of it curdling if boiled. Creams lower than 20% fat should be added to dishes and reheated without boiling. Check labels on creme fraiche some brands contain gelatine.

Buttermilk is the liquid left over after making butter. It is very low in fat and has a mild, tangy flavour. It can be added to scones, batters, breads or cakes. **Smetana** is similar but richer. It is still low in fat, about 10%.

Yoghurt is renowned for its health-giving properties. It is nutritionally rich in vitamins and minerals. The bacteria used in yoghurt have many health benefits to the digestive system, promoting the natural flora in the intestine. Greek yoghurt has the highest fat content, about 10%. This is enough to prevent it curdling when heated so it can make a useful lower-fat substitute for cream or crème fraîche. Check yoghurt labels carefully. Some are set with gelatine, others may be high in sugar or additives. Yoghurt is easy to make at home (see recipe on page 470).

Vegetarian alternatives to dairy products

Soya milk products are the most used vegetarian alternatives to dairy foods. Milk, cream, yoghurt and cheese are all available. Soya milk can be used in the same way as cow's milk. It is thicker and has a nutty flavour. Soya cream is like single cream and cannot be used for whipping. There are other vegetarian alternatives to cream which taste extremely good although the whipping and double versions never whip as firmly as dairy creams. Ice cream made with soya milk will be very hard and needs to be softened at room temperature before serving. Soya milk is a good source of protein, minerals and vitamin E.

Vegetarian rennet is widely used now so most cheeses can be found in vegetarian versions. **Feta** is naturally curdled so no rennet is used. Fresh unripened cheeses are young and creamy. These include **fromage frais**, **ricotta**, **quark**, **cottage** and **cream cheese**. They can be used in cooking in a similar way to yoghurt and are particularly good for dips and desserts. In many of our recipes we refer to generic cheeses but vegetarians should always check – for example when a recipe calls for Parmesan Cheese we would recommend Twineham Grange Italian Style hard cheese.

SPECIAL TECHNIQUES

Peeling tomatoes: Douse the tomatoes in boiling water for 10 seconds. Carefully slit the skin with a sharp knife. It will now peel away easily.

Deseeding chillies: Chilli seeds can be cooked but are seriously hot. For a milder flavour, remove the seeds by slicing off the stalk and cutting the chilli in half lengthways. Cut away the seeds and membrane and wash under cold running water. The membranes and juices are fiery, so take care when preparing chillies not to touch your face or eyes.

Reducing: This means rapidly boiling liquid to reduce the quantity and intensify the flavour. Very reduced sauces will take on a thicker, syrupy consistency.

Dry-frying spices: This brings out the flavour in whole spices. It is a useful technique when using spices that are not going to be cooked, such as in dips, relishes or to scatter on top of dishes at the end of cooking. Use a heavy cast-iron frying pan. Heat the pan, add the spices and shake over the heat until the spices release a 'toasted' aroma and turn a shade or two darker. Watch carefully as there is a fine line between beautifully toasted spices and those that are slightly burnt, which gives a bitter flavour.

Toasting nuts or seeds: Toasting transforms the flavour of nuts and seeds into a subtle richness quite different from the raw ingredient. This can be done in the oven or under the grill. Put the nuts or seeds in a single layer in a baking tin. Bake or grill, shaking from time to time, until evenly golden-brown. Chopped nuts or seeds can be toasted in a dry frying pan in the same way as whole spices. Remove from the heat immediately when the nuts are perfectly golden as over-toasted nuts have a bitter flavour.

Seasoning a frying pan: Pans are seasoned to give them a good finish which distributes the heat evenly. Set the pan over the heat and wipe round with a piece of kitchen paper soaked in oil. When the pan is thoroughly hot, add a teaspoon of salt and rub this around the pan, still over the heat. Remove from the heat and empty out the salt. Heat the pan again, wiping with a fresh wad of kitchen paper soaked in oil. Remove the pan from the heat and allow to cool.

Baking blind: Preheat the oven to 200°C/400°F/gas mark 6. Line the raw pastry case with a sheet of kitchen foil or a double sheet of greaseproof paper and fill it with baking beans, dried lentils, rice or even pebbles or coins. This is to prevent the pastry from bubbling up during cooking. When the pastry is half cooked (after about 15 minutes), remove the 'blind beans' and bake the pastry case for a further 10–15 minutes until it has dried out and is light golden. The beans can be re-used indefinitely.

BRASSICAS AND LEAFY GREENS

Bok Choi • Broccoli • Brussels sprouts • Cabbage • Cauliflower • Kohlrabi • Swiss Chard • Sorrel • Spinach • Spring greens

INTRODUCTION

Brassicas are available all year round. Somehow their strong flavours are best suited to cold weather. Their delicious savoury flavours are only retained by careful cooking. These vegetables often tend to be overcooked, producing the unpalatable flavours so reminiscent of school meals. The addition of a bay leaf during cooking helps reduce the lingering smell. Brassicas have many health-giving properties and are full of B and C vitamins and rich in minerals (raw broccoli has a calcium content that is comparable to that of milk). To retain maximum flavour and nutritional value, brassicas are best cooked rapidly in a small amount of water. As a general rule, choose brassicas that are bright, firm and heavy for their size.

Broccoli: the purple sprouting variety has dark purple flowers and long leafy stems. It is sometimes nicknamed 'poor man's asparagus' and can usually be used as a substitute in asparagus recipes. Strictly speaking, the type of broccoli with the large cauliflower-like head is calabrese, named after its place of origin, Calabria. This is the most widely available variety and keeps longer.

Broccoli is good lightly boiled and served with a drizzle of lemon butter or Parmesan cheese or stir-fried or steamed. Choose bright vegetables with no sign of yellowing. Broccoli can be stored in the refrigerator for up to 5 days.

Brussels sprouts are traditionally best after the first frost. This is because the sugars develop and improve the flavour. Small is best with this vegetable. Choose tightly packed sprouts that are no more than 2.5cm/1in in size. Trim the root and the outer leaves before boiling. Don't be tempted to make a cross on the base as the sprouts will become soggy when cooked. Of all brassicas this is the most displeasing when overcooked. Boil briefly, steam, or shred and stir-fry and serve immediately. The spring greens-like leaves from the top of the plant are trimmed and sold as Brussels tops at the end of the season.

Cabbages are multi-coloured, textured and flavoured. Some are crisp and bland, others dark green with an intense depth of flavour. White cabbage is mild and used raw for making salads. Savoy is a favourite, with good flavour and bright green crinkly leaves. Large leaves are the best for stuffing. Pointed cabbage is another interesting variety. The outer leaves contain the most nutrients and keep the heart of the cabbage fresh. Generally the tightly packed leaf cabbages are the winter varieties and the loose-leafed the spring/summer ones. Choose heavy, bright vegetables with no limp or yellow leaves. Cabbage keeps well in the refrigerator for a week.

Savoy cabbage is good cooked in thick chunks but cabbage should usually be finely shredded. Quarter the cabbage and trim off the tough stalks before slicing. Cook in a smattering of salted water in a pan with a well-fitting lid and shake over the heat for a few minutes only. Serve tossed in butter with plenty of freshly ground black pepper. Whole leaves should be blanched in boiling water prior to stuffing. Cabbage is also very good stir-fried. Red cabbage is the exception to the rule and should be slowly braised with sugar, vinegar and often some fruit. This makes a substantial side dish or a meal in itself. Red cabbage can also be used raw in a salad.

Cauliflower originated in the Middle East where it was a sort of sprouting cabbage. It was first introduced to Europe as coleflower or cabbageflower. Cauliflower is grown throughout the year. As with broccoli, freshness is the essence. The buds should be solid and the stalks firm, with no sign of spots of yellow or black. The stems and leaves are good too.

Cauliflower is best cooked in even-sized florets but can also be cooked whole. Hollow out the stalk so that the heat can penetrate through the middle, then steam or simmer gently in salted water for about 15 minutes until just tender. Parboiled cauliflower can be stir-fried with whole spices, or small florets can be served raw with pre-dinner drinks.

Curly kale is a loose-leaf variety of cabbage that has no heart. It has dark green leaves and a particularly strong flavour. It is a relative of collard greens which are extensively used in the cooking of America's Deep South. Choose kale with bright, springy leaves and use within 2 days of purchase. Kale should be shredded and cooked like cabbage. It can be mashed with potatoes or stir-fried with hot strong spices.

Kohlrabi is bred for its bulbous stem. Choose smooth-skinned bulbs about the size of a tennis ball.

There are two varieties, pale green or purple. Thinly peeled kohlrabi can be simply steamed or boiled and topped with butter or parsley. Wafer-thin slices can be deep-fried into crisps or raw sticks can be coated with remoulade sauce. Wrap in a bag and store in the refrigerator for up to a week.

LEAFY GREENS

All dark green leaves are packed with vitamins and minerals. For information on bok choi and other oriental leaves, see page 169.

Chard and **leaf beet** have experienced a rather dull image in the past. In fact they are interesting leaves, much used in Caribbean, Middle Eastern, Mediterranean and Oriental cookery.

The stems are tender and should be eaten along with the leaves. Rhubarb chard has bright red or yellow stems. Choose leaves with plenty of bounce and store them, unwashed and wrapped in kitchen paper, in the salad drawer of the refrigerator. They will keep for only 2 days. They must be used when full of life to obtain the best flavour. They need thorough washing to remove any grit. The leaves should be folded in half lengthways and stripped from the stalk. Slice both and cook the stems for a few minutes longer than the leaves. The youngest leaves can be eaten raw but most that have found their way to the supermarket shelf will need cooking. These leafy greens need only brief cooking by either boiling, steaming or stir-frying.

Sorrel resembles a form of spinach. It has a lemony bitterness, due to the high acid content, that is more fragrant than the flavour of spinach. It is a good leaf to use raw in salads or lightly cooked in an omelette but take care if using for sauces as the high acid content can cause curdling. Sorrel is not often seen in the supermarket and is best home-grown or bought from a specialist supplier.

Spinach is a powerfully flavoured leaf full of antioxidants and beta-carotene. Choose leaves with fresh, springy stalks. Spinach does not keep well and should be refrigerated for only 2 days. It is available throughout the year. Wash spinach leaves in copious amounts of water to remove any traces of sand. Nutritionally it is best eaten raw. Large leaves can be used like vine leaves. It is staggering how spinach shrinks when cooked, so use a large pan with no additional water. Cover and heat for a few minutes until the leaves wilt. Press well to ensure that all excess water is removed. Young Spinach can be cooked briefly in a little butter.

Spring greens are bright green and open-leaved. The leaves are tender as the greens are picked when young and have little or no heart. Cook them in a dash of boiling salted water and dress with a little butter and plenty of freshly ground black pepper.

BROCCOLI SOUP

This soup is delicious served with a little grated Gruyère or crumbled Stilton cheese.

30g/1oz butter
1 large onion, sliced
450g/1lb broccoli
570ml/1 pint summer vegetable stock (see
    page 530)
salt and freshly ground black pepper
150ml/¼ pint milk
150ml/¼ pint single cream
freshly grated nutmeg

1. Melt the butter in a large saucepan and when foaming, add the onion and cook over a low heat until soft and transparent.
2. Roughly chop the broccoli florets and stalks, discarding the very tough ends of the stalks. Add to the pan with the stock. Season with salt and pepper and simmer for about 30 minutes until the broccoli is tender.
3. Purée in a food processor or blender and return to the rinsed-out pan. Stir in the milk and cream. Adjust the seasoning to taste and add a little grated nutmeg. Reheat without boiling.

INDIVIDUAL SOUFFLÉED BROCCOLI CHEESE

20g/¾oz butter, plus extra for greasing
20g/¾oz plain flour
a large pinch of dry English mustard
290ml/½ pint milk
2 eggs, separated
85g/3oz Cheddar cheese, grated
cayenne pepper
salt and freshly ground black pepper
675g/1½lb cooked broccoli florets
30g/1oz Parmesan cheese, freshly grated

1. Preheat the oven to 200°C/400°F/gas mark 6. Grease 4 individual shallow ovenproof dishes with butter.
2. Melt the butter in a heavy saucepan. Add the flour and mustard. Stir over a low heat for 1 minute.
3. Remove the pan from the heat. add the milk gradually and mix well until smooth. Return to the heat and stir until boiling and thickened. Simmer for 2 minutes.
4. Remove from the heat. Stir in the egg yolks and Cheddar cheese and season well with cayenne, salt and pepper.
5. Transfer the sauce to a large bowl and stir in the broccoli.
6. In a separate bowl, whisk the egg whites until stiff but not dry. Carefully fold into the broccoli mixture, using a large metal spoon.
7. Divide the mixture between the prepared dishes and sprinkle over the Parmesan cheese. Bake in the centre of the preheated oven for 12–15 minutes or until bubbling and slightly risen.

TWICE-BAKED BROCCOLI SOUFFLÉ WITH CRANBERRY SAUCE

45g/1½ oz butter, plus extra for greasing
290ml/½ pint milk
1 small carrot
1 stick of celery
1 slice of onion
1 bay leaf
1 sprig of fresh thyme
parsley stalks
black peppercorns
45g/1½oz plain flour
salt and freshly ground black pepper
170g/6oz cooked broccoli florets
3 eggs, separated
1–2 tablespoons chopped fresh thyme and parsley
30g/1oz hard goat's cheese, grated

For the sauce
1 quantity cranberry sauce (see page 507)

1. Preheat the oven to 200°C/400°F/gas mark 6. Grease 4 ramekin dishes with butter.
2. Place the milk in a saucepan with the carrot, celery, onion, bay leaf, thyme, parsley stalks and peppercorns and bring slowly to simmering point. Remove from the heat and leave to infuse for 8–10 minutes.
3. Melt the butter in a saucepan, stir in the flour and cook over a low heat, stirring, for 1 minute. Remove from the heat. Strain in the infused milk and mix well. Return the sauce to the heat and stir or whisk continuously until boiling. Simmer, stirring well, for 3 minutes. season to taste with salt and pepper.
4. Remove from the heat and transfer to a blender. Add the broccoli and the egg yolks. Process until smooth. Add the herbs and adjust the seasoning to taste. Transfer to a large mixing bowl.
5. Whisk the egg whites until stiff but not dry and carefully fold into the broccoli mixture, using a large metal spoon. Spoon into the prepared ramekin dishes. Stand the ramekins in a roasting pan half filled with boiling water and bake for 15 minutes or until well-risen and golden-brown. Remove from the pan. Run a knife around the edge of each dish to loosen and allow the soufflés to sink.
6. Turn each soufflé out on to the palm of your hand, giving the dish a sharp shake. Place the soufflés upside down in an ovenproof dish, sprinkle with the cheese and return to the oven for 5–10 minutes until the cheese has melted and the soufflés are hot again. Serve immediately with warm cranberry sauce.

BROCCOLI, CHERRY TOMATO AND MUSTARD QUICHE

110g/4oz flour quantity shortcrust or
  wholemeal pastry (see page 521 or 522)
15g/½oz butter
½ medium onion, finely chopped
225g/8oz broccoli florets
150ml/¼ pint Greek yoghurt
150ml/¼ pint milk
1 egg
1 egg yolk
1 heaped teaspoon wholegrain mustard
salt and freshly ground black pepper
1 tablespoon chopped fresh chives
110g/4oz cherry tomatoes
30g/1oz Parmesan cheese, freshly grated

1. Use the pastry to line an 18cm/7in flan dish and prick the base with a fork. Chill for 45 minutes to relax – this prevents shrinkage during baking.
2. Preheat the oven to 190°C/375°F/gas mark 5.
3. Bake the pastry case blind (see page 22) then remove from the oven. Lower the oven temperature to 180°C/350°F/gas mark 4.
4. Melt the butter in a small pan, add the onion and fry over a low heat until soft and golden-brown. Cut the broccoli florets into walnut-sized pieces and cook in boiling salted water for 2 minutes. Refresh under cold running water, drain very thoroughly and pat dry with kitchen paper.
5. Beat together the yoghurt, milk, egg, egg yolk and mustard. Season with salt and pepper and stir in the chives.
6. Spread the onion over the base of the cooked pastry case. Scatter over the broccoli florets. Arrange the cherry tomatoes in between the florets and sprinkle over the cheese. Pour in the yoghurt mixture.
7. Bake in the preheated oven for about 40 minutes until the filling is just set and golden-brown. Leave to stand for 10 minutes before serving.

BROCCOLI AND CAULIFLOWER PUDDING

55g/2oz butter
1 leek, trimmed and finely chopped
salt and freshly ground black pepper
55g/2oz plain flour
290ml/½ pint milk
110g/4oz cooked broccoli florets
340g/12oz cooked cauliflower
4 eggs, separated
2 tablesoons chopped fresh herbs, such as
  parsley or coriander
225g/8oz Lancashire cheese, crumbled
butter or oil, for greasing

1. Melt the butter in a saucepan and add the leek. Season with salt and pepper, cover and cook over a low heat for 5–8 minutes or until the leek is soft. Add the flour and cook for a further 1–2 minutes. Remove from the heat and stir in the milk, then return to the heat and cook, stirring, until the sauce boils and thickens.
2. Pour the sauce into the bowl of a food processor, add the broccoli, cauliflower and egg yolks and process until smooth. Transfer to a large mixing bowl. Add the herbs and cheese. Adjust the seasoning to taste.
3. Preheat the oven to 180°C/350°F/gas mark 4. Grease a large ovenproof dish with butter.
4. Whisk the egg whites until stiff but not dry. Carefully fold into the mixture in the bowl and transfer to the prepared dish.
5. Bake in the preheated oven for 20–25 minutes or until golden and well risen. The pudding should be steady when the dish is given a light shake. Serve immediately.

BROCCOLI AND SAGE GOUGÈRE

butter, for greasing
85g/3oz Cheddar cheese
1 × 3-egg quantity choux pastry (see page 524)
1 tablespoon shredded fresh sage
450g/1lb cooked broccoli florets
1 quantity warm béchamel sauce (see page 525)
salt and freshly ground black pepper
1 teaspoon dried breadcrumbs

1. Preheat the oven to 200°C/400°F/gas mark 6. Grease an ovenproof dish with butter.
2. Cut 55g/2oz of the cheese into cubes and add to the choux pastry with the sage. Mix well. Spoon the mixture around the edge of the prepared dish. Set aside.
3. Add the broccoli to the warm béchamel sauce and mix carefully. Season to taste with salt and pepper. Pile the sauce into the centre of the choux ring. Grate the remaining cheese evenly over the surface and sprinkle with the breadcrumbs. Place the dish on a baking sheet.
4. Bake in the centre of the preheated oven for about 30–40 minutes or until the choux is well risen and golden-brown and the sauce is bubbling hot.

BROCCOLI AND GREENS WITH CITRUS GREMOLATA

340g/12oz sprouting broccoli
450g/1lb kale or spring greens
olive oil
2 teaspoons lemon juice

For the citrus gremolata
1 tablespoon chopped fresh flat-leaf parsley
2 cloves of garlic, crushed
2 shallots, finely chopped
grated zest of 2 lemons
grated zest of 2 oranges
sea salt and freshly ground black pepper

1. First make the citrus gremolata: mix all the ingredients together and season with ½ teaspoon salt and plenty of pepper.
2. Trim the thick stalks from the broccoli, leaving long thin stalks with the florets at the top. Remove any thick stalks and outer leaves from the kale or greens and cut the leaves into thick slices.
3. Bring a saucepan of boiling water to the boil and cook the vegetables for about 2 minutes until *al dente*. Drain and place in a warm bowl. Drizzle over some oil and the lemon juice. Toss with the citrus gremolata.

VEGETABLE FRITTO MISTO WITH CHILLI JAM

The sparkling water used in this recipe makes an especially light and crisp batter.

170g/6oz broccoli
225g/8oz cauliflower
110g/4oz chestnut mushrooms
1 large carrot
1 medium red onion
vegetable or sunflower oil, for deep-frying
salt

For the batter
170g/6oz self-raising flour
a large pinch of salt
425ml/¾ pint sparkling water
2 egg whites

To serve
chilli jam (see page 508)

1. Cut the broccoli and cauliflower into florets about the same size as the mushrooms. Peel the carrot and cut it into quarters lengthways and then into 2.5cm/1in pieces. Peel the onion and slice into thick rings.
2. Make the batter: sift the flour into a large mixing bowl with the salt. Make a well in the centre. Gradually add the water to the well, drawing in the flour from around the sides until all the liquid is added and the mixture is smooth and creamy. Beat the egg whites to soft peaks. Stir a spoonful into the batter, using a large metal spoon, then carefully fold in the remainder.
3. Preheat the oven to 150°C/300°F/gas mark 2. Line a baking tray with kitchen paper. Heat about 5cm/2in oil in a deep frying pan until a drop of batter will sizzle slowly. Dip the vegetables in the batter, a few at a time, and fry until golden-brown. Using a draining spoon, lift the vegetables on to the baking tray. Sprinkle with salt and keep warm in the oven while cooking and frying the remainder in the same way. Pile the vegetables on to a warmed serving dish and serve immediately, with the chilli jam handed separately.

BRUSSELS SPROUTS GRATINÉE

30g/1oz butter, melted, plus extra for greasing
450g/1lb Brussels sprouts
340/12oz new potatoes, unpeeled
salt and freshly ground black pepper
1 teaspoon paprika
a pinch of cayenne pepper
200ml/7fl oz crème fraîche
55g/2oz wholemeal breadcrumbs
15g/½oz Parmesan cheese, freshly grated
1 tablespoon chopped fresh parsley

1. Preheat the oven to 200°C/400°F/gas mark 6. Grease an ovenproof dish with butter.
2. Trim the stalks and outer leaves from the Brussels sprouts. Cook in boiling salted water for about 5 minutes. They should still be very crunchy. Cook the potatoes in boiling salted water for 10 minutes until just tender.
3. Drain the sprouts and cut them in half. Drain and slice the potatoes and mix together with the sprouts. Season with salt and pepper.
4. Stir the paprika and cayenne into the crème fraîche and season with salt and pepper.
5. Put half the sprouts and potatoes into the dish. Spread over half the crème fraîche. Top with the remaining vegetables and then the remaining crème fraîche.
6. Mix the breadcrumbs with the melted butter. Stir in the cheese and parsley and spread on top. Bake in the preheated oven for 15–20 minutes until the vegetables are hot and the crumbs are crisp and brown.

BRUSSELS SPROUTS WITH TOASTED HAZELNUTS

675g/1½lb Brussels sprouts
salt
110g/4oz skinned hazelnuts
45g/1½oz unsalted butter

1. Trim the stalks and outer leaves from the Brussels sprouts. Cook in boiling salted water for 6–10 minutes until just tender.
2. Meanwhile, chop the hazelnuts roughly and toast over the heat in a dry, heavy frying pan. Remove from the pan and set aside.
3. Drain the sprouts. Melt the butter in the frying pan and add the hazelnuts and sprouts. Toss together and serve immediately.

CABBAGE LEAVES STUFFED WITH BEANS AND RICE

1 tablespoon sesame oil
1 large onion, finely chopped
walnut-sized piece of fresh root ginger, peeled
*   and grated*
110g/4oz cooked aduki beans (see page 313)
55g/2oz cooked brown rice
1 carrot, grated
salt and freshly ground black pepper
8 large Savoy cabbage leaves
2 tablespoons sweet soy sauce

To serve
tomato sauce (see page 527) or harissa (see
*   page 510)*

1. Preheat the oven to 180°C/350°F/gas mark 4.
2. Heat the oil in a heavy frying pan, add the onion and fry over a low heat until soft and transparent. Stir in the ginger and cook for 1 further minute. Stir the beans, rice and carrot into the onion mixture and season with salt and pepper.
3. Blanch the cabbage leaves for 1 minute in boiling salted water. Drain, reserving 290ml/½ pint of the water, and pat dry on kitchen paper.
4. Lay the cabbage leaves out on a board, vein side up, and divide the rice mixture between them, placing it in the centre of each leaf. Fold the sides of the leaves inwards and then roll up. Arrange the stuffed cabbage leaves seam side down in an ovenproof dish.
5. Bring the reserved water to the boil, add the soy sauce and pour over the stuffed cabbage leaves. Cover with kitchen foil and bake in the preheated oven for about 40 minutes, until tender. Serve with tomato sauce or harissa and a little of the cooking liquor.

CABBAGE LEAVES STUFFED WITH YELLOW AND GREEN SPLIT PEAS

1 large green cabbage
2 tablespoons sunflower oil
1 onion, chopped
1 large clove of garlic, crushed
1 green chilli, chopped
4 tomatoes, peeled and chopped (see page 22)
1 teaspoon ground turmeric
a pinch of chilli powder
2 teaspoons ground cumin
1 teaspoon mustard seeds
100ml/3½fl oz dry white wine
110g/4oz uncooked weight split yellow peas, cooked
110g/4oz uncooked weight split green peas, cooked
150ml/¼ pint summer vegetable stock (see page 530)
2 teaspoons lime or lemon juice
salt and freshly ground black pepper

For the sauce
1 tablespoon sunflower oil
1 onion, sliced
1 clove of garlic, crushed
1 tablespoon plain flour
570ml/1 pint summer vegetable stock (see page 530)
55ml/2fl oz dry white wine

1. Carefully cut 8 large outer leaves from the cabbage. Remove and discard the thick stalk from the centre of the cabbage leaves, blanch the leaves in a large saucepan of boiling water for 2–3 minutes, remove, then refresh under cold running water and drain well on kitchen paper.
2. Heat the oil in a large saucepan. Add the onion and cook over a low heat for 10 minutes, until softened. Add the garlic and green chilli and cook for a further 5 minutes.
3. Add the tomatoes, turmeric, chilli powder, cumin and mustard seeds to the pan. Cook for 2 minutes, then add the wine, bring to the boil and reduce by half. Add the cooked split peas, stock and lime or lemon juice. Boil to reduce to a thick mixture. Season with salt and pepper. Set aside to cool.
4. Make the sauce: heat the oil in a saucepan, add the onion and cook for 10 minutes until softened and lightly coloured. Add the garlic and stir in the flour, then pour in the stock and wine. Bring to the boil, stirring all the time, then lower the heat and simmer for 5 minutes. Season with salt and pepper.
5. Preheat the oven to 190°C/375°F/gas mark 5.
6. To assemble: lay the cabbage leaves out on a board, vein side up. Divide the split pea mixture between the leaves, placing it in the centre of each leaf. Fold the sides of the leaves inwards and then roll up. Place the stuffed cabbage leaves seam side down in a shallow ovenproof dish and pour over the sauce. Cover with kitchen foil and bake in the preheated oven for 30 minutes. Serve hot.

NOTE: The rest of the cabbage can be used in a soup or stew.

CALDO VERDE

(PORTUGUESE CABBAGE, BEAN AND
POTATO STEW)

SERVES 4–6

225g/8oz dried white beans, such as cannellini,
    soaked overnight
4 tablespoons olive oil
1 onion, halved and thinly sliced
1 large clove of garlic, crushed
1 medium-hot green Dutch chilli, thinly sliced
675g/1½lb potatoes, cut into small chunks
salt and freshly ground black pepper
570ml/1 pint summer vegetable stock (see
    page 530)
450g/1lb Savoy cabbage

To serve
extra virgin olive oil
rustic crusty bread

1. Drain the beans, put them into a large
saucepan and cover them with plenty of fresh
cold water. Bring them to the boil, then lower
the heat and simmer for 45–50 minutes or until
tender. Tip the beans into a colander set over a
bowl to collect the cooking liquor. Measure the
liquor and make it up to 570ml/1 pint with cold
water if necessary. Set aside.
2. Heat the oil in the rinsed-out pan. Add the
onion and cook over a low heat for 7–8 minutes
until soft and lightly golden.
3. Add the garlic, chilli, potatoes, ½ teaspoon
of salt and some pepper and cook for 2 minutes.
Add the reserved bean liquor and the stock,
bring to the boil and simmer for 20 minutes
until the potatoes are just starting to break up.
4. Meanwhile, divide the cabbage into leaves
and strip the leaves from the largest stalks. Cut
the leaves across into strips 2.5cm/1in wide. Stir
the cabbage and beans into the soup, cover and
simmer for a further 7–8 minutes until the
cabbage is tender. Season to taste with salt and
pepper.
5. Ladle the stew into warm bowls and drizzle
over some oil. Serve with rustic crusty bread.

CABBAGE, PARSNIP AND APPLE PIE

1 tablespoon sunflower or vegetable oil
30g/1oz butter
1 medium onion, sliced
340g/12oz parsnips
1 teaspoon plain flour
425ml/¾ pint summer vegetable stock (see
    page 530), reduced to 290ml/½ pint
150ml/¼ pint apple juice
1 bay leaf
salt and freshly ground black pepper
1 dessert apple
2 teaspoons shredded fresh sage
170g/6oz Savoy or spring cabbage, shredded
170g/6oz flour quantity shortcrust or
    wholemeal pastry (see page 521 or 522)
beaten egg or milk, to glaze

1. Heat the oil in a sauté pan. Add the butter
and when foaming, add the onion and fry over
a low heat until soft and golden-brown.
2. Peel the parsnips and cut into 2.5cm/1in
chunks. Add to the pan and fry for 10 minutes
until starting to brown. Stir in the flour and
cook for 1 further minute.
3. Mix the reduced stock and apple juice
together and gradually add to the pan, stirring
all the time. Add the bay leaf and season with
salt and pepper. Simmer very gently for 20–30
minutes until the parsnips are tender and the
liquid reduced.
4. Peel, quarter and core the apple. Cut into
2.5cm/1in chunks. Add to the parsnips with the
sage and cabbage. Leave to cool.
5. Preheat the oven to 190°C/375°F/gas mark 5.
Spoon the cabbage mixture into a 1 litre/1¾
pint pie dish.
6. Roll the pastry out until it is 2.5cm/1in
larger than the pie dish. Cut a strip of pastry
slightly wider than the rim of the dish. Brush
the rim of the dish with water and press on the
strip of pastry. Brush with a little more water
and lay the pastry lid over the pie. Cut away the
surplus pastry with a knife. Press the edges
together and mark a pattern with a small knife,
or crimp with the fingers into a raised border.

Shape the pastry trimmings into leaves for decoration. Make a small hole in the centre of the pastry lid to let the steam escape. Brush the pastry with beaten egg or milk, decorate with the pastry leaves and brush again. Bake in the preheated oven for 30 minutes until the pastry is golden-brown and the filling piping hot.

RED CABBAGE PLATE PIE

340g/12oz red cabbage
30g/1oz butter
1 onion, sliced
1 small cooking apple, peeled and sliced
1 small dessert apple, peeled and sliced
30g/1oz soft light brown sugar
1 tablespoon red wine vinegar
4 cloves
150ml/¼ pint apple juice
salt and freshly ground black pepper
1 quantity wholemeal pastry (see page 522)
beaten egg, to glaze

1. Cut the cabbage into quarters. Remove the outer leaves and tough stalk and shred. Rinse in cold water.
2. Melt the butter in a large saucepan and when foaming, add the onion and fry over a low heat until soft and transparent. Lift the cabbage, without shaking off the water, into the pan and add the apples, sugar, vinegar, cloves, apple juice and salt and pepper. Cover the pan tightly and cook slowly, stirring from time to time, for 40–50 minutes, until the cabbage is very soft.
3. Preheat the oven to 190°C/375°F/gas mark 5.
4. Spoon the cabbage mixture into a 20cm/8in pie plate. Brush the rim with water.
5. Roll the pastry out so that it is large enough to cover the dish with about 2.5cm/1in to spare. Trim the edges, roll into a strip and use to cover the rim of the pie plate. Brush with water. Now cover the whole of the dish with the remaining pastry, pressing the edges firmly together, and trim with a sharp knife.
6. Knock up the edge by slashing with a knife, then crimp by pushing the pastry between thumb and forefinger. Brush with beaten egg and bake in the preheated oven for 35 minutes until the pastry is golden-brown and the filling piping hot.

SAVOY CABBAGE AND THREE-CHEESE PANCAKES

This filling can also be used for cannelloni served with tomato sauce (see page 527).

55g/2oz butter, plus extra for greasing
340g/12oz Savoy cabbage
½ medium onion, finely chopped
salt and freshly ground black pepper
freshly grated nutmeg
110g/4oz ricotta cheese
110g/4oz mozzarella cheese, grated
70g/2½oz Parmesan cheese, freshly grated
12 French pancakes (see page 532)
cayenne paper

1. Preheat the oven to 190°C/375°F/gas mark 5. Grease an ovenproof dish with butter.
2. Cut the cabbage into wedges. Slice away the tough stalk and shred the cabbage thinly. Melt half the butter in a frying pan, add the onion and cook over a low heat until golden. Add the cabbage and toss over the heat until slightly softened but still bright green and crisp. Season with salt, pepper and nutmeg.
3. Put the ricotta into a mixing bowl and beat to soften. Stir in the mozzarella and 55g/2oz of the Parmesan cheese. Season with salt and pepper.
4. Lay the pancakes side by side on a worktop. Divide the cabbage between them, placing it in one quarter of the pancake. Top with a spoonful of the cheese mixture. Fold each pancake in half to form a semi-circle and in half again to form a triangle.
5. Arrange the pancakes in the prepared dish, overlapping each other with the points upwards. Melt the remaining butter and pour over the pancakes. Scatter with the remaining Parmesan cheese and dust with a little cayenne. Bake in the preheated oven for 20–30 minutes until piping hot all the way through.

BUBBLE AND SQUEAK CAKES WITH POACHED EGGS AND MUSTARD SAUCE

This recipe needs to be started a day in advance.

785g/1¾lb floury potatoes, such as Maris Piper
    or King Edwards
salt and freshly ground black pepper
450g/1lb green cabbage
2 tablespoons olive oil
1 leek, trimmed and thinly sliced
30g/1oz butter
1 tablespoon white wine vinegar
8 medium eggs

For the sauce
570ml/1 pint summer vegetable stock (see
    page 530)
150ml/¼ pint dry white wine
4 tablespoons double cream
55g/2oz butter, plus 1 teaspoon
1 heaped teaspoon plain flour
2 teaspoons wholegrain mustard

1. The day before, peel the potatoes and cut them into 5cm/2in chunks. Bring to the boil in well-salted water and simmer for 15 minutes until just tender. Drain and leave to go cold, then cover and chill overnight.
2. The following day, trim the large stalks from the cabbage. Cook the leaves in a large saucepan of boiling salted water for 2 minutes until tender. Drain and refresh under cold running water to set the colour. Drain well again, spread out on a clean tea-towel and leave to dry off thoroughly. (Both the potatoes and the cabbage need to be very dry to make the bubble and squeak crisp.) Chop the cabbage into small pieces.
3. Heat 1 tablespoon of the oil in a small frying pan. Add the leek and cook for 3 minutes or until lightly browned. Put the potatoes into a large bowl and mash them to a coarse purée with a fork. Mix in the cabbage and leek and season well with salt and pepper.
4. Shape the mixture into 8 × 10cm/4in discs

about 2.5cm/1in thick. Cover and chill for 1 hour.
5. Make the mustard sauce: put the stock, wine, cream and 55g/2oz of the butter into a medium saucepan and boil rapidly until reduced by about three-quarters to the consistency of single cream. Blend the remaining butter with the flour into a smooth paste. When the sauce has reached the required consistency, whisk in the flour-and-butter paste. Simmer for 2–3 minutes. Keep warm.
6. Heat the remaining oil and butter in a large frying pan. Add the bubble and squeak cakes and fry over a medium-high heat for 4–5 minutes on each side until crisp and golden-brown.
7. Meanwhile, bring about 2.3 litres/4 pints water to a gently rolling boil in a large saucepan. Add the vinegar. Break the eggs one at a time into a ramekin or teacup and slide them into the water. Lower the heat and poach for 3 minutes, then lift them out with a slotted spoon and drain briefly on kitchen paper.
8. Put the bubble and squeak cakes on to 4 warmed individual plates and top with the poached eggs. Bring the sauce back up to a simmer, whisk in the wholegrain mustard and season to taste with salt and pepper. Pour a little of the sauce over the eggs and the remainder around the outside of each plate.

BLACK CABBAGE STIR-FRY WITH BLACK BEANS AND CASHEW NUTS

*1 head of black cabbage, outer leaves and thick
   stalks removed*
1 tablespoon vegetable oil
55g/2oz unsalted cashew nuts
*1 bunch of spring onions, trimmed and thinly
   sliced*
*1 × 140g/5oz can of black beans, well rinsed and
   drained*
½ tablespoon sesame oil
salt and freshly ground black pepper

1. Shred the cabbage leaves very finely. Bring a
large saucepan of salted water to the boil, add
the cabbage and cook for 1½–2 minutes. Drain
thoroughly.
2. Heat the oil in a wok or heavy frying pan.
Add the cashew nuts and fry until lightly
browned. Remove from the pan with a slotted
spoon and drain on kitchen paper.
3. Lower the heat and add the spring onions to
the pan. Fry gently for 2–3 minutes or until
beginning to soften. Add the beans and
continue to cook for 1 further minute.
4. Increase the heat and stir in the drained
cabbage. Return the cashew nuts to the pan and
pour in the sesame oil. Season to taste with salt
and pepper.

NOTE: Black cabbage is the Italian brassica
cavolo nero.

CABBAGE WITH APPLE AND CARAWAY

450g/1lb white cabbage
2 tablespoons olive oil
1 large onion, sliced
1 teaspoon caraway seeds
290ml/½ pint apple juice
1 dessert apple
salt and freshly ground black pepper
freshly grated nutmeg
4 tablespoons crème fraîche

1. Remove and discard the tough stalk from
the cabbage. Slice the cabbage thickly.
2. Heat the oil in a saucepan. Add the onion
and fry over a low heat until golden-brown. Stir
in the caraway seeds and cook for a further 1–2
minutes. Pour in the apple juice and stir to
remove any sticky sediment from the base of the
pan. Stir in the cabbage.
3. Quarter, core and slice the apple and add to
the pan. Season with salt, pepper and nutmeg.
Mix well. Partially cover and simmer gently for
about 15 minutes until the apple and cabbage
are tender and the liquid reduced.
4. Stir in the crème fraîche and adjust the
seasoning to taste. Bring to the boil, then lower
the heat and simmer for 2 minutes before
serving.

BRAISED RED CABBAGE WITH APPLES AND CLOVES

SERVES 6

900g/2lb red cabbage
3 tablespoons soft light brown sugar
2 cloves of garlic, finely chopped
½ teaspoon ground cinnamon
¼ nutmeg, freshly grated
½ teaspoon whole cloves
30g/1oz butter
450g/1lb onions, halved and thinly sliced
450g/1lb cooking apples, peeled, cored and
    chopped into small pieces
salt and freshly ground black pepper
3 tablespoons red wine vinegar

1. Preheat the oven to 150°C/300°F/gas mark 2. Remove and discard the outer leaves from the cabbage. Cut into quarters, cut out and discard the core and slice the cabbage thinly.
2. Mix together the sugar, garlic, cinnamon, nutmeg and cloves. Rub a little of the butter over the base of a large casserole dish. Layer the cabbage, onions and apple in the casserole, sprinkling over some of the sugar mixture and salt and pepper. Finish with a layer of cabbage.
3. Pour over the vinegar, dot the top layer of cabbage with the remaining butter and cover with a tight-fitting lid. Cover and cook in the preheated oven for 2½ hours, stirring once or twice during cooking. Adjust the seasoning to taste before serving.

BRAISED RED CABBAGE WITH BEETROOT

340g/12oz red cabbage
1 tablespoon olive oil
1 red onion, finely diced
225g/8oz raw beetroot, peeled and diced
2 teaspoons soft light brown sugar
a pinch of ground cloves
1 tablespoon raspberry vinegar
juice of ½ small orange
salt and freshly ground black pepper

1. Cut the cabbage into quarters, remove the hard core and shred.
2. Heat the oil in a large, heavy saucepan, add the onion and fry over a low heat until it begins to soften. Add the cabbage, beetroot and all the remaining ingredients. Season with salt and pepper.
3. Cover the pan tightly and cook over a very low heat, stirring occasionally, for 1½–2 hours, or until soft and reduced in bulk. (During cooking keep an eye on the liquid; there should be enough to prevent sticking but no excess by the end.) Adjust the seasoning to taste.

NOTE: This can be made in advance and reheated. It can also be cooked in an ovenproof container in a low oven if hob space is short.

SAUTÉED SAVOY CABBAGE AND SWEDE

340g/12oz swede
salt and freshly ground black pepper
½ Savoy cabbage
1 tablespoon sunflower or vegetable oil
1 tablespoon walnut oil, plus extra to finish
55g/2oz walnuts, toasted (see page 22)
balsamic vinegar

1. Peel the swede and cut it into thin matchsticks. Blanch in boiling salted water for 2 minutes. Drain and set aside for 20–30 minutes to allow to dry.
2. Remove and discard the outer leaves from the cabbage. Cut the cabbage into quarters and cut out the tough stalk. Cut the quarters in half again and shred.
3. Heat the sunflower or vegetable oil in a wok or large, heavy frying pan. Add 1 tablespoon walnut oil and the swede and toss over the heat until the swede begins to brown and caramelize. Add the cabbage and cook for a few more minutes until it is beginning to soften.
4. Roughly chop the walnuts, stir into the vegetables and season with salt and pepper. Drizzle with a little walnut oil and a few drops of balsamic vinegar and serve immediately.

SAUTÉED RED CABBAGE WITH RAISINS, RED WINE AND HONEY

675g/1½lb red cabbage
2 tablespoons olive oil
55g/2oz butter
1 large red onion, halved and thinly sliced
2 cloves of garlic, finely chopped
1 bay leaf
1 sprig of fresh thyme
55ml/2fl oz red wine
55g/2oz raisins
2 tablespoons balsamic vinegar
2 tablespoons clear honey
salt and freshly ground black pepper

1. Remove and discard the outer leaves from the cabbage. Cut the cabbage into quarters, cut out and discard the core and slice the cabbage thinly.
2. Heat the oil and butter in a large saucepan. Add the onion and cook over a medium to high heat for 6–7 minutes, stirring frequently, until lightly browned. Increase the heat, add the cabbage and garlic and sauté for 5 minutes until the cabbage has wilted down slightly into the base of the pan.
3. Add the bay leaf, thyme, wine and raisins. Lower the heat to medium and continue to cook until the wine has almost evaporated and the cabbage is tender. Add the vinegar and honey and cook for 1–2 minutes. Season to taste with salt and pepper and serve.

MOCK SEAWEED (CRISPY FRIED GREENS WITH TOASTED COCONUT)

340g/12oz spring cabbage or Brussels sprouts
*   *tops*
55g/2oz desiccated coconut
sunflower or vegetable oil, for deep-frying
sea salt

1. Remove the outer leaves from the cabbage, if used. Slice away any tough stalk with a sharp knife. Roll the leaves up into a tight bundle and shred very finely. Shred the Brussels sprouts tops, if used.

2. Put the coconut into a dry, heavy frying pan and toss over the heat until golden-brown. Set aside.

3. Heat about 10cm/4in oil in a saucepan at least 20cm/8in deep until a shred of the greens will sizzle vigorously. Cook the greens in batches for 1–2 minutes until crisp but still bright green. The oil will boil up as the greens are dropped in, because of their high water content, so do not overfill the pan.

4. Drain on kitchen paper and sprinkle with salt and toasted coconut. Serve immediately.

NOTE: Brussels sprouts tops are spring greens-like leaves produced by the plant at the end of the season.

APPLE AND LEMON COLESLAW

SERVES 6–8

1 red-skinned dessert apple
1 green-skinned dessert apple
3 tablespoons lemon juice
finely grated zest of 1 large lemon
6 tablespoons mayonnaise
4 tablespoons Greek yoghurt
salt and freshly ground black pepper
285g/10oz white cabbage, finely shredded
6 spring onions, trimmed and thinly sliced
225g/8oz carrots, coarsely grated
4 sticks of celery, thinly sliced

1. Cut the apples into quarters, cut out the cores and cut the fruit into small pieces. Add 1 tablespoon of the lemon juice and toss together well.

2. Put the lemon zest, mayonnaise and yoghurt into a bowl and mix together well. Gradually mix in the remaining lemon juice and season to taste with salt and pepper.

3. Put the cabbage, spring onions, carrot and celery into the bowl with the apples and toss together well. Stir in the lemon mayonnaise mixture and adjust the seasoning to taste.

AMERICAN CABBAGE AND GREEN PEPPER COLESLAW

SERVES 6–8

285g/10oz white cabbage
2 sticks of celery, thinly sliced
1 green pepper, deseeded and very thinly sliced
4 spring onions, trimmed and thinly sliced
½ tablespoon Dijon mustard
1 teaspoon creamed horseradish
½ teaspoon Tabasco sauce
1 tablespoon red wine vinegar
a pinch of cayenne pepper
2 tablespoons olive oil
2 tablespoons mayonnaise
salt and freshly ground black pepper
3 tablespoons chopped fresh dill

1. Remove and discard the outer leaves from the cabbage. Cut the cabbage into quarters, cut out and discard the core and thinly slice the cabbage. Put into a large bowl with the celery, green pepper and spring onions and toss together well.
2. Mix the mustard, horseradish, Tabasco, vinegar and cayenne together in a small bowl. Gradually whisk in the oil, mayonnaise and salt and pepper to taste.
3. Stir the dressing and dill into the vegetables just before serving so that the cabbage stays nice and crunchy.

GARDEN LEAVES WITH TOMATO AND OLIVES

For the salad
¼ Savoy cabbage
55g/2oz rocket leaves
55g/2oz young spinach leaves
15g/½oz fresh coriander
½ bunch of spring onions
about 12 cherry tomatoes, halved
55g/2oz green olives, pitted and halved

For the dressing
grated zest and juice of ½ lemon
4 tablespoons olive oil
1 clove of garlic, crushed
salt and freshly ground black pepper

1. Remove the outer leaves from the cabbage. Trim away and discard the stalk and shred the cabbage finely. Wash the rocket, spinach and coriander and remove any tough stalks. Cut the spring onions into quarters lengthways, then crossways into 2.5cm/1in strips.
2. Make the dressing: whisk all the ingredients together or shake together in a screwtop jar.
3. Place all the salad ingredients together in a large serving bowl. Toss in the dressing and mix well just before serving.

CAULIFLOWER AND TURMERIC FRITTERS

MAKES 12

1 small cauliflower
salt and freshly ground black pepper
140g/5oz plain flour
2 teaspoons ground turmeric
a good pinch of chilli powder
2 teaspoons ground cinnamon
2 teaspoons cumin seeds, toasted (see page 22)
2 eggs, beaten
170ml/6fl oz cold water
1 medium onion, finely chopped
2 cloves of garlic, crushed
sunflower or groundnut oil, for frying

To serve
Parmender salad (see page 229)

1. Remove the outer leaves from the cauliflower and cut into florets. Blanch in boiling salted water for 3 minutes. Pour into a colander and leave to stand for 10 minutes so that all the water can drain away. Roughly chop the cauliflower.
2. Sift together the flour, turmeric, chilli and cinnamon. Add 1 teaspoon salt and the toasted cumin seeds and make a well in the centre. Put the beaten eggs into the well and whisk to a smooth paste. Gradually whisk in the water to make a smooth batter.
3. Stir the chopped cauliflower, onions and garlic into the batter. Season with salt and pepper.
4. Heat about 1cm/½in oil in a frying pan until a crumb of bread will sizzle vigorously. Drop spoonfuls of the batter mixture into the oil. When the fritters are turning brown at the edges, turn and cook for 1 further minute on the other side. Serve hot with the salad handed separately.

NOTE: Broccoli florets can be used instead of cauliflower.

CHEESE FONDUE WITH CAULIFLOWER AND POLENTA FRITTERS

For the fondue
1 clove of garlic
290ml/½ pint dry white wine
2 teaspoons cornflour
3 tablespoons kirsch
225g/8oz Gruyère cheese, coarsely grated
225g/8oz Emmental cheese, coarsely grated
a pinch of freshly grated nutmeg

For the cauliflower fritters
1 large cauliflower, broken into small florets
salt and freshly ground black pepper
sunflower oil, for deep-frying
85g/3oz plain flour, seasoned
4 medium eggs, beaten
170g/6oz polenta

1. First make the fritters: cook the cauliflower florets in boiling salted water for 3 minutes until just tender. Drain, refresh under cold running water and set aside to drain on a clean tea-towel.
2. Heat oil in a deep-fryer to 180°C/350°F. Coat the cauliflower florets in batches first with the flour, then with the beaten egg and finally with the polenta. Deep-fry them for 2 minutes until crisp and golden. Lift them out with a slotted spoon on to a baking tray lined with kitchen paper and keep hot in a low oven while you fry the remainder in the same way.
3. Make the fondue: cut the clove of garlic in half and rub it over the base and sides of a fondue pan or medium, heavy saucepan. Add the wine and bring to the boil over a high heat. Meanwhile, mix the cornflour with the kirsch.
4. Reduce the wine to a simmer, add the cheeses and stir constantly until they have melted. Stir in the cornflour and kirsch mixture and continue stirring until the wine and cheeses have amalgamated and the mixture is very smooth. Do not let the mixture boil. Add the nutmeg and season to taste with salt and pepper.

5. Lift the pan on to a burner set in the middle of the table. Serve with the hot cauliflower fritters.

NOTE: If the fondue starts to get too thick, add another 55ml/2fl oz wine, return the pan to a low heat, and stir again until smooth.

MALLOREDDUS PASTA WITH A CAULIFLOWER, SAFFRON AND TOMATO CREAM SAUCE

4 tablespoons extra virgin olive oil
1 large cauliflower, broken into small florets
5 cloves of garlic, finely chopped
1 medium-hot red Dutch chilli, deseeded and
    finely chopped (see page 22)
3 tablespoons sun-dried tomato paste
a large pinch of saffron strands
salt and freshly ground black pepper
450g/1lb malloreddus pasta or other shell-
    shaped pasta
5 canned plum tomatoes, roughly chopped
2 tablespoons double cream
2 tablespoons chopped fresh flat-leaf parsley

To serve
freshly grated Parmesan cheese

1. Heat the oil in a large saucepan. Add the cauliflower florets and cook over a medium heat for 5 minutes, stirring from time to time, until the cauliflower begins to soften but does not colour.
2. Add the garlic and chilli and cook for 1 minute, stirring. Mix the sun-dried tomato paste with 110ml/4fl oz water, stir it into the cauliflower, cover and cook over a low heat for 15 minutes or until the cauliflower is tender.
3. Meanwhile, cover the saffron with 55ml/2fl oz warm water and leave it to soak. Bring 2.3 litres/4 pints water and 4 teaspoons salt to the boil in another large saucepan. Add the pasta and cook for 8–9 minutes or until *al dente*.

4. Add the saffron and its soaking liquid to the cauliflower with the tomatoes and season to taste with salt and pepper. Increase the heat slightly and continue to cook, stirring from time to time, until the cauliflower is very soft. Break up the florets slightly, then stir in the cream and parsley.
5. Drain the pasta well, return to the rinsed-out pan and add the sauce. Toss together well, spoon into warmed individual bowls and serve sprinkled with the cheese.

NOTE: Malloreddus is a small, shell-shaped pasta. Any small pasta shapes about 1cm/½in long can be used instead.

CAULIFLOWER AND CHEESE TORTELLINI GRATIN

450g/1lb fresh tortellini pasta, filled with cheese
450g/1lb cauliflower, broken into small florets
salt and freshly ground black pepper

For the cheese sauce
570ml/1 pint milk
1 bay leaf
4 black peppercorns
1 blade of mace
2 shallots, halved
55g/2oz butter
45g/1½oz plain flour
110g/4oz Fontina cheese, coarsely grated
a little freshly grated nutmeg
15g/½oz Parmesan cheese, freshly grated

1. First make the cheese sauce: put the milk, bay leaf, peppercorns, mace and shallots into a pan and bring slowly to the boil. Remove from the heat, cover and set aside for 15–20 minutes to infuse.
2. Bring the milk back to the boil, then strain. Melt the butter in another saucepan, stir in the flour and cook over a low heat, stirring, for about 1 minute. Remove the pan from the heat and gradually add the infused milk, stirring well between each addition.
3. Return the pan to the heat and bring the sauce back to the boil, stirring all the time. Lower the heat once more and leave the sauce to cook very gently for 2 minutes, stirring from time to time.
4. Bring two large saucepans of salted water to the boil. Add the cauliflower to one pan and cook for 3–4 minutes until just tender. Drain and set side. Add the tortellini to the other pan and cook for 4 minutes, or according to the manufacturer's instructions, until *al dente*. Drain well and set aside.
5. Preheat the grill to high. Stir 85g/3oz of the Fontina cheese into the sauce and season to taste with salt, pepper and nutmeg. Gently stir in the tortellini and the cauliflower florets, then spoon into a shallow ovenproof dish. Mix the remaining Fontina cheese with the Parmesan cheese and sprinkle over the top. Grill for 2–3 minutes, turning the dish from time to time, until golden and bubbling.

VEGETABLE PAKORAS WITH A ROASTED CUMIN AND TOMATO RAITA

Pakoras are Indian-style fritters made with a spicy chickpea batter.

285g/10oz small cauliflower florets
225g/8oz small broccoli florets
1 small aubergine, cut into small chunks
110g/4oz okra, trimmed
sunflower oil, for deep-frying

For the batter
170g/6oz chickpea flour (gram flour)
½ teaspoon baking powder
1 teaspoon cornflour
1½ teaspoons ground cumin
1½ teaspoons ground coriander
1½ teaspoons ground turmeric
½ teaspoon cayenne pepper
salt
225ml/8fl oz warm water
1 tablespoon sunflower oil
1 tablespoon lemon juice

For the raita
½ teaspoon cumin seeds
150ml/¼ pint Wholemilk natural yoghurt
2 tablespoons soured cream
2 vine-ripened tomatoes, peeled, deseeded and
   cut into small dice (see page 22)
1 medium-hot green Dutch chilli, deseeded and
   finely chopped (see page 22)
1 tablespoon chopped fresh mint

1. First make the roasted cumin and tomato raita: heat a dry, heavy frying pan over a high heat. Add the cumin seeds and shake them around for a few seconds until they darken slightly and begin to release their aroma. Tip them into a mortar or mug and crush with a pestle or the end of a rolling pin.

2. Put the yoghurt and soured cream into a bowl and stir in the roasted cumin seeds, the tomato, chilli and mint. Cover and set aside in the refrigerator.

3. Make the batter: sift the chickpea flour, baking powder, cornflour, ground spices, cayenne and 1 teaspoon salt into a large mixing bowl. Make a well in the centre and add the water, oil and lemon juice. Gradually draw dry ingredients into the liquid to make a smooth, thin batter.

4. Heat oil in a deep-fryer to 180°C/350°F. Stir a few pieces of the vegetables into the batter, lift out and drop into the hot oil. Cook for 3 minutes until crisp and golden. Lift out with a slotted spoon and drain on kitchen paper. Keep warm in a low oven while you fry the remaining vegetables in the same way.

5. Sprinkle the pakoras with a little salt and pile them on to a warmed serving dish. Serve with the roasted cumin and tomato raita.

STIR-FRIED HOT AND SPICY CAULIFLOWER

3 tablespoons sunflower oil
1 teaspoon ground cumin
1 teaspoon mustard seeds
1 teaspoon garam masala
a large pinch of chilli powder
2 cloves of garlic, chopped
2.5cm/1in piece of fresh root ginger, peeled and grated
450g/1lb cauliflower florets
1 green chilli, finely chopped
100ml/3½fl oz water
½ teaspoon salt
55ml/2fl oz Greek yoghurt

1. Heat the oil in a wok and add the cumin, mustard seeds, garam masala, chilli powder and garlic. Stir-fry until the mustard seeds begin to pop.

2. Add the ginger, cauliflower and green chilli. Stir-fry for 3–5 minutes.

3. Add the water to the wok with the salt, cover and cook for 5 minutes. Do not overcook or the cauliflower will go watery. Remove from the heat, add the yoghurt and serve immediately.

CAULIFLOWER DHAL

225g/8oz green lentils
1 large onion, sliced
5cm/2in piece of fresh root ginger, bruised
1 green chilli, deseeded and sliced (see page 22)
2 tablespoons sunflower oil
1 teaspoon black mustard seeds
2 teaspoons cumin seeds
3 cloves of garlic, chopped
2 teaspoons ground turmeric
1 small cauliflower, cut into florets
110g/4oz creamed coconut
290ml/½ pint boiling water
salt and freshly ground black pepper

1. Put the lentils into a saucepan with the onion, ginger and chilli. Cover with water and simmer for about 30 minutes until tender.
2. Meanwhile, heat the oil in a frying pan, add the mustard and cumin seeds and fry until they begin to pop. Add the garlic and cook over a low heat until soft, then stir in the turmeric. Add the cauliflower florets and stir until coated in the spice mixture.
3. Dissolve the creamed coconut in the boiling water and pour over the cauliflower. Season with salt and pepper. Cover and simmer until the cauliflower is tender.
4. When the lentils are cooked, remove the ginger and drain away any remaining liquid. Toss together with the cauliflower and serve hot.

CAULIFLOWER WITH WATERCRESS SAUCE

1 large cauliflower
salt and freshly ground black pepper
30g/1oz pumpkin seeds, toasted
30g/1oz Parmesan cheese, freshly grated (optional)

For the sauce
110g/4oz watercress
45g/1½oz butter
30g/1oz plain flour
a large pinch of cayenne paper
425ml/¾ pint milk
freshly grated nutmeg

1. Preheat the oven to 190°C/375°F/gas mark 5. Cut away the outer leaves and tough stalks from the cauliflower and break into florets. Boil in salted water for 8–10 minutes until just tender. Pour the cauliflower into a colander and leave to stand to allow the excess water to drain away.
2. Make the sauce: remove any tough stalks from the watercress and wash thoroughly. Chop and leave to dry on kitchen paper.
3. Melt the butter in a saucepan and add the flour and cayenne. Stir over the heat for 1 minute. Gradually add the milk and cook, stirring all the time, until thick and boiling. Stir in the watercress. Season with salt, pepper and nutmeg.
4. Place the cauliflower, stalks down, in an ovenproof dish. Pour over the sauce, covering all the cauliflower. Scatter with the pumpkin seeds and sprinkle with the cheese if used. Bake in the preheated oven for 30 minutes until piping hot and golden-brown on top.

KOHLRABI AND NAVY BEAN STEW

This can be served as an accompaniment to a variety of grains, such as couscous, millet or barley, and can be made in advance and reheated.

2–3 tablespoons olive oil
1 red onion, finely chopped
1 leek, trimmed and diced
1 clove of garlic, crushed
1 bulb of fennel, cored and diced
3 sticks of celery, sliced
1 carrot, diced
1 bay leaf
salt and freshly ground black pepper
2 medium purple kohlrabi, peeled and diced
1 quantity tomato sauce II (see page 527)
1 × 400g/14oz tin navy beans

1. Heat the oil in a large saucepan. Add the onion, leek and garlic, cover and soften for 2–3 minutes. Add the fennel, celery, carrot and bay leaf, season with salt and pepper and cover again. Cook over a low heat for 5–8 minutes or until the vegetables are beginning to soften. Add the kohlrabi and cook for a further 1–2 minutes.
2. Add the tomato sauce and simmer for 15–20 minutes or until the vegetables are tender and the sauce is quite thick. Add the beans and season to taste with salt and pepper. Heat the beans through in the sauce. Remove the bay leaf before serving.

NOTE: If navy beans are unavailable, substitute kidney beans.

KOHLRABI RAGOÛT

2–3 tablespoons olive oil
1 large aubergine, diced
2 red onions, finely diced
1 clove of garlic, crushed
salt and freshly ground black pepper
2 medium purple kohlrabi, peeled and diced
1 quantity tomato sauce II (see page 527)
20 black olives, pitted

1. Heat the oil in a saucepan, add the aubergine, onion and garlic and turn in the oil. Season with salt and pepper. Cover and cook over a low heat for 10 minutes or until soft, stirring regularly.
2. Add the kohlrabi and tomato sauce and simmer for 20 minutes or until the vegetables are tender and the sauce is quite thick. Add the olives and adjust the seasoning to taste.

KOHLRABI, CARROT AND CUMIN SALAD IN A LEMON DRESSING

2 large carrots
1 small kohlrabi, about 225g/8oz
a pinch of salt
2 tablespoons sunflower oil
4 teaspoons cumin seeds
4 teaspoons lemon juice

1. Peel the carrots and kohlrabi and coarsely grate them into long thin shreds, using a mandolin or food processor. Toss them together with the salt in a large bowl.
2. Heat the oil in a small saucepan. Add the cumin seeds and as soon as they begin to sizzle, tip them over the vegetables and add the lemon juice. Toss everything together once more and serve immediately.

BOK CHOI, SPRING ONION AND WATER CHESTNUT WONTONS IN A CLEAR CHINESE BROTH

SERVES 6

6 spring onions, trimmed
1 litre/1¾ pints summer vegetable stock (see page 530)
2.5cm/1in piece of fresh root ginger, peeled and thinly sliced
2 cloves of garlic, thinly sliced
225g/8oz bok choi, trimmed
110g/4oz canned water chestnuts, drained and finely chopped
1 tablespoon light soy sauce
1 teaspoon roasted sesame oil
1 tablespoon chopped fresh coriander
salt and freshly ground black pepper
24 wonton wrappers

1. Trim the white parts from 2 of the spring onions and chop roughly. Put the stock into a large saucepan and add the white spring onion, ginger and garlic. Bring to the boil, then lower the heat and simmer for 10 minutes.
2. Meanwhile, put the bok choi into a large, opened-out petal steamer, with the white stems underneath and the green leaves on top. Bring about 2.5cm/1in water to the boil in a large saucepan with a tight-fitting lid. Lower in the steamer, cover and cook for 4 minutes until the bok choi are tender.
3. Lift the bok choi on to a clean tea-towel and leave to drain and cool. Then slice one head across into strips 2.5cm/1in wide and set aside. Chop the remaining bok choi very finely and put into a mixing bowl. Chop the remaining spring onions finely and add them to the bok choi with the water chestnuts, soy sauce, sesame oil and coriander. Season to taste with salt and pepper.
4. Fill the wontons: put a heaped teaspoon of the bok choi mixture into the centre of each wonton wrapper. Brush very lightly with water around the filling, draw the edges up to make a pouch and twist in the middle to seal.
5. Bring a large saucepan of boiling water to the boil. Add the wontons and simmer for 4 minutes until cooked. Meanwhile, strain the vegetable stock to remove the flavourings, return it to the pan and bring back to the boil. Keep hot.
6. Drain the wontons and divide them between 6 warmed soup bowls. Add some of the reserved bok choi to each bowl, ladle over the hot stock and serve immediately.

STEAMED BOK CHOI WITH SESAME OIL AND SOY SAUCE

12 small heads of bok choi
4 teaspoons roasted sesame oil
2 tablespoons dark soy sauce

1. Remove any damaged leaves from each head of bok choi and neatly trim the bases. Put them into a large, opened-out petal steamer, with the white stems underneath and the green leaves on top.
2. Bring about 2.5cm/1in water to the boil in a large saucepan with a tight-fitting lid. Lower in the steamer, cover and cook for 4 minutes until the bok choi are tender.
3. Put the bok choi on to a warmed serving plate and sprinkle over the sesame oil and soy sauce.

SWISS CHARD QUICHE

110g/4oz shortcrust or wholemeal pastry (see page 521 or 522)
225g/8oz Swiss chard
45g/1½oz butter
1 medium onion, finely chopped
1 clove of garlic, crushed
salt and freshly ground black pepper
85g/3oz soft blue cheese, such as Dolcelatte or Gorgonzola
1 whole egg
1 egg yolk
150ml/¼ pint milk
150ml/¼ pint double cream
about 8 black olives, pitted and halved

1. Preheat the oven to 200°C/400°F/gas mark 6.
2. Roll out the pastry and use to line a 17cm/7in flan ring or dish. Chill for 45 minutes, then bake blind (see page 22). Lower the oven temperature to 180°C/350°F/gas mark 4.
3. Rinse, trim and chop the chard leaves and stalks. Melt the butter in a sauté pan, add the onion and fry over a low heat until soft and golden. Add the garlic and fry for 1 minute. Stir in the chard, season with salt and pepper and fry briskly for 3–4 minutes until just tender. Spoon into the cooked pastry base.
4. Remove the rind from the blue cheese and dot the cheese over the chard. Whisk the egg and egg yolk together with the milk and cream. Season with a little salt and plenty of pepper. Pour into the pastry case. Scatter the olives on top. Bake in the preheated oven for about 20–25 minutes until the filling is just set and golden-brown on top.

STIR-FRIED CHARD WITH GARLIC, BALSAMIC VINEGAR AND OLIVE OIL

This recipe should only be made with very fresh and young chard. It may be served simply as a side dish or scattered with toasted pinenuts or shavings of Parmesan cheese.

450g/1lb young Swiss chard or seakale beet
2 tablespoons olive oil
1 large red onion, chopped
2 cloves of garlic, chopped
2–3 teaspoons balsamic vinegar
salt and freshly ground black pepper

1. Wash the chard or seakale beet and pat dry with kitchen paper. Cut the leaves and stalks into bite-sized pieces, keeping the leaves and stalks separate.
2. Heat the oil in a heavy sauté pan or wok. Add the onion and toss over the heat until softened. Add the garlic and fry for 1 further minute. Add the chard or seakale beet stalks and toss over a medium heat until just tender. Toss in the leaves and cook for 1 minute.
3. Add balsamic vinegar and salt and pepper to taste. Serve immediately.

SWISS CHARD AND PROVOLONE LASAGNE

If you can't get hold of Swiss chard and provolone 'picante' cheese, use spinach and Parmesan cheese instead.

SERVES 6–8

900g/2lb Swiss chard, washed
30g/1oz butter, plus extra for greasing
225g/8oz fresh lasagne sheets
salt and freshly ground white pepper
55g/2oz Parmesan cheese, freshly grated

For the sauce
1 small onion, halved
4 cloves
900ml/1½ pints milk
2 fresh bay leaves
a large pinch of freshly grated nutmeg
2 sprigs of fresh thyme
1 teaspoon black peppercorns
70g/2½oz butter
70g/2½oz plain flour
55ml/2fl oz double cream
110g/4oz provolone 'piccante' cheese, coarsely grated

1. First make the sauce: stud the onion halves with the cloves and put them into a saucepan with the milk, bay leaves, nutmeg, thyme and peppercorns. Simmer for 5 minutes, then remove from the heat and set aside for at least 20 minutes to allow time for the flavours to infuse.

2. Bring the milk back to the boil, then strain through a sieve into a jug or clean pan. Melt the butter in a medium pan, add the flour and cook over a low heat for 2–3 minutes without colouring. Gradually stir in the hot milk and bring to the boil, stirring constantly, then leave to simmer over a very low heat for 10 minutes, stirring now and then, until very slightly reduced.

3. Meanwhile, prepare the Swiss chard: slice the green leaves away from the white stems, roll them up into bunches and cut them across into thin strips. Slice the stems across into pieces 1cm/½in wide and place them in a large, opened-out petal steamer. Bring about 2.5cm/1in of water to the boil in a large saucepan with a tight-fitting lid, lower in the steamer, cover and steam for 5 minutes or until almost tender. Uncover the pan, add the green leaves, cover again and steam for a further 3 minutes until both stems and leaves are cooked. Tip the chard into a colander and set aside. Grease a shallow 2.3 litre/4 pint ovenproof dish with butter.

4. Drop the lasagne sheets into a pan of boiling water, remove from the heat and leave to soak for 5 minutes. Drain well, then separate the sheets and leave to drain on a clean tea-towel.

5. Preheat the oven to 200°C/400°F/gas mark 6. Melt the butter in a pan, add the steamed chard and toss together for 1 minute. Season to taste with salt and pepper. Stir the cream and provolone cheese into the sauce and season with salt and pepper.

6. Layer the lasagne sheets, Swiss chard and cheese sauce in the prepared dish, finishing with a layer of cheese sauce. Sprinkle over the Parmesan cheese and bake in the preheated oven for 30 minutes until golden and bubbling.

SORREL, SPINACH AND ARTICHOKE RAGOÛT

SERVES 6

4 tablespoons olive oil
1 large onion, finely chopped
1 leek, trimmed and finely chopped
110g/4oz carrots, finely chopped
6 medium baby globe artichokes, about 675g/
    1½lb
a dash of lemon juice
4 cloves of garlic, sliced
150ml/¼ pint summer vegetable stock (see
    page 530)
150ml/¼ pint dry white wine
salt and freshly ground black pepper
110g/4oz spinach
110g/4oz sorrel or bok choi
2 tablespoons chopped chervil or tarragon

1. Heat the oil in a large, shallow pan with a
tight-fitting lid. Add the onion, leek and carrot
and cook, uncovered, over a low heat for about
30 minutes until very soft and golden.
2. Prepare the artichokes: slice off the tips and
stems. Pull away the thick outer leaves.
Immerse the artichokes in cold water with the
lemon juice added until ready to use. (See the
instructions on page 270 for the preparation of
medium artichokes.)
3. Stir the garlic into the onion mixture and
cook for 1 further minute. Add the stock and
wine and stir to remove any sediment from the
bottom of the pan. Season with salt and pepper.
Arrange the artichokes in a single layer on top
of the vegetables. Cover with greaseproof paper
and the lid and simmer very gently for about 45
minutes until the artichokes are almost tender.
4. Remove any tough stalks from the spinach
and sorrel or bok choi. Roll the leaves into tight
bundles and cut into 1cm/½in shreds. Scatter
the greens over the top of the artichokes with 1
tablespoon of the herbs. Cover again and cook
for a further 30 minutes until the artichokes are
very tender and the greens have reduced to a
rich sauce. Adjust the seasoning to taste and
sprinkle with the remaining herbs.

SORREL SALAD WITH RAW BEETROOT

2 handfuls of watercress or lamb's lettuce
85g/3oz sorrel
2 raw beetroot
1 tablespoon pumpkin seeds, toasted (see
    page 22)

For the dressing
1 clove of garlic, peeled
2 tablespoons walnut or hazelnut oil
2 tablespoons sunflower oil
1 tablespoon white wine vinegar
½ teaspoon sugar
2–3 teaspoons Dijon mustard
salt and freshly ground black pepper

1. Remove any tough stalks from the
watercress and sorrel. Wash and leave to dry on
kitchen paper.
2. Make the dressing: split the garlic clove with
the back of a knife. Put into a screwtop jar with
all the remaining dressing ingredients and shake
well.
3. Peel the beetroot and grate or shred as finely
as possible. (This is best done with the fine
grating blade of a food processor.) Toss
together with the green leaves and dressing,
discarding the garlic. Scatter with the pumpkin
seeds and serve immediately.

NOTE: Use baby spinach leaves if sorrel is not
available.

SPICY SPINACH AND COCONUT SOUP WITH YOGHURT, FRIED ONIONS, CHILLI AND GARLIC

For the soup
2 teaspoons coriander seeds
2 teaspoons cumin seeds
½ teaspoon black peppercorns
3 cloves
3 green cardamom pods, seeds only
2.5cm/1in cinnamon stick
¾ teaspoon ground turmeric
3 tablespoons clarified butter (see page 529)
1 large onion, quartered and thinly sliced
2.5cm/1in piece of fresh root ginger, peeled and
    finely grated
1 clove of garlic, crushed
2 medium-hot green Dutch chillies, thinly sliced
1.1 litres/2 pints summer vegetable stock (see
    page 530)
450g/1lb fresh spinach, washed and large stalks
    removed
200ml/7fl oz coconut cream
4 teaspoons lemon juice
freshly grated nutmeg
salt and freshly ground black pepper
110ml/4fl oz Greek yoghurt, to serve

For the fried shallot, chilli and garlic mixture
sunflower oil, for shallow-frying
4 large shallots, thinly sliced
2 cloves of garlic, thinly sliced
1 medium-hot red Dutch chilli, deseeded and
    thinly sliced (see page 22)

1. First prepare the fried shallot, chilli and garlic mixture: heat about 1cm/½in of oil in a large, deep frying pan to 180°C/350°F. Add the shallots and fry for about 3 minutes, stirring from time to time until they begin to colour. Add the garlic and chilli and fry for 1 further minute or until the shallots and garlic are crisp and nicely golden. Remove from the heat, lift the shallots, garlic and chilli out with a slotted spoon on to plenty of kitchen paper and leave to drain. Sprinkle with a little salt and set aside.

2. Make the soup: heat a dry, heavy frying pan over a high heat. Add the whole spices and shake them around for a minute or two until they darken slightly and start to release their aroma. Cool. Tip them into a spice grinder, add the turmeric and grind to a fine powder.

3. Heat the clarified butter in a large saucepan, add the onion and ginger and fry over a low heat until the onion is soft and lightly coloured. Stir in the garlic, chillies and ground spices and fry for a further 2 minutes. Add the stock and bring to the boil. Meanwhile, finely shred the spinach leaves.

4. Add the spinach to the pan and simmer for 5 minutes. Stir in the coconut cream, lemon juice and nutmeg, salt and pepper to taste.

5. Ladle the soup into warmed bowls. Add a good spoonful of yoghurt and then sprinkle generously with the fried shallot, chilli and garlic mixture.

NOTE: for a milder flavour, deseed the green chillies.

SPINACH GNOCCHI

450g/1lb spinach
30g/1oz butter
85g/3oz ricotta cheese
30g/1oz plain flour
1 tablespoon double cream
1 egg, beaten
45g/1½oz Parmesan cheese, freshly grated
salt and freshly ground black pepper
freshly grated nutmeg

1. Remove any tough stalks from the spinach and wash thoroughly. Lift the spinach, still wet, into a large saucepan. Cover and shake over the heat for 2 minutes or until tender. Drain well, squeeze out all the moisture and chop finely.
2. Melt half the butter in a heavy pan and add the spinach. Heat until any excess moisture has evaporated. Add the ricotta cheese and stir until melted. Turn the mixture into a bowl and beat in the flour, cream, egg and 30g/1oz of the Parmesan cheese. Season with salt, pepper and nutmeg. Cover and chill for 30 minutes.
3. With floured hands, roll the mixture into balls about the size of a walnut. Bring a large saucepan of water to the boil and turn down the heat. Preheat the grill to high. Drop the gnocchi into the water and simmer very gently for 5–10 minutes until firm. Lift out with a slotted spoon and drain on kitchen paper. Put into an ovenproof dish.
4. Melt the remaining butter and pour over the gnocchi. Scatter over the remaining Parmesan cheese and grill until golden-brown.

SPINACH AND RICOTTA CRESPOLINI

SERVES 4–6

For the pancakes
110g/4oz plain flour, sifted
¼ teaspoon salt
1 medium egg
1 medium egg yolk
290ml/½ pint milk
1 tablespoon oil, plus extra for cooking

For the tomato sauce
2 tablespoons olive oil
1 medium onion, finely chopped
1 large clove of garlic, crushed
1 × 400g/14oz can of chopped tomatoes
1 × 225g/8oz can of chopped tomatoes
2 sprigs of fresh thyme
2 bay leaves
salt and freshly ground black pepper

For the Parmesan cheese sauce
55g/2oz butter
35g/1¼oz plain flour
570ml/1 pint milk
55ml/2fl oz double cream
55g/2oz Parmesan cheese
salt and freshly ground white pepper

For the filling
2 tablespoons olive oil
1 clove of garlic, crushed
450g/1lb fresh spinach, washed and large stalks removed
250g/9oz ricotta cheese
30g/1oz Parmesan cheese, freshly grated
a pinch of freshly grated nutmeg

1. Make the pancakes: sift the flour and salt into a food processor or blender. Add the whole egg, egg yolk and milk and blend together to make a smooth batter with the consistency of single cream. Set aside for 30 minutes.
2. Heat a 17.5cm/7in non-stick frying pan over a medium to high heat. Brush the base with a little oil, pour in a little of the batter and swirl it

around so that it thinly coats the base of the pan. Cook for about 1 minute until lightly golden underneath, then turn the pancake over and cook for a few seconds more until marked with light brown spots. Slide the pancake on to a plate and repeat with the remaining batter to make 12 pancakes.

3. Make the tomato sauce: heat the oil in a medium saucepan. Add the onion and fry over a low heat for 7–8 minutes until soft but not browned. Add the garlic and fry for 1 further minute. Add the chopped tomatoes, thyme and bay leaves and simmer for 20–25 minutes, stirring from time to time, until well reduced and thickened. Discard the thyme and bay leaves and season to taste with salt and pepper.

4. Make the Parmesan cheese sauce: melt the butter in a medium saucepan, add the flour and cook over a low heat for 2–3 minutes without colouring. Gradually stir in the milk, bring to the boil and simmer gently over a very low heat for 2 minutes, stirring from time to time, until slightly reduced and thickened. Stir in the cream, most of the Parmesan cheese and salt and pepper to taste.

5. Make the filling: heat the oil in a large saucepan. Add the garlic and spinach and stir-fry over a high heat until the spinach has wilted down into the bottom of the pan. Tip into a colander and press out the excess liquid. Chop coarsely, transfer to a mixing bowl and leave to cool. Mix in the ricotta cheese, Parmesan cheese and salt, pepper and nutmeg to taste.

6. Preheat the oven to 190°C/375°F/gas mark 5. Spoon 1 heaped tablespoon of the filling in a short line across the centre of each pancake. Fold the sides of the pancakes over the ends of the filling, then roll each one up into a neat parcel.

7. Spread the tomato sauce over the base of a large, shallow ovenproof dish. Arrange the pancakes in the dish and pour over the Parmesan cheese sauce. Sprinkle over the remaining Parmesan cheese and bake in the preheated oven for 30–40 minutes until bubbling and golden-brown.

SPINACH AND FETA FILO PIE

450g/1lb spinach
30g/1oz butter
1 large onion, chopped
1 clove of garlic, crushed
¼ teaspoon ground cumin
¼ teaspoon ground cinnamon
225g/8oz feta cheese, crumbled or grated
110g/4oz pinenuts, toasted
2 eggs, beaten
salt and freshly ground black pepper
freshly grated nutmeg
4 tablespoons olive oil
1 quantity filo or strudel pastry (see page 523)
    or 10 sheets of bought filo pastry

1. Remove any tough stalks from the spinach and wash thoroughly. Lift the spinach, still wet, into a large saucepan, cover and toss over a medium heat for a few minutes until tender. Drain, squeeze out all the excess moisture, chop and put into a large mixing bowl.

2. Heat the butter in a frying pan, add the onions and fry over a low heat until golden-brown. Add the garlic and spices and fry for a further 2 minutes. Stir into the spinach. Add the cheese, pinenuts and eggs. Season with salt, pepper and nutmeg.

3. Preheat the oven to 180°C/350°F/gas mark 4. Brush a 20–22cm/8–9in shallow ovenproof dish with oil.

4. Take 5 sheets of pastry. Brush one side with oil and arrange in an overlapping layer in the dish with the excess pastry hanging over the sides.

5. Spoon the mixture into the pastry. Fold the overlapping pastry on top of the pie. Brush the remaining pastry with oil. Crumple up and arrange over the top so that the spinach filling is completely covered. Bake for about 30 minutes until the filling is set and the pastry is golden-brown.

SAAG (SPINACH) BHAJI WITH TOMATOES AND CUMIN

900g/2lb spinach, washed and large stalks
 removed
4 tablespoons sunflower oil or ghee
1 medium onion, finely chopped
2 medium-hot green chillies, finely chopped
3 cloves of garlic, finely chopped
2.5cm/1in piece of fresh root ginger, peeled and
 finely grated
2 teaspoons ground coriander
1 teaspoon ground cumin
1 teaspoon yellow mustard seeds
1 tomato, peeled, deseeded and diced
salt
cayenne pepper

1. Shred the spinach leaves and remove the excess water in a salad spinner. Heat 2 tablespoons of the oil or ghee in a large saucepan. Add a large handful of the spinach and stir-fry over a high heat until it begins to wilt into the bottom of the pan. Add another handful of spinach and continue in the same way until all the spinach is cooked. Tip it into a colander and press out the excess liquid. Set aside.
2. Heat the remaining oil or ghee in the pan, add the onion and fry over a low heat for 6–7 minutes until lightly golden. Add the chillies, garlic and ginger and fry for 1 minute. Add the spices and fry for 1 further minute.
3. Return the spinach to the pan with the tomato and toss over a high heat for about 1 minute until heated through. Serve as part of an Indian meal, or on its own with some spiced pilau rice (see page 359) and cucumber and mint raita (see page 513).

WILTED SPINACH WITH PINENUTS AND RAISINS

This dish makes a perfect accompaniment to couscous, pasta or baked potatoes for a quick dinner, or simply serve with crusty bread.

900g/2lb spinach
4 tablespoons olive oil
110g/4oz pinenuts
110g/4oz raisins
2–3 cloves of garlic, finely chopped
salt and freshly ground black pepper
freshly grated nutmeg

To serve
shavings of Parmesan cheese

1. Remove any tough stalks from the spinach. Wash thoroughly and shake dry.
2. Heat the oil in a large, shallow pan or wok. Add the pinenuts, raisins and garlic and fry briefly. Throw in the spinach and toss over the heat until it begins to wilt. Season with salt and plenty of pepper and nutmeg. Serve topped with Parmesan shavings.

WILTED SPINACH WITH ONION AND COCONUT MASALA

2 tablespoons groundnut or vegetable oil
55g/2oz butter
2 onions, sliced
3 cloves of garlic, crushed
55g/2oz creamed coconut
a good pinch of cayenne pepper
½ teaspoon ground turmeric
1 teaspoon ground coriander
2 teaspoons garam masala
about 2 tablespoons boiling water
salt and freshly ground black pepper
lemon juice
900g/2lb baby spinach leaves
30g/1oz flaked almonds, toasted, to garnish (see page 22)

1. Heat the oil in a sauté pan. Add the butter and when foaming, add the onions and fry over a low heat until deep golden-brown Add the garlic and fry for 1 further minute.
2. Meanwhile, chop the creamed coconut and add the cayenne, turmeric, coriander and garam masala. Mix to a loose paste with the water. Stir the paste into the onions, season with salt, pepper and lemon juice and cook for 5 minutes.
3. Remove any stalks from the spinach and wash thoroughly. Pile into a large saucepan, cover and shake over a medium heat for about 1 minute until the spinach has wilted. Drain well and season with salt and pepper.
4. Make a bed of spinach on 4 warm individual plates. Spoon the onion and coconut masala on top and scatter with the toasted almonds.

WARM SALAD OF SPINACH AND MUSHROOMS WITH PARMESAN CROÛTONS

450g/1lb baby spinach leaves
2 thick slices of white bread
sunflower or vegetable oil, for frying
30g/1oz Parmesan cheese, freshly grated
225g/8oz chestnut mushrooms
2 tablespoons walnut or hazelnut oil
salt and freshly ground black pepper
balsamic vinegar

1. Remove any tough stalks from the spinach, wash thoroughly and leave to dry on kitchen paper.
2. Remove the crusts from the bread and cut into 5mm/¼in cubes. Heat the oil in a frying pan and fry the bread cubes on both sides until golden-brown. Drain on kitchen paper and toss in the cheese. Set aside.
3. Slice the mushrooms thickly. Heat the nut oil in a heavy frying pan, add the mushrooms and fry briskly. Toss together with the spinach. Season with salt, pepper and vinegar. Add the Parmesan croûtons and serve immediately.

SPINACH SALAD WITH ORANGES AND ROASTED RED PEPPERS

225g/8oz baby spinach leaves
2 red peppers
2 tablespoons olive oil
2 oranges
½ red onion, finely chopped
salt and freshly ground black pepper
a large handful of fresh mint leaves
a dash of balsamic vinegar
a handful of pinenuts, toasted (see page 22)

1. Wash and dry the spinach leaves. Remove any tough stalks.
2. Preheat the grill to high. Cut the peppers in half and remove the stalks, pith and seeds. Rub the skin with a little oil and grill, cut side down, until black and blistered. Cover with a tea-towel and leave to cool, then peel and cut into slices.
3. Using a sharp knife, peel the oranges as you would an apple, removing all the pith and peel and saving the juice. Cut the orange into segments and put into a bowl with the sliced peppers, oil and onion. Season with salt and pepper.
4. Add the spinach and mint leaves to the bowl. Drizzle over a little vinegar and toss together. Transfer to a salad bowl and scatter over the pinenuts just before serving.

SPINACH AND WATERCRESS SALAD WITH PEARS AND PECORINO

about 150g/5oz mixed baby spinach leaves and
*   watercress*
55g/2oz walnut halves
1 pomegranate
1 tablespoon walnut oil
1 teaspoon pomegranate syrup (see page 19)
juice of ½ lemon
1 small clove of garlic, crushed
1 ripe comice pear
salt and freshly ground black pepper
45g/1½oz shavings of Pecorino or Parmesan
*   cheese*

1. Remove the tough stalks from the spinach and watercress, wash and pat dry on kitchen paper. Heat a heavy frying pan, add the walnuts and toast until browned, then chop coarsely and cool.
2. Cut the pomegranate in half and use the back of a teaspoon handle or a cocktail stick to ease the seeds into a large bowl with all the juice.
3. Stir in the walnut oil, pomegranate syrup, lemon juice and garlic. Peel, quarter, core and thickly slice the pear and toss it in the dressing.
4. Add the spinach, watercress and toasted walnuts. Season with salt and pepper and toss well. Scatter the Pecorino or Parmesan shavings on top before serving.

WILTED GREENS WITH SOY SAUCE

450g/1lb spring or mustard greens
4 tablespoons sesame oil
2 cloves of garlic, sliced
sweet soy sauce
salt and freshly ground black pepper
1 tablespoon sesame seeds, toasted (see page 22)

1. Wash the greens and shake dry. Cut into thick slices.
2. Heat the oil in a wok or large, heavy frying pan. Add the garlic and fry for 1 minute. Toss in the greens, taking care as they will crackle and spit. Toss over the heat for a few minutes until wilted but still bright green.
3. Add a good sprinkling of soy sauce, season with salt and pepper and scatter with sesame seeds. Serve immediately.

NOTE: Savoy cabbage is also delicious cooked in this way.

MIXED GREENS WITH BLACK-EYED BEANS

170g/6oz black-eyed beans, soaked overnight
140g/5oz leafy greens, such as baby spinach,
    Swiss chard, lamb's lettuce, nettles, young
    spring greens
2 bulbs of fennel
3 tablespoons olive oil
1 large onion, sliced
2 cloves of garlic, crushed
2 sprigs of fresh coriander, chopped
1 × 225g/8oz can of chopped tomatoes
½ teaspoon fennel seeds, toasted (see page 22)
290ml/½ pint summer vegetable stock (see
    page 530)
salt and freshly ground black pepper

1. Drain the beans, place in a saucepan and cover with fresh cold water. Bring to the boil, then simmer for 30 minutes until tender. Drain.
2. Remove any tough stalks from the greens and wash thoroughly. Trim the roots from the fennel and remove and discard the outer leaves. Slice the fennel thinly.
3. Heat the oil in a large saucepan. Add the onion and fennel and fry over a low heat for about 10 minutes until very soft and lightly coloured. Add the garlic and cook for 1 further minute.
4. Stir in the coriander, tomatoes, fennel seeds, stock and cooked beans. Season with salt and pepper. Partially cover with a lid and simmer for 10 minutes. Add the greens and simmer, uncovered, for 10 minutes until slightly reduced and well flavoured.

ROOTS AND TUBERS

Jerusalem artichokes • Beetroot • Carrots • Celeriac •
Parsnips • Potatoes • Sweet Potatoes • Radishes • Salsify •
Swede • Turnip

INTRODUCTION

In spite of their humble earthy appearance, root vegetables provide a wealth of flavour and substance for the cook. As they can survive the worst growing conditions and can be stored throughout winter, it is no wonder that they have become a staple food synonymous with comforting winter soups, stews and pies. Turnips, swede and carrots are traditional accompaniments to our national dishes and we serve potatoes with almost everything. Young root vegetables from the first crop of the season are thin-skinned and tender and have quite different characteristics to the older vegetables harvested later on. Store in a cool, airy place or in the refrigerator. Remove any plastic wrapping before storing.

Jerusalem artichokes are a delicious treat but they are tiresome to peel and have a bad reputation for inducing flatulence. The name is thought to have derived from the Italian *girasol*, meaning 'towards the sun', as they originated in North America and have no connection with Jerusalem. Choose firm, smooth artichokes for ease of peeling and immerse in acidulated water as once peeled they will turn brown if left standing. They are best used in soups but are also excellent sautéed in nut oil and scattered with herbs or sliced and boiled or steamed. Jerusalem artichokes can be stored in the refrigerator for up to 2 weeks but must be used before sprouting. The best are available between spring and summer.

Beetroot has had a much deserved revival in popularity in recent years. It has a fragrant, earthy flavour suitable for many a gourmet dish. Beetroot is traditionally known for its ruby colour, but depending on the level of the pigment may also be found with gold, white or

pink and white striped flesh. These varieties will probably only be available to keen vegetable gardeners but may be found from a specialist supplier. Mysteriously, beetroot is the only vegetable sold ready-cooked from greengrocers. This may be because of the long cooking time and the staining caused to hands and chopping board. Avoid packaged, vinegared beetroot as the subtle flavour is overpowered.

It is best to buy firm, medium-sized raw beetroots with the stalk attached as this will prevent the colour from bleeding during cooking. When boiling, make sure the beetroots are well covered with salted water and boil gently for 1–1½ hours until the skin will peel away easily. Beetroot can be baked, untrimmed and wrapped in kitchen foil, at 190°C/375°F/gas mark 5 for 1½–2 hours until tender. Finely shredded or grated raw beetroot is a colourful addition to a bowl of salad leaves. Lightly boiled multi-coloured beets, tossed in butter, lemon juice and parsley or with spring onion, black pepper and chilli, make a really special side dish. Beetroot contains iron, calcium and vitamins A and C. It is also high in fibre. Beetroot tops can be eaten as a green vegetable. They will keep in the refrigerator for about 3 days and beetroot for up to a week.

Carrots should be crisp, smooth and bright in colour. When the Romans introduced carrots to Britain they were red, violet or black. The bright orange carrots that we see today were developed by the Dutch. Summer carrots are slender and sweet and do not need peeling. Remove the feathery leaves before storing as they drain the moisture from the root. Older carrots need to be peeled and trimmed into sticks before cooking. Organic carrots are a great success story, costing little more than other carrots and tasting as carrots should. Carrots are rich in vitamin A and beta-carotene.

Celeriac is hard and knobbly with a delicate celery flavour that belies its rugged appearance. It needs to be peeled thickly. Once peeled it will discolour quickly so should be kept in acidulated water. Celeriac can be roasted or puréed with potatoes and is classically cut into fine matchsticks and coated in remoulade sauce.

Jicama is associated with Mexican cooking and is slowly making its way across the Atlantic to UK stores. It has crisp, juicy flesh. Jicama should be peeled and sliced or grated. It can be dressed with lime and chillies or used in salads. It discolours rapidly so cover with acidulated water during preparation. Jicama can be used as a substitute for mooli or kohlrabi. Choose firm, fresh vegetables with no bruises.

Parsnips have a distinctive, sweet flavour. They can be puréed, made into soups and also make excellent chips. Take care when adding parsnips to stews as that sweetness can overpower other flavours. Parsnips roasted in honey and butter are delicious sprinkled with a little lime juice and zest to balance the sweetness. Buy small to medium parsnips as the large ones are woody in the centre. Small parsnips do not need to be peeled.

Potatoes: It is remarkable that such a plain-looking vegetable as the potato can be so delicious. It is one of the most important world crops, easy to grow, cheap to buy and full of substance and energy. Our taste for potatoes appears to be tireless and there are hundreds of potato varieties with subtle differences in flavour and texture. Waxy potatoes hold their shape so are good for boiling and making salads while floury potatoes are more suited to baking and mashing. Choose firm potatoes with unblemished skins. Avoid any with green patches caused by exposure to light which develop toxins under the skin. These are not present in harmful quantities but can cause a bitter flavour. Potatoes are high in carbohydrates and vitamin C and contain some protein, fibre, minerals and vitamin B. Their repuutation for being fattening is due to the oil and butter that tastes so good and is added during the cooking – crisp, buttery baked potatoes and a bagful of freshly fried chips doused in vinegar are two of the great mainstays of British fast food. Plain baked, boiled or steamed potatoes are nutritious and low in fat. Potatoes are also used for thickening and for making bread and pizza bases.

SELECTION OF POTATO VARIETIES

NAME	CROP	USES	COMMENTS
ARRAN PILOT	First early.	Salads, chipped, baked.	White skin and flesh; waxy texture when cooked.
ASPERGE LA RATTE/ CORNICHON	Second early.	Salads, steamed.	Yellow skin; creamy flesh; waxy texture when cooked.
CARA	Main.	All rounder.	Large; round; white skin; pink eyes; creamy flesh; creamy texture when cooked.
CHARLOTTE	Second early	Salads, steamed, boiled.	Pale yellow skin and flesh; good flavour; waxy texture when cooked.

NAME	CROP	USES	COMMENTS
DESIRÉE	Main.	All rounder.	Red skin; pale yellow flesh; waxy texture when cooked.
ESTIMA	Second early.	Baked, chipped, boiled.	Pale yellow skin and flesh; waxy texture when cooked.
GOLDEN WONDER	Main.	Salads, baked, mashed.	Brown skin; pale yellow flesh; floury texture when cooked.
KING EDWARD	Main.	All rounder.	Large; pale skin with pink patches; creamy flesh; floury texture when cooked.
MARIS BARD	First early.	Salads, boiled, baked when mature.	White skin and flesh; waxy texture when cooked.
MARIS PIPER	Main.	All rounder.	Thin white skin; cream-coloured flesh; floury texture when cooked.
PENTLAND DELL	Main.	All rounder.	Long oval shape; white flesh and skin; firm texture when cooked.
PENTLAND JAVELIN	First early.	Salads, boiled, steamed.	Smooth white skin; white flesh; waxy texture when cooked.
PENTLAND SQUIRE	Main.	Baked, roasted, chipped, mashed.	White skin (russeted); white flesh; floury texture when cooked.
PINK FIR APPLE	Main.	Salads, boiled.	Pink skin; pinky-yellow flesh; new potato characteristics; waxy texture when cooked.
ROMANO	Main.	Baked, boiled, roasted, chipped.	Red skin; creamy flesh; waxy texture when cooked.
RECORD	Main.	Grown mainly for processing, such as crisps, waffles, etc.	Short oval; yellow skin; pigments on exposure to light; yellow flesh; firm; slightly waxy texture.
ULSTER SCEPTRE	First early.	Salads, boiled.	Elongated oval shape; white skin and flesh; very waxy; firm texture when cooked.
WILJA	Second early.	Boiled, baked, chipped.	Rough yellow skin; pale yellow firm flesh; slightly dry but firm texture when cooked.

MOST SUITABLE COOKING METHODS

BOILING	MASHING	BAKING	CHIPPING
Cara	Golden Wonder	Arran Pilot	Arran Pilot
Charlotte	King Edward	Cara	King Edward
Desirée	Maris Piper	Estima	Maris Piper
Estima	Pentland Dell	Golden Wonder	Maris Bard
King Edward	Pentland Squire	King Edward	Pentland Dell
Maris Piper	Romano	Maris Piper	Romano
Maris Bard	Wilja	Pentland Dell	Desirée
Pentland Javelin	Desirée	Romano	
Pentland Squire		Wilja	
Pink Fir Apple		Desirée	
Romano			
Ulster Sceptre			
Wilja			

ROASTING	SALADS	STEAMING	PROCESSING
King Edward	Asperge	Asperge	Record
Maris Piper	Desirée	Pentland Javelin	
Pentland Dell	Golden Wonder	Ulster Sceptre	
Romano	Maris Bard	Wilja	
Wilja	Pentland Javelin		
Desirée	Pentland Squire		
	Wilja		
	Charlotte		
	Pink Fir Apple		
	Ulster Sceptre		

Sweet potatoes originated from the Americas. They can have smooth or rough pinkish-brown skins. The flesh is cream to bright orange in colour and is mealy in texture. Sweet potatoes can be used in the same way as ordinary potatoes. Sometimes it is a good idea to mix the two together to balance the sweetness. They blend very well with spices.

Radishes come in many varieties. The best-known in this country is the small red turnip-like radish with crunchy, white juicy, peppery flesh. They are best used raw in crudités or salads. In Asia radishes are highly esteemed. They grow to giant sizes and are extremely pungent. Some come in bright shades of green with red flesh, others are red and green all the way through. These multi-coloured radishes make a beautiful salad but unless grown at home are difficult to find other than in Asian grocers. Mooli or daikon is the most easily available oriental radish. They should be finely sliced or shredded and can be used in stir-fries or to make sharp, refreshing relishes and side dishes.

Horseradish has a fierce pungency that has a reputation for clearing sinuses. It is never eaten as a vegetable but is used grated to make horseradish cream, sauce or relish. It is also used in mustard-making. The flavour of fresh horseradish far surpasses any horseradish in jars.

Salsify and **scorzonera** are discouraging-looking vegetables, but a real delicacy lies beneath their black, earthy exteriors. Boil them with their skins on for about 30 minutes, then peel. After peeling they are best roasted or sautéed with a sprinkling of lemon zest added at the end. Cold salsify or scorzonera can be tossed in French dressing or dipped in horseradish. If home-grown, the bittersweet leaves can be used in salad. The season is autumn to spring. Choose firm vegetables and store in a cool, dark place.

Swede is a very plain-looking vegetable but becomes a vibrant golden colour when cooked. It has a strong taste of winter with its pungent, peppery flavour of mild horseradish. It is a close relative of the turnip and sometimes their names are used interchangeably. In Scotland swedes are called neeps and in America rutabagas. Choose firm swede; size does not generally affect the flavour or texture. Organic swede gives the benefit of the full flavour. Swede can be roasted or mashed and is excellent in hearty soups and stews where it provides robust flavour without too much sweetness. It can be finely grated and used raw in salads.

Turnips are a close relation of swede and have a similar but more bitter peppery flavour. Turnip tops can be treated like spring greens. Turnips are best eaten young and small when they do not need to be peeled and can be simply boiled, glazed or roasted with a little stalk still attached. Main-crop turnips have a purplish tinge on their white skin. If they are larger than a tennis ball the flesh becomes soft and fibrous. They should be peeled and roasted, boiled, shredded and sautéed in butter, stir-fried or used in stews. Take care when blending them with other vegetables as the flavour can be overpowering.

Yams originated in Asia and spread via the slave trade to Africa and the Americas. They vary in colour from white and yellow to pinkish and purple. Small yams can be cooked in their skins but large ones must be peeled as they contain toxins below the skin. The yam is sometimes confused with **taro**, which is a similar tuber. It is a staple food of tropical areas and is known as dasheen in the Caribbean.

JERUSALEM ARTICHOKE SOUP WITH CURRY OIL

85g/3oz butter
1 medium onion, chopped
1 clove of garlic, crushed
560g/1lb 2oz Jerusalem artichokes, peeled and
*   cut into small chunks*
1 stick of celery, thinly sliced
860ml/1½ pints summer vegetable stock (see
*   page 530)*
salt and freshly ground black pepper

For the curry oil
150ml/¼ pint sunflower oil, plus 2 tablespoons
*   for frying*
1 large shallot, finely chopped
1 small clove of garlic, finely chopped
1 teaspoon peeled and finely chopped fresh root
*   ginger*
½ medium-hot red Dutch chilli, finely chopped
½ star anise
2 teaspoons medium curry powder (see
*   page 528)*
1 teaspoon tomato purée
thinly pared zest of ¼ lemon

1. First make the curry oil: heat 2 tablespoons oil in a small saucepan. Add the shallot, garlic, ginger, chilli, star anise and curry powder and fry over a low heat for 5 minutes, stirring from time to time, until the shallot is soft. Add the tomato purée and cook gently for 2 minutes. Stir in the remaining oil and the lemon zest and simmer very gently for 30 minutes. Leave to cool, then strain through a muslin-lined sieve. Store in a screwtop jar in the refrigerator. The oil will keep for up to 4 weeks.
2. Make the soup: melt the butter in a large saucepan. Add the onion and cook over a low heat for 5 minutes until soft but not browned. Add the garlic, artichokes and celery, cover and cook gently for a further 10 minutes. Add the stock and ½ teaspoon of salt to the pan and bring to the boil, then cover and simmer for 20 minutes until the artichokes are very tender.
3. Purée the soup in batches in a food processor or blender. Return the soup to the rinsed-out pan, season to taste with salt and pepper and bring back to the boil. Ladle into warmed soup bowls and swirl 1 tablespoon of the curry oil into each.

BEETROOT, COCONUT AND LIME SOUP

30g/1oz unsalted butter
1 medium onion, sliced
2 stalks of lemon grass, trimmed and sliced
800g/1¾lb cooked beetroot
290ml/½ pint summer vegetable stock (see
*   page 530)*
salt and freshly ground black pepper
1 × 400ml/14oz can of coconut milk
juice of 1 lime

To garnish
4 tablespoons crème fraîche
grated zest of 1 lime

1. Melt the butter in a saucepan and when foaming, add the onion and lemon grass and fry over a low heat until softened.
2. Peel and trim the beetroot. Cut into large chunks. Put into the pan with the stock. Season with salt and pepper and bring to the boil, then lower the heat and simmer for 20 minutes.
3. Purée the soup in a food processor or blender with the coconut milk.
4. Pour the soup into the rinsed-out pan, add the lime juice and season to taste with salt and pepper. Reheat and serve in warmed soup bowls, each topped with a spoonful of crème fraîche and a little lime zest.

BORSCHT WITH CURD CHEESE AND DILL PIROSHKIS

4 large raw beetroot
1 large carrot
1 parsnip
1 leek
3 bay leaves
4 tablespoons lemon juice
4 allspice berries
10 black peppercorns
7g/¼oz dried porcini mushrooms
570ml/1 pint summer vegetable stock (see
    page 530)
1.7 litres/3 pints water
salt and freshly ground black pepper

For the piroshkis
110g/4oz curd cheese
30g/1oz butter, melted and cooled
1 medium egg, beaten
1½ tablespoons chopped fresh dill
225g/8oz flour quantity puff pastry (see
    page 522)
butter, for greasing
plain flour, for rolling

To garnish
4 tablespoons soured cream
4 sprigs of fresh dill

1. First make the soup: peel and quarter the beetroot. Peel the carrot and parsnip and cut them into chunks. Trim and slice the leek. Put the beetroot, carrot, parsnip, the white part of the leek, bay leaves, lemon juice, allspice berries, peppercorns, dried mushrooms and stock into a large saucepan. Add the water and bring to the boil. Lower the heat, partially cover and simmer for 2 hours.

2. Meanwhile, make the piroshkis: put the curd cheese, melted butter and 2 tablespoons of the beaten egg into a small bowl and beat together until smooth. Beat in the dill and salt and pepper to taste. Reserve the remaining beaten egg for glazing.

3. Grease a baking tray lightly with butter. Roll out the pastry thinly on a light floured worktop and cut out 24 × 7.5cm/3in discs. Place a heaped teaspoon of the filling into the centre of each. Dampen half the edge with a little water, bring the edges together and press together well to seal. Crimp the edges between your fingers to give an attractive finish and lay the piroshkis on the prepared baking sheet. Cover loosely with clingfilm and chill.

4. When the soup is almost ready, preheat the oven to 220°C/425°F/gas mark 7. Brush the piroshkis with the remaining beaten egg and bake in the preheated oven for 15 minutes until puffed up and golden.

5. Strain the soup through a fine sieve into a clean pan. Discard the solids left in the sieve. Bring the soup back to a simmer and season to taste with salt and pepper. Ladle into warmed soup bowls and garnish with the soured cream and sprigs of dill. Serve with the warm piroshkis.

BEETROOT AND HORSERADISH MOUSSE

butter, for greasing
200g/7oz cooked beetroot
1 teaspoon ground cumin
2 eggs, beaten
1 egg yolk
85g/3oz fresh white breadcrumbs
2 tablespoons creamed horseradish
290ml/½ pint milk
55ml/2fl oz double cream
salt and freshly ground black pepper

1. Preheat the oven to 170°C/325°F/gas mark 3. Grease an 860ml/1½ pint soufflé dish with butter and line the base with a circle of non-stick baking paper.
2. Peel and grate the beetroot and mix with the cumin.
3. Mix the eggs, egg yolk, breadcrumbs, horseradish, milk and cream together in a bowl. Season well with salt and pepper.
4. Quickly stir in the beetroot and pour into the prepared soufflé dish. Place in a bain-marie and cook in the preheated oven for 45–60 minutes until the centre is set.
5. Remove from the oven and allow to cool. Turn the mousse out and serve with a leafy salad.

RED FLANNEL HASH

450g/1lb potatoes
salt and freshly ground black pepper
2–4 tablespoons sunflower or vegetable oil
1 large red onion, chopped
225g/8oz raw beetroot, peeled and grated
1 red pepper, deseeded and finely chopped

1. Peel the potatoes and cut them into large chunks. Cook in boiling salted water for about 5 minutes. Drain and set aside for about 30 minutes to dry.
2. Heat 2 tablespoons oil in a large frying pan, add the onion and cook on a low heat for 2 minutes to soften. Add the potatoes and fry briskly until starting to brown, then add the beetroot and red pepper.
3. Season well with salt and pepper and continue to fry over a medium heat, stirring from time to time, until the beetroot and pepper are tender. The vegetables should be crisp and slightly mashed together, rather like bubble and squeak. Serve hot.

BABY BEETROOT WITH GINGER, LIME AND MINT

340g/12oz raw baby beetroot
5cm/2in piece of fresh root ginger, peeled and chopped
grated zest and juice of 1 lime
salt
2 tablespoons white wine vinegar
55g/2oz caster sugar
2 tablespoons chopped fresh mint

1. Scrub the beetroot with a stiff brush, trim and cut away any blemishes. Cut them in half and put into a saucepan with the ginger and lime juice. Add enough water barely to cover with a good pinch of salt. Bring to the boil, then lower the heat, cover and simmer for about 20 minutes, stirring occasionally, until the beetroot is tender.
2. Remove the beetroot from the pan, increase the heat and reduce the liquid to 5mm/¼in. Reserve.
3. Put the vinegar and sugar together into a small, heavy pan. Dissolve the sugar over a low heat, then boil until the sugar caramelizes and is dark brown and bubbly. Pour on the reserved beetroot liquor. It will hiss and splutter, so take care. Stir until the lumps of caramel have melted. Add the lime zest and mint and pour over the beetroot. Serve warm or cold.

BALSAMIC-ROASTED BEETROOT WITH GARLIC AND THYME

900g/2lb raw beetroot
6 tablespoons olive oil
3 tablespoons balsamic vinegar
3 tablespoons lemon juice
3 cloves of garlic, finely chopped
1 teaspoon sea salt flakes
1 teaspoon black peppercorns, coarsely crushed
3 sprigs of fresh thyme
6 tablespoons water

1. Preheat the oven to 220°C/425°F/gas mark 7. Trim the stalks and roots from the beetroot, then peel. Leave whole if small or cut in half or into quarters if larger. Put the beetroot into a small roasting tin.
2. Mix the oil, vinegar, lemon juice, garlic, salt and pepper together in a small bowl. Pour the mixture over the beetroot and turn a few times to coat well. Spread the beetroot out in a single layer over the base of the tin and tuck in the sprigs of thyme.
3. Roast the beetroot in the preheated oven for 40 minutes. Remove, turn the beetroot over a few times and then sprinkle over the water. Roast for a further 30–40 minutes until tender. Serve hot.

NOTE: Beetroot cooking times can vary enormously so check for tenderness every so often – they may only take a total of 30 minutes to cook if very young.

HOT ROASTED BEETROOT WITH CRÈME FRAÎCHE AND WHOLEGRAIN MUSTARD DRESSING

675g/1½lb raw baby beetroot
1 tablespoon vegetable oil
2 tablespoons rice wine vinegar
salt and freshly ground black pepper

For the sauce
5 tablespoons crème fraîche
1 tablespoon wholegrain mustard
grated zest and juice of ½ lemon
2 tablespoons finely chopped fresh chives

1. Wash the beetroot and cook in plenty of boiling salted water for 20 minutes. Allow to cool slightly.
2. Preheat the oven to 200°C/400°F/gas mark 6. Peel the beetroot and place them in a roasting tin. Toss with the oil, vinegar, salt and pepper and roast in the preheated oven for 20 minutes or until tender.
3. Mix the crème fraîche, mustard, lemon zest and juice together in a small bowl. Stir in the chives and season to taste with salt and pepper.
4. Transfer the hot beetroot to a warmed serving dish. Drizzle over the dressing and serve.

CRUNCHY BAKED GOAT'S CHEESE ON A BEETROOT AND ROCKET SALAD

4 × 1cm/½in thick slices of firm goat's cheese,
*   such as chèvre log*
55g/2oz fresh white breadcrumbs
2 teaspoons olive oil
6 black olives, pitted and finely chopped
4 finely shredded fresh basil leaves
sea salt flakes and coarsely ground black pepper

For the salad
450g/1lb cooked beetroot
4 teaspoons extra virgin olive oil, plus extra to
*   serve*
4 teaspoons balsamic vinegar, plus extra to serve
30g/1oz rocket leaves

1. Preheat the oven to 230°C/450°F/gas mark 8. Peel and thinly slice the beetroot and spread the slices over the base of a shallow dish. Sprinkle over the oil, vinegar, sea salt flakes and pepper and set aside.
2. Line a baking tray with foil and brush with a little oil. Put the slices of goat's cheese on top and set aside.
3. Put the breadcrumbs into a small bowl, add the oil, olives, basil and salt and pepper and mix well.
4. Spoon the breadcrumb mixture on to the top of each slice of goat's cheese and press it out gently so that it covers the slices in an even layer. Bake at the top of the preheated oven for 7–8 minutes until the crumbs are crisp and golden and the cheese has softened slightly.
5. Overlap the beetroot slices in the centre of 4 large individual plates and drizzle over any remaining dressing. Carefully lift the slices of goat's cheese off the baking tray and place in the centre of the beetroot. Drizzle a little more oil and vinegar around the outside of each plate and sprinkle with a few sea salt flakes and some pepper. Scatter over the rocket leaves and serve warm.

PINK RUSSIAN SALAD

225g/8oz raw beetroot, topped and tailed
225g/8oz waxy new potatoes, scraped
salt and freshly ground black pepper
110g/4oz French beans, topped and tailed
110g/4oz small carrots, peeled
55g/2oz gherkins, finely chopped
1½ tablespoons capers in brine, drained and
  rinsed
2 teaspoons extra virgin olive oil
2 teaspoons red wine vinegar
55ml/2fl oz lemon mayonnaise (see page 512)

1. Put the beetroot and potatoes into separate
pans of cold salted water. Bring to the boil, then
cook the beetroot for 20–30 minutes and the
potatoes for 15 minutes or until both are tender.
Cook the beans in boiling salted water for 2–3
minutes. Transfer to a colander with a slotted
spoon and refresh under cold running water.
Add the carrots to the pan, bring back to the
boil and cook for 10 minutes or until tender.
Drain and refresh under cold running water.
When the potatoes and beetroot are cooked,
drain and leave to cool.
2. Peel the beetroot and cut into 1cm/½in
pieces. Cut the potatoes into similar-sized
pieces. Cut the beans into 2.5cm/1in pieces and
thinly slice the carrots.
3. Put all the cooked vegetables into a bowl
and add the chopped gherkins and capers. Mix
the oil, vinegar and mayonnaise together in a
small bowl and season to taste with salt and
pepper. Gently stir the dressing into the
vegetables, taking care not to break up the
potatoes too much, and adjust the seasoning if
necessary. Chill for 1 hour before serving.

BEETROOT AND RED ONION SALAD

1 tablespoon olive oil
1 red onion, finely chopped
salt and freshly ground black pepper
450g/1lb raw beetroot
4 tablespoons water
balsamic vinegar
roughly chopped fresh thyme
roughly chopped fresh parsley

1. Heat the oil in a frying pan with a lid. Add
the onion, season with salt and pepper and
cook over a low heat for 3–4 minutes, until
softened.
2. Peel and top and tail the beetroot and cut it
into small cubes. Add to the pan, turn in the hot
oil and add the water. Cover and cook over a
low heat until the beetroot is just soft. Remove
the lid and reduce any excess liquid.
3. Add vinegar and salt and pepper to taste.
Mix in plenty of herbs and allow to cool. Serve
at room temperature.

SLICED BEETROOT SALAD WITH APPLE HORSERADISH

4 medium cooked beetroot
1 bunch of watercress
1 teaspoon poppy seeds, toasted (see page 22)
1 tablespoon French dressing (see page 528)

For the apple horseradish
1 small Granny Smith apple
juice of ½ lemon
2 tablespoons double cream, lightly whipped
2 teaspoons freshly grated horseradish
about ¼ teaspoon Dijon mustard
salt and freshly ground black pepper

1. First make the apple horseradish: peel, core and coarsely grate the apple. Toss in the lemon juice. Fold into the cream in a bowl and gently stir in the horseradish and mustard. Season with a little salt and pepper and leave to stand for about 30 minutes to allow the flavours to blend.
2. Peel and slice the beetroot and arrange in an overlapping layer on 4 individual plates.
3. Wash the watercress and remove any tough stalks. Pat dry, then toss together with the poppy seeds and French dressing. Arrange a pile of watercress on each plate and serve with a spoonful of apple horseradish.

NOTE: This recipe is also delicious made with sliced ripe pears, instead of apple.

BEETROOT SALAD WITH SOURED CREAM

450g/1lb small raw beetroot
salt and freshly ground black pepper
white wine vinegar
1 tablespoon walnut or hazelnut oil
a good pinch of ground cumin
a good pinch of paprika
a little caster sugar
5fl oz/¼ pint soured cream
1 tablespoon roughly chopped fresh flat-leaf
*   parsley, to garnish*

1. Top and tail the beetroot and put into a saucepan with enough salted water to cover. Simmer for about 1 hour until tender.
2. Meanwhile, make the dressing by mixing together a dash of vinegar, the oil, cumin and paprika. Season with salt, pepper, and sugar to taste.
3. Drain the beetroot and, when cool enough to handle, peel and quarter. Pour the dressing over while still warm, leave to cool and then chill.
4. Just before serving, arrange the beetroot on a serving plate and drizzle over the soured cream. Sprinkle with the parsley.

BABY BEETROOT WITH CREAM CHEESE AND HERBS

1 tablespoon raspberry vinegar
5 tablespoons olive oil
1 small clove of garlic, crushed
1 tablespoon chopped fresh oregano
salt and freshly ground black pepper
450g/1lb baby or cooked beetroot, peeled
110g/4oz cream cheese
2 tablespoons Greek yoghurt
grated zest of 1 lime
1 tablespoon lime juice
1 tablespoon chopped fresh chives
1 tablespoon chopped fresh mint

1. Mix together the vinegar, 4 tablespoons of the oil, the garlic, oregano, salt and pepper. Add to the beetroot in a bowl and leave to marinate for 1–2 hours.
2. Mix together the cream cheese, yoghurt, lime zest and juice, chives, mint and the remaining oil. Season well with salt and pepper.
3. To serve: put neat spoonfuls of the cream cheese mixture on to each plate and surround with the beetroot. If the beetroot are large, cut into slices and overlap on the plate.

BEETROOT AND SESAME SALAD

450g/1lb cooked beetroot
1 tablespoon sesame seeds, toasted (see page 22),
* to garnish*

For the dressing
1 teaspoon Dijon mustard
2 tablespoons lemon juice
2 tablespoons olive oil
2 tablespoons sesame oil
salt and freshly ground black pepper
1 tablespoon chopped fresh chives
1 tablespoon chopped fresh thyme

1. Peel the beetroot and cut into 1cm/½in cubes. Place in a bowl.
2. Make the dressing: whisk the Dijon mustard, lemon juice, oils, salt and pepper together. Add the chives and thyme.
3. Pour the dressing over the beetroot and mix well. Leave to stand for 1 hour.
4. Serve scattered with the sesame seeds.

CARROT AND CORIANDER SOUP WITH PUFF PASTRY TOPS

675g/1½lb carrots, peeled and sliced
1 onion, finely chopped
15g/½oz butter
1 bay leaf
860ml/1½ pints summer vegetable stock (see
   page 530) or water
salt or freshly ground black pepper
1 tablespoon chopped fresh parsley
1 tablespoon chopped fresh coriander
4 tablespoons double cream
225g/8oz flour quantity puff pastry (see
   page 522)
beaten egg, to glaze

1. Put the carrots and onion into a large, heavy saucepan with the butter. Sweat for 10 minutes or until beginning to soften. Add the bay leaf, stock, salt and pepper. Bring to the boil, then simmer as slowly as possible for 25 minutes. Remove the bay leaf.
2. Purée the soup with the parsley and coriander in a food processor or blender and push through a sieve into a clean saucepan. Check the consistency. If a little thin, reduce by rapid boiling, if a little thick, add extra water.
3. Add the cream and season to taste with salt and pepper. Leave to get completely cold.
4. Preheat the oven to 220°C/425°F/gas mark 7.
5. Put 200ml/7fl oz of the cold soup into 4 large ovenproof soup bowls.
6. Roll out the pastry very thinly and cut out 4 circles a little larger than the rim of the bowl (allowing about 1cm/½in extra). Brush a little of the beaten egg around the edge of each circle and use this to attach the pastry to the bowl, pressing firmly to make a good seal. Trim off any uneven edges. Brush the pastry with remaining egg glaze. Chill well in the refrigerator.
7. Place the soup bowls on a baking sheet and bake near the top of the preheated oven for 20 minutes until well risen and golden-brown.

CARROT AND CELERIAC GRATIN

SERVES 6

450g/1lb carrots
340g/12oz celeriac
55g/2oz butter
2 tablespoons crème fraîche
salt and freshly ground black pepper
freshly grated nutmeg
55g/2oz wholemeal or granary breadcrumbs
110g/4oz goat's cheese
1 tablespoon chopped fresh flat-leaf parsley

1. Peel the carrots and celeriac and cut into 2.5cm/1in cubes. Steam for about 30 minutes until tender. Purée in a food processor or blender, then add the butter, crème fraîche, salt, pepper and nutmeg and process again until smooth. Spoon into a wide gratin dish.
2. Preheat the oven to 190°C/375°F/gas mark 5.
3. Put the breadcrumbs into a bowl and crumble in the goat's cheese. Add the parsley and season with salt and pepper. Scatter over the top of the vegetable purée. Bake in the preheated oven for 20 minutes until the topping is melted and browned and the purée piping hot.

CARROT AND COURGETTE 'PASTA' WITH ROCKET PESTO

3 medium carrots
3 medium courgettes
1 tablespoon olive oil
1 tablespoon lemon juice
4 tablespoons rocket pesto (see page 526)
salt and freshly ground black pepper

1. Peel the carrots and top and tail them. Using a potato peeler, slice them into ribbons.
2. Top and tail the courgettes and using a potato peeler, slice them into ribbons.
3. Heat the oil in a wok or large, heavy frying pan. When very hot, add the carrots and stir-fry for 1 minute. Add the courgettes and stir-fry for 1 further minute. Add the lemon juice and remove from the heat.
4. Stir in the rocket pesto and season well with salt and pepper.

NOTE: Do not cook for too long or the courgettes will become watery.

CARROT AND CORIANDER FRITTERS WITH GREEN YOGHURT SAUCE

2 eggs
85ml/3fl oz milk
15g/½oz butter, melted
100g/3½oz plain flour
½ teaspoon baking powder
1½ teaspoons ground cumin
½ teaspoon ground turmeric
¼ teaspoon cayenne pepper
¾ teaspoon salt
340g/12oz carrots, coarsely grated
2 teaspoons coriander seeds, coarsely crushed
6 spring onions, trimmed and chopped
3 tablespoons chopped fresh coriander
sunflower oil, for shallow-frying

For the sauce
5 tablespoons Wholemilk natural yoghurt
2 shallots, finely chopped
1cm/½in piece of fresh root ginger, finely grated
2 green jalapeño chillies, halved and deseeded (see page 22)
¾ teaspoon caster sugar
20g/¾oz fresh mint leaves
55g/2oz fresh coriander leaves
½ teaspoon salt

1. First, make the green yoghurt sauce: put all the ingredients into a food processor and blend until smooth. Spoon into a bowl, cover and chill for 1 hour.
2. Preheat the oven to 110°C/225°F/gas mark ¼ and line a baking tray with kitchen paper.
3. Make the fritters: beat the eggs, milk and melted butter together in a mixing bowl. Beat in the flour, baking powder, cumin, turmeric, cayenne and salt.
4. Pile the carrots into the centre of a clean tea-towel and squeeze out the excess liquid. Stir them into the batter with the coriander seeds, spring onions and fresh coriander.
5. Pour 1cm/½in oil into a large, deep frying pan and heat it to 180°C/350°F. Drop 4 large

spoonfuls of the batter into the oil and flatten the mixture slightly with a spoon. Fry the fritters for about 1½ minutes on each side until crisp and golden-brown. Lift on to the paper-lined tray and keep warm in the oven while you cook the remainder in the same way. Serve warm with the green yoghurt sauce.

SPICED CARROTS WITH CRÈME FRAÎCHE

450g/1lb carrots
salt and freshly ground black pepper
15g/½oz butter
1 teaspoon ground cumin
3 tablespoons crème fraîche
2 tablespoons milk
1 tablespoon sultanas (optional)
2 teaspoons chopped fresh mint

1. Peel the carrots and cut crossways into 5cm/2in pieces. Slice each piece lengthways. Boil the carrots in salted water until tender but still retaining a little crunch.
2. Drain the carrots. Melt the butter in the pan, add the cumin and fry for 1 minute. Stir in the crème fraîche and milk and heat gently. Return the carrots to the pan and toss in the crème fraîche mixture. Season with salt and pepper. Stir in the sultanas, if used, and serve sprinkled with the mint.

CARROTS WITH CUMIN AND LEMON

900g/2lb large carrots
290ml/½ pint spicy vegetable stock (see page 531)
1 teaspoon cumin seeds, toasted (see page 22)
1 teaspoon black mustard seeds, toasted (see page 22)
grated zest and juice of 1 lemon
2 kaffir lime leaves
1 teaspoon of caster sugar
salt and freshly ground black pepper
1 tablespoon chopped fresh coriander

1. Peel the carrots and cut them in half lengthways, then crossways into 2.5cm/1in pieces. Put into a large saucepan with the stock, which should come about halfway up the carrots. Add the cumin and mustard seeds, lemon zest and juice, lime leaves, sugar and a pinch of salt.
2. Bring to the boil, then lower the heat and simmer, covered, for 10–15 minutes until the carrots are tender but still retaining a little crunch. Season with pepper and toss with the coriander before serving.

STIR-FRIED CARROTS WITH HORSERADISH CREAM

450g/1lb carrots
2–3 tablespoons soured cream
about 1 tablespoon fresh grated horseradish
salt and freshly ground black pepper
1 tablespoon sesame oil
1 tablespoon sunflower or vegetable oil
1 tablespoon poppy seeds
2 teaspoons chopped fresh mint

1. Peel the carrots and cut them into 3cm/1½in pieces crossways, then slice thinly lengthways.
2. Mix together the soured cream and horseradish to taste. Season with salt and pepper.
3. Heat the oils in a wok or large, heavy frying pan. Add the carrots, season with salt and pepper and toss over the heat until tender but still retaining a little crunch. Toss with the poppy seeds and mint. Spoon into a warmed serving dish and dot with spoonfuls of the horseradish cream.

SWEET GLAZED BABY CARROTS WITH GINGER

150ml/¼ pint water
1 teaspoon caster sugar
grated zest and juice of ½ lemon
2 teaspoons peeled and grated fresh root ginger
15g/½oz butter
salt and freshly ground black pepper
350g/12oz baby carrots, washed well or scraped
1 tablespoon chopped fresh mint

1. Put the water, sugar, lemon zest and juice, ginger, butter, salt and pepper into a saucepan. Bring to the boil, then add the carrots, cover and cook for 5 minutes.
2. Remove the lid and reduce the liquid until the carrots are sticky and glazed. Add the mint, adjust the seasoning to taste and serve immediately.

CARROT AND SWEDE MASH WITH ROASTED SEED BUTTER

450g/1lb carrots
675g/1½lb swede
2 teaspoons coriander seeds
1 teaspoon cumin seeds
85g/3oz unsalted butter, melted
15g/½oz pumpkin seeds
15g/½oz sunflower seeds
salt and freshly ground black pepper
2 tablespoons roughly chopped fresh coriander

1. Bring a large saucepan of salted water to the boil. Peel and roughly chop the carrots. Peel and dice the swede. Add the carrots and swede to the pan and return to the boil, then lower the heat to a simmer. Cook for 20–25 minutes or until very tender.
2. Meanwhile, dry-fry the coriander and cumin seeds in a small frying pan until they release their aroma and begin to pop. Transfer the seeds to a bowl and crush lightly with the end of a rolling pin. Add the melted butter and set aside.
3. In the same pan, dry-fry the pumpkin and sunflower seeds until lightly browned. Set aside.
4. Drain the cooked carrots and swede thoroughly and mash roughly with a fork. Strain the roasted seed butter (it may be necessary to reheat it at this stage) through a muslin-lined sieve over the mashed vegetables. Discard the seeds.
5. Stir the pumpkin and sunflower seeds into the mash and season well with salt and pepper. Transfer to a warmed serving dish and sprinkle with the chopped coriander before serving.

CARROT, MINT AND GINGER SALAD

450g/1lb carrots
2 shallots, finely chopped
3 tablespoons chopped fresh mint
2.5cm/1in piece of fresh root ginger, peeled and
*   grated*
2 tablespoons mustard seeds, toasted (see
*   page 22)*
1 tablespoon demerara sugar
4 tablespoons lime juice
2 tablespoons olive oil
salt and freshly ground black pepper

1. Peel and coarsely grate the carrots. Mix with the shallots, mint, ginger, mustard seeds and sugar.
2. Mix the lime juice and oil together and add to the carrots. Season well with salt and pepper.
3. Chill for 30 minutes before serving.

NOTE: If the salad is left for too long it can become watery. If you want to make it in advance, keep it covered and leave out the dressing until 30 minutes before serving.

CARROT, POPPY SEED AND ALMOND SALAD

SERVES 6

110g/4oz blanched almonds
675g/1½lb carrots
1 tablespoon blue poppy seeds

For the dressing
1½ teaspoons white wine vinegar
½ teaspoon Dijon mustard
2 tablespoons olive oil
salt and freshly ground black pepper

1. Put the blanched almonds into a bowl and cover them with hot water. Leave them to soak for 10 minutes.
2. Preheat the grill to high. Drain the almonds and cut them lengthways into long slivers. Spread them over a baking tray and toast them under the grill, shaking them from time to time, until they are nicely golden. Set aside and leave to cool.
3. Peel and coarsely grate the carrots, by hand, on a mandolin or in a food processor, and put them into a mixing bowl. Make the dressing: whisk the vinegar and mustard together in a small bowl, then gradually whisk in the oil and salt and pepper to taste. Stir the almonds, poppy seeds and dressing into the carrots just before serving.

CELERIAC PURÉE

2 medium potatoes
225g/8oz celeriac
150ml/¼ pint milk
55g/2oz butter
salt and freshly ground white pepper

1. Wash and peel the potatoes and place them in a saucepan of cold salted water. Bring to the boil, cover and simmer for about 25 minutes until tender.
2. Meanwhile, wash the celeriac, peel it and cut into chunks. Simmer slowly in the milk for about 20–30 minutes, or until tender.
3. Mash the celeriac with its milk, which should by now be much reduced.
4. Drain the potatoes and mash or sieve them. Place the potatoes and celeriac together in a clean heavy saucepan. Beat over a low heat, adding the butter as you mix. Season to taste with salt and pepper.
5. Pile into a warmed serving dish and serve immediately.

TWICE-BAKED CELERIAC AND STILTON SOUFFLÉS

225g/8oz celeriac
salt and freshly ground black pepper
55g/2oz butter, plus extra for greasing
1 clove of garlic, crushed
55g/2oz plain flour
a pinch of cayenne pepper
290ml/½ pint milk
110g/4oz Stilton cheese, crumbled
4 medium eggs, separated
150ml/¼ pint double cream
30g/1oz Parmesan cheese, freshly grated

1. Peel the celeriac, cut it into quarters and slice. Cook in boiling salted water for about 30 minutes until tender. Drain and purée in a food processor or blender.
2. Preheat the oven to 200°C/400°F/gas mark 6. Grease 8 × 8.5cm/3½in ramekin dishes with butter.
3. Melt the butter in a saucepan, add the garlic and fry for 30 seconds. Stir in the flour and cayenne and fry for 1 minute. Gradually add the milk, stirring all the time, until the mixture is smooth and boiling.
4. Remove the pan from the heat and stir in the Stilton cheese and the celeriac purée. Add the egg yolks and season with a little salt and plenty of pepper.
5. Beat the egg whites to soft peaks. Stir 2 tablespoons of the egg white into the celeriac mixture, then carefully fold in the remainder, using a large metal spoon. Spoon into the prepared ramekin dishes on a baking tray and bake in the preheated oven for 15 minutes. Cool, then chill.
6. To serve, preheat the oven to 200°C/400°F/gas mark 6. Grease a shallow ovenproof dish with butter.
7. Turn the soufflés out of the ramekins into the dish. Season the cream with salt and pepper and spoon over the soufflés. Sprinkle with a little Parmesan cheese and bake in the preheated oven for 10–12 minutes until puffed up and golden-brown. Serve immediately.

CELERIAC TIMBALES WITH TARRAGON BEURRE BLANC

For the timbales
oil, for brushing
340g/12oz celeriac, prepared weight, diced
150ml/¼ pint milk
1 egg, beaten
85g/3oz Lancashire cheese, grated
2 tablespoons double cream
1 tablespoon chopped fresh tarragon
salt and freshly ground white pepper

For the sauce
150ml/¼ pint summer vegetable stock (see page 530)
2 tablespoons gin
1 shallot, thinly sliced
3 tablespoons double cream
110g/4oz unsalted butter, chilled and diced
1 tablespoon chopped fresh tarragon
lemon juice

1. Preheat the oven to 190°C/375°F/gas mark 5. Brush 4 ramekin dishes or dariole moulds lightly with oil and put a disc of oiled greaseproof paper in the bottom of each.
2. Simmer the celeriac in the milk in a small saucepan until it is completely soft but still holding its shape. Drain away any remaining milk. Set aside to cool slightly.
3. Purée the celeriac in a food processor or blender. Add the egg, cheese and cream and process pulse quickly to blend. Add the tarragon and season to taste with salt and pepper. Divide the mixture between the prepared ramekin dishes or moulds.
4. Bake the timbales in a bain-marie in the preheated oven for 10–15 minutes or until the tops are light golden-brown and the mixture is set. Remove from the hot water and keep warm for 5–10 minutes before unmoulding.
5. Make the sauce: put the stock, gin and shallot into a small saucepan. Bring to the boil and reduce by half. Add the cream and boil again to reduce to about 4 tablespoons. Whisk in the chilled butter piece by piece. Add the tarragon and season to taste with salt, pepper

and lemon juice.
6. Turn the timbales out on to 4 warmed individual plates and spoon some of the sauce around. Serve immediately, with the remaining sauce handed separately.

CELERIAC MASH WITH APPLE AND WATERCRESS

900g/2lb celeriac
salt and freshly ground black pepper
lemon juice
85g/3oz butter
2 tablespoons crème fraîche
110g/4oz watercress
2 Cox's apples
55g/2oz walnut halves

1. Peel and slice the celeriac. Boil in salted water with a squeeze of lemon juice for about 30–40 minutes until very tender. Drain and leave to dry.
2. Mash the celeriac by passing it through a vegetable mill, or purée in a food processor or blender. Melt 55g/2oz of the butter in a pan, add the celeriac and reheat gently. Stir in the crème fraîche and season with salt and pepper.
3. Remove any tough stalks from the watercress, rinse and pat dry with kitchen paper. Remove the cores from the apples and slice into rings. Melt the remaining butter in a sauté pan, add the apple and fry over a medium heat until lightly golden and tender. Stir in the watercress and walnuts and season with salt and pepper. Toss over the heat briefly until just wilted.
4. Place a mound of celeriac mash on 4 individual plates and pile the apple and watercress on top.

CELERIAC AND MUSTARD SEED SALAD

1 tablespoon sunflower oil
1 tablespoon yellow mustard seeds
2 tablespoons Dijon mustard
1 teaspoon white wine vinegar
1 teaspoon lemon juice
55ml/2fl oz mayonnaise
55ml/2fl oz soured cream
salt and freshly ground black pepper
1 large head of celeriac
110g/4oz gherkins, cut into long, thin matchsticks
2 tablespoons chopped fresh parsley

1. Heat the oil in a small frying pan with a lid. Add the mustard seeds, cover and cook until they begin to pop. Remove from the heat and as soon as the popping has subsided, uncover and pour the oil and seeds into a mixing bowl. Add the mustard, vinegar, lemon juice, mayonnaise and soured cream and stir together well. Season to taste with salt and pepper.
2. Peel the celeriac and grate it into very long, thin shreds by hand, on a mandolin or in a food processor. You should be left with about 340g/12oz prepared celeriac.
3. Stir the celeriac into the dressing with the gherkins and half the parsley. Sprinkle with the remaining parsley.

SPICY PARSNIP SOUP WITH PARSNIP CRISPS AND SOURED CREAM

For the soup
450g/1lb parsnips
55g/2oz butter
1 medium onion, thinly sliced
1 large clove of garlic, crushed
2 teaspoons mild curry powder
1.1 litres/2 pints summer vegetable stock (see page 530)
150ml/¼ pint single cream
4 heaped tablespoons soured cream
salt and freshly ground black pepper
1 tablespoon chopped fresh parsley, to garnish

For the parsnip crisps
1 teaspoon cumin seeds
1 medium parsnip
sunflower oil, for frying

1. First make the soup: peel the parsnips and cut them into small chunks. Melt the butter in a large saucepan and add the onion, garlic and parsnips. Cover and cook over a low heat for 10 minutes.
2. Uncover the pan, stir in the curry powder and cook for 1 minute. Add the stock and bring to the boil, then cover again and simmer for 30 minutes or until the parsnips are very tender.
3. Meanwhile, make the parsnip crisps: heat a dry, heavy frying pan over a high heat. Add the cumin seeds and shake them around for a few seconds until they darken slightly and begin to release their aroma. Tip them into a mortar or spice grinder and grind them to a fine powder. Set aside.
4. Peel the parsnip and cut it lengthways into long, very thin strips, by hand or on a mandolin. Heat a small amount of oil for deep-frying in a small saucepan to 190°C/375°F. Add the parsnip strips a few at a time and fry for 1–1½ minutes until crisp and golden. Lift out with a slotted spoon and leave to drain on kitchen paper. When cool, toss with some of the roasted ground cumin and salt to taste.

5. Purée the soup in batches in a food processor or blender. Reurn to the pan and stir in the single cream and salt and pepper to taste. Reheat and ladle into warmed soup bowls. Add a spoonful of the soured cream to each bowl and pile a few of the parsnip crisps on top. Serve sprinkled with a little parsley.

PARSNIP AND APPLE SOUP

2 tablespoons olive oil
1 medium onion, chopped
1 clove of garlic, crushed
170g/6oz cooking apple
450g/1lb parsnips
170g/6oz potato
75ml/2½fl oz dry white wine
570ml/1 pint summer vegetable stock (see
  page 530)
salt and freshly ground black pepper
150ml/¼ pint milk
2 tablespoons crème fraîche
chopped fresh chives, to garnish

1. Put the oil into a large saucepan, add the onion and garlic and cook over a very low heat, covered, for 10 minutes, making sure the onion does not brown.
2. Peel and chop the apple, parsnips and potato. Add the apple and parsnips to the pan and cook for a further 5 minutes.
3. Add the wine, bring to the boil and reduce by half, then pour in the stock and add the potato. Season carefully with salt and pepper. Bring to the boil, then lower the heat and simmer gently for about 20 minutes or until the vegetables are very soft.
4. Purée the soup in a food processor or blender and pass through a sieve if a very smooth result is required. Add enough milk to achieve the consistency of thick cream.
5. Adjust the seasoning to taste and stir in the crème fraîche. Serve hot in warmed soup bowls, sprinkled with chives.

GINGERED PARSNIP AND GARLIC SOUP

450g/1lb parsnips
4 cardamom pods
1 teaspoon coriander seeds
a walnut-sized piece of fresh root ginger, peeled
  and chopped
15g/¼oz butter
1 small bulb of garlic, peeled
1 litre/1¾ pints milk
salt
cayenne pepper
150ml/¼ pint soured cream
½ bunch spring onions, trimmed and chopped

1. Peel the parsnips and cut them into chunks.
2. Crush the cardamom pods and remove the seeds. Put them into a mortar with the coriander seeds and crush. Add the ginger and crush to a paste.
3. Melt the butter in a large pan, add the garlic and fry for a few minutes to soften. Stir in the ginger paste and fry for 1 further minute. Add the parsnips and milk. Season with salt and cayenne. Simmer for 30–40 minutes until the parsnips and garlic are very soft.
4. Purée the soup in a food processor or blender. Add the soured cream and reheat without boiling. Adjust the seasoning to taste and stir in the spring onion.

PARSNIP AND PARMESAN SOUFFLÉ

SERVES 6

melted butter, for greasing
dried white breadcrumbs
340g/12oz parsnips
1 tablespoon sunflower oil
45g/1½oz butter
45g/1½oz plain flour
290ml/½ pint milk
55g/2oz Parmesan cheese, freshly grated
3 egg yolks
salt and freshly ground black pepper
4 egg whites

1. Brush 6 ramekin dishes with melted butter and dust with the breadcrumbs.
2. Peel the parsnips and cut into 5mm/¼in dice. Cook in boiling salted water until tender. Drain very well.
3. Mash half the cooked parsnips with a potato masher or fork.
4. Heat the oil in a frying pan, add the remaining diced parsnips and cook until lightly browned and crisp. Drain on kitchen paper.
5. Preheat the oven to 200°C/400°F/gas mark 6.
6. Melt the butter in a saucepan, add the flour and cook over a low heat for about 1 minute, stirring occasionally. Remove from the heat.
7. Gradually add the milk, stirring constantly. Return to the heat and bring to the boil, then lower the heat and cook for 2–3 minutes.
8. Pour the sauce into a large bowl, add the mashed parsnips, Parmesan cheese and egg yolks and mix well. Stir the diced parsnip into the mixture. Season well with salt and pepper.
9. Whisk the egg whites until stiff but not dry. Fold carefully into the parsnip mixture, using a large metal spoon.
10. Pour the mixture into the prepared ramekin dishes. Bake in the preheated oven for 15–20 minutes until well risen and brown on top. Serve immediately.

PARSNIP CAKES WITH GARLIC BORLOTTI BEANS

For the cakes
340g/12oz potatoes, cooked and mashed
340g/12oz parsnips, cooked and mashed
1 tablespoon roughly chopped fresh oregano
2 tablespoons roughly chopped fresh parsley
30–55g/1–2oz Parmesan cheese, freshly grated
salt and freshly ground black pepper
flour, for shaping
1 egg, beaten
dried white breadcrumbs
sunflower oil, for frying

For the sauce
150ml/¼ pint olive oil
2 cloves of garlic, thinly sliced
1 × 200g/7oz tin borlotti beans
6 sprigs of fresh oregano
balsamic vinegar

1. Mix the mashed vegetables together in a bowl, add the herbs and cheese, season to taste with salt and pepper and mix well. Divide into 8 even-sized pieces and with floured hands, shape into cakes. Chill.
2. Dip the cakes first into the beaten egg, then coat evenly with the breadcrumbs. Chill. Repeat the coating once more, then chill for at least 10 minutes.
3. Heat enough oil in a frying pan to come halfway up the parsnip cakes. Fry the cakes on both sides until golden-brown. Drain on kitchen paper and sprinkle lightly with salt. Keep warm in a low oven.
4. Make the sauce: heat the oil in a frying pan with the garlic over a low heat until the garlic just begins to turn golden-brown. Add the cooked beans and heat through. Tear off the oregano leaves and add to the sauce with a dash of vinegar. Season to taste with salt and pepper.
5. Divide the warm beans between 4 individual plates and put 2 parsnip cakes on each plate. Serve immediately.

NOTE: Once fried, the parsnip cakes can be cooked and frozen. To reheat, put into an oven preheated to 200°C/400°F/gas mark 6 for 10–15 minutes.

PARSNIP AND PARSLEY CAKES WITH SUN-DRIED TOMATO SAUCE

For the cakes
675g/1½lb parsnips
225g/8oz floury potatoes, such as Maris Piper
15g/½oz butter
1 egg yolk
30g/1oz fresh white breadcrumbs
15g/½oz Parmesan cheese, finely grated
2 tablespoons chopped fresh flat-leaf parsley
salt and freshly ground black pepper
plain flour, for coating
sunflower oil, for drying

For the sauce
30g/1oz sun-dried tomatoes in oil, drained and
    chopped (oil reserved)
1 medium onion, finely chopped
2 cloves of garlic, crushed
2 tablespoons sun-dried tomato paste
1 × 200g/7oz can of chopped tomatoes
150ml/¼ pint summer vegetable stock (see
    page 530)

1. First make the parsnip and parsley cakes: peel the parsnips and potatoes and cut them into chunks. Cook them in boiling salted water for 20 minutes until tender. Drain and leave until the steam has died down, then return to the pan and mash until smooth. Beat in the butter, egg yolk, breadcrumbs, cheese, parsley and salt and pepper to taste. Chill the mixture for 30 minutes.
2. Meanwhile, make the sun-dried tomato sauce: heat 1 tablespoon of the oil from the jar of sun-dried tomatoes in a saucepan. Add the onion and fry over a low heat for 4–5 minutes until soft. Add the garlic and cook for 2 minutes. Add the sun-dried tomato paste, sun-

dried tomatoes, chopped tomatoes and stock and simmer for 15–20 minutes until slightly thickened. Season to taste with salt and pepper and keep warm.
3. Divide the parsnip and potato mixture into 8 even-sized pieces. Dip each one into a little flour and with well-floured hands, shape into 7.5cm/3in flat discs.
4. Heat a thin layer of oil in a large, non-stick frying pan. Add 4 of the parsnip cakes and fry them for about 3 minutes on each side until crisp and golden. Lift out and keep hot in a low oven while you cook the remainder in the same way. Serve with the sun-dried tomato sauce.

PARSNIP MASH WITH FRIZZLED ONIONS

675g/1½lb parsnips
225g/8oz floury potatoes, such as Maris Piper
30g/1oz butter
½ teaspoon garam masala
salt and freshly ground black pepper

For the onions
150ml/¼ pint sunflower oil
2 medium onions, thinly sliced

1. First make the parsnip mash: peel the parsnips and potatoes and cut them into large chunks. Cook in boiling salted water for 20 minutes until tender.
2. Meanwhile, make the frizzled onions: heat the oil in a large, deep frying pan. Add the onions and fry over a high heat, stirring regularly, until crisp and richly golden. Lift them out with a slotted spoon on to kitchen paper, toss with a little salt and keep warm in a low oven.
3. Drain the parsnips and potatoes and leave them until the steam has died down. Return them to the pan and mash until smooth. Beat in the butter, garam masala and salt and pepper to taste. Pile into a warmed serving dish and serve with the frizzled onions.

NOTE: 110g/4oz Brussels sprouts, finely shredded, may be fried and added to the frizzled onions.

ROASTED HONEY PARSNIPS WITH HORSERADISH GREENS

675g/1½lb parsnips
30g/1oz butter
1 tablespoon clear honey
110g/4oz flat beans or French beans
110g/4oz sprouting broccoli
225g/8oz Brussels sprouts or Savoy cabbage,
    finely shredded
170g/6oz baby spinach leaves
200ml/7fl oz crème fraîche
2 teaspoons grated fresh horseradish
salt and freshly ground black pepper

1. Preheat the oven to 220°C/425°F/gas mark 7.
2. Peel the parsnips. Cut them in half lengthways and then into 1cm/½in sticks. Parboil in salted water for 2 minutes. Drain and set aside to dry.
3. Put the butter into a roasting tin and melt on top of the stove. Stir in the honey and mix together. Toss the parsnips in the honey mixture until coated all over. Bake in the preheated oven for 30 minutes, turning from time to time, until tender and golden-brown.
4. Top and tail the beans and cut on the diagonal into 2.5cm/1in pieces. Trim the rough stalks from the broccoli. Trim and halve the Brussels sprouts. Remove any tough stalks from the spinach and wash thoroughly.
5. Shortly before the parsnips are cooked, steam the Brussels sprouts for 4 minutes. Add the beans and broccoli and steam for a further 4 minutes, then add the spinach and steam for a further 2 minutes.
6. Set the steamed vegetables aside and drain the water from the base of the steamer. Put the crème fraîche, horseradish and 2–3 tablespoons of the vegetable water into the pan and heat through without boiling. Season with salt and pepper.
7. Serve the parsnips on 4 warmed individual plates with the greens piled on top and the creamed horseradish drizzled over.

BUTTERED PARSNIPS WITH LAMB'S LETTUCE AND SPICED KUMQUATS

The kumquats used in this recipe make a very good pickle or side dish.

1 tablespoon white wine vinegar
55ml/2fl oz water
5cm/2in cinnamon stick
½ teaspoon pickling spice
55g/2oz sugar
110g/4oz kumquats
450g/1lb parsnips
55g/2oz unsalted butter
1 teaspoon ground cumin
110g/4oz lamb's lettuce
salt and freshly ground black pepper

1. Preheat the oven to 200°C/400°F/gas mark 6.
2. Put the vinegar, water, cinnamon stick, pickling spice and sugar into a small pan. Heat slowly until the sugar has dissolved, then simmer for 5 minutes. Top and tail the kumquats and slice thickly, discarding the seeds. Put the kumquats into the sugar syrup and simmer for 30 minutes until the fruit is tender and translucent. Leave to stand in the syrup.
3. Peel the parsnips and cut them into wedges. Cook in boiling salted water for 3 minutes, drain and leave to dry in a colander. Melt the butter in a small roasting tin. Add the cumin and fry for 1 minute. Toss the parsnips in the spicy butter until thoroughly coated. Bake in the preheated oven for 30 minutes until golden-brown and tender.
4. Drain the kumquats from any remaining syrup and discard the cinnamon stick. Toss the hot parsnips together with the lamb's lettuce and season with salt and pepper. Serve with a spoonful of spiced kumquats on the side.

POTATO SOUP WITH TRUFFLE OIL AND BLACK OLIVES

900g/2lb floury potatoes, such as Maris Piper
110g/4oz butter
2 large onions, thinly sliced
2 bay leaves
salt and freshly ground white pepper
85ml/3fl oz double cream
55g/2oz black olives, pitted
2 tablespoons truffle oil

1. Peel the potatoes and slice them very thinly by hand, on a mandolin or in a food processor. Melt the butter in a large saucepan, add the onions and bay leaves and cook over a low heat, stirring from time to time, for 7–8 minutes until soft but not browned.
2. Add the sliced potatoes to the pan and stir well. Cook over a low heat for 3–4 minutes until the potatoes start to break up a little. Add 1 teaspoon of salt and 1.1 litres/2 pints of boiling water. Bring back to the boil, cover and simmer for 40 minutes.
3. Remove the bay leaves and liquidize the soup in batches until smooth. Stir in the cream and a little more boiling water if necessary to give the soup a good consistency. Season to taste with salt and pepper.
4. Cut the olives into thin strips. Ladle the soup into warmed soup plates and drizzle over a little of the truffle oil. Scatter with the olive strips and serve.

CHEESY HERB AND POTATO TART IN A WHOLEMEAL SESAME CRUST

255g/9oz floury potatoes, such as Maris Piper
45g/1½oz butter
340g/12oz onions, finely chopped
2 cloves of garlic, crushed
170g/6oz Cheddar cheese, finely grated
3 tablespoons chopped fresh parsley
salt and freshly ground black pepper

For the pastry
110g/4oz plain flour
110g/4oz wholemeal flour
½ teaspoon salt
150g/5oz chilled unsalted butter, diced
15g/½oz sesame seeds, lightly toasted (see page 22)
1½–2 tablespoons cold water
butter, for greasing
plain flour, for rolling
1 egg white

1. First make the pastry: sift the flours and salt into a mixing bowl or food processor. Add the butter and work together until the mixture resembles fine breadcrumbs. Stir in the sesame seeds, add the water and stir with a round-bladed knife until the mixture comes together into a ball.
2. Grease a 20cm/8in loose-based flan tin 4cm/1½in deep with butter. Turn the pastry on to a lightly floured worktop and knead briefly until smooth. Roll out, using a little more flour, into a 25cm/10in disc and use to line the prepared tin. Prick the pastry here and there with a fork and chill for 20 minutes.
3. Preheat the oven to 200°C/400°F/gas mark 6. Bake the pastry case blind in the preheated oven for 15 minutes (see page 22). Remove the paper and beans and return to the oven for 5 minutes. Remove once more and brush the base with a little egg white. Return to the oven for 1 further minute. Remove and increase the oven temperature to 220°C/435°F/gas mark 7.

4. Peel the potatoes and cut them into even-sized chunks. Cook in well-salted boiling water for 20 minutes until tender. Meanwhile, melt the butter in a medium saucepan, add the onions and garlic and cook over a medium heat for 7–8 minutes, stirring from time to time, until very soft but not browned.

5. Drain the potatoes and leave until the steam has died down, then return them to the pan and mash until smooth. Beat in the onions, half the cheese, the parsley and salt and pepper to taste.

6. Spread the mixture into the baked pastry case and sprinkle over the remaining cheese. Bake in the preheated oven for 20–25 minutes until golden.

CREAMY NEW POTATO AND PUFF PASTRY PIE

SERVES 6–8

30g/1oz butter
225g/8oz flour quantity puff pastry (see page 522)
plain flour, for rolling
675g/1½lb large new potatoes, scraped
salt and freshly ground black pepper
1 large egg, beaten
150ml/¼ pint single cream
150ml/¼ pint double cream
4 cloves of garlic, finely chopped
¼ nutmeg, freshly grated
½ small onion, finely chopped
2 tablespoons chopped fresh fines herbes (chervil, tarragon, parsley and chives)

1. Grease a 20cm/8in loose-based sandwich tin 5cm/2in deep with half the butter. Preheat the oven to 230°C/450°F/gas mark 8. Cut the pastry in half and roll one piece out on a lightly floured worktop into a 30cm/12in disc. Use to line the base and sides of the prepared tin.

2. Thinly slice the potatoes by hand, on a mandolin or in a food processor. Drop them into a saucepan of boiling salted water, bring back to a vigorous boil and then drain. Refresh briefly under cold running water to prevent the potatoes from cooking any further.

3. Set aside 1 tablespoon of the beaten egg for glazing. Put the remainder into a jug and beat in the creams, garlic, nutmeg and salt and pepper. Arrange a thin layer of potatoes in the bottom of the pastry-lined tin, sprinkle over a little onion, herbs and salt and pepper, then pour over a little of the egg and cream mixture. Continue to layer up the ingredients in this way, finishing with a layer of potatoes. Dot the top layer of potatoes with small pieces of the remaining butter.

4. Roll out the remaining pastry on a lightly floured worktop into a disc slightly larger than the top of the tin. Brush the edge of the pie with a little water, cover with the disc of pastry and press the edges together well to seal. Trim away the excess pastry and crimp the edges between your fingers to give the pie an attractive finish.

5. Brush the top of the pie with the reserved egg and lightly score into a diamond pattern with the tip of a small, sharp knife, taking care not to cut too deeply into the pastry. Cut a small hole in the centre of the lid.

6. Bake in the centre of the preheated oven for 40 minutes, protecting it with a sheet of greaseproof paper after about 15 minutes to prevent it from getting too brown. Remove the pie from the oven and leave it to rest for 10 minutes. Then carefully remove it from the tin and place on a serving plate. Serve cut into wedges.

RED POTATO BAKE

900g/2lb red potatoes
salt and freshly ground black pepper
150ml/¼ pint olive oil, plus extra for brushing
3 cloves of garlic, chopped
2 teaspoons wholegrain mustard
1 large red onion, cut into wedges
4 tomatoes, peeled and quartered (see page 22)
170g/6oz Brie or Camembert cheese, cut into
*   slices*
torn fresh basil leaves

To serve
crusty bread

1. Preheat the oven to 190°C/275°F/gas mark 5.
2. Scrub the potatoes and parboil in salted water for 10 minutes. Drain and cut into slices. Set aside.
3. Mix together the oil, garlic and mustard and season with salt and pepper. Toss the potato slices in the dressing, making sure that all the slices are coated.
4. Arrange half the potatoes in an ovenproof dish. Scatter over the onions and tomatoes and then arrange the remaining potatoes on top. Brush a sheet of greaseproof paper with oil and use to cover the dish. Bake in the preheated oven for about 1½ hours until the vegetables are very tender.
5. Remove the paper and arrange the cheese on top of the potatoes. Return to the oven for 15–20 minutes until the cheese has melted. Scatter with basil leaves and serve with crusty bread.

POTATO AND CABBAGE GRATIN

For a less rich dish leave out the Gruyère cheese and simply sprinkle the grated Parmesan on top.

675g/1½lb new potatoes
butter, for greasing
1 clove of garlic, crushed
290ml/½ pint double cream
225g/8oz Savoy cabbage, shredded
1 tablespoon chopped fresh marjoram
salt and freshly ground black pepper
55g/2oz Gruyère cheese, grated
1 tablespoon freshly grated Parmesan cheese
cayenne pepper
dry English mustard

1. Wash the potatoes and cook them in boiling water until just tender. Drain and cut into halves or quarters depending on size.
2. Preheat the oven to 200°C/400°F/gas mark 6. Grease an ovenproof dish with butter.
3. Stir the garlic into the cream and mix together with the potatoes, cabbage and marjoram. Season with salt and pepper.
4. Spoon half the potato mixture into the base of the dish. Sprinkle the Gruyère cheese on top and cover with the remaining potato. Season the Parmesan cheese with a pinch each of cayenne and dry English mustard and sprinkle over the top.
5. Cover the dish with kitchen foil and bake in the preheated oven for 30 minutes. Remove the foil and bake for a further 10–15 minutes until the top is golden-brown.

POTATO STOVIES WITH SORREL

To make a main meal of this dish, top with poached eggs and season with a dash of Tabasco.

900g/2lb red potatoes
2 tablespoons olive oil
1 medium onion, sliced
150ml/¼ pint winter vegetable stock (see page 530)
salt and freshly ground black pepper
225g/8oz sorrel
freshly grated nutmeg

1. Peel the potatoes, cut them in half lengthways and slice.
2. Heat the oil in a heavy saucepan, add the onion and fry over a low heat until softened. Stir in the potatoes and turn until coated in oil. Add the stock and season with salt and pepper. Cover with a sheet of greaseproof paper gently pressed down on top of the potatoes and cover tightly with the lid. Cook over a very low heat for 20 minutes until tender. Shake the pan from time to time to make sure that the potatoes do not stick.
3. Meanwhile, remove any tough stalks from the sorrel, wash and shake dry. Add to the potatoes, increase the heat and cook briskly until the sorrel has wilted and any excess moisture has evaporated. Stir occasionally to prevent the potatoes from sticking. Adjust the seasoning to taste and add some grated nutmeg.

NOTE: Use baby spinach leaves or rocket if sorrel is not available.

OVEN-BAKED POTATO CAKES WITH MUSHROOMS AND THYME

The potato cakes make a substantial main course. Serve with a leafy green salad.

oil, for brushing
450g/1lb floury potatoes, such as Maris Piper
55g/2oz butter
1 egg yolk
salt and freshly ground black pepper
freshly grated nutmeg
plain flour, for shaping
chopped fresh flat-leaf parsley, to garnish

For the filling
450g/1lb mushrooms
1 tablespoon olive oil
30g/1oz butter
2 cloves of garlic, chopped
1 teaspoon chopped fresh thyme
lemon juice
1 tablespoon dry sherry

1. Preheat the oven to 200°C/400°F/gas mark 6. Brush a baking tray with oil.
2. Peel and quarter the potatoes and cook them in boiling salted water until tender.
3. Drain the potatoes and return to the pan. Mash over a low heat. Remove from the heat and add the butter and egg yolk. Season with salt, pepper and nutmeg and beat well.
4. Divide the mixture into 8. With floured hands shape into flat cakes about 10cm/4in in diameter. Place on the baking sheet and bake in the preheated oven for 15 minutes. Turn, using a fish slicer, and bake for a further 15 minutes.
5. About 10 minutes before the potato cakes are ready, make the filling: cut the mushrooms into chunky pieces. Heat the oil in a heavy frying pan. Add the butter and when foaming, briskly fry the mushrooms until tender. Add the garlic, thyme and lemon juice to taste and season with salt and pepper. Fry for a further 2

minutes. Add the sherry and bring to the boil, scraping any sediment from the base of the pan.

6. Lift 4 of the potato cakes on to 4 individual plates. Divide the filling between them and top with a second potato cake. Sprinkle with the parsley.

SWISS POTATO RÖSTI WITH BEAUFORT CHEESE

900g/2lb even-sized floury potatoes, such as
  Maris Piper
salt and freshly ground black pepper
2 tablespoons olive oil
30g/1oz butter
110g/4oz Beaufort cheese, coarsely grated

1. Cook the unpeeled potatoes in boiling salted water for 10 minutes. Drain and leave to cool completely (ideally in the refrigerator overnight).
2. Peel the potatoes and grate them coarsely. Season lightly with salt and pepper.
3. Heat a 23cm/9in non-stick, ovenproof frying pan over a high heat. Add half the oil, then cover the base of the pan with half the potatoes. Press them down well with the back of a wooden spatula and neaten up the edges.
4. Cut the butter into small pieces and tuck half the pieces around the outside edge of the pan. Turn the heat down to medium and leave the rösti to cook for 5 minutes or until richly golden underneath.
5. Spread the cheese over the rösti, to within 2.5cm/1in of the edge. Cover with the remaining grated potatoes and press them down. Cover the pan with an inverted plate, hold the two together and turn over, so that the rösti is now on the plate. Return the pan to the heat, add the remaining oil and when hot, carefully slide in the rösti. Tuck the remaining butter pieces around the edge of the pan and cook for a further 5 minutes or until golden. Meanwhile, preheat the oven to 190°C/375°F/gas mark 5.

6. Transfer the frying pan to the preheated oven and bake for 15 minutes until the rösti is richly golden-brown on both sides. Slide it out on to a plate and serve cut into wedges.

VARIATION:

WINTER HERB RÖSTI
Mix 1 teaspoon each of chopped rosemary, thyme and sage into the potato mixture with the seasoning. Press all the potatoes into the pan and cook as before. Serve cut into wedges, topped with fried eggs if you wish.

SWEET OVEN-DRIED TOMATOES ON WATERCRESS AND GREEN PEPPERCORN RÖSTI

6 plum tomatoes
2 teaspoons caster sugar
salt and freshly ground black pepper
sprigs of fresh rosemary

For the rösti
1 Spanish onion, finely chopped
olive oil
675g/1½lb waxy potatoes
85g/3oz watercress, tough stalks removed
2 teaspoons green peppercorns, rinsed and
  chopped
lemon juice

1. Preheat the oven to 100°C/200°F/gas mark ½.
2. Slice the tomatoes thinly lengthwise. Lay them on a baking tray. Sprinkle with the sugar, season with salt and pepper and lay the sprigs of rosemary on top.
3. Cook the tomatoes in the oven for 1½–2 hours until very wrinkled. Discard the rosemary.
4. Make the rösti: cook the onion in 1 tablespoon oil until soft but not coloured. Remove from the heat.
5. Peel the potatoes, grate them coarsely and place in a bowl.

6. Chop one-third of the watercress and carefully fork into the potatoes with the peppercorns. Season with salt.

7. Divide the potato mixture into 8 and shape roughly into flattish rounds.

8. Heat 1cm/½in oil in a large frying pan and fry the rösti over a low heat until the underside is crusty and golden-brown. Turn and repeat on the other side.

9. Roughly chop the remaining watercress and mix with oil and lemon juice to taste. Season with salt and pepper.

10. To serve: place 2 rösti on each individual plate and top with a pile of watercress and an overlapping circle of the tomato slices.

POTATO GNOCCHI WITH PESTO

675g/1½lb even-sized floury potatoes, such as
* Maris Piper*
salt
125g/4½oz plain flour
55ml/2fl oz double cream

For the pesto
45g/1½oz fresh basil leaves
30g/1oz pinenuts
1 large clove of garlic, crushed
70ml/2½fl oz olive oil
30g/1oz Parmesan cheese, freshly grated

To serve
15g/½oz Parmesan cheese, freshly grated

1. Preheat the oven to 200°C/400°F/gas mark 6. Prick the potatoes and place on a baking tray and bake in the preheated oven for 1 hour or until tender.

2. Make the pesto: put the basil, pinenuts, garlic and oil into a food processor and blend to a coarse paste. Transfer to a bowl and stir in the Parmesan cheese and salt to taste.

3. Bring a large pan of lightly salted water to the boil. Remove the potatoes from the oven and when they are cool enough to handle, cut them in half and scoop out the flesh. Pass the flesh through a potato ricer on to a worktop and sprinkle with a little salt. (If you don't have a potato ricer, simply mash the potatoes in the usual way and then tip it on to the worktop.) Gradually sprinkle over the flour, working it in quickly with the heel of your hand until smooth.

4. Shape small amounts of the mixture into ropes, about 15cm/6in long and 2.5cm/1in wide. Cut each into 2cm/¾in pieces. Shape the pieces, one at a time, with a fork; rest them on the inside curve of the fork and press lightly in the centre so that one side takes on a slight dip and the other is marked in ridges. This will help the sauce to cling to the gnocchi.

5. Drop the gnocchi, 16 at a time, into the boiling water and cook until they have all floated to the surface. Leave them to cook for a further 8–10 seconds, then lift them out with a slotted spoon on to a tray lined with kitchen paper.

6. Put 4 heaped tablespoons of the pesto and the cream into a large, heavy saucepan and stir over a low heat without boiling for 1–2 minutes. Add the gnocchi, stir together gently and then divide between 4 warmed individual plates. Serve sprinkled with a little Parmesan cheese.

VARIATIONS:

Gnocchi with Gorgonzola Cheese Sauce: Put 30g/1oz crumbled Gorgonzola cheese, 1½ tablespoons double cream, 1½ tablespoons milk, 15g/½oz butter and salt and pepper into a medium saucepan and stir over a low heat until the cheese has melted. Cook for 1 minute until thick and creamy. Stir in the cooked gnocchi and serve sprinkled with Parmesan cheese.

Gnocchi with warm Sage and Garlic Butter: Put 55g/2oz butter, 6 finely shredded fresh sage leaves, 2 finely chopped garlic cloves and salt and pepper into a medium saucepan and leave over a low heat until the butter has melted and the garlic is beginning to sizzle. Add the cooked gnocchi and toss together gently, then serve.

Gnocchi with a simple Tomato Sauce: Cut 900g/2lb vine-ripened tomatoes in half lengthways. Put them into a medium saucepan, cover and simmer for 10 minutes. Pass them through a vegetable mill or large sieve and return to the pan. Add 55g/2oz butter, 1 peeled and halved onion, ¼ teaspoon caster sugar and some salt. Simmer, uncovered, for 45 minutes, stirring frequently. Discard the onion and season to taste with salt and pepper. Stir in the cooked gnocchi and serve sprinkled with Parmesan cheese.

DRY-SPICED POTATO AND CAULIFLOWER CURRY

450g/1lb floury potatoes, such as Maris Piper
salt and freshly ground black pepper
4–5 tablespoons sunflower oil
1 teaspoon cumin seeds
450g/1lb cauliflower, broken into small florets
1 teaspoon ground cumin
1 teaspoon ground coriander
¼ teaspoon ground turmeric
½ teaspoon cayenne pepper
2 medium-hot green Dutch chillies, deseeded
    and finely chopped (see page 22)
½ teaspoon garam masala

1. Peel the potatoes and cut them into 2.5cm/1in pieces. Cook them in boiling salted water for 6–7 minutes until just tender. Drain and leave to cool slightly.
2. Heat half the oil in a large, heavy frying pan. Add the cumin seeds and as soon as they begin to pop, add the cauliflower florets and fry over a medium to high heat for about 5 minutes, stirring from time to time, until the cauliflower is just tender and lightly browned. Tip on to a plate.
3. Heat the remaining oil in the pan, add the potatoes and sprinkle over the ground cumin, coriander, turmeric, cayenne and chillies. Fry for 8–10 minutes, gently turning from time to time, until the potatoes are coated in a golden spicy crust.
4. Return the cauliflower to the pan and season with salt. Toss together for 2–3 minutes until the cauliflower has heated through, then sprinkle with the garam masala.

SPICY POTATO AND ONION BHAJI WITH POACHED EGGS

2 small onions
4 tablespoons sunflower oil, plus extra for
    shallow-frying
1 tablespoon black mustard seeds
1 medium-hot red Dutch chilli, deseeded and
    chopped (see page 22)
¾ teaspoon ground turmeric
¼ teaspoon cayenne pepper
salt
675g/1½lb main-crop potatoes, peeled and cut
    into 2cm/¾in cubes
4 fresh curry leaves (optional)
225ml/8fl oz water
2 tablespoons white wine vinegar
8 medium eggs
1 tablespoon chopped fresh coriander

To serve
warm paratha or naan bread

1. Make the bhaji: thinly slice half of 1 onion
and set aside. Finely chop the remainder. Heat
the oil in a large, deep frying pan with a lid.
Add the mustard seeds, cover and leave until
they begin to pop. Uncover and quickly add the
chopped onion and chilli. Cook over a medium
heat for 7 minutes or until the onion is soft but
not browned.
2. Stir in the turmeric, cayenne, salt, potatoes,
curry leaves, if used, and water. Cover and cook
over a low heat for 20 minutes, stirring from
time to time, until the potatoes are tender.
3. Meanwhile, heat 1cm/½in oil in a deep,
medium frying pan. Add the reserved sliced
onion and fry until crisp and golden. Lift out
with a slotted spoon on to plenty of kitchen
paper and leave to drain. Toss with a little salt
and set aside.
4. Shortly before the bhaji is ready, bring about
2.3 litres/4 pints water to a rolling boil in a
large saucepan. Add the vinegar. Break the eggs
into a ramekin or teacup and slide them one at
a time into the water. Lower the heat and poach

for 3 minutes, then lift out with a slotted spoon
and leave them to drain briefly on kitchen
paper.
5. Stir the coriander into the bhaji and season
to taste with salt and pepper. Spoon it on to 4
warmed individual plates and put the poached
eggs on top. Sprinkle over the crisp fried onions
and serve with the warm paratha or naan
bread.

MARMITAKO

(SPANISH ROOT VEGETABLE STEW)

110g/4oz dried chickpeas, soaked overnight
450g/1lb red potatoes, scrubbed
3 tablespoons olive oil
1 large onion, sliced
2 green peppers, deseeded and roughly chopped
3 cloves of garlic, crushed
1 teaspoon paprika
1 teaspoon ground cumin
1 red chilli, deseeded and sliced (see page 22)
1 × 200g/7oz can of chopped tomatoes
290ml/½ pint winter vegetable stock (see
    page 530)
1 heaped teaspoon saffron strands
salt and freshly ground black pepper

To serve
rouille (see page 512)
crusty bread

1. Rinse and drain the chickpeas and cook
them in boiling water for 30 minutes. Drain
again. Meanwhile, cut the potatoes into 2.5cm/
1in chunks.
2. Heat the oil in a saucepan, add the onion
and peppers and cook over a low heat until soft.
Add the garlic and spices. Fry for a further 2
minutes. Add the potatoes and stir until well
coated in the spice and onion mixture.
3. Stir in the chilli, tomatoes, stock and saffron.
Season with salt and pepper. Add the chickpeas.
Simmer for 20–30 minutes until the potatoes
and chickpeas are tender. Serve with crusty
bread and hand the rouille separately.

DEEP-FRIED POTATO SKINS WITH THREE-BEAN CHILLI

SERVES 6

For the potato wedges
4 × 340g/12oz baking potatoes
sunflower oil, for deep-frying

For the chilli
170g/6oz dried black beans, soaked overnight
170g/6oz dried red kidney beans, soaked overnight
170g/6oz dried cannellini or haricot beans, soaked overnight
2 large dried red chillies, such as ancho
1 onion, roughly chopped
3 cloves of garlic, roughly chopped
110ml/4fl oz sunflower oil
2 green jalapeño chillies, deseeded and chopped (see page 22)
2 teaspoons ground cumin
1 tablespoon sweet paprika
1 × 400g/14oz can of chopped tomatoes
1 teaspoon dried oregano
290ml/½ pint winter vegetable stock (see page 530)
30g/1oz fresh coriander, coarsely chopped
salt and freshly ground black pepper

To garnish
150ml/¼ pint soured cream
6 sprigs of fresh coriander

1. Preheat the oven to 200°C/400°F/gas mark 6. Prick the potatoes and place on a baking tray and bake in the preheated oven for 1¼ hours until tender.

2. Meanwhile, make the chilli: rinse and drain the beans and put the black beans and red kidney beans into one pan and the cannellini beans into another. Cover both with plenty of fresh water and bring them to the boil. Boil the pan of black and red kidney beans vigorously for 10 minutes, then cover both pans and leave to simmer for 40–50 minutes or until the beans are just tender.

3. Meanwhile, slit open the dried chillies and remove the stems and seeds. Bring a pan of water to the boil. Heat a dry, heavy frying pan over a high heat, add the chillies and dry-roast them for about 2 minutes on each side, shaking the pan constantly and taking care that they don't scorch. Drop them into the pan of boiling water, remove the pan from the heat and place a saucer on top of the chillies to keep them submerged. Leave them to soak for 20–30 minutes until soft.

4. Drain the chillies and put them into a food processor or blender with the onion and garlic. Process to a coarse paste. Heat the oil in a large saucepan. Add the onion and chilli paste and cook, stirring for 5 minutes. Add the jalapeño chillies, cumin and paprika and fry for a further 2 minutes.

5. Drain the beans and add them to the pan with the tomatoes, oregano and stock. Bring to the boil, then lower the heat and simmer gently for 20–30 minutes, until the sauce has reduced and thickened.

6. Shortly before the three-bean chilli is ready, heat oil in a deep-fryer to 190°C/375°F. Remove the potatoes from the oven and cut them into quarters lengthways. Scoop away most of the cooked potato with a spoon to leave skins about 1cm/½in thick. (The cooked potato can be used in potato scones or pastry.) Deep-fry the potato skins in batches for 1½–2 minutes until crisp and golden. Lift out with a slotted spoon and drain briefly on kitchen paper. Keep hot in a low oven.

7. Stir the coriander into the three-bean chilli and adjust the seasoning if necessary. Spoon into warmed serving bowls and garnish each with a spoonful of soured cream and a sprig of coriander. Serve with the hot potato wedges.

CURRIED POTATOES WITH SPINACH AND TOMATOES

This dish is very good topped with poached eggs.

450g/1lb waxy potatoes
salt and freshly ground black pepper
450g/1lb fresh spinach
3 tablespoons sunflower oil
1 teaspoon yellow mustard seeds
½ teaspoon ground turmeric
a good pinch of ground cumin
a good pinch of chilli powder
1 large onion, finely chopped
3 tomatoes, peeled, deseeded and chopped (see page 22)

1. The potatoes can be left with the skins on or peeled. Cut them into quarters and parboil in salted water for 10 minutes until still quite firm. Cool, then cut into 1cm/½in cubes.
2. Wash the spinach thoroughly and remove any tough stalks. Put into a pan with a tight-fitting lid and shake over a medium heat for a few minutes until tender. Drain and squeeze out all the excess moisture, then chop roughly.
3. Heat the oil in a heavy frying pan. Add the mustard seeds and when they begin to pop, add the turmeric, cumin and chilli and fry for 1 minute. Add the onion and cook over a low heat until soft and golden-brown.
4. Stir in the potatoes, season with salt and pepper and continue to fry gently until tender all the way through. Add the tomatoes and spinach, check the seasoning and heat briskly for a few minutes until piping hot.

OLIVE OIL POTATO WEDGES WITH TAPENADE

4 large waxy potatoes
3 tablespoons olive oil
sea salt flakes
tapenade (see page 510)

1. Preheat the oven to 200°C/400°F/gas mark 6.
2. Cut each potato lengthways into 6–8 wedges. Put the oil into a roasting tin and heat on top of the stove. Turn the potatoes in the hot oil until thoroughly coated. Scatter with a little salt. Bake in the preheated oven for 50–60 minutes, turning from time to time, until the potatoes are crisp, golden and tender.
3. Drain the potatoes on kitchen paper and sprinkle with salt. Arrange them on a warmed serving plate with the tapenade in a small dish in the centre.

BABY RED POTATOES WITH GOAT'S CHEESE, BROCCOLI AND CAULIFLOWER

150ml/¼ pint olive oil
1 tablespoon balsamic vinegar
1 clove of garlic, crushed
1 shallot, finely chopped
1 tablespoon capers, rinsed, drained and chopped
salt and freshly ground black pepper
2 teaspoons lemon juice
450g/1lb small red potatoes
110g/4oz broccoli florets
110g/4oz cauliflower florets
140g/5oz mild soft goat's cheese
1 tablespoon chopped fresh flat-leaf parsley, to garnish

1. Preheat the oven to 220°C/425°F/gas mark 7.
2. Mix together the oil, vinegar, garlic, shallot and capers and season with salt, pepper and lemon juice.
3. If the potatoes are large, cut them to about the same size as the broccoli and cauliflower florets. Boil in salted water for about 10 minutes until just tender. Blanch the broccoli and cauliflower florets in boiling salted water for 2 minutes. While still hot, toss them together with the potatoes in the oil mixture and spoon into a shallow ovenproof dish.
4. Dot spoonfuls of the goat's cheese through the vegetables, then bake in the preheated oven for 15 minutes or until the vegetables are tender and the cheese browned. Sprinkle with the parsley before serving.

'PIZZA' BAKED ANYA POTATOES

450g/1lb Anya potatoes, halved lengthways
2 tablespoons olive oil
salt and freshly ground black pepper
1 heaped teaspoon sun-dried tomato paste
3 plum tomatoes, quartered and deseeded (see page 22)
30g/1oz black olives, pitted and halved
2 teaspoons finely chopped fresh oregano
140g/5oz buffalo mozzarella cheese, cubed
2 tablespoons freshly grated Parmesan cheese

To serve
crusty bread

1. Preheat the oven to 200°C/400°F/gas mark 6.
2. Put the potatoes into a large ovenproof dish and pour over the oil. Season with salt and pepper and bake in the preheated oven for 1 hour or until just tender and beginning to brown.
3. Spread the sun-dried tomato paste over the potatoes and add the tomatoes, olives and oregano. Return to the oven for a further 15 minutes.
4. Preheat the grill to its highest setting.
5. Scatter the cubed mozzarella and Parmesan cheese over the potatoes. Place the dish under the grill for 3–5 minutes or until the cheese has melted and is lightly browned. Serve hot with plenty of crusty bread.

JACKET POTATO

A baked potato makes a simple but satisfying lunch or supper. The best baked potatoes are pricked with a fork, then rubbed with oil and salt. They can be baked either for 2 hours at 180°C/350°F/gas mark 4 or for 1 hour at 200°C/400°F/gas mark 6, depending on what else the oven may be being used for. They are cooked when the skin is dry and very crisp and a skewer will pass through the potato easily.

The speed at which a microwave oven can deal with a baked potato is too convenient to ignore even though the results tend to be second-best. A combination oven will produce baked potatoes with a dry and slightly crisp skin. Prick a washed potato and cook on 200°C/high power for 6 minutes. Allow to stand for 3 minutes.

An ordinary microwave oven cannot produce a crisp skin, but if the washed and pricked potato is first wrapped in kitchen paper this will absord some of the moisture. Microwave on high power for 6 minutes and leave to stand for 3 minutes. As a rough guide, if cooking more than one potato increase the cooking and standing time by 50 per cent per potato.

Many of the recipes in this book are suitable to serve as a topping or accompaniment to a baked potato. Stews or casseroles such as ratatouille, chilli beans with whole roasted chillies, Mexican bean pot or Puy lentil casserole could all be used. Toppings for bruschetta or vegetable side dishes such as greens with citrus gremolata or wilted spinach with pinenuts and raisins are also suitable.

Whizzed eggs with mushroom and asparagus would be a good accompaniment, or create a carbohydrate extravaganza by serving a piping-hot jacket potato with parsnip cakes with garlic and borlotti beans, buttered parsnips with lamb's lettuce and spiced kumquats, or roasted honey parsnips with horseradish greens.

A baked potato is equally delicious served with a simple, traditional topping such as grated mature Cheddar cheese, soured cream and chives, or cottage cheese with chopped spring onions.

SUN-DRIED TOMATO AND BLACK OLIVE SOUFFLÉD JACKET POTATOES

4 large baking potatoes, scrubbed
6 sun-dried tomatoes, chopped
45g/1½oz black olives, pitted and chopped
15g/½oz roughly chopped fresh basil leaves
45g/1½oz butter
2 eggs, separated
salt and freshly ground black pepper
55g/2oz Parmesan cheese, freshly grated
fresh basil leaves, to garnish

1. Preheat the oven to 200°C/400°F/gas mark 6.
2. Prick the potatoes all over with a fork and bake in the centre of the preheated oven for 1¼–1½ hours or until very tender when pierced with a knife.
3. Cut the potatoes in half horizontally and scrape the flesh into a bowl, keeping the skins intact.
4. Mash the potato with a fork and stir in the sun-dried tomatoes, olives and basil. Beat in the butter and egg yolks and season with salt and pepper.
5. In a separate bowl, whisk the egg whites until stiff but not dry and carefully fold into the potato mixture, using a large metal spoon.
6. Fill the potato skins with the mixture and sprinkle over the cheese. Place the potatoes on a baking sheet and return to the oven for 10–15 minutes or until hot, puffed up and golden-brown. Serve hot, garnished with basil leaves.

INDIVIDUAL CHRISTMAS BUBBLE AND SQUEAKS

450g/1lb potatoes, cooked and mashed
170g/6oz parsnips, cooked and diced
170g/6oz Brussels sprouts, cooked and roughly
  chopped
1 small Bramley apple, peeled and grated
55g/2oz cooked chestnuts, chopped
salt and freshly ground black pepper
plain flour, for shaping
2 tablespoons vegetable oil

To serve
cranberry sauce (see page 507)

1. Mix together the mashed potato, parsnips, sprouts and grated apples in a large bowl.
2. Stir in the chestnuts and season well with salt and pepper.
3. Divide the mixture into 8 and with floured hands shape roughly into rounds.
4. Heat the oil in a large frying pan and fry the bubble and squeaks on both sides until well browned. Lower the heat annd cook for a further 5–7 minutes or until hot through. Serve immediately with cranberry sauce.

COLCANNON

30g/1oz butter
1 medium onion, sliced
560g/1¼lb cooked potato, mashed
225g/8oz Savoy cabbage, thinly sliced and
  cooked
4 tablespoons double cream or milk
salt and freshly ground black pepper

1. Preheat the oven to 190°C/375°F/gas mark 5.
2. Melt the butter in a medium saucepan, add the onion and cook over a low heat for 3 minutes until lightly browned.
3. Mix the mashed potato, cabbage and onion together. Add the cream or milk and season well with salt and pepper.
4. Put into a 1.4 litre/2 pint pie dish and bake in the preheated oven for 30 minutes or until the top is brown and crispy and the mixture is heated through.

ROASTED NEW POTATOES AND ARTICHOKE HEARTS WITH WARM TARTARE DRESSING

675g/1½lb small new potatoes, scrubbed
2 tablespoons olive oil
salt and freshly ground black pepper
1 × 400g/14oz can of artichoke hearts, rinsed,
  drained and halved
chopped fresh parsley, to garnish

For the sauce
150ml/¼ pint mayonnaise (see page 527)
2 shallots, very finely chopped
1 tablespoon capers, rinsed, drained and
  crushed
1 tablespoon chopped gherkin
juice of ½ lemon
2 tablespoons chopped fresh parsley

1. Preheat the oven to 200°C/400°F/gas mark 6.
2. Put the potatoes into a large roasting pan. Toss them lightly in the oil and season with salt and pepper. Roast in the preheated oven, turning occasionally, for about 1 hour until tender.
3. Add the artichoke hearts to the potatoes and cook for a further 10 minutes.
4. Mix all the ingredients for the sauce together in a small saucepan and heat very gently. Season with salt and pepper.
5. Remove the potatoes and artichokes from the roasting tin with a slotted spoon and drain briefly on kitchen paper. Transfer to a warmed serving bowl, drizzle over the warm dressing and sprinkle with parsley.

CRUSHED COCONUT AND LEMONGRASS POTATOES

675g/1½lb new potatoes, scrubbed and halved if large
2 stalks of lemongrass, trimmed and very finely chopped
425ml/¾ pint unsweetened coconut milk
2 kaffir lime leaves, shredded (optional)
grated zest of 1 lemon
30g/1oz fresh flat-leaf parsley, roughly chopped
salt and freshly ground black pepper

1. Bring the potatoes to the boil in a large saucepan of boiling salted water. Add half the lemongrass and reduce to a simmer. Cook for 20–25 minutes or until the potatoes are just beginning to break up. Drain thoroughly.
2. Meanwhile, put the coconut milk into a small saucepan with the remaining lemongrass and the lime leaves, if used. Bring to a simmer and turn off the heat. Leave to infuse while the potatoes are cooking.
3. Strain the infused coconut milk over the hot potatoes. Add the lemon zest and parsley and season well with salt and plenty of pepper. Transfer to a warmed serving bowl and serve hot.

OLIVE OIL POTATOES WITH HONEY, LEMON AND CHICKPEAS

110g/4oz dried chickpeas, soaked overnight
900g/2lb new potatoes
1 bulb of garlic
1 lemon
3 tablespoons olive oil
salt and freshly ground black pepper
2 teaspoons clear honey
1 tablespoon chopped fresh flat-leaf parsley

1. Rinse and drain the chickpeas. Cover with plenty of cold water in a saucepan and bring to the boil, then lower the heat and simmer for 45–60 minutes until tender. Drain and set aside.
2. Preheat the oven to 200°C/400°F/gas mark 6.
3. Scrub the new potatoes and cut them in half. Slice the top off the bulb of garlic. Grate the zest from the lemon, squeeze the juice and cut each lemon shell into about 6 pieces.
4. Put the oil into a roasting pan and heat on top of the stove. Add the potatoes and turn in the hot oil. Season with salt and pepper. Stir in the lemon zest, juice and chopped lemon. Stand the garlic bulb in the pan and bake in the preheated oven for 40 minutes, stirring from time to time.
5. Remove the garlic and leave to cool slightly. Turn it upside down and squeeze out the cloves. Stir the garlic into the potatoes with the honey and chickpeas. Bake for a further 20–30 minutes until the potatoes are tender and well browned. Sprinkle with the parsley before serving.

SPICED BASHED POTATOES

675g/1½lb red potatoes
salt and freshly ground black pepper
2 teaspoons vegetable oil
½ teaspoon mustard seeds
½ teaspoon cumin seeds
30g/1oz butter
1 green chilli, deseeded and finely chopped (see
    page 22)
2 spring onions, trimmed and chopped
2–3 tablespoons soured cream

1. Peel the potatoes, cut them into quarters and cook in a saucepan of boiling salted water until tender. Drain.
2. Put the oil into the rinsed and dried pan and heat. Add the mustard and cumin seeds and when they begin to pop, return the potatoes to the pan with the butter and mash roughly with a fork or wooden spoon.
3. Stir in the chilli, spring onion and soured cream and stir a couple of times before serving.

BASIL MASH

900g/2lb red potatoes
3 cloves of garlic, chopped
salt and freshly ground black pepper
about 55g/2oz butter or 3 tablespoons olive oil
3 tablespoons soured cream
3–4 teaspoons pesto
freshly grated nutmeg

1. Peel the potatoes and cut them into even-sized pieces. Put into a saucepan with the garlic, cover with water and add a good pinch of salt. Bring to the boil, then lower the heat and simmer for 20–30 minutes until the potatoes are tender.
2. Drain thoroughly. Return the potatoes to the rinsed and dried pan and set over a low heat. Mash with a large fork or potato masher, allowing the steam to evaporate.
3. Beat in the butter or oil, soured cream and pesto to taste. Season with salt, pepper and nutmeg.

NOTE: For rocket mash, use 110g/4oz rocket, washed and shredded, instead of the pesto.

LEMON AND THYME BAKED POTATOES

900g/2lb waxy potatoes
salt and freshly ground black pepper
150ml/¼ pint olive oil
grated zest of 2 lemons
2 teaspoons fresh thyme

1. Quarter the unpeeled potatoes and parboil in salted water for about 10 minutes until still quite firm.
2. Preheat the oven to 220°C/425°F/gas mark 7. Brush a shallow ovenproof dish with a little of the oil.
3. Cut the potatoes into slices 5mm/¼in thick. Arrange in an overlapping layer in the prepared dish.
4. Brush liberally with all the remaining oil and season with salt and pepper. Scatter over the lemon zest and thyme. Bake in the preheated oven for about 30 minutes until the potatoes are tender and golden-brown on top.

POTATO SLICES FOR THE OVEN OR BARBECUE

*900g/2lb large floury potatoes, such as Maris
   Piper*
4 tablespoons olive oil
1 tablespoon white wine vinegar or lemon juice
2 cloves of garlic, chopped
*2 teaspoons chopped fresh oregano or
   marjoram*
salt and freshly ground black pepper

To serve
*roasted garlic mayonnaise (see page 512), mooli
   relish (see page 109) or salsa (see page 514)*

1. If using the oven, preheat it to 230°C/450°F/
gas mark 8.
2. Scrub the potatoes and cut them lengthways
into slices 5mm/¼in thick.
3. Mix together the oil, vinegar or lemon juice,
garlic and herbs and season with salt and
pepper. Pour over the potatoes and mix,
making sure that all the slices are covered in the
oil mixture. Leave to stand for about 1 hour.
4. Put the potato slices on to a baking tray and
bake in the preheated oven for about 15
minutes, turning them halfway through
cooking, until golden-brown. Alternatively,
cook the potatoes on a barbecue for 10 minutes,
turning them from time to time, until cooked
through and brown on the outside. Serve on a
platter with an assortment of dips in small
bowls.

NOTE: For spicy potatoes add 1 level
tablespoon cajun spice (see page 529) to the
marinade.

QUICK DAUPHINOISE POTATOES

SERVES 6

900g/2lb floury potatoes, such as Maris Piper
290ml/½ pint double cream
290ml/½ pint milk
1 clove of garlic, crushed
salt and freshly ground black pepper
¼ nutmeg, freshly grated
15g/½oz butter, for greasing

1. Preheat the oven to 200°C/400°F/gas mark 6.
Peel the potatoes and slice them very thinly by
hand, on a mandolin or in a food processor.
2. Put the cream, milk, garlic, salt and pepper
into a large, non-stick saucepan. Add the
potatoes and simmer for 10 minutes, stirring
them gently from time to time and taking care
not to break up the slices, until they are just
tender when pierced with the top of a small,
sharp knife. Stir in the nutmeg and adjust the
seasoning to taste.
3. Spoon the potatoes into a lightly buttered
1.4 litre/2½ pint shallow ovenproof dish.
Overlap the top layer of potatoes neatly if you
wish. Bake in the preheated oven for 30 minutes
or until golden and bubbling.

VARIATIONS:
Cheesy Dauphinoise potatoes: Sprinkle the
top of the potatoes with 55g/2oz Gruyère
cheese, finely grated, before baking.
Wild mushroom Dauphinoise: Fry 110g/4oz
cleaned and thinly sliced wild mushrooms in
15g/½oz butter over a high heat for 3 minutes
until all the excess moisture has evaporated. Stir
in another 15g/½oz butter, 1 teaspoon fresh
thyme leaves and salt and pepper to taste. Layer
the mixture between the potatoes in the dish
and bake as before.

Dauphinoise Potatoes With Artichokes and Truffle: Layer 110g/4oz thinly sliced artichoke bottoms and 1 teaspoon minced truffle between the potatoes in the dish and bake as before.

BRAISED SAFFRON AND TOMATO POTATOES

900g/2lb main crop potatoes
55ml/2fl oz extra virgin olive oil
4 cloves of garlic, thinly sliced
225g/8oz small vine-ripened tomatoes, peeled and deseeded (see page 22)
290ml/½ pint summer vegetable stock (see page 530)
a good pinch of saffron strands
salt and freshly ground black pepper

1. Peel the potatoes and cut them crossways into slices 2cm/¾in thick. Heat the oil and garlic in a medium saucepan until the garlic begins to sizzle.
2. Add the tomatoes and cook for 2–3 minutes. Add the potatoes, stock, saffron and ½ teaspoon salt. Bring to a simmer and cook, uncovered, over a low heat for 20 minutes or until the potatoes are tender and the liquid is well reduced. Season to taste with salt and pepper.

SAUTÉED NEW POTATOES AND BABY VEGETABLES WITH ORANGE AND CHIVE SAUCE

SERVES 6

450g/1lb even-sized new potatoes
salt and freshly ground black pepper
2–4 tablespoons olive oil
110g/4oz young asparagus
10 baby courgettes
10 baby patty-pan squash

For the sauce
150ml/¼ pint summer vegetable stock (see page 530)
grated zest and juice of ½ orange
1 shallot, thinly sliced
110g/4oz unsalted butter, chilled
1 tablespoon crème fraîche
1 tablespoon chopped fresh chives

1. Parboil the new potatoes in boiling salted water for 5–8 minutes. Drain thoroughly and allow to dry.
2. Heat 1–2 tablespoons oil in a large frying pan and add the potatoes. Season with salt and pepper and fry over a low heat for 20–30 minutes, turning the potatoes occasionally, until they turn a pale nutty brown.
3. Meanwhile, in another frying pan heat 1–2 tablespoons oil. When hot, add the asparagus, courgettes and squash, season with salt and pepper and sauté gently for about 10 minutes or until just soft. (If the patty-pan squash are bigger than 1cm/½in across, cut them in half so they will cook in the same time as the other vegetables.)
4. Make the sauce: bring the stock, orange juice and zest and the shallot to the boil in a small saucepan. Continue to boil until the liquid has reduced to about 4 tablespoons. Gradually whisk in the butter over a low heat. Finish the sauce off with the crème fraîche. Season to taste with salt and pepper and add the chives.
5. Put the vegetables into a warmed serving dish, spoon over some of the sauce and hand the remainder separately.

HOT POTATO SALAD NIÇOISE WITH EGGS AND MUSTARD DRESSING

675g/1½lb new potatoes, scraped
225g/8oz small, vine-ripened tomatoes, halved
salt and freshly ground black pepper
4 medium eggs
110g/4oz French beans, topped, tailed and
  halved
110g/4oz baby broad beans
4 spring onions, trimmed and thinly sliced
4 teaspoons chopped fresh parsley
1 tablespoon chopped fresh basil

For the dressing
3 tablespoons extra virgin olive oil
1 clove of garlic, crushed
1 tablespoon white wine vinegar
2 teaspoons Dijon mustard
55g/2oz small black olives

1. First make the mustard dressing: put the oil, garlic, vinegar, mustard and salt and pepper into a small pan and whisk together lightly. Stir in the olives and set aside.
2. Cook the potatoes in boiling salted water for 15 minutes or until just tender. Meanwhile, bring another 2 saucepans of water to the boil and preheat the grill to high. Arrange the tomatoes cut side up on the grill pan and season lightly with salt and pepper. After the potatoes have been cooking for 5 minutes, add the eggs to one pan of boiling water and hard-boil for 8 minutes. After another 5 minutes, add the French beans and broad beans with a large pinch of salt to the third pan and cook for 3 minutes. Grill the tomatoes for 2 minutes. Place the pan of dressing over a low heat.
3. Remove the eggs and set aside. Drain the potatoes and beans well and put them into a large shallow serving dish. Add three-quarters of the warm dressing, the spring onions, half the parsley, the basil and salt and pepper and mix together gently.
4. Peel the eggs and cut them into quarters. Arrange them on top of the salad with the grilled tomatoes. Drizzle over the remaining dressing, sprinkle over the remaining parsley and serve warm.

SWEET POTATO, PUMPKIN AND GINGER SOUP

450g/1lb sweet potatoes
450g/1lb pumpkin
55g/2oz butter
1 large onion, sliced
5cm/2in piece of fresh root ginger, peeled and
  chopped
1 teaspoon coriander seeds, crushed
860ml/1½ pints summer vegetable stock (see
  page 530)
salt and freshly ground black pepper
150ml/¼ pint double cream
1 level teaspoon freshly grated nutmeg
fresh coriander leaves, to garnish

1. Peel and slice the sweet potatoes. Remove the pumpkin skin and scrape away the seeds and pulp. Chop the flesh.
2. Melt the butter in a large saucepan, add the onion and fry over a low heat until softened. Add the ginger and coriander seeds and fry for a further 5 minutes. Stir in the sweet potatoes, pumpkin and stock. Season with salt and pepper and bring to the boil, then lower the heat, partially cover and simmer for 20–30 minutes until the vegetables are very soft.
3. Purée the soup in a food processor or blender. Pour back into the rinsed-out pan, add the cream and reheat gently without boiling. Adjust the seasoning to taste and add the nutmeg. Pour into warmed soup bowls and scatter with coriander leaves before serving.

SWEET POTATO AND POPPY SEED FLAN

For the pastry
170g/6oz plain flour
a pinch of salt
85g/3oz butter
55g/2oz Cheddar cheese, grated
30g/1oz poppy seeds
cold water, to mix

For the filling
450g/1lb sweet potatoes
salt and freshly ground black pepper
225g/8oz ricotta cheese
2 tablespoons double cream
1 egg, beaten
55g/2oz Parmesan cheese, freshly grated
freshly grated nutmeg

1. First make the pastry: sift the flour with the salt into a large mixing bowl. Rub in the butter until the mixture resembles coarse breadcrumbs. Add the cheese and poppy seeds and with a round-bladed knife mix in sufficient water to make a firm dough. Use to line a 20cm/8in flan dish. Chill for 45 minutes to relax – this prevents shrinkage during baking.
2. Preheat the oven to 200°C/400°F/gas mark 6.
3. Bake the pastry case blind for 10 minutes (see page 22), then lower the oven temperature to 180°C/350°F/gas mark 4.
4. Meanwhile, make the filling: peel the sweet potatoes and cut into dice. Put the sweet potato into a saucepan with sufficient water to come a quarter of the way up the sides of the pan. Season with salt, cover and bring to the boil. Lower the heat and simmer until the sweet potato is soft but still holds its shape. Drain, mash and allow to cool.
5. Mix the ricotta cheese, cream, egg and Parmesan cheese together in a bowl. Add the sweet potato and mix thoroughly. Season to taste with salt, pepper and nutmeg.
6. Pile the mixture into the pastry case and level the surface. Bake in the preheated oven for 25–30 minutes or until the mixture is set and a light golden-brown.

NOTE: The flan is best eaten on the day it is made.

ROASTED SWEET POTATO AND GARLIC SOUFFLÉ

675g/1½lb sweet potatoes
6 cloves of garlic in their skins
2 tablespoons olive oil
salt and freshly ground black pepper
150ml/¼ pint milk
4og/1¼oz butter
30g/1oz plain flour
a pinch of cayenne pepper
55g/2oz Cheddar cheese, grated
4 eggs, separated

1. Preheat the oven to 200°C/400°F/gas mark 6.
2. Peel the sweet potatoes and cut them into 2.5cm/1in slices. Put them into a roasting tin with the garlic. Pour over the oil and, using your hands, mix well with the potatoes and garlic. Season with salt and pepper. Roast in the preheated oven for 25 minutes, turning over once, until the sweet potatoes are tender and the garlic is soft.
3. Put the sweet potatoes into a food processor. Remove the skins from the cloves of garlic, and add to the sweet potatoes. Process until smooth, then add the milk.
4. Melt the butter in a large saucepan and use some to grease a 1.5 litre/2½ pint soufflé dish. Add the flour to the remaining butter with the cayenne.
5. Carefully stir in the sweet potato and garlic purée and bring to the boil. The mixture should be fairly thick. Simmer for 2 minutes, then remove from the heat. Add the cheese and egg yolks. Season well with salt and pepper. Heat a baking sheet in the oven.
6. Whisk the egg whites until stiff but not dry and mix a spoonful into the sweet potato mixture. Fold in the remaining egg whites quickly and carefully, using a large metal spoon,.
7. Pour the mixture into the soufflé dish. It should come three-quarters of the way up the sides of the dish. Run a knife around the top edge: this will give the soufflé a 'top hat' appearance.
8. Place the dish on the preheated baking sheet

and bake in the preheated oven for 25 minutes or until the soufflé is risen and brown. It should still be a little soft inside the centre. Serve immediately.

NOTE: The mixture can be baked in 6–8 individual ramekin dishes, depending on size, for 10–15 minutes.

SWEET POTATO AND GINGER MASH

900g/2lb sweet potatoes
salt and freshly ground black pepper
30g/1oz butter
2 cloves of garlic, crushed
2.5cm/1in piece of fresh root ginger, peeled and
*   finely grated*
1½ tablespoons lemon juice
a small pinch of freshly grated nutmeg

1. Peel the sweet potatoes and cut them into large chunks. Cook in boiling salted water for 10 minutes until tender.
2. Drain the potatoes and leave them until the steam has died down. Meanwhile, put the butter, garlic and ginger into a small pan and leave over a low heat.
3. Mash the potatoes until smooth, then beat in the melted butter mixture with the lemon juice, nutmeg and salt and pepper.

SPICED SWEET POTATO CHIPS

450g/1lb sweet potatoes

For the spice paste
1 teaspoon salt
2 large cloves of garlic
2 teaspoons cumin seeds
2 teaspoons coriander seeds
10 black peppercorns
½ teaspoon ground turmeric
3 tablespoons sunflower oil
1 teaspoon lemon juice

To serve
sweet lime sauce (see page 507)

1. Preheat the oven to 200°C/400°F/gas mark 6.
2. Peel the sweet potatoes and cut them into large chips.
3. Put all the dry ingredients for the spice paste into a mortar and grind together. Add the oil and lemon juice and mix well.
4. Toss the sweet potatoes in the spice paste, making sure they are well coated. Spread in a single layer on a baking tray. Bake in the preheated oven for 30–40 minutes until golden and crisp.

POTATO, SWEET POTATO AND PARSNIP SAUTÉ WITH PARMESAN CHEESE

340g/12oz potatoes
340g/12oz sweet potatoes
340g/12oz parsnips
2 tablespoons sunflower oil
30g/1oz unsalted butter
1 onion, sliced
3 tablespoons freshly grated Parmesan cheese
1 tablespoon chopped fresh rosemary
salt and freshly ground black pepper

1. Peel the potatoes, sweet potatoes and parsnips and cut them into 5cm/2in chunks. Cook them in boiling salted water. The potatoes will take about 15 minutes to cook and the sweet potatoes and parsnips 10 minutes.
2. Heat the oil and butter in a wok or large, non-stick frying pan. Add the onion and cook over a low heat for 5 minutes. Add the potatoes, sweet potatoes and parsnip and cook for 20 minutes, turning the vegetables over occasionally.
3. Increase the heat and allow the vegetables to brown, but do not let them burn.
4. Remove from the heat, scatter over the cheese and rosemary and season with salt and pepper. Mix well and serve immediately.

BAKED SWEET POTATOES WITH CHILLI SOURED CREAM

4 large sweet potatoes
1 tablespoon olive oil
1 red chilli, deseeded and chopped (see page 22)
150ml/¼ pint soured cream
grated zest and juice of 1 lime
salt and freshly ground black pepper
a pinch of ground cumin
55g/2oz butter
1 tablespoon chopped fresh coriander, to garnish

1. Preheat the oven to 200°C/400°F/gas mark 6.
2. Wash the sweet potatoes and prick them all over. Place on a baking tray, rub with a little oil and bake in the preheated oven for about 1 hour until soft all the way through.
3. Meanwhile, put the chilli into a bowl with the soured cream, lime zest and juice. Season with salt, pepper and cumin.
4. When the sweet potatoes are cooked, cut them in half and fluff up the flesh with a fork. Put a knob of butter on each half. Spoon the chilli cream on top and scatter with the coriander.

NOTE: Instead of the soured cream, serve with the spiced butter from the savoury American pancake recipe (see page 490).

WARM SALAD OF SWEET POTATOES WITH GINGER AND GARLIC

The spicy sweet potato mixture without the salad leaves makes an excellent side dish.

900g/2lb sweet potatoes
2 tablespoons olive oil
30g//1oz butter
4 cloves
4 cardamom pods, crushed
3 cloves of garlic, chopped
5cm/2in piece of fresh root ginger, peeled and
*   chopped*
1 teaspoon ground cinnamon
2 teaspoons soft light-brown sugar
salt and freshly ground black pepper
a pinch of cayenne pepper
4 handfuls of salad leaves, such as lamb's
*   lettuce, watercress, young spinach, rocket,*
*   curly endive*
lime juice
balsamic vinegar
2 tablespoons roughly chopped fresh coriander,
*   to garnish*

1. Peel the sweet potato and cut into 1cm/½in cubes. Heat the oil and butter in a large frying pan and when foaming, add the sweet potatoes, cloves and cardamom. Cook over a low heat, stirring occasionally, for about 15 minutes until the sweet potato is just tender.
2. Add the garlic, ginger and cinnamon and fry for a further 5 minutes. Add the sugar and season with salt, pepper and cayenne. Cook over a low heat until the sugar has dissolved and is starting to caramelize.
3. Wash and pat dry the salad leaves. Arrange on 4 individual plates. Cool the sweet potatoes for 1 minute, then toss with a good squeeze of lime juice and a good shake of balsamic vinegar. Pile on top of the salad leaves and scatter with the coriander before serving.

TOSTADAS WITH RADISH AND GUACAMOLE

When cold, the tostadas can be broken into pieces and used with dips in the same way as tortilla chips.

55g/2oz wholemeal flour
55g/2oz plain flour, plus extra for dusting
1 teaspoon mild chilli powder
1 teaspoon cumin seeds
a pinch of ground coriander
salt and freshly ground black pepper
1 tablespoon olive oil
90ml/3fl oz hot water
about 12 radishes, grated
1 tablespoon white wine vinegar
1 teaspoon caster sugar
1 quantity guacamole (see page 213)
a handful of fresh coriander, chopped

1. Mix the flours and spices together in a bowl. Season with ½ teaspoon salt and pepper. Add the oil and mix with a round-bladed knife until the mixture resembles breadcrumbs. Gradually stir in the hot water and bind to a soft but firm dough. Knead until smooth, cover with a clean, damp tea-towel and leave to stand for 5 minutes.
2. Divide the dough into 8 equal-sized pieces. Shape each into a ball, flatten and roll into a circle about 3mm/⅛in thick. Dust each tostada with flour as it is made and pile up under the damp tea-towel.
3. Mix the radishes with the vinegar and sugar. Season with salt and pepper.
4. Heat a heavy frying pan or griddle. Cook the tostadas in batches until they bubble on one side. Turn and cook on the other side.
5. Serve while still warm, with a spoonful of guacamole topped with the radish mixture and sprinkled with fresh coriander on the side.

STIR-FRIED RADISH WITH MUSTARD SEEDS

This recipe can be served as a side dish or with noodles or rice as a main course.

1 bunch of radishes
1 mooli or daikon radish, about 225g/8oz
2 tablespoons chilli or sesame oil
1 tablespoon mustard seeds
1 red chilli, deseeded and chopped (see page 22)
salt and freshly ground black pepper
1–2 tablespoons dark soy sauce
110g/4oz lamb's lettuce or young spinach
1 tablespoon chopped fresh mint, to garnish

1. Top and tail the radishes and quarter them lengthways. Peel the mooli or daikon and cut into chunks about the same size as the radishes.
2. Heat the oil in a wok or large, heavy pan. Add the mustard seeds and fry until they begin to pop. Stir in the radish, mooli and chilli. Toss over the heat for a few minutes until the vegetables have lost their crunch.
3. Season with salt and pepper. Toss in the soy sauce and lamb's lettuce and shake over the heat for 1 minute. Sprinkle with the mint before serving.

RADISH AND KOHLRABI SALAD

1 bunch of radishes
110g/4oz mooli
2 carrots
225g/8oz kohlrabi
2 sticks of celery
2 tablespoons vegetable or sunflower oil
1 teaspoon black mustard seeds
salt and freshly ground black pepper
1 tablespoon sesame oil
balsamic vinegar
1 tablespoon chopped fresh celery leaves

1. Top, tail and scrub the radishes. Scrub the mooli and peel the carrot and kohlrabi. Slice them into very thin rounds, using a mandolin or food processor. Remove any stringy threads from the celery and slice thinly. Toss the vegetables together in a bowl.
2. Heat the oil in a small pan. Add the mustard seeds and fry until they begin to pop. Pour the hot oil over the vegetables and season with salt, pepper, sesame oil and a dash of vinegar. Transfer to a shallow serving dish and sprinkle with the celery leaves.

RADISH AND RED ONION SALAD WITH POMEGRANATE DRESSING

1 tablespoon pomegranate syrup
4 tablespoons olive oil
salt and freshly ground black pepper
½ teaspoon ground cinnamon
1 teaspoon soft light brown sugar
1 pomegranate
2 oranges, peeled and sliced
2 bunches of radishes
1 red onion
fresh mint leaves, to garnish

1. Put the syrup and oil into a salad bowl. Season with salt, pepper, the cinnamon and sugar and whisk together.
2. Cut the pomegranate in half and ease out the seeds with a teaspoon handle or fork and add to the dressing.
3. Wash and top and tail the radishes. Slice them very thinly, using a sharp knife or mandolin. Cut the onion in half and peel and slice very thinly. Toss together with the fruit and dressing in the bowl. Garnish with mint leaves just before serving.

MOOLI RELISH

This relish can be served with any patties or burgers made with pulses.

225g/8oz mooli
3 tablespoons mayonnaise (see page 527)
1 teaspoon French mustard
2 teaspoons white wine vinegar
a little milk (optional)
Tabasco sauce
salt and freshly ground black pepper

1. Peel and grate the mooli.
2. Whisk the mayonnaise together with the mustard and vinegar. The mayonnaise should be thick enough to coat the back of a wooden spoon thickly. If it is too thick, dilute with milk. Fold the grated mooli into the mayonnaise and season with a good dash of Tabasco, salt and pepper. Leave to stand for 30 minutes for the flavours to blend before serving.

ROASTED SALSIFY

675g/1½lb salsify
salt and freshly ground black pepper
olive oil
30g/1oz butter

1. Scrub the salsify but do not peel. Cook in boiling salted water for about 30 minutes until the black skin will peel away easily. Remove the skin and rinse in hot water. Set aside to dry for 20 minutes.
2. Preheat the oven to 200°C/400°F/gas mark 6.
3. Heat the oil and butter in a roasting tin until foaming. Add the salsify and turn until well coated. Roast in the preheated oven for 30 minutes until golden-brown.

NOTE: The salsify can be eaten simply boiled as at the end of stage 1. Serve with melted butter and lemon juice or hollandaise sauce (see page 526).

MASHED SWEDE

675g/1½lb swede
salt and freshly ground black pepper
55g/2oz butter
freshly grated nutmeg

1. Peel the swede and slice thinly. Put into a saucepan, season with salt and pepper and pour about 1cm/½in water into the bottom of the pan. Cover with a tight-fitting lid and simmer gently until the swede is tender and all the water has evaporated.
2. Mash the swede over a low heat with a fork or potato masher. Stir in the butter and season with salt, pepper and nutmeg. Serve hot.

BASHED NEEPS WITH GINGER

675g/1½lb swede
salt and freshly ground black pepper
55g/2oz butter
2.5cm/1in piece of fresh root ginger, peeled and
    grated
2 tablespoons lemon juice
1 tablespoon caster sugar

1. Peel the swede and cut it into chunks. Put into a saucepan of boiling salted water and cook until tender. Drain and put back into the pan over a low heat to steam-dry.
2. Meanwhile, put the butter, ginger, lemon juice, sugar and salt and pepper into a small saucepan. Bring up to the boil, then lower the heat and simmer for 2 minutes.
3. Put the swede into a food processor and process until smooth. With the motor still running, pour in the butter and ginger mixture. Alternatively, push the swede through a sieve or mash with a potato masher, then add the butter and ginger mixture. This will not produce such a smooth result. Serve hot.

SWEDE DAUPHINOISE

30g/1oz butter, plus extra for greasing
1 medium onion, thinly sliced
1 clove of garlic, crushed
2 teaspoons paprika
675g/1½lb swede
150ml/¼ pint double cream
150ml/¼ pint milk
salt and freshly ground black pepper
freshly grated nutmeg

1. Preheat the oven to 180°C/350°F/gas mark 4. Grease an ovenproof dish with butter.
2. Melt the butter, add the onion and fry over a low heat until soft and golden-brown. Add the garlic and half the paprika and fry for 1 further minute.
3. Peel the swede, cut into wedges, then slice thinly by hand or in a food processor. Place in a bowl.
4. Whisk together the cream and milk. Pour over the swede and season with salt, plenty of pepper and nutmeg and mix well.
5. Arrange half the swede in the base of the dish. Top with the onion and garlic mixture. Add the remaining swede, arranging the top in an overlapping layer. Pour any cream left in the bowl over the swede. Cover with kitchen foil and bake in the preheated oven for 1 hour.
6. Sprinkle with the remaining paprika and bake for a further 30 minutes, uncovered, until the top is browned and the swede tender. Serve hot.

SWEDE AND PARSNIP MASH WITH SOURED CREAM AND MUSTARD SEEDS

450g/1lb swede
450g/1lb parsnips
salt and freshly ground black pepper
30g/1oz butter
5 tablespoons soured cream
2 teaspoons black mustard seeds, toasted (see page 22)

1. Peel the swede and parsnips and cut them into chunks.
2. Boil the vegetables in the salted water until tender. Drain very well.
3. Mash the cooked vegetables with a potato masher. Beat in the butter, soured cream and mustard seeds. Season to taste with salt and pepper. Serve hot.

CARAMELIZED TURNIPS WITH ORANGE AND HORSERADISH

675g/1½lb small white turnips
1 tablespoon olive oil
salt and freshly ground black pepper
grated zest and juice of 1 orange
2 tablespoons creamed horseradish
75ml/2½fl oz double cream
1 tablespoon caster sugar

1. Preheat the oven to 200°C/400°F/gas mark 6.
2. Peel the turnips and cut them into 2.5cm/1in chunks. Put into a roasting tin, add the oil and turn the turnips over so that they are coated with oil. Season with salt and pepper. Bake in the preheated oven for 15 minutes.
3. Meanwhile, put the orange zest and juice in a small saucepan with the horseradish and bring to the boil. Boil to reduce by half. Stir in the cream, then remove from the heat.
4. Turn the turnips over and sprinkle with the sugar. Return to the oven for 10 minutes.
5. Pour over the sauce, mix well and cook in the oven for a further 5 minutes. Serve hot.

GLAZED TURNIPS WITH CORIANDER

675g/1½lb small white turnips
salt and freshly ground black pepper
30g/1oz butter
1 teaspoon coriander seeds, crushed
1 tablespoon clear honey
150ml/¼ pint spicy vegetable stock (see page 531)
2 tablespoons chopped fresh coriander

1. If the turnips are very small and young, leave them whole and unpeeled. If not, peel and quarter them. Blanch in boiling salted water for about 3 minutes, then drain and leave to stand for about 30 minutes to allow them to dry.
2. Melt the butter in a sauté pan large enough to hold the turnips in a single layer. Add the coriander seeds, turnips and honey. Give the pan a good shake to coat the turnips in the butter and honey. Cook over a low heat until the turnips begin to caramelize.
3. Pour in the stock and stir to dissolve the caramel. Season with salt and pepper and simmer gently until the turnips are tender and the liquid has reduced to a syrupy glaze. Adjust the seasoning to taste and sprinkle with the coriander. Serve warm.

TURNIPS WITH GARLIC TOMATO

450g/1lb small white turnips
2 tablespoons olive oil
4 shallots, finely chopped
3 cloves of garlic, chopped
1 red chilli, deseeded and chopped (see page 22)
1 × 200g/7oz can of chopped tomatoes
150ml/¼ pint winter vegetable stock (see page 530)
salt and freshly ground black pepper
2 tablespoons chopped fresh flat-leaf parsley

1. Peel and trim the turnips. Cut each turnip into 6–8 thick wedges, depending on size. Heat the oil in a frying pan, add the shallots and cook over a low heat until softened. Add the turnips, garlic and chilli, cover and cook gently for about 10 minutes.
2. Stir in the tomatoes and stock. Season with salt and pepper. Simmer gently for about 20 minutes until the turnips are tender and the sauce reduced. Sprinkle with parsley before serving.

WINTER VEGETABLE PIE WITH ROUGH PUFF PASTRY CRUST

1 red onion
450g/1lb parsnips
340g/12oz swede
3 carrots
2 tablespoons olive oil
salt and freshly ground black pepper
290ml/½ pint winter vegetable stock (see page 530)
30g/1oz pearl barley
1 bay leaf
2 tablespoons mushroom ketchup
1–2 tablespoons finely chopped fresh parsley
225g/8oz chestnuts, cooked
225g/8oz flour quantity rough puff pastry (see page 523)
1 egg, beaten, to glaze

1. Preheat the oven to 190°C/375°F/gas mark 5. Peel and roughly dice the onion and root vegetables.
2. Cook the barley in the stock for 20 minutes.
3. Heat the oil in a saucepan, add the onion and cook over a low heat for 1–2 minutes. Add the root vegetables and season with salt and pepper. Cover and sauté for 2–3 minutes.
4. Add the stock with the pearl barley and bay leaf and simmer gently for 5–8 minutes or until the vegetables are just soft. Remove the bay leaf. Add the mushroom ketchup, parsley and chestnuts to the vegetables, stir well and transfer to a 570ml/1 pint pie dish. Allow to cool.
5. Roll out the pastry to the thickness of a £1 coin. Cut a long strip just wider than the rim of the pie dish, brush the lip of the dish with water and press down the strip.
6. Brush the strip with water and lay over the sheet of pastry. Press down firmly. Cut away any excess pastry. Cut a 1cm/½in hole in the centre of the pastry lid to allow the steam to escape. The excess pastry can be cut into leaves and used to decorate the pie.
7. Brush the pastry with beaten egg and leave in the refrigerator to relax for 10 minutes.
8. Put the pie dish on a baking sheet and bake in the preheated oven for 30 minutes or until the pastry is well risen and golden-brown.

ROOT VEGETABLE CURRY

225g/8oz potatoes
225g/8oz sweet potatoes
225g/8oz carrots
225g/8oz parsnips
2 tablespoons sunflower oil
1 large onion, sliced
3 cloves of garlic, crushed
1 green chilli, chopped
2.5cm/1in piece of fresh root ginger, peeled and
    grated
½ teaspoon ground cloves
a good pinch of chilli powder
2 teaspoons ground cumin
3 teaspoons ground coriander
1 teaspoon ground turmeric
2 teaspoons mustard seeds
6 cardamom pods, crushed
1 × 400g/14oz can of chopped tomatoes
570ml/1 pint water
225g/8oz leeks, trimmed and sliced
salt and freshly ground black pepper
200ml/7fl oz Greek yoghurt
2 tablespoons chopped fresh coriander
55g/2oz almonds, toasted (see page 22)

To serve
fresh lime pickle (see page 508)
mango and lime chilli relish (see page 508)

1. Peel the root vegetables and cut them into
2.5cm/1in cubes.
2. Heat the oil in a large saucepan. Add the
onion and cook over a low heat for 5 minutes.
Add the garlic, chilli and ginger and cook for a
further 2 minutes.
3. Add the cloves, chilli powder, cumin, ground
coriander, turmeric, mustard seeds and
cardamom and cook for a further 2 minutes.
4. Add the tomatoes, water, leeks and root
vegetables. Season well with salt and pepper.
Bring to the boil, then cover the pan, lower the
heat and cook gently for 30–45 minutes until
the vegetables are soft.
5. If there is a lot of liquid left, remove the lid
and allow it to reduce a little.
6. Remove from the heat and stir in the
yoghurt, coriander and almonds. Serve
immediately with fresh lime pickle and mango
and lime chilli relish.

VEGETABLE TAGINE WITH CARDOONS

450g/1lb cardoons or 1 head of celery
lemon juice
salt and freshly ground black pepper
3 carrots
2 small white turnips
3 tablespoons olive oil
1 large onion, sliced
3 cloves of garlic, chopped
2 green chillies, deseeded and chopped (see
    page 22)
1 heaped teaspoon ground cumin
4 tomatoes, peeled and chopped (see page 22)
110g/4oz dried black-eye beans, soaked
    overnight
1 heaped teaspoon saffron strands
570ml/1 pint winter vegetable stock (see
    page 530)
2 tablespoons chopped fresh coriander
2 courgettes
2 tablespoons preserved lemons (see page 510)
110g/4oz green olives, pitted
30g/1oz cracked wheat

1. Remove the stringy threads from the
cardoons or celery and cut into 5cm/2in
lengths. If using cardoons, put them into a pan
with a squeeze of lemon juice and enough salted
water to cover, and simmer for 30 minutes. Peel
the carrots and turnips and cut into 2.5cm/1in
cubes.
2. Heat the oil in a large, heavy saucepan. Add
the onion and fry over a low heat until soft and
transparent. Stir in the garlic, chilli and cumin
and fry for 1 further minute. Add the cardoons
or celery, the carrots, turnip, tomatoes, rinsed
and drained soaked beans and saffron. Stir in
the stock and coriander. Season with salt and
pepper. Bring to the boil, then lower the heat
and simmer for 40 minutes.
3. Cut the courgettes in half lengthways, then
cut into 5cm/2in pieces. Add the preserved
lemons. Halve the olives. Add to the tagine with
the cracked wheat and simmer for a further 20–
30 minutes until all the vegetables are tender.
Serve hot.

ROOT VEGETABLE RÖSTI

450g/1lb waxy potatoes
salt and freshly ground black pepper
110g/4oz swede, peeled
1 small turnip, peeled
110g/4oz carrot
1 medium onion, finely chopped
3 tablespoons olive oil
chopped fresh parsley, to garnish

1. Peel the potatoes, cut them into even-sized pieces and parboil in salted water for 3 minutes. Cut the swede, turnip and carrot into similar-sized pieces. Put them into a separate saucepan of cold water, bring to the boil and boil for 2 minutes. Drain all the vegetables and leave them in a colander covered with a clean tea-towel for at least 2 hours, ideally in the refrigerator overnight.
2. Heat 1 tablespoon of the oil in a heavy or non-stick 20cm/8in frying pan. Add the onion and cook over a low heat until soft and transparent.
3. Meanwhile, coarsely grate all the parboiled vegetables. When the onion is cooked, fork it into the grated vegetables and season with salt and pepper.
4. Wipe out the frying pan with kitchen paper, add another teaspoon of oil and heat. Put the grated vegetables into the pan and press down well with the back of a wooden spoon. Fry over a low heat for about 15 minutes until the underside is crusty and golden-brown. Shake the pan from time to time to make sure that the rösti does not stick.
5. Loosen the rösti round the edge of the pan. Put an inverted plate over the pan and turn the two together so that the rösti is now on the plate. Heat the remaining oil in the pan, carefully slide the rösti back in and cook over a low heat for a further 15 minutes.
6. Slide the rösti on to a warmed serving dish. Sprinkle with chopped parsley and cut into wedges to serve.

ROOT VEGETABLE AND NUT CRUMBLE

SERVES 6

30g/1oz butter
2 leeks, trimmed and sliced
170g/6oz potatoes
170g/6oz carrots
170g/6oz parsnips
170g/6oz swede
170g/6oz butternut squash
1 teaspoon sweet paprika
30g/1oz wholemeal flour
290ml/½ pint winter vegetable stock (see page 530)
150ml/¼ pint milk
1 × 200g/7oz can of chopped tomatoes
2 tablespoons chopped fresh parsley
salt and freshly ground black pepper

For the crumble topping
110g/4oz butter
170g/6oz plain wholemeal flour
110g/4oz Cheddar cheese, coarsely grated
85g/3oz mixed shelled nuts, such as Brazil nuts, almonds, cashew nuts, coarsely chopped
1 tablespoon sunflower seeds
1 tablespoon sesame seeds
1 tablespoon finely chopped fresh parsley

1. Peel the root vegetables and cut them into 2.5cm/1in chunks. Peel the squash, remove the seeds and cut the flesh into similar-sized chunks.
2. Melt the butter in a large saucepan, add the leeks and cook for 3–4 minutes until tender.
3. Add the root vegetables to the pan, cover and cook over a low heat for 10 minutes. Stir in the paprika and cook for 1 further minute. Stir in the flour and cook for 1 further minute. Gradually stir in the stock, milk and tomatoes. Cover and simmer for 15 minutes or until all the vegetables are tender.
4. Preheat the oven to 190°C/375°F/gas mark 5. Make the topping: work the butter into the flour, by hand or in a food processor, until the mixture resembles coarse breadcrumbs. Stir in the cheese,

nuts, sunflower seeds, sesame seeds and parsley. Season to taste with salt and pepper.

5. Spoon the vegetable mixture into a 2.3 litre/ 4 pint shallow ovenproof dish and spoon over the topping. Bake in the preheated oven for 30 minutes or until golden.

ROASTED ROOT VEGETABLES WITH CRANBERRY RELISH

2 tablespoons clear honey
1 tablespoon wholegrain mustard
3 tablespoons olive oil
1 tablespoon white wine or cider vinegar
salt and freshly ground black pepper
2 tablespoons pinenuts
225g/8oz swede
2 parsnips
2 large carrots
16 small new potatoes
16 button onions

To serve
cranberry relish (see page 509)

1. Preheat the oven to 200°C/400°F/gas mark 6.
2. Mix together the honey, mustard, oil and vinegar and season with salt and pepper. Spread the pinenuts out on a baking tray and toast in the preheated oven for a few minutes until golden-brown, then remove from the oven and set aside.
3. Peel the swede, parsnips and carrots and cut them into pieces about the same size as the new potatoes. Parboil all the vegetables in salted water for 5 minutes. Drain, pour over the honey and mustard mixture and leave to cool.
4. Douse the button onions in boiling water for 1 minute, then peel and trim off the roots. Stir into the other vegetables.
5. Carefully thread the vegetables on to skewers or wooden kebab sticks. Suspend the skewers over a roasting tin and cook in the preheated oven for 30 minutes, basting from time to time, until the vegetables are tender and golden-brown. Scatter with pinenuts before serving and hand the cranberry relish separately.

ROASTED ROOT VEGETABLES WITH ROCKET AND GARLIC

about 900g/2lb assorted root vegetables, such as
*   carrots, parsnips, baby beetroot, swede,*
*   baby potatoes, turnip*
1 large red onion
2 bulbs of fennel
2 tablespoons chopped fresh mixed herbs
150ml/¼ pint olive oil
salt and freshly ground black pepper
1 bulb of garlic
grated zest and juice of 1 lemon
2 teaspoons clear honey
110g/4oz rocket
shavings of Parmesan cheese, to garnish

1. Place a large roasting tin in the oven and preheat to 220°C/425°F/gas mark 7.
2. Peel the root vegetables and cut them into walnut-sized pieces. If using baby new potatoes, scrub them and leave whole. Cut the onion into thick wedges. Remove the outer leaves from the fennel and cut into quarters.
3. Mix all the vegetables together in a bowl with the herbs and 2 tablespoons of the oil. Season with salt and pepper and mix well. Spread in a single layer in the hot roasting tin. Slice the top off the bulb of garlic, just exposing the tip of the cloves, and put into the tin. Roast in the preheated oven for about 40–50 minutes, stirring from time to time, until the vegetables are crisp on the outside and tender in the middle.
4. Make a dressing by whisking together the remaining olive oil, lemon zest and juice and the honey. Season with salt and pepper.
5. When the vegetables are cooked, take the garlic from the pan, turn it upside down and squeeze the cloves out into the pan. Toss the vegetables together with the rocket and the dressing. Serve immediately, topped with a few shavings of Parmesan cheese.

SLICED ROOT VEGETABLES WITH SHALLOTS AND GARLIC

2 parsnips
450g/1lb swede
2 small white turnips
salt and freshly ground black pepper
225g/8oz shallots
12 cardamom pods
1 teaspoon coriander seeds
30g/1oz butter
4 tablespoons olive oil
3–4 cloves of garlic, sliced
a pinch of dried red chilli flakes
lemon juice

To serve
lemon wedges

1. Peel and slice the parsnips and swede. Peel the turnips and cut each into 8–12 wedges, depending on size. Put the vegetables into a saucepan of salted water and bring to the boil, then lower the heat and simmer for 5 minutes. Drain and set aside.
2. Blanch the shallots in boiling water. Peel, trim off the roots and cut each shallot into quarters. Crush the cardamom pods, remove the seeds, crush together with the coriander seeds, mix in the chilli flakes, and set aside.
3. Heat the butter and oil in a heavy frying pan. Add the shallots and garlic and fry over a low heat for 15–20 minutes until soft and golden-brown.
4. Increase the heat and add the spices and sliced vegetables. Season with salt and pepper. Toss in the spicy juices until tender and golden-brown. Stir in a little lemon juice before serving and hand the lemon wedges separately.

ROOT VEGETABLE OVEN CHIPS

340g/12oz parsnips
2 carrots
1 medium swede
1 sweet potato
4 tablespoons vegetable oil
6 bay leaves
coarse sea salt and freshly ground black pepper

1. Preheat the oven to 200°C/400°F/gas mark 6.
2. Peel the vegetables and cut them into batons 7.5cm/3in long and 1cm/½in thick.
3. Heat the oil in a large roasting tin and heat in the oven for 3–4 minutes or until very hot. Add the vegetables and bay leaves. Season with salt and pepper and carefully turn in the hot oil.
4. Cook the vegetables on the top shelf of the preheated oven for 45–60 minutes or until crisp, brown and tender when pierced with the tip of a knife.
5. Drain the vegetables on kitchen paper and sprinkle with a little salt. Serve very hot.

Celeriac Mash with Apple and Watercress

Potato Soup with Truffle Oil and Black Olives

Buttered Parsnips with Lamb's Lettuce and Spiced Kumquats

Leek and Stilton Eccles Cakes, Quinoa and Apricot Salad
with Toasted Pinenuts

Leek and Walnut Steamed Pudding, Broccoli and Greens
with Citrus Gremolata

Cauliflower Dahl, Parmender Salad and Lime Pickle

Radish and Red Onion Salad with Pomegranate Dressing

Selection of Oriental Greens (clockwise from bottom right):
Pak Choi, Choi Sum, Bok Choi, Sisho Purple, Chinese Chives, Kang Choi,
Green Mustard, Chinese Convolvulus

THE ONION FAMILY

White, red and Spanish onions • Button onions • Spring onions • Shallots • Leeks • Garlic

INTRODUCTION

The ubiquitous onion is indispensable in cooking. It may have a humble image but it has been highly regarded for both culinary and healing properties by many civilizations. The onion has been cultivated for so long that it is almost unknown in the wild apart from mustard garlic, which appears in hedgerows in May and June and is responsible for the mild garlicky smell that wafts through the air at that time of year. Onions are the foundation of a vast range of dishes, imparting flavours through the spectrum from tearfully fiery to mellow and sweet.

In cooked dishes onion is sweated in butter and oil to take away the harsh, raw flavour. During cooking chemical places take place that make onion many times sweeter than sugar. It is the caramelization of these sugars that turns onion brown. Onions should usually be cooked slowly. Frying them over a fierce heat creates a tough film around the outside. This is fine if the onions are to be crisp and scattered on top of a dish but they will never melt into a purée unless cooked slowly.

Buy rock-hard onions that are dry with no sign of moisture. Avoid any that show signs of sprouting on top. Store them in a dry, airy place.

Brown, **yellow** or **white globe onions** are the medium to large onions that we use in everyday cooking. They are the most fiercely flavoured and are particularly good for hearty soups and stews.

Button or **pickling onions** are baby globe onions picked when the bulb has just formed. They are mostly found in autumn. The onions are used whole for roasting, on kebabs and in casseroles. It is a good idea to leave the root attached and trim it off with a small sharp knife at the end of cooking. This prevents the onion from falling apart. These small onions are especially difficult to peel. Dousing first in boiling water helps to loosen the skin.

Red onions are mild and sweet with ruby-coloured skins and striking red-tinged layers. They are best used raw as they lose colour when cooked. They are wonderful in salads or cut into wedges. Or they may be skewered, brushed with oil and barbecued, and also make a delicious confit.

Spanish onions are large and spherical. Milder and sweeter than globe onions, they can be used raw in salads and are a good choice for roasting or baking whole.

Shallots are not baby onions but have distinctive characteristics of their own. They are oval and can have grey, pinkish or brown skins. They grow in clusters, like garlic, with up to 6 bulbs joined at the root. Shallots are the most delicate member of the onion family and if cooked long and slow, gently melt into a liquid purée. They are used as the base for many a great sauce. Care should be taken when sweating shallots as they develop a bitter flavour when browned. Banana shallots are an elongated oval in shape. The flesh is purple and sweeter than that of other shallots. They are too big to use whole but if halved lengthways the lovely layers can be seen. One banana shallot is the equivalent of about 4 shallots – a great saving on the tiresome peeling process.

Spring onions are also known as scallions, salad onions or green onions. Some are mild-flavoured and others are strong and peppery. They are available all year round. Spring onions are mostly used raw in salads but they are also good for stir-fries or with eggs and in mashed potatoes.

Leeks are found on the periphery of the onion family. Their flavour is very subtle and gives great depth to soups and stews. If cooked for long enough, leeks will disintegrate, thickening the liquid and enriching the flavour. The white part of the leek is most favoured as it has the best flavour and texture. Use as much of the green part as possible and save the rest for the stockpot. Look for leeks with bright green leaves.

Leeks can deteriorate rapidly and can only be stored in the refrigerator for up to a week. They need careful washing as soil is harboured between the layers. Remove the root and outer leaves and trim the dark green leaves at an angle. Cut the leek in half lengthways and hold under cold running water, opening out the layers to make sure that all the dirt has been removed.

Garlic is as well known for its healing properties as it is for its culinary uses. It is known to be an antibacterial agent, to boost the immune system and lower cholesterol levels. It is also reputed to ward off evil spirits.

Garlic is a bulb which is harvested when the tall green shoots are dying down. Most garlic sold has been dried briefly but in June to July fresh or wet garlic is available. This is a real treat with its plump, juicy, mild-flavoured cloves which can be chopped or sliced and eaten raw in salads. Elephant garlic is rare to find but is also mild in flavour with huge cloves that can weigh up to 85g/3oz. Choose garlic that has firm, plump bulbs that show no sign of sprouting. Store it in a cool, airy place. The amount of juice released from the garlic determines the strength of flavour, so whole cloves will impart a mild flavour, chopped a medium flavour and crushed the maximum flavour. As with onion, slow cooking tames the flavour, causing it to become sweet and rich. Be careful not to allow garlic to brown or it will turn very bitter.

FRENCH ONION SOUP WITH GRUYÈRE CHEESE TOASTS

SERVES 6

30g/1oz butter, plus extra for spreading
2 tablespoons sunflower oil
675g/1½lb onions, halved and thinly sliced
2 cloves of garlic, crushed
½ teaspoon caster sugar
1 litre/1¾ pints winter vegetable stock (see page 530)
2 teaspoons yeast extract
290ml/½ pint dry white wine
6 thick slices of fresh French bread
225g/8oz Gruyère cheese, coarsely grated
salt and freshly ground black pepper

1. Heat the butter and oil in a large, heavy saucepan. Add the onions, garlic and sugar and cook over a medium heat for about 30 minutes, stirring from time to time, until the onions are soft and richly caramelized.
2. Add the stock, yeast extract and wine and bring to the boil. Lower the heat, cover and leave to simmer for a further 30 minutes.
3. Preheat the grill to high. Season the soup with salt and pepper and ladle it into 6 flameproof bowls. Place the bowls in the bottom of the grill pan.
4. Lightly toast the slices of bread on both sides and spread with a little butter. Float the toast, buttered side up, on top of each bowl of soup and then cover each slice with grated cheese. Carefully slide the tray under the grill and cook for 2–3 minutes until the cheese is golden and bubbling.

ONION BHAJIS

1 large egg
1½ tablespoons lemon juice
6 tablespoons cold water
170g/6oz chickpea flour (gram flour)
1 medium-hot green Dutch chilli, deseeded and finely chopped (see page 22)
¾ teaspoon cumin seeds
¾ teaspoon garam masala
¾ teaspoon chilli powder
¼ teaspoon ground turmeric
¼ teaspoon cayenne pepper
¾ teaspoon salt
sunflower oil, for deep-frying
340g/12oz onions, thinly sliced

To serve
cucumber and mint raita (see page 513)
mango chutney

1. Break the egg into a mixing bowl and beat in the lemon juice and water. Beat in the chickpea flour, green chilli, spices and salt to make a smooth batter. Set aside for 15 minutes.
2. Heat oil in a deep-fryer to 165°C/310°F. Add the sliced onions to the batter and mix together well.
3. To shape the bhajis, scoop up about one-eighth of the mixture between 2 dessertspoons and form into a roughly shaped ball. Carefully lower 4 balls into the hot oil and cook for 4–5 minutes, turning them from time to time, until they are crisp and golden-brown.
4. Remove the bhajis with a slotted spoon and leave to drain on kitchen paper. Keep hot in a low oven while you cook the remainder in the same way. Serve with the cucumber and mint raita and mango chutney.

AMERICAN-STYLE ONION RINGS IN BUTTERMILK AND CORNMEAL

2 large onions
170g/6oz plain flour
70g/2½oz cornmeal
45g/1½oz cornflour
5 teaspoons baking powder
2 teaspoons salt
cayenne pepper
150ml/¼ pint milk
150ml/¼ pint buttermilk
vegetable oil, for deep-frying

To serve
spicy tomato ketchup (see page 515)

1. Cut the onions crossways into slices 2.5cm/ 1in thick. Carefully separate each slice into rings, discarding those from the very centre of each slice. Put the rings into a large mixing bowl, cover with cold water and leave to soak for 30 minutes.
2. Sift 110g/4oz of the flour, the cornmeal, cornflour, baking powder, salt and a pinch of cayenne into another mixing bowl. Put the milk and buttermilk into a smaller bowl and mix together well. Put the remaining flour into a third bowl.
3. Heat the oil in a deep-fryer to 170°C/325°F. Drain the onion rings well but do not dry them. Dip them one at a time into the flour, then into the buttermilk mixture, and then into the cornmeal mixture. Finally dip once more into the buttermilk and the cornmeal mixture to give them an extra-thick coating.
4. Deep-fry the onion rings 4 at a time for 2 minutes, turning them over halfway through, until crisp and golden. Drain on kitchen paper and keep hot in a low oven while you cook the remainder in the same way. Serve with the spicy tomato ketchup.

ONION LATTE

SERVES 6

55g/2oz butter, plus extra for greasing
2 onions, thinly sliced
30g/1oz plain flour
a large pinch of cayenne pepper
1 bay leaf
150ml/¼ pint milk
150ml/¼ pint double cream
salt and freshly ground black pepper
2 egg yolks
4 egg whites
30g/1oz Parmesan cheese, freshly grated

1. Melt the butter in a heavy frying pan, add the onion and fry over a very low heat for 20–30 minutes until soft, golden and caramelized.
2. Preheat the oven to 200°C/400°F/gas mark 6. Grease 6 ramekin dishes with butter.
3. Stir the flour, cayenne and bay leaf into the onions and fry for 1 further minute. Gradually pour on the milk, stirring all the time, until the mixture is smooth and very thick.
4. Remove from the heat and discard the bay leaf. Gradually stir in the cream. Season with salt and pepper, then beat in the egg yolks.
5. Whisk the egg whites until stiff but not dry. Using a large metal spoon, fold a spoonful of egg white into the onion mixture and then carefully fold in the remainder. Spoon into the ramekin dishes. Sprinkle with the cheese. Bake in the preheated oven for about 10 minutes until just set at the edges but fluffy, golden-brown on top and runny inside. Serve immediately.

FOUR ONION TART WITH POLENTA PASTRY

200g/7oz polenta pastry (see page 524)
12 shallots, peeled and halved
2 tablespoons olive oil
1 onion, sliced
2 cloves of garlic, crushed
8 spring onions, trimmed and sliced
1 egg
1 egg yolk
100ml/3½fl oz milk
55ml/2fl oz double cream
salt and freshly ground black pepper
55g/2oz mature Cheddar cheese, grated

1. Preheat the oven to 200°C/400°F/gas mark 6.
2. Chill the pastry, then roll out and use to line a 20cm/8in flan tin. Chill again for 10 minutes. Bake blind for 15 minutes in the preheated oven (see page 22).
3. Meanwhile, put the shallots into a roasting tin and add half the olive oil. Turn the shallots to coat them with oil. Cook in the oven for 15–20 minutes or until the shallots are softened and slightly caramelized. Remove from the oven and allow to cool. Lower the oven temperature to 170°C/325°F/gas mark 3.
4. Heat the remaining oil in a heavy saucepan, add the sliced onion, cover and sweat over a low heat for 20 minutes or until soft but not coloured. Add the garlic and spring onions. Cook for a further 5 minutes.
5. Mix together the whole egg, egg yolk, milk and cream and season with salt and pepper.
6. Sprinkle half the cheese over the base of the cooked pastry case. Arrange the onions and shallots on top, then add the remaining cheese. Pour over the egg and milk mixture. Bake in the oven for 20 minutes or until the filling is set. Serve hot or cold.

ONION GOUGÈRE WITH BROAD BEANS

For the gougère
1 tablespoon oil
2 onions, thinly sliced
salt and freshly ground black pepper
110g/4oz Cheddar cheese
3-egg quantity choux pastry (see page 524)
butter, for greasing
1 teaspoon dried breadcrumbs

For the sauce
675g/1½lb broad beans, cooked weight
1 quantity béchamel sauce (see page 525)
1–2 tablespoons finely chopped fresh parsley

1. First make the gougère: heat the oil in a heavy saucepan, add the onion, season with salt and pepper and sweat over a low heat for about 10 minutes or until soft and transparent.
2. Cut 85g/3oz of the cheese into cubes and add to the choux together with the softened onion. Mix thoroughly. Spoon the mixture round the edge of a greased ovenproof dish. Set aside.
3. Remove the tough outer skins from the broad beans.
4. Preheat the oven to 200°C/400°F/gas mark 6.
5. Heat the béchamel sauce and add the broad beans together with the parsley. Season to taste with salt and pepper.
6. Pile the broad bean mixture into the centre of the dish. Grate over the remaining cheese and sprinkle the breadcrumbs over the top. Bake near the top of the preheated oven for 25–30 minutes or until the choux is well risen and the sauce is bubbling. Serve immediately.

ONION MARMELADE CHEESECAKE

1 tablespoon olive oil
2 large onions, sliced
1 tablespoon red wine vinegar
1 tablespoon caster sugar

For the base
70g/2½oz butter
1 clove of garlic, crushed
110g/4oz fresh white breadcrumbs
1 tablespoon wholegrain mustard
55g/2oz Cheddar cheese, grated
1 tablespoon chopped fresh chives
1 tablespoon chopped fresh thyme
salt and freshly ground black pepper

For the topping
70g/2½oz soft goat's cheese
100g/3½oz feta cheese
2 eggs
100ml/3½fl oz Greek yoghurt
1 tablespoon chopped fresh thyme
salt and freshly ground black pepper

1. Preheat the oven to 180°C/350°F/gas mark 4.
2. Heat the oil in a medium saucepan. Add the onions, cover and cook over a very low heat for 20–30 minutes, stirring occasionally, until very soft but not browned.
3. Add the vinegar and sugar and boil until pale brown and sticky.
4. Make the base: melt the butter in a medium saucepan, add the garlic and cook over a low heat for 2 minutes. Do not allow the garlic to brown. Remove from the heat and stir in the breadcrumbs, mustard, cheese, chives and thyme. Season well with salt and pepper.
5. Press the mixture into the base and up the sides of a 20cm/8in loose-based flan tin. Bake in the preheated oven for 10 minutes. Lower the oven temperature to 150°C/300°F/gas mark 2.
6. Make the topping: beat the cheeses together and add the eggs, yoghurt, thyme, salt and pepper. Beat well. You can use a food processor for this.
7. Put the onions into the cooked flan case and pour the cheese and egg mixture on top.
8. Place on a baking tray and bake in the oven for 30 minutes or until the cheesecake has set. Serve hot or cold.

NOTE: Strong-flavoured onions are best for this recipe. Mild Spanish onions are not suitable.

PISSALADIÈRE WITH MI-CUIT TOMATOES

SERVES 6

For the bread dough
285g/10oz strong plain flour, plus extra for
*   kneading*
1 teaspoon easy-blend yeast
1 teaspoon sea salt flakes
150ml/¼ pint warm water
2 tablespoons olive oil, plus extra for brushing

For the topping
3 sprigs of fresh thyme
3 sprigs of fresh marjoram or oregano
2 small sprigs of fresh rosemary
55ml/2fl oz olive oil
900g/2lb onions, halved and thinly sliced
6 mi-cuit tomatoes, cut into thin strips
55g/2oz small black olives
salt and freshly ground black pepper

1. First make the bread dough: sift the flour, yeast and salt into a warmed mixing bowl. Make a well in the centre and pour in the water and oil. Gradually mix the flour into the liquid to form a soft dough. Turn the dough on to a lightly floured worktop and knead for 10 minutes until smooth and elastic.

2. Place the dough in a lightly oiled mixing bowl and cover tightly with greased clingfilm. Leave in a warm place for 50–60 minutes until doubled in bulk.

3. Make the topping: tie 2 sprigs of the thyme, the marjoram and 1 sprig of the rosemary into a bundle. Heat the oil in a large, heavy frying pan, add the onions, the herb bundle and salt and pepper and cook over a medium heat for about 30 minutes, stirring from time to time, until the onions are very soft and lightly coloured. Remove from the heat and leave to cool. Then remove the bundle of herbs and adjust the seasoning to taste.

4. Pick the leaves from the remaining thyme and rosemary sprigs and roughly chop the rosemary leaves. Preheat the oven to 230°C/450°F/gas mark 8.

5. Turn the dough out of the bowl on to a lightly floured worktop and knock out the air. Knead briefly until smooth, then roll out to fit a large baking sheet (about 30 × 35cm/12 × 14in). Brush the baking sheet lightly with oil and lift on the dough.

6. Spread the onions over the dough in a thick, even layer, to within 2.5cm/1in of the edges. Scatter over the tomatoes, thyme, rosemary and olives. Season with a little more pepper. Cover loosely with clingfilm and leave in a warm place to rise for 30 minutes.

7. Bake the pissaladière in the preheated oven for 20 minutes until crisp and golden around the edges. Remove, leave for 5 minutes, then cut into squares and serve warm.

NOTE: Mi-cuit (literally 'half-cooked') tomatoes have been only partially sun-dried, which makes them more moist. Sun-dried tomatoes in olive oil, drained, can be used as a substitute.

ZEWELWAI

(ALSACIENNE ONION AND CREAM TART)

SERVES 6

For the filling
30g/1oz butter
450g/1lb onions, halved and thinly sliced
3 large eggs
425ml/¾ pint double cream
¼ nutmeg, freshly grated
salt and freshly ground black pepper

For the pastry case
225g/8oz plain flour, plus extra for rolling
½ teaspoon salt
70g/2½oz chilled butter, cut into small pieces
*70g/2½oz chilled vegetable shortening, cut into
    small pieces*
1½–2 tablespoons cold water
1 egg white

1. First make the pastry case: sift the flour and salt into a food processor or a mixing bowl, add the chilled butter and vegetable shortening and work together until the mixture resembles fine breadcrumbs. Stir in the water with a round-bladed knife until the mixture comes together into a ball. Turn on to a lightly floured worktop and knead briefly until smooth.
2. Dust the worktop with a little more flour, roll the pastry out thinly and use to line a 25cm/10in loose-based flan tin 4cm/1½in deep. Prick the base here and there with a fork and chill for 20 minutes.
3. Make the filling: melt the butter in a large, heavy frying pan. Add the onions and cook them over a low heat for 30 minutes, stirring from time to time, until very soft but not browned.
4. Preheat the oven to 200°C/400°F/gas mark 6. Bake the pastry case blind in the preheated oven for 15 minutes (see page 22). Remove the paper and beans and return it to the oven for 5 minutes. Remove from the oven once more and brush the base with a little of the unbeaten egg white. Return to the oven for 1 minute. Remove and lower the oven temperature to 190°C/375°F/gas mark 5.
5. Spread the cooked onions over the base of the pastry case. Beat the eggs, cream and nutmeg together, then season to taste with salt and pepper. Pour the egg mixture over the onions. Bake the tart in the preheated oven for 25 minutes or until the filling is just set and lightly browned. Remove from the tin, cut into wedges and serve warm.

MACARONI CHEESE WITH CARAMELIZED ONIONS

SERVES 6

100g/3½oz butter
2 tablespoons olive oil
2 medium onions, halved and thinly sliced
a pinch of granulated sugar
55g/2oz plain flour
½ teaspoon cayenne pepper
860ml/1½ pints milk
salt and freshly ground black pepper
350g/12oz macaroni
340g/12oz Cheddar cheese, coarsely grated
55ml/2fl oz double cream
30g/1oz fresh white breadcrumbs

1. Heat 15g/½oz of the butter and the oil in a large, heavy frying pan. Add the onions and sugar and cook over a medium to high heat for 20–30 minutes, stirring from time to time, until soft and richly caramelized.
2. Meanwhile, melt the remaining butter in a medium saucepan. Add the flour and cook over a low heat for 4 minutes, stirring all the time. Stir in the cayenne, remove the pan from the heat and gradually stir in the milk. Return the pan to the heat and bring back to the boil, stirring all the time. Leave to simmer for 10 minutes, stirring from time to time, until the sauce is smooth and slightly reduced.
3. Bring a large saucepan of well-salted water to the boil. Add the macaroni and cook for 8–9 minutes or until *al dente*. Drain well.
4. Stir 225g/8oz of the Cheddar cheese into the sauce and season well with salt and pepper. Stir for 2 minutes until the cheese has melted, then stir in the cream and the macaroni.
5. Preheat the oven to 200°C/400°F/gas mark 6. Spoon one-third of the macaroni mixture over the base of a 2.2 litre/4 pint shallow, ovenproof dish. Spread over half the caramelized onions and sprinkle with 30g/1oz of the remaining cheese. Repeat the layers once more and then spoon over the remaining pasta mixture. Mix the remaining cheese with the breadcrumbs and sprinkle over the top. Bake in the preheated oven for 25–30 minutes until golden and bubbling. Leave to rest for 10 minutes before serving.

NOTE: If macaroni is unavailable use any tubular shaped pasta such as rigatoni or tubetti.

SWEET AND SOUR PICKLED ONIONS ON GRILLED PARMESAN SOURDOUGH BREAD

1cm/½in piece of fresh root ginger, peeled and grated
7g/¼oz blades of mace
7g/¼oz allspice berries
7g/¼oz black peppercorns
7g/¼oz yellow mustard seeds
4 whole cloves
1 dried red chilli
1 cinnamon stick
3 tablespoons olive oil
4 onions, very thinly sliced
a pinch of salt
1½ tablespoons soft light brown sugar
4 tablespoons white wine vinegar
lemon juice
4 thick slices of sourdough bread
85g/3oz Parmesan cheese, freshly grated
55g/2oz Cheddar cheese, grated

1. Tie the ginger and the spices except the cinnamon stick in a piece of muslin. Crush lightly with a rolling pin.
2. Heat the oil in a large saucepan and add the bag of spices, the cinnamon stick, the onions and salt. Cover and cook over a low heat for 45–50 minutes, stirring occasionally, until the onions are very soft and transparent.
3. Increase the heat and continue to cook, uncovered, for a further 5–7 minutes or beginning to brown. Sprinkle over the sugar and cook for 1 further minute.
4. Pour the vinegar and a dash of lemon juice into the pan and bring to the boil, then lower the heat and simmer for 1 minute or until syrupy. Remove the bag of spices and the cinnamon stick and leave to cool completely.
5. Preheat the grill and toast the sourdough bread on both sides.
6. Mix the cheeses together and spread on to one side of the toasted bread. Return to the grill until the cheese is brown and bubbling.
7. Divide the onions between the slices of hot toasted bread and serve immediately.

ROASTED ONIONS WITH CHEDDAR AND MUSTARD

4 medium onions
2–3 tablespoons olive or chilli oil
salt and freshly ground black pepper
110g/4oz mature Cheddar cheese
2 teaspoons Dijon mustard
1 tablespoon chopped fresh parsley

To serve
crusty bread

1. Preheat the oven to 180°C/350°F/gas mark 4. Peel the onions and trim the stalks and roots. Stand the onions on the root end and cut a cross over the top of the stalk end and halfway down the onion.
2. Place the onions in a roasting tin. Drizzle with oil and season with salt and pepper. Cover with kitchen foil and roast in the preheated oven for 45 minutes. Remove the foil and roast for a further 20–30 minutes until the onions are brown and meltingly tender.
3. Cut the cheese into tiny cubes and mix together with the mustard. Squeeze the base of the onion to open out the cross cut on the top and fill with the cheese mixture. Return to the oven until the cheese has melted. Sprinkle with parsley and serve with crusty bread to mop up the juices.

ONIONS STUFFED WITH LANCASHIRE CHEESE, APPLE AND THYME

4 large onions
3 tablespoons olive oil
1 large clove of garlic, crushed
1 dessert apple, peeled and grated
55g/2oz fresh white breadcrumbs
85g/3oz Lancashire cheese, cut into tiny cubes
grated zest of 1 lemon
salt and freshly ground black pepper
570ml/1 pint boiling water
3 tablespoons crème fraîche

1. Preheat the oven to 180°C/350°F/gas mark 4.
2. Trim the hairy roots of the onions but do not cut too much off as the root holds the onion together. Cut off the tops of the onions and remove the outer skin. Using a strong teaspoon and a small, sharp knife, scoop out the inside of each onion, leaving the outer 2–3 layers intact. Reserve the scooped-out onion.
3. Blanch the onions in boiling water for 5 minutes, then drain and allow to dry.
4. Make the filling: chop the reserved onion. Heat 2 tablespoons of the oil in a large saucepan and add the chopped onion. Cook over a low heat for 10–15 minutes until soft. Add the garlic and cook for 2 further minutes. Remove from the heat.
5. Add the apple, breadcrumbs, cheese and lemon zest. Season to taste with salt and pepper.
6. Stuff the onions with the mixture, pressing it down well to ensure there are no air pockets.
7. Place the onions side by side in a deep casserole dish. Add the boiling water.
8. Cover and cook in the preheated oven for 1½ hours until the onions are soft.
9. Remove the lid and drizzle the remaining oil over the onions. Increase the oven temperature to 200°C/400°F/gas mark 6 and cook for a further 20 minutes.
10. Remove the onions from the casserole dish and keep warm.
11. Reduce the cooking liquor by boiling until there is about 200ml/7fl oz left. Stir in the crème fraîche and season with salt and pepper. Serve with the onions.

ROASTED RED ONION AND MADEIRA CRUMBLE

For the filling
2 tablespoons vegetable oil
1.35kg/3lb red onions, quartered
2 bay leaves
salt and freshly ground black pepper
5 tablespoons Madeira
1½ tablespoons soft dark brown sugar
1 tablespoon finely chopped fresh thyme leaves

For the crumble
170g/6oz plain flour
a pinch of salt
85g/3oz butter, diced
2 tablespoons freshly grated Parmesan cheese

1. Preheat the oven to 180°C/350°F/gas mark 4.
2. Heat the oil in a large roasting tin and add the onions and bay leaves. Season with salt and pepper. Roast at the top of the preheated oven for 20 minutes.
3. Pour over the Madeira and sprinkle with the sugar and thyme. Return to the oven for a further 1–1½ hours, stirring occasionally, until the onions are very tender and caramelized and the liquid is syrupy. Remove from the oven and allow to cool.
4. Meanwhile, make the crumble: sift the flour and salt into a bowl and rub in the butter until the mixture resembles coarse breadcrumbs. Stir in the cheese. Chill until needed.
5. Increase the oven temperature to 200°C/400°F/gas mark 6.
6. When the oven mixture is cool, transfer to an ovenproof serving dish and cover with the crumble mixture, pressing down lightly. Bake on the top shelf of the preheated oven for 20–25 minutes or until hot through and the topping brown and crisp. Serve hot.

INDIAN-STYLE TOMATO, RED ONION AND CUMIN SALAD

450g/1lb vine-ripened tomatoes, stalks removed
1 medium red onion
1 tablespoon lemon juice
2 tablespoons chopped fresh coriander
¼ teaspoon ground cumin
salt and cayenne pepper

1. Slice the tomatoes thinly. Cut the onion in half and then crossways into very thin slices.
2. Layer the tomatoes and onions in a shallow serving dish, sprinkling each layer with a little of the lemon juice, coriander, cumin, salt and cayenne.

BAKED SPANISH ONIONS STUFFED WITH LENTILS

4 Spanish onions
290ml/ ½ pint winter vegetable stock (see page 530)
110g/4oz Puy lentils
15g/½oz butter
1 tablespoon chopped fresh parsley
a pinch of dried red chilli flakes
salt and freshly ground black pepper
lemon juice
olive oil, for brushing
1 quantity warm balsamic hollandaise sauce (see page 267)

To serve
salad leaves

1. Peel the onions and remove a slice from the top and base of each so that they will sit nicely. Set aside. Put the onions into a pan into which they will fit tightly and pour over the stock. Cover and simmer for 5 minutes. Lift the onions out with a slotted spoon and drain on kitchen paper. Scoop out 4–5 concentric rings from the centre of each onion and reserve.
2. Cook the lentils in the same stock as the onions for 30 minutes until tender. Drain.
3. Preheat the oven to 190°C/375°F/gas mark 5.
4. Chop the reserved onion centres finely. Melt the butter in a frying pan and when foaming, add the chopped onion and fry over a low heat until soft and transparent. Mix together with the lentils and add the parsley and chilli flakes. Season with salt, pepper and lemon juice. Pile the mixture into the centre of the onions. Brush liberally with oil and bake in the preheated oven for 30–40 minutes until tender and golden-brown.
5. Set the onions on 4 individual plates. Spoon a dollop of hollandaise sauce on top of each and serve with salad leaves on the side.

MIXED ONIONS EN PAPILLOTE

24 baby leeks, outer skin removed
24 spring onions, outer skin removed
24 button onions, peeled
olive oil
4 cloves of garlic, peeled
salt and freshly ground black pepper
4 sprigs of fresh thyme

1. Preheat the oven to 200°C/400°F/gas mark 6.
2. Carefully shave the roots off the leeks, spring onions and button onions, taking care to keep the layers intact.
3. Cut out 4 × 20cm/8in circles of greaseproof paper. Brush the inside of the circles with a little oil, leaving the edges clear.
4. Arrange the leeks, onions and garlic on one half of each of the circles of paper. Drizzle over some oil, season with salt and pepper and add a sprig of thyme. Fold the free half of the papillote paper over to make a parcel, rather like an apple turnover. Fold the edges of the 2 layers of paper over twice together, twisting and pressing hard to seal.
5. Brush a baking tray lightly with oil and put into the preheated oven for 5 minutes. Then put the papillotes on the hot baking tray, taking care that they do not touch each other.
6. Bake in the oven for 15–20 minutes or until the onions feel soft when touched through the paper. The cooking time will depend on the thickness of the vegetables.

NOTE: If the button onions are rather large, they can be cut in half or quartered to ensure they cook in the same time as the thinner leeks and spring onions.

WARM ROASTED ONION AND GARLIC SALAD

450g/1lb button onions
3 tablespoons olive oil
1 bulb of garlic
a handful each of rocket and baby spinach
  leaves
1 heart of romaine lettuce
6 sun-dried tomatoes, chopped
55g/2oz pinenuts, toasted (see page 22)
1 tablespoon balsamic vinegar
salt and freshly ground black pepper

1. Preheat the oven to 190°C/375°F/gas mark 5. Douse the onions in boiling water. Peel and trim off the roots. Put into a roasting tin and turn in the oil. Slice the stalk end of the bulb of garlic, just exposing the tips of the cloves. Stand in the tin with the onions. Roast in the preheated oven for 30–40 minutes until the onions are golden-brown and very soft.
2. Meanwhile, wash the salad leaves and pat dry. Put into a bowl with the sun-dried tomatoes and pinenuts.
3. As soon as the onions are cooked, tip them into the salad leaves with all the cooking oil. Pick the garlic up with a tea-towel, holding it by the root end. Squeeze out the cloves into the salad. Add the vinegar and season with salt and pepper. Serve immediately.

SPRING ONION PLATE SOUFFLÉ

45g/1½oz unsalted butter, plus extra for
  greasing
2 bunches of spring onions, well trimmed and
  sliced on the diagonal
salt and freshly ground black pepper
200g/7oz Parmesan cheese, freshly grated
225g/8oz soft goat's cheese, crumbled
150ml/¼ pint double cream
6 eggs, separated

1. Preheat the oven to 200°C/400°F/gas mark 6.
Lightly grease 4 large shallow ovenproof soup
plates with butter.
2. Melt the butter in a small saucepan. Add the
spring onions and cook over a low heat for 10
minutes until soft and beginning to brown.
Season with salt and pepper and allow to cool.
3. Mix 170g/6oz of the Parmesan cheese, the
goat's cheese, cream and egg yolks together in a
large bowl. Stir in the spring onions. Season
with a little salt and plenty of pepper.
4. In a separate bowl, whisk the egg whites
until stiff but not dry, then fold into the cheese
and onion mixture, using a large metal spoon.
5. Divide the mixture between the soup plates.
Sprinkle over the remaining Parmesan cheese
and bake in the preheated oven for 12–15
minutes or until risen and golden-brown. Serve
immediately.

SHALLOT MARMELADE TARTLETS IN PINENUT AND THYME SABLÉ PASTRY

For the pastry
225g/8oz plain flour
a pinch of salt
140g/5oz cold butter, diced
2 small egg yolks
3 tablespoons very cold water
85g/3oz pinenuts
1½ teaspoons finely chopped fresh thyme

For the filling
2 tablespoons olive oil
450g/1lb shallots, very finely chopped
3 bay leaves
salt and freshly ground black pepper
1½ tablespoons balsamic vinegar
2 tablespoons Parmesan cheese, freshly grated
beaten egg, to glaze

1. Preheat the oven to 200°C/400°F/gas mark 6.
2. First make the pastry: sift the flour with the
salt on to a worktop. Make a large well in the
centre and add the butter, egg yolks and 1
tablespoon of the water. 'Peck' the yolks and
butter together with the fingers of one hand and
gradually draw in the surrounding flour, only
adding the remaining water if required, to make
a softish but not sticky paste.
3. Scatter over the pinenuts and thyme and
bring together with the fingers, kneading
lightly. Wrap and chill for 10 minutes.
4. Use half the pastry to line 4 individual deep
tartlet tins. Chill for 15 minutes, then bake
blind in the prepared oven (see page 22).
5. Cut 4 circles from the remaining pastry to fit
the tops of the tartlet tins and use any leftovers
to cut out leaves for decoration. Place on a
baking sheet and chill until required.
6. Make the filling: heat the oil in a large
saucepan and add the shallots and bay leaves.
Season with salt and pepper. Cover and cook
over a very low heat for 45 minutes, stirring
occasionally.
7. Stir in the vinegar. Increase the heat and

cook, uncovered, for a further 5 minutes until the shallots are lightly browned and the juices syrupy. Remove from the heat, discard the bay leaves and allow to cool completely.

8. Sprinkle the cheese over the base of the cooked pastry cases. Spoon over the shallot marmelade.

9. Brush the edges of the pastry cases with a little water and cover with the pastry tops. Press down firmly and brush with the beaten egg. Decorate the tartlets with the pastry leaves and glaze again.

10. Bake on the top shelf of the hot oven for 10 minutes or until the pastry is crisp and brown. Remove from the tartlet tins and serve hot or warm.

INDIVIDUAL SHALLOT AND SAGE TOAD-IN-THE-HOLE

For the batter
110g/4oz plain flour
a large pinch of salt
2 eggs
150ml/¼ pint milk
150ml/¼ pint water
1½ tablespoons finely chopped fresh sage

For the filling
3 tablespoons olive oil
340g/12oz shallots, peeled and halved lengthways
1½ teaspoons light brown sugar
salt and freshly ground black pepper
1 teaspoon finely chopped fresh sage

1. First make the batter: sift the flour and salt into a large mixing bowl. Make a well in the centre and break the eggs into it, adding a little of the milk.

2. Using a whisk or a wooden spoon, mix the eggs and milk together, very gradually drawing in the surrounding flour to form a thick paste. When all the flour is incorporated, stir in the remaining milk and water. Add the sage. Cover and chill in the refrigerator for at least 30 minutes.

3. Make the filling: heat 2 tablespoons of the oil in a large saucepan and add the shallots. Cover and cook over a low heat for 30 minutes or until the shallots are very soft.

4. Sprinkle over the sugar. Season with salt and pepper. Stir in the sage. Cook, uncovered, for a further 5–10 minutes or until the shallots are lightly caramelized.

5. Preheat the oven to 200°C/400°F/gas mark 6.

6. Pour the remaining oil into 4 shallow individual ovenproof dishes. Heat in the oven until the oil is smoking.

7. Divide the shallots between the dishes and pour over the batter.

8. Bake in the hot oven for 20–25 minutes or until the batter is risen and brown. Serve immediately.

SHALLOTS BAKED WITH TOMATOES, PEPPER AND GARLIC

450g/1lb shallots
340g/12oz plum tomatoes, about the same size
  as the shallots
2 yellow peppers
6 cloves of garlic
2 sprigs of fresh rosemary
3–4 thinly pared strips of orange zest
2 tablespoons balsamic vinegar
salt and freshly ground black pepper
3 tablespoons olive oil
1 tablespoon chopped fresh flat-leaf parsley

1. Preheat the oven to 190°C/375°F/gas mark 5.
2. Douse the shallots and tomatoes in boiling water for 2 minutes. Drain and peel. Trim the roots from the shallots. Remove the pith and seeds from the peppers. Cut the peppers into quarters and then into large pieces about the same size as the shallots. Peel the garlic.
3. Put the shallots, tomatoes, peppers and whole cloves of garlic into an ovenproof dish. Add the rosemary, orange zest and vinegar. Season with salt and pepper and pour in the oil. Turn the vegetables in the oil until well coated. Bake in the preheated oven for 40–50 minutes until very soft and slightly caramelized. Sprinkle with the parsley before serving.

ROAST BANANA SHALLOTS ON MUSTARD AND CREAM SPINACH

4 banana shallots, peeled and halved
  lengthways
75g/2½oz unsalted butter
1 tablespoon olive oil
2 bay leaves
salt and freshly ground black pepper
150ml/¼ pint dry white wine
finely grated zest of 1 lemon
4 tablespoons mascarpone
1 tablespoon wholegrain mustard
675g/1½lb baby spinach leaves

1. Preheat the oven to 180°C/350°F/gas mark 4.
2. Arrange the shallots, cut side up, in a single layer in a large shallow flameproof casserole. Dot with 45g/1½oz of the butter and drizzle over the oil.
3. Add the bay leaves and season with salt and pepper. Roast in the centre of the oven for 45–60 minutes until the shallots are very tender.
4. Remove the dish from the oven and place over a direct heat. Pour over the wine and bring to the boil, scraping the base of the pan to release any sediment. Boil for 2–3 minutes or until syrupy. Place the shallots in a bowl, pour over the juices and keep warm. Discard the bay leaves.
5. Return the dish to the heat and add the remaining butter. Stir in the lemon zest and cook over a very low heat for 30 seconds. Stir in the mascarpone and mustard.
6. Add the spinach and toss quickly to coat with the creamy sauce. Season to taste with salt and pepper and pile into a warmed serving dish.
7. Arrange the shallots on top of the spinach and pour over the juices. Serve immediately.

LEEK AND AVOCADO SOUP

2 medium leeks, trimmed
30g/1oz butter
2 cloves of garlic, crushed
570ml/1 pint summer vegetable stock (see
*   page 530)*
salt and freshly ground black pepper
1 large, ripe avocado
150ml/¼ pint double cream
about 150ml/¼ pint milk
1 tablespoon chopped fresh chives

1. Cut the leeks in half lengthways. Wash thoroughly and slice.
2. Melt the butter in a heavy saucepan and when foaming, add the leeks, cover and sweat for 10 minutes. Add the garlic and cook for 1 further minute. Stir in the stock, season with salt and pepper and simmer for about 20 minutes until the leeks are very tender.
3. Halve the avocado and remove the stone, peel and roughly chop. Put into a food processor or blender with the leeks and blend until smooth.
4. Add the double cream and adjust the seasoning to taste. Reheat without boiling and add enough milk to give the required consistency. Pour into warmed soup bowls and sprinkle with the chives.

CHAR-GRILLED BABY LEEK BRUSCHETTA WITH PARMESAN CHEESE

20 baby leeks, trimmed
55g/2oz Parmesan cheese
1 loaf of ciabatta bread
1 clove of garlic
6 tablespoons extra virgin olive oil
sea salt flakes and coarsely ground black pepper
1 tablespoon chopped fresh chives

For the dressing
1 tablespoon Dijon mustard
1 tablespoon white wine vinegar
4 tablespoons extra virgin olive oil
1 tablespoon water

1. Trim the green part of each leek so that they measure about 17.5cm/7in. Shave thin slices from the cheese, using a sharp potato peeler. Cut the ciabatta in half horizontally as you would a bread roll, then cut crossways to give 4 pieces. Set aside.
2. Make the dressing; whisk the mustard and vinegar together in a small bowl and gradually whisk in the oil. Stir in the water to loosen the texture slightly and season to taste with salt and pepper. Set aside.
3. Cook the leeks in boiling salted water for 2 minutes until just tender. Drain, refresh under cold running water and leave to drain on a clean tea-towel.
4. Heat a ridged cast-iron griddle over a high heat. Toast the bread on the griddle for 1–2 minutes on each side until lightly browned. Peel the garlic and rub over the cut side of each piece of bread. Put a piece of bread on to 4 individual plates, drizzle over a little oil and sprinkle with sea salt flakes and pepper.
5. Place the leeks diagonally across the griddle and cook for 1 minute on each side, pressing down on them lightly with a palette knife so that they get nicely marked by the ridges.
6. Lift the leeks off the griddle and arrange 5 on each piece of bread. Drizzle a little of the dressing over the leeks and over the plate. Sprinkle the leeks lightly with sea salt flakes and pepper, scatter over the Parmesan shavings and chives and serve warm.

LEEK FLAN

110g/4oz flour quantity wholemeal pastry (see page 522)
2 medium leeks
15g/½oz butter
150ml/¼ pint double cream
2 egg yolks
1 heaped teaspoon wholegrain mustard
30g/1oz Parmesan cheese, freshly grated
salt and freshly ground black pepper
55g/2oz mixed chopped nuts and seeds, such as pinenuts, walnuts, pumpkin seeds, sesame seeds

1. Preheat the oven to 200°C/400°F/gas mark 6.
2. Use the pastry to line a 17.5cm/7in flan ring or dish. Chill for 30 minutes, then bake blind in the preheated oven for 15 minutes (see page 22). Lower the temperature to 180°C/350°F/gas mark 4.
3. Trim the dark green leaves from the leeks and slice in half lengthways. Wash thoroughly to remove any dirt between the layers, then slice thinly. Melt the butter in a frying pan, add the leeks and fry over a low heat until tender.
4. Whisk together the cream, egg yolks, mustard and half the cheese. Season with salt and pepper and stir in the leeks. Pour the filling into the pastry cases. Bake in the preheated oven for 25–30 minutes until the filling is just set. Mix the nuts and seeds together with the remaining cheese and scatter over the top of the flan. Bake for a further 5 minutes until golden-brown.

LEEK JALOUSIE

225g/8oz flour quantity puff pastry (see page 522)
plain flour, for dusting

For the filling
290ml/½ pint milk
1 slice of onion
1 carrot, sliced
1 bay leaf
1 stick of celery
black peppercorns
parsley stalks
45g/1½oz butter, plus extra for greasing
3 large leeks, trimmed and thinly sliced
salt and freshly ground black pepper
30g/1oz flour
170–225g/6–8oz spinach, cooked weight
freshly grated nutmeg
2 hard-boiled eggs, sliced
1 egg, beaten, to glaze

1. Roll the pastry into 2 thin rectangles, one about 2.5cm/1in larger all round than the other. Place on to 2 baking sheets and chill for about 20 minutes.
2. Preheat the oven to 200°C/400°F/gas mark 6.
3. Prick the surface of the smaller rectangle all over with a fork and bake in the preheated oven for 10–15 minutes until evenly brown, then turn over and continue to bake until there are no greasy, uncooked areas. Turn the pastry over again and allow to cool on a wire rack.
4. Meanwhile, put the milk into a saucepan and add the onion, carrot, bay leaf, celery, peppercorns and parsley stalks. Bring to boiling point, then remove from the heat and leave to infuse for 10 minutes.
5. Make the sauce: melt 30g/1oz of the butter in a saucepan, add the leeks and season with salt and pepper. Cover and sauté over a low heat until soft but not coloured. Add the flour and stir over the heat for 1 minute. Remove the pan from the heat, strain in the infused milk and mix well. Return the sauce to the heat and bring to the boil, stirring continuously. Lower the heat and simmer for 2–3 minutes until thick. Season to taste with salt and pepper. Remove

from the heat and allow to cool.

6. Melt the remaining butter in a small frying pan, add the spinach and season with salt, pepper and nutmeg. Turn the spinach in the butter until evenly coated and all excess liquid has evaporated. Remove from the heat and allow to cool.

7. Place the cooked pastry on a lightly greased baking sheet and spoon the spinach over the surface, leaving a 2.5cm/1in margin around the edges. Arrange the slices of egg on top of the spinach. Spoon the leek sauce over the surface of the eggs and level carefully.

8. Assemble the jalousie: remove the remaining pastry rectangle from the refrigerator. Lay it on a lightly floured surface and carefully brush the border with beaten egg. Dust the pastry with flour and carefully fold it in half lengthways, do not allow it to stick. Using a sharp knife, cut through the folded side of the pastry at right angles to the edge in parallel lines (as though you were cutting through the teeth of a comb). Leave an uncut margin of about 2.5cm/1in all around the other edges, so that when you open up the pastry there is a solid border like a picture frame.

9. Lay the pastry over the filling. Using a sharp knife, cut the corners off at right angles to the cooked base. Working carefully with a palette knife, lift the base and tuck the pastry blanket underneath it. Brush with beaten egg to seal. Repeat with the other 3 sides. Chill for 10 minutes. Bake the jalousie at the top of the oven for about 20 minutes or until the pastry is well risen and evenly browned.

LEEK, CHEESE AND SAGE PASTIES WITH CLOTTED CREAM

MAKES 6

450g/1lb flour quantity puff pastry (see page 522), chilled
340g/12oz leeks, trimmed and sliced
340g/12oz potatoes, cut into 1cm/½in pieces
340g/12oz Cheddar cheese, cut into 1cm/½in pieces
1 tablespoon chopped fresh sage
salt and freshly ground white pepper
4 tablespoons clotted cream
butter, for greasing
1 small egg, beaten, to glaze

1. Preheat the oven to 200°C/400°F/gas mark 6. Divide the pastry into 6 even-sized pieces. Roll out each piece on a lightly floured surface and cut out a 19cm/7½in disc, using a plate as a template.

2. Make the filling: put the leeks, potatoes, cheese, sage, 1 teaspoon of salt and ½ teaspoon pepper into a mixing bowl and mix together well. Stir in the clotted cream.

3. Divide the filling between the pastry discs. Moisten one half of the pastry edge with a little water, bring the sides together over the top of the filling and pinch together well to seal. Crimp the edge of each pasty decoratively between the fingers.

4. Transfer the pasties to a lightly greased baking tray and brush with beaten egg. Bake in the preheated oven for 35 minutes until golden. Serve warm.

LEEK AND STILTON ECCLES CAKES

These are delicious hot or cold and are perfect for picnics.

1 × 225g/8oz flour quantity puff pastry (see page 522)
plain flour, for rolling

For the filling
1 tablespoon olive oil
340g/12oz leeks, trimmed and thinly sliced
salt and freshly ground black pepper
1–2 tablespoons chopped fresh mixed herbs, such as oregano and parsley
110g/4oz Stilton cheese, crumbled
1 tablespoon dried breadcrumbs

To glaze
1 egg, beaten
mustard seeds
sesame seeds

1. First make the filling: heat the oil in a saucepan. Add the leeks and season with salt and pepper, then cover and cook over a low heat for 5–10 minutes until softened. Add the herbs, Stilton cheese and breadcrumbs. Adjust the seasoning to taste. Tip on to a large plate and leave to cool.
2. Roll the pastry out on to a floured surface to the thickness of a £1 coin. Cut out 4 × 15cm/6in rounds. Chill.
3. Preheat the oven to 200°C/400°F/gas mark 6.
4. Divide the filling between the pastry rounds, placing it in the centre of each. Dampen the edges of the pastry and gather the pastry over the filling. Press the pastry together in the centre, forming a small ball. Turn the balls over and flatten them lightly with a rolling pin.
5. Using a sharp knife, make 3 small parallel cuts in the top of each. Brush the top and sides of the pastry with beaten egg and sprinkle mustard and sesame seeds over the top. Chill.
6. Place on a baking tray and cook at the top of the preheated oven for 20 minutes or until evenly browned.

LEEK AND OLIVE GRATIN

2 tablespoons olive oil
1 large onion, sliced
5 leeks
2 cloves of garlic, crushed
1 × 400g/14oz can of chopped tomatoes
1 × 200g/7oz can of butter beans
½ teaspoon dried oregano
salt and freshly ground black pepper
55g/2oz pitted black olives, halved

For the gratin topping
110g/4oz granary wholemeal breadcrumbs
1 tablespoon shredded fresh basil leaves
1 tablespoon Parmesan cheese, freshly grated
1 red chilli, deseeded and chopped (see page 22)
55g/2oz butter, melted

1. Heat the oil in a saucepan, add the onion and fry over a low heat until soft and transparent.
2. Meanwhile, cut the leeks in half lengthways. Remove the outer leaves, wash thoroughly and cut into 2.5cm/1in pieces. Add the leek to the onion and fry for a further 5 minutes. Add the garlic and cook for 1 further minute.
3. Stir in the tomatoes, butter beans and oregano and season with salt and pepper. Simmer gently for about 20 minutes until the leeks are tender and the mixture reduced. Stir in the olives.
4. Preheat the grill to high. Mix all the gratin ingredients together and season with salt and pepper.
5. Pour the leek mixture into an ovenproof dish. Scatter the gratin mixture over the top and grill until browned.

LEEK AND POTATO CAKE WITH GRILLED TOMATOES AND SPINACH

This is equally good served plainly as an accompaniment to a main course or with fried eggs for breakfast.

225g/8oz leeks, trimmed
675g/1½lb red potatoes
salt and freshly ground black pepper
285g/10oz baby spinach leaves
2 tablespoons olive oil
30g/1oz butter
2 tablespoons chopped fresh coriander
4 plum tomatoes
caster sugar
freshly grated nutmeg

1. Wash the leeks thoroughly between the layers and slice thinly. Peel the potatoes and grate them coarsely. Toss the potatoes with a little salt, put into a colander and press down with a potato masher to squeeze out some of the moisture. Trim any tough stalks from the spinach and wash thoroughly. Leave to drain.
2. Heat a little of the oil and a knob of the butter in a 25cm/10in heavy or non-stick frying pan. Fry the leeks over a low heat for about 5 minutes, stirring from time to time. Spoon into a bowl. Season with salt and pepper and stir in the coriander.
3. Wipe out the frying pan with kitchen paper, add 1 tablespoon of the oil and a knob of the butter and heat. Then lower the heat, add half the potatoes and spread them evenly over the base of the pan, pressing down with the potato masher.
4. Spread the leek mixture evenly over the top and cover with the remaining potatoes, pressing down well. Cook over a medium heat for 5 minutes until beginning to crisp and turn golden-brown. Loosen the cake with a palette knife. Invert a plate over the pan and turn both over together so that the cake is on the plate. Add a little more oil and butter to the pan and heat. Carefully slide the cake back into the pan

and cook for 5–10 minutes until the potatoes are cooked all the way through and the base is crisp and golden-brown. Slide on to the plate.
5. Meanwhile, preheat the grill to high. Cut the tomatoes in half, brush with oil and season with pepper and a sprinkling of sugar. Grill until soft and charred at the edges.
6. Toss the spinach into the frying pan and shake over the heat for 2 minutes until wilted. Season with a knob of butter, salt, pepper and nutmeg. Divide the spinach between 4 individual plates. Top with a wedge of leek and potato cake and the grilled tomatoes.

LEEK AND TAHINI CRUMBLE

1 tablespoon olive oil
2 leeks, trimmed and thinly sliced
salt and freshly ground black pepper
30g/1oz butter
30g/1oz plain flour
290ml/½ pint milk
1 tablespoon tahini
290ml/½ pint tomato sauce I (see page 527),
    well reduced

For the crumble topping
170g/6oz plain flour
85g/3oz butter
1–2 tablespoons chopped fresh mixed herbs,
    such as parsley, basil, thyme
1 tablespoon sesame seeds

1. Heat the oil in a saucepan, add the leeks and season with salt and pepper. Cover and cook over a low heat for 5–8 minutes, stirring occasionally, until softened.
2. Preheat the oven to 200°C/400°F/gas mark 6.
3. Melt the butter into the leeks, then add the flour and stir over the heat for 1–2 minutes. Remove the pan from the heat, pour in the milk and mix well. Return the sauce to the heat and bring to the boil, stirring continuously. Simmer for 2–3 minutes until thickened. Add the tahini and season to taste with salt and pepper. Transfer the mixture to an ovenproof dish. Pour over the tomato sauce.
4. Make the crumble topping: place the flour in a mixing bowl, add the butter and rub in with the fingertips until the mixture resembles breadcrumbs. Add some salt and pepper and the herbs. Sprinkle the mixture evenly over the surface of the dish. Sprinkle over the sesame seeds. Cook near the top of the preheated oven for 20–30 minutes or until evenly browned.

LEEK AND WALNUT STEAMED PUDDING

For the filling
55g/2oz butter, plus extra for greasing
1 large onion, chopped
450g/1lb leeks
110g/4oz walnuts, roughly chopped
1 tablespoon chopped fresh parsley
2 teaspoons chopped fresh thyme or
    ½ teaspoon dried thyme
salt and freshly ground black pepper
freshly grated nutmeg

For the suet pastry
225g/8oz self-raising flour, plus extra for rolling
110g/4oz vegetable suet
about 150ml/¼ pint water, to mix

To serve
mustard gravy (see page 511)

1. Melt the butter in a sauté pan. Add the onion and fry over a low heat until golden-brown.
2. Meanwhile, cut the leeks in half lengthways. Discard the outer leaves, wash the leeks thoroughly and slice. Put into the pan with the onion, cover and cook over a low heat until the leeks are tender. Stir in the walnuts, parsley and thyme and season with salt, pepper and nutmeg. Remove from the heat and set aside.
3. Grease a 1.1 litre/2 pint pudding basin. Make the pastry: mix together the flour and suet. Season with salt and pepper and add enough water to bind to a soft dough.
4. Knead the dough on a lightly floured surface and divide into 3 pieces, one large, one medium and one small. Use the small piece to cover the bottom of the bowl and spoon one-third of the filling mixture on top. Roll the medium piece to cover the filling and press into place. Spoon the remaining filling on top. Finally roll the large piece of pastry to cover the top of the pudding.
5. Cut a piece of greaseproof paper and a piece of kitchen foil to cover the top of the bowl. Butter the greaseproof, lay it buttered side up on top of the foil and make a pleat in the

middle. Cover the pudding with the paper and foil and twist the edges to secure. Steam the pudding for 2 hours.

6. Turn the pudding out of the bowl on to a serving plate and cut into wedges. Serve with the mustard gravy handed separately.

GLAMORGAN SAUSAGES

MAKES 12

30g/1oz butter
1 large leek, trimmed and thinly sliced
salt and freshly ground black pepper
285g/10oz fresh white breadcrumbs
225g/8oz Cheddar cheese, finely grated
1 teaspoon dried thyme
1 tablespoon chopped fresh chives
1 tablespoon chopped fresh parsley
a pinch of freshly grated nutmeg
2 medium eggs, separated
1 teaspoon dry English mustard
1 tablespoon milk
30g/1oz plain flour, plus extra for shaping
110g/4oz fresh white breadcrumbs
sunflower oil, for frying

To serve
spicy tomato ketchup (see page 515)

1. Melt the butter in a medium frying pan. Add the leek, season with salt and pepper and cook over a low heat for 2–3 minutes until soft but not browned. Tip into a large mixing bowl and leave to cool.

2. Add the breadcrumbs, cheese, thyme, chives, parsley and nutmeg to the leek in the bowl and mix together well. Beat the egg yolks with the mustard and milk and stir into the dry ingredients until the mixture starts to combine. It may look a little dry at this point but it will come together when you shape the sausages. Season to taste with salt and pepper.

3. Divide the mixture into 12 even-sized pieces and with floured hands shape into thin sausages about 12.5cm/5in long.

4. Put the egg whites into a shallow dish and whisk lightly until slightly frothy. Put the flour

into another dish and the breadcrumbs into a third. Coat the sausages first in the flour, then in the egg white and finally in the breadcrumbs, making sure they take on a good, even coating.

5. Heat enough oil in a large frying pan to cover the base of the pan. Add half the sausages and cook over a medium heat for 5 minutes, turning from time to time, until they are crisp and golden all over. Lift on to a baking tray lined with kitchen paper and keep hot in a low oven while you cook the remainder in the same way. Serve hot with spicy tomato ketchup.

COCONUT LEEKS

450g/1lb leeks
110g/4oz carrots
1 tablespoon vegetable oil
½ teaspoon yellow mustard seeds
½ medium onion, finely chopped
2.5cm/1in piece of fresh root ginger, peeled and grated
1–2 green chillies, deseeded and sliced (see page 22)
6 cardamom pods, crushed
190ml/⅓ pint coconut cream
salt and freshly ground black pepper

1. Trim the leeks and cut them in half lengthways, wash thoroughly and cut into 2.5cm/1in slices. Peel the carrots and cut into 5cm/2in pieces, then cut into ribbons on the slicing blade of a grater.

2. Heat the oil in a sauté pan. Add the mustard seeds and fry until they begin to pop. Lower the heat, add the onion and fry gently until soft and transparent. Stir in the ginger, chilli and the cardamom pods and fry for a further 2 minutes.

3. Add the leeks, carrots and creamed coconut to the pan. Season with salt and pepper. Simmer for 10–15 minutes until the leeks are tender and the coconut has reduced and thickened. Remove the cardamom pods before serving.

SWEET ROASTED GARLIC SOUP

2 whole bulbs of garlic
salt and freshly ground black pepper
30g/1oz unsalted butter
15g/½oz caster sugar
860ml/1½ pints summer vegetable stock (see
    page 530)
1 egg
30g/1oz Parmesan cheese, freshly grated
½ teaspoon Dijon mustard
1 tablespoon shredded fresh basil

1. Preheat the oven to 190°C/375°F/gas mark 5.
Slice the tops off the bulbs of garlic, just
exposing the cloves. Place the garlic in a small
roasting tin and roast in the preheated oven for
about 25 minutes until completely soft.
2. Leave the garlic to cool slightly, then turn
upside down and squeeze out the cloves.
Sprinkle the garlic with ½ teaspoon salt and
mash to a pulp with a small palette knife.
3. Melt the butter in a saucepan. Stir in the
garlic and sugar and fry over a low heat for a
few minutes until the sugar has caramelized
slightly. Pour on the stock and season with
pepper. Simmer, partially covered, for 30
minutes.
4. Mix the egg with the cheese and mustard.
Pour about 150ml/¼ pint of the hot but not
boiling stock on to the egg mixture, stirring all
the time. Return to the pan and cook over a low
heat until the soup has thickened slightly. On
no account allow to boil or the egg will
scramble. Stir in the basil and serve
immediately.

BROWNED CHEESE WITH GARLIC AND VINEGAR SAUCE

250g/8oz halloumi cheese
olive oil
2 cloves of garlic, thinly sliced
1 teaspoon dried oregano or marjoram
freshly ground black pepper
3–4 tablespoons balsamic vinegar
4 handfuls of salad leaves

To serve
crusty bread

1. Cut the cheese into thick slices. Brush a
heavy frying pan with oil and heat. Add the
cheese, lower the heat and cook for about 2
minutes until lightly browned.
2. Turn the cheese and add the garlic and
herbs. Season with salt and pepper and brown
the other side, then add the vinegar and bring to
the boil.
3. Arrange the salad leaves on 4 individual
plates and set the cheese on top. Pour over the
pan juices and serve immediately with crusty
bread.

MUSHROOMS AND OTHER FUNGI

INTRODUCTION

It is surprising how many mushrooms grow wild in local parks and woodlands. Even urban parks can produce the odd puffball and a few fairy rings. It is a thrill to find these elusive and magical fungi that pop up in the autumn when the weather is perfect for the spores to grow. Extreme care must be taken in selecting which to gather, however, as many fungi are poisonous and some lethal. Be sure to use a guide or take an expert with you. Wild fungi have a deliciously special flavour, a rich earthiness that can provide depth and substance to many dishes. Their cultivated counterparts cannot compete for distinction or pungency but none the less have a lot of character. More and more mushroom varieties are readily available and are worth experimenting with, especially in sauces or stocks. Cultivated mushrooms are best used as soon as possible or may be stored for a few days wrapped in paper or open in the refrigerator.

Mushrooms do not need peeling. Simply wipe or shake to remove any loose dirt or, if they are very gritty, rinse quickly immediately before use. Wild mushrooms are best used on the day they are gathered. Dust away any soil and dirt with a soft brush. Give them a good shake and inspect for any traces of unwanted visitors. Dried wild mushrooms are an excellent substitute for fresh as they retain an intense flavour. The best are morels or ceps. Use them in conjunction with cultivated mushrooms for the best value in bulk and flavour. Soak dried mushrooms in boiling water for 30 minutes before use. Be sure to use or save the liquor as it is full of flavour. Excess fresh mushrooms can be thinly sliced and dried, laid flat on a tray covered with kitchen paper, in the oven or an airing cupboard.

There are thousands of varieties of edible wild fungi. We have noted the most commonly found or varieties that might be found in a supermarket.

WILD MUSHROOMS

Ceps are nicknamed 'penny buns' as this is what their golden caps look like. They have a strong meaty flavour. Ceps are delicious thickly sliced and fried in butter with a squeeze of lemon juice. Unlike many other mushrooms they keep their texture when cooked. They are expensive but a few go a long way. In Italy they are called *porcini* and this is the name that is often used for dried ceps.

Chanterelles or **girolles** are funnel-shaped. They are a distinctive orangey-yellow with a faint scent of apricot and a fragrant flavour.

Morels, unusually, appear in the spring. They have a spongy appearance and vary in colour from beige to very dark brown. They have a good strong flavour. They need to be washed before cooking as it is impossible to remove all the dirt by shaking or brushing.

Puffballs can grow larger than a football. They should be white and feel firm. If there is any sign of yellow they should be discarded. Covered in clingfilm, they can be stored in the refrigerator for several days. Slice into large steaks and fry in butter with a dash of lemon juice and a sprinkling of parsley or dip them in beaten egg and breadcrumbs and fry briskly.

Truffles: A little truffle goes a long way, which is just as well because of the exorbitant cost of these precious nuggets. Truffles have a deliciously intense flavour. A little grated truffle in an omelette, salad or risotto turns a simple dish into a delicacy. A truffle stored in a box of eggs or in a jar of rice will impart its flavour.

CULTIVATED MUSHROOMS

Cultivated mushrooms are all relatives of the field mushroom. Button, closed or open-cap, and flat are all different stages of growth. Flavour develops as the mushroom grows, so button are the mildest while flat have the most flavour and colour. Chestnut mushrooms are cultivated organically and have a deep nutty flavour.

Oyster mushrooms can be white, pink or grey and are thin and 'flappy'. They have a good flavour and a silky texture. Oyster mushrooms have a high water content so they shrink a lot once cooked.

Portobello mushrooms are among the biggest flat mushrooms available. They are deep fawn in colour and have a strong distinctive flavour. These mushrooms are used for their good meaty texture and for holding their size when cooked.

Enoki is a Japanese mushroom with a small cap and elegant stalk. Enoki are sold in clusters. They have a slightly lemony flavour and are good for stir-fries.

Shiitake mushrooms are of Chinese and Japanese origin. They have a rich meaty flavour, ideal for adding to stir-fries. They are easily found in supermarkets.

Quorn is a micro protein that is a natural derivative of the mushroom family. Quorn was discovered and developed in Harlow, Essex, and is now retailed nationally. It is an excellent meat substitute and is available as mince, steaks, and cubes.

MUSHROOM AND FENNEL SOUP

1 bulb of fennel
225g/8oz flat mushrooms
55g/2oz butter
1 teaspoon fennel seeds, crushed
1 clove of garlic, crushed
2 slices of white bread
1 litre/1¾ pints mushroom stock (see page 531)
salt and freshly ground black pepper
150ml/¼ pint double cream or crème fraîche
1 tablespoon chopped fresh flat-leaf parsley

1. Remove the outer leaves from the fennel. Trim off the root and slice the fennel. Reserve and chop the feathery tops. Chop the mushrooms.
2. Melt the butter in a large saucepan and when foaming, add the fennel and fennel seeds and fry for a few minutes until softened. Stir in the mushrooms and fry until soft and mushy. Add the garlic and cook for 1 further minute, then stir in the bread until it is soaked in the mushroom juices. Pour in the stock and season with salt and plenty of pepper. Simmer for 20 minutes.
3. Purée the soup in a food processor or blender and pour back into the rinsed-out pan. Add the cream and parsley and reheat without boiling. Check the seasoning and serve in warmed soup bowls, sprinkled with the reserved fennel tops.

MUSHROOM PÂTÉ

55g/2oz butter
1 small onion, finely chopped
1 teaspoon coriander seeds, crushed
340g/12oz mushrooms, sliced
salt and freshly ground black pepper
30g/1oz creamed coconut
1 tablespoon dark soy sauce
55g/2oz wholemeal breadcrumbs

1. Melt the butter in a saucepan and when foaming, add the onion and fry over a low heat until soft and transparent. Add the coriander seeds and fry for 1 further minute, then add the mushrooms and fry for about 10 minutes until very soft.
2. Season with salt and pepper and stir in the creamed coconut, soy sauce and breadcrumbs. Put into a food processor or blender and process until smooth. Spoon into 4 ramekin dishes and chill.

NOTE: Any kind of mushrooms can be used.

WILD MUSHROOM TART WITH OATMEAL PASTRY

170g/6oz quantity oatmeal pastry (see page 522)
15g/½oz butter
1 shallot, chopped
1 clove of garlic, crushed
15g/½oz dried porcini mushrooms, soaked in 150ml/¼ pint milk
110g/4oz oyster mushrooms, diced
110g/4oz shiitake mushrooms, diced
2 tablespoons chopped fresh sage
2 tablespoons chopped fresh parsley
2 eggs, beaten
2 tablespoons crème fraîche
salt and freshly ground black pepper

1. Preheat the oven to 200°C/400°F/gas mark 6.
2. Roll out the pastry and use to line a 20cm/8in flan tin. Chill for 20 minutes, then bake blind in the preheated oven for 15 minutes (see page 22). Lower the oven temperature to 170°C/325°F/gas mark 3.
3. Melt the butter in a sauté pan, add the shallot and garlic and cook over a low heat for 5 minutes.
4. Drain the porcini mushooms, reserving the milk. Turn up the heat and add the oyster, shiitake and porcini mushrooms to the pan and cook until softened, making sure the shallot does not burn. Add the sage and parsley, then remove from the heat and allow to cool.
5. Mix the eggs with the porcini mushroom soaking milk. Add the crème fraîche and season with salt and pepper. Add the cooled mushrooms.
6. Pour into the baked pastry case and place on a baking sheet. Bake in the preheated oven for 20–25 minutes or until the filling is just set in the middle.

MUSHROOM KOULIBIAC

225g/8oz flour quantity puff pastry (see page 522)

For the sauce
30g/1oz butter
200g/7oz button mushrooms, finely sliced
1 bay leaf
salt and freshly ground black pepper
30g/1oz plain flour
290ml/½ pint milk

For the filling
30g/1oz butter
125g/4½oz oyster mushrooms, roughly sliced

For the base
85g/3oz couscous
100ml/3½fl oz water
30g/1oz butter
1 clove of garlic, crushed
salt and freshly ground black pepper
1–2 tablespoons chopped fresh herbs, such as tarragon, thyme, parsley
1 egg, beaten, to glaze

1. First make the sauce: melt the butter in a saucepan, add the mushrooms, bay leaf, salt and pepper and cook over a medium heat until the mushrooms are soft. Remove the bay leaf and add the flour. Cook for 1–2 minutes, stirring. Remove the pan from the heat, pour in the milk and mix well.
2. Return the pan to the heat and bring to the boil, stirring continuously. Simmer for 2–3 minutes, then remove from the heat, season with salt and pepper and allow to cool thoroughly.
3. Make the filling: melt the butter in a frying pan. Add the mushrooms and season with salt and pepper. Cook over a high heat until soft and slightly browned. Remove from the heat and allow to cool.
4. Make the base: soak the couscous in the water for 5 minutes. Meanwhile, melt the butter in a saucepan, add the garlic and cook over a low heat until the garlic is soft. Add the

couscous (there should be no liquid) and turn in the hot garlic butter over a low heat for 1–2 minutes. Season with salt and pepper and mix in the herbs. Set aside.

5. Preheat the oven to 200°C/400°F/gas mark 6.

6. On a floured surface roll out one-third of the puff pastry into an oblong roughly 20 × 30cm/8in × 12in. Place on a damp baking sheet and prick the surface all over with a fork. Chill for 5–10 minutes, then bake at the top of the preheated oven for 15 minutes, until golden-brown. Turn the pastry base over and, if necessary, cook the underside for a further few minutes to make sure there are no raw or greasy patches.

7. Spread the couscous mixture evenly over the pastry base, leaving a narrow margin around the edge. Place spoonfuls of the thick mushroom sauce over the couscous and scatter the oyster mushrooms on top of the sauce. Brush the edge of the pastry with beaten egg.

8. Roll out the remaining pastry to a rectangle large enough to cover the mixture with an overlap of 2.5cm/1in. Using a sharp knife, cut the corners off the pastry rectangle at right angles to the cooked base. Working carefully with a palette knife, lift the base and tuck the uncooked pastry underneath it. Brush with beaten egg to seal. Repeat with the other 3 sides. Chill for 10 minutes.

9. Meanwhile, shape the trimmed corners into leaves, marking the veins and stems with the back of the knife.

10. Brush the koulibiac with more beaten egg, decorate with the pastry leaves and brush again with egg. Bake in the preheated oven for 30 minutes until the pastry is golden-brown. Serve hot or cold.

MUSHROOM AND MASCARPONE PIZZA

30g/1oz dried ceps
55g/2oz unsalted butter
2 tablespoons olive oil
110g/4oz each chestnut, oyster and field
*   mushrooms, sliced*
salt and freshly ground black pepper
200g/7oz quantity pizza dough (see page 533)
flour for rolling and dusting
150g/5oz mascarpone
110g/4oz Gorgonzola cheese
4 tablespoons sweet white dessert wine
1½ tablespoons finely chopped fresh marjoram
55g/2oz Parmesan cheese, freshly grated

1. Soak the ceps in warm water for 15 minutes, then drain and discard the liquid.

2. Meanwhile, heat the butter and 1 tablespoon of the oil in a large frying pan. Add the fresh mushrooms and fry briskly until browned. Stir in the soaked ceps and cook for a further 1–2 minutes until all the liquid has evaporated. Season with salt and pepper and allow to cool.

3. Preheat the oven to 200°C/400°F/gas mark 6. Roll the pizza dough on a lightly floured work surface into a 30cm/12in circle. Place on a floured baking sheet.

4. Spread the pizza base with the mascarpone, leaving a 1cm/½in border.

5. Spoon the cooled mushrooms on to the mascarpone and crumble over the Gorgonzola cheese. Sprinkle with the wine and marjoram.

6. Drizzle over the remaining oil and finish with the Parmesan cheese. Bake in the preheated oven for 20–25 minutes. Serve hot.

MUSHROOM AND SHALLOT GOUGÈRE

30g/1oz butter, plus extra for greasing
110g/4oz shallots
225g/8oz flat mushrooms
½ medium onion, finely chopped
15g/½oz plain flour
290ml/½ pint mushroom stock (see page 531)
salt and freshly ground black pepper
30g/1oz pinenuts, toasted (see page 22)
freshly grated Parmesan cheese

For the choux pastry
105g/3¾oz plain flour
a large pinch of dry English mustard
a large pinch of cayenne pepper
85g/3oz butter
225ml/7½fl oz water
a pinch of salt
2–3 eggs, beaten
30g/1oz Parmesan cheese, freshly grated

1. Preheat the oven to 200°C/400°F/gas mark 6. Grease a 1 litre/1¾ pint ovenproof dish with butter.
2. Douse the shallots in boiling water. Peel and trim off the stalks and roots. Cut the mushrooms into quarters or eighths so that they are roughly the same size as the shallots.
3. Heat the butter in a saucepan, add the shallots and shake over the heat until they are browned all over. Lift the shallots from the pan and set aside. Fry the onion in the same butter until beginning to brown. Add the mushrooms and fry until tender.
4. Stir in the flour and cook for 1 minute. Gradually add the stock and bring to the boil, stirring all the time until the mixture is smooth. Season with salt and pepper. Return the shallots to the pan. Simmer for 5 minutes, then remove from the heat and set aside.
5. Make the pastry: sift the flour with the mustard and cayenne on to a sheet of kitchen paper. Put the butter and water into a pan and bring slowly to the boil. Immediately the mixture boils, slip in all the flour mixture, remove from the heat and beat until thick and coming away from the sides of the pan. Leave to cool, then beat in enough egg to give a consistency that will drop easily from the spoon. Beat in the Parmesan and season with salt and pepper.
6. Spread the choux pastry around the sides of the dish. Pour the filling into the middle. Bake in the preheated oven for about 40 minutes until the pastry is risen and golden-brown. Scatter with toasted pinenuts and Parmesan before serving.

MUSHROOM, SPRING ONION AND GRUYÈRE PANCAKE PIE

6 French pancakes (see page 532)

For the filling
450g/1lb assorted mushrooms
55g/2oz butter, plus extra for greasing
½ medium onion, finely chopped
1 bunch of spring onions, trimmed and chopped
15g/½oz plain flour
150ml/¼ pint mushroom stock (see page 531)
salt and freshly ground black pepper
2 tablespoons chopped fresh flat-leaf parsley
110g/4oz Gruyère cheese, grated
4 tablespoons milk
a pinch of cayenne pepper
a pinch of dry English mustard
15g/½oz Parmesan cheese, freshly grated

1. Preheat the oven to 190°C/375°F/gas mark 5.
2. Cut the mushrooms into 1cm/½in pieces.
Melt the butter in a large sauté pan, add the
onion and fry over a low heat until golden. Add
the mushrooms and continue to fry until tender.
3. Stir in the spring onions and flour and cook
for 1 further minute. Gradually add the stock
and bring to the boil, stirring continuously,
until thick. Season with salt and pepper and stir
in the parsley.
4. Mix the Gruyère cheese with the milk and
season with cayenne and mustard.
5. Grease the base of a small roasting tin or
baking dish with butter. Place 2 pancakes, one
on top of the other, on the base of the tin or
dish. Spread one-third of the mushroom
mixture over the pancakes and top with one-
third of the cheese mixture. Cover with a single
pancake. Make 2 further layers of the
mushroom and cheese mixture, finishing the
top layer off with double pancakes.
6. Cover with kitchen foil and bake in the
preheated oven for 20 minutes. Remove the foil
and scatter the top pancake with the Parmesan
cheese. Return to the oven for about 10 minutes
until the top is golden and crisp and the pie
piping hot.

OYSTER MUSHROOM AND LEEK PITHIVIERS

For the stock
½ onion, roughly chopped
1 medium carrot, roughly chopped
1 stick of celery, roughly chopped
1 clove of garlic, crushed
6 black peppercorns
290ml/½ pint water
150ml/¼ pint dry white wine

For the filling
15g/½oz butter
110g/4oz leeks, trimmed and sliced
1 clove of garlic, crushed
110g/4oz oyster mushrooms
75ml/2½ fl oz dry white wine
½ tablespoon chopped fresh sage
½ tablespoon chopped fresh thyme
1 tablespoon crème fraîche
1 teaspoon Dijon mustard
salt and freshly ground black pepper
*425g/15oz flour quantity puff pastry (see
  page 522)*
1 egg, beaten, to glaze

For the sauce
150ml/¼ pint double cream
*a handful of watercress, fresh sage and mint,
  stalks removed*
lemon juice
1 tablespoon chopped fresh chives

1. First make the stock: put the onion, carrot,
celery, garlic and peppercorns into a medium
saucepan with the water and wine. Bring to the
boil, then lower the heat and simmer,
uncovered, for 30–40 minutes until reduced to
about 150ml/¼ pint. Reserve.
2. Meanwhile, make the filling: melt the butter
in a saucepan, add the leeks and garlic, cover
and sweat over a low heat for 15 minutes or
until the leeks are soft. Stir occasionally to
ensure the leeks do not brown.
3. Tear the oyster mushrooms into pieces, add
to the leeks and cook for 2–3 minutes. Add the
wine and bring to the boil. Cook over a high

heat until the wine has nearly evaporated. Add the sage, thyme, crème fraîche and mustard. Bring to the boil again and cook until the sauce just coats the leeks. Remove from the heat, season with salt and pepper and allow to cool.

4. Preheat the oven to 200°C/400°F/gas mark 6.

5. Divide the puff pastry in half. Roll out one piece into a 22.5cm/9in square. Cut out 4 × 10cm/4in circles, using a saucer or small plate as a template.

6. Roll out the second piece of pastry slightly larger than the first and cut out 4 × 12.5cm/4½in circles.

7. Divide the filling into 4 and put on to the smaller circles, leaving a narrow border around the edges.

8. Wet the edges with a little water and place the remaining circles of pastry on top of the filling. Carefully press out any air bubbles and seal the edges together. Crimp the edges with finger and thumb and using a blunt knife, mark a criss-cross pattern on the top of the pastry. Place on a baking sheet, brush with beaten egg and chill for 10 minutes.

9. Brush again with egg and bake in the preheated oven for 20 minutes or until the pastry has risen and is golden-brown.

10. Meanwhile, make the sauce: put the reserved stock and the cream into a saucepan, bring to the boil and reduce by half. Pour boiling water over the watercress, sage and mint, then dip in cold water. Squeeze out the excess water. Chop roughly and put into a blender. Pour over the reduced stock and cream and liquidize until a bright green sauce is achieved. Pour back into the pan and add lemon juice, salt and pepper to taste. Stir in the chives.

11. To serve: place the pithiviers on 4 individual plates and pour a little sauce beside each.

MUSHROOM AND PECAN RISOTTO STRUDEL

150ml/¼ pint boiling mushroom stock (see page 531)
55g/2oz dried porcini mushrooms
110g/4oz unsalted butter, plus extra for greasing
1 small onion, chopped
225g/8oz assorted mushrooms, sliced
55g/2oz arborio or carnaroli rice
55g/2oz pecan nuts
1 tablespoon chopped fresh flat-leaf parsley
55g/2oz Parmesan cheese, freshly grated
1 teaspoon Dijon mustard
salt and freshly ground black pepper
lemon juice
225g/8oz flour quantity filo or strudel pastry, rolled (see page 523) or 4 sheets of bought filo pastry

1. Pour the stock over the dried mushrooms and leave to soak. Melt half the butter in a sauté pan, add the onion and fry over a low heat until soft and transparent. Add the sliced mushrooms and cook until tender. Stir in the rice and turn in the buttery juices for a few minutes.

2. Drain the dried mushrooms and strain and reserve the soaking liquid. Gradually add the liquid to the rice mixture, and cook, stirring continuously, until the rice is creamy and *al dente*. Stir in the soaked mushrooms, pecan nuts, parsley, cheese and mustard. Season to taste with salt, pepper and lemon juice. Set aside.

3. Preheat the oven to 200°C/400°F/gas mark 6. Grease a baking sheet with butter. Melt the remaining 55g/2oz butter. Cut the pastry into 4 rectangles about 20 × 30cm/8 × 12in. Place one sheet on a worktop and brush with melted butter. Cover with another sheet and brush again. Repeat with the third sheet and finally top with the fourth.

4. Spread the filling over the pastry, leaving about 5cm/2in uncovered at one end. Roll the strudel up towards the uncovered 5cm/2in of pastry. Place, seam side down, on the baking sheet. Brush with butter and bake in the preheated oven for 20–25 minutes until the pastry is golden-brown.

MUSHROOM TURNOVERS WITH CREAM CHEESE PASTRY

2 tablespoons olive oil
2 shallots, chopped
450g/1lb mushrooms, chopped
1 teaspoon plain flour
100ml/3½fl oz soured cream
1 tablespoon chopped fresh dill
salt and freshly ground black pepper
250g/9oz flour quantity cream cheese pastry
  (see page 524)
1 egg, beaten

1. Heat the oil in a sauté pan, add the shallots and cook over a low heat for 5 minutes. Add the mushrooms and cook rapidly for about 5 minutes until all the liquid has evaporated.
2. Stir in the flour and cook for 1 minute, then add the soured cream, bring to the boil and remove from the heat. Add the dill and season with salt and pepper. Allow to cool completely.
3. Preheat the oven to 200°C/400°F/gas mark 6.
4. Cut the pastry into 4 even-sized pieces and roll each piece into a 15cm/6in round, using a saucer or small plate as a template.
5. Spoon the filling into the centre of each round. Brush around the edge with water. Carefully bring the sides up and over the filling and seal the edges together. Using a finger and thumb, crimp the edges. Place the turnovers on a baking sheet, brush with beaten egg and chill for 10 minutes.
6. Brush again with beaten egg. Bake near the top of the preheated oven for 20 minutes. Serve hot.

MUSHROOM CROUSTADE WITH QUAIL'S EGGS

For the base
110g/4oz bread, crusts removed
55g/2oz porridge oats
30g/1oz walnuts, roughly chopped
55g/2oz Cheddar cheese, grated
55g/2oz butter, melted

For the filling
55g/2oz butter
1 onion, finely chopped
1 clove of garlic, crushed
450g/1lb assorted mushrooms, such as button,
  oyster, chestnut, finely chopped
4 tablespoons double cream
salt and freshly ground black pepper
1–2 tablespoons chopped fresh tarragon
12 quail's eggs
freshly grated Parmesan cheese

1. Preheat the oven to 200°C/400°F/gas mark 6.
2. First make the base: put the bread and the porridge oats into a food processor and process until the mixture resembles breadcrumbs. Transfer to a large bowl, add the chopped walnuts, cheese and melted butter and mix well. Place the mixture in a 23–25cm/9–10in loose-bottomed flan tin. Press the mixture evenly over the base and up the sides of the tin, using the back of a wooden spoon.
3. Bake the case on the top shelf of the preheated oven for 10–15 minutes or until set and evenly browned. Remove from the oven and set aside.
4. Make the filling: melt the butter in a large saucepan, add the onion and garlic and cook over a low heat until the onion is softened and transparent. Increase the heat and add the mushrooms. Turn them in the butter and cook over a medium heat until soft (the heat may need to be increased further to evaporate any excess moisture). Add the cream and reduce by boiling to a thick sauce. Season with salt and pepper. Add the tarragon and mix thoroughly.
5. Pile the mushroom mixture into the baked

case and spread out evenly. Using a teaspoon, make 12 small pockets in the filling mixture. Crack one quail's egg at a time into a cup and slip an egg into each pocket. Sprinkle the Parmesan cheese over the surface of the croustade and bake on the top shelf of the oven for 5–10 minutes until the eggs are set and the cheese is lightly browned. Serve hot.

WILD MUSHROOM SAUTÉ WITH HORSERADISH RÖSTI TOPPING

85g/3oz unsalted butter, plus extra for brushing
6 shallots, finely chopped
1 tablespoon olive oil
225g/8oz field mushrooms, peeled, stalks
 removed and sliced
170g/6oz oyster mushrooms, roughly torn into
 pieces
110g/4oz shiitake mushrooms, halved
5 tablespoons sherry or dry white wine
1 tablespoon Dijon mustard
5 tablespoons crème fraîche
salt and freshly ground black pepper
a large handful of parsley, very finely chopped
675g/1½lb waxy potatoes
2 tablespoons creamed horseradish
1 teaspoon freshly grated horseradish

1. Melt 55g/2oz of the butter in a frying pan, add the shallots and cook over a low heat for 10–12 minutes until softened. Remove from the pan and set aside.
2. Add the remaining butter and the oil to the pan, increase the heat and fry the mushrooms briskly for 5–7 minutes until browned.
3. Return half the shallots to the pan, pour in the sherry or white wine and boil rapidly until the liquid is reduced by two-thirds.
4. Stir in the mustard, crème fraîche, salt, pepper and parsley. Transfer to an 850ml/1½ pint shallow casserole dish. Allow to cool slightly.
5. Preheat the oven to 200°C/400°F/gas mark 6.
6. Peel the potatoes and cut into 5cm/2in chunks. Cook the potatoes in a pan of boiling,

salted water for 5 minutes, then drain thoroughly.
7. Grate the potatoes. Carefully fork through the creamed horseradish, grated horseradish, salt, pepper and the remaining shallots.
8. Spoon the potato mixture on top of the mushroom mixture in the dish. Do not press it down. Brush over a little melted butter and bake in the preheated oven for 15–20 minutes or until brown and crusty on top.

WILD MUSHROOM RAGOÛT, SERVED ON A MUSTARD CROÛTE

For the croûte
1 tablespoon Dijon mustard
3 tablespoons olive oil
8 slices of baguette, cut on the diagonal

For the ragoût
2 tablespoons olive oil
2 shallots, finely chopped
1 clove of garlic, crushed
125g/4½oz shiitake mushrooms
125g/4½oz oyster mushrooms
250g/9oz field mushrooms
10g/½oz dried porcini mushrooms, soaked in
    150ml/¼ pint warm milk
1 teaspoon tomato purée
1 teaspoon Dijon mustard
150ml/¼ pint dry white wine
salt and freshly ground black pepper
chopped fresh chervil or chives, to garnish

1. Preheat the oven to 180°C/350°F/gas mark 4.
2. First make the croûte: mix the mustard with
the oil and brush both sides of the slices of
baguette with the mixture. Lay the slices flat on
a baking tray and bake in the preheated oven
for 10 minutes or until pale brown and crisp.
3. Make the ragoût: heat the oil in a sauté pan.
Add the shallots and cook over a low heat for 5
minutes. Add the garlic and cook for 1 further
minute.
4. Meanwhile, wipe the shiitake, oyster and
field mushrooms and cut them into thick slices.
Drain the porcini mushrooms and reserve the
milk.
5. Add all the mushrooms to the shallots and
garlic and cook over a medium heat for 5
minutes or until the liquid has evaporated.
6. Add the tomato purée, mustard and wine.
Bring to the boil and reduce to a couple of
tablespoons of liquid. Add the reserved milk
and boil again until the mushrooms are lightly
coated with the sauce. Season carefully with salt
and pepper.

7. Spoon the ragoût on to the warm mustard
croûte. Garnish with chervil or chives.

NOTE: As an alternative to the croûte, serve
the ragoût on fried polenta slices (see page 524).

MUSHROOM CROQUETTES

1 tablespoon olive oil
250g/9oz button mushrooms, wiped and
    quartered
1 clove of garlic, crushed
salt and freshly ground black pepper
290ml/½ pint milk
1 small carrot
1 stick of celery
1 bay leaf
1 slice of onion
black peppercorns
parsley stalks
55g/2oz butter
70g/2½oz plain flour
1–2 tablespoons chopped fresh mixed herbs

For the coating
seasoned plain flour
2 eggs, beaten
dried white breadcrumbs
oil, for deep-frying

1. Heat the oil in a frying pan, add the
mushrooms and garlic and cook over a high
heat until the mushroms are nutty brown and
all the liquid has evaporated.
2. Put the milk and the carrot, celery, bay leaf,
onion, peppercorns and parsley stalks into a
saucepan and bring up to simmering point.
Remove from the heat and leave to infuse for at
least 10 minutes, preferably longer, then strain.
3. Melt the butter in a heavy saucepan and
stir in the flour. Cook for 1–2 minutes, then
remove from the heat and gradually stir in the
infused milk. Return to the heat and bring
slowly to the boil, stirring continuously.
Simmer for 2–3 minutes until thickened, then
add the herbs, mushrooms and garlic.
Transfer to a blender and process until
smooth. Season to taste with salt and pepper.

Allow to cool completely. The sauce should be very thick.

4. With floured hands, shape the mixture into cylinders about 4cm/1½in long. Dip first into the flour, then into the beaten egg and finally coat evenly with breadcrumbs. Chill, then repeat the process to ensure that the croquettes are well protected. Chill again.

5. Heat oil in a deep-fat fryer to 180°C/350°F.

6. Deep-fry the croquettes until crisp and golden-brown, turning them from time to time. Drain well on kitchen paper, sprinkle lightly with salt and serve immediately.

NOTE: If a deep-fryer is not available, shape the mixture into discs or patties and shallow-fry or grill instead.

DEVILLED MUSHROOM CRUMBLES

30g/1oz butter
450g/1lb button mushrooms, sliced
1 clove of garlic, crushed
1 tablespoon Dijon mustard
1 teaspoon Tabasco sauce
1 tablespoon double cream
salt and freshly ground black pepper

For the crumble topping
45g/1½oz butter
1 clove of garlic, crushed
1 tablespoon Dijon mustard
1 tablespoon chopped fresh thyme
55g/2oz fresh white breadcrumbs

1. Preheat the oven to 200°C/400°F/gas mark 6.

2. Melt the butter in a large saucepan, add the mushrooms and fry for 2 minutes. Add the garlic and cook until all the liquid has evaporated. Remove from the heat and stir in the mustard, Tabasco, cream, salt and pepper. Divide between 4 ramekin dishes.

3. Make the crumble topping: melt the butter in a saucepan, add the garlic and cook over a low heat for 1 minute. Remove from the heat and stir in the mustard, thyme, breadcrumbs, salt and pepper. Spoon the mixture evenly over the mushrooms.

4. Place on a baking tray and bake in the preheated oven for 10 minutes. Serve hot.

THAI YELLOW MUSHROOM CURRY WITH SPINACH AND POTATOES

For the yellow curry paste
1 yellow Scotch Bonnet chilli, deseeded and
    chopped (see page 22)
1 stalk of lemongrass, trimmed and chopped
1 tablespoon chopped fresh coriander
1 teaspoon cumin seeds, crushed
1 teaspoon ground turmeric
2.5cm/1in piece of fresh root ginger or galengal,
    peeled and chopped
1 small onion, finely chopped
1 teaspoon coriander seeds, crushed
2 cloves of garlic, chopped
grated zest and juice of 1 lime

For the curry
340g/12oz assorted mushrooms, stalks removed
450g/1lb baby new potatoes
2 tablespoons vegetable oil
1 medium onion, chopped
290ml/½ pint spicy vegetable stock (see
    page 531)
150ml/¼ pint coconut cream
4 kaffir lime leaves, finely chopped
170g/6oz baby spinach leaves, washed and
    drained
1 tablespoon chopped fresh basil

To serve
Thai fragrant rice (see page 352)

1. First make the curry paste: put all the
ingredients together into a food processor or
blender and process to a paste.
2. Cut the mushrooms into pieces about the
same size as the potatoes. Wash and scrub the
potatoes.
3. Heat the oil in a heavy pan, add the
mushrooms and fry briskly until softened.
Remove from the pan and set aside. Add the
onion to the pan and fry over a low heat until
soft and golden-brown. Stir in the curry paste
and fry for 1 minute. Gradually pour in the
stock and coconut cream. Add the potatoes and

lime leaves. Season with salt and pepper and
bring to the boil, then simmer gently for 20
minutes.
4. Return the mushrooms to the pan and add
the spinach leaves. Cover and cook for 5
minutes. Scatter with the basil and serve with
Thai fragrant rice.

NOTE: For a milder curry add half the curry
paste. If the potatoes are not very small they
should be cut into halves or quarters.

FIELD MUSHROOMS IN A BUN

4 large field mushrooms, about the size of a
    burger
4 tablespoons olive oil, preferably chilli- or
    basil-flavoured
salt and freshly ground black pepper
150g/5oz mozzarella cheese
4 crusty bread rolls
about 6 sun-dried tomatoes, chopped
1 tablespoon shredded fresh basil

1. Preheat the grill to high. Brush the caps of
the mushrooms with oil and grill for 5 minutes.
Spoon the remaining oil into the gill sides of the
mushrooms and grill until tender.
2. Slice the cheese. Cut the crusty rolls in half
and grill on the cut side until lightly browned.
Arrange the cheese over one half of the rolls and
grill until melting. Scatter with the sun-dried
tomatoes, season with salt and pepper, and top
with a grilled mushroom. Sprinkle with the
basil and cover the rolls with the lids.

TOASTED SAGE AND LEMON MUSHROOM SANDWICHES

4 portobello mushrooms, peeled and stalks
    removed
3 tablespoons lemon-flavoured olive oil
juice of ½ lemon
grated zest of 2 lemons
salt and freshly ground black pepper
10 large fresh sage leaves, roughly chopped
8 slices of brioche, cut into rounds large enough
    to fit the mushrooms
3 tablespoons freshly grated Parmesan cheese

1. Preheat the oven to 200°C/400°F/gas mark 6.
2. Put the mushrooms into a large roasting tin,
gill side up.
3. Pour over 2 tablespoons of the oil, the lemon
juice and half the zest. Season to taste with salt
and pepper and sprinkle with the sage leaves.
4. Bake the mushrooms on the top shelf of the
preheated oven for 10–15 minutes or until
tender.
5. Meanwhile, drizzle the remaining oil over
one side of the brioche rounds and divide the
remaining lemon zest evenly between them. Put
the brioche under the grill and toast until lightly
browned. Sprinkle over the cheese and grill
again until it begins to melt.
6. To serve, put the brioche, toasted side down,
on 4 warmed individual plates. Put a mushroom
on top of each round and finish with a second
round of brioche, toasted side uppermost. Serve
immediately.

WELSH RAREBIT-TOPPED PORTOBELLO MUSHROOMS

170g/6oz Gruyère cheese, grated
170g/6oz Cheddar cheese, grated
1 teaspoon wholegrain mustard
3 tablespoons beer
1 egg, beaten
cayenne pepper
salt and freshly ground black pepper
30g/1oz butter
1 tablespoon olive oil
4 very large portobello mushrooms, peeled and
    stalks removed
2 tablespoons finely chopped fresh chives
55g/2oz Parmesan cheese, freshly grated
sprigs of watercress, to garnish

1. Mix the Gruyère and Cheddar cheeses
together in a small bowl. Stir in the mustard,
beer, egg, cayenne, salt and pepper. Set aside.
2. Preheat the grill.
3. Heat the butter and oil in a small saucepan
and use half to brush the cap sides of the
mushrooms. Place the mushrooms on a baking
sheet and put them under the grill for 2–3
minutes or until browned.
4. Turn the mushrooms over, brush the gill
side with the remaining butter and oil and
season with salt and pepper. Grill for a further
2 minutes.
5. Divide the chives between the mushrooms
and spoon over the cheese mixture. Sprinkle
with the Parmesan cheese and return to the grill
until set and nicely browned.
6. Serve garnished with sprigs of watercress.

BLUE CHEESE MUSHROOMS

4 large flat mushrooms
55g/2oz butter, melted
juice of ½ lemon
salt and freshly ground black pepper
110g/4oz soft blue cheese, such as Brie or
Cambozola

1. Preheat the oven to 190°C/375°F/gas mark 5.
Wipe the mushrooms and set them gill side
down in an ovenproof dish. Mix the butter and
lemon juice together and spread over the
mushrooms. Season with salt and pepper and
bake in the preheated oven for 10 minutes.
2. Cut the cheese into small pieces. Turn the
mushrooms over and put the cheese inside the
cups. Bake for a further 5–10 minutes until the
mushrooms are tender and the cheese has
melted. Serve immediately.

MUSHROOM AND COURGETTE SAUTÉ WITH BASIL AND MUSTARD

450g/1lb flat mushrooms, stalks removed
2 courgettes
1 tablespoon vegetable oil
30g/1oz butter
150ml/¼ pint mushroom stock (see page 531)
4 tablespoons crème fraîche
2 tablespoons Dijon mustard
2 tablespoons shredded fresh basil

To serve
basmati rice (see page 352) or couscous (see
page 382)

1. Slice the mushrooms. Cut the courgettes on
the diagonal into 5mm/¼in slices.
2. Heat the oil in a sauté pan, add the butter
and when foaming, add the courgettes and fry
briskly until beginning to soften and brown.
Lift out with a slotted spoon and set aside on
kitchen paper.
3. Add the mushrooms and fry over a medium
heat until they are cooked and plenty of juice is
left in the pan.
4. Stir in the courgettes, stock, crème fraîche
and mustard. Season with salt and pepper. Mix
carefully and simmer for a few minutes until the
cream has thickened. Stir in the basil and serve
immediately with rice or couscous.

STIR-FRIED MUSHROOMS WITH GREEN VEGETABLES IN SWEET AND SOUR SAUCE

To make this dish more substantial top with deep-fried tofu or add some toasted cashew nuts.

225g/8oz assorted mushrooms
110g/4oz broccoli florets
1 green pepper
2 tablespoons sesame oil
½ onion, thinly sliced
1 clove of garlic, crushed
1 green chilli, deseeded and finely chopped (see page 22)
a walnut-sized piece of fresh root ginger, peeled and finely chopped
110g/4oz mangetout, topped and tailed
110g/4oz sugar-snap peas, topped and tailed
salt and freshly ground black pepper

For the sauce
150ml/¼ pint water
½ teaspoon cornflour
1 tablespoon soft light brown sugar
1 tablespoon red wine vinegar
1 tablespoon soy sauce
1 tablespoon tomato ketchup

1. Halve or quarter the mushrooms so that they are about the same size as the broccoli florets. Cut the pepper into quarters and remove the pith and seeds, then slice.
2. Make the sauce: add a little of the water to the cornflour in a bowl and blend to a smooth paste. Gradually stir in the remaining water, sugar, vinegar, soy sauce and ketchup. Set aside.
3. Heat the oil in a wok or large, heavy frying pan. Add the onion and fry for a few minutes. Stir in the mushrooms and pepper and fry until beginning to soften, then add the garlic, chilli and ginger, and stir over the heat for 1 minute. Finally add the mangetout, sugar-snap peas and broccoli florets. Season with salt and pepper and toss over the heat for a few more minutes

until the green vegetables are beginning to soften but are still crunchy and brightly coloured.
4. Pour in the sauce and stir until boiling. Simmer for about 2 minutes. Check the seasoning and serve immediately.

MUSHROOM AND CORIANDER SEED SALAD

225g/8oz button mushrooms
French dressing (see page 528)
2 teaspoons coriander seeds, lightly toasted
1 onion, sliced
sunflower oil
freshly ground black pepper

1. Wipe the mushrooms, slice fairly thinly and leave to marinate in the French dressing.
2. Crush the coriander seeds extremely well in a pestle and mortar and add to the mushrooms. Leave for 2 hours.
3. Cook the onion until soft but not brown in a minimum amount of oil in a non-stick frying pan. Remove from the heat and cool, then add to the mushrooms and season well with salt and pepper.

QUORN HERB CRUMBLE

3 tablespoons sunflower oil
1 onion, chopped
1 stick of celery, chopped
1 red pepper, deseeded and chopped
110g/4oz carrot, chopped
1 clove of garlic, crushed
350g/12½oz Quorn mince
2 tablespoons plain flour
1 × 400g/14oz can of chopped tomatoes
150ml/¼ pint mushroom stock (see page 531)
1 tablespoon tomato purée
salt and freshly ground black pepper

For the crumble
85g/3oz butter
170g/6oz plain flour
3 tablespoons chopped fresh mixed herbs, such
    as parsley, mint, thyme, rosemary
55g/2oz Cheddar cheese, grated

1. Heat 2 tablespoons of the oil in a frying pan.
Add the onion, celery and pepper and fry for 2
minutes, then add the carrot and garlic and
cook over a low heat for 3 minutes. Transfer to
a saucepan.
2 Heat the remaining oil in the frying pan and
add the Quorn. Fry for a few minutes, then add
to the vegetables in the pan.
3. Add the flour to the Quorn and vegetable
mixture and mix well. Add the tomatoes, stock
and tomato purée and bring to the boil, stirring
continuously. Season with salt and pepper,
lower the heat and cook for 15 minutes, then
remove from the heat and allow to cool.
4. Meanwhile, make the crumble topping: rub
the butter into the flour in a large bowl until the
mixture resembles coarse breadcrumbs. Mix in
the herbs, cheese and salt and pepper.
5. Preheat the oven to 180°C/350°F/gas mark 4.
6. Put the Quorn mixture into a pie dish and
cover evenly with the crumble topping. Place on
a baking sheet and cook in the preheated oven
for 25–30 minutes.

QUORN AND LEEK PIE

3 tablespoons olive oil
500g/1lb 2oz leeks, trimmed and sliced
1 clove of garlic, crushed
2 tablespoons plain flour
150ml/¼ pint dry white wine
425ml/¾ pint mushroom stock (see page 531)
450g/1lb Quorn pieces
85g/3oz Cheddar cheese, grated
salt and freshly ground black pepper

For the topping
560g/1¼lb potatoes
170g/6oz sweet potatoes
85ml/3fl oz milk
45g/1½oz butter

1. Preheat the oven to 200°C/400°F/gas mark 6.
2. Heat 2 tablespoons of the oil in a large
saucepan. Add the leeks, cover and cook over a
low heat for 10 minutes.
3. Add the garlic and stir in the flour, then
gradually add the wine, stirring continuously.
Bring to the boil and cook for 2 minutes. Add
the stock and bring to the boil again, then lower
the heat and simmer for 5 minutes.
4. Heat the remaining oil in a frying pan and
add the Quorn. Stir-fry for 2 minutes, then add
to the leek sauce. Stir in all but 2 tablespoons of
the cheese and season with salt and pepper.
Pour into a pie dish.
5. Make the topping: peel the potatoes and
sweet potatoes and cut them into even-sized
chunks. Put them into separate pans of boiling
water (the sweet potatoes will take less time to
cook). When cooked, drain the potatoes and
sweet potatoes and put them both back into one
pan. Pour in the milk and heat it over a low
heat. Mash the potato, add the butter and
season with salt and pepper. Spread over the
leeks and Quorn mixture and use a fork to
mark a pattern on the top. Sprinkle over the
remaining cheese.
6. Place on a baking sheet and bake in the
preheated oven for 20 minutes.

QUORN SHEPHERD'S PIE WITH ROOT MASH

2 tablespoons olive oil
1 red onion, finely chopped
1 red pepper, deseeded and diced
2 carrots, diced
1 leek, trimmed and thinly sliced
salt and freshly ground black pepper
300g/11oz Quorn mince
1 × 400g/14oz can of tomatoes
290ml/½ pint mushroom stock (see page 531)
2 tablespoons tomato purée
2 tablespoons mushroom ketchup

For the mash
450g/1lb sweet potatoes
450g/1lb potatoes
450g/1lb parsnips
2 tablespoons milk
30g/1oz butter
salt and freshly ground black pepper

1. Heat the oil in a large saucepan. Add the onion, pepper, carrots and leek. Season with salt and pepper, cover and cook for 10–15 minutes until softened.

2. Add the Quorn mince to the vegetables and mix thoroughly with a wooden spoon. Increase the heat and allow the Quorn to colour slightly.

3. Add the tomatoes (these can be liquidized for a smoother consistency, if liked), stock, tomato purée and mushroom ketchup. Cover and simmer gently for 20–30 minutes, stirring occasionally to prevent sticking, until the liquid is well reduced. Adjust the seasoning to taste.

4. Preheat the oven to 180°C/350°F/gas mark 4.

5. Peel the sweet potatoes, potatoes and parsnips and cut into even-sized chunks. Cook the sweet potatoes and potatoes together in boiling salted water for 10 minutes, then add the parsnips and cook for a further 10 minutes or until soft. Drain thoroughly

6. Push the vegetables through a sieve or vegetable mill. Return them to the dry saucepan. Heat carefully, stirring, to allow the mash to steam-dry.

7. Push the mash to one side of the saucepan.

Set the exposed part of the pan over direct heat and pour in the milk. Add the butter, salt and pepper. Tilt the pan to allow the milk to boil and the butter to melt. When the milk is boiling, beat it into the mash. Adjust the seasoning to taste.

8. Transfer the Quorn mixture to an ovenproof dish. Spread the mash over the top and fork it up to leave the surface rough, or draw the fork over the surface to mark with a pattern. Place on a baking tray and cook in the preheated oven for 20–30 minutes or until very hot. If necessary, brown the top under a hot grill.

QUORN AND RED ONION BOLOGNESE

2 tablespoons olive oil
1 red onion, finely chopped
1 red pepper, deseeded and chopped
2 carrots, finely chopped
1 leek, thinly sliced
salt and freshly ground black pepper
300g/11oz Quorn mince
1 × 400g/14oz can of tomatoes
290ml/½ pint mushroom stock (see page 531)
2 tablespoons tomato purée
2 tablespoons mushroom ketchup

To serve
340g/12oz spaghetti
freshly grated Parmesan cheese

1. Heat the oil in a large saucepan and add the onion, pepper, carrots and leek. Season with salt and pepper, cover and cook over a low heat for 10–15 minutes until softened.
2. Add the Quorn mince to the vegetables and mix thoroughly with a wooden spoon. Increase the heat and allow the Quorn to colour slightly.
3. Add the tomatoes (these can be liquidized for a smoother consistency, if liked), stock, tomato purée and mushroom ketchup. Cover and simmer for 20–30 minutes, stirring occasionally to prevent sticking, until the liquid is well reduced. Adjust the seasoning to taste.
4. Meanwhile, bring a large saucepan of salted water to the boil. Add the spaghetti and cook, uncovered, for 10–12 minutes until *al dente*. Drain thoroughly and rinse the spaghetti under hot running water. Drain well.
5. Place the spaghetti in a warmed serving dish and pour over the Quorn bolognese sauce. Serve with Parmesan cheese sprinkled on top of the sauce or handed separately.

QUORN THAI CURRY

2 tablespoons sunflower oil
2 onions, sliced
1 red pepper, deseeded and sliced
600g/1lb 5oz Quorn pieces
1 red chilli, deseeded and chopped (see page 22)
2 cloves of garlic, chopped
2.5cm/1in piece of fresh root ginger, peeled and finely chopped
1 tablespoon green Thai curry paste
1 stalk of lemongrass, halved and bruised
3 kaffir lime leaves
290ml/½ pint spicy vegetable stock (see page 531)
200g/7oz French beans, cut into 5cm/2in lengths
200g/7oz baby sweetcorn, cut into 5cm/2in lengths
400ml/14fl oz coconut milk
salt and freshly ground black pepper
3 tablespoons chopped fresh coriander

To serve
boiled or steamed rice

1. Heat the oil in a wok and add the onions and pepper. Fry for 5 minutes without colouring.
2. Add the Quorn and stir-fry for 2 minutes. Add the chilli, garlic and ginger and cook for a further 2 minutes.
3. Add the curry paste, lemongrass, lime leaves, stock, beans, sweetcorn, coconut milk, salt and pepper. Bring to the boil, then lower the heat and simmer for 15 minutes.
4. Add the coriander and serve with boiled or steamed rice.

NOTE: If you cannot find lime leaves, use the grated zest of 1 lime instead.

QUORN AND CASHEW NUT BALLS

These make a substantial supper dish. The balls will fall apart a little but are nevertheless delicious.

2 tablespoons sunflower oil
350g/12½oz Quorn mince
1 medium onion, chopped
1 clove of garlic, crushed
85g/3oz Cheshire cheese, grated
1 tablespoon chopped fresh mint
2 tablespoons chopped fresh parsley
85g/3oz fresh white breadcrumbs
85g/3oz cashew nuts, chopped and toasted (see
*   page 22)*
salt and freshly ground black pepper
3 eggs, beaten

For the sauce
1 tablespoon sunflower oil
1 onion, chopped
1 clove of garlic, crushed
2 × 400g/14oz cans of chopped tomatoes
1 tablespoon tomato purée
1 teaspoon white wine vinegar
1 teaspoon caster sugar
1 tablespoon chopped fresh thyme
salt and freshly ground black pepper
150ml/¼ pint water

1. Heat half the oil in a frying pan, add the Quorn and fry over a low heat for 2–3 minutes. Tip it into a large bowl.
2. Heat the remaining oil in the pan, add the onion and garlic and fry until it is just beginning to brown. Put into the bowl with the Quorn.
3. Add the cheese, mint parsley, breadcrumbs and cashew nuts. Season with salt and pepper. Mix in the eggs to bind.
4. Make the tomato sauce: heat the oil in a saucepan, add the onion and garlic and cook over a low heat for 10 minutes. Add the tomatoes, tomato purée, vinegar, sugar, thyme, a little salt and pepper and the water. Bring to the boil, then lower the heat and simmer for 5 minutes. Taste and add more salt and pepper if necessary.
5. Preheat the oven to 180°C/350°F/gas mark 4.
6. Using wet hands, shape the Quorn mixture into balls the size of a ping-pong ball. Put half the sauce into a casserole dish. Add some of the Quorn balls, then some more sauce, and so on. Finish with a layer of sauce, cover and bake in the preheated oven for 45 minutes. Serve immediately.

QUORN WITH SAMBAL SAUCE

340g/12oz Quorn pieces

For the marinade
2 cloves of garlic, crushed
1 teaspoon ground coriander
1 teaspoon ground ginger
3 tablespoons dark soy sauce
juice of 1 small lemon
2 teaspoons soft light brown sugar
freshly ground black pepper

To serve
2 teaspoons olive oil
1 red pepper, deseeded and thinly sliced
1 orange pepper, deseeded and thinly sliced
1 small bulb of fennel, cored and thinly sliced
1 leek, quartered and cut into 5cm/2in lengths
110g/4oz fine green beans, topped and tailed
salt and freshly ground black pepper
sambal sauce
sprigs of fresh flat-leaf parsley

1. Mix together the ingredients for the marinade and add the Quorn pieces. Leave to marinate for at least 1 hour.
2. Heat the oil in a large frying pan and add the peppers and fennel. Cover and cook for 3–4 minutes. Add the leeks and green beans and cook for a further 3–4 minutes.
3. Increase the heat and add the drained marinated Quorn. Cook until the Quorn is evenly coloured and the edges turn a nutty brown. Season with salt and pepper.
4. To serve: pile the Quorn and the vegetables into the centre of 4 warmed individual plates, spoon some sambal sauce on top and garnish each with a sprig of flat-leaf parsley. Hand the remaining sauce separately.

QUORN WITH CHILLI, TOMATO AND CORIANDER

1 tablespoon olive oil
30g/1oz butter
450g/1lb Quorn, cubed
5 large tomatoes, peeled and chopped (see page 22)
2 green chillies, deseeded and chopped (see page 22)
2 tablespoons chopped fresh coriander
150ml/¼ pint spicy vegetable stock (see page 531)
salt and freshly ground black pepper
200g/7oz crème fraîche or Greek yoghurt

1. Heat the oil in a large sauté pan. Add the butter and when foaming, add the Quorn in batches and fry until golden.
2. Return all the Quorn to the pan and add the tomatoes, chilli, coriander and stock. Season with salt and pepper. Simmer for 20–30 minutes until the tomatoes are cooked and the sauce has reduced.
3. Stir in the crème fraîche or yoghurt. Reheat and adjust the seasoning to taste.

SALAD LEAVES

Chicory • Endive • Lettuce • Oriental leaves • Rocket and fresh herbs • Vine leaves • Watercress

INTRODUCTION

Over the last decade there has been an explosion in the variety of salad leaves available on supermarket shelves. The bitter leaves that have recently become so fashionable in this country have been used in the Mediterranean for many years. Oriental leaves such as mizuna, Japanese mustard greens or bok choi are now commonly found in major stores as well as ethnic greengrocers. These multi-coloured, frilly leaves have deep, intricate, bittersweet flavours. Using mixed leaves has never been so easy. A handful is often the perfect accompaniment to transform a snack into a meal or to make a refreshing side salad to balance the richness of a main course. Some salad leaves can be lightly cooked: grilled radicchio; lettuce in soup or braised with chicory; peas with shredded rocket tossed through pasta just before serving. Discard any blemished leaves before storing in the refrigerator and eat as fresh as possible. Avoid cutting leaves with a knife as this causes bruising and discoloration. All salad leaves are best washed and torn into pieces. Dress salads just before serving and toss carefully by hand before lifting into a clean salad bowl.

Chicories are the most bitter of the salad leaves and add bite to a good mixed salad. Witloof Chicory is the tightly packed, bullet-shaped variety grown in the dark to produce white leaves tinged with green. The root should be hollowed out before cooking so that the heat can penetrate to the centre. Radicchio (Italian for chicory) is a ruby-red chicory that looks like a small lettuce. Radicchio may also be pink and variegated. Chicories can also be cooked, baked, sautéed, braised or added to pasta and risottos.

Endive belongs to the chicory family and is sometimes known as Belgian endive or frisée because of its frilly, fine, deep-cut leaves which make it resemble lettuce. Escarole or batavia is similar but broader-leaved. These are the traditional leaves for warm salads and should be served with a robust dressing.

Cos and **Romaine** lettuces are long and pointed. Both the leaves and the crisp hearts are excellent for flavour. The small whole leaves make a perfect vehicle to scoop up garlic mayonnaise or dips. **Little Gem** is a small variety that is useful if buying in small quantities but the leaves lack the crispness of the larger lettuces.

Iceberg and **Webbs** are round lettuces with tightly packed leaves. They are accused of blandness but this is compensated by their refreshing crispness. Combine with stronger-tasting leaves such as spinach or rocket to spike up the flavour.

Oak leaf and **lollo rosso** have frilly leaves tinged with red. They have a delicate flavour and add colour and texture to a salad.

Lamb's lettuce, also known as **corn salad** or **mâche**, grows in clusters of dark green leaves which should be washed thoroughly as sand collects in between the leaves. The leaves are decorative and have a nutty flavour that blends well with sweeter lettuces.

Oriental leaves are the most recent arrivals in the salad bowl. Among those to be found are mizuna, mustard greens, Chinese cabbage, bok choi, pak choi or tatsoi. Chinese cabbage and bok choi are crunchy, clean-tasting and refreshing while the other leaves have a pungent, peppery flavour. They provide the cook with a palette of colour, flavour and texture to add to salads and hot dishes. Chinese cabbage should be firm and heavy for its size. It will keep in the salad drawer of the refrigerator for 2 weeks. The other leaves should be crisp, firm and undamaged and should be used within a few days of purchase. Many are available in supermarkets but a wider variety will be found in Asian stores.

Watercress is a wonderfully spicy leaf. It must be used very fresh. It is a soothing accompaniment to rich dishes. If used as a salad, watercress requires a powerful dressing. It also makes excellent soup and is good for garnishes.

Rocket falls somewhere between a herb and a leaf. Home-grown or wild rocket has the best peppery flavour. A handful will lift the flavour of any salad and it is a useful garnish.

It is easy to grow in herb pots or on a window sill.

Fresh herbs are widely available and some are easy to grow: ideally, grow those that you use a lot. The leaves have great subtlety of flavour and are a good addition to any salad. Herbs in packets will keep in the refrigerator for 3–4 days. Frozen herbs have good flavour if used in hot dishes. Dried herbs taste quite different to fresh and have a more intense flavour, so should only be used sparingly in robust soups or stews.

Vine leaves: Fresh vine leaves can be eaten when young. They have a mild lemony flavour. If cooking with fresh vine leaves blanch them in boiling salted water first. Vine leaves can be bought from delicatessens and some supermarkets and are usually vacuum-packed in brine. They need to be immersed in boiling water, rinsed, drained and carefully separated before use.

GRILLED CHICORY AND GORGONZOLA TOPPING FOR POLENTA OR BRUSCHETTA

This is also good simply served on toast like a Welsh rarebit.

4 heads of chicory
2 tablespoons olive oil, plus extra to finish
lemon juice
salt and freshly ground black pepper
½ teaspoon chopped fresh oregano
110g/4oz Gorgonzola cheese

To serve
polenta (see page 390) or bruschetta (see
    page 532)

1. Preheat the grill to high. Trim the root ends from the chicory and rinse the heads in cold water. Cut into quarters lengthways.
2. Season the oil with lemon juice, salt, pepper and oregano. Brush a baking tray with the mixture. Arrange the chicory on the tray and brush liberally with the oil mixture. Grill until the chicory is tender and beginning to char at the edges.
3. Crumble the cheese on top of the chicory and grill briefly to melt. Use a fish slice to lift the chicory and place on top of the hot polenta or bruschetta. Drizzle with a little olive oil and add a twist of black pepper before serving.

NOTE: Radicchio can be used instead of chicory. Blue Brie, Dolcelatte or Roquefort can be used instead of Gorgonzola.

BRAISED CHICORY AND LETTUCE HEARTS WITH BEANS

110g/4oz dried green flageolet or black-eyed
    beans, soaked overnight
2 bay leaves
4 heads of chicory
2 Little Gem lettuce hearts
1 tablespoon olive oil
1 medium onion, sliced
290ml/½ pint summer vegetable stock (see
    page 530)
3 sprigs of fresh thyme
freshly grated nutmeg
salt and freshly ground black pepper
15g/½oz butter

1. Rinse and drain the beans and put them into a saucepan. Cover with cold fresh water, add the bay leaves and bring to the boil, then lower the heat and simmer for about 1 hour until the beans are tender. Drain.
2. Preheat the oven to 190°C/375°F/gas mark 5.
3. Trim the root ends from the chicory and using a sharp knife, hollow out the tough base of the root. Remove the base and outer leaves of the lettuce and cut into quarters lengthways. Arrange the chicory and lettuce in a single layer in the base of an ovenproof dish.
4. Heat the oil in a frying pan, add the onion and fry over a low heat until softened. Add the stock and cooked beans and bring to the boil. Pour over the lettuce and chicory, add the thyme and season with nutmeg, salt and pepper.
5. Cover and bake in the preheated oven for 40 minutes until the vegetables are tender. Remove the thyme. Stir in the butter and adjust the seasoning to taste before serving.

CHICORY TARTE TATIN

This dish should be cooked in a frying pan or tin that is suitable for use on top of the stove and in the oven.

For the pastry
140g/5oz plain flour
55g/2oz ground rice
½ teaspoon salt
140g/5oz butter
1 egg, beaten

For the topping
110g/4oz unsalted butter
2 large onions, finely chopped
6 heads of chicory
30g/1oz caster sugar
salt and freshly ground black pepper
juice of ½ lemon

To serve
150ml/¼ pint soured cream
1 tablespoon wholegrain mustard

1. First make the pastry: sift the flour, ground rice and salt into a large bowl. Rub in the butter until the mixture resembles breadcrumbs. Bind to a stiff dough with the beaten egg. Cover and set aside.
2. Make the topping: melt half the butter in a sauté pan, add the onion and fry over a low heat for 30–40 minutes until soft and golden-brown.
3. Preheat the oven to 200°C/400°F/gas mark 6.
4. Trim the root ends from the chicory and using a sharp knife, hollow out the tough base of the root. Cut the chicory in half lengthways. Melt the remaining butter in a 25cm/10in heavy frying pan with a metal handle, add the sugar and heat until dissolved.
5. Put the chicory heads into the pan and cook gently in the buttery juices until they begin to caramelize. Remove from the heat and arrange the chicory in the pan, cut side down, in a circle, with the tips pointing outwards. Season with salt and pepper. Spoon the onion on top and sprinkle with the lemon juice.

6. Roll the pastry to a circle about 5mm/¼in thick, to fit the top of the pan. Lay it over the chicory and press down. Crimp the edges of the pastry and bake in the preheated oven for 25–30 minutes until lightly browned.
7. Mix the soured cream with the mustard and season with salt and pepper. When the tart is cooked, loosen the edges, then turn upside down on to a plate. Hand the mustard sauce separately.

CHICORY, RADISH AND WALNUT SALAD WITH CREAMY MUSTARD DRESSING

3 heads of chicory
1 bunch of radishes
110g/4oz walnuts
1–2 tablespoons chopped fresh flat-leaf parsley, to garnish

For the dressing
3 tablespoons olive oil
1 tablespoon white wine or tarragon vinegar
1 heaped teaspoon wholegrain mustard
2 tablespoons soured cream
salt and freshly ground black pepper
a pinch of caster sugar

1. Trim the roots from the chicory and separate the leaves. Wash and leave to dry on kitchen paper. Trim the stalks and roots from the radishes and slice into thin rounds.
2. Heat a heavy frying pan, add the walnuts and toss over a medium heat until toasted. Cool and chop.
3. Arrange the chicory leaves in a circle with the tips pointing outwards. Scatter over the radishes and then the walnuts.
4. Make the dressing: whisk all the ingredients together in a small bowl and drizzle over the salad. Garnish with the parsley.

CHICORY AND WATERCRESS SALAD WITH TOASTED HAZELNUTS

55g/2oz hazelnuts
4 small heads of chicory
55g/2oz watercress
1 tablespoon chopped fresh flat-leaf parsley

For the dressing
2 tablespoons hazelnut oil
1 tablespoon balsamic vinegar
a pinch of dry English mustard
salt and freshly ground black pepper
lemon juice

1. Preheat the oven to 190°C/375°F/gas mark 5. Put the hazelnuts on a baking tray and bake in the preheated oven until dark brown. Alternatively, heat the grill to medium and toast the hazelnuts until dark brown. Tip the nuts into a clean tea-towel and rub to remove the skins. Leave to cool, then chop roughly.
2. Trim the root ends from the chicory and using a sharp knife, hollow out the tough base of the roots. Separate the leaves. Remove any tough stalks from the watercress. Wash and drain well on kitchen paper.
3. Make the dressing: whisk the oil and vinegar together and season with the mustard, salt, pepper and lemon juice to taste. Put the washed leaves, hazelnuts and parsley together in a salad bowl, pour over the dressing and toss. Serve immediately.

WALDORF SALAD IN CHICORY LEAVES

3 crisp, red-skinned dessert apples
1 tablespoon lemon juice
1 teaspoon caster sugar
3 sticks of celery
55g/2oz walnut pieces
110ml/4fl oz lemon mayonnaise (see page 512)
1 tablespoon milk
salt and freshly ground black pepper
2 large heads of chicory

To serve
quick walnut bread (see page 502)

1. Cut the apples into quarters, remove the cores and cut the fruit into small chunks. Place in a bowl with the lemon juice and sugar and toss together well.
2. Slice the celery thinly and add to the apples with the walnuts. Mix again.
3. Mix the lemon mayonnaise with the milk until smooth. Stir into the apple mixture and season to taste with salt and pepper.
4. Break the chicory into separate leaves. Spoon some of the Waldorf salad into each leaf and serve with slices of walnut bread.

CHICORY AND RAISIN SALAD IN A CURRIED DRESSING

3 heads of red chicory
3 heads of green chicory
85g/3oz raisins

For the dressing
1 teaspoon Dijon mustard
1 teaspoon white wine vinegar
½ teaspoon mild curry paste
½ teaspoon clear honey
2 tablespoons extra virgin olive oil
salt and freshly ground black pepper

1. Trim the root ends from the chicory and slice the heads crossways into 2.5cm/1in wide strips. Discard the bases. Put the chicory into a bowl with the raisins.
2. Whisk the mustard, vinegar, curry paste and honey together in a small bowl. Gradually whisk in the oil to make a thick dressing. Season to taste with salt and pepper. Add the dressing to the chicory and raisins and toss together well. Serve immediately.

FRISÉE IN WARM SHERRY DRESSING WITH POMEGRANATE

1 small head of curly endive (frisée)
1 head of chicory
1 pomegranate
1 tablespoon olive oil
1 small clove of garlic, sliced
1 tablespoon dry sherry
1 teaspoon white wine vinegar
2 tablespoons walnut oil
2 tablespoons roughly chopped walnuts
salt and freshly ground black pepper

1. Separate the leaves of the curly endive. Wash thoroughly and dry. Trim the root end from the chicory and separate the leaves. Place the endive and chicory leaves in a serving bowl.
2. Cut the pomegranate in half. Scoop the seeds into a small bowl, using the handle of a teaspoon or a cocktail stick, discarding any membrane. Reserve any juice that is released.
3. Heat the oil in a small pan, add the garlic and fry over a low heat for a few minutes. Add the sherry and vinegar and bring to the boil. Pour over the endive and chicory. Add the walnut oil, walnuts, pomegranate seeds and juice and season with salt and pepper. Mix well and serve immediately.

GRILLED RADICCHIO SALAD

*2 large heads of radicchio, each cut into 8
   wedges*

For the dressing
3 tablespoons hazelnut or walnut oil
*1 tablespoon balsamic, sherry or raspberry
   vinegar*
chopped fresh chives

1. Preheat the grill.
2. Mix the oil with the vinegar. Toss the
radicchio in this dressing.
3. Grill half the radicchio wedges until brown
around the edges but pink in the middle.
4. Toss the grilled radicchio with the ungrilled
radicchio and add the chives. Serve
immediately.

EVERYTHING GREEN SALAD

1 lettuce (any kind)
French dressing (see page 528)
choice of the following:
cucumber
fennel
celery
chicory
spring onions
watercress
green beans
peas
*1 teaspoon chopped fresh mint, parsley or
   chives*

1. Prepare the salad ingredients.
Lettuce: Wash, drain and shake to allow to drip
dry. Do not twist or wring the leaves together,
which bruises them, but tear each lettuce leaf
individually and place in a salad bowl.
Cucumber: Peel or not, as desired. Slice thinly.
Fennel: Wash and shave into thin slices.
Celery: Wash and chop together with a few
young leaves.
Chicory: Wipe with a damp cloth. Remove the
tough core with a sharp knife and cut each head
on the diagonal into 3–4 pieces.
Spring onions: Wash and peel. Chop half the
green stalks finely. Keep the white part with the
rest of the salad.
Watercress: Wash and pick over, discarding the
thick stalks and any yellow leaves.
Beans and peas: Cook in boiling salted water
until just tender and cool under cold running
water. Drain well and pat dry in a tea-towel.
2. Add the herbs and the spring onion tops to
the dressing.
3. Mix the salad ingredients together and just
before serving toss them in French dressing.

FRILLY BITTER SALAD

slightly bitter leaves: watercress; young kale; curly endive; young spinach; chicory; lamb's lettuce; radicchio; rocket

For the dressing
3 tablespoons salad oil
1 tablespoon olive oil
1 tablespoon red wine vinegar
1 teaspoon French mustard
salt and freshly ground black pepper

1. Put the dressing ingredients into a screw-top jar and shake well.
2. Wash and dry the salad leaves, discarding any tough stalks.
3. Toss the salad in the dressing and tip into a clean bowl.

AVOCADO, APPLE AND LETTUCE SALAD

1 green-skinned dessert apple, washed
French dressing (see page 528)
1 ripe avocado
1 small cos or round lettuce

1. Cut the unpeeled apple into chunks, and put straight into the French dressing.
2. Peel and cut the avocado into cubes and turn carefully with the apple in the French dressing until completely coated.
3. Toss the lettuce with the avocado and apple.

ICEBERG LETTUCE WEDGES WITH A CREAMY BLUE CHEESE AND SPRING ONION DRESSING

1 iceberg lettuce

For the dressing
110g/4oz Danish blue cheese, crumbled
1 teaspoon lemon juice
150ml/¼ pint soured cream
2 tablespoons mayonnaise (see page 527)
2 tablespoons extra virgin olive oil
1 teaspoon Dijon mustard
salt and freshly ground black pepper
2 spring onions, trimmed and freshly chopped

1. Make the dressing: put the cheese, lemon juice, soured cream, mayonnaise, oil and mustard into a blender and process until smooth. Transfer to a bowl, season to taste with salt and pepper and stir in the spring onions.
2. Halve the iceberg lettuce and neatly cut out the core. Discard the outside leaves and cut each half into 4 thin wedges.
3. Overlap 2 wedges of lettuce on each individual plate and spoon over some of the dressing. Sprinkle with a little black pepper and serve.

LITTLE GEM LETTUCE HEARTS WITH A COOKED GARLIC AND SHERRY VINEGAR DRESSING

5 Little Gem lettuce hearts
6 tablespoons extra virgin olive oil
4 cloves of garlic, very finely chopped
4 teaspoons sherry vinegar
1 tablespoon chopped fresh flat-leaf parsley
salt and freshly ground black pepper

1. Cut the lettuce hearts lengthways into quarters through the stem and place them cut side up in a large shallow serving dish.
2. Put the oil and garlic into a small pan and cook over a low heat until the garlic begins to sizzle and colour very slightly. Remove the pan from the heat and leave to cool, then whisk in the vinegar, parsley and salt and pepper.
3. Spoon the warm dressing over the lettuce hearts and sprinkle with a little pepper.

CAESAR-STYLE SALAD WITH A CREAMY GARLIC DRESSING

3 romaine lettuce hearts
45g/1½oz Parmesan cheese shavings

For the croûtons
3 tablespoons olive oil, plus extra for greasing
1 clove of garlic, crushed
110g/4oz day-old white bread (French if possible)

For the dressing
1 small clove of garlic, crushed
2 teaspoons lemon juice
½ teaspoon Dijon mustard
1 large egg yolk
salt and freshly ground black pepper
150ml/¼ pint olive oil
1 teaspoon double cream

1. First make the croûtons: preheat the oven to 180°C/350°F/gas mark 4. Brush a baking tray lightly with oil. Mix the oil with the garlic in a large mixing bowl. Cut the bread into 1cm/½in pieces, add to the garlicky oil and toss together well. Spread the bread out on the prepared baking tray and bake in the preheated oven for 10–12 minutes until crisp and golden. Remove from the oven and leave to cool.
2. Make the dressing: whisk together the garlic, lemon juice, mustard, egg yolk and salt and pepper in a small bowl. Using a hand-held electric mixer, very slowly whisk in the oil to make a thick, creamy dressing. Stir in the cream and adjust the seasoning to taste. Set aside.
3. Remove and discard the outer leaves of the lettuce. Wash the remaining lettuce leaves, dry them well and then tear them into small, chunky pieces. Put them into a large bowl, drizzle over some of the dressing and toss together well.
4. Divide the dressed lettuce leaves between 4 individual plates. Drizzle over a little more of the dressing, scatter over the croûtons and the Parmesan cheese shavings and serve immediately.

THAI LETTUCE SALAD WITH FRIED TOFU AND A CHILLI AND LIME DRESSING

225g/8oz firm tofu
3–4 tablespoons sunflower oil
salt and freshly ground black pepper

For the marinade
1cm/½in piece of fresh root ginger
1 small clove of garlic, crushed
1 tablespoon dark soy sauce
1 tablespoon Chinese rice wine or dry sherry
1½ teaspoons rice vinegar
1 teaspoon sweet chilli sauce

For the salad
1 romaine lettuce heart
4 spring onions, trimmed and halved
a handful of small fresh mint leaves
a handful of small sprigs of fresh coriander

For the dressing
2 tablespoons lime juice
2 tablespoons light soy sauce
*1 stalk of lemongrass, outer leaves removed and
    very finely chopped*
1 small clove of garlic, very finely chopped
*½ medium-hot red Dutch chilli, deseeded and
    very thinly sliced (see page 22)*
½ teaspoon caster sugar

1. Wrap the tofu in a few sheets of kitchen paper. Put it into a shallow dish, cover with a board and weight down. Leave to drain for 20 minutes.
2. Unwrap the tofu and cut it into 2.5cm/1in squares about 1cm/½in thick. Make the marinade: peel and finely grate the ginger and squeeze the juice into a shallow dish. Mix in the remaining marinade ingredients. Add the pieces of tofu, stir once or twice until they are well coated and leave to marinate for 20 minutes.
3. Meanwhile, make the salad: cut the romaine lettuce crossways into strips 2.5cm/1in wide. Cut the spring onion pieces lengthways into fine shreds and toss them in a bowl with the lettuce strips, mint leaves and sprigs of coriander. Cover and chill. Mix together all the ingredients for the dressing.
4. Cook the tofu: heat the oil in a large, non-stick frying pan. Lift the pieces of tofu out of the marinade, add them to the hot oil and cook over a medium heat for 3 minutes, turning them from time to time, until crisp and golden-brown all over. Transfer them to a plate lined with kitchen paper and leave to drain briefly. Season to taste with salt and pepper.
5. Divide the salad between 4 individual plates and arrange the pieces of tofu among the leaves. Spoon over the dressing and serve immediately.

GADO GADO SERVED IN ICEBERG LETTUCE CUPS

This is a chunky Indonesian vegetable salad served with a warm, spicy peanut dressing.

225g/8oz small new potatoes, scrubbed
4 medium eggs
110g/4oz French beans, topped and tailed
1 large carrot, peeled
110g/4oz cucumber
170g/6oz cauliflower
55g/2oz fresh bean sprouts
1 small iceberg lettuce
salt and freshly ground black pepper

For the dressing
110g/4oz crunchy peanut butter
3 tablespoons sesame oil
1 medium-hot red Dutch chilli, deseeded and
  chopped (see page 22)
1 clove of garlic, crushed
1 tablespoon sweet chilli sauce
4–5 tablespoons warm spicy vegetable stock
  (see page 531)
2 teaspoons soft light brown sugar
2 teaspoons dark soy sauce
1 tablespoon lemon juice
1 tablespoon sesame seeds, lightly toasted (see
  page 22), to garnish

1. Cook the potatoes in boiling salted water for 10–15 minutes until tender, then drain. Cut into thick slices. Hard-boil the eggs for 8 minutes, then drain, cover with cold water and leave to cool. Put the peanut butter for the dressing into a small bowl set over a pan of simmering water to warm through.
2. Halve the beans. Cut the carrot and the cucumber into similar-sized matchsticks and break the cauliflower into very small florets. Drop the beans, carrot and cauliflower into boiling salted water, bring back to the boil and cook for 1 minute or until just cooked but still crunchy. Drain and refresh under cold running water. Leave to drain on kitchen paper. Peel the eggs and cut each into quarters.
3. Gently mix together the potatoes, beans, carrots, cauliflower, cucumber and bean sprouts and season with salt and pepper. Discard the outer leaves of the iceberg lettuce and select 4 large, crisp, cup-shaped leaves in which to serve the salad. Spoon the vegetables into the lettuce leaves and top with the pieces of hard-boiled egg.
4. Heat the sesame oil in a small pan, add the chilli and fry for a few seconds. Beat this into the peanut butter with the garlic, sweet chilli sauce, stock, sugar, soy sauce and lemon juice to make a smooth dressing. Drizzle the dressing over the salad, sprinkle over the sesame seeds and serve while the dressing is still warm.

SALAD LEAVES WITH ROASTED RED PEPPER AND PESTO BUTTER SAUCE

4 large handfuls of assorted salad leaves, such
 as baby spinach, watercress, rocket, lamb's
 lettuce, romaine lettuce hearts, curly endive,
 sorrel, radicchio
1 thin baguette
olive oil, for frying
1–2 cloves of garlic
3 red peppers
55g/2oz pinenuts, toasted (see page 22)
salt and freshly ground black pepper
shavings of Parmesan cheese, to garnish

For the sauce
290ml/½ pint summer vegetable stock (see
 page 530)
110g/4oz butter, diced
2 teaspoons pesto (see page 526)
lemon juice

1. Separate the salad leaves and remove any
tough stalks. Wash the leaves and shake dry,
then drain on kitchen paper.
2. Cut the baguette into 1cm/½in thick slices
and cut each slice in half crossways. Heat about
1cm/½in oil in a frying pan until a crumb of
bread sizzles vigorously. Fry the bread until
crisp and golden. Drain the croûtes on kitchen
paper, then rub with garlic.
3. Preheat the grill to the highest setting. Cut
the peppers in half and remove the pith and
seeds. Rub with a little oil, then grill, skin side
up, until black and charred. Place in a plastic
bag, seal and leave to cool, then remove the skin
and cut into strips.
4. Meanwhile, make the sauce: boil the stock
to reduce by three-quarters, then gradually
whisk in the butter. Set aside.
5. Toss the salad leaves with the pinenuts and
croûtes and pile on to 4 individual plates. Pile
the red pepper on top. Gently reheat the butter
sauce, whisking all the time. Whisk in the pesto
and season to taste with salt, pepper and lemon
juice. Drizzle the sauce over the salad. Scatter
with Parmesan shavings and serve immediately.

BITTERLEAF SALAD WITH PINK GRAPEFRUIT AND PASSION-FRUIT DRESSING

4 handfuls of assorted bitter salad leaves, such
 as rocket, baby spinach, lamb's lettuce, curly
 endive, chicory, radicchio, watercress
½ bunch of spring onions
2 pink grapefruit

For the dressing
2 passion-fruit
4 tablespoons walnut or hazelnut oil
lime juice
½ teaspoon soft light brown sugar
salt and freshly ground black pepper

1. Separate the salad leaves, remove any tough
stalks and wash and pat dry with kitchen paper.
Trim the spring onions and remove the outer
leaves. Slice lengthways into thin strips about
2.5cm/1in long. Place the leaves and spring
onions in a salad bowl.
2. Peel the grapefruit as you would an apple,
removing all the pith and peel and catching any
juice in a bowl. Cut the grapefruit into
segments and discard the membrane. Cut the
segments in half crossways. Place in the salad
bowl.
3. Make the dressing: cut the passion-fruit in
half and use a spoon to scoop out the juice and
seeds. Put them into the bowl with the
grapefruit juice and whisk in the oil. Add a dash
of lime juice and the sugar and season with salt
and pepper. Pour over the salad ingredients and
toss together. Serve immediately.

LATE SUMMER SALAD

1 head of oakleaf lettuce
110g/4oz lamb's lettuce
4 ripe tomatoes
1 thin baguette
2 × 110g/4oz logs of goat's cheese
110g/4oz girolles or other wild mushrooms
olive oil, for frying
12 black olives
55g/2oz pecan nuts

For the dressing
2 tablespoons walnut or hazelnut oil
2 tablespoons olive oil
1 tablespoon white wine vinegar
juice of ½ lemon
1 teaspoon Dijon mustard
1 clove of garlic, crushed
salt and freshly ground black pepper

1. Separate the leaves of the oakleaf and lamb's lettuce and pat dry with kitchen paper. Cut the tomatoes into eighths.
2. Make the dressing: whisk all the ingredients together and season with salt and pepper.
3. Cut the baguette and goat's cheese into about 12 thin slices. Trim off the girolle stalks and quarter the caps. Heat 2 tablespoons oil in a frying pan, add the girolles and sauté. Drain and sprinkle with salt. Add a little more oil to the pan and fry the baguette slices on both sides until golden. While still hot, spread a piece of goat's cheese on each slice.
4. Toss the lettuce, tomatoes, girolles, olives and pecan nuts in the dressing. Transfer to a serving bowl and top with the goat's cheese croûtes.

CARAMELIZED PEAR, PECAN AND ROQUEFORT SALAD

4 tablespoons olive oil
2 tablespoons sherry vinegar
2 tablespoons demerara sugar
4 ripe pears
55g/2oz pecan nuts, chopped

For the salad
½ tablespoon lemon juice
2 tablespoons olive oil
salt and freshly ground black pepper
4 large handfuls of mixed salad leaves
170g/6oz Roquefort cheese, crumbled

1. Preheat the oven to 200°C/400°F/gas mark 6.
2. Put the oil, vinegar and half the sugar into a small saucepan. Heat gently to dissolve the sugar, then cook over a low heat for 3 minutes.
3. Peel, quarter and core the pears. Lay them on a non-stick Swiss roll tin or a baking tray lined with non-stick baking paper. Pour over the oil and vinegar mixture, ensuring that each piece of pear is well coated. Cook in the preheated oven for 5 minutes.
4. Turn the pear pieces over, sprinkle with the remaining sugar and cook for a further 5 minutes.
5. Scatter over the pecan nuts and return to the oven for 3 minutes.
6. Meanwhile, make the salad: mix the lemon juice and oil together and season with salt and pepper. Put the salad leaves into a big bowl, pour over the dressing and mix well. Divide between 4 individual plates and add the cheese.
7. Remove the pears from the oven and divide them between the plates. Scatter over the pecan nuts and pour over the sticky dressing. Serve immediately.

VEGETABLE SALAD NIÇOISE

To make this a more substantial main course dish, add 225g/8oz cooked baby new potatoes.

8 whole baby carrots
170g/6oz green beans, topped and tailed
1 red pepper
1 romaine lettuce heart
8 radishes, trimmed and halved
3 plum tomatoes
*1 × 290g/10oz jar of artichoke hearts marinated
    in oil*
12 black olives
balsamic vinegar
salt and freshly ground black pepper
6 spring onions, trimmed
4 hard-boiled eggs, peeled and quartered

To serve
roasted garlic mayonnaise (see page 512)

1. Cook the carrots in boiling salted water until just tender. Blanch the beans in the same water. Refresh both under cold running water.
2. Preheat the grill to high. Cut the peppers into quarters and remove the pith and seeds. Grill, skin side up, until black and charred. Place in a plastic bag, seal and leave to cool, then remove the skins and cut into strips.
3. Wash the lettuce. Break up the large leaves and leave the smaller ones whole. Trim the radishes, leaving a little of the green stalks. Cut each tomato into six wedges. Drain the artichoke hearts and reserve the oil.
4. Toss the carrots, beans, pepper, lettuce, tomatoes, artichoke hearts and olives together. Add 2 tablespoons of the reserved artichoke oil and a good sprinkling of vinegar. Season with salt and pepper and mix well. Turn into a salad bowl and arrange the spring onion and hard-boiled eggs on the top. Hand the mayonnaise separately.

ORIENTAL CABBAGE SALAD WITH SWEET SOY DRESSING

1 red pepper
¼ cucumber
1 small head of Chinese leaves
1 medium raw beetroot
110g/4oz bean sprouts

For the dressing
1 clove of garlic, crushed
*2.5cm/1in piece of fresh root ginger, peeled and
    grated*
*1 piece of lemongrass, outer leaves removed and
    finely chopped*
1 teaspoon soft light brown sugar
2 tablespoons sesame oil
1 tablespoon rice wine vinegar
1 tablespoon sweet soy sauce
a small pinch of dried red chilli flakes
salt and freshly ground black pepper

1. Core the pepper and remove the seeds and pith. Cut into quarters and slice thinly. Peel the cucumber and halve it lengthways, scoop out the seeds with a melon-baller or teaspoon, then slice crossways. Discard the outer leaves from the Chinese leaves and slice thinly. Peel the beetroot and cut into very fine matchsticks, either by hand or in a food processor.
2. Make the dressing: put all the ingredients together in a small pan and bring to the boil. Season lightly with salt and pepper.
3. Toss all the vegetables together with the hot dressing and either serve immediately while still warm or leave to stand for 20 minutes.

ROCKET AND MOZZARELLA TEMPURA

4 × 125g/4½oz buffalo mozzarella cheeses
85g/3oz rocket, roughly torn
1 teaspoon black onion seeds
salt and freshly ground black pepper
1 × 225g/8oz packet of tempura mix
oil, for frying

1. Drain the cheese and cut into 1cm/½in cubes. Dry well on kitchen paper.
2. Mix the cheese, rocket and onion seeds together in a large bowl and season with salt and pepper.
3. Make up the tempura mix according to the packet instructions and stir in the cheese and rocket mixture.
4. Heat 7.5cm/3in oil in a large, heavy saucepan and when a drop of batter sizzles vigorously, carefully lower in heaped tablespoons of the mixture. Fry for 2–3 minutes or until the fritters rise to the surface and are crisp and brown.
5. Drain on kitchen paper, sprinkle with salt and keep warm in a low oven. Fry the remaining mixture in the same way. Serve hot.

ROCKET AND HAZELNUT SALAD WITH OVEN-DRIED MANGO

2 large ripe mangoes
85g/3oz rocket
55g/2oz baby spinach leaves
55g/2oz baby red chard
1 small frisée lettuce
85g/3oz hazelnuts, toasted and skinned (see
  page 22)

For the dressing
1½ tablespoons salad oil
1½ tablespoons hazelnut oil
2 tablespoons raspberry vinegar
salt and freshly ground black pepper

1. Preheat the oven to 100°C/200°F/gas mark ½.
2. Peel the mangoes and slice the flesh into thin slices as close to the flat stone as possible.
3. Lay half the mango slices on a baking tray and place in the oven for 1–1½ hours, turning occasionally, until slightly shrivelled. (This will intensify the flavour.) Cut into small dice.
4. Wash and dry the salad leaves. Chop the hazelnuts roughly.
5. Mix all the dressing ingredients together.
6. Toss the salad leaves with the hazelnuts, salad dressing and diced dried mango. Transfer to a serving bowl and arrange the fresh mango slices on top.

ROCKET SALAD TOPPED WITH COURGETTE AND NEW POTATO FRITTERS

This recipe would make a feast served with lemony chickpeas (see page 327) and a tomato salad.

225g/8oz waxy new potatoes, scrubbed
2 medium courgettes
55g/2oz Parmesan cheese, freshly grated
sunflower or vegetable oil, for frying
225g/8oz rocket
balsamic vinegar
walnut or hazelnut oil
salt and freshly ground black pepper
shavings of Parmesan cheese, to garnish

For the batter
110g/4oz plain flour
½ teaspoon salt
2 eggs, beaten

1. Put the new potatoes into a saucepan of cold salted water. Bring to the boil and cook for 2 minutes. Drain and cool. Grate the potatoes and courgettes coarsely. Put into a colander and leave to drain for 10–15 minutes.
2. Make the batter: sift the flour and salt into a large mixing bowl and make a well in the centre. Add the beaten egg and mix, gradually drawing in the flour from around the sides, until the batter is smooth, creamy and very thick. Season with salt and pepper.
3. Fold the grated vegetables and cheese into the batter. Heat a little oil in a heavy frying pan until a drop of batter will sizzle slowly. Drop tablespoonfuls of batter into the pan and fry on both sides until golden-brown. Transfer to a baking tray lined with kitchen paper and keep warm while you cook the remaining fritters in the same way. There should be 8 fritters in all.
4. Meanwhile, wash and pat the rocket dry. Drizzle over a little vinegar and nut oil and divide between 4 individual plates. Top each with 2 fritters and scatter with a few shavings of Parmesan cheese.

RICOTTA, MOZZARELLA AND HERB FILO PARCELS

MAKES 12 SMALL PARCELS

30g/1oz butter
110g/4oz ricotta cheese
110g/4oz mozzarella cheese, grated
1 egg, beaten
1 tablespoon chopped fresh flat-leaf parsleey
2 tablespoons chopped fresh chives
1 tablespoon chopped fresh mint
30g/1oz pistachio nuts, chopped
salt and freshly ground black pepper
freshly grated nutmeg
8 sheets of bought filo pastry

1. Preheat the oven to 200°C/400°F/gas mark 6. Brush a baking sheet with a little of the melted butter.
2. Mix the ricotta and mozzarella cheeses with the beaten egg. Stir in the herbs and pistachio nuts and season with salt, pepper and nutmeg.
3. Lay 4 sheets of pastry side by side on a worktop and brush with melted butter. Cover with the remaining 4 sheets of pastry so that there are now 4 pairs of 2 sheets each. Brush with more melted butter. Cut each pair into 4–5 strips.
4. Place a spoonful of the cheese mixture at one end of each strip. Form a triangle by folding the right-hand corner across to the opposite side. Then fold across from the left to the right. Keep folding in this way until the strip of pastry is used up.
5. Lay the parcels on the baking sheet and brush again with melted butter. Bake in the preheated oven for about 10 minutes until golden-brown.

HERB SOUFFLÉ WITH FETA CHEESE CENTRE

85g/3oz feta cheese, crumbled
2 tablespoons crème fraîche
2 tablespoons double cream
salt and freshly ground black pepper
55g/2oz butter, plus extra for greasing
dried white breadcrumbs
55g/2oz plain flour
½ teaspoon dry English mustard
a pinch of cayenne pepper
200ml/½ pint milk
85g/3oz Gruyère cheese, grated
4 eggs, separated
1 tablespoon each freshly chopped chives,
    chervil and flat-leaf parsley

1. Mix the feta cheese, crème fraîche and double cream together in a small bowl. Season with salt and pepper and set aside.
2. Preheat the oven to 200°C/400°F/gas mark 6. Lightly grease a 570ml/1 pint soufflé dish with butter and coat with breadcrumbs. Tap out the excess.
3. Melt the butter in a saucepan. Add the flour, mustard and cayenne. Cook over a low heat for 30 seconds. Add the milk and bring to the boil, stirring continuously. Lower the heat and simmer for 1 minute.
4. Remove the sauce from the heat. Stir in the Gruyère cheese, egg yolks and herbs. Season well with salt and pepper. Transfer to a large bowl.
5. In a separate bowl, whisk the egg whites until stiff but not dry. Fold a spoonful of the egg white into the same mixture, using a large metal spoon. Carefully fold in the remainder.
6. Pour half the mixture into the prepared dish and cover with the feta cheese mixture. Top with the remaining soufflé mixture.
7. Bake in the centre of the preheated oven for 20–25 minutes or the soufflé is well risen, browned and wobbles slightly when the dish is shaken gently. Serve immediately.

GRIDDLED VINE LEAVES WITH MARINATED GOAT'S CHEESE

3 × 110g/4oz goat's cheeses
4 tablespoons olive oil
1 red chilli, deseeded and chopped (see page 22)
2 cloves of garlic, crushed
grated zest and juice of ½ lemon
about 6 fresh basil leaves
salt and freshly ground black pepper
12 preserved vine leaves

1. Cut each round of goat's cheese into 4 triangles and place in a shallow dish. Mix together the oil, chilli, garlic, lemon zest and juice. Shred the basil leaves and add to the marinade with salt and pepper. Pour over the goat's cheese, cover and chill for at least 2 hours or overnight.
2. Rinse the vine leaves and carefully pat dry with kitchen paper. Lay the leaves vein side up on a worktop. Place a wedge of goat's cheese towards one end of each leaf. Fold in the sides and roll up. Brush with the remaining marinade.
3. Heat a ridged griddle pan and cook the vine leaves in batches for 2 minutes on each side. Serve immediately.

GRIDDLED VINE LEAVES WITH BULGHAR WHEAT STUFFING

110ml/4fl oz boiling water
85g/3oz bulghar wheat
1 tablespoon olive oil, plus extra for brushing
1 medium onion, finely chopped
1 clove of garlic, chopped
¼ teaspoon ground fenugreek
¼ teaspoon paprika
¼ teaspoon ground cumin
1 orange
2 beefsteak tomatoes, peeled, chopped and
    deseeded (see page 22)
1 tablespoon chopped fresh mint
1 tablespoon chopped fresh parsley
salt and freshly ground black pepper
20 preserved vine leaves
110g/4oz feta cheese, cut into cubes (optional)

To serve
harissa (see page 510)

1. Pour the boiling water over the bulghar
wheat in a bowl. Cover with a clean tea-towel
and leave to soak for 15 minutes.
2. Heat the oil in a frying pan, add the onion
and fry over a low heat until very soft and
transparent. Add the garlic and spices and fry
for a further 2 minutes.
3. Peel the orange as you would an apple,
removing all the pith and pips. Cut into
segments, discarding any membrane. Put any
juice collected into the bowl with the bulghar
wheat and roughly chop the segments.
4. Break up the bulghar wheat with a fork and
stir in the onion mixture and the orange with
the tomatoes, mint and parsley. Season with
salt and pepper.
5. Rinse the vine leaves and carefully pat dry
with kitchen paper. Place the leaves vein side up
on a worktop. Divide the stuffing equally
between the vine leaves and add a cube of feta
cheese to each, if used. Fold in the sides of the
leaves and roll up into flat parcels. Brush with
oil. Heat a ridged griddle and cook the vine
leaves in batches for 2 minutes on each side
until crisp on the outside and hot in the middle.
Hand the harissa separately.

CREAM OF WATERCRESS SOUP

450g/1lb floury potatoes, such as Maris Piper
55g/2oz butter
1 litre/2 pints boiling water
225g/8oz watercress, large stalks removed
salt and freshly ground white pepper
110ml/4fl oz double cream
4 small sprigs of watercress, to garnish

1. Peel the potatoes and slice them thinly.
2. Melt the butter in a large saucepan, add the
potatoes and stir until well coated in the butter.
Cover and cook over a low heat for about 6
minutes until they are beginning to soften and
break up.
3. Add the water and bring to the boil, then
cover and leave the soup to simmer for 20
minutes until the potatoes are very soft.
4. Stir in the watercress and cook for no longer
than 3 minutes, otherwise it will lose its bright
green colour. Purée the soup in batches in a
food processor or blender, return to the rinsed-
out pan, stir in half the cream and season to
taste with salt and pepper. Reheat gently
without boiling, ladle into warmed soup bowls
and garnish each bowl with a swirl of the
remaining cream and a sprig of watercress.

WATERCRESS AND GOAT'S CHEESE SOUFFLÉ

30g/1oz butter, plus extra for greasing
85g/3oz Parmesan cheese, freshly grated
85g/3oz watercress
15g/½oz plain flour
cayenne pepper
225g/8oz mascarpone
170g/6oz firm goat's cheese, crumbled
5 eggs, separated
salt and freshly ground white pepper

1. Preheat the oven to 200°C/400°F/gas mark 6. Heat a baking tray in the oven. Grease a 1.25 litre/2 pint soufflé dish or 4 × 170ml/6fl oz ramekin dishes with butter and dust the sides with a little of the Parmesan cheese.
2. Wash the watercress thoroughly, remove any thick stalks and pat dry on kitchen paper. Chop roughly.
3. Melt the butter in a small saucepan. Add the flour and a pinch of cayenne and stir over a low heat for 1 minute. Remove the pan from the heat and stir in the mascarpone, goat's cheese, the remaining Parmesan cheese, the egg yolks and chopped watercress. Season to taste with salt and pepper.
4. Whisk the egg whites until stiff but not dry. Stir 2 spoonfuls of the egg white into the goat's cheese mixture, then carefully fold in the remainder, using a large metal spoon. Spoon into the prepared soufflé or ramekin dishes and run a knife around the rim. Set on the hot baking tray and bake in the preheated oven for 30–40 minutes for a large soufflé and for 15–20 minutes for individual soufflés.

FETA ROULADE WITH WATERCRESS AND OLIVE FILLING

This roulade is perfect for a summer lunch. Serve with crusty bread and tomato salad with basil and red onion.

For the roulade
olive oil, for brushing
5 eggs, separated
225g/8oz feta cheese, crumbled
2 tablespoons double cream
freshly ground black pepper
55g/2oz Parmesan cheese, freshly grated

For the filling
110g/4oz watercress
55g/2oz Kalamata olives, pitted and quartered
55g/2oz walnuts, roughly chopped
sea salt
1 tablespoon walnut oil

1. Preheat the oven to 200°C/400°F/gas mark 6. Brush a Swiss roll tin about 23 × 31cm/9 × 13in with oil. Line the base and sides of the tin with greaseproof paper, then oil the paper as well.
2. Beat the egg yolks in a bowl and mix in the feta and cream. Season with plenty of pepper. Whisk the egg whites until stiff but not dry. Fold 2 tablespoons of the egg white into the cheese mixture, then carefully fold in the remainder, using a large metal spoon. Pour the mixture into the prepared tin and bake in the preheated oven for 10–12 minutes until the centre feels firm when pressed with the fingertips. Cover with a clean damp tea-towel and leave until cold.
3. Trim the tough stalks from the watercress. Chop the watercress and mix with the olives and walnuts. Season with a little salt and pepper and toss in the walnut oil.
4. Sprinkle a sheet of greaseproof paper with the Parmesan cheese. Turn the roulade on to the paper. Spread the watercress salad over the roulade and roll up lengthways.

CHEESE BAPS WITH WATERCRESS

MAKES 8

225g/8oz *wholemeal flour*
225g/8oz *strong plain flour, plus extra for dusting*
1 *teaspoon salt*
1 *teaspoon caster sugar*
55g/2oz *chilled butter, diced*
1½ *teaspoons easy-blend yeast*
30g/1oz *sunflower seeds*
290ml/½ *pint milk, plus extra for brushing*
1 *medium egg*
110g/4oz *mature Cheddar cheese, coarsely grated*
225g/8oz *soft, full-fat cheese, such as Crowdie, Caboc or St Chevrier Ash*
2 *bunches of watercress, tough stalks removed*

1. First make the baps: sift the flours, salt and sugar into the bowl of a food processor. Add the butter and process briefly until the mixture resembles fine breadcrumbs. Tip the mixture into a bowl and stir in the yeast and sunflower seeds.

2. Pour the milk into a small saucepan and warm gently over a low heat. Remove and beat in the egg. Stir the mixture into the dried ingredients until they come together into a soft dough that will leave the sides of the bowl. Tip the dough on to a lightly floured worktop and knead for 10 minutes until smooth and elastic.

3. Put the dough back into the bowl and cover with a piece of lightly greased clingfilm. Leave in a warm place for about 1 hour until doubled in bulk.

4. Remove the dough from the bowl, punch down and knead for 5 minutes until smooth again. Divide into 8 even-sized pieces and shape each one into a flattish round. Place well spaced apart on 1 large or 2 smaller lightly floured baking sheets, cover loosely in clingfilm, and leave in a warm place until almost doubled in size. Meanwhile, preheat the oven to 200°C/400°F/gas mark 6.

5. Brush the tops of the baps with milk and sprinkle generously with the Cheddar cheese. Bake in the preheated oven for 20 minutes. Remove from the oven and leave to cool on a wire rack.

6. Split the baps in half and spread the bottom half with some of the soft cheese. Fill generously with watercress and serve.

WATERCRESS, ROCKET AND FETA TART

225g/8oz shortcrust pastry (see page 521)
15g/½oz butter
2 shallots, chopped
100g/3½oz feta cheese, crumbled
2 eggs, beaten
150ml/¼ pint milk
4 tablespoons Greek yoghurt
2 tablespoons freshly grated Parmesan cheese
15g/½oz watercress leaves, chopped
15g/½oz rocket, chopped
salt and freshly ground black pepper

1. Preheat the oven to 200°C/400°F/gas mark 6.
2. Roll out the pastry and use to line a 20cm/8in flan tin. Chill for 20 minutes, then bake blind in the preheated oven for 15 minutes (see page 22). Remove from the oven and lower the temperature to 150°C/300°F/gas mark 2.
3. Melt the butter in a small saucepan and add the shallots. Cook over a low heat for 10 minutes without browning.
4. Put the feta cheese into a bowl and add the eggs, milk, yoghurt, half the Parmesan cheese, the watercress, rocket, shallots, salt and pepper. (Feta cheese can be very salty, so be careful when adding the salt.)
5. Pour the mixture into the prepared flan case and sprinkle over the remaining Parmesan cheese. Place on a baking sheet and bake in the preheated oven for 30–35 minutes or until the filling is set. Remove from the oven and serve hot or cold.

WATERCRESS RAREBIT

1½ bunches of watercress
110g/4oz Gorgonzola cheese, crumbled
110g/4oz ricotta cheese
1 tablespoon fresh white breadcrumbs
a large pinch of cayenne pepper
4 thick-cut slices of white bread

1. Twist the watercress to remove the top from the tough bottom part of the stalks. Wash thoroughly and pat dry with kitchen paper. Chop two-thirds of the watercress.
2. Mix the Gorgonzola cheese with the ricotta, breadcrumbs and chopped watercress. Season with cayenne.
3. Preheat the grill to high. Toast the bread on both sides. Top with the cheese and watercress mixture and grill until melted and golden-brown. Serve with the remaining watercress on the side.

NOTE: This recipe can also be made as a canapé. Toast medium-sliced bread and cut into small rounds with a pastry cutter. Top with the watercress mixture and grill until golden-brown.

VEGETABLE FRUITS

Aubergines • Avocados • Peppers and Chillies • Tomatoes • Fruits

INTRODUCTION

Vegetable fruits are a colourful reflection of their native sunny climates. They are packed full of vitamins, especially Vitamin C. Vegetable fruits need careful choosing and storing to gain the maximum flavour. All are best if ripened naturally. That is a tall order when so many vegetables are harvested under-ripe to satisfy retailers' demands but it is sometimes possible to find freshly ripened produce from local smallholdings, markets or greengrocers. Vegetable fruits should all be bright and glossy with smooth skins and no sign of wrinkling. Store them in the refrigerator for up to a week. If they need ripening keep them at room temperature.

Aubergines should have taut, glossy skins. They are mostly a deep purplish-black but some are violet and others mottled with cream. Some miniature varieties are available now which are lovely cooked whole with a little stuffing or dressing and served as a first course. Aubergines are no longer bitter so there is no need to degorge them with salt. This spoils the texture and the finished dish is inevitably over salty. Aubergines soak up vast amounts of oil when fried. Generally it is better to brush them with oil and grill. Because of their substance and texture, aubergines are a particularly good substitute for meat in many dishes. Store in a plastic bag in the refrigerator for 1–2 weeks.

Avocado pears are considered one of the most complete foods. They have a high mono-unsaturated fat content. They also contain substantial amounts of vitamins C and E plus the mineral potassium. Avocados can be baked and are good in grilled sandwiches but they are at their best when eaten raw. The secret is to judge the ripeness. Even a bullet-hard avocado can be perfectly ripened. Sitting in a fruit bowl it will ripen in about a week; placing it next to bananas or leaving it in the warmth of an airing cupboard speeds up the process. The avocado is ripe if the flesh gives a little when squeezed. Do this gently or the pear will be bruised. Avocados can now be bought ready-ripened at a premium price. They are usually reliable and of good quality. There are three kinds of avocado that appear in stores according to the season: Hass, which is rough-skinned; Eltinger, which is smooth and a much brighter green; and Fuerte, which is in between.

Peppers: All peppers are members of the capsicum family. In this country we mostly buy bell peppers but there are varieties of sweet pepper that are long and pointed. The various colours of peppers span the spectrum. First growing into green fruit, they ripen to red and some to yellow and orange. The flavour mellows with the colour: green peppers have a slight bitterness but red are sweet and oily. Creamy-white and purple-black peppers are similar to green in flavour. Their colour is not related to ripeness but to a lack of chlorophyll. Peppers are equally good raw or cooked. When roasted or grilled the sweetness and oiliness are intensified and the pepper takes on a quite different, richer flavour. Choose bright, shiny peppers with smooth skins. Peppers keep well in the refrigerator.

Chillies are also members of the capsicum family and are native to South America. They contain large amounts of vitamin C. Capsaicin is responsible for their fiery heat. There are in the region of 200 varieties of all colours, shapes and sizes. The degree of heat is usually disproportionate to the size – it is the small, inoffensive-looking chillies that are the hottest.

The heat is in the membrane and seeds of the chilli. The basic red and green chillies sold loose are quite mild, while the plump Scotch Bonnet or Habañero chillies are at the opposite end of the spectrum. Check the heat chart if venturing into other varieties. Prepare chillies with care as the juice will burn the skin and eyes if contact is made. Hands and kitchen utensils should be carefully washed after preparation. There is also a whole range of dried chillies. These develop more intense and intricate flavours in the drying process. Chilli aficionados will blend a combination of fresh and dried for ultimate flavour and heat combination. Chillies are a truly addictive ingredient and their use is a fascinating subject.

CHILLIES – KEY: [1] = MILD [2] = FAIRLY HOT [3] = MEDIUM HOT
[4] = VERY HOT [5] = FIERCELY HOT

Fresh Chillies

NAME/CHARACTERISTICS	COLOURS	USES	SUBSTITUTES	HEAT SCALE
Aji or Orange Thai chilli (*Capsicum baccatum*) Aji is a generic name for any chilli in South America. It measures 7–13cm/3–5in long and 1cm/½in wide with thin flesh. It has a fruity flavour and is quite hot. When dried it is called canagueño.	Yellow to orange.	In all Peruvian dishes, particularly ceviches. It is also good pickled in any Thai or Malayan dishes.	Brazilian malagueta (smaller and hotter) or 2 Indian chillies to 1 Aji.	[4]
ANAHEIM or New Mexican (*Capsicum chinense*) 10–15cm/4–6in long, 2.5cm/1in wide and flattish. Smooth medium-thick flesh and a mild, sweet, vegetable flavour. The red Anaheim is sweeter than the green and is also known as chilli Colorado.	Green and red.	Very versatile chilli. Flavour is improved by roasting, a delicious addition to roasted sweet pepper salads, sandwich fillings and green chilli sauces.	New Mexico green or red are a little bit hotter, but a good substitute.	[2]
CAYENNE (*Capsicum annuum*) 7–13cm/3–5in long. Long, thin, sharply pointed. The many varieties include Hot Portugal or Ring of Fire, grown for their heat.	Green, red, yellow.	Primarily used for grinding into cayenne pepper or in bottled sauces.	Thai or Indian.	[4]
DUTCH or HOLLAND RED chilli, or Red or Green Westland chilli 10cm/4in long with a curved, tapering point; it has a thick flesh with a strong, fresh flavour.	Bright red or green.	Salsas, pickles, stews and soups.	Red Thai or frescos.	[3]
FRESNO or Kenyan (*Capsicum chinense*) 5cm/2in long, 2.5cm/1in wide on the shoulders, tapering to a round end. Sometimes mistaken for a red jalapeño, fresno has a medium-thick flesh with a sweet flavour.	Light green, red.	Good in everything, raw, cooked or grilled. Used in salsas, ceviches, soups and stir-fries.	Jalapeño, red or green, although less hot, make a perfect substitute.	[3]

Fresh Chillies—contd

NAME/CHARACTERISTICS	COLOURS	USES	SUBSTITUTES	HEAT SCALE
HABAÑERO, or Jamaican hot, Scotch Bonnet, rocoto, rocotillo (*Capsicum chinense*) These chillies are all of the same family and have a very similar shape and taste. They are 5cm/2in long and roundish with an irregular shape which resembles a bonnet. The habañero and its cousins are the hottest chillies in the world with an intense, fruity flavour.	Deep green to orange and light red.	Its fierce heat goes really well with seafood and shellfish. Good for flavouring oils, vinegars, salsas and pickles.	Any *Capsicum chinenser* will be a perfect substitute, although the heat varies slightly.	[5]
JALAPEÑO (*Capsicum chinense*) The most used chilli in the USA. About 5–7cm/2–3in long, 2.5cm/1in wide and tapered to a round end. Juicy, thick-fleshed and rather stringy, with a clean, fresh vegetable flavour.	Grass green to dark green or red.	A very popular and versatile chilli which can be stuffed or grilled and used in anything from salsas to pickles, marinades to curries.	Fresno, even though slightly hotter, is a good substitute when roasted for salsas.	[3]
PIMIENTO (*Capsicum annuum*) 10cm/4in long, 7.5cm/3in wide, with almost a heart shape. It is a mild chilli, with thick flesh and found mostly canned or pickled. Once powdered it becomes paprika, a well-known spice.	Scarlet.	As a substitute for red peppers, pimiento can be stuffed, used in sauces and marinades, or grilled and cut into strips for sandwich fillings, salads or pasta dishes.	Hungarian sweet chilli has a paler colour but similar flavours and uses.	[1]
POBLANO (*Capsicum annuum*) 12cm/5.5in long, 7.5cm/3in wide on the shoulders, looking like a triangle with a tapered point. The poblano has a thick flesh with a mild but rich flavour. It is the most popular of the fresh chillies in Mexico.	The green-fleshed poblano has an aubergine skin colour, this becomes deep red brown when ripe.	The green variety is not eaten raw, but is always roasted and skinned and used mainly for stuffing.	Although hotter, New Mexico red can be used.	[1]
RED SNUB CHILLIES 4–5cm/1½–2in long. Short and dumpy, fat at the top with a rounded point at the bottom.	Red and shiny.	Good in rice dishes, stews, etc.	There are no substitutes for the mildness of these chillies but as they are the standard chillies sold loose in supermarkets they are nearly always available.	[1]
SERRANO or Mountain Chilli (*Capsicum annuum*) Small, bullet-shaped chillies with a rounded end. Measuring 3–5cm/1–2in long, serranos have a thick, smooth flesh with a hard appearance. They are high in acidity with a pungent flavour.	Bright green and scarlet red.	Used in salsas, pickles and relishes; thinly sliced to flavour stews, curries and other slow-cooking dishes, and also as a decoration chilli.	Thai chillies or ajis (1 Thai to 3 serranos)	[3]

Fresh Chillies—contd

NAME/CHARACTERISTICS	COLOURS	USES	SUBSTITUTES	HEAT SCALE
TABASCO (*Capsicum frutescens*) 2.5cm/1in long, these small tapered chillies have a smooth skin and thin flesh. With a very hot and sharp flavour, they constitute the main ingredient of the world-famous McIlhenny Tabasco pepper sauce.	Bright yellow, orange or red.	Soups, stews and flavouring oils.	Brazilian malagueta or Thai chillis (Indian in the UK).	[4]
THAI or Indian chilli in the UK (*Capsicum annuum*) 2.5–5cm/1–2in long, slender with a pointed end. These are thin-fleshed with lots of seeds.	Bright red and dark green.	Used extensively in Asian cuisines, the Thai chilli is very good for flavouring oils and as a decorative element in soups, stews, stir-fries and noodle dishes.	Serranos or Brazilian malagueta (a bit hotter than the Thai).	[4]
WAX chillies (*Capsicum annuum*) Includes chillies with very different characteristics, such as Hungarian wax, banana, caribe, Santa Fé, Cera, Gierro. Sizes vary from 7.5–10cm/3–4in long and the heat varies from medium to hot. They usually have a sweetish, waxy taste.	Pale yellow green to pale yellow.	Good for salsas (grilled, skinned and cut into strips) and for chilli purées.	Use any light yellow chilli with thick flesh, but make sure to taste a small piece before using any of them, as hotness can vary.	[2]

Dried Chillies

NAME/CHARACTERISTICS	USES	HEAT SCALE
ANCHO or DRIED POBLANO Dark mahogany in colour, 10–12cm/4–5in long and 7cm/3in on the shoulders. It is the sweetest dried chilli, with a mild flavour of prunes.	Stuffed rajas (strips), moles, salsas, soups, stews, chilli paste.	[2]
BIRD'S EYE, Pequin, Chilli Pequeño or Piquin 1cm/½in long, small, bright orange to bright red, usually oval or arrowhead-shaped. Thin-fleshed with a smoky, sweet flavour.	Ideal for flavouring oils and vinegars, or in stews and soups.	[5]
CASCABEL, Little Rattle or Chilli Bola Round in shape, about 3.5cm/1½in long. Dark reddish-brown in colour, thick-fleshed and smooth-skinned with lots of seeds. Nutty, woody flavour, slightly acidic and tannic.	Soups, salsas, chilli paste with nuts.	[2]
CAYENNE, Ginnie Pepper 5–10cm/2–4in long, tapering to a point. Bright red, thin-fleshed. Cayenne peppers have an acidic, tart flavour.	Most used in powdered form and in bottled sauces. Good for flavouring oils and vinegars.	[4]

Dried Chillies—contd

NAME/CHARACTERISTICS	USES	HEAT SCALE
CHIPOTLE, Chilli Ahumado or Meco Chipotle is a smoked, dried red jalapeño, 2.5cm/1in long, 1cm/½in wide, dark brick to coffee colour with cream veins and ridges. A distinctive smoky and hot flavour.	Chipotle is good with everything; its smoky flavour gives an interest to all dishes, especially soups, salsas and stews.	[3]
GUAJILLO 10–15cm/4–6in long, 3.5cm/1in wide, slightly curved and tapered at the end. Shiny dark cherry in colour with thin skin and slightly tannic taste.	Guajillo is widely used in Mexico, mainly in sauces, soups and stews.	[5]
HABAÑERO 2.5cm/1in-round, golden orange in colour. Thin-fleshed with intense heat, aroma and flavour. Dried or fresh, the habañero is the hottest chilli available. Its rich fruity flavour can be tasted even through all its heat.	It goes particularly well with fish soups and in stews, salsas and in chilli pastes. A little goes a long way.	[5]
MULATO 10–13cm/4–5in long, 5–7cm/2–3in wide. Dark brown in colour, the mulato is similar to the ancho, but larger and flatter. It has a medium-thick flesh and a smoky, pungent flavour with hints of tobacco and liquorice.	Very good stuffed in salsas and mixed wth mulato and pasilla for mole sauces.	[5]
PASILLA or Chilli Negro 13–15cm/5–6in long, 2.5cm/1in across. Shiny graphite colour, with twisted, tapered body. Liquorice and earthy flavour. It can be used instead of ancho, but it has a more pungent flavour.	Ideal chilli for any seafood. Pasilla is also used in powdered form and can be used in any salsa.	[2]

Tomatoes are second only to onions for versatility and all-round ability to add flavour. They have been one of the first casualties of modern production, with flavour being sacrificed for uniformity of size and harvesting when under-ripe. Flavour always reaches its full potential on the vine and is the result of the right balance of sweetness and acidity. **Vine-ripened tomatoes** and locally bought produce are likely to be tastiest. **Plum tomatoes** are richly flavoured and the variety used for canning. They are also very good in salads. **Cherry tomatoes** are sweet and useful for side dishes, salads and garnishes. Tomatoes can come in a variety of colours when ripe – green, yellow, orange and striped as well as red. Sun-dried tomatoes are literally that – the moisture has been dried in the heat of the sun, intensifying the flavour. Fresh tomatoes are best eaten at room temperature and should only be stored in the refrigerator once they are ripe.

AUBERGINE APPETIZERS

MAKES ABOUT 12

2 small aubergines
3 tablespoons flavoured olive oil, such as chilli
    or basil
salt and freshly ground black pepper
1 quantity hummus (see page 325)
1 tablespoon fresh coriander leaves

1. Preheat the grill to high. Trim the stalks
from the aubergines and slice each lengthways
into about 6 slices 1cm/¼in thick. Brush
liberally with oil and grill until golden. Turn,
brush again with oil, season with salt and
pepper and grill until golden and tender.
2. Spread the aubergine slices with the
hummus. Roll up and secure with cocktail
sticks. Arrange on a colourful plate and scatter
with coriander leaves.

NOTE: Green or red pesto (see pages 526 and
527) can be substituted for the hummus.

AUBERGINE BRUSCHETTAS

8 tablespoons olive oil
2 cloves of garlic, sliced
2 aubergines
½ large baguette (you will need about 12 slices)

For the tomato topping
1 tablespoon balsamic vinegar
1 tablespoon chopped fresh basil
1 tablespoon pinenuts, toasted (see page 22)
salt and freshly ground black pepper
3 tomatoes, chopped

For the pepper topping
1 red pepper
1 yellow pepper
½ tablespoon fresh thyme leaves
salt and freshly ground black pepper

1. Put the oil and the garlic into a bowl and
allow to infuse for at least 30 minutes.
2. Trim the stalks from the aubergines and cut
them on the diagonal into 1cm/½in slices.
3. Preheat the grill to high. Cut the baguette on
the diagonal into about 12 slices of similar size
to the aubergines. Grill the baguette slices very
lightly on both sides.
4. Place the aubergines on the grill rack and
brush with the infused oil. Grill until brown
then turn, brush again with oil and grill until
brown and cooked through. Remove from the
grill and allow to cool.
5. Make the tomato topping: add the vinegar, 1
tablespoon of the infused oil, the basil, pinenuts
and salt and pepper to the chopped tomatoes.
6. Make the pepper topping: cut the peppers
into quarters and remove the pith and seeds.
Grill, cut side down, until the skin is blackened
and blistered. Put the peppers into a bowl,
cover with a plate and leave for 10–15 minutes.
Remove the stalks and skin, cut the flesh into
strips and add 1 tablespoon of the infused oil,
the thyme, salt and pepper.
7. To assemble: put the slices of the toasted
baguette on a large plate and drizzle over the
remaining infused oil. Cover with a slice of
aubergine and top half the slices with the
tomatoes and the remainder with the peppers.

AUBERGINE CROQUETTES

2 medium aubergines
1 tablespoon olive oil
2 cloves of garlic
140g/5oz ricotta cheese
1 egg, beaten
110g/4oz dry white breadcrumbs
85g/3oz Parmesan cheese, freshly grated
salt and freshly ground black pepper
freshly grated nutmeg

For the coating
55g/2oz plain flour
1 egg, beaten
225g/8oz dry white or wholemeal breadcrumbs
oil, for frying

To serve
tomato salsa (see page 514)

1. Preheat the oven to 190°C/375°F/gas mark 5.
2. Brush the aubergines with oil and place in a small roasting tin. Bake in the preheated oven for 20 minutes, then add the garlic to the tin. Bake for a further 20–30 minutes until the aubergines are soft, then remove from the oven and leave to cool.
3. Scoop the aubergine flesh into a strainer set over a bowl and drain off the excess moisture. Peel the garlic. Purée the aubergine and garlic in a food processor or blender.
4. Beat the aubergine purée into the ricotta cheese. Add the egg, breadcrumbs and Parmesan cheese. Season with salt, pepper and nutmeg. Chill for 30 minutes–1 hour until firm.
5. Form the aubergine mixture into sausage shapes about 5cm/2in long. Roll first in the flour, then in the beaten egg and then in the breadcrumbs. Heat about 1cm/½in of oil in a frying pan until a crumb of bread will sizzle vigorously. Fry the croquettes on all sides until golden-brown. Drain on kitchen paper and sprinkle with a little salt. Serve immediately with the salsa on the side.

AUBERGINE AND COURGETTE FRITTERS WITH TAHINA CREAM AND YOGHURT DIP

170g/6oz plain flour
1 teaspoon baking powder
salt and freshly ground black pepper
1 egg, separated
1 tablespoon olive oil, plus extra for deep-frying
150ml/¼ pint cold water
2 aubergines
3 large courgettes

For the dip
2 cloves of garlic
150ml/¼ pint Greek yoghurt
3 tablespoons tahina (sesame seed paste)
1½ tablespoons lemon juice
1 tablespoon chopped fresh flat-leaf parsley, to garnish

1. Make the batter: sift together 110g/4oz of the flour, the baking powder and ½ teaspoon salt. Tip into a food processor or blender, add the egg yolk, oil and water and blend together until smooth. Set aside for 30 minutes.
2. Meanwhile, make the tahina cream and yoghurt dip: crush the garlic cloves on a chopping board with a little salt to make a smooth paste. Scrape into a bowl, add the yoghurt and tahina and mix together well. Stir in the lemon juice, season to taste with salt and pepper and set aside.
3. Top and tail the aubergines and courgettes and cut each one into slices crossways. Heat olive oil in a deep-fryer to 190°C/375°F.
4. Season the aubergine and courgette slices on both sides with salt and pepper. Whisk the egg white to soft peaks and fold gently into the batter, using a large metal spoon.
5. Dip a few aubergine and courgette slices at a time into the remaining flour. Shake off the excess, dip the slices into the batter and then lower them into the hot oil. Cook for 2 minutes on each side until crisp and a rich golden-brown. Lift out with a slotted spoon and drain briefly on kitchen paper. Keep hot in a low oven

while you cook the remainder in the same way.

6. Pile the aubergine and courgette fritters on to a serving plate. Sprinkle the parsley over the tahina cream and yoghurt dip and serve with the hot fritters.

AUBERGINE AND SMOKED TOFU PARCELS WITH WARM SAFFRON DRESSING

1 large aubergine
3 tablespoons olive oil
salt and freshly ground black pepper
200g//7oz smoked tofu

For the dressing
150ml/¼ pint olive oil
2 tablespoons mixed fresh herbs, such as basil,
    chives, coriander, marjoram, oregano
1 clove of garlic, sliced
1 red chilli, deseeded and chopped
1 teaspoon saffron threads
grated zest and juice of 1 lemon
1 tablespoon capers, rinsed and chopped

To garnish
1 teaspoon chopped fresh mint
55g/2oz pinenuts, toasted (see page 22)

1. Preheat the grill to high. Trim the stalks from the aubergine and cut it in half lengthways. Lay cut side down on a board and cut lengthways into thin slices. Brush with oil and grill until golden-brown on both sides. Season with salt and pepper.

2. Make the dressing: mix together the oil, herbs, garlic, chilli and saffron. Heat gently in a small saucepan and whisk in the lemon zest and juice and capers. Season with salt and pepper.

3. Slice the tofu into the same number of pieces as the aubergine. Lay each piece in the centre of a grilled aubergine slice and roll the aubergine around it. Grill the parcels again for a few minutes until piping hot. Lift into a warmed serving dish and pour over the hot dressing. Scatter with mint and pinenuts.

AUBERGINE SOUFFLÉ

45g/1½oz butter, plus extra for greasing
290ml/½ pint milk
1 carrot, sliced
1 stick of celery
1 bay leaf
1 onion, sliced
1 sprig of fresh thyme
sprigs of fresh parsley
black peppercorns
1 small aubergine, roughly diced
1–2 tablespoons olive oil
2 cloves of garlic
45g/1½oz plain flour
3 eggs, separated
fresh thyme leaves
salt and freshly ground black pepper

1. Preheat the oven to 200°C/400°F/gas mark 6. Grease 8 ramekin dishes or a 1.1 litre/2 pint soufflé dish with butter.

2. Pour the milk into a small saucepan and add the carrot, celery, bay leaf, onion, herbs and peppercorns. Bring to boiling point, then remove from the heat and set aside for at least 10 minutes.

3. Arrange the aubergine cubes in a single layer on a baking tray and drizzle over the oil. Bake on the top shelf of the preheated oven for about 5 minutes. Add the garlic and cook for a further 5–10 minutes, stirring frequently to prevent sticking, until the aubergine is soft and lightly browned. Remove from the oven and allow to cool.

4. Melt the butter in a saucepan, add the flour and stir over the heat for 1 minute. Remove the pan from the heat, strain in the infused milk and mix well. Return the sauce to the heat and stir continually until boiling. Simmer for 2–3 minutes to thicken. Remove from the heat and add the aubergine and the egg yolks. Liquidize until smooth. Add thyme leaves and salt and pepper to taste.

5. Whisk the egg whites until stiff but not dry and fold into the aubergine mixture, using a large metal spoon. Spoon into the prepared ramekins or soufflé dish and bake in the hot oven for 15 minutes for ramekins or 25–30 minutes for a single dish. Serve immediately.

BAKED AUBERGINE SLICES WITH CRÈME FRAÎCHE AND BASIL

2 large aubergines
olive oil
30g/1oz Parmesan cheese, freshly grated
200ml/7fl oz crème fraîche
a pinch of cayenne pepper
salt and freshly ground black pepper
2 tablespoons shredded fresh basil leaves

1. Preheat the grill to high and preheat the oven to 200°C/400°F/gas mark 6.
2. Trim the stalks from the aubergines and cut each lengthways into 4–5 slices. Brush with oil and grill on both sides until golden-brown.
3. Arrange the slices in an ovenproof dish. Stir the cheese into the crème fraîche and season with cayenne, salt and pepper. Spoon evenly over the aubergines. Bake in the preheated oven for 15 minutes until bubbling. Scatter with the basil before serving.

BAKED AUBERGINE STEAKS WITH COUSCOUS AND 'SEAWEED' TOPPING

110g/4oz couscous
225ml/8fl oz boiling water
150ml/¼ pint olive or chilli-flavoured oil
1 clove of garlic, crushed
2 shallots or spring onions, finely chopped
grated zest of 1 lemon
juice of ½ lemon
salt and freshly ground black pepper
2 medium to large aubergines
30g/1oz butter, melted
110g/4oz mock seaweed (see page 39)
a walnut-sized piece of fresh root ginger, peeled and finely chopped

1. Preheat the grill to high and preheat the oven to 190°C/375°F/gas mark 5.
2. Place the couscous in a bowl, pour over the boiling water and leave to soak. Warm the oil in a small saucepan and stir in the garlic, shallot or spring onion and half the lemon zest and the juice. Season with salt and pepper.
3. Trim the stalks from the aubergines and cut each lengthways into 4–5 thick slices. Brush liberally with the infused oil and grill on both sides until golden-brown.
4. Using a fork, mix the couscous with the melted butter, mock seaweed, ginger and the remaining lemon zest. Season with salt and pepper. Arrange the aubergine slices in a single layer in an ovenproof dish. Pile the couscous mixture on top and bake in the preheated oven for about 15 minutes or until the couscous topping is hot and roasted on top.

AUBERGINE STEAKS WITH GINGER AND CHILLI CRUST

2 large aubergines
150ml/¼ pint olive oil

For the buttered crust
110g/4oz white breadcrumbs
2 fresh red chillies, deseeded and finely chopped
   (see page 22)
2.5cm/1in piece of fresh root ginger, peeled and
   finely chopped
grated zest of 1 lime
2 tablespoons chopped fresh coriander
85g/3oz butter, melted
salt and freshly ground black pepper

1. Preheat the grill to the highest setting. Trim the stalks from the aubergines and cut each in half lengthways, then in half again to make 4 thick slices. Brush each slice liberally with oil and grill on both sides until golden-brown.
2. Meanwhile, make the crust: mix all the ingredients together and season with salt and pepper. Spread the mixture evenly over the aubergine steaks and continue to grill until browned. Serve immediately.

BAKED HALLOUMI WITH ROASTED AUBERGINE AND TOMATO

4 small aubergines
4 plum tomatoes
1 red onion
150ml/¼ pint olive oil
salt and freshly ground black pepper
110g/4oz assorted salad leaves, such as lettuce,
   watercress, rocket, baby spinach
8 slices of halloumi cheese
a handful of fresh coriander or basil leaves, to
   garnish

For the dressing
1 tablespoon red wine vinegar
1 teaspoon wholegrain mustard
2 tablespoons Greek yoghurt

1. Preheat the oven to 200°C/400°F/gas mark 6.
2. Cut the aubergines and tomatoes in half lengthways. Place in a roasting tin, cut side up. Peel the onion and cut it into eighths. Scatter into the pan with the other vegetables. Brush the vegetables with 4 tablespoons of the oil and season with salt and pepper. Roast in the preheated oven for 30 minutes.
3. Meanwhile, wash and dry the salad leaves. Make the dressing: put the remaining oil into a small mixing bowl. Whisk in the vinegar, mustard, yoghurt, and season with salt and pepper.
4. Lay the halloumi slices on top of the roasted aubergines and tomatoes. Return to the oven for a further 15 minutes until melted.
5. Arrange the salad leaves on 4 individual plates. Spoon the vegetables and melted cheese on top and drizzle over the yoghurt dressing. Garnish with fresh basil or coriander leaves.

BAKED AUBERGINE WITH CORIANDER AND CHILLI CHUTNEY

The coriander and chilli chutney also makes a good dip. Serve with potato chips or poppadums.

4 small aubergines
olive oil

For the chutney
85g/3oz fresh coriander
1 small red onion
4 cloves of garlic
2 green chillies, deseeded (see page 22)
2 teaspoons coarse salt
2 teaspoons caster sugar
2 tablespoons lemon juice

1. Preheat the oven to 190°C/375°F/gas mark 5.
2. Make the coriander and chilli chutney: reserve a few sprigs of coriander to garnish. Remove any tough stalks from the remainder and roughly chop the leaves. Peel the onion and garlic and chop roughly. Put the coriander, onion, garlic and chilli into a food processor or blender. Add the salt, sugar and lemon juice and process until smooth.
3. Leave the stalks attached to the aubergines. Cut each lengthways into 4–5 slices but not right through to the stalk, so that the slices are still all held together. Spread the coriander and chilli chutney between the slices and press the aubergines back together again. Place in a baking dish and brush generously with oil. Cover with kitchen foil and bake in the preheated oven for 45 minutes until tender. Garnish with sprigs of coriander before serving.

BAKED STUFFED AUBERGINES

4 small aubergines
1 red pepper
1 green pepper
4 tablespoons olive oil
1 large onion, chopped
2 cloves of garlic, chopped
5 ripe tomatoes, peeled and chopped (see page 22)
salt and freshly ground black pepper
2 tablespoons chopped fresh flat-leaf parsley
2 tablespoons water

To serve
150ml/¼ pint Greek yoghurt
2 tablespoons chopped fresh mint

1. Preheat the oven to 190°C/375°F/gas mark 5.
2. Cut the aubergines in half and scoop out the flesh, using a teaspoon, being careful to leave the shells intact. Set the shells aside. Remove the pith and seeds from the peppers and chop roughly.
3. Heat 3 tablespoons of the oil in a frying pan, add the onion and cook over a low heat until soft and golden. Stir in the garlic and peppers and fry for a few minutes to soften. Add the tomatoes and the aubergine flesh and season with salt and pepper. Simmer for 5–10 minutes until the aubergine is cooked. Adjust the seasoning to taste and stir in the parsley.
4. Brush the outside of the aubergine shells with oil and place them in a large roasting tin. Divide the filling between the shells. Drizzle with a little extra oil and put the water into the base of the roasting tin. Cover with kitchen foil and bake in the preheated oven for 40–45 minutes until tender.
5. Mix the yoghurt and mint together and season with salt and pepper. Serve with the stuffed aubergines.

AUBERGINE AND RED PEPPER PIE WITH A BRIOCHE CRUST

125ml/4½fl oz olive oil
1 Spanish onion, sliced
2 aubergines
2 red peppers
1 bulb of fennel, sliced
2 cloves of garlic, crushed
100ml/3½fl oz dry white wine
140g/5oz cream cheese
1 tablespoon chopped fresh chives
fresh lemon juice
salt and freshly ground black pepper
5 medium tomatoes, peeled and sliced (see
   page 22)
2 tablespoons chopped fresh basil
1 quantity brioche dough (see page 503), using
   only 2 teaspoons sugar
beaten egg, to glaze

1. Heat 3 tablespoons of the oil in a saucepan. Add the onion, cover and cook over a very low heat for 10 minutes, stirring occasionally. Do not allow the onion to brown.

2. Trim the stalks from the aubergines and cut them into slices. Cut the peppers into quarters and remove the pith and seeds.

3. Add the fennel to the onion in the pan and continue to cook slowly for 15 minutes. Add the garlic and cook for 1 further minute.

4. Preheat the grill to high and preheat the oven to 190°C/375°F/gas mark 5.

5. Lay the aubergine slices on the grill rack. Brush with oil and grill until brown, then turn them over, brush with oil and grill again until brown.

6. Grill the pepper quarters until the skin is black and blistered. Put into a bowl and cover with a plate. Leave for 10 minutes.

7. Add the wine to the fennel and onion and reduce by half. Remove from the heat and stir in the cream cheese, chives and 1 tablespoon lemon juice. Season with salt and pepper. Taste and add more lemon juice, salt and pepper as necessary.

8. Peel the peppers and cut them into slices.

9. Arrange a layer of the grilled aubergine slices in the base of a 1.7 litre/3 pint pie dish. Cover with half the peppers and tomatoes, season with salt and pepper and sprinkle with half the basil. Put in all the onion and fennel mixture and cover with the remaining peppers and tomatoes. Sprinkle with the remaining basil, season with salt and pepper and finally top with the remaining aubergines.

10. Roll out the brioche dough and use to cover the pie dish. Use the trimmings to decorate the pie and crimp the edges with thumb and forefinger.

11. Brush with beaten egg and bake in the preheated oven for 10 minutes. Lower the oven temperature to 170°C/325°F/gas mark 4 and bake for a further 30 minutes.

AUBERGINE AND TOMATO COBBLER

3 medium aubergines
7 tablespoons olive oil
1 large red onion, chopped
2 red peppers, deseeded and cut into slices
1 clove of garlic, crushed
450g/1lb ripe tomatoes, peeled and chopped
    (see page 22)
1 tablespoon chopped fresh oregano
1 tablespoon chopped fresh basil
½ teaspoon sugar
salt and freshly ground black pepper
55g/2oz stale brown bread, cut into 1cm/½in
    cubes
225ml/8fl oz Greek yoghurt

For the cobbler
170g/6oz self-raising flour
45g/1½oz butter
55g/2oz Cheddar cheese, grated
1 tablespoon chopped fresh basil
150ml/¼ pint milk

1. Trim the stalks from the aubergines and cut them into slices.
2. Preheat the oven to 200°C/400°F/gas mark 6.
3. Heat 1 tablespoon of the oil in a medium saucepan. Add the onion, cover and cook over a low heat for 10 minutes until soft, stirring occasionally to prevent it from browning. Add the sliced peppers and cook for a further 5 minutes.
4. Add the garlic, tomatoes, oregano, basil, sugar, salt and pepper. Cover again and cook until the tomatoes are soft. Add the brown bread and remove from the heat.
5. Preheat the grill to high. Place the aubergine slices on the grill rack and brush with oil. Grill until brown, then turn them over, brush with oil and grill again until brown and softened.
6. Arrange a layer of aubergine slices in the base of a 2.3 litre/4 pint casserole dish. Cover with one-third of the tomato mixture and spread half the yoghurt on top. Cover with another layer of aubergine slices, then with half the remaining tomato mixure and the remaining

yoghurt. Finish with a final layer of aubergine slices topped with the remaining tomato mixture.
7. Preheat the oven to 200°C/400°F/gas mark 6.
8. Make the cobbler: sift the flour into a mixing bowl and rub in the butter until the mixture resembles fine breadcrumbs. Stir in the cheese and herbs. Make a well in the centre, pour in the milk and mix to a soft, spongy dough with a knife.
9. Knead the dough very lightly on a floured surface until it is just smooth. Roll or press out to about 2.5cm/1in thick and stamp out into rounds with a 5cm/2in biscuit cutter.
10. Arrange the rounds on top of the tomato mixture. Bake, uncovered, in the preheated oven for 25–30 minutes or until the scones are risen and brown. Serve immediately.

NOTE: Although the vegetable layers can be prepared in advance and refrigerated, the scone dough needs to be cooked immediately after mixing and shaping.

AUBERGINE AND POTATO MOUSSAKA

6 tablespoons olive oil
1 large onion, chopped
2 cloves of garlic, crushed
2 × 400g/14oz cans of chopped tomatoes
1 cinnamon stick
2 sprigs of fresh thyme
2 fresh bay leaves
salt and freshly ground black pepper
785g/1¾lb floury potatoes, peeled
2 aubergines
85g/3oz butter
85g/3oz plain flour
570ml/1 pint milk
55g/2oz Cheddar cheese, grated
a pinch of freshly grated nutmeg
2 eggs, beaten

1. Heat 2 tablespoons of the oil in a medium saucepan. Add the onion and fry over a low heat for 5 minutes until soft but not browned. Add the garlic, tomatoes, cinnamon, thyme and bay leaves and simmer for 20–25 minutes until well reduced and thickened. Discard the cinnamon and herbs and season to taste with salt and pepper. Set aside.
2. Slice the potatoes thickly and cook them in boiling salted water for 7 minutes. Drain and set aside. Trim the stalks from the aubergines and cut them lengthways into slices 1cm/½in thick.
3. Heat a large, heavy frying pan over a high heat. Brush the aubergine slices on both sides with oil and fry for 3 minutes on each side until a rich golden-brown. Lift on to kitchen paper and leave to drain.
4. Preheat the oven to 180°C/350°F/gas mark 4. Lay half the potato slices over the base of a shallow 2.3 litre/4 pint ovenproof dish and cover with half the tomato sauce and half the aubergines. Season with salt and pepper. Repeat the layers once more.
5. Melt the butter in a saucepan. Add the flour and cook over a low heat for 1 minute, stirring. Remove the pan from the heat and gradually stir in the milk. Return to the heat and bring to the boil, stirring. Simmer for 5 minutes, then remove from the heat and stir in the cheese, nutmeg and salt and pepper. Leave to cool slightly, then gradually whisk in the beaten eggs.
6. Pour the sauce over the top layer of aubergines. Bake in the preheated oven for 30 minutes until golden-brown and bubbling.

SICILIAN AUBERGINE PARMIGIANA

SERVES 6

150ml/¼ pint olive oil
2 cloves of garlic, crushed
2 × 400g/14oz cans of chopped tomatoes
salt and freshly ground black pepper
900g/2lb aubergines
45g/1½oz plain flour
85g/3oz Parmesan cheese, freshly grated
55g/2oz currants
55g/2oz pinenuts, lightly toasted (see page 22)
170g/6oz provolone or mozzarella cheese,
   thinly sliced
12 fresh basil leaves, torn into pieces

1. Make the tomato sauce: put 2 tablespoons of
the oil and the garlic into a large, deep frying
pan. Put over a medium to high heat and as
soon as the garlic starts to sizzle, add the
tomatoes and simmer for 30 minutes until well
reduced and thickened. Remove from the heat,
season to taste with salt and pepper and set
aside.
2. Trim the stalks from the aubergines and cut
them crossways into thin slices. Season them
well on both sides with salt and pepper. Mix
the flour and 45g/1½oz of the Parmesan cheese
together in a shallow dish.
3. Preheat the oven to 200°C/400°F/gas mark 6.
Heat 2 tablespoons of the oil in a frying pan.
Dip a few aubergine slices into the flour and
cheese mixture, shake off the excess, and fry
over a medium to high heat for 1–2 minutes on
each side until crisp and golden. Lift on to
kitchen paper and leave to drain. Fry the
remaining aubergine slices in the same way.
4. Layer half the aubergines, tomato sauce,
currants, pinenuts, provolone or mozzarella
cheese slices and basil in the bottom of a 2.2
litre/4 pint shallow ovenproof dish. Season with
pepper, then repeat the layers once more,
ending with a layer of cheese.
5. Sprinkle over the remaining Parmesan cheese
and bake in the preheated oven for 25–30
minutes until golden and bubbling.

AUBERGINE CURRY

785g/1¾lb aubergines
150ml/¼ pint sunflower oil
2.5cm/1in piece of fresh root ginger, peeled and
   roughly chopped
8 cloves of garlic, roughly chopped
1 tablespoon ground coriander
½ teaspoon ground turmeric
4 tablespoons water
1 medium-hot red Dutch chilli, finely chopped
1½ teaspoons fennel seeds, lightly crushed
1 teaspoon black onion seeds (kalonji)
1 × 400g/14oz can of chopped tomatoes
1 tablespoon chopped fresh coriander
1 tablespoon chopped fresh mint
salt
cayenne pepper

To serve
spiced pilau rice (see page 359) or warm naan
   bread

1. Trim the stalks from the aubergines and cut
each one in half crossways, then cut each piece
lengthways into 6–8 wedges.
2. Heat a large frying pan over a high heat.
Pour the oil into a shallow dish. Dip some of
the aubergine wedges briefly into the oil, then
put them into the frying pan and cook for 3–4
minutes on each side until a rich golden-brown.
Transfer to a sieve set over a bowl and leave to
drain. Repeat with the remaining aubergines.
3. Put the ginger, garlic, coriander, turmeric
and water into a food processor or blender and
process to a smooth paste. Put 2 tablespoons of
the oil drained from the cooked aubergines
back into the frying pan and add the chilli,
fennel and onion seeds. Fry for 1 minute, then
add the ginger and garlic paste and the
tomatoes and season with salt and pepper.
Simmer for 8–10 minutes until reduced and
slightly thickened.
4. Return the fried aubergines to the pan and
stir well to coat in the sauce. Simmer for 5
minutes, then stir in the coriander, mint and
salt and cayenne to taste. Serve with pilau rice
or warm naan bread.

AUBERGINE AND POTATO CURRY

½ teaspoon chilli powder
1 teaspoon ground turmeric
2 teaspoons ground cumin
1 teaspoon ground coriander
1 teaspoon sea salt
3 tablespoons sunflower or vegetable oil
1 teaspoon cumin seeds
1 teaspoon black mustard seeds
1 large onion, chopped
2 cloves of garlic, crushed
2.5cm/1in piece of fresh root ginger, peeled and grated
1 green chilli, deseeded and chopped (see page 22)
450g/1lb red potatoes, peeled
1 large aubergine, diced
1 × 225g/8oz can of tomatoes or 3 fresh tomatoes, peeled and deseeded (see page 22)
290ml/½ pint spicy vegetable stock (see page 531)
2 tablespoons chopped fresh coriander
fresh lime juice
salt and freshly ground black pepper
2–3 tablespoons Greek yoghurt

1. Mix the chilli powder, turmeric, cumin, coriander and salt to a paste with 1 tablespoon of the oil. Heat the remaining oil in a large, heavy saucepan, add the cumin and mustard seeds and fry until they begin to pop. Lower the heat and allow the pan to cool a little, then fry the onion slowly until very soft and golden-brown.
2. Add the garlic, ginger and chilli to the pan and fry for 2 minutes. Stir in the spice paste and fry for 1 further minute. Meanwhile, cut the potatoes into 2.5cm/1in cubes and add to the pan with the aubergine, tomatoes and stock. Stir gently, scraping any sticky sediment from the base of the pan.
3. Cover and simmer gently for about 30 minutes until the potato is tender. Stir in the fresh coriander, add lime juice to taste and adjust the seasoning. Swirl over a little Greek yoghurt before serving.

AUBERGINE WITH PINENUTS, MINT AND CAPERS

2 large aubergines
150ml/¼ pint olive oil, plus a little extra to serve
1 shallot, finely chopped
1 clove of garlic, crushed
grated zest and juice of 1 lemon
1 tablespoon capers, well rinsed and chopped
salt and freshly ground black pepper
55g/2oz pinenuts, toasted (see page 22)
1 tablespoon chopped fresh mint

1. Preheat the grill to high or heat a ridged cast-iron griddle pan. Trim the stalks from the aubergines and cut them lengthways into slices 5mm/¼in thick.
2. Mix together the oil, shallot, garlic, lemon zest and juice and capers. Season with salt and pepper. Brush the aubergine slices liberally with the dressing and grill until deep golden on both sides, brushing with more dressing when they are turned.
3. Lift the aubergine into a warmed shallow serving dish. Season with more salt and pepper. Scatter over the pinenuts and mint and pour over any of the remaining oil mixture. Drizzle with a little extra oil and serve warm.

GRILLED AUBERGINE SANDWICH WITH HUMMUS

1 large aubergine
150ml/¼ pint olive oil
2 onions, thinly sliced
4 ciabatta or crusty rolls
½ quantity hummus (see page 325)
110g/4oz rocket
a little freshly grated Parmesan cheese
salt and freshly ground black pepper

1. Preheat the grill to high. Trim the stalk from the aubergine and cut it crossways into 8 thick slices. Brush with oil and grill on each side until golden-brown.
2. Heat 3 tablespoons of the oil in a heavy frying pan, add the onions and fry until crisp and golden.
3. Cut the rolls in half and toast the cut side. Warm 4 individual plates.
4. Spread the bottom half of the rolls with the hummus and top with rocket. Sprinkle with grated cheese, salt and pepper. Top each one with 2 grilled aubergine slices and some of the onion and cover with the lid of the roll.

SWEET AND SOUR AUBERGINE SALAD WITH MINT

5 tablespoons olive oil
6 cloves of garlic, finely chopped
170ml/6fl oz white wine vinegar
4 tablespoons caster sugar
450g/1lb small aubergines
salt and freshly ground black pepper
6 tablespoons chopped fresh mint

1. Heat 1 tablespoon of the oil in a medium saucepan. Add the garlic and fry over a low heat for 1–2 minutes without letting it brown. Add the vinegar and sugar and stir over a low heat until the sugar has dissolved. Bring to the boil, then boil for 7–8 minutes until the mixture has reduced by half. Set aside.
2. Cut the aubergines in half lengthways through the stalks. Brush them generously with oil and season well with salt and pepper. Heat a ridged, cast-iron griddle or a heavy frying pan over a medium-high heat. Brush the griddle or pan with a little oil, add a single layer of aubergines, and cook for about 3–4 minutes on each side until nicely browned and tender. Transfer to a shallow serving dish and cook the remaining aubergines in the same way.
3. Stir the mint into the vinegar syrup and spoon it over the aubergines. Serve warm or cold.

CAPONATA

(SICILIAN AUBERGINE SALAD)

Serve this hot, warm or cold as a side dish or as a main course with fresh crusty bread.

150ml/¼ pint olive oil
1 onion, chopped
450g/1lb ripe tomatoes, peeled, deseeded and chopped (see page 22)
2 tablespoons white wine vinegar
1 tablespoon sugar
salt and freshly ground black pepper
450g/1lb aubergine, chopped
½ head of celery, chopped
8 green olives, halved
1 tablespoon capers, rinsed and roughly chopped
2 tablespoons pinenuts, toasted (see page 22)
1 tablespoon chopped fresh flat-leaf parsley

1. Heat half the oil in a medium saucepan, add the onion and fry over a low heat until golden-brown. Add the tomatoes and simmer gently for about 20 minutes until pulpy. Stir in the vinegar and sugar and season with salt and pepper. Lower the heat and continue to cook until reduced and thickened.
2. Heat the remaining oil in a frying pan, add the aubergine and celery and sauté briskly until golden, then stir into the tomato sauce. Simmer gently for a further 20 minutes, stirring from time to time. Add a little water if the mixture becomes dry.
3. Stir in the olives, capers and pinenuts and cook for a further 15 minutes. Check the seasoning and sprinkle with the parsley before serving.

AVOCADO AND ROCKET GAZPACHO

2 ripe avocados
1 red pepper
1 small cucumber
3 medium, ripe tomatoes
3 spring onions
1 clove of garlic, crushed
200ml/7fl oz water
55g/2oz rocket, roughly chopped
juice of 1 lime
6 drops of Tabasco sauce
1 tablespoon white wine vinegar
1 teaspoon ground coriander
150ml/¼ pint Greek yoghurt
4 tablespoons olive oil
salt and freshly ground black pepper
150ml/¼ pint crème fraîche
2 tablespoons toasted flaked almonds

1. Cut the avocados in half and remove the stones, then peel. Cut 1 half into small dice and reserve. Roughly chop the remaining 3 halves.
2. Cut the red pepper into quarters and remove the pith and seeds. Cut 1 quarter into small dice and reserve. Roughly chop the remaining 3 quarters.
3. Peel the cucumber, cut it in half lengthways and remove the seeds with a melon-baller or teaspoon. Cut a quarter of the cucumber into small dice and reserve. Roughly chop the remaining cucumber.
4. Cut one of the tomatoes into quarters and remove the seeds, then cut the flesh into small dice and reserve. Roughly chop the remaining 2 tomatoes.
5. Trim and slice the spring onions, then place in a food processor or blender with the roughly chopped avocado, pepper, cucumber, tomatoes, garlic and water.
6. Start to liquidize, then add the rocket, lime juice, Tabasco, vinegar, coriander, yoghurt, oil and season with salt and pepper. Process until smooth. This may need to be done in several batches, depending on the size of the machine.
7. Sieve the soup into a large bowl. Adjust the seasoning to taste and add the reserved chopped vegetables. Chill for a couple of hours, then pour into chilled soup bowls and top each with a spoonful of crème fraîche sprinkled with toasted almonds just before serving.

BAKED AVOCADOS WITH HERB AND GARLIC CREAM CHEESE

2 avocados
85g/3oz herb and garlic cream cheese

For the dressing
juice of ½ lemon
½ teaspoon Dijon mustard
2 tablespoons olive oil
salt and freshly ground black pepper

To serve
85g/3oz cherry tomatoes, halved
4 handfuls of rocket
warm crusty bread

1. Preheat the oven to 200°C/400°F/gas mark 6.
2. Cut the avocados in half and remove the stones, then peel.
3. Stuff the avocado halves with the cream cheese. Line a baking tray with non-stick baking paper and place the pears cut side down on top.
4. Make the dressing: mix together the lemon juice, mustard and oil and season with salt and pepper. Brush the avocados with some of the dressing and season with more salt and pepper. Bake in the preheated oven for 10 minutes.
5. Add the cherry tomatoes to the rocket and mix with the remaining dressing. Place the hot avocados on 4 individual plates and garnish with the salad. Serve with warm crusty bread.

AVOCADO AND MANGO SALAD WITH PAPAYA DRESSING

For the dressing
1 quantity French dressing (see page 528)
1 ripe papaya, peeled and deseeded
1 small lime

For the salad
55g/2oz rocket
55–85g/2–3oz watercress, tough stalks removed
2 large ripe avocados, peeled, stoned and sliced
1 ripe mango, peeled, stoned and sliced

1. First make the dressing: liquidize the French dressing with the papaya and lime juice in a food processor or blender.
2. Put the rocket and watercress into a serving bowl and arrange the avocado and mango slices on top. Pour over the dressing and serve immediately.

AVOCADO AND NEW POTATO SALAD IN PAPRIKA DRESSING

For the dressing
6 tablespoons olive oil
2 teaspoons hot paprika
55g/2oz sun-dried tomatoes in oil, finely
    chopped
3 tablespoons balsamic vinegar
1 green chilli, deseeded and finely chopped (see
    page 22)
salt and freshly ground black pepper

For the salad
450g/1lb baby new potatoes
1 × 225g/8oz can of kidney beans
1 large, ripe avocado
225g/8oz cherry tomatoes, halved
1 red onion, thinly sliced
a few basil leaves, to garnish

1. First make the dressing: heat 1 tablespoon of
the oil in a small, heavy-based pan. Add the
paprika and sun-dried tomatoes and fry for 1
minute. Pour into a mixing bowl and whisk in
the remaining oil with the vinegar and chilli.
Season with salt and pepper.
2. Boil the potatoes in salted water for about 15
minutes or until just tender. Drain and toss in
the dressing. Rinse and drain the kidney beans
and add to the potatoes.
3. Cut the avocado in half and remove the
stone, then peel. Cut the flesh into chunks
about the same size as the potatoes. Add the
cherry tomatoes and red onion. Toss together,
pile into a salad bowl and garnish with the basil
leaves.

AVOCADO, TOMATO AND MOZZARELLA SALAD WITH A BASIL DRESSING

For the dressing
55g/2oz fresh basil leaves
1 tablespoon lemon juice
sea salt and freshly ground black pepper
5 tablespoons extra virgin olive oil

For the salad
2 ripe but firm avocados
285g/10oz buffalo mozzarella cheese
3 ripe but firm beef tomatoes

To serve
ciabatta bread

1. First make the dressing: pack the basil leaves
into the bowl of a food processor and add the
lemon juice, salt and pepper. With the machine
running, gradually add the oil through the lid to
make a smooth dressing. Adjust the seasoning
to taste.
2. Cut the avocados in half and remove the
stones. Carefully peel away the skin, then cut
each half across into half-moon-shaped slices.
3. Slice the mozzarella cheese and the tomatoes
thinly. Arrange the avocado, mozzarella and
tomato slices overlapping on 4 individual
plates, then drizzle over the dressing. Sprinkle
with a little more salt and pepper and serve
with the ciabatta bread.

Individual Roasted Pepper Terrines

Baked Halloumi with Roasted Aubergine and Tomato

Boiled Eggs with Spinach Salad and Parmesan Croûtes

Fig and Goat's Cheese Tartlets with Sesame Seed Pastry

Welsh Rarebit-topped Portobello Mushrooms

Rocket and Mozzarella Tempura

Stuffed Acorn Squash

Caramelized Pear, Pecan and Roquefort Salad

GUACAMOLE WITH BLUE CORN CHIPS

3 large, ripe but firm avocados
2 jalapeño chillies, deseeded and finely chopped
  (see page 22)
1 small onion, finely chopped
5 tablespoons chopped fresh coriander
1 vine-ripened tomato, peeled, deseeded and
  finely diced (see page 22)
1 tablespoon lemon or lime juice
salt

To serve
blue corn tortilla chips

1. Cut the avocados in half and remove the stones. Scoop out the flesh into a bowl.
2. Mash the avocado up against the sides of the bowl with a fork to make a coarse paste (it should not be too smooth).
3. Stir in the chilli, onion, 4 tablespoons of the coriander, the tomato, lemon or lime juice and salt to taste. Spoon the mixture into a serving bowl and sprinkle over the remaining coriander. Serve with the blue corn tortilla chips.

AVOCADO AND ROQUEFORT TOASTS

4 thick slices of quick walnut bread (see page 502)
olive oil
2 large, ripe avocados
110g/4oz Roquefort cheese
110g/4oz rocket or watercress
balsamic vinegar
salt and freshly ground black pepper

1. Preheat the grill to high. Toast the walnut bread lightly on both sides. Drizzle one side with oil.
2. Cut the avocados in half, remove the stones and peel. Slice thickly lengthways and arrange the slices on the toasted bread. Crumble over the Roquefort cheese and grill until bubbling.
3. Put the rocket or watercress into a bowl and toss in a little vinegar. Place the Roquefort toasts on 4 individual plates and serve with the leaves on the side.

ROASTED RED PEPPER SOUP

6 tomatoes
2 red peppers, deseeded and quartered
2 cloves of garlic
2 tablespoons olive oil
salt and freshly ground black pepper
570ml/1 pint summer vegetable stock (see
  page 530)

To garnish
4 slices of white bread, crusts removed
oil for frying
2 cloves of garlic
1–2 tablespoons finely chopped fresh parsley

1. Preheat the oven to 190°C/375°F/gas mark 5.
2. Place the tomatoes on a baking tray together with the pepper quarters. Tuck the garlic underneath the peppers for protection. Drizzle with the oil and season with salt and pepper. Roast in the preheated oven for about 30 minutes or until the peppers are soft and the tomato skins have split. Peel the garlic cloves.
3. Tip the vegetables into a saucepan and add the stock. Bring to the boil, then lower the heat and cook for 5 minutes. Purée the soup in a food processor or blender and adjust the seasoning to taste. Adjust the consistency if required by adding more stock or water or reduce by boiling. Keep the soup warm.
4. Make the croûtons for the garnish: cut the bread into even-sized cubes. Heat sufficient oil in a frying pan to allow the bread to float. Add the garlic and cook over a low heat until golden-brown (the garlic can be removed at this stage if preferred). Add the cubes of bread and fry until golden-brown. Put a metal sieve over a china bowl and pour the oil and croûtons into the sieve. Drain the croûtons on kitchen paper. Sprinkle with salt and keep warm if necessary.
5. Serve the soup in warmed soup bowls, sprinkled with the croûtons and the parsley.

ROASTED RED PEPPER GAZPACHO

2 large red peppers
675g/1½lb vine-ripened tomatoes, peeled (see page 22)
1 cucumber
½ loaf of ciabatta bread
4 tablespoons sherry vinegar
1 clove of garlic, crushed
150ml/¼ pint olive oil
2 teaspoons caster sugar
salt and freshly ground white pepper

To garnish
2 teaspoons extra virgin olive oil
2 vine-ripened tomatoes, peeled (see page 22)
¼ cucumber
3 spring onions, trimmed

To serve
about 10 ice cubes, crushed

1. Preheat the oven to 220°C/425°F/gas mark 7. Place the peppers on a baking tray and roast in the preheated oven for about 25 minutes, turning them from time to time, until the skins are black and blistered. Place the peppers in a plastic bag, seal and leave to become cold. Break the peppers open, pull out and discard the stalks, pith and seeds and peel off the skin. Roughly chop the flesh and put it into a large mixing bowl.

2. Lower the oven temperature to 200°C/400°F/gas mark 6. Cut each tomato into quarters, scoop out the seeds into a sieve set over a small bowl, and roughly chop the flesh. Work the juice out of the seeds with a spoon and add to the red pepper with the tomato flesh. Discard the seeds left in the sieve.

3. Peel the cucumber, cut it in half lengthways and scoop out the seeds with a melon-baller or teaspoon. Chop the flesh roughly and add to the bowl.

4. Cut 2 slices off the ciabatta loaf and reserve for the garnish. Remove the crusts from the remainder and process it into breadcrumbs in a food processor or blender. Add 55g/2oz of the breadcrumbs to the tomato and cucumber mixture with the vinegar, garlic, oil, sugar and salt and pepper. Stir together well.

5. Purée the mixture in batches in the food processor or blender. Pour it into another bowl and thin to the required consistency with a little cold water if necessary. Cover and chill for at least 2 hours.

6. Meanwhile, prepare the garnishes: tear the reserved slices of ciabatta into small pieces and toss them with the oil. Spread over a baking tray and bake in the preheated oven for 8–10 minutes until crisp and golden. Remove from the oven and leave to cool. Cut the tomatoes into quarters, remove the seeds and cut the flesh into small dice. Cut the cucumber in half lengthways, scoop out the seeds with a melon-baller or teaspoon and cut into small dice. Slice the spring onions thinly. Put the croutons, tomato, cucumber and spring onions into separate bowls.

7. Ladle the soup into chilled soup bowls and add ice to each. Serve sprinkled with the garnishes.

INDIVIDUAL ROASTED PEPPER TERRINES

2 red peppers
2 yellow peppers
1 orange pepper
3 tablespoons olive oil
2 medium red onions, sliced
2 cloves of garlic, crushed
1 tablespoon chopped fresh thyme
salt and freshly ground black pepper
3 plum tomatoes
1 tablespoon shredded fresh basil

To serve
tomato, garlic and basil sauce (see page 507)
crusty bread

1. Preheat the oven to 200°C/400°F/gas mark 6.
2. Cut the peppers into quarters and remove the pith and seeds. Grease 2 baking trays with 1 tablespoon of the oil or line them with non-stick baking paper.
3. Lay the peppers, skin side down, on the baking sheets. Bake in the preheated oven for 30 minutes until the skins are blackened and blistered. Remove the peppers from the baking trays and place in a bowl. Cover with a plate and leave until cold.
4. Heat the remaining oil in a saucepan. Add the onions and garlic and cook over a low heat for 20–30 minutes or until softened but not browned. Boil off any liquid left in the pan. Add the thyme and season with salt and pepper.
5. Peel and quarter the tomatoes and remove the seeds. Peel the peppers.
6. Line 4 large ramekin dishes with clingfilm, leaving it overhanging the sides of the dishes.
7. Place 2 red pepper quarters side by side in the bottom of each ramekin. Press down well. Add a spoonful of onion and then 1 orange pepper quarter. Arrange 3 tomato quarters on top of the pepper and sprinkle with basil. Season with salt and pepper. Add another spoonful of onion and finish with yellow pepper quarters laid side by side.
8. Pull over the clingfilm to seal the tops of the ramekins and press down well. Chill for at least 1 hour before serving.

9. To serve: carefully pull back the clingfilm and turn each terrine out on to an individual plate. Pour a little tomato, garlic and basil sauce around it and serve with crusty bread.

BAKED GUACAMOLE PEPPERS

4 red peppers
2 tomatoes, peeled (see page 22)
2 cloves of garlic
salt and freshly ground black pepper
4 tablespoons olive oil
2 ripe avocados
juice of 1 lime
2 green chillies, deseeded and finely chopped
1 teaspoon ground cumin
1 shallot, finely chopped
85g/3oz Cheddar, Gruyère or mozzarella
    cheese, grated
a handful of chopped fresh coriander, to
    garnish

To serve
soured cream
tostadas (see tostadas with radish and
    guacamole, page 107)

1. Preheat the oven to 190°C/375°F/gas mark 5. Cut the peppers in half through the stalks and remove the pith and seeds but leave the stalks in place.
2. Cut the tomatoes into quarters and cut the garlic into slivers. Put 2 tomato quarters into each pepper half on a baking tray. Scatter with the garlic and season with salt and pepper. Drizzle each pepper half with 2 teaspoons of oil. Bake in the preheated oven for 30 minutes.
3. Meanwhile, cut the avocados in half, remove the stone and peel. Mash the flesh with the lime juice. Stir in the chillies, cumin and shallot and season with salt and pepper. Divide the mixture between the peppers and sprinkle with the grated cheese. Bake in the oven for a further 15 minutes.
4. Sprinkle with the coriander before serving and hand the soured cream and tostadas separately.

MEDITERRANEAN SLOW-BAKED PEPPERS

4 large red peppers
4 vine-ripened tomatoes, peeled (see page 22)
2 large cloves of garlic, thinly sliced
8 black olives, pitted and cut lengthways into
    thin strips
8 fresh basil leaves, shredded
8 tablespoons extra virgin olive oil
sea salt and freshly ground black pepper
a few small fresh basil leaves, to garnish

To serve
warm ciabatta or foccacia bread

1. Preheat the oven to 180°C/350°F/gas mark 4. Cut the peppers in half through the stalks and remove the pith and seeds but leave the stalks in place. Lay the pepper halves cut side up in a shallow roasting tin.
2. Cut each tomato into 6 wedges and divide between the pepper halves with the garlic, olives and basil. Spoon 1 tablespoon of oil into each pepper half and season well with salt and pepper. Bake in the preheated oven for 50 minutes.
3. Place the pepper halves on 4 warmed individual plates and spoon over the juices from the tin. Garnish with the basil leaves and serve with the bread.

ROASTED PEPPERS WITH MUSHROOM COUSCOUS

85g/3oz dried mushrooms
290ml/½ pint boiling water
4 Romano (long-pointed) peppers
2 bulbs of fennel
3 tablespoons olive oil
140g/5oz couscous
a large handful of fresh flat-leaf parsley
2 cloves of garlic, chopped
lemon juice
salt and freshly ground black pepper

For the sauce
2 tablespoons summer vegetable stock (see
    page 530) or dry white wine
1 teaspoon ground cumin
1 teaspoon ground coriander
½ teaspoon ground chilli
2 tablespoons tomato purée or sun-dried
    tomato paste

1. Preheat the grill to high. Soak the mushrooms in the boiling water for 15 minutes.
2. Cut the peppers in half lengthways and remove the pith and seeds but leave the stalks in place. Remove the outer leaves from the fennel bulbs and reserve the tops. Cut each fennel bulb into 3–4 thick slices. Brush the pepper and fennel liberally with 1 tablespoon oil. Grill the pepper cut side up only and the fennel on both sides until charred on the edges.
3. Meanwhile, drain the mushrooms, strain their soaking liquid over the couscous and leave to soak.
4. Make the sauce: boil the stock or wine in a small pan for 2 minutes. Pour on to the spices and tomato purée in a small bowl and mix well. Season with salt if necessary.
5. Roughly chop the parsley and the fennel tops, keeping them separate. Heat the remaining oil in a frying pan, add the garlic and fry over a low heat for 1–2 minutes. Fork the couscous through to separate the grains and add to the pan with the mushrooms and parsley. Cook gently, stirring, until piping hot. Stir in the parsley and season with a dash of lemon juice, salt and pepper.
6. Arrange the roasted peppers and fennel on 4 warmed individual plates. Spoon the mushroom couscous into the peppers and scatter over the fennel tops. Drizzle with the tomato sauce.

STUFFED RED PEPPERS WITH SOUFFLÉ TOPS

4 red peppers

For the stuffing
1 tablespoon olive oil
1 red onion, finely chopped
2 carrots, finely chopped
1 clove of garlic, crushed
110g/4oz red lentils
1 × 400g/14oz can of chopped tomatoes
tomato purée
1 bay leaf
mango chutney
Tabasco sauce
salt and freshly ground black pepper

For the top
110g/4oz fromage frais
55g/2oz Cheddar cheese, grated
1 egg
1 tablespoon finely chopped fresh parsley

1. Cut the tops off the peppers and remove the stalks, pith and seeds. Finely dice the tops and reserve.
2. Bring a saucepan of water to the boil. Add the peppers and cook for 5 minutes. Drain and refresh under cold running water. Leave upside down to drain.
3. Make the stuffing: heat the oil in a saucepan, add the onion and carrots and sauté for 2–3 minutes. Add the garlic and cook for 1 further minute. Add the lentils, tomatoes, tomato purée and bay leaf. Stir and allow to simmer for 1–2 minutes. Add chutney, Tabasco and salt and pepper to taste, then cover and cook gently for 10–15 minutes until the lentils are cooked and all the liquid has evaporated. Adjust the seasoning to taste.
4. Preheat the oven to 200°C/400°F/gas mark 6.
5. Place the peppers in an ovenproof dish and three-quarters fill them with the lentil stuffing.
6. Make the topping: mix all the ingredients together, reserving a little of the cheese, and spoon on to the lentil mixture. Sprinkle with the reserved cheese.

7. Bake in the centre of the preheated oven for 20 minutes or until the topping has puffed up and is golden-brown. Serve immediately.

SWEET PEPPER FAJITAS WITH GUACAMOLE, TOMATILLO SALSA AND SOURED CREAM

1 quantity guacamole (see page 213)
150ml/¼ pint soured cream
2 red peppers
1 green pepper
1 yellow pepper
1 large Spanish onion
1 large red onion
3 courgettes
4 tablespoons sunflower oil

For the tomatillo salsa
170g/6oz tomatillos or green tomatoes
2 jalapeño chillies
1 small onion, roughly chopped
1 clove of garlic, roughly chopped
2 tablespoons chopped fresh coriander
1 teaspoon lime juice, if green tomatoes are
* used*
salt and freshly ground black pepper

To serve
8–12 flour tortillas

1. First make the tomatillo salsa: peel the papery husk from the tomatillos, if used. Drop the tomatillos or green tomatoes and the chillies into a saucepan of boiling water and simmer for 10 minutes. Drain and leave to cool.
2. Roughly chop the tomatillos or green tomatoes and the chillies and put them into a food processor with the onion, garlic, coriander and lime juice if green tomatoes are used. Process, using the pulse button, to a coarse paste. Season to taste with salt and pepper and spoon into a small serving bowl.
3. Spoon the guacamole and the soured cream into 2 small serving bowls.

4. Warm the tortillas: stack them on a plate, cover with a clean tea-towel and microwave on high for about 30 seconds. Or heat a dry frying pan over a high heat, add 1 tortilla, cook for a few seconds, then turn it over and add another to the pan. After a few seconds turn them over together and add another to the pan. Continue like this until all the tortillas are in the pan. Reserve, wrap in kitchen foil and keep warm in a low oven.

5. Make the fajitas: cut the peppers in half and remove the stalks, pith and seeds. Cut the flesh into long thin strips. Cut the onions into quarters and then through the stalk into thin wedges. Top and tail the courgettes and cut them in half crossways, then lengthways into short, chunky strips.

6. Heat 2 tablespoons of the oil in a large frying pan. Add the onions and fry over a high heat, stirring, until they are nicely caramelized. Tip them on to a large plate and keep warm. Add another tablespoon of oil to the pan and fry the peppers until just soft and nicely browned around the edges. Add to the onions. Add the remaining oil to the pan with the courgettes and fry until nicely browned but still slightly crunchy. Return the onions and peppers to the pan, season to taste with salt and pepper and toss together over a high heat for 1 minute.

7. Spoon the vegetables into a warmed serving dish and serve with the bowls of guacamole, soured cream and tomatillo salsa and the warm tortillas. Spoon some of the vegetables and a little of the guacamole, soured cream and salsa down the centre of each tortilla, then roll up.

NOTE: For information on tomatillos, see page 231.

MIXED PEPPER PIZZA

For the topping
2 tablespoons olive oil
1 red pepper, deseeded and cut into strips
1 orange pepper, deseeded and cut into strips
1 yellow pepper, deseeded and cut into strips
1 leek, trimmed and thinly sliced
1 red onion, thinly sliced
2 sprigs of fresh thyme
salt and freshly ground black pepper
125g/4½oz mozzarella cheese, evenly sliced
olives (optional)

For the base
110g/4oz butter
*450g/1lb self-raising flour, plus extra for
    kneading*
*2 tablespoons chopped fresh mixed herbs, such
    as parsley and thyme*
290ml/½ pint milk or water

1. Preheat the oven to 200°C/400°F/gas mark 6.

2. Make the topping: heat the oil in a large saucepan, add the vegetables and the sprigs of thyme and season with salt and pepper. Cover and cook over a low heat for 10 minutes, stirring frequently to prevent burning. Remove from the heat, discard the thyme and allow to cool slightly.

3. Make the dough base: rub the butter into the flour in a mixing bowl until it resembles fine breadcrumbs. Add the herbs and mix thoroughly.

4. Add enough milk or water to form a soft but not sticky dough. Turn on to a floured worktop and knead very lightly to form a rough circle.

5. Lightly flour a baking sheet and put the dough in the centre. With floured fingertips, gently but quickly press the dough into a circle about 1cm/½in thick.

6. Spoon the vegetables over the surface, leaving a narrow rim around the edge. Arrange the cheese and olives, if used, on the top. Bake on the top shelf of the preheated oven for 25–30 minutes. If the top becomes very brown before the base is cooked through, transfer to a lower shelf.

PICKLED MEDITERRANEAN VEGETABLES

225ml/8fl oz white wine vinegar
120ml/4fl oz extra virgin oil
3 tablespoons soft light brown sugar
1 teaspoon coarse sea salt
2 red peppers, cored, deseeded and cut into
  thick strips
2 orange peppers, cored, deseeded and cut into
  thick strips
2 yellow peppers, cored, deseeded and cut into
  thick strips
225g/8oz courgettes, trimmed and cut into
  batons
200g/7oz kalamata black olives, pitted
1 tablespoon roughly chopped fresh sage
freshly ground black pepper

To serve
crusty bread

1. Put the vinegar, oil, sugar and salt into a large saucepan. Bring to the boil and add the prepared vegetables, then reduce to a simmer and cook for 5 minutes.
2. Add the olives and sage to the pan and season with pepper. Turn off the heat and allow to cool.
3. Drain the vegetables in a colander and discard the liquid. Chill the vegetables lightly before serving with crusty bread.

ROASTED VEGETABLES WITH PINENUTS

2 medium red onions
3 courgettes
2 red peppers
2 large potatoes
4 sprigs of fresh marjoram or thyme
salt and freshly ground black pepper
150ml/¼ pint olive oil
4 tomatoes, halved
55g/2oz pinenuts

1. Preheat the oven to 190°C/375°F/gas mark 5.
2. Peel and halve the onions. Trim off the stalks and roots and cut each half into quarters.
3. Wash the remaining vegetables. Trim the courgettes and cut them into quarters. Cut the peppers in half through the stalks and remove the pith and seeds. Cut the potatoes into quarters.
4. Put all the vegetables into a roasting tin. Sprinkle with the herbs and season with salt and pepper. Pour over the oil and turn the vegetables until evenly coated.
5. Bake in the preheated oven for 40 minutes, turning the vegetables from time to time. Add the tomatoes and sprinkle the pinenuts over the top. Return to the oven for a further 20 minutes until the vegetables are well cooked and charred at the edges.

YOGHURT SOUP WITH CHILLIES, CORIANDER AND BLACK MUSTARD SEEDS

200ml/7fl oz Wholemilk natural yoghurt
2½ tablespoons chickpea flour (gram flour)
350ml/12fl oz summer stock (see page 530)
2 tablespoons sunflower oil
1 tablespoon black mustard seeds
2.5cm/1in piece of fresh root ginger, peeled and
    finely grated
1 clove of garlic, crushed
1 medium-hot red Dutch chilli, deseeded and
    finely chopped (see page 22)
1 medium-hot green Dutch chilli, deseeded and
    finely chopped (see page 22)
1 × 400ml/14fl oz can of coconut milk
1 fresh curry leaf
salt
3 tablespoons coarsely chopped fresh coriander

To serve
warm naan bread

1. Put the yoghurt and flour into a bowl and
mix together to a smooth paste. Gradually stir
in the stock and set aside.
2. Heat the oil in a medium saucepan. Add the
mustard seeds, cover and as soon as the seeds
begin to pop, uncover and add the ginger, garlic
and the red and green chillies. Fry for a few
seconds, then pour in the yoghurt mixture and
bring to a simmer, stirring constantly. Add the
coconut milk, curry leaf and ½ teaspoon salt
and simmer for 3–4 minutes. Stir in the
coriander and serve with the warm naan bread.

CHILE CON QUESO

(ANAHEIM CHILLI AND MELTED CHEESE
DIP)

6 mild green Anaheim chillies
2 tablespoons sunflower oil
1 medium onion, finely chopped
2 cloves of garlic, finely chopped
450g/1lb Cheddar cheese, coarsely grated
1 tablespoon soured cream

To serve
tortilla chips

1. Grill the chillies over a naked gas flame or
under a hot grill, turning them from time to
time, until their skins are black and blistered all
over. Alternatively roast them at 220°C/425°F,
gas mark 7 for 10 minutes. Place the chillies in a
plastic bag, seal and leave to cool.
2 Remove the chillies from the bag and peel off
the skins. Slit them open lengthways and
remove and discard the stalks and seeds. Chop
the flesh coarsely.
3. Heat the oil in a large, deep frying pan. Add
the onion and garlic and cook over a low heat
for 10 minutes until the onion is very soft but
not browned. Stir in the chillies and cook gently
for a further 5 minutes.
4. Stir in the cheese and leave it to melt over a
low heat. Stir in the soured cream until the
mixture is smooth and creamy, then pour into a
warmed gratin dish. Serve immediately, with
the tortilla chips.

CHILES RELLENOS

(ANAHEIM CHILLI AND CHEESE FRITTERS WITH RED CHILLI SAUCE)

8 large mild green Anaheim chillies or small red
    Romano peppers
450g/1lb Monterey Jack or Cheddar cheese
4 medium eggs
sunflower oil, for frying
55g/2oz plain flour, seasoned

For the sauce
20g/¾oz dried, mild red chillies, such as New
    Mexico
110g/4oz plum tomatoes
1½ tablespoons sunflower oil
½ small onion, roughly chopped
1 large clove of garlic, crushed
½ teaspoon ground cumin
salt
1–1½ teaspoons caster sugar
salt and freshly ground black pepper

To serve
warm flour tortillas

1. First make the sauce: slit open the dried chillies and remove the stalks and seeds. Bring a saucepan of water to the boil. Heat a dry, heavy frying pan over a high heat, add the chillies and dry-roast them for about 2 minutes on each side, shaking the pan constantly to prevent them from scorching. Remove the pan of water from the heat, add the chillies and place a saucer on top to keep them submerged. Leave them to soak for 20 minutes until they are soft.
2. Meanwhile, preheat the grill to high. Cut the tomatoes in half and grill them, cut side down, for 5 minutes until the skins are black. Heat 1 tablespoon of the oil in a small frying pan, add the onion and fry over a medium to high heat, stirring from time to time, until a rich golden-brown.
3. Drain the chillies, reserving the soaking liquid. Put the chillies, tomatoes, onion, garlic, cumin and ½ teaspoon salt into a blender with 110ml/4fl oz of the chilli soaking liquid and

process to a smooth paste. Pass through a sieve into a bowl.
4. Heat the remaining oil in a medium saucepan. Add the sieved sauce and the sugar and simmer for 10 minutes, stirring from time to time, until reduced and thickened. Season to taste with salt and pepper and keep hot.
5. Make the chilli and cheese fritters: grill the chillies over a naked gas flame or under the hot grill, turning from time to time, until their skins are black and blistered all over. Alternatively roast them at 220°C/425°F, gas mark 7 for 10 minutes. Place the chillies in a plastic bag, seal and leave to cool.
6. Remove the chillies from the bag and peel off the skins. Make a slit down one side, leaving the stalks in place, and carefully scoop out the seeds, taking care not to tear the flesh. Season well inside and out.
7. Cut the cheese into thick slices, then into sticks about 7.5cm/3in long and 2.5cm/1in wide. Poke one stick of cheese into each chilli, then push the chillis back into shape.
8. Separate the eggs into 2 medium bowls. Beat the egg yolks until smooth and creamy. Whisk the egg whites with a pinch of salt into soft peaks, then fold into the egg yolks, using a large metal spoon.
9. Heat 1cm/½in oil in a large, deep frying pan. Dip the chillies first into the seasoned flour, then into the whisked egg mixture and fry a few at a time for 1–1½ minutes on each side until crisp and a rich golden-brown. Lift them out carefully with a fish slice and drain briefly on kitchen paper. Serve with the red chilli sauce and the warm flour tortillas.

RED CHILLI OATCAKES WITH GRILLED RED PEPPERS AND BAKED CAMEMBERT

For the oatcakes
225g/8oz medium oatmeal, plus extra for
   rolling and dusting
55g/2oz plain flour
¼ teaspoon bicarbonate of soda
a large pinch of salt
30g/1oz butter
30g/1oz white vegetable fat
1 small red chilli, deseeded and very finely
   chopped
4–5 tablespoons boiling water

For the peppers
3 large red peppers, halved and deseeded
1 tablespoon chopped fresh marjoram
2 tablespoons olive oil
1½ tablespoons red wine vinegar
salt and freshly ground black pepper
2 whole Camembert cheeses

1. Preheat the oven to 190°C/375°F/gas mark 5.
2. Put the oatmeal and flour into a mixing
bowl with the bicarbonate of soda and the salt.
3. Rub in the butter and vegetable fat until the
mixture resembles coarse breadcrumbs. Stir in
the chopped chilli and, using a knife, mix
together with enough boiling water to make a
fairly firm dough.
4. Sprinkle a worktop with oatmeal. Roll the
dough out about 5mm/¼in thick. Using a
7.5cm/3in pastry cutter, stamp out rounds.
5. Place the oatcakes on a baking tray and dust
with a little oatmeal. Bake in the preheated oven
for 20 minutes or until dry and crisp at the edges.
Cool on a wire rack. Do not turn the oven off.
6. Preheat the grill. Grill the peppers until they
are black and blistered. Place in a plastic bag,
seal and leave until cool, then peel away the
skin.
7. Cut the peppers into strips and toss with the
marjoram, oil and vinegar. Season with salt and
pepper.

8. Remove the lids from the Camembert
cheeses. Prick several holes in the top of each
cheese and cover with a piece of kitchen foil.
9. Bake the Camembert in the hot oven for 7–
10 minutes or until soft to the touch.
10. Divide the peppers between 4 individual
plates. Top with a spoonful of the baked
Camembert and hand the oatcakes separately.

NOTE: These cheeses are baked in their boxes.

FRESH VINE TOMATO SOUP

30g/1oz butter
1 large onion, chopped
675g/1½lb vine-ripened tomatoes, chopped
1 clove of garlic, crushed
½ teaspoon sugar
1 sprig of fresh thyme
1 teaspoon tomato purée
salt and freshly ground black pepper
150ml/¼ pint summer vegetable stock (see
   page 530)
5 tablespoons double cream
chopped fresh chives, to garnish

1. Melt the butter in a large saucepan and add
the onion, then cover and sweat over a very low
heat, stirring occasionally, for 15 minutes. Do
not allow the onion to brown.
2. Add the tomatoes, garlic, sugar, thyme,
tomato purée and salt and pepper to taste.
Cook over a medium heat for 10 minutes or
until the tomatoes and onions are soft.
3. Add the stock and cook for a further 5
minutes.
4. Purée the soup in a food processor or
blender, then pass through a sieve. Pour back
into the rinsed-out pan. Add the cream and
more salt, pepper and sugar as necessary.
5. Serve in warmed soup bowls, sprinkled with
chives.

TOMATO AND FENNEL SOUP WITH CHIVE MASCARPONE

2 tablespoons olive oil
1 onion, chopped
1 clove of garlic, crushed
1 bulb of fennel
450g/1lb fresh tomatoes, peeled and chopped (see page 22)
720ml/1¼ pints summer vegetable stock (see page 530)
1 tablespoon red pesto (see page 527)
salt and freshly ground black pepper
6 fresh basil leaves
sugar
lemon juice
4 tablespoons mascarpone
1 tablespoon chopped fresh chives

1. Heat the oil in a large saucepan, add the onion and fry over a low heat until softened, then add the garlic and fry for 1 further minute.
2. Trim and slice the fennel, reserving the feathery tops. Add the fennel to the pan, cover and cook over a low heat for about 10 minutes. Add the tomatoes, stock and pesto and season with salt and pepper. Bring to the boil, then lower the heat and simmer for 30 minutes.
3. Add the basil, then purée the soup in a food processor or blender. Reheat in the rinsed-out pan and adjust the seasoning to taste, adding a little sugar and lemon juice if necessary. Chop the reserved fennel tops and stir into the mascarpone with the chives. Swirl into the soup just before serving in warmed soup bowls.

SAVOURY TOMATOES

This is a substantial first course. To serve as a main course or supper dish, set the tomatoes on toasted chunks of crusty bread or on potato cakes (see page 89).

hazelnut or walnut oil
4 large tomatoes
salt and freshly ground black pepper
4 small eggs
55g/2oz Parmesan cheese, freshly grated
about 55g/2oz rocket
balsamic vinegar

1. Preheat the oven to 200°C/400°F/gas mark 6. Brush a baking tray with oil.
2. Cut a small slice from the top of each tomato, just enough to expose the seeds. Using a teaspoon, remove the seeds and hollow out the inside. Season with salt and pepper, place on the baking tray and cook in the preheated oven for 8 minutes.
3. Separate the eggs and slip the yolks inside the tomato shells. Whisk the egg whites in a large mixing bowl until very stiff. Fold in the cheese, using a large metal spoon, and season with salt and pepper. Pile on top of the tomatoes.
4. Bake in the oven for 10 minutes until the topping is golden-brown and slightly crisp. Season the rocket with a drizzle of oil and vinegar. Arrange the tomatoes on 4 individual plates and garnish with the rocket.

BAKED STUFFED TOMATOES WITH LEMON DRESSING

2 tablespoons groundnut oil, plus extra for
  brushing
55g/2oz dried aduki beans, soaked overnight
55g/2oz couscous
4 ripe beefsteak tomatoes
8 spring onions
1 small red onion, chopped
1 clove of garlic, crushed
2 tablespoons finely chopped fresh mint
55g/2oz unsalted peanuts
salt and freshly ground black pepper
chopped fresh coriander, to garnish

For the dressing
grated zest and juice of 1 lemon
3 tablespoons olive oil
1 teaspoon Dijon mustard

1. Preheat the oven to 200°C/400°F/gas mark 6.
Brush a small roasting tin with a little oil.
2. Rinse and drain the aduki beans and cook
them in boiling water for 30–40 minutes until
tender, then drain and set aside. Pour 150ml/¼
pint boiling water over the couscous and leave
to soak.
3. Place the tomatoes stem side down on a
chopping board. Slice a 1cm/½in lid off the top
of each. Chop the lids. Scoop the seeds out of
the centre of the tomatoes and discard. Remove
the outer skin from the spring onions and slice
on the diagonal.
4. Heat the oil in a heavy frying pan. Add the
red onion and fry over a low heat until soft and
beginning to colour. Add the garlic, mint,
peanuts, chopped tomato and spring onion into
the pan together. Fry briefly. Fork the couscous
through to separate the grains and stir into the
pan together with the cooked aduki beans.
Season to taste with salt and pepper.
5. Spoon the stuffing into the tomatoes and
place them in the prepared roasting tin. Cook in
the preheated oven for 10–15 minutes until the
tomatoes are soft and the skins slightly charred.

6. Meanwhile, whisk all the dressing
ingredients together and season with salt and
pepper. Pour over the tomatoes just before
serving and sprinkle with coriander.

BAKED BABY PLUM TOMATOES AND BABY LEEKS

400g/14oz baby leeks
2 tablespoons olive oil
1 clove of garlic, crushed
salt and freshly ground black pepper
250g/9oz baby plum tomatoes, peeled (see
  page 22)
juice of ½ lemon
a pinch of sugar
1 tablespoon shredded fresh basil

1. Preheat the oven to 180°C/350°F/gas mark 4.
2. Top and tail the leeks and remove the outer
layer. Wash very well.
3. Heat the oil in a small saucepan over a low
heat. Add the garlic and infuse very carefully
for about 5 minutes, taking care not to let it
brown.
4. Place the leeks in a shallow, ovenproof dish,
pour over the oil and garlic and season with salt
and pepper. Cover and bake in the preheated
oven for 15 minutes. Turn the leeks over and
add the tomatoes, then pour over the lemon
juice and sprinkle with the sugar and more salt
and pepper. Return to the oven, uncovered, for
10 minutes.
5. Just before serving, scatter over the basil.

NOTE: Leave the tomatoes unpeeled if
preferred.

OVEN-DRIED TOMATOES WITH BAKED FETA CHEESE AND BLACK OLIVES

340g/12oz feta cheese
4 teaspoons extra virgin olive oil, plus extra to
  serve
1 teaspoon dried red chilli flakes
110g/4oz small black olives

For the oven-dried tomatoes
675g/1½lb vine-ripened plum tomatoes
oil, for brushing
1½ teaspoons sea salt flakes
coarsely ground black pepper
1 teaspoon fresh thyme leaves

To serve
warm Turkish flat bread

1. Prepare the oven-dried tomatoes: preheat the oven to 240°C/475°F/gas mark 9. Remove the cores from the tomatoes with the tip of a small, sharp knife, then cut them in half lengthways. Brush a roasting tin lightly with oil and lay the tomatoes, cut side up, in the tin. Sprinkle salt, pepper and thyme leaves on each tomato, then roast in the preheated oven for 15 minutes.
2. Lower the oven temperature to 150°C/300°F/gas mark 2 and roast the tomatoes for a further 1½ hours or until they have shrivelled to about half their original size and are concentrated in flavour. Remove from the oven and set aside.
3. Increase the oven temperature to 200°C/400°F/gas mark 6. Cut the feta cheese into 4 large slices and lay them on 4 large squares of lightly oiled kitchen foil. Sprinkle each piece of cheese with 1 teaspoon oil and a few chilli flakes. Seal the foil loosely around the cheese, crimping the edges together well. Lift the foil parcels on to a baking tray and bake the cheese in the oven for 10 minutes.
4. Remove the cheese from the oven and unwrap each parcel. Carefully lift the cheese on to 4 individual plates and arrange the oven-dried tomatoes and black olives alongside.

Drizzle some oil over the cheese and around the edge of the plate and garnish with sea salt flakes and pepper. Serve with warm Turkish flat bread.

METBOUKHA TARTLETS

This rich and spicy tomato and green pepper marmelade has its origins in North Africa. It can be served in tartlet cases as a first course or in smaller ones as a canapé.

MAKES 8–12

170g/6oz flour quantity shortcrust pastry (see page 521)
2 green peppers
340g/12oz tomatoes
2 tablespoons sunflower oil
1 red onion, chopped
1 clove of garlic, crushed
1 red chilli, chopped
½ teaspoon paprika
100ml/3½fl oz red wine
1 teaspoon sugar
salt

1. Preheat the oven to 200°C/400°F/gas mark 6.
2. Roll out the pastry and use to line patty tins. Bake blind in the preheated oven for 10–15 minutes (see page 22).
3. Preheat the grill. Cut the peppers into quarters and remove the pith and seeds. Grill the peppers skin side up until blistered and blackened. Place in a plastic bag, seal and leave to cool, then remove the skin and discard the stalks and seeds. Bring a saucepan of water to the boil, add the peeled peppers and cook for 3 minutes to remove any bitterness. Drain and cut into small dice.
4. Peel the tomatoes and chop them finely (see page 22).
5. Heat the oil in a medium saucepan. Add the onion and sweat gently for 10 minutes. Add the garlic, diced peppers, chilli and paprika and cook for 2 minutes.
6. Add the tomatoes, wine, sugar and a little salt. Bring to the boil and cook for 2 minutes. Lower the heat, cover and cook gently for 30 minutes.
7. Remove the lid and allow any liquid to evaporate. Taste and add more salt or sugar as required.
8. Serve in the tartlet cases, warm or cold.

TOMATO AND VODKA GALETTES WITH CRÈME FRAÎCHE PASTRY

SERVES 6

For the pastry
170g/6oz plain flour, plus extra for rolling
a pinch of salt
45g/1½oz butter, diced
12 large fresh basil leaves, shredded
2 tablespoons crème fraîche
1 egg yolk
1–2 tablespoons very cold water

For the topping
8 ripe plum tomatoes, sliced lengthways
3 tablespoons vodka
1½ tablespoons olive oil
salt and freshly ground black pepper
fresh basil leaves, to garnish

1. Make the pastry: sift the flour and salt into a mixing bowl.
2. Rub in the butter until the mixture resembles coarse breadcrumbs. Stir in the basil.
3. Mix the crème fraîche with the egg yolk and 1 tablespoon of the water. Add the flour and mix to a firm dough, first with a round-bladed knife, then with one hand. It may be necessary to add more water but the pastry should not be too damp.
4. Roll out the pastry on a floured worktop to the thickness of a £1 coin. Using a plate as a template, cut out 6 × 10cm/4in discs. Place on a baking tray and chill for 30 minutes.
5. Preheat the oven to 200°C/400°F/gas mark 6.
6. Arrange the tomato slices in overlapping circles on the pastry discs. Mix the vodka and oil together and drizzle over the tomatoes. Season with salt and pepper and lay a large basil leaf on top of each slice.
7. Bake on the top shelf of the preheated oven for 15 minutes or until the pastry is brown and crisp. Serve hot or warm.

TOMATO TARTE TARTIN

This recipe needs to be made in a tin or frying pan that is suitable for use both on the hob and in the oven.

For the topping
45g/1½oz butter
30g/1oz soft light brown sugar
1½ tablespoons balsamic vinegar
5 plum tomatoes, peeled
a handful of fresh basil leaves

For the scone dough
110g/4oz self-raising flour
a pinch of baking powder
a pinch of dry English mustard
a pinch of cayenne pepper
2 tablespoons olive oil
6 green or black olives, pitted and roughly
   chopped
salt and freshly ground black pepper
1 egg
1–2 tablespoons milk

1. First make the topping: melt the butter in 1 20cm 8in flame proof and ovenproof pan, add the sugar and cook over a low heat until the mixture begins to caramelize. Add the venegar and boil for 30 seconds. Cut the tomatoes in half lengthways. Scatter some of the basil leaves on top of the sugar mixture and then arrange the tomatoes, cut side down, to cover the base of the pan completely.
2. Preheat the oven to 220°C/425°F/gas mark 7.
3. Make the scone dough: sift the flour with the baking powder, mustard and cayenne pepper into a large mixing bowl. Add the oil and mix together with a round-bladed knife until the mixture resembles breadcrumbs. Stir in the olives and season with salt and pepper. Bind to a spongy dough with the egg and milk.
4. Turn the dough on to a floured surface and knead gently until smooth. Roll to a circle about 5mm/¼in thick, to fit the top of the pan. Lay it on top of the tomatoes and press down lightly.

5. Bake in the preheated oven for 10–15 minutes until the scone dough feels firm and is slightly golden. Loosen the edges with a knife, cover with a serving plate and invert to turn out. Garnish with the remaining basil leaves and serve immediately.

SPICED TOMATOES

8 large tomatoes, peeled (see page 22)
1 teaspoon salt
1 teaspoon chilli powder
1 tablespoon oil
½ teaspoon fennel seeds
1 teaspoon mustard seeds
1 large onion, chopped
1 clove of garlic
½ teaspoon ground cinnamon
225ml/8fl oz coconut milk
freshly ground black pepper

To serve
boiled rice

1. Cut the tomatoes into thick slices. Lay them on a plate. Mix together the salt and chilli powder and sprinkle over the tomatoes. Leave for 20 minutes.
2. Heat the oil in a frying pan and add the fennel and mustard seeds. Fry until they begin to pop, then add the onion. Fry over a low heat for 5 minutes until the onion begins to brown. Add the garlic and cinnamon and cook for 1 further minute.
3. Add the tomato slices and cook for 10 minutes or until they have pulped down and some of the juice has evaporated. Pour in the coconut milk and season with pepper. Bring to the boil, then serve immediately with boiled rice.

FRIED BEEF TOMATOES IN A PARMESAN AND POLENTA CRUST WITH SALSA VERDE

6 ripe but firm beef tomatoes
55g/2oz plain flour
140g/5oz polenta
30g/1oz Parmesan cheese, freshly grated
3 medium eggs, beaten
olive oil, for shallow frying

For the salsa verde
30g/1oz fresh flat-leaf parsley leaves
15g/½oz fresh mint leaves
3 tablespoons capers in brine drained and
  rinsed
1 large clove of garlic, crushed
1 teaspoon Dijon mustard
1½ tablespoons lemon juice
120ml/4fl oz extra virgin olive oil
salt and freshly ground black pepper

1. First make the salsa verde: chop the parsley, mint and capers together on a board into a coarse paste. Scrape into a small bowl and stir in the garlic, mustard, lemon juice, oil and salt and pepper to taste. Cover and set aside.
2. Remove the core of each tomato with the tip of a small, sharp knife. Cut each one across into 1cm/½in thick slices, then season them well on both sides with salt and pepper.
3. Lightly season both the flour and the polenta and mix the cheese with the polenta. Put the flour, polenta and beaten eggs into 3 separate shallow dishes. Pour 1cm/½in oil into a large, deep frying pan and place over a medium to high heat.
4. Coat the tomato slices a few at a time in flour, then in egg and then in the polenta mixture, pressing it on well to make a thick, even coating.
5. Carefully lower the tomato slices into the hot oil and fry them for 2 minutes on each side until crisp and golden. Drain briefly on kitchen paper and keep hot in a low oven while you cook the remainder in the same way. Serve warm with the salsa verde.

TOMATO CURRY WITH BLACK MUSTARD SEEDS AND CURRY LEAVES

900g/2lb vine-ripened tomatoes, peeled (see
  page 22)
6 tablespoons sunflower oil
4 cloves of garlic, thinly sliced
2.5cm/1in piece of fresh root ginger, peeled and
  finely grated
1 medium onion, halved and thinly sliced
1 medium-hot red Dutch chilli, finely chopped
½ teaspoon hot paprika
½ teaspoon ground turmeric
½ teaspoon ground cumin
½ teaspoon ground coriander
1 teaspoon tomato purée
10 fresh curry leaves
150ml/¼ pint hot water
½ teaspoon salt
1 teaspoon black mustard seeds

To serve
lemon rice (see page 357)

1. Finely chop half the tomatoes and cut the remainder into quarters. Heat half the oil in a large, deep frying pan. Add half the garlic and as soon as it starts to sizzle, add the ginger, onion and chilli and fry over a low heat for 5–6 minutes until softened.
2. Add the paprika, turmeric, cumin and coriander and fry for 2 minutes. Add the chopped tomatoes, tomato purée, half the curry leaves and the hot water and simmer for 5 minutes. Add the quartered tomatoes and the salt and simmer for a further 5 minutes.
3. Heat the remaining oil in a small saucepan. Add the remaining garlic, curry leaves and the mustard seeds and as soon as the mustard seeds begin to pop and the garlic has started to colour, pour the mixture into the tomato curry and stir together well. Serve with lemon rice.

SALAD OF ROASTED TOMATOES AND SPRING ONIONS

10 ripe plum tomatoes
olive oil
salt and freshly ground black pepper
caster sugar to taste
sprigs of fresh thyme
30g/1oz butter
½ bunch of spring onions, trimmed and
  cleaned, sliced on the diagonal

For the dressing
1 teaspoon Dijon mustard
2 teaspoons tarragon vinegar
2 teaspoons white wine vinegar
2 tablespoons olive oil

To garnish
½ bunch of flat-leaf parsley, chopped

1. Preheat the oven to 200°C/400°F/gas mark 6. Cut the tomatoes in half vertically and scoop out the seeds. Drain the tomatoes thoroughly on absorbent kitchen paper.
2. Brush a baking sheet with oil. Arrange the tomatoes cut side up on the sheet. Season with salt, pepper and sugar. Scatter with sprigs of thyme and drizzle over more oil.
3. Roast in the preheated oven for 10–15 minutes until the tomato flesh just gives when touched.
4. Arrange 5 tomato halves, cut side down, on each individual serving plate.
5. Melt the butter in a frying pan and sauté the spring onions for about 2 minutes. Scatter around the roasted tomatoes.
6. Whisk the dressing ingredients together, check the seasoning, and drizzle over the tomatoes. Sprinkle with parsley.

PARMENDER SALAD

This delicious yoghurty salad is perfect to serve as part of a summer buffet or as a refreshing side dish with fiery stews or curries.

SERVES 6

6 ripe tomatoes, peeled
½ cucumber
1 medium red onion, thinly sliced
2 teaspoons garam masala
½ teaspoon ground turmeric
290ml/½ pint Greek yoghurt
2 tablespoons chopped fresh coriander
salt and freshly ground black pepper
juice of ½ lime
a few fresh coriander leaves, to garnish

1. Quarter and deseed the tomatoes. Cut the flesh into slivers. Peel the cucumber, cut in half and scoop out the seeds with a melon-baller or teaspoon, then slice thinly. Mix the tomatoes, cucumber and red onion together in a bowl.
2. Whisk the garam masala and turmeric into the yoghurt. Stir in the chopped coriander and pour over the vegetables.
3. Season with salt, pepper and lime juice. Spoon into a serving dish and scatter with coriander leaves.

PANZANELLA

(TUSCAN TOMATO AND BREAD SALAD)

1 loaf of ciabatta bread
15cm/6in piece of cucumber
1 small red pepper
675g/1½lb vine-ripened tomatoes, peeled (see
  page 22)
2 large cloves of garlic
sea salt flakes and coarsely ground black pepper
2 tablespoons red wine vinegar
4 tablespoons extra virgin oil, plus extra to serve
1 small red onion, halved and thinly sliced
2 tablespoons capers in brine, rinsed
110g/4oz small black olives
30g/1oz fresh basil leaves, torn into pieces

1. Preheat the grill to high. Cut the bread into
slices 1cm/½in thick and toast them very lightly
on both sides until just beginning to colour.
Leave to cool, then break into rough 2.5cm/1in
pieces and set aside.
2. Peel the cucumber, cut in half lengthways
and scoop out the seeds with a melon-baller or
teaspoon. Cut the cucumber crossways into
half-moon slices. Grill the pepper over a naked
gas flame or under the grill, turning from time
to time, until the skin is black and blistered all
over. Place in a plastic bag, seal and leave to
cool. Then break the pepper open and discard
the stalk and seeds. Peel off the skin and cut the
flesh into chunky strips.
3. Working over a sieve set over a large salad
bowl, deseed the tomatoes and cut the flesh into
1cm/½in pieces, taking care not to lose any of
the juices. Rub the juice from the seeds through
the sieve and discard the seeds.
4. Crush the garlic on a board with a little salt
and stir into the tomato juice with the vinegar,
oil and salt and pepper to taste.
5. Five minutes before serving, add the bread
pieces to the dressing in the bowl and toss
together well. Add the cucumber, red pepper,
tomatoes, onion, capers, olives and basil and
toss together briefly. Adjust the seasoning if
necessary and set aside for 5 minutes to allow
the bread to soften slightly.
6. Divide the mixture between 4 large individual

plates and drizzle over a little more oil. Sprinkle
with sea salt flakes and black pepper.

GREEK SALAD SAMOSAS WITH MINT AND YOGHURT DIPPING SAUCE

For the samosas
4 plum tomatoes, peeled, deseeded and diced
  (see page 22)
½ cucumber, peeled, deseeded and diced
110g/4oz feta cheese, crumbled
8 kalamata black olives, pitted and chopped
5½ tablespoons extra virgin olive oil
2 tablespoons fresh flat-leaf parsley, roughly
  chopped
salt and freshly ground black pepper
6 sheets of bought filo pastry
1 tablespoon lemon juice
2 teaspoons very finely chopped fresh thyme
  leaves
1 egg, beaten
fresh flat-leaf parsley, to garnish

For the dipping sauce
150ml/¼ pint Greek yoghurt
juice of ½ lemon
1 tablespoon finely chopped fresh mint
salt and freshly ground black pepper

1. Preheat the oven to 200°C/400°F/gas mark 6.
2. Mix the tomatoes, cucumber and feta cheese
together in a large bowl. Stir in the olives, 1½
tablespoons of the oil and the parsley. Season
with salt and pepper. Set aside.
3. Lay a sheet of filo pastry on a work surface.
Mix the remaining oil with the lemon juice and
thyme leaves and brush the pastry with the
mixture. Cover with a second sheet and brush
again. Cut in half lengthways.
4. Place a large spoonful of the tomato,
cucumber and cheese mixture at one end of
each pastry strip. Form a triangle by folding the
right-hand corner to the opposite side, then
folding across from the left-hand corner to the
edge. Continue folding until the strip of pastry

is used up. Brush with the beaten egg and repeat with the remaining pastry and tomato, cucumber and cheese mixture.

5. Place the pastry triangles on a baking sheet and bake on the top shelf of the preheated oven for 10–12 minutes until crisp and golden-brown.

6. Meanwhile, make the dipping sauce: put the yoghurt, lemon juice and mint into a bowl and season with salt and pepper.

7. Serve the hot samosas with a spoonful of the sauce on each plate, garnished with flat-leaf parsley.

GRIDDLED TOMATILLOS

Tomatillos deserve a special mention. They are an intrinsic part of Mexican and Californian dishes. Although the name implies that they are a relative of the tomato they are in fact a member of the physalia family and have the same papery jacket as the Cape gooseberry. They are difficult to find fresh in this country but are gradually appearing on the lists of specialist mail order suppliers. Their flavour has a distinctive pungency that cannot be duplicated. Canned tomatillos bear no resemblance to fresh and are best left on the shelf. Tomatillos are ready for eating when they fill the husk and the flavour is best before the husk is broken. They can be stored, covered, in a refrigerator for up to 2 weeks but should be cooked before freezing. Tomatillos can be added to any tomato sauce recipe or substituted for tomatoes in salsa. These griddled tomatillos can be used to make a smoky-flavoured tomato sauce by following the recipe for baked tomato relish on page 509.

450g/1lb tomatillos
sunflower or vegetable oil
salt and freshly ground black pepper

To serve
roasted garlic mayonnaise (see page 512)
warm crusty bread

1. Remove the husks from the tomatillos and wash briefly to remove the sticky film. Brush with oil.

2. Heat a griddle or heavy frying pan. Cook the tomatillos briskly on both sides for about 3 minutes, sprinkling with salt and pepper while they are cooking. Serve immediately with a dollop of roasted garlic mayonnaise and warm crusty bread.

TOMATILLO AND COCONUT SALSA

6 fresh tomatillos
2 tablespoons chopped fresh coriander
¼ small red onion, finely chopped
1–2 green chillies, deseeded and finely chopped
  (see page 22)
1 clove of garlic, crushed
grated zest and juice of 1 lime
15g/½oz creamed coconut
½ teaspoon ground cumin
½ teaspoon salt
freshly ground black pepper

1. Roughly chop the tomatillos and mix with the coriander, onion, chilli, garlic and lime zest and juice.

2. Grate the creamed coconut and stir into the mixture. Add the cumin, salt and several twists of black pepper. Leave to stand for 1 hour before serving.

MEZZE PLATE

This is a selection of traditional Greek salads, served with hot sesame pitta bread.

For the baba ghannouj
2 small aubergines, each about 225g/8oz
2 tablespoons extra virgin olive oil
1 clove of garlic, crushed
2 tablespoons tahina (sesame seed paste)
2 tablespoons lemon juice
2 tablespoons chopped fresh flat-leaf parsley
salt and freshly ground black pepper
1 tablespoon pomegranate seeds, to garnish
   (optional)

For the hummus
1 × 400g/14oz can of chickpeas, drained and
   rinsed
1½ teaspoons ground cumin
2 small cloves of garlic, crushed
1 tablespoon tahina
4 tablespoons lemon juice
4 tablespoons extra virgin olive oil

For the tzatziki
½ cucumber
200g/7oz Greek yoghurt
2 cloves of garlic, crushed
1 tablespoon lemon juice

For the tomato salad
5 small vine-ripened tomatoes, peeled
4 spring onions, trimmed and thinly sliced
3 tablespoons coarsely chopped fresh flat-leaf
   parsley
1 small red onion, finely chopped
1 tablespoon lemon juice
2 tablespoons extra virgin olive oil

To serve
55g/2oz kalamata olives
1 quantity garlic and sesame pitta bread (see
   page 492)

1. Make the baba ghannouj: heat a ridged cast-iron griddle over a high heat. Pierce the aubergines near the stem end with a fork and rub them all over with a little oil. Place them on the griddle and cook for 20 minutes, turning from time to time, until the skin is black all over and the flesh is very soft. Cut the aubergines in half lengthways and scoop the flesh out into a bowl. Mash to a rough purée with a fork and stir in the garlic, tahina, lemon juice, parsley, oil and salt and pepper to taste. Cover and chill.

2. Make the hummus: put the chickpeas into a food processor with the cumin, garlic, tahina, lemon juice and 1 teaspoon of salt. Process to a smooth paste, then, with the machine still running, gradually add the oil through the hole in the lid. Season to taste with pepper.

3. Make the tzatziki: grate the cucumber coarsely. Pile it into a clean tea-towel and squeeze out the excess water. Mix in a bowl with the yoghurt, garlic, lemon juice and salt and pepper to taste.

4. Make the tomato salad: remove the seeds from the tomatoes and cut the flesh into small pieces. Place in a bowl and stir in the spring onions, parsley, onion, lemon juice, oil and salt and pepper to taste.

5. To serve, spoon a portion of each salad on to individual plates. Garnish the baba ghannouj with the pomegranate seeds, if used, and scatter around a few olives. Serve with the garlic and sesame pitta bread.

BRIE AND RATATOUILLE JALOUSIE

When making the ratatouille for this recipe, cut the vegetables into 1-cm/½in-chunks and simmer until most of the liquid has evaporated.

450g/1lb flour quantity puff pastry (see
  page 522)
1 quantity ratatouille (see page 234)
225g/8oz Brie or Camembert cheese
plain flour, for dusting
beaten egg or milk, to glaze

1. Preheat the oven to 230°C/450°F/gas mark 8.
2. Cut the pastry in half and roll each piece into a rectangle, one about 17.5 × 30cm/7 × 12in, and the other a little larger. Cover with a clean tea-towel and leave to rest for 20 minutes.
3. Put the smaller pastry rectangle on to a wet baking sheet. Prick with a fork and bake in the preheated oven for 20 minutes until crisp and brown. When cooked, loosen it from the baking sheet and leave to cool.
4. Lower the oven temperature to 220°C/425°F/gas mark 7.
5. Trim the edges from the cooked pastry base and place on a clean baking sheet. Spoon the ratatouille on top. Cut the rind from the Brie or Camembert and slice. Arrange the cheese over the top of the ratatouille.
6. Take the uncooked sheet of pastry, dust with flour and fold in half lengthways. Cut diagonal lines from the folded side towards the edge, leaving a margin of about 5cm/2in around the edge. Carefully lift the pastry and lay the folded edge down the centre of the filling. Unfold the pastry to form a cover with 'V'-shaped slashes down the centre. Tuck the excess pastry under the jalousie. Brush with beaten egg or milk, then bake in the preheated oven for 20–30 minutes until the pastry is golden-brown on top.

ROAST RATATOUILLE HOT POT

450g/1lb red potatoes
1 red pepper
1 green pepper
1 aubergine
1 courgette
4 tablespoons olive oil
1 large red onion, sliced
2 cloves of garlic, crushed
1 × 400g/14oz can of chopped tomatoes
salt and freshly ground black pepper
a pinch of caster sugar
2 tablespoons chopped fresh basil
grated zest of 1 lemon

1. Scrub the potatoes and cut them in half. Put into a saucepan of salted water and bring to the boil, then boil for 2 minutes. Drain and leave to cool.
2. Preheat the grill to high and preheat the oven to 200°C/400°F/gas mark 6.
3. Cut the peppers in half and remove the stalks and seeds. Cut the aubergine in half lengthways, then slice. Cut the courgette into diagonal slices.
4. Rub the pepper halves with a little oil and grill, cut side down, until black and charred. Cover with a clean tea-towel and leave to cool. Brush the aubergine and courgette with oil and grill on both sides until golden-brown.
5. Peel and slice the peppers and put them into an ovenproof casserole with the aubergine and courgette.
6. Heat 1 tablespoon of the oil in a frying pan, add the onion and fry over a low heat until browned. Add the garlic and fry for 1 further minute. Pour in the tomatoes and bring to the boil. Season with salt, pepper and sugar and stir in the basil. Pour into the casserole and mix.
7. Cut the potato into 5mm/¼in slices and arrange in an overlapping layer on top. Brush liberally with oil and sprinkle over the lemon zest. Cover and cook in the preheated oven for 30 minutes.
8. Lower the oven temperature to 190°C/375°F/gas mark 5. Uncover and cook for 1 further hour until the potatoes are browned and tender.

RATATOUILLE AND CHEESE PASTRY PIE

For the pastry
170g/6oz plain flour
a pinch of salt
85g/3oz butter
55g/2oz Cheddar cheese, grated, or 2
    tablespoons freshly grated Parmesan cheese
about 2 tablespoons cold water
beaten egg or milk, to glaze

For the filling
2 tablespoons olive oil
1 onion, sliced
1 clove of garlic, crushed
1 green pepper, deseeded and chopped
1 yellow pepper, deseeded and chopped
1 courgette, sliced
1 small aubergine, diced
1 × 225g/8oz can of chopped tomatoes
salt and freshly ground black pepper
1 teaspoon dried basil
1 × 225g/8oz can of chickpeas or kidney beans

1. First make the filling: heat the oil in a frying pan, add the onion and fry over a low heat until softened. Stir in the garlic and fry for 1 further minute. Add the peppers, courgette, aubergine and tomatoes. Season with salt and pepper, stir in the basil and simmer for about 40 minutes until the vegetables are tender and the liquid reduced. Stir in the beans or chickpeas. Leave to cool.
2. Meanwhile, make the pastry: sift the flour and salt into a mixing bowl. Rub in the butter until the mixture resembles fine breadcrumbs. Stir in the cheese and season with salt and pepper. Add enough cold water to bind to a stiff dough.
3. Preheat the oven to 200°C/400°F/gas mark 6.
4. Roll out the pastry to a 30cm/12in circle and use to line a 20cm/8in spring-release cake tin. Press the pastry well into the corners and up the sides and allow the excess to overlap the edge of the tin.
5. When the ratatouille is cold, spoon it into the pastry case and fold the excess pastry over the edges. Brush with egg or milk, then bake in the preheated oven for 30 minutes until the pastry is browned and the ratatouille hot.

RATATOUILLE PIE WITH LEEK MASH

1 large aubergine, cut into small chunks
salt and freshly ground black pepper
3 tablespoons olive oil
1 medium onion, sliced
2 cloves of garlic, sliced
1 red pepper, deseeded and cut into small
    chunks
2 small courgettes, thickly sliced
1 heaped teaspoon coriander seeds, well
    crushed
450g/1lb vine-ripened tomatoes, peeled,
    deseeded and coarsely chopped (see page 22)
1 tablespoon chopped fresh flat-leaf parsley

For the leek mash
900g/2lb floury potatoes such as Maris Piper,
    cut into chunks
30g/1oz butter
1 large leek, trimmed and sliced
85g/3oz Cheddar cheese, coarsely grated

1. Toss the aubergine in a colander with ½ teaspoon of salt. Rest a plate on the top and leave to drain for 1 hour.
2. Pat the aubergine dry with kitchen paper. Heat the oil in a large saucepan, add the onion and fry over a low heat for 10 minutes. Stir in the garlic, aubergine and pepper, then cover and cook over a low heat for 20 minutes.
3. Add the courgettes to the pan with the coriander seeds, tomatoes and black pepper. Leave to simmer, uncovered, for 40 minutes or until the vegetables are tender and all the excess moisture has evaporated.
4. Meanwhile, make the topping: cook the potatoes in boiling salted water for 20 minutes or until tender. Melt the butter in a medium saucepan, add the leek and cook over a low heat for 3–4 minutes until tender.
5. Preheat the oven to 200°C/400°F/gas mark 6. Drain the potatoes and leave them until the steam has died down. Return them to the pan and mash until smooth. Beat in the cooked leek and cheese and season to taste with salt and pepper.
6. Stir the parsley into the ratatouille and

season to taste with salt and pepper. Turn it into a 1.1 litre/2 pint shallow ovenproof dish then spoon the leek mash evenly over the top. Bake in the preheated oven for 20–25 minutes until the top is crisp and golden.

FIG AND GOAT'S CHEESE TARTLETS

For the pastry
110g/4oz plain flour
a pinch of salt
55g/2oz butter, diced
1½ tablespoons sesame seeds
1 egg yolk
1–1½ tablespoons very cold water

For the filling
140g/5oz soft, rindless goat's cheese
4 tablespoons crème fraîche
2 tablespoons milk
2 egg yolks
4 dried figs, finely chopped
freshly grated nutmeg
salt and freshly ground black pepper
4 fresh figs, cut into quarters

1. Preheat the oven to 200°C/400°F/gas mark 6.
2. Make the pastry: sift the flour with the salt into a mixing bowl. Rub in the butter until the mixture resembles coarse breadcrumbs. Stir in the sesame seeds.
3. Make a well in the centre. Mix the egg yolk and water together and pour into the well. Bring the mixture together with a round-bladed knife to form a soft paste and use to line 4 deep, loose-based tartlet cases. Chill for 10 minutes.
4. Bake the tartlet cases blind in the preheated oven for 10–12 minutes (see page 22), then remove the baking beans and return to the oven for a further 2–3 minutes or until the pastry is crisp and dry. Lower the oven temperature to 180°C/350°F/gas mark 4.
5. Meanwhile, make the filling: mash the goat's cheese with a fork in a mixing bowl. Beat in the crème fraîche, milk and egg yolks. Stir in the chopped dried figs and season with a little

nutmeg, salt and pepper.
6. Divide the mixture between the pastry cases and arrange the fresh figs on top. Bake in the centre of the preheated oven for 12–15 minutes, or until the filling is just set. Allow to cool slightly before serving.

BAKED GOAT'S CHEESE WITH MANGO AND POMEGRANATE SALSA

olive oil, for brushing
4 × 110g/4oz goat's cheeses
2 handfuls of rocket
walnut or hazelnut oil
4 slices of quick walnut bread (see page 502)

For the salsa
1 small ripe mango
1 pomegranate
1 fresh red chilli, deseeded and finely chopped (see page 22)
½ red onion, finely chopped
juice of 1 lime
1 tablespoon chopped fresh coriander or mint
salt and freshly ground black pepper

1. Preheat the oven to 190°C/350°F/gas mark 5. Brush a baking tray with oil.
2. Place the goat's cheeses on the baking tray and bake in the preheated oven for 15–20 minutes until soft all the way through.
3. Meanwhile, make the mango and pomegranate salsa: peel the mango, slice the flesh neatly away from the stone and chop. Cut the pomegranate in half and ease out the seeds with a spoon handle or fork. Mix the mango and pomegranate seeds together and add the chilli, onion, lime juice and coriander. Season with salt and pepper and set aside.
4. Toss the rocket in a little walnut or hazelnut oil and arrange on 4 individual plates. Toast the bread lightly. Set the baked cheeses on top of the toast. Place one on each plate with a spoonful of salsa to the side.

PINEAPPLE WITH TARRAGON SABAYON

1 fresh pineapple
caster sugar

For the tarragon sabayon dressing
1 egg
3 tablespoons tarragon vinegar
2 tablespoons caster sugar
a pinch of salt
2 tablespoons cream, lightly whipped

1. Slice the pineapple in half lengthways, cutting through the fruit and the leaves. Using a grapefruit knife, cut out the flesh in one piece from each pineapple half. Remove and discard the woody core. Slice the flesh and return it rounded side up to the pineapple shell. Sprinkle with sugar and leave to stand while preparing the dressing.
2. Put the egg into a heatproof bowl with the vinegar, sugar and salt. Stand the bowl over a pan of simmering water and stir slowly until lightly thickened, then whisk continuously until thick and creamy. Allow to cool.
3. Stir in the cream and spoon the dressing over the pineapple.

WATERMELON AND FETA CHEESE SALAD

450g/1lb watermelon
110g/4oz feta cheese
1 bunch of watercress
½ red onion, thinly sliced
about 12 black kalamata olives
1 tablespoon pumpkin seeds, toasted (see page 22), to garnish

For the dressing
4 tablespoons olive oil
1 tablespoon lemon juice
a pinch of caster sugar
salt and freshly ground black pepper
1 tablespoon finely chopped fresh mint leaves

1. Cut the watermelon into wedges. Remove the rind and many of the seeds and cut the flesh into slices. Arrange the slices in an overlapping layer on a round serving plate.
2. Mix the dressing ingredients together.
3. Cut the feta cheese into small cubes. Trim and wash the watercress. Toss together with the onion and olives. Spoon the mixture over the watermelon slices. Grind over plenty of pepper and scatter with the pumpkin seeds before serving.

SQUASH

Acorn squash • Butternut squash • Patty pan squash •
Pumpkin • Vegetable marrow • Courgettes • Cucumbers

INTRODUCTION

Squash are fascinating for their wonderful variety of colour and diverse shapes. There are both summer and winter varieties. Winter squash appear in a bright splash of autumnal colour near Hallowe'en. Squash is a popular vegetable in the USA where it is roasted with butter and sugar and baked in pies for the traditional Thanksgiving dessert, and we are now seeing many more varieties regularly stocked in supermarkets in this country.

Squash have a mild but distinctive flavour. They are excellent for pairing with strong herbs and spices and give plenty of bulk in soups and stews. Winter varieties can have rock-hard skins and the flesh tends to be more fibrous. The tough skin can be left on for baking or roasting but if peeling is necessary it is best removed in segments. Winter squash should be hard, heavy, and sound hollow when knocked. If the skin is undamaged the squash can be stored in a cool place for several months.

Summer squash are young and eaten whole with skins. Choose small summer squash that are heavy for their size with smooth, unmarked skins. They will keep in the refrigerator for up to a week. Neither winter nor summer squash is suitable for freezing because of the high water content.

Many of the flowers of the squash family are edible and can be stuffed or shredded and added to eggs and soups, made into fritters or used raw in salads. They are not readily available but delicious if they can be found. Buy and eat the flowers on the same day.

Acorn squash is sweet-flavoured. It has a pretty, fluted shape and is just the right size and shape for stuffing.

Butternut squash is one of the most readily available varieties. It is pear-shaped with a cream-coloured skin and orange, nutty-flavoured flesh. Butternut is versatile but tastes best when baked. It is a good substitute for pumpkin.

Little Gem is dark green and about the size of a tennis ball. It matures to a rich yellow and has a delicate-flavoured flesh. Boil or steam whole and serve with butter and fresh herbs, or cut in half and stuff.

Patty pan or **custard marrows** come in a variety of delicate cream, green and yellow colours. They are similar in flavour to courgettes and can be used in the same way. Buy small firm patty pans no larger than 5cm/ 2in in diameter.

Pumpkins are native to America. They can grow to an enormous size, leaving hollows in the earth where they have grown. Medium-sized pumpkins are the best with a mild, sweet flavour. Puréed pumpkin can be frozen and used for soups or pies. Canned pumpkin purée is also good for pies. Pumpkin seeds are very nutritious and can be toasted and scattered in salads, on cereal or used in cakes or bread.

Spaghetti squash is rather like a plump marrow, growing to about 25cm/10in long. It has cream-coloured skin and flesh that resembles spaghetti. It is usually boiled in its skin and the flesh scooped out and served with butter and a spicy sauce.

Vegetable marrows tend to be bland but are good vehicles for stuffing or for carrying a well-flavoured sauce or spice mixture.

Courgette is a small, immature marrow. The flavour is more intense when the courgettes are young. They are available all year but are noticeably livelier-looking in summer. Most courgettes have dark green, shiny skins but they can also be yellow or lime green.

Cucumbers were cultivated as long ago as 10,000 BC. They have been bred to remove their natural bitterness but are still considered indigestible. They can be pickled or cooked but their refreshing qualities are best enjoyed raw.

Cucumbers are perfect for salads or in side dishes with yoghurt where their cooling effect will take the heat off spicy dishes. Choose firm, bright cucumbers and store in the refrigerator for up to a week.

Some **edible gourds** can be used like cucumber. Bitter melons, angled loofahs and chayote can be found in ethnic stores and specialist supermarkets. The tough skins are best removed. Excessive bitterness can be removed by salting.

ACORN SQUASH AND COURGETTE SOUP WITH PESTO AND CRÈME FRAÎCHE

SERVES 6

110g/4oz butter
2 medium onions, chopped
560g/1¼lb peeled acorn squash, deseeded and
    cut into small chunks
3 courgettes, trimmed and sliced
1.1 litres/2 pints summer vegetable stock (see
    page 530)
3 tablespoons pesto (see page 526)
1 tablespoon lemon juice
salt and freshly ground black pepper

To garnish
4 tablespoons crème fraîche
1 tablespoon pinenuts, toasted (see page 22)
a handful of small fresh basil leaves

1. Melt the butter in a large saucepan. Add the onions and cook over a low heat for 5–7 minutes until soft and lightly golden. Add the squash, courgettes and stock and bring to the boil, then lower the heat, cover and simmer for 20–25 minutes until the vegetables are soft.
2. Liquidize the soup in batches in a food processor or blender, briefly, so that it retains a slightly chunky texture. Return the soup to the pan and add the pesto and lemon juice. Season to taste with salt and pepper.
3. Ladle the soup into warmed soup bowls. Garnish each with a spoonful of the crème fraîche, toasted pinenuts and basil leaves.

ROASTED WEDGES OF ACORN SQUASH WITH FENNEL SEEDS AND GARLIC

2 × 450–675g/1–1½lb acorn squash
2 teaspoons coriander seeds
½ teaspoon fennel seeds
1 clove of garlic, finely chopped
1 teaspoon fresh thyme leaves
1 teaspoon chopped fresh rosemary
½ teaspoon dried red chilli flakes
1 teaspoon sea salt flakes
1 teaspoon black peppercorns, coarsely crushed
3 tablespoons olive oil

1. Preheat the oven to 200°C/400°F/gas mark 6. Cut each squash into 6–8 wedges and scoop out the seeds and fibres with a teaspoon.
2. Put the coriander and fennel seeds into a mortar or a spice grinder and work to a coarse powder. Tip into a roasting tin and add the garlic, thyme, rosemary, chilli flakes, salt, pepper and oil. Mix together well.
3. Add the wedges of squash to the roasting tin and turn them over a few times in the spice mixture until well coated. Turn them all cut side up and roast in the preheated oven for 30–40 minutes until tender. Serve hot.

STUFFED ACORN SQUASH

30g/1oz butter, plus extra for greasing
2 medium acorn squash
85ml/3fl oz summer vegetable stock (see
    page 530)
55g/2oz couscous
1 medium onion, chopped
1 clove of garlic, crushed
a pinch of ground cinnamon
¼ teaspoon ground cumin
1 × 150g/5oz can of prunes
1 tart green dessert apple
15g/½oz raisins
30g/1oz pinenuts, toasted (see page 22)
1 teaspoon fresh thyme leaves
lemon juice
salt and freshly ground black pepper

1. Preheat the oven to 180°C/350°F/gas mark 4.
Grease a baking sheet with butter.
2. Cut the squash in half crossways and remove
all the seeds and fibres with a teaspoon. Place
the squash cut side down on a baking tray. Bake
in the preheated oven for 30 minutes. Meanwhile,
pour the stock over the couscous and leave to
soak.
3. Melt the butter in a frying pan and when
foaming, add the onion and fry over a low heat
until softened. Add the garlic and spices and fry
for 1 further minute. Drain the prunes, remove
the stones and chop the flesh roughly. Quarter,
core and chop the apple. Stir the prunes, apple
and raisins into the onion mixture and cook for
a few more minutes until the apple is soft.
4. Fork through the couscous to loosen it and
stir into the pan. Stir in the pinenuts and thyme.
Season with lemon juice and salt and pepper to
taste and spoon the mixture into the squash
halves. Place the squash on the baking tray and
cover with kitchen foil. Bake in the hot oven for
20 minutes until piping hot.

AMERICAN-STYLE BAKED SQUASH

2 small acorn or butternut squash or ½
    pumpkin
55g/2oz butter
55g/2oz soft light brown sugar or 2 tablespoons
    clear honey
a pinch of dried red chilli flakes
salt and freshly ground black pepper
lime juice

1. Preheat the oven to 190°C/375°F/gas mark 5.
2. Cut the squash or pumpkin in half or into
quarters, depending on size. Use a teaspoon to
scrape out the seeds and fibres. Place the squash
or pumpkin cut side up in a roasting tin.
3. Melt the butter together with the sugar or
honey in a small pan. Stir in the chilli flakes and
season with salt and pepper. Pour over the
squash and bake in the preheated oven for
about 40 minutes, basting from time to time,
until the squash is tender and the outside is
caramelized and golden-brown. Add a dash of
lime juice before serving.

CURRIED BUTTERNUT SQUASH AND PEANUT BUTTER SOUP

900g/2lb butternut squash
30g/1oz butter
1 medium onion, thinly sliced
2 sticks of celery, thinly sliced
2 teaspoons mild curry powder
860ml/1½ pints summer vegetable stock (see page 530)
5 tablespoons crunchy peanut butter
290ml/½ pint milk
1–2 tablespoons lemon juice
salt and freshly ground black pepper
55g/2oz salted roasted peanuts, coarsely chopped, to garnish

1. Cut the squash into wedges and scoop out the seeds and fibres with a teaspoon. Peel off the skin and cut the flesh into small chunks.
2. Melt the butter in a large saucepan. Add the onion and celery and cook over a low heat for 5 minutes until soft and lightly browned. Stir in the curry powder and cook for 1 further minute. Add the squash and stock and bring to the boil. Cover and simmer for 20 minutes or until the squash is very tender.
3. Purée the soup in batches with the peanut butter in a food processor or blender. Return the soup to the rinsed-out pan and stir in the milk, lemon juice and salt and pepper to taste. Bring slowly back to the boil then lower the heat and leave to simmer for 5 minutes. Serve in warmed soup bowls, sprinkled with the peanuts.

SQUASH TOAD IN THE HOLE

450g/1lb butternut squash, peeled and deseeded
2 tablespoons olive oil
1 red onion, sliced

For the batter
170g/6oz plain flour
a large pinch of salt
2 eggs
425ml/¾ pint milk and water, mixed half and half
2 teaspoons chopped fresh thyme

To serve
baked tomato relish (see page 509)

1. Preheat the oven to 220°C/425°F/gas mark 7.
2. First make the batter: sift the flour and salt into a mixing bowl and make a well in the centre. Break the eggs into the well, add a little of the milk and mix with a wooden spoon or whisk. Gradually add more of the milk, drawing in the flour from the sides until the mixture reaches the consistency of thick cream. Beat well and stir in the remaining milk. (The batter can also be made by whizzing all the ingredients together in a food processor or blender.) Stir in the thyme and set aside.
3. Slice the squash. Put the oil into a small roasting tin and heat on top of the stove. Add the onion and cook over a low heat until soft. Increase the heat, add the squash and toss for 2 minutes. Pour in the batter and bake in the preheated oven for 30–40 minutes until risen and golden-brown. Serve immediately, with the baked tomato relish handed separately.

BUTTERNUT SQUASH AND RED PEPPER STEW

2 tablespoons olive oil
340g/12oz butternut squash, peeled, deseeded
  and chopped
1–2 cloves of garlic, crushed
1 small red chilli, deseeded and roughly
  chopped (see page 22)
1–2 tablespoons caraway seeds
salt and freshly ground black pepper
½ red onion, roughly chopped
½ bulb of fennel, cored and roughly diced
1 red pepper, deseeded and diced
110g/4oz carrots, cut on the diagonal
290ml/½ pint spicy vegetable stock (see
  page 531)
1 tablespoon roughly chopped fresh coriander
1 tablespoon roughly chopped fresh parsley

1. Heat the oil in a large saucepan, add the squash, garlic, chilli and caraway seeds and season with salt and pepper. Turn in the oil for a few minutes. Add the remaining vegetables, cover and cook over a low heat for 5–8 minutes until beginning to soften.
2. Add the stock, cover again and continue to simmer until the vegetables are soft but still holding their shape.
3. Remove the lid and reduce some of the liquid, leaving enough to provide a thin gravy. Season to taste and add the herbs.

NOTE: This is delicious with hot buttered couscous.

ROASTED BUTTERNUT SQUASH WITH SOFT GOAT'S CHEESE

2 small butternut squash or similar
1 tablespoon oil
salt and freshly ground black pepper

For the filling
85–140g/3–5oz soft goat's cheese
3 sun-dried tomatoes, roughly chopped
30g/1oz pinenuts

1. Preheat the oven to 220°C/425°F/gas mark 7.
2. Peel the squash and cut it in half lengthways. Scoop out the seeds and score a trellis pattern on the cut surface of each piece of squash, then brush with oil and season well with salt and pepper. Place on a baking tray.
3. Roast at the top of the preheated oven for 45–50 minutes until the squash is soft.
4. Make the filling: combine the filling ingredients together in a small bowl and season to taste with salt and pepper. Spoon the mixture into the cavities of the squash and return to the oven for a further 10–15 minutes or until the pinenuts begin to brown. Serve immediately.

NOTE: Plain goat's cheese or goat's cheese flavoured with celery seeds may be used.

BUTTERNUT SQUASH WITH COCONUT AND MANGO

2 tablespoons olive oil
1 red onion, thinly sliced
2 cloves of garlic, crushed
1 red chilli, deseeded and sliced (see page 22)
1 leek, trimmed and thinly sliced
4 sticks of celery, thinly sliced
340g/12oz butternut squash, peeled, deseeded and cut into chunks
salt and freshly ground black pepper
1 teaspoon korma curry powder
150ml/¼ pint spicy vegetable stock (see page 531)
425ml/¾ pint coconut milk
1 large mango, peeled and sliced
30g/1oz blanched almonds, toasted (optional) (see page 22)
1 tablespoon roughly chopped fresh coriander
1 tablespoon roughly chopped fresh basil

1. Heat the oil in a large saucepan, add the onion, garlic and chilli and cook over a low heat for 3–4 minutes. Add the leek, celery and squash and season with salt and pepper. Cover and cook for 8–10 minutes, stirring regularly.
2. Add the curry powder and cook for a few more minutes, stirring carefully. Add the stock and simmer gently for 5–10 minutes.
3. Add the coconut milk and continue to simmer until the vegetables are soft and the sauce has reduced. (If the vegetables are cooked first, they can be removed to a warmed serving bowl while the sauce is reducing to prevent the squash from breaking up.)
4. Add the mango slices, toasted almonds, if used, and some of the chopped herbs and warm through.
5. Place in a warmed serving bowl and garnish with the remaining herbs before serving.

SAUTÉED BUTTERNUT SQUASH WITH MINT

450g/1lb butternut squash
olive oil, for frying
3 cloves of garlic, chopped
salt and freshly ground black pepper
cayenne pepper
1 teaspoon paprika
2 tablespoons chopped fresh mint
2 teaspoons caster sugar
2 tablespoons tarragon or white wine vinegar

1. Peel the squash and scoop out the seeds and fibres with a teaspoon. Cut the flesh into slices about 5mm/¼in thick.
2. Heat about 3–4 tablespoons oil in a heavy frying pan. Add the squash in batches and sauté briskly until golden-brown and tender, seasoning with a sprinkling of garlic, salt, pepper, cayenne and paprika. When the squash is cooked, transfer it to a shallow serving dish and scatter the mint over the top.
3. When all the squash is cooked, add the sugar to the pan juices and set over a medium heat until it has melted and caramelized. As soon as the sugar has turned golden-brown, pour in the vinegar and allow to boil up. Stir to remove all the juices and sediment from the base of the pan and pour over the cooked squash. Serve hot at room temperature.

SAUTÉED PATTY PAN SQUASHES WITH PINENUTS

450g/1lb yellow and green patty pan squashes
2 tablespoons olive oil
1 clove of garlic, crushed
3 tablespoons pinenuts, toasted (see page 22)
1 tablespoon chopped fresh savory or thyme
1 tablespoon chopped fresh mint
1 tablespoon lemon juice
salt and freshly ground black pepper

1. Wash, top and tail the squashes. Cut them in half or into quarters, depending on the size.
2. Heat the oil in a large frying or sauté pan. Add the garlic and squash and cook over a low heat for 5–10 minutes or until just cooked and beginning to take on a little colour.
3. Add the pinenuts, herbs and lemon juice. Mix well and season with salt and pepper. Serve immediately.

TWO WAYS WITH PATTY PAN SQUASH

These recipes also work well with baby aubergines.

450g/1lb patty pan squash

Wash the squash and steam for about 15 minutes or microwave on high power for about 5 minutes until tender.

With herbs and butter
55g/2oz butter
grated zest and juice of ½ lemon
1 tablespoon chopped fresh chives
1 tablespoon chopped fresh chervil
salt and freshly ground black pepper

Melt the butter in a saucepan. Add the lemon zest, juice and herbs. Season to taste with salt and pepper, pour over the squash and serve immediately.

With tomatoes, basil and fromage frais
30g/1oz butter
110g/4oz cherry tomatoes, halved
salt and freshly ground black peper
caster sugar
2 tablespoons fromage frais
1 tablespoon shredded fresh basil leaves

Melt the butter in a heavy frying pan. Add the cooked squash and tomatoes and fry briskly for about 5 minutes. Season to taste with salt, pepper and sugar. Stir in the fromage frais and basil and cook briefly. Serve immediately.

ROASTED PATTY PAN SQUASH AND SWEET POTATO

225g/8oz patty pan squash
225g/8oz sweet potato
1 red onion, quartered
3 tablespoons olive oil
2 tablespoons soy sauce
1 teaspoon ground cumin
salt and freshly ground black pepper

To garnish
30g/1oz pumpkin seeds
chopped fresh mint

To serve
lime soured cream (see chilli beans, page 340) or
*   roasted garlic mayonnaise (see page 512)*

1. Preheat the oven to 220°C/420°F/gas mark 7.
2. Cut the squash in half lengthways. Cut the sweet potato into chunks about the same size as the squash.
3. Put a roasting tin to heat in the oven. Whisk the oil, soy sauce and cumin together in a large bowl. Add all the vegetables and toss until they are completely coated. Season with salt and pepper.
4. Spread the vegetables in a single layer in the hot roasting tin and bake in the preheated oven for 20–30 minutes until tender, caramelized and slightly charred at the edges. Scatter with pumpkin seeds and mint and hand the lime soured cream or garlic mayonnaise separately.

PUMPKIN SOUP WITH BUTTERMILK

55g/2oz butter
1 large onion, sliced
450g/1lb pumpkin, peeled, deseeded and
*   chopped*
salt and freshly ground black pepper
freshly grated nutmeg
290ml/½ pint summer vegetable stock (see
*   page 530)*
2 teaspoons chopped fresh tarragon
570ml/1 pint buttermilk

To garnish
150ml/¼ pint double cream
chopped fresh parsley

1. Melt the butter in a large saucepan. Add the onion and fry over a low heat until softened. Add the pumpkin, cover and cook gently for 10 minutes. Season with salt, pepper and nutmeg. Pour in the stock and bring to the boil, then lower the heat and simmer for 30 minutes.
2. Purée the soup in a food processor or blender. Return to the rinsed-out pan and bring to the boil. Add the tarragon and buttermilk and reheat without boiling. Adjust the seasoning to taste and serve in warmed soup bowls, each topped with a swirl of cream and a sprinkling of parsley.

PUMPKIN AND TARRAGON COBBLER

675g/1½lb pumpkin
30g/1oz butter
1 large onion, sliced
1 × 400g/14oz can of tomatoes
1 tablespoon black treacle
2 tablespoons soy sauce
1 × 400g/14oz can of cannellini beans, rinsed and drained
290ml/½ pint winter vegetable stock (see page 530)
salt and freshly ground black pepper
1 tablespoon chopped fresh tarragon

For the cobbler
170g/6oz self-raising wholemeal flour, plus extra for rolling
½ teaspoon salt
85g/3oz butter
about 150ml/¼ pint milk or buttermilk, plus extra to glaze

1. Peel the pumpkin and remove the seeds and fibres with a teaspoon. Cut the flesh into 2.5cm/1in cubes.
2. Heat the butter in a saucepan. Add the onions and fry over a low heat until soft and golden-brown. Stir in the pumpkin, tomatoes, treacle, soy sauce, beans and stock. Season with salt and pepper and simmer until the beans and pumpkin are tender and the liquid reduced and well flavoured. Stir in the tarragon. Spoon the pumpkin mixture into an ovenproof dish.
3. Preheat the oven to 200°C/400°F/gas mark 6.
4. Make the cobbler: put the flour and salt into a mixing bowl and rub in the butter until the mixture resembles breadcrumbs. Bind to a soft dough with the milk or buttermilk. On a floured worktop press the dough out to a 2.5cm/1in thickness. Cut out rounds with a 5cm/2in pastry cutter. Arrange the rounds in an overlapping layer on top of the pumpkin. Brush with a little milk or buttermilk and bake in the preheated oven for 20–30 minutes until the cobbler is well risen and golden-brown.

THAI RED PUMPKIN AND COCONUT CURRY

675g/1½lb pumpkin
3 tablespoons sunflower oil
1 × 397ml/14fl oz can of coconut milk
2 tablespoons light soy sauce
2 teaspoons soft light brown sugar
juice of 1 lime
2 kaffir lime leaves (optional)
salt
1 × 200g/7oz can of bamboo shoots, rinsed and drained
15g/½oz fresh basil leaves, Thai holy basil if possible

For the red curry paste
5 medium-hot red Dutch chillies, stalks removed and roughly chopped
2.5cm/1in piece of fresh root ginger, peeled and roughly chopped
2 stalks of lemongrass, outer leaves discarded and the core roughly chopped
6 cloves of garlic, roughly chopped
3 shallots, roughly chopped
1 teaspoon ground coriander
1 teaspoon ground cumin
2 teaspoons paprika
1 tablespoon sunflower oil

To serve
lemongrass and coconut rice (see page 357) or plain steamed basmati or Thai jasmine rice (see page 352)

1. First make the red curry paste: put all the ingredients into a food processor and blend until smooth.
2. Peel the pumpkin, scoop out the seeds and fibres with a teaspoon and cut the flesh into thick, neat slices.
3. Heat the oil in a large saucepan. Add the curry paste and fry over a low heat for 1–2 minutes, stirring from time to time, until the paste begins to separate from the oil. Add the coconut milk, soy sauce, sugar, lime juice and kaffir lime leaves, if used, and bring to the boil.
4. Stir in the prepared pumpkin and ½

teaspoon salt, cover and simmer for 10–12 minutes or until the pumpkin is tender.

5. Add the bamboo shoots and simmer for 1 minute. Add the basil leaves and adjust the seasoning if necessary. Serve with lemongrass and coconut rice or plain steamed rice.

WHOLE BAKED SQUASH

This dish is perfect to serve on Bonfire Night and is ideal for a buffet.

1 × 900g/2lb pumpkin or other large round
   squash
225g/8oz ricotta cheese
225g/8oz mascarpone
55g/2oz Parmesan cheese, freshly grated
½ teaspoon freshly grated nutmeg
½ teaspoon salt
½ teaspoon freshly ground pepper

1. Preheat the oven to 180°C/350°F/gas mark 4. Wash the squash and bake in the preheated oven for about 45–60 minutes until almost tender.

2. Beat the ricotta, mascarpone and three-quarters of the Parmesan cheese together with the nutmeg, salt and pepper.

3. When the squash is cooked, cut a slice off the top to expose the seeds. Hollow out the centre, discarding all the seeds and fibres. Fill the centre with the ricotta mixture and sprinkle the remaining Parmesan cheese on top. Bake for another 30–40 minutes until the squash is completely cooked and the filling is golden and just set. Leave to stand in a warm place for 10 minutes before serving.

THREE SQUASH LASAGNE

2 tablespoons olive oil
2 onions, sliced
1 small butternut squash
450g/1lb pumpkin
2 courgettes
2 cloves of garlic, crushed

4 cardamom pods, crushed
salt and freshly ground black pepper
1 tablespoon bottled green peppercorns,
   drained
225g/8oz soft goat's cheese
4–5 sheets of fresh of ready-to-use lasagne

For the topping
30g/1oz cornflour
150ml/¼ pint milk
150ml/¼ pint Greek yoghurt
150ml/¼ pint double cream
freshly grated nutmeg
1 tablespoon freshly grated Parmesan cheese

1. Heat the oil in a frying pan with a lid. Add the onions and fry over a low heat until soft and golden-brown.

2. Meanwhile, peel the butternut squash and pumpkin and remove all the seeds and fibres with a teaspoon. Cut the squash, pumpkin and courgettes into 1cm/½in cubes.

3. Add the garlic and cardamom pods to the pan and fry for 1 minute. Stir in the squash, pumpkin and courgettes and season with salt and pepper. Cover and cook over a low heat for 20–30 minutes until the vegetables are tender. Remove the cardamom pods and stir in the green peppercorns.

4. Preheat the oven to 190°C/375°F/gas mark 5.

5. Cut away any rind from the cheese and slice as thinly as possible. Spoon one-third of the vegetable mixture over the base of a deep ovenproof dish. Arrange half of the cheese on top of this and cover with sheets of lasagne. Repeat the layers and finish with a layer of squash.

6. Make the sauce: blend the cornflour and 2 tablespoons of the milk together in a saucepan. Stir in the yoghurt and then the remaining milk. Bring to the boil, stirring all the time, and allow to bubble for 2 minutes. Stir in the cream and reheat. Season wih salt, pepper and nutmeg. Pour over the lasagne and sprinkle with the Parmesan cheese. Bake in the preheated oven for 30–40 minutes until bubbling and golden-brown on top.

SQUASH AND SPINACH GRATIN WITH RICOTTA CUSTARD

1 tablespoon olive oil
1 leek, trimmed and thinly sliced
1 clove of garlic, crushed
1 bay leaf
salt and freshly ground black pepper
225g/8oz pumpkin or butternut squash, peeled, deseeded and cut into chunks
340g/12oz courgettes, trimmed and thickly sliced
30g/1oz butter
900g/2lb spinach
freshly grated nutmeg

For the custard
225g/8oz ricotta cheese
2 eggs, beaten
55g/2oz Parmesan cheese, freshly grated

1. Cook the spinach (see page 25)
2. Heat the oil in a saucepan and add the leek, garlic and bay leaf. Season with salt and pepper and cook over a low heat for 1–2 minutes. Add the squash and courgettes and cook for a further 5–8 minutes or until the vegetables are soft but still holding their shape. Discard the bay leaf and transfer the vegetables to an ovenproof dish.
3. Preheat the oven to 180°C/350°F/gas mark 4.
4. Melt the butter in a small frying pan, reheat the spinach in the hot butter for 1–2 minutes and season with salt, pepper and nutmeg to taste. Spoon over the vegetables in the dishes.
5. Make the custard: mix the ricotta cheese and eggs together in a bowl. Add all but 15g/½oz of the Parmesan cheese, season with salt and pepper and mix thoroughly. Pour evenly over the vegetables in the dish and sprinkle with the remaining Parmesan cheese.
6. Bake in the centre of the preheated oven for about 20 minutes or until the custard has risen and is golden-brown. Leave to stand in a warm place for 10 minutes before serving.

MARROW DAUPHINOISE AU GRATIN

1 medium marrow
salt and freshly ground black pepper
15g/½oz butter
1 medium onion, sliced
1 large clove of garlic, crushed
150ml/¼ pint double cream
45g/1½oz Cheddar cheese, grated

1. Preheat the oven to 200°C/400°F/gas mark 6.
2. Peel the marrow and cut it in half, then cut each half in half lengthways. Scoop out the seeds and fibres, using a teaspoon, and discard. Cut the flesh into 1cm/½in slices. Lay them on a wire rack over a tray and sprinkle with a little salt. Leave for 30 minutes to degorge, then rinse well.
3. Steam the marrow slices for 7 minutes or until just beginning to soften. Do not overcook.
4. Meanwhile, melt the butter in a small saucepan, add the onion and garlic and cook over a low heat for 10 minutes or until the onion has softened. Do not allow it to brown.
5. Season the cream with salt and pepper.
6. Put a layer of the steamed marrow slices in the base of a shallow gratin dish, cover with the onion and garlic mixture and cover with the remaining marrow slices. Pour over the seasoned cream and scatter with the cheese.
7. Bake in the preheated oven for 15–20 minutes until the cream is bubbling and the cheese is golden-brown.

MARROW STUFFED WITH COUSCOUS

85g/3oz couscous
85g/3oz sultanas
scant 150ml/¼ pint boiling water
1 marrow, weighing about 900g/2lb
1 tablespoon olive oil
1 medium onion, chopped
2 cloves of garlic, crushed
2.5cm/1in piece of fresh root ginger, peeled and
    finely chopped
1 teaspoon ground cinnamon
1 teaspoon ground cumin
1 teaspoon paprika
1 teaspoon ground turmeric
450g/1lb ripe tomatoes, peeled and deseeded
    (see page 22)
salt and freshly ground black pepper
2 teaspoons clear honey
30g/1oz pinenuts, toasted (see page 22)

1. Preheat the oven to 190°C/375°F/gas mark 5.
2. Soak the couscous and sultanas in the
boiling water for about 10 minutes, until all the
liquid is absorbed.
3. Meanwhile, cut the marrow in half
lengthways and scoop out the seeds and fibres,
using a teaspoon. Lay the two halves skin side
down in an ovenproof dish or roasting tin.
4. Heat the oil in a frying pan, add the onion
and fry over a low heat until soft and
transparent. Add the garlic and ginger and fry
for a further 2 minutes. Stir in the cinnamon,
cumin, paprika and turmeric and fry for a few
minutes longer.
5. Chop the tomatoes and add to the pan.
Season with salt and pepper and simmer for 5
minutes to allow the juice to evaporate. Add the
honey, pinenuts and soaked couscous. Adjust
the seasoning to taste.
6. Pile the couscous mixture into the marrow
halves. Cover with kitchen foil and bake in the
preheated oven for 40–50 minutes until the
marrow is tender. Serve hot.

CARAMELIZED MARROW WITH ROASTED PUMPKIN SEEDS

3 tablespoons pumpkin seeds
1 tablespoon soft light brown sugar
1 tablespoon olive oil
2 onions, thinly sliced
30g/1oz butter
30g/1oz caster sugar
1 marrow, about 900g/2lb, peeled, deseeded
    and cut into 2.5cm/1in cubes
3 tablespoons white wine vinegar
1 tablespoon finely chopped fresh sage
salt and freshly ground black pepper

1. Preheat the oven to 180°C/350°F/gas mark 4.
Mix the pumpkin seeds and brown sugar
together and spread out on a baking tray. Roast
in the oven for 7–10 minutes or until lightly
browned. Remove from the oven and allow to
cool.
2. Heat the oil in a large frying pan with a lid.
Add the onions, cover and cook over a low heat
for 10–15 minutes until soft but not coloured.
3. Add the butter, caster sugar and marrow to
the pan and mix well. Cook covered for 10–15
minutes until the marrow is just tender.
4. Increase the heat and pour the vinegar into
the pan. Cook over a high heat until the excess
moisture has evaporated and the marrow is
lightly browned.
5. Add the sage, salt, pepper and roasted
pumpkin seeds and serve immediately.

COURGETTE SOUP WITH PASTA AND HERBS

450g/1lb courgettes, trimmed
2 tablespoons olive oil
1 large onion, finely chopped
3 cloves of garlic, chopped
720ml/1¼ pints summer vegetable stock (see page 530)
150ml/¼ pint white vermouth or dry white wine
salt and freshly ground black pepper
½ teaspoon dried red chilli flakes
1 tablespoon chopped fresh oregano
55g/2oz small pasta shapes
1 tablespoon chopped fresh chives
1 tablespoon shredded fresh basil

To serve
Parmesan cheese shavings
Parmesan scones (see page 533)

1. Cut the courgettes into 1cm/½in cubes. Heat the oil in a large saucepan, add the onion and garlic and fry over a low heat until soft and transparent. Add the courgettes, cover and leave to sweat for 5 minutes.
2. Pour in the stock and vermouth or wine. Season with salt and pepper and add the chilli flakes and oregano. Simmer for 15–20 minutes until the courgettes are tender. Stir in the pasta shapes and simmer for a further 5–10 minutes until cooked.
3. Add the chives and basil to the soup and check the seasoning. Serve topped with a few Parmesan cheese shavings and hand the scones separately.

COURGETTE AND WATERCRESS SOUP

SERVES 4–6

2 tablespoons olive oil
900g/2lb courgettes, trimmed and sliced
1 onion, sliced
1 leek, trimmed and sliced
salt and freshly ground black pepper
1.1 litres/2 pints summer vegetable stock (see page 530)
85g/3oz watercress, washed, tough stalks removed

1. Heat the oil in a large saucepan and add the courgettes, onion and leek. Season with salt and pepper, cover and cook over a low heat for 5–8 minutes until soft.
2. Add the stock and bring to the boil, then lower the heat and simmer gently for 10–15 minutes.
3. Add the watercress to the hot soup. Cook for a further 2–3 minutes, then purée in a food processor or blender and adjust the seasoning to taste. Do not reheat the soup or keep it warm for too long or the courgettes and watercress will lose their colour.

COURGETTE STICKS WITH TOASTED SESAME SEEDS AND GINGER DIPPING SAUCE

These are ideal for serving with pre-dinner drinks.

2 courgettes
55g/2oz sesame seeds

For the dipping sauce
1 tablespoon sweet soy sauce
juice of ½ lemon
1 tablespoon water
1cm/½in piece of fresh root ginger, peeled and grated
1 tablespoon soft light brown sugar
½ red chilli, deseeded and finely chopped (see page 22)
2 teaspoons chopped fresh coriander

1. First make the dipping sauce: mix all the ingredients together and leave to stand for 30 minutes.
2. Trim the courgettes and cut them lengthways into sticks about 5cm/2in long.
3. Toast the sesame seeds in a dry, heavy frying pan until light golden-brown. If they become too dark the flavour will be bitter and overpowering.
4. Put the dipping sauce and sesame seeds in two small bowls and set in the middle of a serving dish. Arrange the courgette sticks around them. The courgettes are eaten like crudités, first dipped in the sauce and then the sesame seeds.

COURGETTE TIMBALES

oil, for brushing
55g/2oz butter
340g/12oz courgettes, grated
1 leek, trimmed and thinly sliced
1 clove of garlic, crushed
salt and freshly ground black pepper
1 tablespoon roughly chopped fresh basil
freshly grated nutmeg
55g/2oz Parmesan cheese, freshly grated
4 eggs, beaten
150ml/¼ pint milk

1. Preheat the oven to 180°C/350°F/gas mark 4. Brush 4 ramekin dishes or dariole moulds lightly with oil and put a disc of oiled greaseproof paper in the bottom of each.
2. Melt the butter in a saucepan and add the courgettes, leek and garlic. Season with salt and pepper, cover and cook over a low heat for 3–4 minutes until softened but not browned. Increase the heat a little and allow any remaining liquid to evaporate, stirring continuously to prevent burning.
3. Add the basil and season with nutmeg, then stir in the cheese. Set aside to cool slightly.
4. Add the eggs to the mixture and mix thoroughly, gradually adding the milk as you do so. Divide the mixture equally between the prepared moulds.
5. Bake in a bain-marie in the preheated oven for 10–15 minutes or until the timbales are set and an even golden-brown. Once cooked, remove from the water and carefully run a knife around the edge of the mould. Leave to cool for a few minutes before turning out on to 4 individual plates. Remove the greaseproof paper discs.

CARIBBEAN COURGETTE, PUMPKIN AND SPINACH COCONUT CURRY

3 courgettes, trimmed
450g/1lb pumpkin or squash, peeled and
 deseeded
340g/12oz spinach
3 tablespoons vegetable oil
290ml/½ pint coconut milk
150ml/¼ pint spicy vegetable stock (see
 page 531)
salt and freshly ground black pepper

For the spice paste
1 teaspoon fennel seeds
1 teaspoon cumin seeds
1 teaspoon coriander seeds
½ cinnamon stick
1 red chilli, deseeded (see page 22)
4 cloves of garlic
1 medium onion, quartered

To serve
basmati rice (see page 352) or couscous (see
 page 382)

1. First make the spice paste: grind the dry
spices in a mortar or spice grinder. Roughly cut
up the chilli and garlic. Put into a food
processor or blender together with the spices
and onion and process to a smooth paste.
2. Cut the courgettes in half lengthways and
then crossways into 2.5cm/1in pieces. Cut the
pumpkin or squash into pieces about the same
size as the courgettes. Remove any tough stalks
from the spinach and wash thoroughly. Young
leaves can be left whole but large leaves should
be torn up roughly.
3. Heat the oil in a large saucepan. Add the
spice paste and fry for 2 minutes. Add the
coconut milk and stock and bring to the boil,
then lower the heat, stir in the pumpkin and
courgette, season with salt and pepper and
simmer for 15 minutes until tender. Add the
spinach and reheat. Serve with basmati rice or
couscous.

COURGETTE, PEPPER AND POTATO EMPANADILLA

An empanadilla is a Spanish pie or pastry. This
recipe is for a large one but it can also be made
into small empanadillas to serve as a snack or
tapa.

For the filling
1 medium potato
2 tablespoons olive oil
½ medium onion, sliced
1–2 cloves of garlic, crushed
½ teaspoon ground allspice
½ teaspoon ground turmeric
½ teaspoon paprika
1 courgette, trimmed and diced
1 red pepper, deseeded and thinly sliced
1 red chilli, deseeded and chopped (see page 22)
salt and freshly ground black pepper
1 tablespoon roughly chopped flat-leaf parsley
lemon juice

For the pastry
butter, for greasing
285g/10oz plain flour
½ teaspoon salt
4 tablespoons olive oil
2 tablespoons milk
150ml/¼ pint water
flour, for rolling
beaten egg, to glaze

1. First make the filling: peel the potato and cut
into 5mm/¼in dice. Heat the oil in a frying
pan, add the onion and fry until softened, then
add the garlic and spices and fry for 1 further
minute. Stir in the potato and fry gently until
almost cooked. Stir in the courgette, pepper and
chilli. Season with salt and pepper and continue
to cook over a low heat, stirring from time to
time until all the vegetables are soft. Add the
parsley and a dash of lemon juice and leave to
cool.
2. Preheat the oven to 200°C/400°F/gas mark 6.
Grease a baking tray with butter.
3. To make the pastry: sift the flour and salt
into a mixing bowl and make a well in the

centre. Put the oil, milk and water into a small saucepan and heat to blood temperature Gradually pour into the flour, working together to form a soft dough. Knead briefly until smooth and elastic.

4. Roll out the pastry thinly on a well-floured worktop and cut out 2 × 20cm/8in circles, using a plate as a template. Place one circle on the baking tray and pile the filling on top. Dampen the edges with water. Cover with the second circle and seal the edges with a fork. Make two slashes on top to allow the steam to escape. Brush with beaten egg and bake in the preheated oven for 35 minutes until golden-brown.

NOTE: For small empanadillas, cut the pastry into 10cm/4in rounds, add a spoonful of filling and fold in half and bake for about 20 minutes.

COURGETTE, PARMESAN AND SAGE PASTIES

MAKES 6

225g/8oz flour quantity shortcrust pastry (see page 521)
flour, for rolling
beaten egg, to glaze
sesame seeds

For the filling
1 tablespoon oil
1 onion, very finely chopped
1 medium potato, cut into 5mm/¼in dice
2–3 tablespoons summer vegetable stock (see page 530) or water
225g/8oz courgettes, trimmed and cut into 5mm/¼in dice
about 12 fresh sage leaves, shredded
salt and freshly ground black pepper
110g/4oz Parmesan cheese, freshly grated

1. Preheat the oven to 190°C/375°F/gas mark 5.
2. First make the filling: heat the oil in a frying pan, add the onion and cook over a low heat for 5 minutes. Add the potato and stock or water

and cook for a further 10 minutes.
3. Stir in the courgettes and sage and season with salt and pepper. Cook for about 10 minutes until the courgettes are tender and the liquid has evaporated. Remove from the heat, stir in the Parmesan cheese and allow to cool completely.
4. Roll the pastry out on a floured worktop. Divide into 6 equal pieces. Roll each piece out fairly thinly and cut into a 12.5cm/5in circle, using a plate as a template.
5. Spoon the filling down the centre of each pastry circle. Dampen the edges with water and bring together to join at the top. Seal, crimping the edges with the fingers and thumb.
6. Brush the pasties with beaten egg and sprinkle with sesame seeds. Bake in the preheated oven for 20–25 minutes or until crisp and brown.

COURGETTE AND CHEESE FLAN

225g/8oz flour quantity shortcrust pastry (see page 340)
340g/12oz courgettes
salt and freshly ground black pepper
55g/2oz butter
1 clove of garlic, crushed
grated zest of 1 lemon
2 teaspoons lemon juice
2 tablespoons plain flour
290ml/½ pint milk
110g/4oz Cheddar cheese, grated
1 egg, separated
2 tablespoons fresh white breadcrumbs
chopped fresh chives, to garnish

1. Preheat the oven to 190°C/375°F/gas mark 5.
2. Use the pastry to line a 22cm/9in flan ring. Bake blind in the preheated oven (see page 22).
3. Wash, trim and slice the courgettes. Place on a wire rack set over a tray and sprinkle with 1 teaspoon salt. Leave to degorge for 30–60 minutes, then rinse well.
4. Melt the butter in a large frying pan and add the garlic, lemon zest, courgettes, salt and

pepper. Sauté for 2 minutes until the courgettes begin to soften. Add the lemon juice. Lift out the courgettes and put them on to a plate.

5. Stir the flour into the buttery juices in the pan, adding a little more butter if necessary. Cook for 1 minute, then gradually add the milk. Bring the sauce to the boil, then lower the heat and simmer for 2 minutes. Remove from the heat and add three-quarters of the cheese. Adjust the seasoning to taste and beat in the egg yolk.

6. Whisk the egg white stiffly, fold into the sauce, using a large metal spoon, and spread the mixture into the baked flan case. Arrange the courgettes on top and sprinkle with the remaining cheese mixed with the breadcrumbs. Bake in the preheated oven for 15 minutes and garnish with chopped chives before serving.

COURGETTE AND TOMATO TART

225g/8oz flour quantity puff pastry (see page 522)
3 tablespoons olive oil
1 onion, chopped
1 clove of garlic, chopped
150g/5oz mozzarella cheese
6 ripe tomatoes
2 courgettes
1 teaspoon fresh oregano leaves
6 fresh basil leaves
salt and freshly ground black pepper

1. Preheat the oven to 220°C/425°F/gas mark 7.
2. Roll the pastry to a large rectangle about 2mm/⅛in thick. Place on a damp baking tray, prick all over with a fork and chill for 30 minutes.
3. Bake the pastry in the preheated oven for 10 minutes. Using a palette knife or fish slice, carefully turn the pastry over and bake for a further 10 minutes on the other side. Turn the oven temperature down to 200°C/400°F/gas mark 6.
4. Heat 2 tablespoons of the oil in a frying pan, add the onion and cook over a low heat until

soft and golden-brown. Add the garlic and fry for a further 2 minutes. Allow to cool, then scatter over the top of the pastry. Slice the cheese and arrange on top of the onion.
5. Cut the tomatoes and courgettes into slices 1cm/½in thick. Arrange the tomatoes and courgettes in alternate overlapping rows over the tart. Scatter over the herbs, season with salt and pepper and drizzle with the remaining oil. Bake for 20 minutes.

NOTE: Alternative toppings can be made with marinated artichoke hearts, grilled peppers, fennel or aubergine, sautéed mushrooms. Soft mild goat's cheese can be substituted for the mozzarella.

SUMMER VEGETABLE FILO PIE

2 tablespoons olive oil
1 onion, sliced
1 red pepper, deseeded and sliced
1 yellow pepper, deseeded and sliced
1 bulb of fennel, cored and sliced
1 clove of garlic, crushed
55ml/2fl oz dry sherry
125g/4½oz baby sweetcorn, cooked and cut into 2.5cm/1in pieces
110g/4oz baby carrots, topped, tailed, cooked and cut into 2.5cm/1in pieces
grated zest of 1 lemon
2 tablespoons lemon juice
1 tablespoon chopped fresh chives
1 tablespoon fresh thyme leaves
200ml/7fl oz crème fraîche
salt and freshly ground black pepper
200g/7oz baby courgettes, sliced and blanched in boiling water for 30 seconds
450g/1lb new potatoes, boiled and sliced
6 sheets of filo pastry
30g/1oz melted butter, or 2–3 tablespoons olive oil
beaten egg, to glaze
1 tablespoon sesame or poppy seeds

1. Preheat the oven to 190°C/375°F/gas mark 5.

2. Heat the oil in a large saucepan and add the onion, peppers, fennel and garlic. Stir to coat with the oil, cover and cook over a low heat for 30 minutes, stirring occasionally to prevent the vegetables from browning.

3. Add the sherry and bring to the boil. Simmer for 2 minutes. Add the sweetcorn, carrots, lemon zest and juice, chives, thyme and crème fraîche. Season with salt and pepper.

4. Put the courgettes into a large, shallow ovenproof dish. Season with salt and pepper. Cover with the vegetable mixture and arrange the sliced new potatoes on top.

5. Brush a sheet of filo pastry with the butter or oil and place over the top. Repeat with each sheet of filo pastry, but brush the top sheet with beaten egg. Trim the edges of the pastry and score a lattice pattern on the top. Scatter over the sesame seeds or poppy seeds.

6. Bake in the preheated oven for 30 minutes. Serve hot.

BAKED COURGETTES WITH A LEMON PEPPER CRUST AND WATERCRESS SALAD

2 tablespoons olive oil
450g/1lb small courgettes
finely grated zest of 2 lemons
2 tablespoons dried white breadcrumbs
1 tablespoon chopped fresh parsley
2 tablespoons freshly grated Parmesan cheese
1 teaspoon black peppercorns, cracked
salt
1 tablespoon melted butter

For the salad
2 tablespoons olive oil
1 tablespoon hazelnut oil
1 tablespoon sherry vinegar
a dash of lemon juice
85g/3oz watercress, tough stalks removed,
  roughly chopped
55g/2oz pinenuts, toasted (see page 22)

1. Preheat the oven to 200°C/400°F/gas mark 6. Heat the oil in a flameproof shallow dish on top of the stove.

2. Cut the courgettes in half lengthways. Lay them cut side down in the hot oil and cook briefly until browned. Remove from the heat.

3. In a small bowl, mix together the lemon zest, breadcrumbs, parsley, cheese and cracked black peppercorns. Season with salt and stir in the melted butter.

4. Press the mixture on to the cut, browned side of the courgettes. Bake in the preheated oven, crust side uppermost, for 15–20 minutes or until the courgettes are tender and the crust brown (it may be necessary to finish them under a hot grill).

5. Make the watercress salad: whisk the oils, vinegar, lemon juice, salt and pepper together. Pour over the watercress and add the pinenuts. Toss together.

6. To serve: put the watercress salad on a large flat serving plate and arrange the courgettes on top in a diagonal line.

CHARGRILLED COURGETTES WITH YELLOW PEPPER, SHALLOT AND CHIVE SALSA

3 yellow peppers
4 tablespoons olive oil
4 shallots, very finely chopped
3 tablespoons balsamic vinegar
1 bunch of fresh chives, finely chopped
salt and freshly ground black pepper
6 courgettes, trimmed

1. Remove the seeds and pith from the peppers and cut the flesh into tiny dice. Set aside.
2. Heat 2 tablespoons of the oil in a frying pan. Add the shallots and cook over a low heat for 5 minutes or until beginning to soften. Add the vinegar and bring to the boil, then transfer to a bowl.
3. Stir the peppers into the warm shallot mixture. Add the chives, reserving 1 tablespoon for the garnish, and season with salt and pepper. Leave to marinate for 30 minutes.
4. Cut the courgettes lengthways into wafer-thin strips. Season with salt and pepper.
5. Heat some of the remaining oil on a griddle pan and fry the courgettes a few at a time for 1 minute on each side or until lightly browned. Remove from the pan and drain on kitchen paper. Repeat with the remaining courgettes.
6. Arrange the warm courgettes on a serving dish and spoon over the salsa. Garnish with the reserved chives and serve.

SAUTÉED COURGETTES WITH BASIL AND ROCKET

6 medium courgettes, trimmed
30g/1oz butter
4 tablespoons olive oil
juice of 1 lemon
a handful of fresh basil leaves
a handful of rocket
salt and freshly ground black pepper
freshly grated nutmeg

1. Cut the courgettes on the diagonal into thick slices. Heat the butter and oil in a large, heavy frying pan, add the courgettes and fry over a low heat for about 10 minutes until very tender and just beginning to brown.
2. Add the lemon juice and remove from the heat, scraping any sediment from the base of the pan. Tear up the basil and rocket leaves and toss in the pan juices. Season with salt, pepper and nutmeg. Cool slightly before serving.

COURGETTE AND CARROT RIBBONS TWO WAYS

For the ribbons
2 medium courgettes
2 medium carrots

Wash and trim the courgettes. Peel the carrot. Using a potato peeler, peel strips off the vegetables to make long thin slices or 'ribbons'. Alternatively this can be done in a food processor: cut the vegetables into lengths that will lay flat in the feeder. Fit the slicing blade in the food processor and stack the vegetables lengthways in the feeder, then slice.

Method 1
30g/1oz butter, melted
grated zest and juice of ½ lime
salt and freshly ground black pepper

Mix the carrots and courgettes together and steam for about 5–8 minutes until tender: the carrots should be a little crunchy. Alternatively microwave on high power for 2–3 minutes. Toss the ribbons in the butter, lime juice and zest. Season well with a little salt and plenty of pepper. Serve as a vegetable accompaniment.

Method 2
These deep-fried ribbons make a very good garnish for other dishes.

oil, for deep-frying
seasoned flour
salt
1 quantity sweet lime sauce (see page 507)

Heat the oil in a deep-fryer until a crumb sizzles vigorously. Mix the carrot and courgette ribbons together in a little of the flour, shake off excess and fry in batches for a few minutes until crisp. Drain on kitchen paper and sprinkle with salt. Drizzle with the sweet lime sauce before serving.

COURGETTE, PINENUT AND RAISIN SALAD

450g/1lb courgettes, trimmed
3 tablespoons olive oil
55g/2oz pinenuts
55g/2oz raisins
2 cloves of garlic, crushed
salt and freshly ground black pepper
2 tablespoons chopped fresh mint
1–2 tablespoons balsamic vinegar

1. Cut the courgettes into thin slices on the diagonal. Heat the oil in a large frying pan, add the courgettes and fry briskly for a few minutes. Add the pinenuts and raisins and just as the pinenuts begin to turn brown, toss in the garlic and fry for 1 further minute.
2. Remove the pan from the heat and season with salt and pepper. Stir in the mint and vinegar to taste. Serve warm or cold.

COURGETTE AND CASHEW NUT SALAD

675g/1½lb courgettes, trimmed
85g/3oz cashew nuts, toasted (see page 22)

For the dressing
1 large clove of garlic, crushed
2 tablespoons lime juice
4 tablespoons olive oil
1 tablespoon sesame oil
1 tablespoon chopped fresh mint
1 tablespoon chopped fresh chives
1 tablespoon chopped fresh oregano
salt and freshly ground black pepper

1. Slice the courgettes very thinly on the diagonal.
2. Make the dressing: mix all the ingredients together.
3. Mix the dressing with the courgettes and leave to marinate for 1 hour. Add the toasted cashew nuts just before serving and adjust the seasoning to taste.

COURGETTE SALAD WITH MUSTARD DRESSING

675g/1½lb courgettes, yellow and green if
available

For the dressing
1 tablespoon olive oil
1 tablespoon vegetable oil
1 tablespoon walnut or hazelnut oil
1 clove of garlic, chopped
1 heaped teaspoon wholegrain mustard
a good dash of lemon juice
2 dill pickles, chopped
1 tablespoon shredded fresh basil
salt and freshly ground black pepper

To garnish
a few courgette flowers, if available, or 1
tablespoon fresh flat-leaf parsley leaves

1. Slice the courgettes thinly and place in a
serving bowl.
2. Mix all the dressing ingredients together in a
screwtop jar and shake well. Pour over the
courgettes and toss gently but thoroughly.
Cover and chill for 1–2 hours. Garnish with
courgette flowers or parsley before serving.

COURGETTE, PINENUT AND MINT SALAD

450g/1lb courgettes, trimmed
1½ tablespoons chopped fresh mint
1 teaspoon lemon juice
1 clove of garlic, finely chopped
1 tablespoon extra virgin olive oil
30g/1oz pinenuts, lightly toasted (see page 22)
salt and freshly ground black pepper

1. Cut each courgette crossways into 4 equal
pieces. Cut each piece lengthways into slices,
then cut each slice crossways into small batons.
2. Just before serving, toss the courgettes with
the mint, lemon juice, garlic, oil, pinenuts and
salt and pepper to taste. Pile into a shallow
serving dish and serve immediately.

WARM DILL PICKLED CUCUMBER WITH SOURED CREAM BAGELS

1 small cucumber
150ml/¼ pint white vinegar
½ teaspoon dill seeds, crushed
½ teaspoon salt
1 teaspoon caster sugar
freshly ground black pepper
1 tablespoon chopped fresh dill
grated zest of 1 lemon
225ml/8fl oz soured cream
4 onion bagels, split
1 bunch of watercress, roughly chopped
sprigs of fresh dill, to garnish

1. Cut the cucumber in half lengthways and slice it thinly on the diagonal.
2. Put the vinegar, dill seeds, salt and sugar into a saucepan and season with pepper. Bring to the boil, then stir in the cucumber and chopped dill. Turn off the heat and allow to cool for 5 minutes. Strain the cucumber and discard the liquid.
3. Stir the lemon zest into the soured cream and season with pepper.
4. Toast the bagels on both sides and spread half of the soured cream over the cut sides.
5. Divide the watercress between the bagels. Top with the warm pickled cucumber and spoon over the remaining soured cream. Garnish with sprigs of dill and serve.

SCANDINAVIAN CUCUMBER AND DILL SALAD

1 large cucumber
3 tablespoons white wine vinegar
1 tablespoon chopped fresh dill
1½ teaspoons caster sugar
salt and freshly ground black pepper

1. Peel the cucumber and cut it into thin slices by hand or on a mandolin.
2. Spread a layer of the cucumber slices over the base of a shallow dish and sprinkle over a little of the vinegar, dill, sugar, salt and pepper. Continue to layer up the cucumber slices in this way until all the ingredients are used up.
3. Cover the dish with clingfilm and chill the salad for 30 minutes before serving.

STALKS AND SHOOTS

Globe artichokes • Asparagus • Celery • Fennel

INTRODUCTION

This group of vegetables encompasses a distinctive range of flavour and texture – luxurious, sweet asparagus, aromatic, aniseedy fennel, crunchy celery and cardoons.

Globe artichokes are loved or hated. In China they are considered weeds; indeed, they are a member of the thistle family. Eating a globe artichoke takes a certain amount of determination. The person who originally discovered the delicious tender heart must have been hungry enough to persevere with the slightly spiky outer leaves. Peeling off the outer leaves, using them to scoop up a little sauce, biting the meat from the tips and finally reaching the heart is satisfying, if not filling. Globe artichokes with dips make an enjoyable lunchtime dish to eat *al fresco*.

Cook artichokes in acidulated water as this prevents discoloration. The choke itself is very thistle-like. It is purple-white and feathery and quite inedible. Baby artichokes, harvested before the choke has formed, can be thinly sliced and griddled. These little delicacies can be found in Mediterranean vegetable markets and are gradually finding their way to this country although they are still difficult to find. Globe artichokes can be green or purple. They should be brightly coloured, firm and fleshy with leaves that are tightly packed. Canned artichoke hearts, though they have a slightly different flavour, are good for including in sauces or sautés. Italian artichokes for antipasti bottled in olive oil with herbs are a useful addition to salads.

Asparagus crops take 3–5 years to mature before harvesting, hence the high price of this treat. Break a spear with both hands and it should snap at the point where the stalk becomes tough. The tough part can be peeled with a potato peeler and is still good for making soup. The tender part is best if cooked upright so that the stalks can be simmered while the tips steam. If asparagus spears are to be cooked horizontally, simmer them gently in salted water for about 5 minutes. To grill or griddle asparagus, brush the spears with oil and turn frequently during cooking. Asparagus cooked in this way is good for salads but gives a slightly tougher result. Green asparagus is most readily available in this country but it can also be purple and white. The season is from April to June. Asparagus is best cooked as fresh as possible. Choose upright, sprightly spears with tightly packed heads. Use within a day or two.

Cardoons resemble celery in shape but are a member of the thistle family and their flavour is more like that of a globe artichoke. The inner stalks and heart are edible and can be braised or included in a casserole. Cardoons are not very much in fashion nowadays but can be found in ethnic greengrocers. Look for thick, fleshy stems and crisp leaves with plump ribs. Cardoons are best eaten very fresh. If unavailable, celery can be substituted.

Celery: crisp and crunchy, this is very good raw and fresh celery sticks are the perfect accompaniment to a sharp Cheddar cheese or hot buttery crumpets spread with Marmite. Celery can also be braised or added to casseroles. Most of our supermarket celery is bright green and forced. Celery with the best flavour is usually clad with a little earth and looks slightly untidy. Outer celery stalks will need destringing. Cut off the end and pull upwards to remove any tough strings. The leaves are tangy and can be added to a hot dish at the end of cooking or used like a herb.

Fennel is a pale green, aniseed-flavoured bulb. The feathery leaves are a herb. The root and outer leaves should be trimmed and can be used in stocks. Raw fennel has a very pungent flavour and can be thinly sliced and used in salads. Cooked fennel is used in a host of dishes, especially from the Mediterranean; it is good roasted or braised. Choose firm, bright-coloured bulbs. The English season is May to September.

ARTICHOKE AND GOAT'S CHEESE TOPPING FOR POLENTA OR BRUSCHETTA

½ × 285g/10oz jar of marinated artichoke hearts
8 plum tomatoes
salt and freshly ground black pepper
1 × 150g/5oz log of goat's cheese
2 tablespoons shredded fresh basil

To serve
polenta (see page 390)
bruschetta (see page 532)

1. Preheat the grill to high. Drain and reserve some of the oil from the artichokes, leaving just enough to moisten, and tip them into a bowl. Brush a baking tray with some of the reserved oil.
2. Cut each tomato into 6 wedges and add to the artichokes. Toss together with a little salt and plenty of black pepper. Spread the mixture on the baking tray and grill until the tomato skins begin to char.
3. Cut the cheese into chunks and add to the tomatoes with the basil. Continue to grill until the cheese browns. Scoop up with a fish slice and pile on top of warm polenta or bruschetta.

GLOBE ARTICHOKES WITH THREE DIPS

4 large fresh globe artichokes
1 lemon, quartered
salt and freshly ground black pepper
1 tablespoon olive oil

Coriander and chilli chutney
½ small red onion
1 clove of garlic
1 green chilli, deseeded (see page 22)
2 tablespoons chopped fresh coriander
1 teaspoon coarse salt
1 teaspoon caster sugar
1 tablespoon lemon juice

Mustard dip
2 tablespoons mayonnaise (see page 527)
2 tablespoons soured cream or crème fraîche
2 teaspoons wholegrain mustard
a dash of lemon juice

Balsamic hollandaise
2 teaspoons balsamic vinegar
1 egg yolk
55g/2oz unsalted butter

1. Cut the stalk, close to the leaves, off the base of the artichokes. Remove a few of the very tough outer leaves. Bring a large saucepan of water to the boil. Add the lemon, a pinch of salt and the oil. Simmer the artichokes for about 45 minutes until a leaf will pull out easily.
2. Meanwhile, make the coriander and chilli chutney: peel the onion and garlic and cut up roughly with the chilli. Put into a food processor or blender with the coriander, salt, sugar and lemon juice and process until smooth.
3. Make the mustard dip: blend all the ingredients together with salt and pepper.
4. Make the balsamic hollandaise: put the vinegar and egg yolk into a small bowl with a pinch of salt and a knob of the butter. Set over a pan of simmering water and whisk until the mixture begins to thicken. Gradually whisk in the remaining butter and remove from the heat.
5. When the artichokes are cooked, drain them upside down on a wire rack set over a tray until cool enough to handle. Prise open the centre of each artichoke and use a teaspoon to scrape out the fibrous choke. Serve the artichokes on 4 individual plates with the dips handed separately.

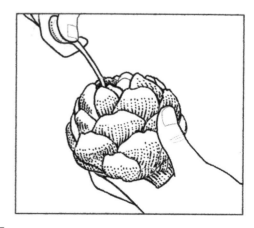

ARTICHOKE TART

*170g/6oz flour quantity herb pastry (see
page 522)*

For the filling
1 tablespoon olive oil
30g/1oz butter
1 shallot, sliced
3 sticks of celery, thinly sliced
1 small bulb of fennel, cored and thinly sliced
1 large clove of garlic, crushed
salt and freshly ground black pepper
4 tablespoons dry white wine
150ml/¼ pint double cream
55g/2oz Parmesan cheese, freshly grated
*1 × 400g/14oz tin artichoke hearts, drained and
quartered*
6 sprigs of fresh thyme
1 teaspoon dried white breadcrumbs

1. Line a 20cm/8in flan dish with the thyme
pastry and chill for at least 10 minutes.
2. Preheat the oven to 200°C/400°F/gas mark 6.
3. Bake the pastry case blind in the preheated
oven (see page 22). Lower the oven temperature
to 190°C/375°F/gas mark 5.
4. Make the filling: heat the oil and butter
together in a saucepan and add the shallot,
celery, fennel and garlic. Season with salt and
pepper, cover and cook over a low heat for 5
minutes.
5. Add the wine and increase the heat. Reduce
by half. Add the cream and reduce again to
make a thick sauce of coating consistency.
6. Add nearly all the cheese, the artichoke
hearts and the thyme. Season to taste with salt
and pepper and pour into the baked pastry case.
Sprinkle the remaining cheese over the top, then
sprinkle with the breadcrumbs.
7. Bake in the preheated oven for 15–20
minutes or until the surface is bubbling and
golden-brown. Serve warm.

NOTE: Canned artichokes may be used if fresh
are not available. Drain thoroughly, then gently
squeeze to remove excess brine.

ARTICHOKE AND GREEN OLIVE PIE

SERVES 6–8

10 fresh globe artichokes
lemon juice
30g/1oz butter
10 shallots, finely diced
2 small cloves of garlic, crushed
chopped fresh thyme
chopped fresh sage
*4 tablespoons dry white vermouth or white
wine*
150ml/¼ pint double cream
170g/6oz green olives, pitted and chopped
salt and freshly ground black pepper
*225g/8oz flour quantity puff pastry (see
page 522)*
1 egg, beaten, to glaze

1. Peel the artichokes to the core and put them
immediately into water acidulated with a dash
of lemon juice, to prevent discoloration.
2. Preheat the oven to 190°C/375°F/gas mark 5.
3. Cut the artichokes into 5mm/¼in cubes and
cook very slowly in the butter, with the
shallots, garlic, thyme and sage, until soft.
4. Add the vermouth or wine. Add the cream
and reduce, by boiling, to a coating consistency.
Stir the sauce every so often to prevent it from
catching on the bottom of the saucepan.
5. Add the olives and season carefully to taste
with salt and pepper. Leave to cool.
6. Roll out the pastry and use half to line a
20cm/8in flan ring. Pile in the artichoke and
olive mixture and cover the pie with the
remaining pastry.
7. Brush with beaten egg and bake in the centre
of the preheated oven for 15–20 minutes or until
golden-brown.

NOTE: If fresh artichokes are not available,
canned artichoke hearts may be used.

ARTICHOKES AND LEMON EN CROÛTE

8 fresh globe artichokes or 8 canned artichoke
    hearts
salt and freshly ground black pepper
grated zest and juice of 1 lemon
1 tablespoon olive oil
3 shallots, chopped
125g/4½oz oyster mushrooms, sliced
55ml/2fl oz dry white wine
150ml/¼ pint double cream
1 tablespoon chopped fresh chives
1 tablespoon chopped fresh thyme
8 green olives, pitted and halved
340g/12oz flour quantity puff pastry (see
    page 522)
beaten egg, to glaze

1. Prepare the fresh artichokes if used. Cut off the stalks and remove the outer leaves. Wash the artichokes and cook in a large saucepan of boiling salted water acidulated with a dash of lemon juice for 30–40 minutes or until the leaves will pull away easily. Remove from the pan and leave to drain upside down on a wire rack set over a tray, until cold. Peel away all the leaves and using a teaspoon, scrape out the fibrous chokes. Chop the artichoke hearts into 1.75cm/½in cubes.

2. Heat the oil in a saucepan, add the shallots and sweat gently for 5 minutes. Add the mushrooms and artichokes and cook for a further 3–4 minutes.

3. Add the wine and reduce to 1 tablespoon. Add the cream and boil rapidly for a few minutes until the sauce has thickened sufficiently to coat the artichokes.

4. Add the lemon zest and juice, the chives, thyme and olives. Season with salt and pepper. Taste and add more lemon juice if necessary. The sauce should taste lemony and be quite thick. Allow to cool completely.

5. Preheat the oven to 210°C/425°F/gas mark 7.

6. Roll out half the puff pastry and cut out a 22.5cm/9in circle, using a plate as a template. Roll out the remaining pastry and cut out a 25cm/10in circle. Put the smaller circle on a

baking sheet and prick all over with a fork. Chill both pastry circles for 10 minutes.

7. Bake the smaller circle in the preheated oven for 10 minutes. Check that the pastry is not rising too much – prick it again if necessary to flatten it. Remove from the oven and allow to cool.

8. Put the artichoke filling on the cooked pastry base, leaving a 1cm/½in border around the edge. Brush the edge with water. Put the remaining pastry on top and ease carefully over the edges. Crimp the edges with thumb and forefinger. Glaze with the beaten egg and lightly score a lattice pattern on top. Chill in the refrigerator for 10 minutes. Brush with more beaten egg and bake in the oven for 25 minutes. Lower the oven temperature if the pastry shows signs of browning too much. Serve immediately.

ARTICHOKE HEARTS STUFFED WITH RICOTTA CHEESE

8 fresh globe artichokes or 8 canned artichoke
*   hearts*
salt and freshly ground black pepper
lemon juice
oil, for brushing
250g/9oz ricotta cheese
1 egg, beaten
45g/1½oz Parmesan cheese, freshly grated
1 tablespoon chopped fresh chives
1 tablespoon chopped fresh thyme

1. Prepare the fresh artichokes, if used. Cut off the stalks and remove the outer leaves. Wash the artichokes and cook them in a large saucepan of boiling salted water acidulated with a dash of lemon juice for about 30–40 minutes or until the leaves will pull away easily. Remove from the pan and leave to drain, upside down on a wire rack over a tray, until cold. Peel away all the leaves and using a teaspoon, scrape out the fibrous chokes. If using canned artichoke hearts, drain and leave to dry on kitchen paper.
2. Preheat the oven to 190°C/375°F/gas mark 5. Brush a shallow ovenproof dish with oil.
3. Mix together the ricotta cheese, egg, Parmesan cheese, chives and thyme. Season with salt and pepper.
4. Season the artichoke hearts with salt and pepper and sprinkle with a few drops of lemon juice. Pile the ricotta cheese mixture on top of the artichoke hearts. Place them in the prepared dish and bake in the preheated oven for 20 minutes. Serve warm.

GRIDDLED ARTICHOKES

This recipe can be served as a side dish or as part of antipasti or mezze. It can only be made with very young artichokes that are harvested before the choke has formed. They are delicious served plain or with melted butter or roasted garlic mayonnaise (see page 512).

12 fresh baby artichokes
150ml/¼ pint olive oil
lemon juice
salt and freshly ground black pepper

1. Trim the stalks and spiky tops from the artichokes. Slice lengthways as thinly as possible. Brush liberally with oil.
2. Brush a griddle pan or heavy frying pan with oil and heat until a haze rises. Cook the artichoke slices for a few minutes on each side until charred and tender. Pile on to a serving plate, drizzle with oil and lemon juice and season with salt and pepper.

SPICED ARTICHOKE HEARTS

1 tablespoon olive oil
1 onion, chopped
2 sticks of celery, thinly sliced
1 large clove of garlic, crushed
salt and freshly ground black pepper
½ teaspoon ground turmeric
½ teaspoon paprika
½ teaspoon ground cumin
150ml/¼ pint spicy vegetable stock (see page 531)
2 tablespoons tomato purée
a pinch of sugar
8 fresh artichoke hearts, cooked and quartered
12 green or black olives, pitted and chopped
1–2 tablespoons roughly chopped fresh mixed herbs, such as parsley, coriander, thyme

1. Heat the oil in a saucepan and add the onion, celery and garlic. Season with salt and pepper, cover and cook over a low heat for 5 minutes. Add the spices and cook for a further 1–2 minutes.
2. Add the stock, tomato purée and sugar. Increase the heat and slowly reduce to a thick sauce. Remove from the heat.
3. Add the artichoke hearts, olives and herbs and allow to cool.

NOTE: This can be served cold as a salad or reheated and served hot as an accompaniment to couscous. Canned artichoke hearts may be used if fresh are not available. Drain thoroughly, then gently squeeze to remove excess brine.

ARTICHOKE AND POTATO SALAD WITH HERB MAYONNAISE

450g/1lb small new potatoes
2 tablespoons French dressing (see page 528)
1 × 400g/14oz can of artichoke hearts, drained
150ml/¼ pint mayonnaise (see page 527)
2 tablespoons melted butter
2 tablespoons mixed chopped fresh tarragon, chives and flat-leaf parsley
salt and freshly ground black pepper
lemon juice

To garnish
chopped fresh chives

1. Boil or steam the new potatoes until tender. Cut them in half and toss in the French dressing in a bowl.
2. Drain the artichoke hearts and leave to dry on kitchen paper. Reserve 2 artichoke hearts and cut the remainder into quarters. Toss together with the potatoes and leave to cool.
3. Put the mayonnaise into a blender, add the reserved artichoke hearts and process until smooth. Gradually stir in the melted butter. Stir gently into the potatoes and artichokes with the herbs and season with salt, pepper and lemon juice. Pile into a serving dish and scatter with chives.

SUNSHINE SALAD

1 × 400g/14oz can of artichoke hearts
2 red peppers
2 yellow peppers
2 tablespoons olive oil
4 ripe tomatoes
½ cucumber
1 small red onion, sliced
1 clove of garlic, chopped
8 Kalamata olives
8 cracked green olives (see page 20)
1 tablespoon balsamic vinegar
salt and freshly ground black pepper
12 fresh basil leaves

1. Drain the artichoke hearts and leave to dry on kitchen paper. Cut into quarters. Preheat the grill to high.
2. Cut the peppers into quarters and remove the pith and seeds. Rub with a little of the oil and grill cut side down until black and charred. Cover with a tea-towel and leave to cool, then remove the skins and slice. Cut each tomato into 8 wedges. Slice the cucumber lengthways, then cut into sticks about 5cm/2in long.
3. Toss the artichoke hearts, peppers, tomatoes and cucumber with the onion, garlic and olives. Dress with the remaining oil and the vinegar. Season with salt and plenty of pepper, pile into a serving bowl and scatter with the basil leaves.

SAUTÉED ASPARAGUS WITH MOZZARELLA AND QUAIL'S EGGS

12 quail's eggs
2 × 150g/5oz mozzarella cheeses
110g/4oz baby spinach leaves
450g/1lb asparagus spears
2 tablespoons olive oil
85g/3oz pinenuts
1 tablespoon balsamic vinegar
salt and freshly ground black pepper
about 6 fresh basil leaves

1. Boil the quail's eggs for 1 minute, then cool under cold running water. When cold, peel and slice in half lengthways. Cut the mozzarella cheeses in half and then into slices. Wash and dry the spinach and put into a large bowl.
2. Trim the woody stalks from the asparagus and cut into 5cm/2in lengths. Heat the oil in a heavy frying pan, add the asparagus and sauté for about 2 minutes. Add the pinenuts and cook until golden. Stir in the vinegar and allow to bubble up, then tip the contents of the pan into the bowl with the baby spinach.
3. Add the quail's eggs and mozzarella to the spinach and asparagus mixture and turn gently. Season with salt and pepper and tear in the basil leaves.

NOTE: To serve as a main course, accompany with crusty bread or new potatoes, or serve on a bed of couscous.

SAUTÉED ASPARAGUS WITH OYSTER MUSHROOMS

1–2 tablespoons olive oil
250g/8oz young asparagus
12 baby leeks
salt and freshly ground black pepper
1 yellow pepper, deseeded and cut into strips
225g/8oz oyster mushrooms, sliced

For the sauce
150ml/¼ pint summer vegetable stock (see
  page 530)
1 tablespoon gin
3 sprigs of fresh thyme
juice and grated zest of ½ orange
1 shallot, thinly sliced
110g/4oz unsalted butter, chilled and diced
1 tablespoon crème fraîche
1 tablespoon chopped fresh chives

1. Heat the oil in a large frying pan and add the asparagus and leeks. Season with salt and pepper and fry over a low heat for 4–5 minutes, turning occasionally.
2. Add the pepper and cook for 1–2 minutes. Increase the heat and add the mushrooms. Cook briskly for 2–3 minutes until all the vegetables are just soft. Keep warm.
3. Make the sauce: put the stock, gin, thyme, orange juice, zest and the shallot into a small saucepan. Bring to the boil and reduce to about 4 tablespoons. Remove the thyme.
4. Gradually add the butter over a low heat, whisking all the time, then stir in the crème fraîche. Season to taste with salt and pepper and add the chives. Divide the sautéed vegetables between 4 warmed individual plates and hand the sauce separately.

ASPARAGUS WITH FRIED QUAIL'S EGGS AND PARMESAN

450g/1lb asparagus
salt and freshly ground black pepper
lemon juice
55g/2oz butter
8 quail's eggs
55g/2oz Parmesan cheese shavings

To serve
warm crusty bread

1. Trim the woody stalks from the asparagus. Fill a sauté pan with water and bring to the boil. Add a pinch of salt and a dash of lemon juice. Cook the asparagus for about 5 minutes until the stalks are just tender.
2. Meanwhile, heat 15g/½oz of the butter in a small frying pan and gently fry the quail's eggs.
3. Drain the asparagus and divide between 4 individual serving plates. Top each serving with 2 quail's eggs. Melt the remaining butter and add a squeeze of lemon juice. Pour over the asparagus and top with the Parmesan shavings. Serve with crusty bread.

NOTE: As quail's egg shells are difficult to crack, it is best to break them carefully with a knife.

ASPARAGUS AND LEEK FILO PIE

450g/1lb asparagus
6 tablespoons olive oil
450g/1lb leeks, trimmed and sliced
2 tablespoons plain flour
150ml/¼ pint dry white wine
290ml/½ pint summer vegetable stock (see page 530)
2 tablespoons chopped fresh thyme
1 tablespoon lemon juice
85g/3oz Emmenthal cheese, grated
3 tablespoons double cream
salt and freshly ground black pepper
4 large sheets of filo pastry (see page 523) or bought filo pastry
1 tablespoon sesame seeds

1. Preheat the oven to 190°C/375°F/gas mark 5.
2. Trim the ends off the asparagus and using a potato peeler, pare off the tough outer skin at the base of the stalks. Bring a large shallow pan of water to the boil. Cook the asparagus for about 5–7 minutes, depending on the thickness of the spears. Remove the asparagus from the cooking water, drain carefully and set aside.
3. Heat 2 tablespoons of the oil in a large saucepan, add the leeks and sweat gently for 10 minutes or until softened. Add the flour and cook for 30 seconds, then add the wine and bring to the boil. Add the stock and bring back to the boil. Lower the heat and simmer for 5–10 minutes or until the sauce is thick. Remove from the heat and add the thyme, lemon juice, cheese, cream, salt and pepper.
4. Cut the asparagus into 5cm/2in lengths.
5. Pour half the sauce into a shallow ovenproof dish. Cover with the asparagus and pour the remaining sauce on top.
6. Brush each sheet of filo pastry with the remaining oil and place on top of the vegetables in layers. Trim off the excess pastry round the edges; brush the top with oil and score with a lattice pattern. Scatter with the sesame seeds.
7. Bake in the preheated oven for 20–25 minutes, lowering the oven temperature if the pastry shows signs of browning too much. Serve hot or warm.

NOTE: The top of the pie can also be finished by laying 2 sheets of pastry on the vegetables and then ripping the remaining sheets, crumpling them up slightly and laying them over the surface. Brush very carefully with oil and scatter over the sesame seeds. This pastry will brown quite quickly so you may need to turn the oven down after 10 minutes.

CREAMY ASPARAGUS TART

170g/6oz flour quantity shortcrust pastry (see page 521) or wholemeal pastry (see page 522)
450g/1lb asparagus
salt and freshly ground black pepper
15g/½oz butter
2 shallots or ½ medium onion, finely chopped
30g/1oz Parmesan cheese, freshly grated
grated zest of 1 lemon
290ml/½ pint double cream
2 tablespoons Greek yoghurt or fromage frais
2 eggs
½ teaspoon freshly grated nutmeg

1. Preheat the oven to 200°C/400°F/gas mark 6. Use the pastry to line a 22.5cm/9in flan dish. Prick the base with a fork. Chill for 30 minutes, then bake blind in the preheated oven (see page 22).
2. Trim the tough stalks from the asparagus and cut the spears into 2.5cm/1in pieces. Simmer for a few minutes in salted water until only just tender. Drain and dry thoroughly on kitchen paper.
3. Melt the butter in a small pan and when foaming add the shallot or onion and fry over a low heat until soft and transparent. Spoon the onion into the base of the cooked flan case and scatter the asparagus evenly over the top. Sprinkle over the cheese and lemon zest.
4. Whisk together the cream, yoghurt or fromage frais, eggs and nutmeg. Season with salt and pepper. Pour into the flan dish and bake for 30–40 minutes until just set. Cool slightly before serving.

ASPARAGUS WITH LEMON AND CAPER SAUCE

This sauce does not reheat without separating and so cannot be made in advance.

24 asparagus spears
salt and freshly ground black pepper

For the sauce
grated zest of 1 lemon
2 tablespoons lemon juice
85ml/3fl oz dry white wine
110g/4oz unsalted butter, chilled and diced
85ml/3fl oz double cream
1 tablespoon capers, rinsed and drained

1. Wash the asparagus and trim off the ends. Using a potato peeler, pare off the tough outer skin at the base of the stalks.
2. Put the asparagus into a steamer and sprinkle with a little salt. Cover and cook for 5–7 minutes, depending on the thickness of the spears. Alternatively, boil the asparagus carefully in a large, shallow pan.
3. Meanwhile, make the sauce: put the lemon zest and juice into a small saucepan with the wine. Bring to the boil and reduce to 2 tablespoons.
4. Gradually whisk the butter, piece by piece, into the reduction, over a low heat. When all the butter has been incorporated, add the cream and capers. Season carefully with salt and pepper (capers can be very salty). Add more lemon juice if necessary.
5. Put the asparagus on to a serving plate and pour some of the sauce over the tips. Serve immediately, with the remaining sauce handed separately.

WARM ROASTED ASPARAGUS SALAD

20 asparagus spears
2 long red peppers
2 tablespoons olive oil
200g/7oz sugar-snap peas
4 handfuls assorted salad leaves
150g/5oz feta cheese, cut into cubes

For the dressing
1 tablespoon lime juice
3 tablespoons olive oil
salt and freshly ground black pepper

To serve
warm crusty bread

1. Preheat the oven to 200°C/400°F/gas mark 6.
2. Wash and trim the asparagus. Using a potato peeler, pare off the tough outer skin at the base of the stalks.
3. Cut the peppers in half lengthways and remove the stalks, pith and seeds.
4. Put the asparagus into a roasting tin, pour over the oil and turn the asparagus to ensure that every piece is coated. Put the peppers into the tin, cut side down. Roast in the preheated oven for 10–15 minutes, depending on the thickness of the spears.
5. Meanwhile, blanch the sugar-snap peas in boiling water for 1 minute, then drain, refresh under cold running water and drain again.
6. Arrange the salad leaves on 4 individual plates and scatter over the feta cheese.
7. Make the dressing: whisk the lime juice with the oil. Season well with salt and pepper.
8. Cut the asparagus into 5cm/2in lengths and cut the pepper into 5cm/2in strips. Arrange over the salad with the sugar-snap peas. Drizzle over the dressing and serve immediately with warm crusty bread.

SAUTÉED ASPARAGUS, RED PEPPER AND ROCKET SALAD

2 tablespoons olive oil, plus extra to finish
340g/12oz asparagus
salt and freshly ground black pepper
1 red pepper, deseeded and cut into strips
55g/2oz rocket
balsamic vinegar
Parmesan cheese shavings

1. Heat the oil in a large frying pan. Trim the tough ends off the asparagus and lay the tips flat in the pan. Season with salt and pepper. Cook over a low heat for 5 minutes, turning carefully occasionally.
2. Add the red pepper and cook for a further 4–5 minutes, depending on the thickness of the asparagus spears and the pepper strips. Check with a sharp knife to see if they are cooked.
3. Pile the asparagus and red pepper in the centre of 4 individual plates. Place a mound of rocket on the top of each pile and drizzle over some vinegar and a little more olive oil. Season with salt and pepper and scatter over Parmesan cheese shavings. Serve warm.

DEEP-FRIED CELERY HEARTS IN CIDER BATTER

For the batter
225g/8oz plain flour
1 teaspoon salt
1 egg
1 egg yolk
290ml/½ pint dry cider

For the celery hearts
4 fresh celery hearts
4 tablespoons plain flour
2 teaspoons ground fennel seeds
salt and freshly ground black pepper
oil, for deep-frying
fresh celery leaves or flat-leaf parsley, to garnish

1. First make the batter: sift the flour and salt into a bowl. Make a well in the centre, add the whole egg and egg yolk and 1 tablespoon of the cider. Beat together to form a smooth thick paste. Slowly beat in the remaining cider, cover and leave to stand in the refrigerator for 30 minutes.
2. Cut the celery hearts into quarters lengthways and trim the root ends.
3 Mix the flour, fennel seeds, salt and pepper together. Dust the celery hearts with the seasoned flour and pat off the excess.
4. Heat 5cm/2in oil in a deep, heavy frying pan. Put the celery into the batter and stir to coat well. Using a slotted spoon, lift the celery from the batter and lower into the hot oil. Fry in batches until brown.
5. Drain the fried celery on kitchen paper and sprinkle with salt. Serve very hot, garnished with celery leaves or parsley.

CELERY AND CELERIAC NUT CRUMBLE

450g/1lb celeriac
1 large red potato
4 sticks of celery with leaves
55g/2oz butter
1 large onion, thinly sliced
290ml/½ pint apple juice
1 tablepoon roughly chopped fresh sage
salt and freshly ground black pepper
freshly grated nutmeg
3 tablespoons crème fraîche

For the crumble topping
30g/1oz butter
55g/2oz wholemeal plain flour
a pinch of cayenne pepper
30g/1oz Parmesan cheese, freshly grated
  (optional)
110g/4oz mixed nuts, roughly chopped

1. Peel the celeriac, cut into pieces and slice thinly. Peel and slice the potato. Remove any stringy threads from the celery. Slice the sticks and chop the leaves.
2. Melt the butter in a saucepan. Add the onion and cook over a low heat until softened. Add the celeriac, potato and celery. Cover and leave to cook gently for 15 minutes.
3. Add the apple juice and sage and season with salt and pepper. Simmer, partially covered, for a further 15 minutes or until the celeriac and potato are tender and the liquid has reduced a little. Stir in the créme fraîche and bring to the boil, then lower the heat and simmer until thickened. Adjust the seasoning to taste and add some nutmeg. Spoon into an ovenproof dish.
4. Preheat the oven to 190°C/375°F/gas mark 5.
5. Make the crumble: rub the butter into the flour in a bowl until the mixture resembles fine breadcrumbs. Season with salt, pepper and cayenne and stir in the cheese, if used, and the nuts. Sprinkle over the celeriac and bake in the preheated oven for 30 minutes until browned. Serve hot.

CELERY, STILTON AND PARMESAN QUICHE WITH HAZELNUT PASTRY

SERVES 6–8

For the hazelnut pastry
55g/2oz blanched hazelnuts
110g/4oz plain flour, plus extra for rolling
110g/4oz wholemeal flour
140g/5oz chilled butter, diced, plus extra for
  greasing
2–3 tablespoons cold water
1 egg white

For the filling
3 eggs
290ml/½ pint double cream
340g/12oz celery, very finely diced
110g/4oz mature Stilton cheese, finely grated
30g/1oz Parmesan cheese, freshly grated
salt and freshly ground black pepper

1. First make the hazelnut pastry: preheat the oven to 200°C/400°F/gas mark 6. Spread the hazelnuts over a baking tray and roast them in the preheated oven for 4–5 minutes until golden-brown. Remove and leave to cool. Put the roasted hazelnuts into a food processor and pulse for a few seconds until they are finely chopped but not greasy. Tip them into a mixing bowl and set aside.
2. Sift the flours and ½ teaspoon salt into the bowl of the food processor, add the butter and process until the mixture resembles fine breadcrumbs. Tip the mixture into the bowl of chopped hazelnuts and stir together well. Add the water and stir with a round-bladed knife until the mixture comes together into a ball.
3. Grease a 25cm/10in loose-bottomed flan tin 4cm/1½in deep with butter. Turn the pastry on to a lightly floured worktop and knead briefly until smooth. Roll out into a 30cm/12in circle and use to line the flan tin. Prick the base here and there with a fork, then chill for 20 minutes.
4. Bake the pastry case blind in the preheated oven for 15 minutes (see page 22). Remove the paper and beans and return to the oven for 5

minutes. Remove once more, brush the base of the pastry case with a little of the egg white and return it to the oven for 1 further minute. Remove from the oven and lower the temperature to 190°C/375°F/gas mark 5.

5. Make the filling: beat the eggs and cream together in a bowl. Stir in the celery and Stilton cheese and season to taste with salt and pepper. Pour the mixture into the pastry case and sprinkle the top with the Parmesan cheese. Bake in the preheated oven for 30 minutes or until just set. Remove from the oven and leave to cool. Serve warm, cut into wedges.

CELERY AND STILTON PASTIES

225g/8oz flour quantity shortcrust pastry (see page 521)
plain flour, for rolling

For the filling
1 tablespoon olive oil
½ head of celery, thinly sliced
2 leeks, trimmed and thinly sliced
110–170g/4–6oz Stilton cheese, crumbled
salt and freshly ground black pepper
1 egg, beaten, to glaze

1. Chill the pastry in the refrigerator.
2. Make the filling: heat the oil in a saucepan, add the celery and leeks, cover and cook over a low heat for 5 minutes or until the vegetables are soft but not coloured. Remove from the heat and allow to cool.
3. Add the cheese and season to taste with salt and pepper.
4. Preheat the oven to 200°C/400°F/gas mark 6.
5. Divide the chilled pastry into 4 equal pieces and roll each piece out to the thickness of a £1 coin on a floured worktop. Cut out 4 × 20cm/ 8in diameter circles, using a plate as a template.
6. Spoon the filling into the centre of each circle. Brush around the edge with water. Carefully bring the sides up and over the filling so that the pasties resemble closed purses. With floured fingers, crimp the edges. Place on a floured baking sheet and brush with beaten egg. Chill for 5–10 minutes.
7. Brush again with beaten egg. Bake near the top of the oven for 10–15 minutes or until the pastry is golden-brown and cooked through. Serve hot or cold.

AROMATIC BRAISED CELERY WITH SWEET POTATO

55g/2oz butter, plus extra for greasing
1 onion, sliced
½ head of celery
450g/1lb sweet potatoes
1 teaspoon ground mace
½ teaspoon ground allspice
1 teaspoon caraway seeds
1 clove of garlic, chopped
salt and freshly ground black pepper
190ml/⅓ pint cider or apple juice

To serve
Greek yoghurt

1. Preheat the oven to 190°C/375°F/gas mark 5.
2. Grease an ovenproof dish with butter. Melt half the remaining butter in a frying pan, add the onion and cook over a low heat until softened. Meanwhile, remove any stringy threads from the celery and cut it into 2.5cm/1in pieces. Peel the sweet potatoes and cut into slices about 2mm/⅛in thick.
3. Mix together the mace, allspice and caraway seeds. Arrange one-third of the sweet potato in a layer in the base of the prepared dish and sprinkle with some of the spice mixture and a little of the garlic. Season with salt and pepper, then add half the celery and top with the onion. Repeat the layers with half the remaining sweet potato and the remaining spice mixture and celery. Arrange the remaining sweet potato in an overlapping layer on top.
4. Pour in the cider or apple juice. Dot the top with the remaining butter. Cover with buttered greaseproof paper and bake in the preheated oven for 40 minutes. Remove the paper and continue to cook until the sweet potatoes are soft and slightly browned. Serve hot, with yoghurt.

STIR-FRIED CELERY WITH SHIITAKE MUSHROOMS

450g/1lb large shiitake mushrooms
2 fresh celery hearts
4 tablespoons sunflower oil
2 cloves of garlic, finely chopped
2 tablespoons Chinese rice wine or dry sherry
1 teaspoon caster sugar
2 tablespoons mushroom soy sauce or dark soy sauce
salt and freshly ground black pepper

To serve
steamed rice

1. Trim off the tougher ends of the mushroom stalks, then cut the mushrooms crossways into thick slices. Cut the celery hearts into thin slices on the diagonal.
2. Heat a wok over a high heat. Add the oil, garlic and celery and stir-fry for 1½ minutes. Add the mushrooms and stir-fry for 1 further minute.
3. Add the rice wine or sherry, sugar and soy sauce and toss together over a high heat for a few seconds. Season to taste with salt and pepper and serve with steamed rice or as part of a more complex Chinese meal.

MARINATED CELERY AND BEAN SALAD

1 head of celery
1 × 400g/14oz can of pinto beans
1 × 400g/14oz can of cannellini beans

For the dressing
4 tablespoons olive oil
2 tablespoons lemon juice
1 teaspoon Dijon mustard
2 tablespoons chopped fresh chives
1 tablespoon chopped fresh oregano
2 tablespoons chopped fresh celery leaves
3 tablespoons Greek yoghurt
salt and freshly ground black pepper

1. Trim the celery and reserve the leaves. Wash the celery well and remove any strings. Cut into thin slices.
2. Drain the beans and rinse them well under cold running water. Mix with the celery.
3. Mix all the dressing ingredients together and combine with the celery and beans. Season well with salt and pepper and leave to marinate for at least 1 hour before serving.
4. Garnish with the celery leaves.

FENNEL, POTATO AND BROAD BEAN SOUP WITH DILL CREAM

45g/1½oz butter
1 medium onion, chopped
½ teaspoon fennel seeds, crushed
2 small bulbs of fennel, coarsely chopped
225g/8oz floury potatoes, thinly sliced
565ml/1 pint summer vegetable stock (see page 530)
110g/4oz shelled fresh broad beans
85ml/3fl oz double cream
salt and freshly ground white pepper

For the dill cream
55ml/2fl oz double cream
1½ tablespoons chopped fresh dill
small sprigs of fresh dill, to garnish

1. Melt the butter in a large saucepan. Add the onion and cook over a low heat for 10 minutes, stirring from time to time, until very soft. Add the fennel seeds and cook for a further 2–3 minutes. Stir in the fennel and potatoes. Press a large crumpled sheet of wet greaseproof paper on top of the vegetables and cover with a lid. Cook over a low heat for a further 10 minutes until the vegetables are very soft.
2. Remove the lid and paper and add the stock to the pan. Bring to the boil, then lower the heat and simmer, covered, for 20 minutes. Stir in the broad beans and simmer for a further 10 minutes.
3. Purée the soup in batches in a food processor or blender. Return the soup to the rinsed-out pan and stir in the cream and salt and pepper to taste. Reheat gently but do not allow to boil.
4. Make the dill cream: whip the cream to soft peaks. Stir in the dill and season to taste with salt and pepper. Ladle the soup into 4 warmed soup plates and top each with a spoonful of the dill cream. Garnish with the sprigs of dill.

ROASTED FENNEL, RED PEPPER AND MOZZARELLA PIZZAS WITH GARLIC BUTTER AND ROCKET

MAKES 2 × 20cm/8in PIZZAS

For the pizza dough
140g/5oz strong plain flour, plus extra for
    kneading
1 teaspoon easy-blend yeast
½ teaspoon salt
110ml/4fl oz warm water
1 teaspoon olive oil
a little polenta, semolina or fine cornmeal, for
    dusting

For the topping
olive oil
2 large red peppers
2 bulbs of fennel, trimmed
salt and freshly ground black pepper
340ml/12fl oz tomato passata
1 tablespoon chopped fresh basil
140g/5oz mozzarella cheese, coarsely grated
85g/3oz Parmesan cheese, freshly grated
30g/1oz butter
1 clove of garlic, crushed
30g/1oz rocket

1. First make the pizza dough: sift the flour, yeast and salt into a warmed mixing bowl. Make a well in the centre, add the water and oil and gradually mix the flour into the liquid until everything comes together into a soft dough. Turn the dough on to a lightly floured worktop and knead for 10 minutes until smooth and elastic.
2. Place the dough back in a lightly oiled mixing bowl and brush the top of the dough lightly with a little more oil. Cover the bowl tightly with clingfilm and leave in a warm place for 40–50 minutes or until the dough has doubled in bulk.
3. Meanwhile, preheat the oven to 240°C/475°F/gas mark 9 and oil a baking tray. Place the peppers directly on to one of the oven

shelves and roast for 20 minutes.
4. While the peppers are roasting, cut the fennel bulbs lengthways through the root into thin slices. Cook in boiling salted water for 1 minute, then drain well. Lay the fennel on the prepared baking tray, sprinkle with a little more oil and some salt and pepper and roast in the oven alongside the peppers for 10 minutes.
5. Pour the passata into a large saucepan and simmer vigorously for about 5 minutes, stirring frequently, until it is well reduced and thickened. Cool slightly, then stir in the basil and season to taste with salt and pepper.
6. Remove the red peppers and fennel from the oven. When the peppers are cool enough to handle, break them open, discard the stalks, pith and seeds and peel off the skin. Cut the flesh into wide strips.
7. Put 2 baking trays into the oven to heat. Sprinkle another 2 baking sheets with a little polenta, semolina or fine cornmeal. Uncover the dough and turn it on to a lightly floured surface. Punch out the air and knead for 2 minutes until smooth. Cut the dough in half and roll each piece out into a 20cm/8in round. Transfer the pizza bases to the dusted baking trays. This will make it easier to transfer them to the hot baking trays for cooking.
8. Spread the reduced passata sauce over the pizza bases to within 2.5cm/1in of the edges. Arrange the roasted fennel, red pepper and grated mozzarella cheese over the sauce, then sprinkle with the Parmesan cheese. Brush the edges of the dough with a little more oil.
9. Slide the pizzas off the baking sheets on to the hot baking sheets and bake them in the preheated oven for 10 minutes, turning them around and switching them over from one shelf to the other if necessary, so that they brown evenly. Meanwhile, put the butter and the garlic into a small saucepan and leave over a very low heat to melt.
10. Remove the pizzas from the oven and spoon over the hot garlic butter. Pile the rocket leaves into the centre of each pizza and serve.

FENNEL AND WALNUT FILO PIE

This is an especially good dinner-party recipe. Serve with new potatoes and a crisp salad with a walnut oil dressing.

SERVES 6

4 bulbs of fennel
3 tablespoons olive oil
3 cloves of garlic, chopped
2 teaspoons fennel seeds
1 teaspoon paprika
grated zest of 1 orange
110g/4oz walnuts, roughly chopped
salt and freshly ground black pepper
1 teaspoon caster sugar
85g/3oz butter, melted
2 eggs
225g/8oz Greek yoghurt or fromage frais
150ml/¼ pint milk
2 tablespoons chopped fresh flat-leaf parsley
225g/8oz strudel pastry (see page 523) or filo
    pastry sheets

1. Trim the roots from the fennel and discard the outer leaves. Cut each bulb in half and slice thinly.
2. Heat the oil in a sauté pan. Add the fennel and cook over a low heat for about 10 minutes until soft. Add the garlic, fennel seeds and paprika seeds and fry for a further 2 minutes. Turn off the heat and stir in the orange zest and walnuts. Season with salt, pepper and sugar. Cool.
3. Preheat the oven to 190°C/375°F/gas mark 5. Brush a 20cm/8in shallow ovenproof dish with a little of the melted butter.
4. Whisk together the eggs, yoghurt, milk and parsley. Pour into the fennel mixture.
5. Use several sheets of pastry to line the prepared dish, overlapping the sheets and letting the edges hang over the side of the dish. Brush liberally with melted butter. Pour in the fennel mixture. Crumple the overlapping edges of pastry on to the dish. Brush the remaining sheets of filo with butter. Crumple up and place in bundles over the top of the pie until it is completely covered. Bake

in the preheated oven for 30 minutes until the filling is set and the pastry is well browned. Cool slightly before slicing.

VEGETABLE UPSIDE-DOWN CAKE

For the base
2 tablespoons olive oil
1 small bulb of fennel, thinly sliced
1 small red onion, thinly sliced
2 cloves of garlic, crushed
½ red pepper, deseeded and thinly sliced
½ green pepper, deseeded and thinly sliced
½ yellow pepper, deseeded and thinly sliced
85g/3oz baby sweetcorn, halved lengthways
85g/3oz baby asparagus spears
salt and freshly ground black pepper
1 tablespoon dried white breadcrumbs
110–140g/4–5oz feta or other cheese

For the topping
225g/8oz self-raising flour
salt and freshly ground black pepper
3–4 tablespoons roughly chopped mixed fresh
    herbs, such as parsley, basil, thyme
2 eggs, beaten
290ml/½ pint buttermilk
85g/3oz butter, melted and cooled

1. Heat the oil in a large frying pan with a lid. Add all the vegetables and season with salt and pepper. Cover and cook over a low heat for 10–15 minutes, stirring occasionally, until softened.
2. Preheat the oven to 190°C/375°F/gas mark 5.
3. Transfer the vegetables to a deep, round ovenproof dish. Sprinkle evenly with the breadcrumbs and then crumble over the cheese.
4. Make the topping: combine the flour, salt, pepper and herbs in a mixing bowl. In a separate bowl, mix the eggs, buttermilk and butter together. Add to the dry ingredients and mix quickly but thoroughly. Pour over the vegetables and spread out evenly. Bake immediately in the centre of the preheated oven for 20–30 minutes until the cake is golden-brown and firm to the touch.

5. Run a knife around the edge of the dish and leave for a few minutes before turning out on to a flat serving plate. Serve warm or cold.

NOTE: This works very well using a moule manqué cake tin or a frying pan with high sides that can go into the oven.

FENNEL AND BRIE RISOTTO WEDGES

This recipe is best started a day in advance.

2 bulbs of fennel
1 tablespoon olive oil
85g/3oz unsalted butter
1 onion, thinly sliced
450g/1lb arborio rice
860ml/1½ pints hot summer vegetable stock
(see page 530)
grated zest and juice of 1 lemon
salt and freshly ground black pepper
55g/2oz Parmesan cheese, freshly grated
225g/8oz soft Brie cheese, rind removed and cut
into 1cm/½in pieces
seasoned plain flour
2 eggs, beaten
dried white breadcrumbs
oil, for shallow-frying
fresh fennel tops or sprigs of fresh flat-leaf
parsley, to garnish

1. Discard any damaged outer leaves from the fennel and cut each bulb in half. Remove the cores and reserve the feathery tops. Chop the fennel very finely.
2. Heat the oil and butter in a large shallow saucepan and add the fennel and onion. Cover and cook over a low heat for 20–25 minutes or until soft but not coloured.
3. Add the rice to the pan and stir to absorb the buttery juices. Add the stock a little at a time, stirring continuously and allowing the stock to become absorbed between each addition, until the rice is tender (about 30 minutes). Stir in the lemon zest and juice and season with salt and pepper.

4. Carefully fold the Parmesan and Brie cheeses into the risotto and allow to cool.
5. Turn the cooled mixture on to a baking tray lined with non-stick baking paper and using a plate as a guide, shape the mixture into a circle about 2.5cm/1in thick. Chill in the refrigerator for 3–4 hours or overnight until very firm.
6. Cut the cold risotto mixture into 8 wedges and dust with seasoned flour. Dip the wedges first into the beaten egg and then into the breadcrumbs.
7. Heat 2.5cm/1in oil in a large, heavy frying pan and fry the risotto wedges for 2–3 minutes on each side until hot, brown and crisp. Drain on kitchen paper and sprinkle with a little salt. Serve hot, garnished with the fennel tops or sprigs of flat-leaf parsley.

NOTE: Leftover risotto can be used for similar dishes.

BAKED FENNEL WITH HOT LEMON DRESSING

4 bulbs of fennel
225g/8oz button onions or shallots
150ml/¼ pint olive oil
salt and freshly ground black pepper
1 teaspoon caster sugar

For the dressing
1 bunch of spring onions
5cm/2in piece of fresh root ginger, peeled and
*   finely chopped*
2 cloves of garlic, chopped
1 red chilli, deseeded and chopped (see page 22)
1 tablespoon walnut oil
grated zest and juice of ½ lemon
chopped fresh flat-leaf parsley, to garnish

1. Preheat the oven to 200°C/400°F/gas mark 6.
2. Trim the roots from the fennel and remove the outer leaves. Cut each fennel bulb into quarters. Douse the button onions or shallots in boiling water. Peel and trim the roots. Put the vegetables together in an ovenproof dish with 2 tablespoons of the oil and mix well. Season with salt and pepper and sprinkle with the sugar. Cover with kitchen foil and bake in the preheated oven for about 1 hour until the vegetables are very soft.
3. Meanwhile, make the dressing: trim the spring onions and cut them on the diagonal into 2.5cm/1in slices. When the fennel and onions are cooked, heat the remaining oil in a frying pan. Add the ginger and garlic and fry for 1 minute. Stir in the spring onion and chilli and fry for 1 further minute.
4. Remove from the heat and stir in the walnut oil. Add the lemon zest and juice and season with salt and pepper. Pour the dressing over the baked fennel and scatter with the parsley.

FENNEL AND TOMATO SAUTÉ WITH CHEDDAR CHEESE

450g/1lb plum tomatoes, peeled and quartered
*   (see page 22)*
450g/1lb large bulbs of fennel
2 tablespoons extra virgin olive oil
15g/½oz butter
1 clove of garlic, crushed
1 teaspoon fennel seeds, crushed
1½ teaspoons chopped fresh thyme
1 bay leaf
2 tablespoons Pernod
55g/2oz small black olives, pipped
85g/3oz Cheddar cheese, coarsely grated
salt and freshly ground black pepper

1. Put the tomatoes into a food processor and pulse for a few seconds until they are coarsely chopped. Set aside. Lightly trim the base of each fennel bulb and then cut them into chunky wedges through the root so that the slices stay held together at the base.
2. Heat the oil and butter in a large, deep frying pan. Add half the fennel wedges and fry them for 5–6 minutes, turning once, until lightly browned on both sides. Lift on to a plate and repeat with the remaining wedges.
3. Add the garlic and fennel seeds to the remaining butter in the pan and fry for 1 minute. Return the fennel to the pan with the thyme, bay leaf, Pernod and tomatoes and stir together well, distributing the wedges of fennel evenly over the base of the pan. Cover and simmer for 4–5 minutes until the fennel is *al dente*.
4. Uncover the pan, raise the heat a little and cook for 5 minutes until the sauce has reduced and thickened slightly. Meanwhile, preheat the grill to high.
5. Sprinkle the olives and cheese over the fennel mixture and slide the pan under the grill for 3 minutes or until the cheese is golden and bubbling.

ROASTED FENNEL WITH PARMESAN

4 bulbs of fennel
salt and freshly ground black pepper
2 tablespoons olive oil
freshly grated nutmeg
30g/1oz butter
55g/2oz Parmesan cheese, freshly grated

1. Preheat the oven to 200°C/400°F/gas mark 6.
2. Trim the base of the fennel and remove the outer leaves. Cut each bulb into quarters. Cook in a saucepan of boiling salted water for 2 minutes. Drain.
3. Heat the oil in a roasting tin on top of the stove. Turn the fennel in the hot oil and season with salt and pepper. Roast in the preheated oven for about 20 minutes until the fennel is *al dente*.
4. Season with nutmeg and dot with butter. Sprinkle with the cheese and bake for a further 10 minutes until golden-brown.

WARM PINK GRAPEFRUIT AND FENNEL SALAD

2 tablespoons sunflower oil
1 tablespoon hazelnut oil
1 tablespoon sherry vinegar
salt and freshly ground black pepper
1 head of fennel, very thinly sliced
3 pink grapefruits, peeled and segmented
1 tablespoon soft light brown sugar
85g/3oz hazelnuts, toasted, skinned and
  roughly chopped
85g/3oz rocket

1. Mix the oils and vinegar together in a small bowl. Season with salt and pepper.
2. Pour the dressing over the sliced fennel and leave to marinate for at least 30 minutes.
3. Preheat the grill and line 2 baking trays with kitchen foil.
4. Drain the fennel, using a slotted spoon and reserving the marinade. Place the fennel slices on one of the baking trays. Grill for 1–1½ minutes. Return the warm fennel to the marinade.
5. Lay the grapefruit segments on the second baking tray and sprinkle over the sugar. Grill for 1½–2 minutes or until beginning to caramelize.
6. Meanwhile, add the hazelnuts and rocket to the warm fennel and toss everything together thoroughly. Divide between 4 individual plates.
7. Carefully remove the grapefruit segments from the baking tray and arrange them on top of the salads. Serve immediately.

FENNEL SALAD WITH ORANGES, LEMONS AND GARLIC

1 bulb of fennel
3 oranges
1 lemon
1 clove of garlic, crushed
3 tablespoons olive oil
salt and freshly ground black pepper
8 Kalamata olives

1. Trim the root and top from the fennel, reserving some of the feathery tops. Remove the outer leaves and slice the fennel thinly.
2. Peel the oranges and lemon with a sharp knife, removing all the pith and peel. Slice the flesh thinly, discarding any seeds. Arrange the fennel and fruit in a shallow serving dish.
3. Stir the garlic into the oil and season with salt and pepper. Pour over the salad. Cover and chill for 1 hour. Scatter with the olives and chopped reserved fennel tops before serving.

PODS AND BEANS

*Broad beans • Green beans • Okra • Peas • Sweetcorn •
Bean sprouts*

INTRODUCTION

Pods are very nutritious, containing plenty of protein, carbohydrate, fibre, vitamins and minerals. The freshest pods are bright green and plump with smooth cases. Seasonally they are the vegetables of summer, their deliciously fragrant flavours blending well with herbs. Many varieties of beans are available all year round, however, and those imported out of season are good quality. Peas, sweetcorn and broad beans are very good frozen and retain their nutritional value.

Fresh beans are bouncy and will snap cleanly. They will keep well in the refrigerator for up to a week. They require boiling or steaming for a few minutes only so that they are still bright green and crunchy.

Broad beans are also known as **fava beans**. This is the only bean that comes in a pod. The pods are edible if the broad beans are very young. As the season is very short – June to September – almost the only way to find beans this young and tender is to grow them. The beans that find their way to the supermarket shelf tend to be the older ones. These need podding. The beans inside have a pale green skin, which can be very tough. When cooked, squeeze the skin gently and the bright green beans inside will pop out. This might sound tedious but is definitely worth the effort. Broad beans are full of fibre and are also sold dried or frozen.

Haricot, **dwarf**, **bobby** and **Kenyan** are short round beans. To top and tail them, line them up in a bundle and trim all together. They can be cooked whole or in smaller lengths. The skin of haricot beans can be green, yellow or purple. When cooked, the purple ones turn green. If the beans are allowed to complete their reproductive cycle they produce the dry edible seeds that we use as pulses.

Runner beans epitomize the English summer and are best from July to October. Very young beans can be eaten raw and included with their flowers in salads. Older beans require topping and tailing and the side strings need to be removed. This can be done by snapping the ends and pulling them back or by slicing the sides away with a knife. **Flat beans** look similar to runners. They are light green and crisper with no side strings.

Yard long beans are found in ethnic stores. They are up to 45cm/18in long and have a lemony flavour.

Okra was spread by the slave trade to the southern states of the USA. It is popular in Indian, Caribbean annd Creole dishes. Some find the gooey insides unpleasant but this feature has been made an intrinsic part of the Creole dish gumbo where it thickens the stew. The best okra to buy are young, crisp pods about 5–7.5cm/2–3in long. Okra can be sliced or cooked whole. The flavour goes well with tomato, garlic and chilli. Young okra are good stir-fried or can be dipped in flour and deep-fried.

Peas are the earliest known cultivated vegetable. Buy fresh peas with smooth pods that will snap easily. They can be stored in the refrigerator for up to a week. Boil fresh peas for 2–3 minutes in 2.5cm/1in water with a sprig of mint. Longer cooking will toughen the peas. Very fresh peas are delicious raw in salads. Two varieties, **mangetout** and **sugar-snaps**, have edible pods. They can be eaten raw, boiled or steamed for 3 minutes. The shells should still be crunchy and have no hint of sogginess.

Sweetcorn, as the name suggests, is full of sugars and is a good source of carbohydrate. It is the third most important cereal in the world. In some countries it is used as animal fodder and is passed by for the human table. The Americans took to corn in a big way and it was they who dried it and discovered popcorn. Fresh corn cobs should have plump, smooth kernels and silky husks. Store the corn with the husks intact as they will keep the kernels moist. Older cobs look dry and wrinkled, the sugars turn to starch and the kernels become tough and tasteless.

To cook sweetcorn, trim the ends and remove the husks. Cook the cobs whole in boiling water for about 10 minutes until tender or slice into small pieces to boil or grill. The cobs are extremely hard so it takes a large sharp knife or cleaver to cut through. Corn cobs also cook well in a microwave oven. Put into a container with a splash of water and cover. Cook on high for 10 minutes and leave to stand for a further 10 minutes. Cobs can also be barbecued whole in their husks and wrapped in kitchen foil. Sweetcorn can be served with melted butter and plenty of freshly ground black pepper. It is also good scattered with dried chilli flakes, lime juice and fresh coriander. If the kernels only are needed they can be removed from the cob by slicing with a sharp knife. Baby corn lacks the flavour of sweetcorn but is very decorative and good for grilling or for use in stir-fries.

BROAD BEAN PÂTE

450g/1lb shelled fresh broad beans
salt and freshly ground black pepper
150ml/¼ pint olive oil
1 clove of garlic, crushed
1 teaspoon chopped fresh thyme
lemon juice

To serve
hot toast

1. Cook the broad beans in boiling salted water
for 8–10 minutes until tender. Remove the
tough outer skins.
2. Mash the beans to a purée with a fork. Add
a good pinch of salt and gradually beat in half
the oil. Season with pepper, garlic, thyme and a
dash of lemon juice. Now add the remaining oil
in a thin stream. Alternatively, put the beans
and seasoning into a food processor and
gradually pour in the oil with the motor
running. Serve with hot toast.

BROAD BEAN POLO

2 tablespoons olive oil
1 bulb of fennel, finely diced
1 yellow pepper, deseeded and finely diced
1 leek, trimmed and thinly sliced
1 bay leaf
salt and freshly ground black pepper
225g/8oz long-grain rice
425ml/¾ pint summer vegetable stock (see
  page 530)
a good pinch of saffron strands
340g/12oz shelled broad beans, cooked weight
30–55g/1–2oz pistachio nuts
1–2 tablespoons chopped fresh mixed herbs,
  such as dill, parsley, coriander, thyme

1. Heat the oil in a saucepan, add the fennel,
pepper, leek and bay leaf and season with salt
and pepper. Cover the pan and soften for 10
minutes.
2. Add the rice to the pan and turn in the hot
oil. Add the stock and saffron and bring to the
boil, then cover and simmer gently for 10–15
minutes, until the rice is cooked. Remove the lid
and allow any excess liquid to evaporate if
necessary. Remove the bay leaf.
3. Meanwhile, remove the tough outer skins
from the cooked broad beans. Add to the
cooked rice, then add the pistachio nuts and the
herbs. Mix carefully so as not to damage the
broad beans. Season to taste with salt and
pepper.

NOTE: This dish can be served hot or cold as a
main dish or accompaniment.

BROAD BEAN SUCCOTASH WITH CHEESE AND CHILLI CORNBREAD

110g/4oz dried butter beans
30g/1oz unsalted butter
1 medium onion, finely chopped
290ml/½ pint summer vegetable stock (see
    page 530)
3 cobs of fresh sweetcorn
225g/8oz shelled fresh broad beans
55ml/2fl oz double cream
a little freshly grated nutmeg
salt and freshly ground black pepper
2 tablespoons chopped fresh chives, to garnish

For the cornbread
55g/2oz melted butter, plus extra for greasing
100g/3½oz plain flour
1 tablespoon baking powder
¼ teaspoon salt
100g/3½oz dried polenta
70g/2½oz Cheddar cheese, finely grated
¼ teaspoon dried red chilli flakes
2 medium eggs, beaten
290ml/½ pint milk

1. Put the butter beans into a saucepan and cover with plenty of cold water. Bring to the boil, then remove from the heat and leave to soak for 2 hours.

2. Melt the butter in a medium saucepan. Add the onion and cook over a low heat for 7–8 minutes until soft but not browned. Drain the butter beans and add them to the pan with the stock. Bring to the boil, partially cover and leave to simmer gently for 45–50 minutes or until the beans are tender and the stock is well reduced.

3. Make the cornbread: preheat the oven to 200°C/400°F/gas mark 6. Grease a 900g/2lb loaf tin with a little butter and base-line with greased greaseproof paper. Sift the flour, baking powder and salt into a mixing bowl and stir in the polenta, grated cheese and dried chilli flakes. Make a well in the centre and add the eggs, milk and melted butter. Mix everything together well until smooth. Pour the mixture into the prepared loaf tin and bake in the preheated oven for 40–45 minutes until well risen, firm to the touch and golden-brown. Remove from the oven and leave to cool in the tin for 10 minutes. Then turn out on to a wire rack.

4. Meanwhile, remove the papery husks and silky strands from the outside of the sweetcorn. Stand each cob upright on a large plate and carefully slice away the kernels of corn with a large, sharp knife, keeping the blade as close as you can to the core of the cob.

5. Cook the broad beans in a saucepan of boiling salted water for 3 minutes. Drain, refresh under cold running water and then carefully remove the tough outer skins.

6. Stir the sweetcorn kernels and the cream into the pan of butter beans and simmer gently for 4 minutes without boiling. Add the broad beans and simmer for 1 further minute. Add the nutmeg and salt and pepper to taste. Spoon into warmed soup plates and garnish with the chives. Serve with thick slices of warm cornbread.

BROAD BEANS WITH ARTICHOKES

450g/1lb shelled fresh or frozen broad beans
salt and freshly ground black pepper
1 × 400g/14oz can of artichoke hearts or 12
   baby artichokes
2 tablespoons olive oil
1 medium onion, chopped
2 cloves of garlic, chopped
1 teaspoon cumin seeds, crushed
a large pinch of ground turmeric
a pinch of saffron strands
2 tablespoons summer vegetable stock (see
   page 530)
2 tablespoons dry white wine
2 tablespoons fresh flat-leaf parsley leaves

1. Cook the broad beans in boiling salted water
until just tender. Drain, then remove the tough
outer skins. If using canned artichokes, drain
them, cut in half and dry on kitchen paper. If
using fresh artichokes, trim off the spiky leaf
ends, then trim off the stalks and outer leaves
and cut the artichokes into quarters.
2. Heat the oil in a sauté pan, add the onion
and fresh artichokes, if used, and fry over a low
heat until the artichokes are soft and the onion
golden-brown. (If using canned artichoke
hearts, add to the pan in step 3.) Add the garlic,
cumin and turmeric and cook for 1 further
minute.
3. Add the beans, saffron, stock and wine to
the pan, and the canned artichoke hearts, if
used. Season to taste with salt and pepper.
Cover and simmer gently for 10 minutes until
the liquid is reduced and syrupy. Sprinkle with
the parsley before serving.

BROAD BEAN SALAD

450g/1lb shelled fresh or frozen broad beans
200g/7oz sugar-snap peas
finely grated zest of 1 orange
2 tablespoons fresh orange juice
150ml/¼ pint soured cream
1 tablespoon lemon juice
1 clove of garlic, crushed
1 tablespoon chopped fresh thyme
1 tablespoon chopped fresh chives
1 tablespoon Dijon mustard
1 shallot, finely chopped
salt and freshly ground black pepper

1. Bring a saucepan of water to the boil, add
the broad beans, bring back to the boil and
cook for 5–6 minutes for fresh beans, 3 minutes
for frozen. Drain and refresh under cold
running water. Remove the tough outer skins
from the broad beans.
2. Put the sugar-snap peas into a saucepan of
boiling water, bring back to the boil and cook
for 1–2 minutes. Drain and refresh under cold
running water.
3. Mix together the orange zest and juice, the
soured cream, lemon juice, garlic, thyme,
chives, Dijon mustard and shallot. Season to
taste with salt and pepper.
4. Mix the dressing with the beans and peas,
pile into a salad bowl and serve.

NOTE: If you find it too much of an effort to
skin the broad beans, leave them on. The
texture will be chewier and the flavour a little
different.

BROAD BEAN AND FETA SALAD WITH MINT

450g/1lb shelled fresh broad beans
salt and freshly ground black pepper
55g/2oz small Greek black olives
2 tablespoons finely shredded fresh mint
3 tablspoons extra virgin olive oil
1 tablespoon lemon juice
170g/6oz feta cheese, broken into small pieces

To garnish
extra virgin oil
Maldon sea salt flakes
small fresh mint leaves

To serve
warm Turkish flat bread

1. Cook the broad beans in a saucepan of well-salted boiling water for 4–5 minutes until just tender. Drain, refresh under cold running water and leave to drain. Remove the tough outer skins.
2. Tip the beans into a bowl and stir in the olives, mint, oil and lemon juice. Season with pepper. Mix together well, then carefully stir in the feta cheese making sure it does not break up too much.
3. Spoon the salad into a shallow serving bowl. Drizzle with a little oil, some coarsely ground black pepper, sea salt flakes and mint leaves. Serve with warm Turkish flat bread.

SPICY GREEN BEAN, POTATO AND CARROT TOSTADAS

225g/8oz French beans
1 large red potato
2 tablespoons vegetable oil
1 teaspoon cumin seeds
1 small onion, finely chopped
½ teaspoon paprika
½ teaspoon ground turmeric
2 cloves of garlic, chopped
1 green chilli, deseeded and chopped (see
    page 22)
salt and freshly ground black pepper
1 large carrot, grated
2 tomatoes, peeled (see page 22)
2 tablespoons fresh coriander leaves

To serve
tostadas (see page 107), flour tortillas or tacos
1 quantity refried beans (see page 339)
1 quantity lime soured cream (see Chilli Beans,
    page 340)

1. Top and tail the French beans and cut into 1cm/½in pieces. Peel the potato and cut into 5mm/¼in cubes.
2. Heat the oil in a heavy frying pan. Add the cumin seeds and cook until they begin to pop. Lower the heat, add the onion and fry until soft and transparent. Stir in the paprika, turmeric, garlic and chilli and cook for a further 2 minutes. Turn the potatoes in the spicy mixture and season with salt and pepper. Add the beans, cover and fry over a low heat for 10–15 minutes, tossing from time to time, until almost tender. Add the carrot and cook for a few minutes longer.
3. Halve and deseed the tomatoes and chop the flesh. Add to the vegetable mixture with the coriander leaves. Check the seasoning. Warm the tostadas and refried beans. Put a spoonful of the beans into the tostada. Top with the piping hot vegetables and a dollop of lime soured cream.

THAI VEGETABLE CAKES

110g/4oz French beans
225g/8oz firm, waxy potatoes, grated
4 spring onions, trimmed and chopped
110g/4oz radishes or mooli, grated
grated zest of 1 lime
2 tablespoons chopped fresh coriander
1 green chilli, deseeded and chopped (see
    page 22)
½–1 tablespoon Thai red curry paste
2 medium eggs, beaten
30g/1oz chickpea flour (gram flour)
salt and freshly ground black pepper
sunflower or groundnut oil, for frying
sprigs of fresh coriander, to garnish

To serve
sweet lime sauce (see page 507)
ginger dipping sauce (see Courgette Sticks with
    Sesame Seeds, page 253)

1. Top and tail the French beans and chop into
small pieces. Mix together with the potatoes,
spring onions, radishes or mooli, lime zest,
coriander, chilli and curry paste. Stir in the eggs
and chickpea flour. Season with plenty of salt
and pepper.
2. Heat a little oil in a heavy frying pan or
griddle. Fry spoonfuls of the mixture for a few
minutes on each side until golden-brown. Serve
garnished with sprigs of coriander and hand the
dipping sauces separately.

PIEDMONT BEANS

900g/2lb French beans, topped and tailed
salt and freshly ground black pepper
30g/1oz butter
1 clove of garlic, crushed
1 egg
55g/2oz Edam or Gruyère cheese, grated

To finish
freshly grated Parmesan cheese
dried white breadcrumbs

1. Preheat the oven to 180°C/350°F/gas mark 4.
Butter an ovenproof serving dish.
2. Cook the beans in a saucepan of boiling
salted water until just tender. Drain well and
chop finely.
3. Melt the butter and, when foaming, add the
beans and garlic. Shake over direct heat for 1
minute. Tip into a mixing bowl.
4. Separate the egg and beat the yolk and Edam
or Gruyère cheese into the bean mixture. Taste
and season with salt and pepper. Be careful not
to over-season as cheese is salty.
5. Whisk the egg white until stiff but not dry,
then using a large metal spoon, fold into the
beans.
6. Turn the mixture into the prepared dish and
sprinkle with the Parmesan cheese and
breadcrumbs. Bake in the preheated oven for 40
minutes.

SAUTÉED GREEN BEANS WITH ALMONDS AND GARLIC

450g/1lb green beans, such as haricots verts,
dwarf beans or flat beans
3 tablespoons olive oil
2 cloves of garlic, chopped
55g/2oz flaked almonds
salt and freshly ground black pepper

1. Top and tail the beans and cut into 2.5cm/ 1in pieces. Cook in boiling salted water for 2 minutes, then drain.
2. Heat the oil in a frying pan. Add the garlic and almonds and fry for 1–2 minutes until lightly golden. Stir in the beans, season with salt and pepper and continue to cook gently until the beans are tender. Serve immediately.

STIR-FRIED GREEN BEANS WITH ONIONS AND TOMATOES

2 tablespoons olive oil
2 large red onions, sliced
½ tablespoon Chinese five-spice powder
1 clove of garlic, crushed
1 teaspoon peeled and grated fresh root ginger
225g/8oz runner or Romano beans, cut on the
diagonal into 5cm/2in lengths
1 × 400g/14oz can of chopped tomatoes
75ml/2½fl oz water
3 tablespoons light soy sauce
salt and freshly ground black pepper

1. Heat the oil in a wok or large frying pan and add the onions. Stir-fry for 3 minutes. Add the Chinese five-spice, garlic and ginger and cook for 1 further minute.
2. Add the beans and stir-fry over a medium heat for 5 minutes.
3. Add the tomatoes, water and soy sauce and continue to cook for about 5–10 minutes until the beans are tender and the sauce is thick. Serve with boiled rice.

RUNNER BEANS WITH TARRAGON CREAM

340g/12oz runner beans
15g/½oz butter
1 bunch of spring onions, trimmed and chopped
150ml/¼ pint soured cream
2 tablespoons chopped fresh tarragon
salt and freshly ground black pepper
freshly grated nutmeg

1. Top and tail the runner beans and trim off the tough edges, then cut the beans into 2.5cm/ 1in slices. Cook the beans in boiling salted water for about 5 minutes until just tender. Drain.
2. Melt the butter in a frying pan, add the onions and fry for 3–4 minutes. Stir in the soured cream, tarragon and cooked beans. Season with salt, pepper and nutmeg. Heat without boiling and serve immediately.

HOT LEMON AND HORSERADISH DRESSED RUNNER BEANS

450g/1lb runner beans
salt and freshly ground black pepper
1 tablespoon olive oil
grated zest of 1 lemon
2 tablespoons grated fresh horseradish

1. Top and tail the runner beans, trim off the tough edges and slice the beans on the diagonal.
2. Bring a saucepan of salted water to the boil, add the beans and cook for 2–3 minutes or until tender. Drain well.
3. Heat the oil in the empty, still hot saucepan. Add the lemon zest and horseradish and stir for 30 seconds. Add the beans and season with salt and pepper. Cover the pan and shake vigorously to mix well. Tip into a warmed serving dish and serve immediately.

MIXED BEAN SALAD WITH SHALLOTS AND A MUSTARD DRESSING

225g/8oz shelled fresh or frozen broad beans
225g/8oz French beans, trimmed and halved
1 × 400g/14oz can of haricot beans, rinsed and
  drained
1 clove of garlic, finely chopped
2 shallots, finely chopped
1 tablespoon chopped fresh fines herbes
  (tarragon, parsley, chervil and chives)

For the dressing
1½ teaspoons Dijon mustard
1½ teaspoons white wine vinegar
2 tablespoons extra virgin olive oil
salt and freshly ground black pepper

1. First make the mustard dressing: whisk the mustard and vinegar together in a small bowl. Gradually whisk in the oil to make a smooth, thick dressing. Season to taste with salt and pepper.
2. Bring a saucepan of boiling water to the boil. Add the broad beans and French beans and cook for 2–3 minutes until just tender. Drain, refresh under cold running water and leave to drain well. Remove the tough outer skins from the broad beans.
3. Put the broad beans, French beans and haricot beans into a bowl and add the garlic, shallots, herbs and mustard dressing. Toss together well and adjust the seasoning to taste.

MIXED POD SALAD

110g/4oz baby sweetcorn
110g/4oz runner or flat beans
170g/6oz shelled fresh broad beans
110g/4oz cherry tomatoes, halved
½ small red onion, thinly sliced
30g/1oz Parmesan or Pecorino cheese, thinly
  shaved
1 tablespoon shredded fresh basil leaves
55g/2oz alfalfa sprouts

For the dressing
2 tablespoons olive oil
1 tablespoon vegetable oil
1 tablespoon white wine vinegar
1 clove of garlic, finely chopped
a pinch of dry English mustard
a pinch of soft light brown sugar
salt and freshly ground black pepper

1. First make the dressing: put all the ingredients together in a screwtop jar and shake well.
2. Trim the baby sweetcorn. Top and tail the beans and remove the tough edges if using runner beans. Cook the sweetcorn and beans in boiling salted water for a few minutes until tender but still crunchy. Drain, put into a bowl and while hot pour over the dressing.
3. Cook the broad beans until tender. Drain and remove the tough outer skins. Add the broad beans to the other vegetables and toss.
4 Add the cherry tomatoes, onion, cheese, basil leaves and alfalfa sprouts. Toss well and transfer to a salad bowl, draining away any excess dressing.

OKRA À LA GRECQUE

2 tablespoons olive oil
1 medium red onion, chopped
1 large clove of garlic, crushed
450g/1lb tomatoes, peeled and chopped (see page 22)
1 teaspoon sugar
1 tablespoon lemon juice
1 tablespoon chopped fresh oregano
55ml/2fl oz red wine
salt and freshly ground black pepper
340g/12oz okra, topped and tailed and cut into 2.5cm/1in lengths
3 tablespoons chopped fresh parsley

1. Heat half the oil in a large frying pan. Add the onion and cook over a low heat until soft.
2. Add the garlic, tomatoes, sugar, lemon juice, oregano, wine, salt and pepper and cook for 5 minutes.
3. Heat the remaining oil in a frying pan with a lid, add the okra and fry until lightly browned. Add to the onion and tomato mixture.
4. Cover and cook over a very low heat for 30–45 minutes, stirring occasionally, until the okra is tender but not falling apart.
5. Check the seasoning and add the parsley. Serve hot or cold.

BHINDI BHAJI

(SWEET AND SOUR STIR-FRIED OKRA)

450g/1lb okra, topped and tailed
3 tablespoons ghee, clarified butter (see page 529) or sunflower oil
¼ teaspoon cumin seeds
¼ teaspoon black mustard seeds
¼ teaspoon black onion (kalonji) seeds
¼ teaspoon fenugreek seeds
¼ teaspoon fennel seeds
1 small onion, finely chopped
1 medium-hot green Dutch chilli, deseeded and chopped (see page 22)
2 teaspoons ground coriander
1 teaspoon ground cumin
½ teaspoon ground turmeric
1 large tomato, peeled, deseeded and chopped (see page 22)
1 teaspoon sugar
4 teaspoons lemon juice
4–5 tablespoons water
½ teaspoon salt
½ teaspoon garam masala

To serve
warm chapatis or spiced pilau rice (see page 359)

1. Wash the okra in cold water and pat dry on a clean tea-towel.
2. Heat the ghee, clarified butter or oil in a large, deep frying pan with a lid. Add the seeds, cover and fry over a medium to high heat until the mustard seeds begin to pop. Uncover the pan, quickly stir in the onions and fry over a low heat for 5 minutes until the onion is soft and lightly browned.
3. Stir in the chilli and ground spices and fry for 1 further minute. Add the tomato, okra, sugar, lemon juice, water and salt. Bring back to a simmer, cover and cook over a low heat for about 8–10 minutes until the okra are *al dente*.
4. Spoon the okra into a warmed serving dish and sprinkle over the garam masala. Serve with warm chapatis or spiced pilau rice.

OKRA AND TOMATO CURRY

2 tablespoons olive oil
1 onion, roughly chopped
1 clove of garlic, crushed
1 leek, trimmed and sliced
1 red pepper, deseeded and roughly diced
1 aubergine, roughly cubed
2 tablespoons curry powder (see page 528)
140–200g/5–7oz okra, topped and tailed
2 tablespoons tomato purée
150ml/¼ pint spicy vegetable stock (see page 531)
salt and freshly ground black pepper

To serve
brown rice

1. Heat the oil in a large saucepan, add the onion and garlic, cover and cook over a low heat for 5 minutes until softened.
2. Add the leek, pepper and aubergine. Cover and cook for 10–15 minutes, stirring regularly to prevent burning, until the vegetables have softened. Add the curry powder and cook for a further 2 minutes.
3. Slice the okra roughly and add to the other vegetables together with the tomato purée and stock. Allow to simmer for 10–15 minutes until the sauce has thickened and the okra are tender. Season to taste with salt and pepper. Serve with brown rice.

SUMMER GREEN SOUP

450g/1lb fresh peas in the pods
1 litre/1¾ pints summer vegetable stock (see page 530)
2 large courgettes
½ cucumber
225g/8oz baby new potatoes, scrubbed
55g/2oz butter
1 bunch of spring onions, cleaned and chopped
salt and freshly ground black pepper
a handful of lettuce, finely shredded
1 tablespoon chopped fresh mint

1. Shell the peas and set aside. Put the pods into a large saucepan with the stock and bring to the boil, then lower the heat and simmer for 20 minutes.
2. Using a potato peeler, peel strips of skin from the courgettes and cucumber to give a striped effect. Cut the courgettes and cucumber into quarters lengthways, then into 1cm/½in pieces crossways. Cut the potatoes into halves or quarters so that they are a similar size.
3. Melt the butter in a large saucepan and when foaming, add the courgettes, cucumber, spring onions and potatoes. Cover and cook over a low heat for 15 minutes. Strain the stock from the other pan on to the vegetables. Season with salt and pepper and simmer for 15 minutes.
4. Stir the peas and lettuce into the soup and simmer for a further 5 minutes until the peas are tender. Add the mint and adjust the seasoning to taste. Serve immediately in warmed soup bowls.

PEA, BROAD BEAN AND GOAT'S CHEESE FLAN

170g/6oz flour quantity shortcrust pastry (see page 521)
110g/4oz shelled fresh or frozen broad beans
55g/2oz shelled fresh or frozen peas
100g/3½oz soft goat's cheese
2 tablespoons chopped fresh chives
1 egg
150ml/¼ pint milk
2 tablespoons double cream
salt and freshly ground black pepper
1 tablespoon freshly grated Parmesan cheese

1. Preheat the oven to 200°C/400°F/gas mark 6.
2. Roll out the pastry and use to line a 20cm/8in flan tin. Bake blind in the preheated oven for 15 minutes (see page 22). Remove from the oven and allow to cool. Lower the oven temperature to 160°C/300°F/gas mark 2.
3. Bring a saucepan of water to the boil, add the broad beans, then lower the heat and simmer for 5 minutes. Drain and refresh the beans under cold running water. Remove the tough outer skins.
4. Put the peas into boiling water and simmer for 3 minutes. Drain and refresh under cold running water.
5. Mix the goat's cheese, chives, egg, milk and cream and season with salt and pepper.
6. Put the peas and beans into the cooked pastry case and pour over the cheese and egg mixture. Sprinkle over the Parmesan cheese and bake in the preheated oven for 25 minutes or until the filling has set.

SPICY PEA AND POTATO SAMOSAS

MAKES 18

4 tablespoons groundnut oil
2 teaspoons black mustard seeds
1 onion, finely chopped
2 medium-hot green Dutch chillies, deseeded and chopped (see page 22)
¾ teaspoon ground turmeric
½ teaspoon ground cumin
¼ teaspoon cayenne pepper
450g/1lb potatoes, such as King Edward's, peeled and cut into 1cm/½in pieces
4 fresh curry leaves
230ml/8fl oz water
170g/6oz shelled fresh or frozen peas
2 tablespoons chopped fresh coriander

For the samosa dough
285g/10oz plain flour, plus extra for kneading
salt
150ml/¼ pint warm water
2 tablespoons sunflower oil, plus extra for deep-frying

To serve
mango chutney, sweet chilli sauce or cucumber and mint raita (see page 513)

1. First make the dough: sift the flour and ¼ teaspoon salt into a mixing bowl. Make a well in the centre and add the water and oil. Mix together to a dough, then turn on to a lightly floured worktop and knead for 3–4 minutes until smooth. Place the dough in the bowl, cover with clingfilm and set aside for 30 minutes.
2. Make the spicy pea and potato filling: heat the oil in a large, deep frying pan with a lid. Add the mustard seeds, cover and leave over the heat until they begin to pop. Quickly add the onion and fry uncovered over a medium to high heat for 6 minutes until soft and lightly browned. Add the chillies and cook for a further 2 minutes.
3. Stir in the turmeric, cumin, cayenne,

½ teaspoon salt, the potatoes, curry leaves and water. Cover and cook over a low heat for 20–25 minutes, stirring from time to time, until the potatoes are tender.

4. Stir in the peas and cook for a further 5–6 minutes if using fresh and 3–4 minutes if using frozen, until the peas are tender. Remove from the heat, season well with salt and pepper and leave to cool completely.

5. Heat oil in a deep-fryer to 180°C/350°F. Divide the dough into 18 pieces and set them to one side, covered with a sheet of clingfilm to prevent them from drying out. Roll each piece into a thin 15cm/6in disc, keeping each one separate with a small sheet of clingfilm.

6. Take one disc of dough and fold it in half. Put a heaped tablespoon of the filling mixture into the centre of each semi-circle and lightly brush the edge of the dough with water. Fold first one side of the dough and then the other over the filling to make a triangular-shaped parcel, pressing the edges together well to seal. Repeat with the remaining discs of dough.

7. Deep-fry the samosas 4 at a time for 4–5 minutes, turning them halfway through cooking, until crisp and golden. Lift them out with a slotted spoon and leave to drain on plenty of kitchen paper. Serve warm with mango chutney, sweet chilli sauce or cucumber and mint raita.

PETITS POIS À LA FRANÇAISE

225g/8oz shelled fresh or frozen peas
1 large mild onion, very thinly sliced
1 small lettuce, shredded
150ml/¼ pint water
30g/1oz butter
a handful each of fresh mint and parsley
½ clove of garlic, crushed (optional)
salt and freshly ground black pepper
1 teaspoon caster sugar

1. Mix the peas, onion and lettuce together in a flameproof casserole. Add the water, butter, mint, parsley, garlic (if using), salt, pepper and sugar.

2. Cover tightly. Put a double seal of greaseproof paper over the casserole before pressing down the lid to make a good seal.

3. Cook for about 30 minutes over a very low heat until the peas are almost mushy or, better still, bake in the oven preheated to 170°C/325°F/gas mark 3 for 1–2 hours.

PEA AND CUCUMBER SAUTÉ

1 cucumber
salt and freshly ground black pepper
caster sugar
15g/½oz unsalted butter
225g/8oz shelled fresh peas
½ bunch of spring onions, peeled and chopped
1 tablespoon chopped fresh chervil or flat-leaf parsley

1. Cut the cucumber in half lengthways and scoop out the seeds, using a melon-baller or teaspoon. Cut the flesh into 5mm/¼in cubes. Put into a bowl and toss with a pinch each of salt and sugar. Leave to stand for 15 minutes.

2. Bring a small saucepan of water to the boil and add a pinch of salt and sugar. Blanch the peas for 2 minutes, then drain.

3. Pat the cucumber dry on kitchen paper. Heat the butter in a sauté pan and when foaming, add the peas and spring onion and fry briskly for a few minutes until the peas are tender. Add the cucumber and fry briskly for a further 2 minutes. Season with salt and pepper and stir in the herbs.

PEA SALAD WITH RED PEPPER

55g/2oz mellow black olives such as Kalamata,
*   pitted*
1 red pepper
340g/12oz shelled fresh or frozen peas
1–2 cloves of garlic, chopped
2.5cm/1in piece of fresh root ginger, peeled and
*   finely chopped*
3 tablespoons olive oil
grated zest and juice of 1 orange
½ teaspoon paprika
salt and freshly ground black pepper
1 heaped tablespoon chopped fresh mint
1 heaped tablespoon chopped fresh flat-leaf
*   parsley*
2 teaspoons white wine vinegar
a few drops of balsamic vinegar
a pinch of sugar

1. Slice the olives. Deseed the pepper, removing all the pith, and slice finely. Put the olives and pepper into a saucepan with the peas, garlic, ginger, oil, orange juice and paprika and season with salt and pepper. Heat over a low heat and simmer for 15 minutes, stirring occasionally. Remove from the heat and leave to cool completely.

2. Stir in the herbs and adjust the seasoning to taste. Add the orange zest, vinegars and sugar to taste. Pile into a salad bowl and serve at room temperature.

SUGAR-SNAP PEAS WITH PAN-FRIED PARMESAN CROÛTONS

100g/3½oz unsalted butter
½ ciabatta loaf, crust removed and roughly
*   crumbled*
55g/2oz Parmesan cheese, freshly grated
salt and freshly ground black pepper
450g/1lb sugar-snap peas, topped and tailed

1. Melt 85g/3oz of the butter in a large frying pan and when foaming, add the crumbled bread. Lower the heat and fry slowly until the butter is absorbed and the bread is golden-brown.

2. Sprinkle over the cheese and stir to coat the croûtons. Continue to cook for a further 2–3 minutes, stirring occasionally, until the cheese has browned. Remove the croûtons from the pan and set aside.

3. Bring a saucepan of salted water to the boil, add the sugar-snap peas and cook for 1 minute. Drain well.

4. Melt the remaining butter in the frying pan, add the peas and season with salt and pepper. Return the croûtons to the pan, stir briefly to mix and serve.

PEA AND BEAN SPROUT SALAD WITH SOY DRESSING

285g/10oz shelled fresh or frozen peas
1 bunch of spring onions
225g/8oz fresh bean sprouts
55g/2oz alfalfa sprouts
30g/1oz sesame seeds, toasted (see page 22)
1 tablespoon chopped fresh coriander

For the dressing
a walnut-sized piece of fresh root ginger, peeled
1 red chilli
2 tablespoons sweet soy sauce
3 tablespoons lemon juice
grated zest and juice of 1 small orange
1 tablespoon clear honey
3 tablespoons vegetable oil
1 tablespoon sesame oil

1. First make the dressing: peel the ginger and cut it into fine shreds. Cut the chilli in half lengthways, remove the seeds and slice thinly. Put the soy, lemon juice, orange zest and juice and the ginger and chilli into a small saucepan and simmer over a medium heat for 5 minutes to reduce the liquid by one-third. Remove from the heat and stir in the honey and oils. Leave to cool.

2. If using fresh peas, cook in boiling salted water for 5 minutes until tender. Refresh under cold running water and set aside. If using frozen peas, douse in boiling water and cool. Trim the spring onions and cut in half lengthways, then cut on the diagonal into 1cm/½in pieces.

3. Toss the peas, spring onions, bean sprouts, alfalfa sprouts and sesame seeds together with the dressing. Pile into a salad bowl. Sprinkle with the coriander.

SUGAR-SNAP PEAS, MANGETOUT AND BROAD BEAN SALAD

110–170g/4–6oz shelled fresh or frozen broad beans, cooked
310g/11oz sugar-snap peas, blanched and refreshed
170g/6oz mangetout, blanched and refreshed
salt and freshly ground black pepper
1 quantity of French dressing (see page 528)
1–2 tablespoons roughly chopped fresh mint and basil

1. Remove the tough outer skins from the broad beans, leaving the tender, bright green beans.

2. Drain the blanched and refreshed vegetables thoroughly and put into a bowl with the broad beans. Pour over the French dressing, add the herbs and toss carefully. Transfer to a salad bowl.

SWEETCORN SOUP WITH BASIL

2 cobs of fresh sweetcorn
30g/1oz butter
1 onion, finely chopped
1 teaspoon ground cumin
1 clove of garlic, finely chopped
1 red chilli, deseeded and chopped (see page 22)
860ml/1½ pints summer vegetable stock (see page 530)
salt and freshly ground black pepper
150ml/¼ pint double cream
1 tablespoon shredded fresh basil leaves, to garnish

1. Remove the papery husks and silky strands from the outside of the sweetcorn. Stand each cob upright on a large plate and carefully slice away the kernels of corn with a large, sharp knife, keeping the blade as close as you can to the core of the cob.

2. Melt the butter in a large saucepan. Add the onion and fry over a low heat until soft and transparent. Add the cumin, garlic and chilli and fry for 1 further minute. Add the stock and sweetcorn kernels. Season with salt and pepper. Simmer for 10–20 minutes.

3. Stir in the cream, reheat without boiling and serve in warmed soup bowls, sprinkled with the basil.

CHINESE SWEETCORN AND NOODLE SOUP

1 litre/1¾ pints summer vegetable stock (see
    page 530)
1 teaspoon peeled and finely chopped fresh
    ginger
2 cobs of fresh sweetcorn
15g/½oz dried rice vermicelli noodles
2 spring onions, trimmed
4 teaspoons cornflour
1 tablespoon light soy sauce
2 tablespoons Chinese rice wine or dry sherry
salt and freshly ground white pepper
1 egg, beaten

1. Bring the stock and ginger to the boil in a
large saucepan. Meanwhile, remove the papery
husks and silky strands from the outside of the
sweetcorn. Stand each cob upright on a large
plate and slice away the kernels with a large,
sharp knife, keeping the blade as close to the
core as you can.
2. Add the sweetcorn to the stock and simmer
for 5 minutes. Break the noodles into shorter
pieces, put them into a bowl and cover them
with boiling water. Leave to soak for 2 minutes,
then drain. Cut each spring onion into 3 pieces,
then cut each piece lengthways into very fine
shreds.
3. Mix the cornflour to a smooth paste with a
little water, stir into the soup and simmer for 2
minutes. Stir in the soy sauce, Chinese rice wine
and three-quarters of the shredded spring
onions and season to taste with salt and pepper.
4. Bring the soup back to a gentle simmer. Give
it a really good stir in one direction, then
remove the spoon and slowly trickle in the
beaten egg so that it forms long, thin strands in
the soup. Stir in the noodles, then ladle the soup
into warmed soup bowls and serve garnished
with the remaining shredded spring onions.

SWEETCORN, SWEET POTATO AND CASHEW NUT CHOWDER

2 tablespoons vegetable oil
55g/2oz unsalted cashew nuts, roughly chopped
30g/1oz butter
2 onions, finely chopped
2 sticks of celery, finely chopped
salt and freshly ground black pepper
1½ tablespoons plain flour
720ml/1¼ pints summer vegetable stock (see
    page 530)
1 large potato, cut into 1cm/½in pieces
1 sweet potato, cut into 1cm/½in pieces
4 large, fresh sage leaves, very finely chopped
4 cobs of sweetcorn, kernels removed

1. Heat the oil in a large, heavy saucepan. Add
the cashew nuts and fry over a low heat for 1
minute or until lightly browned. Remove the
nuts with a slotted spoon and drain on kitchen
paper. Set aside.
2. Add the butter to the pan and when
foaming, stir in the onions and celery. Season
with salt and pepper and cook over a very low
heat for 10–15 minutes or until the onion is soft
and transparent.
3. Stir in the flour and cook for 1 minute until
it turns a pale biscuit colour. Add the stock and
bring to the boil.
4. Add the potato to the pan, lower the heat
and cook for 3 minutes. Add the sweet potato
and sage and continue to cook for a further 5
minutes.
5. Stir in the sweetcorn and simmer gently for a
further 2–3 minutes until the potatoes are
beginning to break up. Adjust the seasoning to
taste.
6. Serve the chowder in warm soup bowls with
the cashew nuts sprinkled over the top.

ROASTED SWEETCORN SOUP WITH CARAMELIZED ONION AND CURRY BUTTER

4 cobs of fresh sweetcorn
55g/2oz butter, melted
salt and freshly ground black pepper
1 medium onion, finely chopped
1 clove of garlic, crushed
1 small leek, trimmed and thinly sliced
1 carrot, chopped
1 litre/1¾ pints summer vegetable stock (see
  page 530)
caster sugar
lemon juice

For the caramelized onion and curry butter
1 teaspoon sunflower oil
30g/1oz onion, finely chopped
a pinch of caster sugar
½ teaspoon cumin seeds
½ teaspoon coriander seeds
55g/2oz butter, softened
½ teaspoon ground turmeric
½ teaspoon paprika
1 medium-hot red Dutch chilli, deseeded and
  finely chopped (see page 22)
2 tablespoons chopped fresh coriander
fresh coriander leaves, to garnish

1. Preheat the oven to 220°C/425°F/gas mark 7. Remove the papery husks and silky strands from the outside of the sweetcorn and lay the cobs in a small roasting tin lined with kitchen foil. Drizzle with a little of the melted butter, season well with salt and pepper and turn once or twice until well coated in the butter. Roast in the preheated oven for 20 minutes until tender and lightly browned.

2. Make the caramelized onion and curry butter: heat the oil in a small saucepan, add the onion and sugar and fry over a low heat for 6–8 minutes until a deep golden-brown. Set aside to cool completely.

3. Heat a dry, heavy frying pan over a high heat. Add the cumin and coriander seeds and toss for a few seconds until they darken slightly and start to release their aroma. Tip them into a spice grinder and grind them to a fine powder.

4. Put the butter into a bowl and mix in the caramelized onion, roasted spices, turmeric, paprika, red chilli, chopped coriander and a little salt. Set aside in a cool place but do not chill.

5. Remove the sweetcorn from the oven and leave to cool. Then stand each cob upright on a large plate and slice off the kernels with a large, sharp knife, keeping the blade as close to the core as you can.

6. Heat the remaining melted butter in a large saucepan. Add the onion, garlic, leek and carrot and stir well. Cover and cook over a low heat for 10 minutes until all the vegetables begin to soften.

7. Add the stock to the pan and bring to a simmer, then cover and cook for 5 minutes until the vegetables are soft. Add the sweetcorn to the pan and simmer for a further 3 minutes.

8. Purée the soup in batches in a food processor or blender. Return the soup to the rinsed-out pan and season to taste with sugar, lemon juice, salt and pepper. Reheat gently.

9. Ladle the soup into warmed soup bowls and swirl a spoonful of the curry butter into each. Sprinkle with the coriander leaves and serve.

CORN AND CEREAL GRIDDLE CAKES

The griddle cakes can be served for breakfast or as a snack. Spread them with plain or spiced butter (Savoury American Pancakes, see page 490).

MAKES 16

55g/2oz wild rice
55g/2oz pearl barley
2 cobs of fresh sweetcorn
110g/4oz self-raising flour
112ml/4fl oz milk
4 eggs
sea salt
cayenne pepper
oil for frying

1. Cook the wild rice and barley together in boiling water for 30 minutes. Drain and leave to cool. Remove the papery husks and silky strands from the sweetcorn. Stand each cob upright on a large plate and slice away the kernels with a large, sharp knife, keeping the blade as close to the core as you can.
2. Put two-thirds of the sweetcorn kernels into a food processor or a blender. Add the flour, milk and eggs and season with salt and cayenne. Process for about 2 minutes to a very smooth purée.
3. Pour the sweetcorn purée into a large jug and stir in the remaining sweetcorn and the wild rice and barley.
4. Heat 1 teaspoon oil in a heavy frying pan or griddle. Wipe dry with kitchen paper. Drop tablespoons of the corn mixture on to the pan and fry for a few minutes on each side until golden-brown and set. Serve hot.

SWEETCORN AND RED PEPPER FRITTERS

1 tablespoon oil
1 onion, finely diced
1 stick of celery, finely diced
1 red pepper, deseeded and finely diced
1 small red chilli, deseeded and finely chopped
    (optional, see page 22)
salt and freshly ground black pepper
110g/4oz sweetcorn, cooked weight
1 tablespoon finely chopped fresh parsley

For the batter
225g/8oz self-raising flour
½ teaspoon salt
290ml/½ pint milk
1 egg, beaten

1. First make the batter: sift the flour and salt into a large bowl. Make a well in the centre and pour in half the milk. Add the egg and beat well with the milk. Stir the liquid and gradually draw in the flour from the sides of the bowl. Stir in the remaining milk until the batter is the consistency of thick cream and will just run from the spoon. Cover and leave to stand for 10 minutes.
2. Heat the oil in a saucepan. Add the onion, celery, red pepper and chilli and sauté for 4–5 minutes or until just soft. Season with salt and pepper. Add the sweetcorn and parsley and cool slightly before adding to the batter mix.
3. Lightly grease a griddle or heavy frying pan and heat. When really hot, drop 2–3 tablespoons of the batter on to the surface, keeping them well separated.
4. Cook for 2–3 minutes until the undersides of the fritters are brown and bubbles rise to the surface. Lift the fritters with a fish slice, turn them over and brown the other side. Serve warm.

SWEETCORN PUDDING

Serve the pudding with a crisp green salad tossed in a sharp dressing such as bitterleaf salad with pink grapefruit and passion fruit dressing (see page 180).

2 cobs of fresh sweetcorn
55g/2oz butter, plus extra for greasing
1 medium onion, finely chopped
1 clove of garlic, crushed
570ml/1 pint milk
4 large eggs
110g/4oz fresh white breadcrumbs
45g/1½oz Parmesan cheese, freshly grated
1 red chilli, deseeded and chopped (see page 22)
salt and freshly ground black pepper
cayenne pepper

1. Preheat the oven to 190°C/375°F/gas mark 5. Grease a 1 litre/1¾ pint ovenproof dish with butter.
2. Remove the papery husks and silky strands from the outside of the sweetcorn. Place each cob upright on a large plate and slice off the kernels with a large, sharp knife, keeping the blade as close to the core as you can.
3. Melt the butter in a saucepan and when foaming, add the onion and fry over a low heat until soft and transparent. Add the garlic and fry for 1 further minute. Pour in the milk and heat gently until just beginning to steam.
4. Beat the eggs in a bowl. Pour the milk and butter mixture on to the eggs, stirring all the time. Stir in the breadcrumbs, sweetcorn kernels, Parmesan cheese and chilli. Season with salt, pepper and a pinch of cayenne. Leave to stand for 5 minutes to allow the breadcrumbs to swell.
5. Turn the mixture into the prepared dish and bake in the preheated oven for about 40 minutes until golden and set. Serve immediately.

CHARGRILLED SWEETCORN WITH A HOT GARLIC, GREEN CHILLI AND CHIVE DRESSING

The sweetcorn for this dish can also be cooked on a barbecue.

8 small cobs of fresh sweetcorn
170g/6oz clarified unsalted butter (see page 529)
4 green jalapeño chillies, deseeded and finely
  chopped (see page 22)
sunflower oil, for frying
salt and freshly ground black pepper
1 tablespoon dark soy sauce
1 clove of garlic, finely chopped
1 tablespoon lemon juice
2 tablespoons chopped fresh chives

To serve
warm crusty bread or naan bread

1. Pull away the papery husks and silky strands from the outside of the sweetcorn. Drop the cobs into a large saucepan of boiling salted water and cook for 2 minutes. Drain well.
2. Put the clarified butter into a saucepan, add the chillies and keep warm.
3. Heat a ridged cast-iron griddle until smoking hot. Rub the cobs of sweetcorn with oil and season well with salt and pepper. Place them diagonally across the ridges of the griddle and cook them for 8–10 minutes, turning them as each side browns. Lift them on to warmed plates as soon as they are cooked.
4. Stir the soy sauce, garlic, lemon juice, chives and salt and pepper to taste into the clarified butter. Spoon some of the warm mixture over the sweetcorn and serve with warm crusty bread or naan bread.

STIR-FRIED BABY SWEETCORN AND CARROTS WITH SWEET GLAZED TOFU

285g/10oz tofu

For the glaze
2 tablespoons hoisin sauce
1 tablespoon clear honey
3 tablespoons lime juice
2 tablespoons light soy sauce
1 tablespoon sesame oil
1 clove of garlic, crushed

For the stir-fry
2 tablespoons sunflower oil
2.5cm/1in fresh root ginger, peeled and grated
1 clove of garlic, sliced
1 onion, sliced
250g/9oz baby carrots, topped, tailed and scrubbed
300g/11oz baby sweetcorn
290ml/½ pint spicy vegetable stock (see page 531)
1 tablespoon cornflour
2 tablespoons water
1 tablespoon sesame seeds, toasted (see page 22)
1 tablespoon sunflower seeds, toasted (see page 22)

1. Drain the tofu and place on a piece of kitchen paper for 10 minutes. Cut into 2.5cm/1in cubes and put into a bowl.
2. Preheat the oven to 200°C/400°F/gas mark 6.
3. Mix all the ingredients for the glaze together. Pour half of the mixture on to the tofu and mix well to coat. Leave to soak for 10 minutes.
4. Line a baking tray with non-stick baking paper and lay the tofu on it. Bake in the preheated oven for 20–25 minutes, turning the tofu halfway through the cooking time.
5. Meanwhile, heat the oil in a wok, add the ginger and garlic and cook for 1–2 minutes. Add the onion and stir-fry until slightly softened.
6. Add the carrots and sweetcorn and stir-fry for 5 minutes.
7. Add the remaining glaze with the stock. Bring to the boil, then cover and cook for 3 minutes.
8. Slake the cornflour with the water and add to the wok. Bring to the boil, stirring well. Add the tofu and sesame and sunflower seeds and serve immediately.

JAMS CALIFORNIAN VEGETABLES

This recipe was inspired by Jams Restaurant, New York, where they serve a similar beautifully colourful selection of attractively prepared vegetables.

12 small new potatoes, washed but not peeled
12 baby carrots, or 3 carrots peeled and sliced on the diagonal
¼ red pepper, deseeded and cut into 4 strips
¼ yellow pepper, deseeded and cut into 4 strips
4 baby sweetcorn
4 button turnips
16 French beans, topped and tailed
4 broccoli florets
2 courgettes, each cut into 6 diagonal slices
12 radishes
12 strips of cucumber, deseeded
30g/1oz butter
freshly ground black pepper

1. Cook the potatoes and carrots in boiling salted water until just tender. Drain.
2. Blanch all the remaining vegetables except the cucumber in boiling salted water for 2 minutes. Drain.
3. Melt the butter in a sauté pan, add the cucumber and toss all the vegetables in it until lightly glazed. Pile on to a warmed serving dish or divide between 4 individual plates and serve immediately.

Chargrilled Courgettes with Yellow Pepper, Shallot and Chive Salsa

Thai Vegetable Cakes

Thai Red Pumpkin and Coconut Curry, Steamed Bok Choi

Spiced Black-eyed Beans and Potatoes, Spicy Pea and Potato Samosas.

Brown Rice Pilaff with Cajun Vegetables

Broad Bean Succotash with Cheese and Chilli Cornbread

Sautéed Asparagus with Mozzarella and Quail's Eggs

Members of the Squash Family: (clockwise from bottom right) Long Island Cheese, Baby Butternut, Pumpkin, Yellow Pattypans, Green Pattypans, Round Courgettes, Acorn, Blue Onion, Ornamental Gourd, Kaboucha, Onion Squash, Baby Courgettes, Crown Prince, Harlequin, Gem, Marrow, Kerrachi

WARM ORIENTAL SPICED HALLOUMI SALAD

225g/8oz halloumi cheese
2 tablespoons olive oil

For the marinade
½ red onion, thinly sliced
1 clove of garlic, crushed
2 teaspoons unrefined caster sugar
2.5cm/1in fresh root ginger, peeled and grated
1 teaspoon mustard seeds
½ teaspoon Chinese five-spice powder
a good pinch of ground cumin

For the salad
sesame oil
1 red pepper, deseeded and cut into strips
1 orange pepper, deseeded and cut into strips
110g/4oz baby sweetcorn, halved lengthways
110g/4oz broccoli spears
225g/8oz mangetout
110g/4oz bean sprouts
soy sauce
salt and freshly ground black pepper
sesame seeds, lightly toasted (see page 22), to
  garnish

1. Cut the halloumi cheese into 2.5cm/1in cubes.
2. Mix the marinade ingredients together in a large bowl and add the cubes of cheese. Cover and chill for at least 2 hours, turning regularly.
3. Heat the olive oil in a large frying pan, add the cheese and fry over a low heat until the sides begin to brown. Remove and keep warm.
4. Add the sesame oil to the pan with the peppers and sweetcorn. Toss in the hot oil and sauté for 3–4 minutes, then add the broccoli and mangetout. Cook for a further 2–3 minutes. Finally add the bean sprouts and cook for 1 minute before returning the cheese to the pan. Drizzle over some soy sauce and season to taste with salt and pepper. Serve in a warmed serving dish or on individual plates, sprinkled with sesame seeds.

GIANT SPRING ROLLS WITH PODS AND TOFU

225g/8oz firm tofu

For the marinade
2 tablespoons dark or sweet soy sauce
2 tablespoons water
1 tablespoon dry sherry
2.5cm/1in piece of fresh root ginger, peeled and
  grated
1 tablespoon sesame oil
2 cloves of garlic, crushed
1 teaspoon soft light brown sugar

For the filling
1 tablespoon sesame oil
3 bunches of spring onions, trimmed and
  chopped
1 clove of garlic, chopped
55g/2oz alfalfa or bean sprouts
1 small carrot, grated
55g/2oz sugar-snap peas or mangetout, sliced
salt and freshly ground black pepper
vegetable or sesame oil, for brushing
8 sheets of filo pastry
1 quantity sweet lime sauce (see page 507)

1. Cut the tofu into 1cm/½in cubes. Mix together all the marinade ingredients and pour over the tofu. Cover and leave to marinate for at least 2 hours. Drain well, reserving the liquid.
2. Make the filling: heat the oil in a wok or heavy frying pan, add the spring onion and garlic and fry briefly. Add the sprouts, carrot, sugar-snap peas or mangetout and the tofu and toss over the heat for 3–4 minutes until the vegetables are tender. Season with salt and pepper.
3. Preheat the oven to 200°C/400°F/gas mark 6. Brush a baking tray with oil.
4. Lay 4 sheets of filo pastry on a board and brush with oil. Cover each sheet with another sheet of filo. Spoon a quarter of the filling on to the centre of each sheet, at the top. Fold the sides in over the filling and then roll up. Brush again with oil.
5. Place the spring rolls on the prepared baking tray and bake in the preheated oven for about 20 minutes until golden. Serve with the reserved marinade and sweet lime sauce on the side.

PULSES AND LEGUMES

Black beans • Black-eyed beans • Borlotti beans • Butter beans • Cannellini beans • Chickpeas • Flageolet beans • Ful medames • Haricot beans • Kidney beans • Lentils • Pinto beans • Split peas • Tofu • Bean sprouts

INTRODUCTION

Legumes are the family of vegetables producing beans and peas. Pulses are the dried edible seeds. Both are among the earliest cultivated crops. This food group, being low in fat and high in protein, carbohydrate, dietary fibre and complex B vitamins, is beneficial to any diet but especially to the vegetarian diet. If combined with a cereal, pulses produce a meal that will match animal proteins in value. All pulses are of a similar nutritional value although they come in a wide variety of sizes, colours, flavours and textures. Each culture has its favourite pulse. Sweet-flavoured black beans are associated with the Caribbean, refried kidney beans with Mexico, black-eyed beans with the Southern American states, aduki and mung beans with the Orient.

Buy pulses that are plump and shiny. They should be stored in an airtight container in a cool, dark place. Pulses will keep for up to a year but toughen with time. It is best to buy in small quantities from a shop with a high turnover.

Pulses can be cooked to retain their shape or boiled until pulpy and used as a thickening agent. Canned pulses are very good, particularly for making purées, patties or dips. However, they never have quite as good a flavour or texture as dried, soaked and boiled pulses.

Soaking overnight helps pulses to cook evenly. They increase in size and weight by approximately three times, so put them into a large bowl with plenty of room to swell and cover with at least 10cm/4in of water. To quick-soak pulses put them into a pan and cover with plenty of water. Bring to the boil for 10 minutes, then remove from the heat and leave to stand in the hot water for 30–60 minutes. Drain before using. Soaked pulses usually take 1–1½ hours to boil. A pressure cooker is useful for speeding up the cooking process. Lentils and split peas are cooked without soaking and take 30–40 minutes to become tender depending on their size. Pulses retain their nutritional value even after the lengthy soaking and cooking process. Salt toughens their skin, so add salt for the last 10 minutes of cooking only. Pulses have the ability to take on flavour so are equally delicious cooked in homely potages or in highly spiced curries. If cooking pulses to make a salad, soak them in the dressing while still hot so that they gain maximum flavour.

Good as pulses are for vegetarians, they are infamous for their side effects. These are caused by gases produced in the gut during digestion. To minimize the effects, rinse pulses well after soaking – never cook them in the soaking water – and skim off any scum that forms on top during cooking. Digestive spices such as a few slices of fresh root ginger or some dill or caraway can be added during boiling.

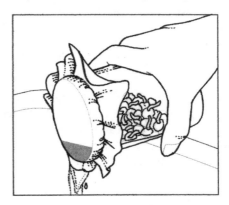

Many pulses can be sprouted. Once the seed has germinated the nutritional value rises dramatically. Sprouts can be bought but they have a short shelf life. Fresh sprouts have a much better flavour and are easy to grow in the required quantity. A jam jar covered with a piece of muslin secured with an elastic band works well. The beans should be doused in water and drained through the muslin lid daily. Make sure that the pulses stay well drained or they may start to ferment. Tiered sprouters are available that enable more than one type of bean to be sprouted at a time. Black-eyed beans and mung beans make large crunchy sprouts that are good in sandwiches; aduki and chickpea sprouts are substantial and have a nutty flavour. Lentils make spicy, peppery sprouts. Seeds and grains can also be sprouted. Try various sorts to find a favourite. Alfalfa is sprouted from small seeds. The sprouts are fine with an earthy, peppery flavour that is a cross between mustard and cress and bean sprouts. They are very nutritious, containing 40% protein and assorted vitamins and minerals. Sprouts take 2–4 days to grow depending on the size of the bean grain or seed.

Aduki beans originated in Japan. These small, deep red beans have a sweet, nutty flavour and are frequently used in oriental dishes. They make very good salads.

Borlotti, **cannellini**, **black-eyed**, **kidney**, **pinto**, **flageolet**, **haricot** and **black beans** all behave in much the same way but have slightly different flavours. Kidney beans should be red and glossy. They have a very good texture and mash well. Care should be taken to boil kidney beans for at least 15 minutes to destroy toxins they produce which can cause food poisoning. Pinto beans are most succulent in casseroles and stews. Haricot beans are sometimes called navy or Boston beans. Flageolets are a beautiful pale green and have a similarly delicate flavour.

Butter beans are hearty and filling. They need to be well soaked before cooking. The larger beans tend to fall apart easily, so choose smaller butter beans if they are to be served whole when cooked. **Lima beans** are similar to butter beans. They are pale green and smaller, with an excellent texture and flavour. It is a pity that they are so difficult to find dried. Look for them in wholefood shops.

Chickpeas have a robust, nutty flavour and good texture. They blend well with other vegetables and are useful to add more substance to a dish. Chickpeas are used prolifically in Mediterranean and Middle Eastern cooking. In India they are ground into gram flour to make bhajis and flat breads.

Ful medames are small Egyptian brown beans with a strong, nutty flavour. They can also be difficult to find. Dried broad beans, sometimes known as **fava beans**, make a good substitute.

Lentils can be yellow, green, brown or red. Yellow and green lentils are larger and have more substance than red. Red lentils are very fine and cook in about 20 minutes. They can be a useful thickening agent if allowed to cook down to a thick purée. Brown lentils are red lentils retaining the outer husk. Lentils can be cooked without soaking although some believe that a short soak will make them more digestible. **Puy lentils** are grown in the Auvergne region of France. They are valued for their peppery flavour and for retaining their shape even after cooking. **Dried peas** are available whole or split. Split peas do not hold their shape so are ideal for purées, mashing and thickening casseroles or, classically, mushy peas.

Mung beans are best known for bean sprouts but they can also be cooked whole. They are sweet and soft, making them excellent in purées and dhal. They can be cooked soaked or unsoaked and will take 30–40 minutes.

Soya beans have all the nutritional benefits of animal protein with none of the disadvantages of saturated fat content. For thousands of years the Chinese have called soya beans the 'meat of the earth'. They are small and oval and can be yellowish-brown or black. Their texture is very dense and they need to be soaked for at least 12 hours before cooking like any other bean. It is for the many products that are soya-based that the bean is best known. It is used as texturized vegetable protein, milk is extracted, it is fermented into soy sauce and ground into flour, and the curds are made into tofu.

Tofu is made, rather like cheese, with the pressed curds of soya milk. It is available in different textures – firm, medium and soft. Silken tofu is soft and creamy like cream cheese. Smoked tofu has a flavour similar to bacon. It is best to buy an organic, medium-textured tofu, which will be suitable for most recipes. Tofu has little flavour so use it marinated, cubed and added to spicy soups and stews or mashed with other flavourings and made into burgers.

MIXED BEAN PÂTÉ ON BRUSCHETTA

100g/3½oz canned borlotti beans, drained
  weight
100g/3½oz canned black-eyed beans, drained
  weight
100g/3½oz canned flageolet beans, drained
  weight
2 tablespoons tahini
55ml/2fl oz water
1 clove of garlic, crushed
1 tablespoon chopped fresh mint
1 tablespoon chopped fresh chives
150ml/¼ pint olive oil
juice of 1–2 lemons
salt and freshly ground black pepper

For the bruschetta
1 baguette
1 clove of garlic
olive oil
1 tablespoon chopped fresh chives, to garnish

1. Rinse the beans very well under cold running water and put into a food processor or blender with the tahini, water, garlic, mint and chives. Process until smooth.
2. With the motor still running, pour in the oil slowly. Add lemon juice, salt and pepper to taste. If the mixture is very thick, add more water. Chill, covered, for 3–4 hours to allow the flavours to develop.
3. Preheat the grill. Slice the baguette on the diagonal and toast both sides. Cut the garlic in half and rub one side of the toast with it. Drizzle with a little oil.
4. Spoon the pâté on to the bruschetta and sprinkle with the chives before serving.

BLACK BEAN HASH

170g/6oz dried black beans, soaked overnight
1 tablespoon olive oil
½ medium onion, finely chopped
110g/4oz chestnut mushrooms, sliced
1 clove of garlic, crushed
1 red chilli, deseeded and chopped (see page 22)
2 tablespoons chopped fresh coriander
1 egg, beaten
salt and freshly ground black pepper
4 pitta breads

To serve
salad leaves, tomato and red onion slices
Greek yoghurt or hummus (see page 325) or
  roasted garlic mayonnaise (see page 512)

1. Rinse and drain the beans and place in a saucepan. Cover with plenty of fresh water and simmer for about 1 hour until tender, then drain.
2. Heat the oil in a frying pan, add the onion and mushrooms and fry until soft. Stir in the garlic and chilli and fry for 1 further minute.
3. Lightly mash the beans and stir in the mushroom mixture, coriander and egg. Season to taste with salt and pepper.
4. Wipe out the frying pan and heat a little more oil. Fry the bean mixture briskly until hot all the way through and beginning to crisp.
5. Meanwhile, warm the pitta bread in the oven or under the grill. Arrange some salad in the pitta bread and top with some of the bean mixture and a generous spoonful of yoghurt, hummus or mayonnaise.

NOTE: The egg can be left out of the mixture, in which case the result will be similar to refried beans.

JAMAICAN BLACK BEAN POT

225g/8oz black beans, soaked overnight
2 tablespoons vegetable or sunflower oil
1 large onion, sliced
1 red pepper, deseeded and sliced
1 green pepper, deseeded and sliced
1 yellow pepper, deseeded and sliced
2 cloves of garlic, crushed
a walnut-sized piece of fresh root ginger, peeled
    and grated
½ teaspoon each ground cinnamon and ground
    allspice
1 teaspoon paprika
425ml/¾ pint spicy vegetable stock (see
    page 531)
a large pinch of dried red chilli flakes
1 × 225/8oz can of plum tomatoes
4 sprigs of fresh thyme
salt and freshly ground black pepper
450g/1lb butternut squash or pumpkin
30g/1oz butter
55g/2oz soft dark brown sugar

1. Rinse and drain the beans.
2. Heat the oil in a large saucepan. Add the onion and fry over a low heat until soft and golden-brown. Stir in the peppers and cook until beginning to soften. Add the garlic, ginger, cinnamon, allspice and paprika and stir over the heat for a further 2–3 minutes.
3. Pour in the stock and stir to remove any sticky sediment from the base of the pan. Add the chilli flakes, tomatoes and thyme. Stir in the beans and season with pepper. Simmer for about 1 hour until the beans are tender.
4. Peel the squash or pumpkin and remove the seeds and fibres, using a teaspoon. Cut the flesh into 2cm/¾in cubes. Heat the butter in a sauté pan, add the squash and fry until beginning to brown. Add the sugar and shake over the heat until it has melted. Spoon the squash into the bean pot. Put a little stock or liquid from the beans into the sauté pan and stir to remove all the sticky sediment. Add to the bean pot.
5. Season with salt and simmer for a further 20–30 minutes until the squash is cooked, the beans are very tender and the liquid is syrupy and well flavoured. Remove the sprigs of thyme before serving.

AUBERGINE AND BLACK-EYED BEAN CURRY

2 tablespoons olive oil
1 red onion, roughly chopped
1 leek, trimmed and thinly sliced
1 large aubergine, cubed
1 bulb of fennel, cored and diced
2 tablespoons korma curry powder
290ml/½ pint spicy vegetable stock (see
    page 531)
2 tablespoons tomato purée
400g/14oz black-eyed beans, cooked weight
salt and freshly ground black pepper

1. Heat the oil in a saucepan, add the onion and the leek and sauté for 1–2 minutes. Add the aubergine and fennel and season with salt and pepper. Cover and cook over a low heat for 10–15 minutes until softened, stirring occasionally. The vegetables should be very soft but still holding their shape. Add the curry powder and cook for a further 2–3 minutes.
2. Add the stock and the tomato purée. Increase the heat slightly and bring to the boil, then reduce to a simmer. Add the cooked beans and simmer gently for 10–15 minutes or until the sauce has thickened. Season to taste with salt and pepper.

NOTE: Any 'earthy'-tasting beans, such as pinto, borlotti or butter beans, can be substituted if black-eyed beans are not available.
Like all spicy dishes, the flavours develop if the curry is made in advance. It freezes and reheats well.

BLACK-EYED BEAN FAJITAS

225g/8oz black-eyed beans, soaked overnight and cooked (see page 313)
2 tablespoons sesame oil
2 teaspoons cumin seeds
2.5cm/1in piece of fresh root ginger, peeled and grated
4 tablespoons sweet, dark soy sauce
2 teaspoons muscovado sugar
1 teaspoon dried red chilli flakes
2 tablespoons water
1 tablespoon chopped fresh mint
salt and freshly ground black pepper
lime juice

To serve
flour tortillas
shredded lettuce, sliced tomato, slivers of spring onion, sliced cucumber
soured cream
guacamole (see page 213)

1. Drain the beans and dry on kitchen paper. Heat the oil in a heavy frying pan and add the cumin seeds and ginger. Fry briskly until the seeds begin to pop. Add the beans and fry in the spicy mixture for a few minutes.
2. Warm the tortillas and prepare the salad ingredients.
3. Mix together the soy sauce, sugar and chilli flakes and add the water. Pour the mixture into the pan with the beans, add the mint and mix, mashing slightly. Season with salt and pepper and sharpen with a dash of lime juice. Spoon some of the mixture into the tortillas. Top with soured cream, guacamole and salad.

SPICED BLACK-EYED BEANS AND POTATOES

225g/8oz black-eyed beans, soaked overnight
1 tablespoon sunflower oil
1 large onion, sliced
2.5cm/1in piece of fresh root ginger, finely chopped
2 cloves of garlic, crushed
2 teaspoons garam masala
½ teaspoon each ground cumin, coriander and turmeric
4 fresh green chillies, deseeded and chopped (see page 22)
860ml/1½ pints spicy vegetable stock (see page 531)
salt and freshly ground black pepper
1 large waxy potato
2 tomatoes, peeled and chopped (see page 22)
a large handful of fresh coriander, roughly chopped

1. Rinse and drain the beans.
2. Heat the oil in a heavy saucepan, add the onion and fry over a low heat until soft and golden-brown. Add the ginger and garlic and fry for 1 further minute. Add the spices and chillies and stir over the heat for 1 further minute.
3. Pour in the stock and season with pepper. Bring to the boil, then lower the heat, add the beans and simmer for 1–1½ hours until the beans are tender.
4. Peel the potato and cut into 1cm/½in cubes. Add to the beans and season with salt. Cook for about 15 minutes until the potatoes are tender. Stir in the tomato and coriander, adjust the seasoning to taste, and reheat before serving.

BORLOTTI BEAN, PARSLEY AND LIME FRITTERS

For the batter
125g/4½oz plain flour
a pinch of salt
2 egg yolks
3 egg whites
150ml/¼ pint milk

For the beans
1 × 400g/14oz can of borlotti beans, rinsed and
    drained
a large handful of fresh flat-leaf parsley,
    chopped
grated zest of 2 limes
a pinch of cayenne pepper
salt and freshly ground black pepper
oil, for shallow-frying
fresh flat-leaf parsley, to garnish

1. First make the batter: sift the flour with a
pinch of salt into a bowl. Make a well in the
centre.
2. Put the egg yolks into the well and mix with
a wooden spoon. Gradually add the milk to
form a smooth, thick batter. Chill for 30
minutes.
3. Put the borlotti beans into a bowl. Add the
parsley, lime zest and cayenne. Season with salt
and pepper. Stir into the batter.
4. Whisk the egg whites until they form
medium peaks and fold into the bean mixture,
using a large metal spoon.
5. Heat 5mm/¼in oil in a large, heavy frying
pan. Carefully lower large spoonfuls of the
bean mixture into the pan. Fry for 2–3 minutes
on each side, then drain on kitchen paper and
sprinkle with a little salt. Repeat with the
remaining mixture.
6. Serve hot, garnished with parsley.

BUTTER BEAN AND SWEETCORN CHOWDER

85g/3oz dried butter beans, soaked overnight
30g/1oz butter
1 large onion, sliced
2 sticks of celery
3 sprigs of fresh marjoram
570ml/1 pint summer vegetable stock (see
    page 530)
1 medium red potato
2 cobs of sweetcorn
290ml/½ pint milk
salt and cayenne pepper

To serve
rouille (see page 512)
2 tablespoons double cream
fresh flat-leaf parsley

1. Rinse and drain the beans.
2. Melt half the butter in a large saucepan. Add
the onions and fry over a low heat until
beginning to soften. Remove any stringy
threads from the celery and slice. Put into the
pan with the onion and fry until both are
softened. Add the marjoram and fry briefly.
3. Put the beans and stock into the pan. Bring
to the boil, then lower the heat and simmer
gently for about 1 hour until the beans are
almost mushy.
4. Meanwhile, peel the potato and cut into
1cm/½in cubes. Melt the remaining butter in a
saucepan, add the potato, cover and fry gently
for about 10 minutes. Slice the kernels from the
cobs and add to the pan. Pour in the milk,
season with salt and a small pinch of cayenne
pepper and simmer for 5–10 minutes until the
potato is tender.
5. Purée the cooked bean mixture in a food
processor or blender. Stir in the sweetcorn and
potato mixture. Reheat and serve in warmed
soup bowls with a spoonful of rouille and a
swirl of cream on each, scattered with parsley.

BUTTER BEAN CASSOULET

SERVES 6

285g/10oz butter beans, soaked overnight
2 tablespoons olive oil
1 large onion, sliced
1 whole bulb of garlic, peeled
2 medium leeks, trimmed and sliced
1 red pepper, deseeded and sliced
1 × 400g/14oz can of tomatoes
570ml/1 pint summer vegetable stock (see
    page 530)
2 sprigs of fresh thyme
salt and freshly ground black pepper
1 large red potato

For the crust
110g/4oz fresh white breadcrumbs
85ml/3fl oz olive oil
2 cloves of garlic, chopped
2 tablespoons chopped fresh flat-leaf parsley

1. Rinse and drain the beans. Put into a
saucepan and cover with plenty of fresh water.
Simmer for about 1 hour until tender. Drain.
2. Heat the oil in a large saucepan, add the
onion and fry over a low heat until soft and
golden. Add the whole cloves of garlic, leeks
and pepper. Cover and fry gently for about 10
minutes, shaking the pan from time to time.
Add the tomatoes, butter beans, stock and
thyme and season with salt and pepper. Simmer
for a further 10 minutes.
3. Preheat the oven to 180°C/350°F/gas mark 4.
4. Peel the potato and cut into 2.5cm/1in cubes.
Stir into the tomato mixture. Pour into a large
casserole, cover and cook in the preheated oven
for 1–1½ hours until the butter beans and
potatoes are tender.
5. Increase the oven temperature to 200°C/
400°F/gas mark 6. Mix the breadcrumbs
together with the oil, garlic and parsley. Season
with salt and pepper. Scatter the crumb mixture
on top of the cassoulet and bake for a further 15
minutes until golden-brown and crisp.

BUTTER BEAN CROUSTADE

For the base
170g/6oz fresh white breadcrumbs
55g/2oz butter, melted
1 clove of garlic, crushed
55g/2oz Cheddar cheese, grated
2 tablespoons roughly chopped fresh mixed
    herbs, such as parsley, oregano, thyme
1 teaspoon mustard seeds
1 teaspoon caraway seeds

For the filling
1 tablespoon olive oil
1 onion, finely chopped
1 clove of garlic, crushed
1 × 400g/14oz can of chopped tomatoes
2 tablespoons tomato purée
salt and freshly ground black pepper
a pinch of sugar
225g/8oz broad beans, cooked weight
110g/4oz butter beans, cooked weight

For the topping
110ml/4fl oz crème fraîche
1 egg, beaten
55g/2oz Cheddar cheese, grated

1. Preheat the oven to 200°C/400°F/gas mark 6.
2. First make the base: mix the breadcrumbs,
melted butter, garlic, cheese, herbs and seeds
together in a large bowl. Put the mixture into a
23cm/9in flan dish and press it evenly over the
base and up the sides of the dish, using the back
of a tablespoon.
3. Bake on the top shelf of the preheated oven
for 10–15 minutes or until set and evenly
browned. Set aside.
4. Make the filling: heat the oil in a large
saucepan, add the onion and garlic and cook
over a low heat until the onion is soft and
transparent. Increase the heat and add the
tomatoes and the tomato purée. Season with a
little salt and pepper and the sugar, then reduce
by boiling to make a very thick sauce.
5. Pop the broad beans out of their tough skins
and add to the sauce together with the butter
beans. Season to taste with salt and pepper.

319

Spoon into the baked croustade base and level the surface with a palette knife.

6. Make the topping: mix the crème fraîche, egg and cheese together in a bowl and season to taste with salt and pepper. Pour over the tomato filling. Bake the croustade in the hot oven for 15–20 minutes or until the top is evenly browned. Serve warm or cold.

BUTTER BEAN TART WITH CRÈME FRAÎCHE

225g/8oz flour quantity shortcrust pastry (see page 521)

For the filling
2 tablespoons olive oil
½ red onion, thinly sliced
1 clove of garlic, crushed
1 yellow pepper, deseeded and thinly sliced
1 small leek, trimmed and thinly sliced
½ bulb of fennel, cored and finely diced
1 bay leaf
salt and freshly ground black pepper
1 × 400g/14oz can of tomatoes, chopped
1–2 tablespoons tomato purée
a pinch of sugar
110g/4oz butter beans, cooked weight

For the topping
150ml/¼ pint crème fraîche
55g/2oz Cheddar cheese, grated
1–2 teaspoons dried breadcrumbs

1. Line a 20cm/8in flan ring with the pastry. Chill thoroughly.
2. Preheat the oven to 200°C/400°F/gas mark 6.
3. Make the filling: heat the oil in a large saucepan, add the onion and garlic and sauté for 1–2 minutes. Add the pepper, leek, fennel and bay leaf and season with salt and pepper. Cover and cook for a further 10 minutes or until the vegetables are soft.
4. Add the tomatoes, tomato purée and sugar. Increase the heat and allow the sauce to reduce to a very thick consistency. Add the butter beans and season to taste with salt and pepper.

Set aside.
5. Bake the pastry case blind in the preheated oven for 10 minutes (see page 22). Lower the oven temperature to 180°C/350°F/gas mark 4.
6. Pour the tomato sauce into the case. Spoon teaspoons of crème fraîche on to the surface of the tart and sprinkle over the cheese, followed by the breadcrumbs. Bake in the oven for 15–20 minutes or until bubbling and golden-brown.

BUTTER BEAN AND BUTTERNUT BAKE

2 tablespoons olive oil
1 small red onion, finely chopped
1 clove of garlic, crushed
2 sticks of celery, thinly sliced
1 small bulb of fennel, cored and thinly sliced
1 small butternut squash, peeled, deseeded and diced
1 small red pepper, deseeded and diced
salt and freshly ground black pepper
290ml/½ pint summer vegetable stock (see page 530)
1 heaped tablespoon tomato purée
55g/2oz dried apricots, roughly chopped
225g/8oz butter beans, cooked weight
55g/2oz egg vermicelli
30g/1oz hard goat's cheese, grated

1. Heat the oil in a saucepan, add the onion and garlic and sauté for 1–2 minutes. Add the celery, fennel, squash and pepper and season with salt and pepper. Cover and cook over a low heat for 8–10 minutes or until the vegetables are beginning to soften, stirring occasionally.
2. Add the stock together with the tomato purée, cover and cook over a low heat for 15–20 minutes until the sauce has reduced slightly.
3. Preheat the oven to 180°C/350°F/gas mark 4.
4. Add the apricots, butter beans and vermicelli to the pan and mix carefully. Season to taste with salt and pepper. Transfer the mixture to an ovenproof dish and sprinkle the cheese over the surface. Bake near the top of the preheated oven for 20 minutes or until the top is golden-brown.

BAKED HONEY AND DIJON BUTTER BEANS

2 tablespoons Dijon mustard
2 tablespoons clear honey
2 tablespoons olive oil
finely grated zest and juice of 1 lemon
2 × 400g/14oz tins of butter beans, rinsed and
    drained
4 sprigs of fresh thyme
salt and freshly ground black pepper

1. Preheat the oven to 200°C/400°F/gas mark 6.
2. Mix the mustard, honey, oil, lemon zest and juice together in a large mixing bowl. Season with salt and pepper.
3. Add the butter beans to the bowl and stir well to coat thoroughly in the dressing.
4. Place the beans in a roasting tin or ovenproof dish and scatter over the thyme. Bake on the top shelf of the preheated oven for 25–30 minutes, stirring occasionally, or until the beans are hot and beginning to brown.
5. Remove the thyme and transfer the beans to a warmed serving dish.

CANNELLINI BEAN PÂTÉ

1 × 400g/14oz can of cannellini beans
3 tablespoons olive oil
3 shallots or ½ medium onion, finely chopped
3 cloves of garlic
a large pinch of cayenne pepper
150ml/¼ pint summer vegetable stock (see
    page 530)
salt and freshly ground black pepper
1 tablespoon fresh coriander leaves

1. Rinse and drain the beans and set aside. Heat 2 tablespoons of the oil in a frying pan, add the shallots or onion and fry over a low heat until softened. Crush 2 cloves of the garlic and add to the pan with the cayenne and fry for 1 further minute. Stir in the stock and beans, season with salt and pepper and simmer for about 10 minutes until the stock has reduced by half.

2. Mash or purée in a food processor or blender. Adjust the seasoning to taste and spoon into a serving dish. Cut the remaining cloves of garlic into fine slivers. Heat the remaining oil in a small pan and cook the garlic briefly until golden. Pour the hot garlic and oil over the top of the pâté and scatter with coriander leaves.

CANNELLINI BEAN SALAD WITH LEMON AND SAGE

2 × 400g/14oz cans of cannellini beans
6 spring onions, trimmed and chopped
1 yellow pepper, deseeded and finely diced
grated zest and juice of 1 lemon
4 tablespoons olive oil
1 clove of garlic, crushed
2 tablespoons chopped fresh sage
salt and freshly ground black pepper

1. Rinse the cannellini beans and put into a bowl. Add the spring onions and yellow pepper.
2. Mix together the lemon zest and juice, the oil, garlic, sage, salt and pepper. Check the seasoning and add more oil if the dressing is too sharp, but it should taste lemony.
3. Pour the dressing over the beans and mix well. Allow to stand for 1 hour before serving.

CHICKPEA AND FENNEL SOUP WITH ROUILLE

1 large onion
2 bulbs of fennel
2 tablespoons olive oil
100ml/3½fl oz dry white wine
1 × 400g/14oz can of chickpeas
570ml/1 pint summer vegetable stock (see
    page 530)
juice of ½ lemon
salt and freshly ground black pepper
4 tablespoons double cream
1 tablespoon chopped fresh fennel or dill leaves
½ quantity rouille (see page 512)

To serve
crusty bread

1. Preheat the oven to 180°C/350°F/gas mark 4.
2. Cut the onion into wedges. Cut the fennel in half, remove any feathery leaves and reserve. Remove the hard core and cut each half into 4 wedges.
3. Put the onion and fennel into a flameproof casserole dish and add the oil. Cover and cook in the preheated oven for 1–1½ hours, stirring occasionally, until the vegetables are soft. Remove from the oven.
4. Add the wine and bring to the boil on the top of the stove, then reduce rapidly until about 2 tablespoons of liquid remain.
5. Drain the chickpeas and rinse very well. Add half of them to the fennel mixture with the stock, lemon juice, salt and pepper. Bring to the boil, then lower the heat and simmer for 15 minutes.
6. Purée the soup in a food processor or blender and return it to the rinsed-out pan. Add the cream, the remaining chickpeas and the fennel or dill leaves. Add more water or stock if the soup is very thick.
7. Serve the soup in warmed soup bowls, each topped with a generous spoonful of rouille. Hand the bread separately.

CURRIED CHICKPEA BURGERS

These can be served traditional burger-style in a bap or ciabatta roll. Alternatively, pile into pitta bread with plenty of salad.

MAKES 8

1 red chilli, deseeded and finely chopped (see
    page 22)
a walnut-sized piece of fresh root ginger, peeled
    and finely chopped
2 sticks of celery, chopped
1 small onion, finely chopped
1 × 400g/14oz can of chickpeas
2 teaspoons curry paste
1 egg
85g/3oz fresh white breadcrumbs
salt and freshly ground black pepper
oil to shallow-fry

1. Put the chilli, ginger, celery and onion into a food processor or blender and process until smooth.
2. Drain the chickpeas, put into the food processor or blender with the curry paste and process briefly. Add the egg and breadcrumbs and process again. Season with salt and pepper.
3. Shape the mixture into 8 patties. Heat about 5mm/¼in oil in a heavy frying pan. Add the burgers and fry until golden-brown on each side.

CHICKPEA AND OLIVE PANCAKE

It is important to cook the batter in a large tin so that the pancake is very thin and crisp. It can be served as a side dish or with vegetable purées or pâtés.

140g/5oz chickpea flour (gram flour)
½ teaspoon salt
400ml/14fl oz tepid water
4 tablespoons olive oil, plus extra for brushing
2 heaped teaspoons chopped fresh rosemary

1. Sift the flour and salt into a mixing bowl and make a well in the centre. Gradually whisk in the water, drawing the flour in from the sides of the well, until the batter is smooth. Cover and set aside for 1 hour.
2. Preheat the oven to 250°C/425°F/gas mark 7 and put a baking sheet in the oven to heat.
3. Using a wooden spoon, stir the oil and rosemary into the batter. Brush a 30cm/12in pizza or Swiss roll tin with oil and heat in the oven. Pour the batter into the tin and set on the hot baking sheet. Bake in the oven for 20 minutes until crisp and golden-brown.
4. Cool for 5 minutes, then slice into wedges.

CHICKPEA AND SPINACH CURRY

This curry can be served topped with peeled and quartered hard-boiled eggs.

225g/8oz dried chickpeas, soaked overnight
1 tablespoon vegetable oil
2 teaspoons mustard seeds
55g/2oz unsalted butter
1 large onion, sliced
3 cloves of garlic, crushed
2 green chillies, chopped
1 teaspoon ground cumin
1 teaspoon ground coriander
1 teaspoon ground turmeric
¼ teaspoon cayenne pepper
425ml/¾ pint spicy vegetable stock (see page 531)
450g/1lb tomatoes, peeled (see page 22)
salt and freshly ground black pepper
450g/1lb fresh spinach

To serve
Greek yoghurt
chopped coriander

1. Rinse and drain the chickpeas.
2. Heat the oil in a heavy frying pan. Add the mustard seeds and fry until they begin to pop. Add the butter and when melted, add the onion and fry over a low heat until very soft and brown. Stir in the garlic, chillies and spices and fry for 1 further minute.
3. Spoon the mixture into a large saucepan. Pour the stock into the frying pan and bring to the boil, stirring and scraping any sediment from the base of the pan. Pour into the saucepan.
4. Chop the tomatoes and add to the pan with the chickpeas. Season with pepper and bring to the boil, then lower the heat and simmer for about 1 hour until the chickpeas are tender.
5. Remove any tough stalks from the spinach and wash thoroughly. Add the spinach to the pan and season with salt. Simmer for a further 5 minutes. Swirl a portion of yoghurt on each serving and scatter with coriander.

CHICKPEA AND SQUASH COUSCOUS

110g/4oz dried chickpeas, soaked overnight
4 tablespoons olive oil
2 onions, sliced
½ teaspoon ground cinnamon
1 teaspoon ground turmeric
1 teaspoon ground cumin
2 red chillies, deseeded and chopped (see page 22)
2 cloves of garlic, crushed
4 ripe tomatoes, peeled and chopped (see page 22)
2 tablespoons chopped fresh coriander
salt and freshly ground black pepper
1 litre/1¾ pints summer vegetable stock (see page 530)
225g/8oz carrots
3 courgettes
450g/1lb butternut squash or pumpkin
a pinch of saffron strands
570ml/1 pint water
285g/10oz couscous
a handful of fresh coriander leaves, to garnish

To serve
harissa (see page 510)

1. Rinse and drain the chickpeas. Heat the oil in a large saucepan, add the onions and cook over a low heat until soft and golden. Stir in the cinnamon, turmeric, cumin, chillies and garlic and cook for 1 further minute.
2. Add the tomatoes, chickpeas and coriander to the pan, season with pepper and pour in the stock. Bring to the boil, then lower the heat and simmer for about 40 minutes until the chickpeas are tender.
3. Meanwhile, prepare the vegetables: peel the carrots, trim the courgettes and cut both in half lengthways, then crossways into 2.5cm/1in lengths. Peel the squash, remove the seeds and fibres with a teaspoon and cut the flesh into 2.5/1cm cubes. When the chickpeas are cooked, add the vegetables and the saffron. Season with salt and simmer for a further 30 minutes until the vegetables are cooked.

4. Pour the water over the couscous in a bowl and leave to soak for 10 minutes. Line a colander with a piece of muslin or a clean 'J'-cloth. Place the couscous in the colander and set over the simmering vegetables. Cover and steam for 20 minutes. Alternatively, heat for 5 minutes in a microwave oven on full power.
5. Pile the couscous on to a large serving platter and make a well in the centre. Spoon in the vegetables and chickpeas and scatter with the coriander leaves. Hand the harissa sauce separately.

FALAFEL

MAKES 16–20

225g/8oz dried chickpeas, soaked overnight
1 red onion, roughly chopped
3 cloves of garlic, crushed
1 slice of bread, roughly cubed
a large handful of fresh parsley, tough stalks removed
a large handful of fresh coriander, tough stalks removed
1 teaspoon ground cumin
salt and freshly ground black pepper
oil, for frying

1. Rinse and thoroughly drain the chickpeas. Put into a food processor or blender with the onion, garlic, bread, herbs and cumin. Process to a very smooth paste. Season well with salt and pepper.
2. Divide the mixture evenly to the size required and mould between the palms of your hands to form smooth discs.
3. In a large frying pan, heat enough oil for shallow frying. Fry 4–5 falafel at a time in the hot oil, allowing them to brown evenly before turning over and browning on the other side. Use as required.

NOTE: If you are making falafel in quantity, once they have been browned in the frying pan they can be transferred to a baking tray and cooked in a preheated moderate oven (180°C/350°F/gas mark 4) for 10–15 minutes.

FALAFEL WITH RED RATATOUILLE

1 quantity falafel (see page 324)

For the ratatouille
olive oil
2 red onions, sliced
1 clove of garlic, crushed
1 red pepper, deseeded and diced
1 medium aubergine, diced
1 small bulb of fennel, cored and diced
2 sticks of celery, sliced
1 × 400g/14oz can of chopped tomatoes
1 tablespoon tomato purée
a pinch of sugar
salt and freshly ground black pepper
1–2 tablespoons roughly chopped fresh
*   coriander, to garnish*

1. Heat the oil in a large saucepan, add the onions and garlic, cover and cook over a low heat for 10 minutes or until soft but not coloured. Add the pepper, aubergine, fennel and celery, cover and cook for a further 5–8 minutes, stirring regularly.
2. Add the tomatoes, tomato purée and sugar and season to taste with salt and pepper. Cover and cook gently for about 20 minutes until reduced and the vegetables are completely soft but have not lost their shape. Uncover the pan and cook to reduce if there is too much liquid.
3. Put the cooked falafel on to the surface of the ratatouille and warm through gently. Garnish with the coriander before serving.

NOTE: Cauldron Foods produce excellent organic falafel which can be substituted for the home-made recipe when time is short, making this a wonderful, quick supper dish.

HUMMUS WITH CUMIN AND VEGETABLE CHUNKS

Make a meal of this dish with a green salad and olive oil potato wedges (see page 95) on the side.

1 bunch of radishes
¼ cucumber
1 yellow pepper
12 cherry tomatoes
a handful of fresh mint leaves
a handful of fresh coriander leaves

For the hummus
200g/7oz chickpeas, soaked overnight and
*   cooked (see page 313), or 1 × 400g/14oz can*
*   of chickpeas*
2 tablespoons olive oil
150ml/¼ pint tahina
1–2 cloves of garlic, chopped
juice of 1 lemon
1 teaspoon ground cumin seeds, toasted (see
*   page 22)*
salt and freshly ground black pepper
a pinch of cayenne pepper

To serve
warm pitta bread, naan or crusty bread

1. Wash the radishes. Trim the roots and leave about 5mm/¼in of the stalks. Cut the cucumber into sticks 5cm/2in long. Core and deseed the pepper and cut into sticks the same size as the cucumber. Wash the tomatoes and remove the stalks.
2. Make the hummus: drain the chickpeas and put into a food processor or blender. Add the oil and process to a purée. Add the tahina, garlic, lemon juice and cumin and process until smooth. Season with salt, pepper and cayenne. Serve the hummus in 4 pasta or shallow soup plates with the mint and coriander leaves scattered over the top and the vegetables arranged on the side. Hand the bread separately.

CHICKPEA MASH

This is a substantial alternative to potato to accompany a main course or it may be served as a lunch dish with a tomato salad and a leafy green salad tossed in a robust dressing.

225g/8oz dried chickpeas, soaked overnight, or
*   2 × 400g/14oz cans of chickpeas*
2 bay leaves
5cm/2in cinnamon stick
2 tablespoons olive oil
55g/2oz butter
2 cloves of garlic, chopped
¼ teaspoon cayenne pepper
1 teaspoon ground cumin
salt and freshly ground black pepper

1. If using dried chickpeas, rinse and drain and put them into a large saucepan. Cover with plenty of fresh water. Add the bay leaves and cinnamon stick and bring to the boil, then lower the heat and simmer for about 1 hour until tender. Drain and remove the flavourings. If using canned chickpeas, rinse and drain well.
2. Heat the oil in a saucepan. Add the butter and when foaming, add the garlic, cayenne and cumin and fry for 2 minutes. Add the chickpeas and crush with a potato masher to a rough purée. Stir over the heat until hot all the way through. Season with plenty of salt and pepper. Serve hot.

CHICKPEA PURÉE WITH A GARLIC AND CHILLI CRUST

225g/8oz dried chickpeas, soaked overnight
85g/3oz unsalted butter, melted
4 tablespoons olive oil
1 large red onion, sliced
a pinch of caster sugar
½ teaspoon freshly grated nutmeg
salt and freshly grated black pepper
55g/2oz granary breadcrumbs
2 cloves of garlic, chopped
1 red chilli, deseeded and chopped (see page 22)
2 tablespoons chopped fresh coriander

1. Rinse and drain the chickpeas, put them into a large saucepan and cover with plenty of fresh water. Bring to the boil, then lower the heat and simmer for about 45 minutes until completely soft.
2. Meanwhile, heat 30g/1oz of the butter in a heavy frying pan with half the oil. Add the onion and fry over a low heat until very soft but not browned.
3. Preheat the oven to 200°C/400°F/gas mark 6.
4. Drain the chickpeas, reserving a cupful of the cooking liquid. Purée in a food processor or blender with the remaining butter and a tablespoon of the reserved hot cooking liquid. Season with the sugar, nutmeg, and salt and pepper. Stir in the onion with all the oil and butter and spoon into an ovenproof dish.
5. Put the breadcrumbs, garlic, chilli and coriander into a bowl. Season with salt and pepper and mix with the remaining oil. Scatter on top of the chickpea purée and bake in the preheated oven for about 20 minutes until browned on top.

ROASTED CHICKPEAS

170g/6oz dried chickpeas, soaked overnight
1 bay leaf
3 tablespoons olive oil
½ teaspoon cumin seeds
salt and freshly ground black pepper
lemon juice
1 clove of garlic, crushed
110g/4oz feta cheese, crumbled
2 tablespoons chopped fresh flat-leaf parsley, to garnish

To serve
warm crusty bread

1. Rinse and drain the chickpeas and put them into a large saucepan. Cover with plenty of fresh water and add the bay leaf. Bring to the boil then lower the heat and simmer for about 45 minutes until tender. Discard the bay leaf, drain the chickpeas and leave to stand for an hour or more to dry.
2. Preheat the oven to 200°C/400°F/gas mark 6. Put the oil into a roasting tin and heat on top of the stove. Toss the chickpeas in the oil with the cumin seeds and season with salt and pepper. Roast in the preheated oven for 20 minutes.
3. Season the chickpeas with plenty of lemon juice and toss with the garlic and feta cheese. Scatter with the parsley and serve with crusty bread.

LEMONY CHICKPEAS

170g/6oz dried chickpeas, soaked overnight
½ onion, cut into quarters
2 bay leaves
½ cinnamon stick
150ml/¼ pint olive oil
1 teaspoon cumin seeds
2 cloves of garlic, chopped
1 green chilli, deseeded if liked, and thinly sliced (see page 22)
grated zest and juice of 1 lemon
2 tablespoons chopped fresh flat-leaf parsley
2 tablespoons chopped fresh coriander
salt and freshly ground black pepper

1. Rinse and drain the chickpeas and put them into a large saucepan with the onion, bay leaves and cinnamon stick. Cover with plenty of fresh water and bring to the boil, then lower the heat and simmer for about 45 minutes until tender. Drain and discard the flavourings.
2. Heat 2 tablespoons of the oil in a frying pan, add the cumin seeds and fry until they begin to pop. Add the garlic and chilli and fry briefly. Add the chickpeas and stir to coat in the spicy oil. Cook gently for 5 minutes, stirring occasionally, but taking care not to break up the chickpeas.
3. Spoon the chickpeas into a bowl and dress with the remaining olive oil and lemon zest and juice. Season with salt and pepper and toss in the herbs. Transfer to a serving dish and serve immediately.

DEEP-FRIED CHICKPEA SALAD IN WARM LEMON PITTA BREAD

200g/7oz dried chickpeas, soaked overnight
4 tablespoons extra virgin lemon-flavoured
*   olive oil*
finely grated zest and juice of 2 lemons
salt and freshly ground black pepper
4 pitta breads, cut in half lengthways
groundnut oil, for deep-frying
½ teaspoon paprika
85g/3oz watercress, washed, dried and roughly
*   chopped*
55g/2oz rocket, roughly chopped

1. Rinse and drain the chickpeas and put them into a large saucepan. Cover with plenty of fresh water and bring to the boil, skimming occasionally. Lower the heat and simmer for 50–60 minutes or until tender. Drain on kitchen paper and allow to dry thoroughly.
2. Preheat the oven to 180°C/350°F/gas mark 4.
3. Mix the lemon oil, lemon zest and juice together in a small bowl. Season with salt and pepper.
4. Use two-thirds of the dressing, reserving the remainder, to brush the insides of the pitta bread. Place on a baking tray and bake in the preheated oven for 10–12 minutes or until hot and lightly browned.
5. Half fill a large, heavy saucepan with the groundnut oil and heat until a cube of bread sizzles and browns in 30 seconds. Deep-fry the chickpeas in batches for 2–3 minutes or until crisp and golden-brown. Drain on kitchen paper and sprinkle with the paprika. Season with salt and pepper.
6. Mix the hot chickpeas, watercress, rocket and the remaining dressing together in a large bowl. Divide the mixture between the warm lemon pitta breads. Serve immediately.

FLAGEOLET FALAFELS

These falafels are lighter and moister than the traditional recipe made with chickpeas.

MAKES ABOUT 16

1 × 400g/14oz can of flageolet beans
2 tablespoons olive oil
1 egg, beaten
2 cloves of garlic, crushed
2 teaspoons ground cumin
1 teaspoon coriander seeds, crushed
grated zest and juice of ½ lemon
2 tablespoons chopped fresh flat-leaf parsley
salt and freshly ground black pepper
7 water biscuits or similar, finely crushed
wholemeal flour, for rolling
oil, for frying

To serve
pitta bread
lettuce, tomato, cucumber, red onion
lemon wedges

1. Rinse and drain the beans and dry on kitchen paper. Purée in a food processor or blender. Add the oil, egg, garlic, cumin, coriander, lemon zest and parsley. Season to taste with lemon juice, salt and pepper and blend again until smooth.
2. Put the purée into a bowl and work in the biscuit crumbs. Cover and leave to stand for 20 minutes. Dust a worktop and your hands with flour and shape the purée into about 16 small patties.
3. Heat about 1cm/½in oil in a frying pan until a crumb of bread sizzles vigorously. Fry the patties in batches until golden-brown on both sides. Drain on kitchen paper. Serve immediately inside pitta bread with the salad and topped with a dash of lemon juice. Hand the lemon wedges separately.

FUL MEDAMES WITH SPINACH AND EGGS

Ful medames are small Egyptian brown beans that belong to the broad bean family. Use dried broad beans or lima beans if they are not available.

200g/7oz ful medames, soaked overnight
6 tablespoons olive oil
2 cloves of garlic, chopped
½ teaspoon ground cumin
1 tablespoon chopped fresh flat-leaf parsley
juice of ½ lemon
salt and freshly ground black pepper
4 large eggs
110g/4oz baby spinach leaves
2 teaspoons tahina
2 teaspoons boiling water

1. Rinse and drain the ful medames. Put them into a large saucepan, cover with plenty of fresh water and simmer for 1 hour until tender. Drain and toss in the oil, garlic, cumin, parsley and lemon juice. Season with salt and pepper. Spoon into a serving dish and set aside.
2. Put the eggs into boiling water and simmer for 6 minutes. Cool and shell.
3. Remove any tough stalks from the spinach. Roll the leaves up into a tight bundle and shred finely. Mix the tahina and water together. Toss with the spinach and season with salt and pepper. Pile the spinach on top of the beans. Quarter the eggs and arrange on top of the spinach.

GREEK BEAN SOUP

450g/1lb haricot beans, soaked overnight
5 tablespoons olive oil
1 Spanish onion, very thinly sliced
4 sticks of celery, thinly sliced
2 bay leaves
2 tablespoons sun-dried tomato paste
6 plum tomatoes, peeled, quartered and deseeded (see page 22)
55g/2oz fresh flat-leaf parsley, roughly chopped
55g/2oz fresh basil leaves, roughly torn
salt and freshly ground black pepper

1. Rinse and drain the beans.
2. Heat the oil in a large saucepan, add the onion and celery and cook over a low heat for 10–15 minutes until beginning to soften.
3. Add the beans to the pan. Cover with cold water and bring to the boil, skimming off any froth with a slotted spoon.
4. Add the bay leaves, sun-dried tomato paste and the tomatoes. Lower the heat and simmer gently for 1–1½ hours or until the beans are very tender.
5. Stir in the parsley and basil and season with salt and pepper. Serve immediately in warmed soup bowls.

HARICOT BEANS WITH RED DRESSING

1 × 400g/14oz tin haricot beans

For the dressing
1–2 tablespoons olive oil
balsamic vinegar to taste
½ red onion, thinly sliced
1 red chilli, deseeded and finely diced (see page 22)
1 tablespoon roughly chopped fresh purple basil
1 tablespoon finely chopped fresh parsley
salt and freshly ground black pepper

1. Combine all the dressing ingredients in a large bowl. Leave for at least 30 minutes, longer if possible, to allow the flavours to combine.
2. Add the beans and mix thoroughly. Season to taste with salt and pepper and chill until ready to serve.

HARICOT BEAN COBBLER

1–2 tablespoons oil
1 small leek, trimmed and thinly sliced
1 small red onion, finely chopped
1 red pepper, deseeded and diced
1 yellow pepper, deseeded and diced
1 green chilli, deseeded and finely diced (see
    page 22)
1 red chilli, deseeded and finely diced (see
    page 22)
1–2 carrots, diced
1 bay leaf
salt and freshly ground black pepper
1 × 400g/14oz can of tomatoes, chopped
1 tablespoon tomato purée
a pinch of sugar
1 × 400g/14oz tin haricot beans

For the cobbler
110g/4oz butter
225g/8oz self-raising flour, plus extra for rolling
1 tablespoon finely chopped fresh parsley
1 tablespoon chopped fresh thyme
150ml/¼ pint milk

1. Heat the oil in a saucepan, add the leek and onion and cook over a low heat for 1–2 minutes. Add the peppers, chillies, carrot and bay leaf and season with salt and pepper. Cover and cook gently for 8–10 minutes or until the vegetables have softened, stirring occasionally.
2. Add the tomatoes, tomato purée and sugar. Cover and simmer gently for a further 10 minutes. Remove the bay leaf. Add the haricot beans and transfer to an ovenproof dish. Allow to cool.
3. Preheat the oven to 200°C/400°F/gas mark 6.
4. Make the cobbler dough: in a large bowl, rub the fat into the flour until it resembles coarse breadcrumbs. Add the herbs and season with salt and pepper. Add the milk and mix to a soft but not sticky dough.
5. On a lightly floured worktop, gently press or roll out the dough until it is 1cm/½in thick. Cut out 5cm/2in circles of dough with a pastry cutter and lay on the surface of the bean mixture. Bake in the top shelf of the preheated oven for 15–20 minutes or until the cobbler is

risen and a golden-brown and the sauce is bubbling.

NOTE: The bean mixture can be made well in advance but the cobbler topping has to be cooked immediately.

HARICOT BEANS WITH SHALLOTS

2 tablespoons olive oil
8–12 small shallots, peeled
1 red pepper, deseeded and cut into short strips
1 clove of garlic, crushed
1 leek, trimmed and thinly sliced
4 bay leaves
225g/8oz button mushrooms, washed
290ml/½ pint summer vegetable stock (see
    page 530)
2–3 tablespoons mushroom ketchup
1 × 400g/14oz tin haricot beans
salt and freshly ground black pepper

1. Heat the oil in a saucepan. Add the shallots and turn them in the hot oil for 5–8 minutes until they begin to brown evenly all over. Add the pepper, garlic, leek and bay leaves and season lightly with salt and pepper. Cover and cook gently for a further 5 minutes until softened.
2. Trim the mushroom stalks level with the caps. Add to the vegetables in the pan and increase the heat slightly. Cook briskly for 4–5 minutes, stirring regularly.
3. Add the stock and ketchup and allow to reduce slightly to the consistency of a thin gravy.
4. Add the haricot beans and lower the heat to allow the beans to reheat without breaking up. Season to taste carefully with salt and pepper and remove the bay leaves.

NOTE: Button onions can be substituted for the shallots.
The reduced sauce can be quite salty, so take care not to overseason.
This dish can be made in advance and reheated, in which case do not over-reduce the sauce.

SPICED LENTIL SOUP WITH GARLIC CROÛTONS

For the soup
1–2 tablespoons olive oil
1 leek, trimmed and thinly sliced
1 small red onion, finely chopped
1 red pepper, deseeded and diced
1–2 carrots, diced
1 clove of garlic, crushed
1 bay leaf
110g/4oz red lentils
1 × 400g/14oz can of chopped tomatoes
570ml/1 pint spicy vegetable stock (see page 531)
salt and freshly ground black pepper
Tabasco sauce
1 tablespoon finely chopped fresh parsley, to garnish

For the croûtons
4 slices of white bread
3–4 tablespoons olive oil
1 clove of garlic, crushed

1. First make the soup: heat the oil in a large saucepan. Add the leek, onion, pepper, carrot, garlic and bay leaf, and season with salt and pepper. Cover and cook gently for 8–10 minutes, stirring occasionally, until the vegetables have softened.
2. Add the lentils, tomatoes and stock to the pan and bring to the boil, then lower the heat for 10–15 minutes or until the vegetables and lentils are completely soft. Season to taste with salt, pepper and a dash of Tabasco. Process in a food processor or blender until smooth. More liquid can be added if required. Return to the rinsed-out pan and keep warm.
3. Make the croûtons: remove the crusts from the bread and cut into 1cm/½in cubes. Heat the oil in a frying pan with the garlic until deep brown but not burnt. Remove the garlic from the pan. Add the bread and fry in the hot oil until golden-brown. Drain on kitchen paper and sprinkle lightly with salt.
4. Serve the soup in warmed soup bowls garnished with warm croûtons and sprinkled with the parsley.

LENTIL AND MUSTARD POTTAGE

1 large leek
1 carrot
1 tablespoon olive oil
1 onion, sliced
2 teaspoons dry English mustard
2 teaspoons Dijon mustard
225g/8oz green lentils
860ml/1½ pints summer vegetable stock (see page 530)
1 bay leaf
salt and freshly ground black pepper

1. Trim the leek, cut in half lengthways, wash thoroughly and slice. Peel and chop the carrot. Heat the oil in a large saucepan, add the onion and fry over a low heat until soft. Add the leek and carrot and fry gently for about 5 minutes to soften. Stir in the mustards and cook for 1 further minute.
2. Add the lentils, stock and bay leaf to the pan and season with pepper. Simmer for about 45 minutes until the lentils are tender and the liquid has reduced and thickened. Season to taste with salt.

LENTIL AND MUSHROOM BAKE WITH SEED TOPPING

SERVES 6

2 tablespoons olive oil, plus extra for brushing
1 large onion, sliced
1 carrot, chopped
2 sticks of celery, chopped
225g/8oz chestnut mushrooms, sliced
140g/5oz brown lentils
290ml/½ pint mushroom stock (see page 531)
1 × 225g/8oz can of chopped tomatoes
salt and freshly ground black pepper

For the topping
55g/2oz fresh wholemeal breadcrumbs
30g/1oz pinenuts, chopped
30g/1oz pumpkin seeds
30g/1oz butter, melted
1 tablespoon chopped fresh parsley

1. Heat the oil in a large saucepan, add the onion and fry over a low heat until beginning to brown. Add the carrot, celery and mushrooms and continue to fry gently until soft. Stir in the lentils, stock and tomatoes. Season with salt and pepper, cover and simmer for 30 minutes until the lentils are tender and the liquid has reduced to a syrupy sauce binding the ingredients together. Adjust the seasoning to taste.
2. Preheat the oven to 190°C/375°F/gas mark 5. Brush an ovenproof dish with oil.
3. Make the topping: mix together the breadcrumbs, pinenuts, pumpkin seeds, butter and parsley. Season with salt and pepper.
4. Spoon the lentil mixture into the prepared dish. Scatter the crumbs and seeds over the top and bake in the preheated oven for 20–30 minutes until piping hot and golden-brown.

BROWN LENTIL AND RED PEPPER PATTIES

These patties are equally good served with hot vegetables or with pitta or crusty bread, salad and a spoonful of Greek yoghurt.

225g/8oz brown lentils
4 tablespoons olive oil
1 large onion, finely chopped
2 cloves of garlic, crushed
½ teaspoon ground cumin
2 red chillies, deseeded and finely chopped (see page 22)
1 red pepper
1 tablespoon chopped fresh parsley
1 tablespoon chopped fresh mint
3 sun-dried tomatoes, finely chopped
salt and freshly ground black pepper

1. Cook the lentils in a large saucepan of simmering water for 30 minutes until tender. Drain well and cool.
2. Meanwhile, heat half the oil in a heavy frying pan, add the onion and fry over a low heat until soft and golden-brown. Add the garlic, cumin and chillies and fry for 1 further minute.
3. Preheat the grill to high. Remove the pith and seeds from the pepper and cut into quarters. Rub the skin with a little oil and grill, skin side up, until charred and blistered. Cover with a tea-towel and leave to cool, then peel and chop finely.
4. Put the lentils into a food processor or blender with the onion mixture, the pepper, parsley, mint and sun-dried tomatoes. Season well with salt and pepper, then process briefly. Alternatively, mash together with a potato masher.
5. Shape the mixture into 4 patties. Chill for 1–2 hours until firm. Wipe out the frying pan and heat a little more oil. Fry the patties gently on both sides until browned.

PUY LENTIL LATTICE

225g/8oz flour quantity puff pastry (see page 522)
plain flour, for rolling and dusting
1 egg, beaten, to glaze

For the filling
290ml/½ pint summer vegetable stock (see page 530)
110–170g/4–6oz Puy lentils
2 tablespoons olive oil
1 clove of garlic, crushed
1 small red chilli, deseeded and roughly chopped (see page 22)
2–3 tablespoons roughly chopped fresh coriander
225g/8oz crumbly cheese, such as feta or Cheshire
salt and freshly ground black pepper

1. Roll the pastry into 2 thin rectangles, one about 2.5cm/1in bigger all round than the other. Put on to 2 baking trays and chill for about 20 minutes.
2. Preheat the oven to 200°C/400°F/gas mark 6.
3. Prick the surface of the smaller rectangle all over with a fork and bake in the preheated oven for 10–15 minutes until evenly brown. Loosen and allow to cool on the baking tray.
4. Bring the stock to the boil in a saucepan, add the lentils and simmer gently for 15–20 minutes or until soft but still holding their shape. Drain thoroughly.
5. Heat the oil in a small frying pan, add the garlic and chilli and sauté carefully for 2–3 minutes. Add the contents of the frying pan to the lentils together with the coriander and allow to cool. Add the cheese, mix thoroughly and season to taste with salt and pepper.
6. Arrange the lentil mixture on the surface of the cooked pastry base, leaving a 2.5cm/1in margin around the edge. Carefully brush the margin with beaten egg. Lay the larger pastry rectangle on a lightly floured worktop. Dust the surface of the pastry with flour and carefully fold it in half lengthways; do not allow it to stick. Using a sharp knife, cut through the folded side of the pastry at right angles to the

edge, in parallel lines (as though you were cutting through the teeth of a comb). Leave an uncut margin of about 2.5cm/1in all around the other edges, so that when the pastry is opened up there is a solid border like a picture frame.
7. Lay the opened pastry top over the filling. Cut the corners of the raw pastry at right angles to the cooked base. Using a palette knife to support the base, carefully tuck the raw edges underneath. Seal the edges down well. Brush the surface with beaten egg glaze and bake at the top of the hot oven for about 20 minutes or until the pastry is well risen and evenly browned. Serve warm.

SPICED LENTILS WITH BUTTERNUT SQUASH

225g/8oz Puy lentils
2 tablespoons olive oil
2 red onions, sliced
1 clove of garlic, crushed
2 teaspoons mustard seeds
2 teaspoons garam masala
1 teaspoon ground cumin
a good pinch of cayenne pepper
1 tablespoon tomato purée
100ml/3½fl oz red wine
150ml/¼ pint water
1 butternut squash, peeled, deseeded and diced
2 tablespoons chopped fresh thyme
salt and freshly ground black pepper
2 tablespoons finely chopped fresh parsley

1. Wash the lentils well and cook them in a large saucepan of gently simmering water until they are tender.
2. Heat the oil in a large saucepan and add the onions and garlic. Sweat over a low heat for 10 minutes. Add the mustard seeds, garam masala, cumin and cayenne. Cook for 2 minutes, stirring constantly.
3. Add the tomato purée, wine, water, squash, thyme, salt and pepper. Bring to the boil, then lower the heat and simmer for 20 minutes, stirring occasionally, until the butternut squash is tender.
4. Add the cooked lentils and the parsley, heat through and season well with salt and pepper.

CREAMY SPICED LENTILS

Serve this dish with rice or use it as a filling for a pie or crumble.

225g/8oz green lentils
55g/2oz unsalted butter
1 large onion, sliced
2–3 cloves of garlic, chopped
2.5cm/1in piece of fresh root ginger, peeled and grated
1 red chilli, deseeded and chopped (see page 22)
150ml/¼ pint double cream
3 tomatoes, peeled, deseeded and chopped (see page 22)
1 heaped tablespoon chopped fresh coriander
salt and freshly ground black pepper

1. Put the lentils into a large saucepan, cover with plenty of water and bring to the boil, then simmer for about 20–30 minutes until tender.
2. Meanwhile, melt the butter in a frying pan and when foaming, add the onion and fry over a low heat until golden-brown. Add the garlic, ginger and chilli and fry for a further 2 minutes.
3. Stir in the cream, scraping any sticky sediment from the base of the pan. Add the tomatoes and coriander and season with salt and pepper. Simmer gently for 10 minutes.
4. Stir in the cooked lentils, reheat and adjust the seasoning to taste.

BROWN LENTILS WITH CHILLI AND OIL

170g/6oz brown lentils
2 bay leaves
570ml/1 pint water
2 green chillies
3 cloves of garlic, chopped
2 tablespoons roughly chopped fresh coriander
290ml/½ pint olive oil
salt and freshly ground black pepper
lemon juice

1. Put the lentils into a saucepan with the bay leaves and water. Bring to the boil, then lower the heat and simmer gently for 20 minutes. Add a little extra water if the lentils become too dry. Cover with a tight-fitting lid and remove from the heat. Allow the lentils to stand for about 15 minutes until they are completely tender but not mushy.
2. Drain away any remaining liquid and discard the bay leaves. Chop the chillies (see page 22), retaining a few of the seeds. Add to the lentils with the garlic and coriander and toss in the oil. Season with salt, pepper and lemon juice to taste.

NOTE: ¼ onion, finely chopped, and 1 large beefsteak tomato, chopped, may be added.

PUY LENTILS WITH ROASTED SHALLOTS

4 tablespoons olive oil
1 leek, trimmed and thinly sliced
2 sticks of celery, thinly sliced
225g/8oz Puy lentils
290ml/½ pint summer vegetable stock (see
    page 530)
2 bay leaves
2–3 tablespoons mushroom ketchup
340g/12oz shallots, peeled
salt and freshly ground black pepper
1–2 tablespoons roughly chopped mixed fresh
    parsley and oregano

1. Preheat the oven to 200°C/400°F/gas mark 6.
2. Heat 1–2 tablespoons of the oil in a
saucepan, add the leek and celery and season
with salt and pepper. Cover and cook over a
low heat for 4–5 minutes until softened.
3. Add the lentils, stock and bay leaves, cover
and simmer for 20–30 minutes or until the
lentils are soft and the stock has nearly
evaporated. Add the ketchup and keep warm.
4. Put the shallots on to a baking tray, drizzle
over 2 tablespoons oil and season with salt and
pepper. Roast in the preheated oven for 20–30
minutes or until a rich, nutty brown, and soft
right the way through.
5. Add the roasted shallots to the lentils and
remove the bay leaves. Season to taste with salt
and pepper and sprinkle with the herbs.

PICKLED VEGETABLES WITH PUY LENTILS

225g/8oz courgettes, trimmed
3 sticks of celery
1 bulb of fennel
2 tablespoons olive oil
2 medium onions, sliced
1 clove of garlic, crushed
salt and frshly ground black pepper
170g/6oz Puy lentils
720ml/1¼ pints spicy vegetable stock (see
    page 531)
2 teaspoons pickling spice
85ml/3fl oz any white vinegar
30g/1oz soft light brown sugar
225g/8oz cherry tomatoes
chopped fresh celery leaves, to garnish

1. Cut the courgettes on the diagonal into 1cm/
½in slices. Cut the celery into 1cm/½in slices.
Remove the outer leaves from the fennel, cut in
half, remove the core and slice, including the
feathery tops.
2. Heat the oil in a saucepan, add the onion
and cook over a low heat until soft and
transparent. Add the garlic and cook for 1
further minute, then add the courgettes, celery
and fennel. Season with salt and pepper. Cover
and cook gently for about 15 minutes until
tender.
3. Meanwhile, put the lentils in a large
saucepan, add the stock and simmer for 15
minutes until soft but not split. Drain and
reserve the stock.
4. Add the spice, vinegar and sugar to the stock
in a saucepan. Bring to the boil, then lower the
heat and simmer for 5 minutes. Remove from
the heat and leave to stand for 5 minutes. Strain
and discard the spice.
5. Put the lentils, spiced stock and tomatoes
into the pan with the vegetables. Adjust the
seasoning to taste and simmer for 5 minutes.
Scatter with celery leaves before serving.

LENTIL, AUBERGINE, PEPPER AND TOMATO SALAD

1 large aubergine
4 tablespoons olive oil
1 red pepper
2 yellow peppers
225g/8oz green lentils
1 onion, halved
1 bay leaf
4 large tomatoes, peeled and cut into segments
   (see page 22)

For the dressing
juice of 1 lemon
100ml/3½fl oz olive oil
salt and freshly ground black pepper
2 tablespoons chopped fresh parsley
2 tablespoons chopped fresh mint

1. Preheat the oven to 200°C/400°F/gas mark 6.
2. Cut the aubergines into quarters lengthways then cut into 2.5cm/1in chunks. Mix with the oil and put into a roasting tin. Roast in the preheated oven for 20–30 minutes, turning after 15 minutes, until the aubergines are soft and brown.
3. Cut the peppers in half and remove the pith and seeds. Place side down on a baking tray and roast in the oven for 30 minutes or until the skins have blackened. Remove from the oven, place the peppers in a bowl and cover with a plate. Leave for 15 minutes, then peel the peppers and cut into 2.5cm/1in chunks.
4. Wash the lentils well and put into a saucepan of cold water. Add the onion and bay leaf and bring to the boil, then lower the heat and simmer for 20–30 minutes until the lentils are soft. Strain through a sieve, discard the onion and bay leaf and run cold water through the lentils to rinse.
5. Make the dressing: put the lemon juice into a bowl, whisk in the oil and season with salt and pepper. Stir in the herbs.
6. Assemble the salad: mix everything together in a serving bowl, add the dressing and toss.

Taste and add more salt, pepper and lemon juice as required. Allow to stand for 30 minutes before serving.

CURRIED LENTIL SALAD

170g/6oz green or Puy lentils
2 bay leaves
2 sticks of celery, chopped
1 shallot, finely chopped
2 carrots, grated
30g/1oz pinenuts, toasted (see page 22)
1 tablespoon chopped fresh coriander
2 teaspoons chopped fresh mint

For the dressing
4 tablespoons groundnut or sunflower oil
1 tablespoon white wine vinegar
grated zest and juice of ½ orange
1 teaspoon red curry paste (see page 529)
salt and freshly ground black pepper

1. Put the lentils and bay leaves into a saucepan and cover with plenty of water. Bring to the boil, then lower the heat and simmer gently for about 30 minutes.
2. Meanwhile, make the dressing: mix all the ingredients together in a jar and shake well.
3. When the lentils are tender, drain and toss them in the dressing. Leave to cool. Mix with all the remaining ingredients and season with salt and pepper.

PUY LENTIL SALAD WITH LEEKS AND QUAIL'S EGGS

85g/3oz Puy lentils
450g/1lb young leeks
12 quail's eggs
a handful of lamb's lettuce
2 tablespoons chopped fresh coriander

For the dressing
3 tablespoons olive oil
1 tablespoon balsamic vinegar
2 teaspoons Dijon mustard
salt and freshly ground black pepper

1. Wash the lentils and cook them in gently simmering water for 20–30 minutes until tender.
2. Trim the leeks and wash them thoroughly. Cut them into 2.5cm/1in lengths and steam for 5 minutes until *al dente*. Drain on kitchen paper to remove all excess moisture.
3. Whisk all the dressing ingredients together and season with salt and pepper. While still hot, toss the lentils and leeks together with the dressing and leave to cool.
4. Put the quail's eggs into a pan of cold water and simmer for 5 minutes. Cool in cold water. Shell and cut in half. Wash and dry the lamb's lettuce.
5. When the leeks and lentils are cool, toss in the lamb's lettuce and coriander. Adjust the seasoning to taste, then gently fold the quail's eggs through the lentils.

TUSCAN BEAN SOUP

110g/4oz pinto beans, soaked overnight
3 tablespoons olive oil
1 large onion, sliced
2 carrots, chopped
2 cloves of garlic, chopped
570ml/1 pint winter vegetable stock (see page 530)
1 courgette, trimmed and diced
1 × 400g/14oz can of plum tomatoes
1 teaspoon dried basil
225g/8oz chard or cavolo nero

To serve
2 tablespoons pesto (see page 526)

1. Rinse and drain the beans.
2. Heat the oil in a large saucepan. Add the onion and carrot and cook over a low heat until soft. Stir in the garlic and cook for a further 2 minutes.
3. Add the stock, stirring to remove any sticky sediment from the base of the pan. Add the courgette to the soup with the tomatoes and basil, then add the beans. Season with pepper and simmer for 1–1½ hours, partially covered, until the beans are tender and the liquid reduced.
4. Remove any tough stalks fom the chard or cavolo nero. Roll into a tight bundle and shred. Stir into the soup and season to taste with salt and more pepper if required. Simmer for a further 5 minutes. Serve in warmed soup bowls each topped with a spoonful of pesto.

ARMENIAN BEAN CASSEROLE WITH YOGHURTY ONIONS

225g/8oz pinto beans, soaked overnight
3 tablespoons olive oil
2 onions, sliced
1 clove of garlic, crushed
2.5cm/1in pieces of fresh root ginger, peeled and finely chopped
1 teaspoon ground cumin
½ teaspoon ground cinnamon
1 litre/1¾ pints winter vegetable stock (see page 530)
1 × 400g/14oz can of tinned tomatoes
85g/3oz no-soak dried apricots
30g/1oz sultanas

To serve
basmati rice (see page 352) or couscous (see page 382)
yoghurty onions (see page 516)

1. Rinse and drain the beans.
2. Heat the oil in a large saucepan. Add the onions and fry over a low heat until soft and golden-brown. Stir in the garlic and ginger and fry for a further 2 minutes. Add the cumin and cinnamon and fry for 1–2 minutes.
3. Pour the stock into the pan and add the tomatoes and beans. Season with pepper and simmer for 45 minutes.
4. Quarter the apricots and add them to the casserole with the sultanas. Season with salt and more pepper if necessary and simmer for a further 30 minutes until the beans are tender and the liquid is reduced and syrupy. Serve with rice or couscous and top with the yoghurty onions.

CARIBBEAN RED BEAN STEW WITH BROCCOLI

225g/8oz red kidney or pinto beans, soaked overnight
2 tablespoons vegetable or groundnut oil
2 medium onions, chopped
3 cloves of garlic, chopped
2 green chillies, deseeded and chopped (see page 22)
2.5cm/1in piece of fresh root ginger, peeled and grated
2 teaspoons paprika
1 teaspoon ground mixed spice
1 × 400g/14oz can of tomatoes
570ml/1 pint spicy vegetable stock (see page 531)
salt and freshly ground black pepper
225g/8oz broccoli
55g/2oz creamed coconut, chopped
1 tablespoon smooth peanut butter
lemon juice
1 tablespoon chopped fresh coriander, to garnish

1. Rinse and drain the beans.
2. Heat the oil in a large saucepan, add the onion and fry over a low heat until softened and beginning to brown. Add the garlic, chillies, ginger and spices and fry for a further 2 minutes. Stir in the tomatoes and stock. Add the beans and season with pepper. Simmer for 1–1½ hours until the beans are nearly tender. Season with salt and more pepper if required.
3. Trim a little of the tough stalks from the broccoli. When the beans are cooked, stir in the creamed coconut and peanut butter. Add the broccoli florets and simmer until tender. Add lemon juice to taste, adjust the seasoning and scatter with the coriander before serving.

MEXICAN BEAN POT

225g/8oz pinto beans, soaked overnight
2 tablespoons olive oil
2 medium onions, sliced
2 cloves of garlic, crushed
2 teaspoons ground cumin
2 green peppers, deseeded and sliced
2 red peppers, deseeded and sliced
3 green chillies, deseeded and sliced (see page 22)
290ml/½ pint black coffee
2 × 400g/14oz cans of tomatoes
1 tablespoon black treacle
1 teaspoon dried oregano
salt and freshly ground black pepper

1. Rinse and drain the beans.
2. Heat the oil in a large saucepan, add the onion and fry over a low heat until soft and beginning to brown. Add the garlic and cumin and cook for a further 2 minutes.
3. Stir in the peppers and chillies. Cover the pan and fry gently for about 10 minutes until soft.
4. Add the beans to the pan with the coffee, tomatoes, treacle and oregano. Season with pepper. Simmer for 1–1½ hours until the beans are tender and the liquid reduced and syrupy. Season to taste with salt and more pepper if required.

REFRIED BEANS

Refried beans are a staple of Mexican cooking. They can be served as a snack with tortilla chips and vegetable wedges or as part of a breakfast or supper.

225g/8oz red kidney, pinto or borlotti beans,
    soaked overnight
1 large onion, halved
2 cloves of garlic
2 green chillies
olive or vegetable oil
salt and freshly ground black pepper
sugar

1. Rinse and drain the beans, put them into a large saucepan and cover with plenty of fresh water. Take half of the onion and cut it into quarters. Add to the pan with the whole cloves of garlic and chillies. Simmer for about 2 hours until the beans are very tender and crush easily between the fingers. Drain and discard the onion, garlic and chilli.
2. Heat 2 tablespoons oil in a large, heavy frying pan. Take the remaining onion half and cut into 8 pieces. Fry in the oil until dark brown and caramelized. When the oil is flavoured, discard the onion and add the beans to the pan. Stir and mash as you would potatoes, adding extra oil if they show signs of sticking. Season to taste with salt, pepper and sugar.

CHILLI BEANS WITH LIME SOURED CREAM

285g/10oz pinto beans, soaked overnight
4 mild red chillies, such as red snub
2 tablespoons olive oil
2 large onions, chopped
2 cloves of garlic, crushed
4 green chillies, deseeded and chopped (see
    page 22)
½ teaspoon chilli powder
2 teaspoons ground cumin
2 × 400g/14oz cans of tomatoes
570ml/1 pint spicy vegetable stock (see page 531)
salt and freshly ground black pepper

To serve
grated zest of 1 lime
1 tablespoon chopped fresh coriander
150ml/¼ pint soured cream

1. Preheat the oven to 190°C/375°F/gas mark 5. Rinse and drain the beans. Rub the chillies with a little oil and roast in the preheated oven for 30–40 minutes until very soft. Set aside.
2. Meanwhile, heat the oil in a large pan, add the onions and fry over a low heat until soft and golden-brown. Add the garlic, chillies, chilli powder and cumin and fry for 1 further minute. Stir in the tomatoes and stock.

3. Add the beans to the pan and season with pepper. Bring to the boil, then lower the heat and simmer for 45 minutes. Season with salt and more pepper if required and simmer for a further 30–40 minutes until the beans are very tender and the liquid reduced and syrupy.

4. Stir the lime zest and coriander into the soured cream. Add the roasted chillies to the beans and heat briefly. Adjust the seasoning to taste and hand the lime soured cream separately.

ROASTED GARLIC AND PEASE PUDDING PATTIES

1 bulb of garlic
225g/8oz yellow split peas, soaked, rinsed and drained
2 sticks of celery, strings removed and finely diced
1 onion, finely chopped
summer vegetable stock (see page 530)
30g/1oz butter, softened
1 egg
1 tablespoon chopped fresh parsley
salt and freshly ground black pepper
plain flour, for shaping
oil, for frying
fresh flat-leaf parsley, to garnish

1. Preheat the oven to 180°C/350°F/gas mark 4. Put the whole garlic in its papery skin on to a baking tray and roast in the preheated oven for 20 minutes or until completely soft. Separate the cloves and squeeze gently to extract the soft pulp.

2. Place the split peas, celery and onion in a large saucepan with enough stock to cover. Bring to the boil, then lower the heat and simmer for 1–1¼ hours or until very tender.

3. Drain the peas, reserving some of the cooking liquid. Put the peas and vegetables into a food processor or blender and process until fairly smooth, adding some of the cooking liquid if necessary. The purée should be quite firm.

4. Transfer the purée to a mixing bowl and beat in the butter, egg, parsley and garlic pulp. Season to taste with salt and pepper.

5. With lightly floured hands, shape the mixture into small flat discs. Chill the patties for 15 minutes.

6. Heat 2.5cm/1in oil in a frying pan and when very hot, fry the patties for 2–3 minutes on each side until brown and crisp. Remove from the pan with a slotted spoon or fish slice and drain on kitchen paper. Serve garnished with flat-leaf parsley.

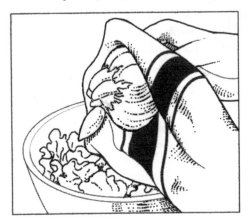

SPLIT PEA AND SHALLOT MASH

225g/8oz yellow split peas
570ml/1 pint summer vegetable stock (see
* page 530)*
55g/2oz unsalted butter
110g/4oz shallots, finely chopped
1 teaspoon cumin seeds
salt and freshly ground black pepper

1. Place the split peas in a sieve and rinse under cold running water. Tip into a saucepan, add the stock and bring to the boil, then lower the heat and simmer for 20–30 minutes until the stock is absorbed and the peas are tender.
2. Meanwhile, melt the butter in a frying pan, add the shallots and fry over a low heat until very soft. Add the cumin seeds and cook for a further 2 minutes.
3. When the peas are cooked, crush with a fork or a potato masher. Beat in the shallots and butter and season with salt and pepper.

CHILLED CUCUMBER SOUP WITH TOFU AND GREEK YOGHURT

2 cucumbers, peeled
1 medium onion, sliced
570ml/1 pint summer vegetable stock (see
* page 530)*
1 bay leaf
2 cloves
salt and freshly ground black pepper
225g/8oz medium tofu, diced
2 tablespoons Greek yoghurt
1½ tablespoons chopped fresh dill

1. Reserve about a quarter of one cucumber and slice the remainder and put into a saucepan with the onion, stock, bay leaf and cloves. Season with salt and pepper. Bring to the boil, then lower the heat and simmer for 20 minutes until the cucumber is tender.

2. Cool slightly, then discard the bay leaf and cloves. Purée the soup, together with the tofu and yoghurt, in a food processor or blender. Stir in 1 tablespoon of the dill and chill.
3. Adjust the seasoning to taste. Roughly chop the reserved cucumber and scatter on top of the soup with the remaining dill.

MARINATED AND FRIED TOFU

This is delicious and quick to make and perfect to add substance to many of the recipes in this book. Fry it off at the last minute and arrange on top of a vegetable dish.

450g/1lb firm tofu
olive oil, for frying
30g/1oz sesame seeds

For the marinade
a walnut-sized piece of fresh root ginger, peeled
* and grated*
2 tablespoons dark soy sauce
1 tablespoon sunflower, vegetable or groundnut
* oil*
a dash of lemon juice
a pinch of caster sugar
freshly ground black pepper

1. First make the marinade: press the ginger and all its juice through a sieve and use the juice only. Combine with all the other ingredients in a dish and season with pepper.
2. Slice the tofu into about 20 thick slices. Stir into the marinade and set aside for at least 30 minutes.
3. Heat a little oil in a heavy or non-stick frying pan. Fry the tofu in batches, scattering each batch with sesame seeds. Serve with the pan juices and the remaining seeds spooned over the top.

TOFU AND MUSHROOM SATÉ WITH PEANUT SAUCE

225g/8oz smoked tofu
24 chestnut mushrooms

For the marinade
2 tablespoons vegetable or groundnut oil
1–2 cloves of garlic, crushed
½ small onion, sliced
2 teaspoons soft light brown sugar
2 tablespoons dark soy sauce
½ lemon
1 stalk of lemongrass, outer leaves removed and
  crushed
a pinch of cayenne pepper

For the peanut sauce
¼ onion, finely chopped
2 tablespoons crunchy peanut butter
1 clove of garlic, crushed
1 stalk of lemongrass, outer leaves removed and
  finely chopped
a pinch of dried red chilli flakes
a walnut-sized piece of fresh root ginger, peeled
  and grated
55g/2oz creamed coconut
150ml/¼ pint water

To serve
cubes of cucumber, slices of raw onion and
  halved cherry tomatoes

1. Cut the tofu into cubes about the same size as the mushrooms.
2. Make the marinade: mix together the oil, garlic, onion, sugar and soy. Squeeze in the juice from the lemon. Cut the lemon flesh and skin into chunks and add to the marinade. Mix the mushrooms and tofu together and toss in the marinade. Cover and chill for several hours or overnight.
3. Make the saté sauce: combine all the ingredients together in a small saucepan and simmer gently for 2 minutes, stirring all the time.
4. Soak some wooden saté sticks in water. Preheat the grill to high. Thread the

mushrooms and tofu on to the skewers with the pieces of lemon from the marinade. Grill for about 5 minutes on each side until the tofu is browned and the mushrooms are tender. Serve with the salad and the saté sauce handed separately.

SWEET AND SOUR TOFU

1–2 tablespoons sunflower oil
2 cloves of garlic, crushed
2.5cm/1in piece of fresh root ginger, peeled and
  grated
1 onion, thinly sliced
½ red pepper, deseeded and sliced
½ yellow pepper, deseeded and sliced
½ orange pepper, deseeded and sliced
4 spring onions, trimmed and sliced on the
  diagonal
250g/9oz firm tofu, cubed
1 × 200g/7oz can of pineapple chunks in natural
  juice
grated zest and juice of 1 orange
1–2 tablespoons caster sugar
1–2 tablespoons white wine, rice or cider
  vinegar
2 tablespoons soy sauce
2 tablespoons cornflour
salt and freshly ground black pepper

To garnish
25–55g/1–2oz cashew nuts, toasted (see page 22)
fresh flat-leaf parsley

To serve
fried rice (see page 356)

1. Heat the oil in a large frying pan or wok. Add the garlic, ginger and onion and fry over a low heat until the onion is transparent.
2. Add the peppers and spring onion and increase the heat slightly. Cook until the peppers are soft, then add the tofu and allow to brown slightly, stirring occasionally to prevent the tofu from breaking up.
3. Add the pineapple chunks and juice, reserving 2 tablespoons, the orange zest and juice, sugar, vinegar and soy sauce. Increase the

heat and allow to simmer gently for a few minutes.

4. Mix the cornflour with the reserved pineapple juice, then add sufficient to the pan to create a light coating sauce. Season to taste with salt and pepper. Serve immediately, garnished with cashew nuts and parsley.

FRIED TOFU WITH SICHUAN PEPPER AND CABBAGE

340g/12oz firm tofu
150ml/¼ pint sunflower oil
grated zest of 1 lemon
225g/8oz green cabbage
1 tablespoon Sichuan peppercorns, crushed
2 cloves of garlic, chopped
170g/6oz beansprouts
1 tablespoon dark soy sauce
2 tablespoons water

1. Cut the tofu into slices about 5mm/¼in thick and put into a dish. Mix the oil and lemon zest together. Pour over the tofu and leave to marinate for at least 30 minutes. Remove the tough stalk from the cabbage and shred finely.
2. Heat 2 tablespoons of the marinade in a heavy frying pan or wok. Add the tofu and fry briskly, scattering over the Sichuan pepper, until golden-brown. Remove from the pan and keep warm.
3. Add the garlic to the pan and fry briefly for 1 minute. Add the cabbage and beansprouts and toss over the heat for a few minutes until the cabbage is bright green but still crunchy. Stir in the soy sauce and water and season with salt. Allow to bubble up and boil for a minute until reduced to a syrupy consistency. Spoon the cabbage into a warmed serving dish and arrange the tofu on top. Pour over the pan juices.

TOFU AND MUSHROOM STROGANOFF

55g/2oz dried porcini mushrooms
290ml/½ pint boiling summer vegetable stock
  (see page 530)
340g/12oz firm tofu
2 tablespoons olive oil
15g/½oz butter
3 shallots or ½ medium onion, thinly sliced
1 clove of garlic, crushed
225g/8oz assorted mushrooms, sliced
55ml/2fl oz dry white wine
salt and freshly ground black pepper
2 tablespoons crème fraîche
1 heaped teaspoon Dijon mustard
a handful of chopped fresh parsley

1. Soak the dried mushrooms in the stock for 1 hour. Drain and boil the stock until reduced to 150ml/¼ pint.
2. Cut the tofu into strips about the size of a little finger. Heat half the oil in a sauté, add the tofu and fry briskly until golden-brown. Remove from the pan and set aside.
3. Add the remaining oil to the pan with the butter. When the butter is foaming, add the shallots or onion and fry over a low heat until softened. Stir in the garlic and fry for 1 further minute.
4. Add the sliced mushrooms and fry gently until soft. Stir in the soaked dried mushrooms and the tofu. Add the wine and allow to boil up while scraping any sticky sediment from the bottom of the pan. Strain in the reduced stock, season to taste with salt and pepper and simmer for 10 minutes.
5. Stir in the crème fraîche and mustard. Check the seasoning and serve sprinkled with the parsley.

TOFU AND SWEETCORN BURGERS

1 tablespoon olive or chilli-flavoured oil, plus
    extra for frying
½ medium onion, finely chopped
1 large cob of sweetcorn
2 cloves of garlic, crushed
225/8oz firm tofu
2 teaspoons chilli relish
1 tablespoon chopped fresh parsley
110g/4oz rolled oats
1 egg, beaten
salt and freshly ground black pepper
30g/1oz wholemeal flour, sifted

1. Heat the oil in a frying or sauté pan, add the onion and fry until softened. Slice the kernels from the sweetcorn cobs and add to the pan with the onions. Fry until the sweetcorn is tender and most of the liquid has evaporated. Stir in the garlic and cook for 1 further minute.
2. Crumble and then mash the tofu. Stir it into the onion and sweetcorn mixture and add the chilli relish, parsley, oats and egg. Season well with salt and pepper.
3. Shape into 4 burgers and dust with the flour. Shallow-fry in hot oil for about 5 minutes on each side until golden-brown.

STIR-FRIED TOFU WITH BROCCOLI AND MANGETOUT

250g/9oz firm tofu
2 tablespoons seasoned plain flour
1 egg, beaten
5 tablespoons sesame seeds
8 tablespoons sunflower oil
1 onion, sliced
1 clove of garlic, chopped
2.5cm/1in piece of fresh root ginger, peeled and
    chopped
300g/10½oz broccoli, blanched
200g/7oz mangetout, blanched
2 tablespoons dry sherry
2 tablespoons soy sauce
2 tablespoons hoisin sauce
3 tablespoons water
10 spring onions, trimmed and sliced
1 tablespoon sesame oil

1. Drain the tofu and place on kitchen paper. Leave to dry for 15 minutes, then cut into 1cm/½in cubes. Dip into the seasoned flour, then into the beaten egg and finally into the sesame seeds.
2. Heat the oil in a wok or large frying pan with a lid. Add the tofu and fry over a low heat until brown. Drain on kitchen paper. Pour off the oil and wipe out the pan.
3. Return 2 tablespoons of the oil to the pan and add the onion, garlic and ginger. Stir-fry for 5 minutes.
4. Add the broccoli, mangetout, sherry, soy sauce, hoisin sauce, water and spring onions to the pan. Then add the fried tofu, cover and cook for 3–5 minutes. Add the sesame oil just before serving.

CHINESE VEGETABLE SPRING ROLLS WITH CHILLI SOY DIPPING SAUCE

2 small carrots, peeled
225g/8oz bok choi
6 spring onions, trimmed and halved
1 tablespoon sunflower oil
1 tablespoon roasted sesame oil
2 cloves of garlic, finely chopped
2.5cm/1in piece of fresh root ginger, peeled and
   very finely shredded
1 medium-hot red Dutch chilli, deseeded and
   thinly sliced (see page 22)
170g/6oz fresh bean sprouts
2 tablespoons dark soy sauce
1 teaspoon sugar
salt and freshly ground black pepper
2 tablespoons plain flour
2 tablespoons water
12 large spring roll wrappers or 25cm/10in
   squares of filo pastry
oil, for deep-frying

For the dipping sauce
2 tablespoons ketchup manis (sweet soy sauce)
2 teaspoons Chinese rice wine or dry sherry
½ teaspoon sambal oelek or minced red chilli
   from a jar

1. Cut the carrots in half crossways, then cut lengthways into thin slices. Stack up a few slices at a time and cut them lengthways into fine shreds. Slice the bok choi across into 1cm/½in wide strips, discarding the bases. Cut the spring onion pieces lengthways into fine shreds.
2. Heat a well-seasoned wok over a high heat. Add the sunflower and sesame oils, followed by the garlic, ginger and chilli, and stir-fry for 30 seconds. Add the carrots and bean sprouts and stir-fry for 1 minute. Add the bok choi and spring onions and stir-fry for a further 30 seconds until all the vegetables are just tender. Add the soy sauce, sugar and salt and pepper. Toss together once, then tip the mixture into a large sieve set over a bowl and leave to drain and cool. Mix the flour with the water to make a smooth paste.

3. To fill the spring rolls, place one wrapper or square of filo pastry on a board, with one corner facing you. Keep the other wrappers or squares of pastry covered with a slightly damp cloth to prevent them from drying out. Place 1 heaped tablespoon of the mixture in a short, horizontal line about 5cm/2in in from the corner.
4. Fold the corner of the wrapper or square of pastry over the filling and give it a little roll, making sure that the filling stays in place. Now fold over first the right and then the left hand side of the wrapper or square of pastry so that they just overlap in the centre. Continue to roll the spring roll up tightly, holding the sides in place as you do so. Seal the end with a little of the flour and water paste. Repeat with the remaining wrappers or squares of pastry.
6. Heat oil in a deep-fryer to 190°C/375°F. Deep-fry the spring rolls 4 at a time for 6 minutes until crisp and golden, turning them over from time to time so that they brown evenly. Drain on kitchen paper.
7. Mix together the ingredients for the dipping sauce and pour it into 4 small saucers or ramekins. Serve with the hot spring rolls.

MALAYSIAN LAKSA WITH BEAN SPROUTS AND NOODLES

Laksa is a mildly spicy, wet noodle dish flavoured with coconut milk, ginger, chillies and lemongrass.

4 tablespoons sunflower oil
860ml/1½ pints summer vegetable stock (see page 530)
225g/8oz dried rice vermicelli noodles
1 × 400ml/14fl oz can of coconut milk
2 teaspoons light muscovado sugar
salt

For the laksa spice paste
4 shallots, roughly chopped
2 cloves of garlic, crushed
2.5cm/1in piece of galangal or fresh root ginger, peeled and roughly chopped
2 medium-hot red Dutch chillies
1 large stalk of lemongrass, outer leaves removed and discarded
30g/1oz unsalted cashew nuts
1 teaspoon ground turmeric
1 teaspoon ground coriander
1 teaspoon paprika
1 tablespoon water

To garnish
½ small cucumber
4 spring onions, trimmed and halved
225g/8oz fresh bean sprouts
a small handful of small sprigs of fresh coriander

1. Make the laksa spice paste: put all the ingredients into a food processor and process until smooth.
2. Heat the oil in a large saucepan. Add the spice paste and fry it over a low heat for 6–7 minutes, stirring frequently, until it starts to split away from the oil. Add the stock and bring to the boil. Cover and simmer for 15 minutes.
3. Meanwhile, cut the cucumber in half lengthways and scoop out the seeds, using a melon-baller or teaspoon. Cut each half into 5cm/2in lengths, then lengthways into long thin strips. Cut the spring onion pieces lengthways into long thin shreds.
4. Bring a large saucepan of water to the boil and add the noodles, then remove from the heat. Leave the noodles to soak for 2 minutes, then drain. Add the coconut milk, sugar and 1 teaspoon of salt to the soup and simmer for 3 minutes.
5. Divide the noodles between 4 deep, warmed soup bowls. Ladle over the hot coconut soup, then garnish each bowl with cucumber, spring onions, bean sprouts and sprigs of coriander.

CARAMELIZED VEGETABLE STIR-FRY WITH BEAN SPROUTS

340g/12oz shallots
3 cloves of garlic
2 tablespoons sesame oil
2–3 tablespoons balsamic vinegar
1 red pepper
1 yellow pepper
vegetable oil, for brushing
170g/6oz mangetout or sugar-snap peas
1 courgette
1 red chilli, deseeded and chopped (see page 22)
salt and freshly ground black pepper
170g/6oz bean sprouts
55g/2oz alfalfa sprouts, to garnish

To serve
crusty bread or basmati rice (see page 352)

1. Douse the shallots in boiling water and then plunge them into cold water. Peel, top and tail and halve the shallots. Peel the cloves of garlic and cut in half. Heat the oil in a wok or heavy frying pan. Add the shallots and garlic, cover and cook over a low heat for 20–30 minutes, stirring and shaking the pan from time to time, until tender, golden-brown and caramelized. Add 2 tablespoons balsamic vinegar and cook for a further 10 minutes.
2. Meanwhile, preheat the grill to high. Cut the peppers in half, remove the pith and seeds and rub the skins with a little oil. Grill until the skins are black and blistered. Cover the peppers with a tea-towel and leave until cool, then remove the skins and slice. Top and tail the mangetout or sugar-snap peas. Cut the courgette in half lengthways. Cut each half into long thin strips, then cut each strip into 3 so that they are about the same length as the mangetout.
3. When the shallots are cooked, add the sliced pepper, courgette, mangetout or sugar-snap peas and the chilli. Season with salt and pepper, turn up the heat and stir-fry briskly until the vegetables are tender but crunchy. Drizzle with a little balsamic vinegar.
4. Make a bed of bean sprouts on 4 individual plates. Top with the caramelized vegetables and garnish with alfalfa sprouts. Serve with crusty bread or rice.

347

RICE

INTRODUCTION

by Roz Denny

It is said that around two-thirds of the world's population are nourished daily with rice. Unlike any other major food, rice is central to the cultures and in some cases, the religion of many countries, particularly in Asia. The cultivation of rice requires great skills of irrigation which in turn has demanded levels of social organization unknown in the West. Rice farmers had to co-operate amicably if their paddy fields were to receive sufficient water for the two or more crops a year needed to sustain their families and fellow villagers. Small wonder, then, that the rice-growing nations of the world hold rice in great esteem and consider it central to their exciting and sophisticated cuisines. Unfortunately, we in the West have barely exploited the potential of rice in the kitchen, relegating it frequently to a small side accompaniment on a plate and requiring only that it should not stick!

In fact, the beauty of rice is that it has very many qualities, and it is well worth learning to discriminate between different types and brands. Texture and flavour play an important part in assessing the culinary worth of rice. This depends on the variety and growing conditions. Good rice can be compared to fine wine in that it can take on the characteristics of the soil and climate where it is grown. Unfortunately, there is no equivalent of an *appellation contrôlée* for rice sold in the West and therefore little way of knowing which is the best quality. Even higher prices are no guide. Whilst cheaper supermarket own-brand rices may well be of poorer quality than well-known brands, a well-advertised brand may lack finesse of flavour and simply be milled to a consistent, bland, non-stick standard. You are merely paying more for marketing and advertising costs.

The best guide to buying quality rices is to seek out brands bought by rice-eating people – Indians, Chinese, Thais, Arabs, and so on. Another assurance of quality is to look for the country of origin on the pack. Rice sold without a country of origin may well be a blend of grains milled to a basic standard with little to commend it to the cook.

TYPES OF RICE

Estimates on the varieties of rice grown vary, but there are believed to be approximately 7,000, all with their own individual styles of taste, texture, colour and cooking quality. Rice is categorized botanically into either long-grain (*Oryza indica*) or short-grain (*Oryza japonica*). Indica rices (e.g. basmati) are higher in amylose starch, which keeps the grains more separate after cooking, whilst Japonica rices (e.g. sushi or risotto) are higher in amylopectin, which makes them appear more starchy. And some grains fall in between the two categories. Long-grain rices are generally more slender and longer. Short-grain rices have plumper grains and cook to a more starchy consistency, either more creamy or more sticky.

LONG-GRAIN RICES

Originally called Patna, after the city on the river Ganges in India, little rice is now sold under this name. Generally it will be classified simply as long-grain. One of the biggest exporters of long-grain rice is the USA. American long-grain rice is a high-quality grain giving excellent results, sometimes said to have a natural 'popcorn' flavour. The best American long-grain is grown in Arkansas, on the delta of the Mississippi, but production is also prolific in California and Texas. Long-grain rice may also come from Spain, India, Surinam, Thailand and Australia.

When rice is sold with the bran layer intact it is known as wholegrain or brown rice.

USES: General accompaniment for casseroles and curries. Good for chilli con carne, Caribbean dishes, salads and pilafs.

Basmati

The Prince of Rices. An elegant long-grain rice with a legendary flavour. The name basmati means 'the fragrant one' in Hindi, and good basmati will smell deliciously aromatic even in its uncooked state. The smell of basmati cooking is even better. There are very many varieties and qualities of basmati, which is grown in Iran, Pakistan and Northern India. The best comes from the Punjab in the foothills of the Himalayas and is sold under various brand names for export to the Middle East, Europe and the USA. Good basmati will lengthen to three times its dried length once cooked and retain a white, delicate, separate fluffiness.

Basmati is also available as wholegrain or brown basmati.

USES: For curries, pilaffs and kedgerees as well as salads, casseroles, koulibiacs, to serve with sauces and even as rice puddings.

Thai rice

Thailand, known as the rice bowl of Asia, is the world's greatest exporter of rice. (The great rice-eating nations of China, Japan and India produce most of their own rice to support their billion-plus populations and export relatively little.) Many rices are produced in Thailand but rice known specifically as Thai rice is lightly sticky or glutinous, displaying some characteristics of short-grain rices, yet retaining a good bite to the grain. This is the rice Chinese cooks like to serve at home and it is becoming increasingly popular in the West. High-quality Thai rices have a silky sheen and a wonderful natural fragrance, like a milky, sweet nuttiness, often likened to the smell of jasmine flowers. It can be sold as Thai Fragrant or specifically Thai Jasmine.

USES: An ideal accompaniment to all Thai and Indonesian dishes as well as Indian food, Chinese and other Oriental dishes. It is excellent, too, as a stir-fry rice as the light stickiness separates out during re-frying. It also makes excellent rice puddings and rice cakes, and is good as a sushi rice.

SHORT-GRAIN RICES

Varieties include risotto and pudding rices (both from Italy) and sticky rices from China and Japan.

Risotto rices

As with basmati, there are different qualities of risotto rices, and choosing the right one can make or break a dish. Risotto rices are grouped into superfini and semifini qualities. The most highly rated risotto rices are Carnaroli and Arborio, which are superfini quality, although the semifino Vialone Nano grain is highly prized by risotto connoisseurs because of its smaller, firmer grain. A good risotto should absorb up to five times its volume in stock and impart a creaminess to the dish while still retaining a good *al dente* bite. When risotto is left to cool it becomes solid and can be shaped into rissoles or savoury cakes. The arborio grain is particularly suitable for this use. Risottos are made differently from pilaffs in that hot stock is stirred gradually into the rice, allowing each addition to be absorbed, thus encouraging the starch in the grain to give a natural creaminess to the dish. Risottos, like soufflés, should always be served immediately.

USES: Risottos, paella, puddings, rissoles/fritters, cakes.

Paella rice

The Moors brought rice-growing into Spain and from there it was introduced into the lush valleys of the Po river in Italy during medieval times. Paella rice is similar to risotto rice in that it is a medium-short grain rice with a creamy texture. A classic paella is shaken, not stirred, in the pan, so the right grain should be not quite as creamy as a risotto rice. However, true paella rices, such as Valencia and Bomba, are not easy to buy in the UK and USA and an arborio grain is fine as a substitute.

Pudding rice

Most of this short-grain rice comes from Italy, although at one stage the Carolinas in North America were abundant producers, hence the one-time term Carolina rice, which is not now used in the industry. Pudding rice imparts a lot of creaminess to a dish, but the grain breaks down completely on cooking and so has little else to offer the cook in the way of flavour or texture. Increasingly, chefs and cooks are experimenting with using other more flavoursome grains such as risotto, Thai or basmati rices in desserts.

USES: Puddings either baked in a slow oven or stirred in a saucepan, to be served hot or cold.

OTHER RICES

Wild rice

Botanically not a true rice at all, but an aquatic grass that is native to Canada and the USA, producing dark brown grains with a delicious nutty flavour and texture. During cooking, good wild rice imparts a wonderful smell like that of new-mown grass. This is a grain that helped sustain the early settlers of North America and consequently is particularly popular in the USA around Thanksgiving and Christmas, served with turkey and game as a 'dressing' or stuffing. The best-quality wild rice has long, unbroken, dark brown, glossy grains and is grown organically around lakes in Canada where it is still hand-harvested by native Americans in canoes. Again, look for good branded wild rice rather than grains sold loose or as own-label. 'Wild' rice is also cultivated and these grains are smaller and paler in colour. Cultivated grains can be passed through a system of rollers that scratches the outside of the grain (known as scarified rice), enabling water to enter the grain quicker during cooking and so shorten the otherwise long cooking time. This grain is increasingly sold blended with basmati or white long-grain rice.

USES: As a dressing/stuffing for turkey, also good with fish, mixed with white rice as an accompaniment, and for salads.

Red Camargue rice

A hybrid rice discovered as a happy accident by a member of the Griotto family of rice farmers in the traditional rice-growing region of the Camargue, southern France. It has a reddish-brown colour and a rather pleasant flavour slightly reminiscent of buckwheat. The texture is nutty but breaks down somewhat in cooking. It is good as an accompaniment and should be treated as a cross between wild rice and brown rice.

USES: Similar to wild rice, for stuffings, as an accompaniment and in salads.

Glutinous black rice

This rice from South East Asia is used primarily as a pudding rice, cooked with sugar, coconut milk and lemon grass. It has a nice nutty texture and a delicious, sweet, milky taste.

USES: As a dessert served with sliced mango, star fruits, etc.

Wehani rice

A reddish-brown, nutty-style rice from the USA, developed by the Lundburg family in California. It should be treated as brown rice and is good as an accompaniment or for stuffings and puddings.

Green rice

A new season's rice from China, this cooks to a soft, sticky consistency. It is used for a Chinese porridge eaten with pickles at breakfast.

EASY-COOK RICES

The rice-milling process called par-boiling is actually based on an ancient Persian technique of treating rice grains so that they could be stored for longer. In Europe we call these rices 'easy-cook'; in the USA the term used is 'par-boiled'. After the removal of the outer bran layer, rice grains are subjected to short bursts of intense steam which hardens the outside of the grain, causing the gelatinization of the starch. The process also has the benefit of driving the vitamins on the outside of the grain into the centre, thus making it marginally more nutritious. Manufacturers claim this makes the rice non-stick, but par-boiling deprives the grain of a lot of its natural flavour, and some would say makes the rice seem quite chewy. Easy-cook rice takes longer to cook than some varieties and the par-boiling makes the grains look yellowish, although the rice is more resistant to careless cooking. An easy-cook basmati rice seems to survive the process quite well, and much of the original flavour continues to shine through.

COOKING METHODS

Allow 55g/2oz uncooked rice per person
Choosing the right grain for a dish is the secret of successful rice cooking. It is hard to make a pilaf with a risotto rice, or a risotto with an easy-cook rice. Also, many grains need differing amounts of water and cooking times: most brown rice, for example, needs considerably longer cooking than white. The best guide is to follow instructions on the pack. There are four main methods (see below) of cooking rice, apart from risotto and pudding rices. The first method, the open-pan, is quick and easy and so ideal for inexperienced cooks. For specific rice recipes, see pages 356–73. Note that all rice benefits from a standing time of about 5 minutes after cooking and draining so that excess water is absorbed back into the grain. Allow for this before serving. In addition, basmati rice benefits from rinsing and sometimes a little pre-soaking. This is not essential but does give a lighter, more traditional result (see box below).

1. OPEN-PAN/FAST BOILING
Suitable for basmati, easy-cook basmati, brown basmati and other brown rices, long-grain, wild rices and wild rice blends.
Allow 1.2 litres/2 pints of water and 1 teaspoon salt for each 110g/4oz rice.

Bring a saucepan of water to a rolling boil. Add salt, then stir in the rice. Return to a medium boil and cook for the following times:

- Basmati and Thai rices: 10 minutes
- American long-grain: 12 minutes

- Easy-cook basmati and easy-cook long-grain: 15 minutes
- Brown basmati and wild rice with white rice blends: 20–25 minutes
- Brown long-grain rices: 25–30 minutes
- Wild rice: 40–50 minutes

Drain in a large sieve and rinse in hot water. Allow to stand in the sieve for 5 minutes before forking through with melted butter or oil.

2. COVERED PAN/ABSORPTION METHOD
Suitable for Thai rice, sushi rice, basmati (rinsed), brown basmati, brown rice, wild rice, wild rice with white rice blends, easy-cook rices. A measured amount of water is absorbed during cooking, so there is no need to drain. Follow the instructions below according to the rice variety.

- Put rice, water and salt to taste into a saucepan. Bring to the boil, stir once, then cover and lower the heat to a gentle simmer. Do not lift the lid.
- After the calculated cooking time (see below) remove from the heat, still uncovered, and allow to stand 5 minutes before forking through with butter or oil.

For each (225ml/8fl oz) cup of rice allow:
Thai and sushi rice: 1¼ cups of water. Cook for 10–12 minutes.
Basmati rice: 1½ cups water. Cook for 10–12 minutes.
Brown basmati wild rice with white rice blends, easy-cook rices: 2 cups water. Cook for 20–25 minutes.
Wild rice and brown long-grain rice: 2½–3 cups water. Cook for 40–50 minutes.

3. STEAMING/MICROWAVE
Suitable for basmati, long-grain and Thai rices.

- Rinse first if using basmati. Par-boil in plenty of boiling salted water for 5 minutes. Drain in a sieve and rinse under cold running water for a good minute or two. Drain again.
- Place in a non-metallic heatproof bowl.

Cover with clingfilm and vent the side very slightly.

- Microwave on full power (100%) for 5 minutes (Thai and basmati), 7 minutes for long-grain rice.
- Allow to stand (still covered) for 5 minutes before forking through with butter or oil.

4. PILAF

Suitable for basmati, easy-cook basmati and long-grain rices. Rinse first if using basmati.

- Fry 1 chopped onion and 2 crushed cloves of garlic in 3 tablespoons sunflower or olive oil for 5 minutes.
- Stir in 250g/9oz rice and cook gently for 1–2 minutes, stirring occasionally.
- Pour in 450ml/¾ pint stock or water for basmati, 600ml/1 pint for other rices.
- Add salt and pepper to taste. Bring to the boil, then cover and simmer gently for 10 minutes for basmati, 12–14 minutes for long-grain rices and 20 minutes for easy-cook basmati.
- Allow to stand, still covered, for 5 minutes, then fork through with butter or oil.

RINSING AND SOAKING BASMATI

For a traditional, light and fluffy grain.

- Place the rice in a deep bowl. Cover with cold water and stir well with your hand. Tip out the water (the grains sink to the bottom, so there is no need for a sieve).
- Fill with more cold water, and repeat the process three more times until the water becomes clearer.
- Fill again with cold water and leave to stand for 10–15 minutes. This also helps shorten the cooking time slightly. Drain well before cooking.

RICE AND YOUR HEALTH

Rice is an excellent food for a well-balanced, healthy diet. For a start, it is a complex carbohydrate starchy food, and as such one of the foods nutritionists and doctors tell us we must eat more of. In fact, half our daily calorie intake should come from starchy foods such as rice. A good 50g/2oz portion (uncooked weight) which swells to 150g/5oz cooked weight provides approximately 170 calories, with useful amounts of B group vitamins, a small amount of easy-to-digest protein, the minerals iron and zinc and useful amounts of fibre. The starchy carbohydrate in rice does not give the body immediate energy. Rather, the energy is released slowly into the bloodstream. In other words, it is better-value energy and keeps us going longer. Rice is therefore an invaluable food for athletes and sportsmen and women.

BOILED RICE

55g/2oz long-grain white rice per person, rinsed

1. Fill a large saucepan with salted water (1 cup of rice will need at least 6 cups of water, but the exact quantities do not matter as long as there is plenty of water). Bring to the boil.
2. Tip in the rice and stir until the water returns to the boil.
3. Boil for 10 minutes and then test: the rice should be neither hard nor mushy, but firm to the bite: *al dente*.
4. Drain the rice in a colander or sieve. Allow to stand for 5 minutes.

BOILED BROWN RICE

Brown rices vary enormously, and though this method is suitable for the majority of them, some may require longer, slower cooking.

55g/2oz brown rice per person
salt

1. Cook the rice in a large amount of boiling salted water for 20 minutes. Drain well. Allow to stand for 5 minutes.

FRIED RICE

salt and freshly ground black pepper
170–225g/6–8oz white or brown rice
1 tablespoon sesame oil
1–2 tablespoons sunflower oil
2.5cm/1in piece of fresh root ginger, peeled and
    sliced
1 clove of garlic, sliced
110g/4oz bok choi, spinach or spring greens,
    shredded
4 spring onions, trimmed and sliced on the
    diagonal
110g/4oz fresh or frozen peas, cooked
1 × 250g/9oz can of bamboo shoots, drained
2 eggs, beaten
soy sauce

1. Bring a large quantity of salted water to the boil in a large saucepan. Add the rice and boil until the rice is tender (about 10 minutes for white, 20–40 minutes for brown). Drain thoroughly and pour over boiling water, then cold water. Set aside.
2. Heat the oils in a wok or large frying pan. Add the ginger and garlic and allow to brown slowly, then remove and discard.
3. Increase the heat and add the shredded greens and spring onions. Cook for 1–2 minutes. Add the cooked rice, peas and bamboo shoots and reheat, stirring regularly to prevent sticking.
4. When hot, add the eggs, mix thoroughly and cook for a further 2–3 minutes. Season with soy sauce and salt and pepper to taste. Serve immediately.

THAI-STYLE FRIED RICE WITH CUCUMBER AND LIME

225g/8oz jasmine rice
2 tablespoons sunflower oil
1 stalk of lemongrass, outer leaves removed and
    cut lengthways through the centre, then
    crossways into quarters
2 shallots, thinly sliced
2 cloves of garlic, chopped
1 medium green chilli, chopped
110g/4oz fresh or frozen peas, cooked
juice of 2 limes
1 cucumber, peeled, deseeded and diced
2 tablespoons light soy sauce
2 tablespoons chopped fresh coriander
salt and freshly ground black pepper

1. Cook the rice 2 hours before required and leave to cool.
2. Heat the oil in a wok or heavy frying pan, add the lemongrass and cook over a low heat for 5 minutes to allow the flavours to infuse. Discard the lemongrass.
3. Add the shallots, garlic and chilli to the pan and stir-fry for 3 minutes. Add the rice and stir-fry to heat through.
4. Add the peas, lime juice, cucumber, soy sauce and coriander. Season to taste with salt and pepper and serve immediately.

CHILLI AND LIME RICE

30g/1oz butter or 1 tablespoon vegetable oil
225g/8oz basmati rice
290ml/½ pint summer vegetable stock (see
    page 530) or water
salt and freshly ground black pepper
1 green chilli, sliced
½ lime, quartered
a handful of fresh coriander leaves

1. Melt the butter or oil in a heavy saucepan.
Add the rice and stir until well coated.
2. Pour in the stock or water, taking care as it
may hiss and splutter. Season with salt and
pepper. Boil vigorously until craters appear on
the surface of the rice. Scatter the chilli, lime and
coriander leaves on top of the rice. Cover with a
piece of kitchen foil and a tight-fitting lid.
3. Leave to stand for 15 minutes. Discard the
lime and fork the chilli and coriander through
the rice before serving.

LEMON RICE

340g/12oz basmati rice
2 tablespoons sunflower oil
1 tablespoon black mustard seeds
6 fresh curry leaves
½ teaspoon ground turmeric
salt
570ml/1 pint boiling water
finely grated zest of ½ lemon

1. Put the rice into a bowl and cover with cold
water. Wash the rice, changing the water from
time to time until it stays clear, then cover with
fresh water and leave to soak for 7 minutes.
2. Tip the rice into a sieve and leave it to drain
well. Heat the oil in a medium saucepan, add the
mustard seeds and curry leaves and allow them
to sizzle for a few seconds. Tip in the rice and
add the turmeric, ½ teaspoon of salt and the
water. Bring to the boil, then cover and reduce
the heat. Cook for 10–12 minutes until all the
liquid has been absorbed and the rice is tender.
3. Uncover the rice, fork in the lemon zest and
serve.

LEMONGRASS AND COCONUT RICE

1 tablespoon clarified butter (see page 529)
1 kaffir lime leaf
1 stalk of lemongrass, halved and bruised with a
    rolling pin
1 medium-hot red Dutch chilli, deseeded and
    finely chopped (see page 22)
285g/10oz Thai jasmine rice
1 × 397ml/14fl oz can of coconut milk
salt
175ml/6fl oz boiling water

1. Gently heat the clarified butter in a large
saucepan. Add the kaffir lime leaf, lemongrass
and chilli and cook over a medium heat for a
few seconds.
2. Stir in the rice, coconut milk, ½ teaspoon of
salt and the water. Bring to the boil, then cover,
lower the heat and cook for 15 minutes until all
the liquid has been absorbed and the rice is
tender.
3. Remove the kaffir lime leaf and lemongrass
and fluff up the rice with a fork, to separate the
grains, before serving.

GREEK RICE WITH SPINACH AND FETA

225g/8oz spinach
3 tablespoons olive oil
30g/1oz butter
1 bunch of spring onions, sliced
1 medium onion, chopped
110g/4oz basmati rice
225ml/8fl oz water or summer vegetable stock
   (see page 530)
1 × 225g/8oz can of chopped tomatoes
salt and freshly ground black pepper
1 tablespoon chopped fresh mint
110g/4oz feta cheese
about 10 black olives

1. Wash the spinach thoroughly and remove any tough stalks. Drain on kitchen paper, then shred.
2. Heat the oil and butter in a sauté pan. Add the spring onions and chopped onion, cover and fry over a low heat for about 10 minutes. Add the rice and stir until well coated in the juices. Pour in the water or stock and the tomatoes. Season with salt and pepper. Cover and cook for 10 minutes.
3. Spread the spinach over the top of the rice, cover with a tight-fitting lid and cook for a further 10 minutes. Turn off the heat and leave the rice mixture to stand for 10 minutes.
4. Add the mint and gently turn through the rice. Crumble the cheese on top and scatter with olives before serving.

MEXICAN GREEN RICE

1 small onion, roughly chopped
2 cloves of garlic
15g/½oz fresh chives, roughly chopped
15g/½oz fresh coriander, roughly chopped
15g/½oz fresh flat-leaf parsley, roughly chopped
1 teaspoon cumin seeds
3 tablespoons olive oil
225g/8oz basmati rice
290ml/½ pint summer vegetable stock (see page 530)
salt and freshly ground black pepper

1. Put the onion, garlic, herbs and cumin seeds into a food processor or blender and process to a paste. Heat 1 tablespoon of the oil in a frying pan and fry the paste for a few minutes.
2. Heat the remaining oil in a saucepan and turn the rice in the hot oil until well coated. Stir in the cooked herb paste. Add the stock and season with salt and pepper. Cover and simmer gently for 30 minutes.
3. Turn off the heat and leave the rice to stand for 10 minutes. It should be tender but still moist.

SPICED PILAU RICE

sunflower oil, for shallow-frying
8 large shallots, thinly sliced
340g/12oz basmati rice
15g/½oz butter
½ teaspoon cumin seeds
4 cloves
4 green cardamom pods, cracked
5cm/2in piece of cinnamon stick
1 bay leaf
salt
570ml/1 pint boiling water

1. Heat 1cm/½in oil in a large, deep frying pan. Add the shallots and fry, stirring from time to time, until golden-brown. Remove with a slotted spoon and leave to drain on plenty of kitchen paper.
2. Put the rice into a bowl and cover with cold water. Wash the rice, changing the water from time to time until it stays clean, then cover with fresh water and leave to soak for 7 minutes.
3. Tip the rice into a sieve and leave it to drain well. Melt the butter in a medium pan and add the cumin seeds, cloves, cardamom pods, cinnamon stick and bay leaf. Allow to sizzle for a few seconds, then tip in the rice and add ½ teaspoon of salt and the water. Bring to the boil, then cover and lower the heat. Cook for 10–12 minutes until all the liquid has been absorbed and the rice is tender.
4. Uncover the rice and remove the cinnamon stick and bay leaf. Fork through the fried shallots before serving.

PERSIAN RICE WITH FRUIT AND PISTACHIOS

This recipe is also very good made with plain boiled rice.

170g/6oz basmati rice
salt and freshly ground black pepper
85g/3oz butter
1 tablespoon cold water
1 tablespoon clear honey
55g/2oz currants
85g/3oz no-soak dried apricots, sliced
110g/4oz pistachio nuts, shelled and roughly
  chopped
½ teaspoon saffron strands
1 tablespoon boiling water

1. Rinse the rice and soak in lukewarm water with 1 tablespoon salt for 2 hours.
2. Bring a large saucepan of water to the boil. Drain the rice and stir into the water. Boil for 5 minutes, then lower the heat and simmer for 5 minutes until the rice is half cooked. Drain well. Wash and dry the pan.
3. Melt 55g/2oz of the butter in the clean pan. Set over the heat and add the cold water. Stir in the rice, season with salt and cook over a very low heat for 10 minutes. Cover the pan with a clean tea-towel and a tightly fitting lid. Fold the corners of the tea-towel back over the lid to keep out of the way. Continue to cook over a very low heat for 5 minutes, then remove from the heat and leave to steam for 20 minutes until the rice is cooked through. The cloth will absorb the steam and the bottom of the rice should turn to a golden crust.
4. Meanwhile, melt the remaining butter in a frying pan and add the honey, dried fruit and nuts. Cook for a few minutes. Put the saffron into the boiling water and leave to soak.
5. When the rice is cooked, fork through the fruit and honey mixture, breaking up the crust at the bottom of the pan. Spoon into a warmed serving dish and drizzle the saffron liquid over the top.

PECAN RICE WITH ASPARAGUS AND GREEN PEA SAUCE

450g/1lb asparagus
110g/4oz pecan nuts
55g/2oz butter
1 medium onion, finely chopped
170g/6oz basmati rice
720ml/1¼ pints summer vegetable stock (see page 530)
110g/4oz frozen peas
2 sprigs of fresh mint
salt and freshly ground black pepper
a pinch of caster sugar
2–3 tablespoons double cream or crème fraîche
2 tablespoons chopped fresh dill or chervil

1. Remove the tough lower part of the asparagus stalks and discard. Trim the tips to about 5cm/2in. Chop the remaining stalks and set aside. Heat a heavy frying pan, add the pecan nuts and toast. Cool and chop roughly.
2. Heat half the butter in a medium saucepan, add half the onion and fry over a low heat until soft and transparent. Add the rice and fry until well coated in the buttery juices. Reserve 150ml/¼ pint of the stock. Add the remainder to the rice and boil until small craters appear on the top. Scatter the asparagus tips over the top of the rice. Remove from the heat, cover with a sheet of kitchen foil and a tight-fitting lid and leave to stand for 15 minutes.
3. Melt the remaining butter in a small pan. Add the remaining onion and fry over a low heat until softened. Add the chopped asparagus stalks and fry for a further 5 minutes. Stir in the peas, mint and the reserved stock. Season with salt, pepper and sugar. Cover and simmer for 15 minutes. Purée in a food processor or blender. Return to the pan, add the cream and reheat without boiling.
4. Gently fork the herbs through the rice. Drizzle the sauce over the rice and serve immediately.

RED CAMARGUE RICE PILAFF

Red Camargue rice takes longer to cook than other rice but has a wonderfully nutty taste and texture.

2 tablespoons olive oil
1 large onion, chopped
1 clove of garlic, crushed
225g/8oz red Camargue rice
860ml/1½ pints summer vegetable stock (see page 530)
1 × 400g/14oz can of chopped tomatoes
170g/6oz carrots, chopped
110g/4oz parsnips, chopped
½ tablespoon chopped fresh sage
2 tablespoons chopped fresh parsley
1 tablespoon chopped fresh thyme
salt and freshly ground black pepper
grated zest of 1 lemon

1. Preheat the oven to 200°C/400°F/gas mark 6.
2. Heat the oil in a flameproof casserole dish, add the onion and cook over a low heat for 10 minutes until beginning to soften and take on a little colour.
3. Add the garlic and rice and cook for 1 minute. Add the stock, tomatoes, carrots, parsnips, sage, half the parsley, the thyme, salt, pepper and lemon zest. Bring to the boil, then lower the heat and simmer for 10 minutes. Cover and cook in the preheated oven for 1 hour or until the rice is tender. Check occasionally to ensure it is not drying out and add more water if necessary.
4. If the rice is still quite wet, set over a medium heat to allow the moisture to evaporate. Taste and adjust the seasoning if required. Serve sprinkled with the remaining parsley.

RED CAMARGUE RICE PILAFF WITH BROCCOLI AND GOAT'S CHEESE

340g/12oz broccoli florets
2 tablespoons sunflower oil
1 large onion, thinly sliced
2 cloves of garlic, thinly sliced
1 red chilli, deseeded and thinly sliced (see
  page 22)
170g/6oz red Camargue rice
55g/2oz raisins
freshly ground black pepper
150g/5oz goat's cheese
lemon juice
shavings of Parmesan cheese, to garnish

1. Blanch the broccoli in boiling salted water for 2 minutes. Drain, reserving the cooking water, and refresh under cold running water.
2. Heat the oil in a sauté pan. Add the onion and fry until soft and golden. Add the garlic and chilli and fry for a further 2 minutes. Add the rice and stir until well coated in the oil and onion mixture.
3. Add 570ml/1 pint of the reserved broccoli cooking water. Stir in the raisins and season with pepper. Cover and cook for about 1 hour until the rice is tender.
4. Roughly cut up the goat's cheese and gently fold into the rice with the broccoli. Season with pepper and lemon juice to taste and heat through gently. Serve topped with shavings of Parmesan cheese.

RICE WITH PEAS AND PLANTAIN CHIPS

110g/4oz aduki beans, soaked overnight
30g/1oz creamed coconut
290ml/½ pint boiling water
170g/6oz basmati rice
2 curry leaves
grated zest of ½ lime
salt and freshly ground black pepper
110g/4oz shelled, fresh or frozen peas
1 plantain
vegetable oil, for deep-frying

1. Rinse and drain the aduki beans. Put them into a saucepan, cover with water and boil for 30–40 minutes until tender. Drain and set aside.
2. Dissolve the creamed coconut in the boiling water and put into a pan with the rice. Add the curry leaves and lime zest and season with salt. Bring to the boil and then lower the heat and simmer gently until craters appear on the surface of the rice. Scatter the cooked beans and the peas on top. Cover the pan with kitchen foil and then a tight-fitting lid. Turn off the heat and leave the rice mixture to stand for 20 minutes.
3. Meanwhile, make the plantain chips: peel the plantain and slice very thinly. Heat about 5cm/2in oil in a small pan until a slice of plantain sizzles vigorously. Fry the plantain in small batches until lightly golden.
4. When the rice is ready, season with pepper and fork through. Serve topped with the plantain chips.

POD PILAFF

an assortment of any of the following, total
weight about 340g/12oz: sugar-snap peas,
French beans, mangetout, topped and tailed,
baby sweetcorn, trimmed, fresh broad beans
3 cardamom pods
1 tablespoon olive oil
30g/1oz unsalted butter
2 teaspoons coriander seeds
2 teaspoons cumin seeds
1 large onion, finely chopped
2 green chillies, deseeded and chopped (see
page 22)
2–4 cloves of garlic, crushed
170g/6oz basmati rice
570ml/1 pint spicy vegetable stock (see page 531)
salt and freshly ground black pepper
chopped fresh flat-leaf parsley, to garnish

1. Cut the French beans into 2.5cm/1in pieces.
If the broad beans are very young, use the
whole pods, topped and tailed and cut into
2.5cm/1in pieces. If the beans are older, shell
them and cook in boiling salted water until
tender. Cool, then slip off the tough outer skins.
Use the sugar-snap peas, mangetout and
sweetcorn whole. Split the cardamom pods and
remove the seeds.
2. Heat the oil in a sauté pan with a lid, add the
butter and when foaming, toss in the
cardamom, coriander and cumin seeds. Fry
until the seeds begin to pop. Add the onion and
fry until golden-brown.
3. Stir in the chillies and garlic and fry for 1
further minute. Stir the rice into the onion and
garlic mixture and fry for 2 minutes. Pour in the
stock, season with salt and pepper and simmer,
uncovered, for about 15 minutes.
4. Add the vegetables, cover partially with the
lid and simmer for a further 10 minutes or until
the rice is cooked and the vegetables are tender
but still crunchy. Sprinkle with parsley before
serving.

RICE AND SPINACH BURGERS

140g/5oz brown rice
425ml/¾ pint water
salt and freshly ground black pepper
vegetable or sunflower oil, for frying
1 onion, finely chopped
55g/2oz frozen leaf spinach, defrosted
1 clove of garlic, finely chopped
2.5cm/1in piece of fresh root ginger, peeled and
grated
30g/1oz fresh coriander, chopped
85g/3oz wholemeal breadcrumbs
1 egg, beaten
freshly grated nutmeg

To serve
tomato sauce I (see page 527) or baked tomato
relish (see page 509)

1. Put the rice and water into a saucepan,
season with salt and simmer until all the liquid
has been absorbed and the rice is nearly dry.
2. Heat a little oil in a frying pan. Add the
onion and fry over a low heat until softened.
Add the spinach and cook until all the moisture
has evaporated. Stir in the garlic and ginger and
cook for 1 further minute. Remove the mixture
from the heat and cool, then chop roughly.
3. Stir the spinach mixure into the cooked rice
and add the coriander, breadcrumbs and egg.
Season well with salt, pepper and nutmeg.
Shape into burgers.
4. Heat about 2mm/⅛in oil in a heavy frying
pan. Fry the burgers for about 3 minutes on
each side until lightly browned. Serve with the
tomato sauce or relish handed separately.

LENTIL KEDGEREE

110g/4oz Puy lentils
1 bay leaf
4 cloves
1 tablespoon vegetable or nut oil
1 teaspoon yellow mustard seeds
1 teaspoon cumin seeds
1 teaspoon ground turmeric
a pinch of chilli powder
170g/6oz basmati rice
425ml/¾ pint spicy vegetable stock (see
*   page 531)*
salt and freshly ground black pepper
55g/2oz butter
2 tablespoons chopped fresh coriander
lemon juice
4 eggs, hard-boiled and quartered

1. Put the lentils into a large saucepan of water
with the bay leaf and cloves and simmer for
about 30 minutes until tender. Drain and
discard the flavourings.
2. Meanwhile, heat the oil in a saucepan, add
the mustard and cumin seeds and fry until they
begin to pop. Stir in the turmeric and chilli
powder and fry for 1 further minute. Add the
rice and stir until coated in the spicy oil. Pour in
the stock and add a good pinch of salt. Boil
vigorously until little craters appear on top of
the rice. Cover the pan with kitchen foil and
then a tight-fitting lid. Turn off the heat and
leave to stand for 15 minutes.
3. Return the lentils to the pan they were
cooked in and set over a low heat. Add the rice
and butter and gently mix together with a fork
until piping hot. Stir in the coriander and
season with salt, pepper and lemon juice. Pile
into a a warmed serving dish and top with the
hard-boiled eggs.

VEGETABLE JAMBALAYA WITH ROASTED CHILLIES AND SPICED NUTS

2 tablespoons sesame oil
3 sticks of celery with leaves trimmed and sliced
1 large onion, finely chopped
1 green pepper, deseeded and sliced
1 red pepper, deseeded and sliced
1 yellow pepper, deseeded and sliced
3 cloves of garlic, chopped
2 red chillies, deseeded and chopped (see
*   page 22)*
a walnut-sized piece of fresh root ginger, peeled
*   and finely chopped*
1 teaspoon ground turmeric
1 teaspoon paprika
110g/4oz basmati rice
290ml/½ pint summer vegetable stock (see
*   page 530)*
4 tomatoes, peeled and chopped (see page 22)
salt and freshly ground black pepper
110g/4oz okra

To garnish
6 red snub chillies
2 tablespoons sesame oil
170g/6oz whole blanched almonds or cashew
*   nuts*
55g/2oz granulated sugar
1 teaspoon ground cumin

1. First make the roasted chillies for the
garnish: preheat the oven to 190°C/375°F/gas
mark 5. Place the chillies on a baking tray, brush
with half the oil and roast in the preheated oven
for 30–40 minutes until very soft.
2. Make the jambalaya: heat the oil in a sauté
pan, add the celery and onion and fry until
golden-brown. Add the peppers and fry until
they begin to soften. Stir in the garlic, chillies,
ginger, turmeric and paprika and fry for 1
further minute.
3. Add the rice and fry until coated in the spicy
oil. Pour in the stock, add the tomatoes and
season with salt and pepper. Simmer for 15
minutes.
4. Meanwhile, make the spiced nuts: heat the

remaining oil in a heavy frying pan. Add the nuts and sprinkle the sugar over. Fry gently until the sugar caramelizes. Spoon the nuts on to a plate and sprinkle with the cumin.

5. Scatter the okra on top of the jambalaya and simmer for a further 5–10 minutes until the okra is tender and the rice cooked and all the liquid has been absorbed. Garnish with the roasted chillies and spiced nuts before serving.

BASIC RISOTTO ALLA MILANESE

85g/3oz unsalted butter
1 large onion, finely chopped
400g/14oz arborio rice
150ml/¼ pint dry white wine
1.75 litres/3 pints vegetable stock (see page 530)
about 15 saffron strands
salt and freshly ground black pepper
30g/1oz unsalted butter
55g/2oz Parmesan cheese, freshly grated, plus
extra for serving (optional)

1. Melt the butter in a large saucepan, add the onion and cook over a low heat until soft and lightly coloured. Add the rice and wine and bring to the boil, cook for about 3 minutes until the wine is absorbed, then reduce the heat and stir gently and continuously.

2. Meanwhile, reheat the stock in a second pan and add the saffron. Allow the stock to simmer gently.

3. Start adding the hot stock to the rice a little at a time, stirring gently. Allow the stock to become absorbed after each addition, stirring all the time. Season with salt and pepper, and keep adding the stock until the rice is cooked but still *al dente* (about 30 minutes).

4. Remove the pan from the heat, add the butter and the cheese and mix well with a wooden spoon until the butter is melted and the cheese absorbed. Serve immediately, with additional grated Parmesan cheese handed separately if desired.

ASPARAGUS, PEA AND LEMON RISOTTO

340g/12oz asparagus
1 litre/1¾ pints hot summer vegetable stock (see
page 530)
2 tablespoons olive oil
55g/2oz butter
1 large onion, finely chopped
2 cloves of garlic, chopped
340g/12oz arborio or carnaroli rice
150ml/¼ pint dry white wine
110g/4oz fresh or frozen peas
grated zest and juice of 1 lemon
55g/2oz Parmesan cheese, freshly grated
1 tablespoon fresh thyme leaves, plus extra to
garnish
salt and freshly ground black pepper
freshly grated nutmeg
200g/7oz mascarpone

1. Trim the woody stalks from the asparagus and set aside to use in stock or soup. Cut the spears into pieces about 5cm/2in long. Bring the stock to the boil, add the asparagus spears and cook for 2 minutes. Drain, reserve the stock and set aside.

2. Heat the oil in a large sauté pan, add the butter and when foaming, stir in the onion and fry over a low heat until softened. Add the garlic and cook for 1 further minute. Stir in the rice until well coated with oil and butter.

3. Pour in the wine and cook until it has all been absorbed. Gradually add the hot stock a little at a time, allowing the liquid to be absorbed before adding more and stirring all the time. When half the stock has been added, add the peas. Continue to add the stock, stirring constantly, until the risotto is creamy and the rice is cooked *al dente*.

4. Add the lemon zest and juice, Parmesan cheese and thyme leaves and season with salt, pepper and nutmeg. Stir in three-quarters of the mascarpone and the asparagus and cook for a further 1–2 minutes. Serve with the remaining mascarpone dotted on top, with a sprinkling of thyme leaves and pepper.

BEAN AND ROCKET RISOTTO

3 tablespoons olive oil
1 large onion, chopped
2–3 cloves of garlic, chopped
1 × 400g/14oz can of green flageolet beans, drained and rinsed
4 tomatoes, peeled, deseeded and cut into slivers (see page 22)
2 bay leaves
salt and freshly ground black pepper
85g/3oz unsalted butter
285g/10oz arborio or carnaroli rice
720ml/1¼ pints hot summer vegetable stock (see page 530)
a handful of mixed chopped fresh parsley and basil
55g/2oz Parmesan cheese, freshly grated

To garnish
freshly grated Parmesan cheese
55g/2oz rocket, roughly chopped

1. Heat the oil in a saucepan, add the onion and fry over a low heat until soft and golden-brown. Add the garlic and beans and fry for a further 1–2 minutes. Stir in the tomatoes and bay leaves and season with salt and pepper. Turn the heat down to very low and leave to simmer gently.
2. Meanwhile, melt the butter in a large sauté pan, add the rice and turn in the butter until well coated. Gradually add the hot stock, a ladleful at a time. Allow the stock to become absorbed before adding the next ladleful and stir constantly until the rice is cooked *al dente* and the risotto is creamy.
3. Add the tomato and bean mixture to the rice. Season with salt and pepper and add the herbs and cheese. Serve with shavings of Parmesan cheese and the rocket scattered on top.

BUTTERNUT SQUASH RISOTTO WITH TOASTED WALNUTS AND DEEP-FRIED SAGE

85g/3oz walnuts
oil, for frying
about 25 fresh sage leaves
55g/2oz unsalted butter
1 medium onion
1 clove of garlic, chopped
2 red chillies, deseeded and chopped (see page 22)
1 teaspoon fresh thyme leaves
1 small butternut squash, about 450g/1lb, peeled, deseeded and sliced
340g/12oz arborio or carnaroli rice
salt and freshly ground black pepper
860ml/1½ pints summer vegetable stock (see page 530)
150ml/¼ pint double cream
55g/2oz Parmesan cheese, freshly grated
shavings of Parmesan cheese, to garnish

1. Heat a heavy frying pan. Add the walnuts and toast over the heat, then chop roughly. Heat about 1cm/½in oil in a small pan until a crumb of bread sizzles vigorously. Fry the sage leaves in batches, flipping them over to cook on both sides. Drain on kitchen paper.
2. Melt the butter in a large sauté pan, add the onion and fry over a low heat until very soft and transparent but not at all coloured. Add the garlic, chillies and thyme and fry for 1 further minute. Add the squash and rice and stir until coated in the buttery juices. Season with salt and pepper.
3. Bring the stock to the boil and add to the rice a ladleful at a time, allowing the liquid to become absorbed before adding more, and stirring all the time. The rice should be *al dente* and the risotto should be creamy when it is cooked. Check the risotto for seasoning. Stir in the cream and grated cheese.
4. Scatter the chopped walnuts and fried sage leaves on top of the risotto. Top with a few Parmesan cheese shavings and serve immediately.

CAPER RISOTTO WITH SPINACH AND POACHED EGGS

For the risotto
55g/2oz butter
1 onion, finely chopped
1 stick of celery, thinly sliced
2 leeks or 6 baby leeks, trimmed and thinly
    sliced
1 clove of garlic, crushed
110g/4oz arborio or carnaroli rice
570ml/1 pint hot summer vegetable stock (see
    page 530)
6 spring onions, trimmed and sliced
1 tablespoon capers, rinsed and roughly
    chopped
55g/2oz Parmesan cheese, freshly grated
salt and freshly ground black pepper
1 tablespoon finely chopped fresh parsley
1 tablespoon shredded fresh basil

To serve
30g/1oz butter
225g/8oz spinach, washed
freshly grated nutmeg
4 very fresh, cold eggs

1. Melt the butter in a large saucepan and add
the onion, celery and leeks. Cover and cook
over a low heat for 10 minutes or until the
vegetables are soft but not coloured. Add the
garlic and rice and turn in the butter for 1–2
minutes.
2. Gradually add the hot stock a little at a time,
allowing each addition to become absorbed
before adding more and stirring all the time.
Continue to add enough stock to cook the rice
until it is *al dente*. With the last addition of
stock, add the spring onions and the capers and
allow any remaining liquid to evaporate. Add
the cheese and season to taste with salt and
pepper. Stir in the herbs. Keep warm.
3. Melt the remaining butter in a frying pan,
add the spinach and allow to wilt over a
medium heat. Season to taste with salt, pepper
and nutmeg.
4. Meanwhile, poach the eggs (see page 434).

5. Divide the caper risotto between 4 warmed
individual plates. Make a coil of spinach and
place this in the centre of the rice. Top with a
poached egg and serve immediately.

CHICORY AND SUN-DRIED TOMATO RISOTTO

3 heads of chicory
10 sun-dried tomatoes
2 tablespoons olive oil
55g/2oz butter
1 medium onion, finely chopped
340g/12oz arborio or carnaroli rice
1.1 litres/2 pints hot summer vegetable stock
    (see page 530)
salt and freshly ground black pepper
55g/2oz Parmesan cheese, freshly grated

1. Trim the roots and outer leaves from the
chicory. Slice the chicory thinly. Slice the sun-
dried tomatoes.
2. Heat the oil in a large sauté pan. Add half
the butter and when foaming, add the onion
and chicory and fry over a low heat until soft
and golden. Stir in the sun-dried tomatoes.
3. Add the rice and cook gently until coated in
the pan juices. Gradually add the hot stock a
ladleful at a time, allowing the liquid to become
absorbed before adding more and stirring all
the time. The rice should be *al dente* and the
risotto should be creamy when it is cooked.
4. Season with salt and pepper. Stir in the
remaining butter and the cheese. Serve
immediately.

COURGETTE AND DOLCELATTE RISOTTO

85g/3oz unsalted butter
1 large onion, finely chopped
2 cloves of garlic, chopped
340g/12oz arborio or carnaroli rice
150ml/¼ pint dry white wine
860ml/1½ pints hot summer vegetable stock
(see page 530)
2 courgettes, grated
30g/1oz Parmesan cheese, freshly grated
salt and freshly ground black pepper
110g/4oz Dolcelatte or other soft blue cheese
a handful of fresh basil leaves, to garnish
freshly grated Parmesan cheese, to serve

1. Melt the butter in a large sauté pan and
when foaming, add the onion and fry over a
low heat until softened. Add the garlic and rice
and turn in the buttery juices for a few minutes.
2. Pour in the wine and stir until it has been
absorbed by the rice. Gradually add the hot
stock a ladleful at a time, allowing the liquid to
become absorbed before adding more and
stirring all the time. The rice should be *al dente*
and the risotto should be creamy when it is
cooked.
3. Stir in the courgettes and Parmesan cheese.
Season to taste with salt and pepper. Cook for a
few minutes longer to allow the rice to absorb
the courgette juices.
4. Cut the Dolcelatte cheese into small pieces
and fold briefly through the risotto. Scatter
with torn basil leaves before serving and hand
the Parmesan cheese separately.

MELON AND FENNEL RISOTTO

1 medium, ripe cantaloupe or galia melon
2 bulbs of fennel
1 tablespoon olive oil, plus extra to finish
85g/3oz butter
1 large onion, finely chopped
340g/12oz arborio or carnaroli rice
290ml/½ pint dry white wine, vermouth or
white port
570ml/1 pint hot summer vegetable stock (see
page 530)
salt and freshly ground black pepper
85g/3oz Parmesan cheese, freshly grated
Parmesan cheese shavings, to garnish

1. Cut the melon into quarters. Scoop out the
seeds and peel away the skin. Purée half the
flesh in a food processor or blender. Cut the
remaining melon into 1cm/½in cubes. Set
aside.
2. Cut the tops off the fennel and reserve the
feathery fronds. Remove the outer fennel leaves
and discard. Cut the fennel in half and slice
finely.
3. Heat the oil in a large sauté pan. Add the
butter and when foaming, add the onion and
fennel and fry over a low heat until softened.
Add the rice and stir until well coated in the
butter and oil.
4. Pour in the wine, vermouth or port and stir
until it has been absorbed. Add the puréed
melon and cook, stirring until it has been
absorbed. Now add the hot stock a ladleful at a
time, stirring until it is all absorbed, the rice is
cooked *al dente*, and the risotto is creamy.
5. Season to taste with salt and pepper. Stir in
the grated cheese and diced melon and cook for
a further few minutes. Serve topped with
shavings of Parmesan cheese, the fennel tops
and a drizzle of oil.

RED PESTO RISOTTO WITH CARAMELIZED ONIONS

For the caramelized onions
1 tablespoon olive oil
30g/1oz unsalted butter
2 large onions, thinly sliced
1 tablespoon soft light brown sugar

For the risotto
85g/3oz unsalted butter
1 tablespoon olive oil
1 onion, finely chopped
340g/12oz arborio or carnaroli rice
150ml/¼ pint dry white wine
*1 litre/1¾ pints hot summer vegetable stock (see
    page 530)*
2½ tablespoons good-quality red pesto
4 sun-dried tomatoes, finely chopped
5 tablespoons mascarpone
a small handful of fresh basil leaves, shredded
55g/2oz Parmesan cheese, freshly grated
salt and freshly ground black pepper
fresh basil leaves, to garnish

1. Heat the oil and butter in a frying pan. Add the onions and cook over a low heat for 15 minutes or until soft and transparent.
2. Sprinkle over the sugar and increase the heat. Cook briskly for 2–3 minutes, stirring occasionally, until the onions are a good caramel colour. Remove from the pan and set aside.
3. Make the risotto: heat the butter and oil in a large flameproof casserole over a medium heat. Add the onion and cook until soft but not coloured. Add the rice and wine, bring to the boil and cook for about 3 minutes until the wine is absorbed.
4. Lower the heat. Add the hot stock to the pan a little at a time, allowing it to be absorbed between each addition and stirring all the time. Keep adding the stock until the rice is cooked *al dente* (about 30 minutes).
5. Stir in the pesto, sun-dried tomatoes, mascarpone, basil and cheese. Season to taste with salt and pepper.
6. Pile the risotto into a warmed serving dish, spoon over the caramelized onions and garnish with basil.

SAFFRON AND TOMATO RISOTTO

85g/3oz butter
1 medium onion, finely chopped
340g/12oz arborio or carnaroli rice
85ml/3fl oz dry white wine
a large pinch of saffron strands
*1 litre/1¾ pints hot summer vegetable stock (see
    page 530)*
salt and freshly ground black pepper
55g/2oz Parmesan cheese, freshly grated
*450g/1lb tomatoes, peeled and deseeded and cut
    into thin strips (see page 22)*
1 tablespoon chopped fresh parsley

1. Melt the butter in a large flameproof casserole. Add the onion and cook over a low heat for 10 minutes without browning.
2. Add the rice and cook over a low heat for 2 minutes. Pour in the wine and reduce by half.
3. Put the saffron into the boiling stock and start to add to the rice, about 85ml/3fl oz at a time. Stir and when the stock has been absorbed, add some more. Continue in the same way, stirring all the time, until the rice is cooked *al dente* (15–20 minutes). If necessary, add extra boiling water.
4. Season with salt and pepper and stir in the remaining butter, the cheese and the tomatoes. Scatter with the parsley and serve immediately.

SUMMER VEGETABLE RISOTTO

You can use any summer vegetables in this risotto. They should be cooked just before you need them. Make sure they do not overcook.

30g/1oz unsalted butter or 2 tablespoons olive oil
1 onion, chopped
340g/12oz arborio or carnaroli rice
85ml/3fl oz dry white wine
860ml/1½ pints hot summer vegetable stock (see page 530)
450g/1lb mixed summer vegetables, such as baby courgettes, trimmed and thickly sliced, sugar-snap peas, baby carrots, green beans, asparagus tips, patty pan squash, baby broad beans, all cooked briefly
2 large handfuls of baby spinach, rocket and basil leaves mixed together and roughly chopped
salt and freshly ground black pepper
3 tablespoons freshly grated Parmesan cheese

1. Melt the butter or heat the oil in a large saucepan, add the onion and cook over a low heat until soft but not coloured. Add the rice and fry gently for 3 minutes, stirring.
2. Add the wine and cook until it is absorbed, stirring all the time.
3. Add the hot stock to the rice, about 85ml/3fl oz at a time, stirring constantly. When the stock has been absorbed, add some more. Continue in the same way, stirring all the time, until all the stock has been absorbed and the rice is cooked *al dente* (about 20 minutes). If necessary add hot water.
4. Add the blanched vegetables and stir in carefully. Add the spinach, rocket and basil and allow to wilt.
5. Season with salt and pepper and add the cheese. Serve immediately.

RISOTTO KIEVS

This is a great way of using up leftover risotto. As a rough guide, one portion of risotto will make enough kievs to serve 2 as a main course or 4 as a first course. Serve with salad or a hot vegetable. Wilted spinach with pinenuts and raisins (see page 54) is an especially good accompaniment.

55g/2oz butter
1 tablespoon chopped fresh flat-leaf parsley
1–2 cloves of garlic, crushed
grated zest of ½ lemon and juice to taste
salt and freshly ground black pepper
2 portions of risotto, made with 170g/6oz rice (see basic risotto milanese, page 364)
55g/2oz plain flour, sifted
1 egg, beaten
sunflower, vegetable or groundnut oil, for frying

1. Beat the butter to soften, then mix in the parsley, garlic and lemon zest. Season with salt, pepper and lemon juice. Spoon the butter on to a piece of greaseproof paper or kitchen foil. Roll up into a narrow cylinder and twist the ends to secure. Chill until firm.
2. Cut the butter into 8 even slices. Divide the risotto into 8 portions and mould into patties around each piece of chilled butter. Dust with flour, then dip in beaten egg and dust again with flour.
3. Shallow-fry the kievs in a little hot oil for 2–3 minutes on each side until golden-brown. Drain on kitchen paper and sprinkle with salt before serving.

BROWN RICE SALAD WITH CASHEW NUTS AND SPRING ONIONS

225g/8oz brown rice
2 tablespoons sunflower oil
1 medium onion, chopped
2 cloves of garlic, chopped
2 teaspoons ground turmeric
2 teaspoons garam masala
1 teaspoon sugar
3 tablespoons light soy sauce
2 tablespoons lemon juice
100g/3½oz cashew nuts, toasted (see page 22)
6 spring onions, trimmed and sliced
1 tablespoon chopped fresh coriander
1 tablespoon chopped fresh parsley
1 tablespoon chopped fresh mint
salt and freshly ground black pepper

1. Wash the rice well and cook in a saucepan of salted boiling water for 35–40 minutes. Drain and pour boiling water through the rice. Leave in a sieve to drain completely.
2. Meanwhile, heat the oil in a large saucepan, add the onion and garlic and cook over a low heat for about 15 minutes until soft.
3. Add the turmeric and garam masala and cook for a further 2 minutes. Add the sugar, soy sauce, lemon juice, cashew nuts, spring onions, herbs, salt and pepper. Mix well and stir in the rice. Taste and adjust for seasoning if necessary. Serve hot or cold.

BROWN RICE SALAD WITH TOASTED SEEDS

140g/5oz brown rice
55g/2oz sunflower seeds
30g/1oz sesame seeds
55g/2oz pumpkin seeds
½ bunch of spring onions, trimmed and chopped
110g/4oz mixed dried fruit, chopped
1 tablespoon mixed chopped fresh parsley and chives

For the dressing
4 tablespoons sunflower or groundnut oil
1 tablespoon tahina
1 tablespoon clear honey
grated zest and juice of ½ lemon
salt and freshly ground black pepper

1. Cook the rice in plenty of boiling salted water for about 25 minutes until *al dente*.
2. Meanwhile, make the dressing: whisk all the ingredients together and season with salt and pepper. Drain the rice and toss in the dressing. Leave to cool.
3. Preheat the oven to 190°C/375°F/gas mark 5. Put the sunflower, pumpkin seeds and sesame seeds into a roasting tin and cook in the preheated oven for 10–15 minutes until lightly toasted. Alternatively, heat the grill to high, spread the seeds in a baking tray and toast lightly.
4. Add the spring onions to the rice together with the seeds, dried fruit and herbs and toss.

BROWN RICE PILAFF WITH CAJUN VEGETABLES

30g/1oz butter
1 large onion, finely chopped
170g/6oz brown rice
860ml/1½ pints spicy vegetable stock (see page 531)
1 × 400g/14oz can of chopped tomatoes
salt and freshly ground black pepper
1 courgette
1 red pepper, deseeded and sliced
110g/4oz baby sweetcorn, trimmed
1 medium red onion, thickly sliced
2–3 teaspoons Cajun spice (see page 529)
2 tablespoons olive oil
lemon juice
1 tablespoon chopped fresh flat-leaf parsley, to garnish

1. Melt the butter in a large pan, add the onion and fry over a low heat until soft and golden. Add the rice and stir to coat well in the buttery juices. Pour in the stock and tomatoes and season with salt and pepper. Bring to the boil, then lower the heat and simmer gently for 45 minutes or until the rice is tender and all the liquid absorbed. If the liquid is absorbed before the rice is cooked, add a little more stock or water.
2. While the rice is cooking, cut the courgettes in half lengthways and then crossways into 1cm/½in slices. Toss together with the pepper, sweetcorn, onion and the Cajun spice. Heat the oil in a wok or heavy frying pan. Add the vegetables and toss over the heat for a few minutes until hot but still very crunchy.
3. When the rice is cooked, add to the pan with the vegetables. Turn together, adjust the seasoning to taste and add some lemon juice. Serve scattered with the parsley.

WILD RICE POT

Wild rice is an aquatic grass that is costly to buy. If preferred, 55g/2oz of the wild rice in this recipe can be replaced by the same quantity of basmati rice. This makes the casserole lighter in texture and the nutty flavour of the wild rice will still come through.

1 tablespoon olive oil
30g/1oz unsalted butter
1 large onion, finely chopped
1 red pepper, deseeded and chopped
170g/6oz flat mushrooms, sliced
140g/5oz wild rice
1 × 230g/8oz can of chopped tomatoes
570ml/1 pint summer vegetable stock (see page 530)
salt and freshly ground black pepper
½ teaspoon chopped fresh marjoram
3 tablespoons chopped fresh flat-leaf parsley, to garnish

1. Preheat the oven to 190°C/375°F/gas mark 5.
2. Heat the oil in an ovenproof casserole, add the butter and when foaming, add the onion and cook over a low heat until golden-brown. Add the pepper and mushrooms and cook until soft.
3. Stir in the rice until covered in the buttery juices. Add the tomatoes and stock and bring to the boil. Season with salt and pepper. Stir in the marjoram, then cover and bake in the preheated oven.
4. Cook for 20 minutes, then reduce the oven temperature to 130°C/325°F/gas mark 3. Continue to cook for another 40–50 minutes until the rice is tender but there is still a little stock left. Taste and adjust the seasoning if necessary and scatter with the parsley before serving.

WILD RICE WITH STIR-FRIED VEGETABLES IN LEMON AND GINGER SAUCE

30g/1oz butter
55g/2oz wild rice
85g/3oz basmati rice
570ml/1 pint water
salt and freshly ground black pepper
¼ cucumber
1 tablespoon sunflower or groundnut oil
½ bunch of spring onions, trimmed and
   chopped
110g/4oz cashew nuts
1 yellow pepper, deseeded and sliced
110g/4oz sugar-snap peas or mangetout, topped
   and tailed
1 clove of garlic, crushed
2 tablespoons chopped fresh coriander

For the sauce
1 red chilli, deseeded and finely chopped (see
   page 22)
2.5cm/1in piece of fresh root ginger, peeled and
   grated
1 stalk of lemongrass, outer leaves removed and
   finely chopped
juice of 1 lemon
1 tablespoon rice vinegar
2 teaspoons caster sugar

1. Melt the butter in a medium saucepan and when foaming, add the rices and fry for 2–3 minutes until coated in the butter. Pour on the water and season with salt and pepper. Boil vigorously until little craters appear on top of the rice. Turn off the heat, cover the pan with a sheet of kitchen foil and a tight-fitting lid and leave to stand for 20 minutes.
2. Make the sauce: mix all the ingredients together and leave to stand for 30 minutes.
3. Cut the cucumber in half lengthways, then slice crossways. Heat the oil in a wok or heavy frying pan. Add the spring onions and cashew nuts and toss over the heat until the cashews have browned. Add the cucumber, pepper,

sugar-snap peas and garlic and fry briefly until hot but still very crunchy. Add the coriander and season with salt and pepper.
4. Pile a portion of rice on to each individual plate, top with some vegetables and hand the sauce separately.

WILD RICE LOAF

This bread can be buttered and served as a snack, or is excellent with mild goat's cheese or a good sharp Cheddar.

MAKES A 900G/2LB LOAF

85g/3oz wild rice
570ml/1 pint water
2 tablespoons black treacle
30g/1oz butter, plus extra for greasing
½ medium onion, finely chopped
2 cloves of garlic, crushed
1 red chilli, deseeded and chopped (see page 22)
1 teaspoon coriander seeds, crushed
2 tablespoons olive oil
225g/8oz wholemeal self-raising flour
½ teaspoon salt and freshly ground black
   pepper
55g/2oz walnuts, toasted and chopped (see
   page 22)
1 carrot, grated
2 eggs, beaten

1. Put the rice into a saucepan with the water and bring to the boil. Cover the pan and simmer the rice for about 45 minutes until the water has been absorbed and the rice is very soft and split. Put the rice into a mixing bowl, stir in the treacle and leave to cool.
2. Meanwhile, melt the butter in a frying pan, add the onion and fry over a low heat until very soft and golden. Add the garlic, chilli and coriander seeds and fry for 1 further minute. Set aside.
3. Preheat the oven to 160°C/325°F/gas mark 3. Grease a 900g/2lb loaf tin with butter and line the base with greased greaseproof paper.
4. Add the oil to the rice, then beat in the flour, salt, walnuts and carrot. Beat in the onion

mixture and the eggs. Spoon the mixture into the prepared tin and smooth the top. Bake in the preheated oven for 1 hour or until the top of the loaf feels firm when pressed with the fingertips and a skewer comes out clean when inserted into the centre.

5. Turn the loaf on to a wire rack and leave to cool.

BLACK RICE SALAD

2–4 tablespoons olive oil
1 medium aubergine, cut into 1cm/½in dice
1 red onion, roughly diced
200g/7oz button mushrooms, washed and
    quartered
salt and freshly ground black pepper
110g/4oz Nanjing black rice
225ml/8fl oz summer vegetable stock (see
    page 530)
soy sauce
30g/1oz sultanas or raisins
1–2 tablespoons roughly chopped fresh thyme
    and parsley

1. Heat the oil in a frying pan, add the aubergines and sauté over a medium heat until the aubergine is soft and well browned. Put into a bowl.

2. Put the onion into the frying pan (more oil may be needed) and sauté for a few minutes, then add the mushrooms. Season with salt and pepper. Contine to cook until the vegetables are soft and any liquid has evaporated. Add to the aubergines.

3. Meanwhile, cook the rice: put the rice and stock into a saucepan and bring to the boil, then lower the heat and simmer for about 10 minutes until the rice is cooked. Increase the heat and allow the excess stock to evaporate, stirring regularly to prevent sticking. Add a dash of soy sauce.

4. Combine the rice with the vegetables and mix in the sultanas and herbs. Season to taste with salt and pepper and leave to cool.

GRAINS AND NUTS

Barley • Couscous • Cracked and bulghur wheat • Millet •
Polenta • Quinoa • Nuts

INTRODUCTION

GRAINS

If one group of foods could epitomize 'food of the world' it would be grains. They have been grown for many thousands of years and still sustain many countries worldwide. Grains are packed full of carbohydrate, vitamins, minerals and protein and can be produced at low cost. They are one of the few food groups to contain both soluble and insoluble fibre. Many grains come in various forms – rolled, ground into flour, crushed: sometimes part of the grain is removed and separated, as with wheat bran and germ. Grains make filling and comforting dishes. Whole grains will have a thickening effect on a soup or stew as will grain meals or flours. Plain flour is the traditional thickening agent but wholemeal, cornmeal, chickpea (gram) or barley flour will work just as well, giving extra body and flavour. Grains are inexpensive to buy and if stored in an airtight container will keep for several months.

Wheat is the most important grain crop in the world. All parts of the grain are used. When wheat grain is milled it is separated into bran, wheat germ and endosperm. Stone-grinding produces the best-quality flour. Wholemeal and wholewheat flour are the same. White flour is made from the starchy endosperm. **Wheat berries** are wholewheat grains with the outer husk removed. They have a sweet, nutty flavour and can be added to soup, stews or breads. If sprouted they grow into wheat grass which is recognized for its excellent healing properties (see page 313 for sprouting instructions). They can be bought in good health food shops or purchased through mail order.

Bran is the outer husk of the wheat kernel and is removed before the kernel is ground into flour. It is very high in dietary fibre and can be added to bread, muffins, cakes and breakfast cereals.

Wheat germ is the highly nutritious heart of the grain. It is used in the same way as bran.

Cracked wheat is crushed wheat berries. All the nutrients are retained. It can be cooked like rice or used in pilaffs.

Bulghur wheat derives from cooked wheat berries. The bran is removed and the berries are dried or crushed. It is often confused with cracked wheat but it is bulghur that is used for salads, notably tabouleh, where only soaking is required. Bulghur can also be cooked and served hot.

Semolina, made from the first milling of the endosperm of wheat, is halfway between wheat and flour. Semolina is used commercially to make pasta. **Couscous** is made from floured semolina grains.

Buckwheat is grown in northern Europe. It is a coarse grain traditionally used to make blinis. It should be mixed with lighter flours for breadmaking.

Barley is mostly used as a highly polished grain known as pearl barley. It contains little bran. Pearl barley is delicious and comforting in soups and stews and will thicken the liquid slightly.

Corn was once an all-encompassing name for grains but has come to mean maize. There are many different types – hard, soft, golden-yellow, red or black. Corn is predominantly used in the cooking of America's Deep South and in Central and South America. Hominy is the Native American name for dried white corn and when ground it is called grits. Finely ground grits are used in cakes, cornbread and spoonbread, giving a pleasant, grainy texture.

Unless corn is stone-ground the germ is usually removed. **Cornmeal** often contains black and red specks from the outer husk. In Mexico and South America corn is made into masa harina. This is the cooked whole grain, which is ground into flour and used to make numerous varieties of tortillas and flat breads. In Italy cornmeal is used to make **polenta**. **Popcorn** is made from a separate variety of corn with a hard outer husk. **Cornflour** is the white heart of the kernel. It is ground to a fine silky powder. This is used as a thickening and also in biscuits or shortbread to give a light, melt-in-the-mouth texture.

Millet is rich in magnesium and easy to digest. It has a bland, nutty texture and swells many times during cooking so the cooking water should be five times the volume of the grain. Toasting millet in a dry frying pan before cooking will improve the flavour and reduce the cooking time. Millet is a good accompaniment to spicy stews and curries. Store in a tightly closed container.

Quinoa, pronounced 'keen-wa', was used by South American Indians in ancient times. It has been revived by interested Americans and has been appearing in health food shops and recipes over the past ten years. It is surprising that it disappeared from use as it has a well-balanced protein content and is rich in calcium. Quinoa has a mild, slightly bitter flavour. It can be cooked like rice or made into a salad. When cooked, the grains quadruple in size and become translucent with a white outer ring.

NUTS

Nuts are the fruit of trees or occasionally, like peanuts, a legume that grows underground.

They are rich in protein, calcium, iron and vitamins, especially vitamin E. In the autumn, when freshly harvested, nuts are sweet and milky. Fresh filberts and green walnuts can be bought when young but most nuts are sold dried. There are several dozen varieties of nuts, each with a unique flavour and texture. Nuts take many roles in cooking and are useful as an addition to vegetarian dishes because of their high nutritional value. Traditionally nuts are served as a snack for pre-dinner drinks or at Christmas. They may be roasted or salted or whole in the shell. Nuts can also be ground coarsely or finely into flour to add to cakes, pastries or for thickening sauces. Whole, chopped or flaked nuts can be used for decoration and added to salads or stews or curries.

Chestnuts are very low in fat wth a soft floury texture. They can be a chore to peel. The following method works well with hot but not undercooked chestnuts: make a slit in the skin of each chestnut and put them into a pan of cold water. Bring to the boil, then lower the heat and simmer for 15 minutes. Remove the pan from the heat and remove one or two chestnuts at a time for peeling. Vacuum-packed chestnuts are nearly as good as fresh and save the chore of peeling. They are usually only available in supermarkets at Christmas-time but may be bought throughout the year at specialist delicatessens or through mail order suppliers. Chestnuts are also available whole or puréed in cans. Dried chestnuts are excellent for adding to casseroles or to fry in butter and toss with green vegetables. They need soaking overnight before use.

To skin **hazelnuts**: toast under the grill or in a warm oven until dark brown. Then put into a paper bag or tea-towel to remove the skins.

BARLEY SOUP

30g/1oz butter
1 large onion, chopped
2 leeks, trimmed and chopped
1 carrot, finely chopped
45g/1½oz pearl barley
2 bay leaves
1 litre/1¾ pints summer vegetable stock (see
page 530)
salt and freshly ground black pepper
30g/1oz rocket, shredded
55ml/2fl oz double cream
1 tablespoon chopped fresh parsley, to garnish

1. Melt the butter in a large saucepan and
when foaming, add the onion and fry over a
low heat until soft and golden-brown. Add the
leeks and carrot, cover and cook gently for 10
minutes. Stir in the barley, bay leaves and stock
and season with salt and pepper. Cover
partially with the lid and simmer for about
1–1½ hours until the barley is tender.
2. Stir in the rocket and cream. Adjust the
seasoning to taste, reheat and serve in warmed
soup bowls, sprinkled with the parsley.

PEARL BARLEY WITH TARRAGON MUSHROOMS

For the barley
570ml/1 pint summer vegetable stock (see
page 530)
225g/8oz pearl barley
1 tablespoon olive oil
1 stick of celery, thinly sliced
1 clove of garlic, crushed
½ bulb of fennel, cored and finely diced
1 small leek, trimmed and thinly sliced
salt and freshly ground black pepper
1–2 tablespoons crème fraîche
30–55g/1–2oz Stilton cheese

For the mushrooms
30g/1oz butter
1 clove of garlic, sliced
450g/1lb button mushrooms, wiped and
quartered
1 tablespoon finely chopped fresh tarragon
1 tablespoon finely chopped fresh parsley, to
garnish

1. Prepare the barley: bring the stock to the
boil in a saucepan. Add the barley and simmer
for 1 hour or until it is just soft. Drain and set
aside.
2. In a separate saucepan, heat the oil and add
the celery, garlic, fennel and leek. Season to
taste with salt and pepper, cover and sauté over
a low heat for 5–8 minutes until soft. Add the
barley together with the crème fraîche. Crumble
in the cheese and allow to melt. Adjust the
seasoning to taste and keep warm.
3. Prepare the mushrooms: melt the butter in a
frying pan, add the garlic and soften for 1–2
minutes. Add the mushrooms and season lightly
with salt and pepper. Cook briskly over a high
heat, turning occasionally. Adjust the seasoning
to taste and add the tarragon.
4. Spoon the barley mixture into a warmed
serving dish, scatter the mushrooms over the
top, then sprinkle generously with the parsley.
Serve immediately.

PEARL BARLEY WITH SPINACH, TOMATO AND POACHED EGGS

570ml/1 pint summer vegetable stock (see
    page 530)
340g/12oz pearl barley
55g/2oz butter
2–3 cloves of garlic, crushed
5cm/2in piece of fresh root ginger, peeled and
    finely grated
4 tomatoes, peeled, deseeded and thickly sliced
    (see page 22)
450g/1lb spinach, washed
freshly grated nutmeg
salt and freshly ground black pepper
4–8 very fresh, cold eggs

1. Bring the stock up to the boil in a large
saucepan. Add the barley and simmer for 1
hour or until soft. Drain and leave to cool.
2. Melt the butter in a large saucepan. Add the
garlic, ginger and tomato slices and soften over
a very low heat for about 5 minutes. Add the
spinach and toss in the hot butter until wilted.
Add the cooked barley and stir carefully.
Season to taste with nutmeg, salt and pepper
and leave to heat through thoroughly over a
very low heat.
3. Meanwhile, poach the eggs (see page 434).
4. Divide the barley mixture between 4 warmed
individual plates. Set 1–2 poached eggs on the
top of each and serve immediately.

HEARTY BEAN AND BARLEY STEW WITH CHILLI AND PEANUT BUTTER SALSA

55g/2oz dried beans, such as pinto, cannellini,
    black-eye, soaked overnight
2 tablespoons olive oil
1 large onion, chopped
1 red chilli, deseeded and chopped (see page 22)
1 green pepper, deseeded and chopped

½ teaspoon ground cumin
½ teaspoon paprika
425ml/¾ pint winter vegetable stock (see
    page 530)
1 × 400g/14oz can of tomatoes
110g/4oz pearl barley
salt and freshly ground black pepper
110g/4oz spinach
110g/4oz French beans
55g/2oz fresh or frozen peas

For the peanut butter salsa
2 tablespoons peanut butter
2 tablespoons boiling water
1 large ripe tomato, peeled and chopped (see
    page 22)
1 green chilli, deseeded and chopped (see
    page 22)
1 tablespoon chopped fresh coriander

1. Rinse and drain the beans.
2. Heat the oil in a large saucepan, add the
onion and fry over a low heat until soft and
golden-brown. Add the chilli and pepper and
fry for a further few minutes. Stir in the spices
and cook for 1 minute. Pour in the stock and
add the tomatoes, barley and beans. Season
with pepper and simmer gently for 1–1½ hours
until the beans and barley are tender.
3. Meanwhile, remove any tough stalks from
the spinach, wash the leaves thoroughly and
tear into smaller pieces. Top and tail the French
beans and cut into 2.5cm/1in pieces.
4. Make the salsa: gently mix the peanut butter
with the water. Carefully fold in the tomato
and chilli and season with salt. Fold in the
coriander leaves.
5. When the stew is cooked, add the spinach,
French beans and peas and season with salt.
Simmer for a further 10 minutes. Serve in
warmed soup bowls, each topped with a
spoonful of salsa.

BARLEY AND ROOT VEGETABLE STEW WITH PARSLEY DUMPLINGS

2 leeks
2 large carrots
225g/8oz swede
1 turnip
1 medium parsnip
2 tablespoons sunflower or vegetable oil
1 large onion, thickly sliced
860ml/1½ pints winter vegetable stock (see page 530)
110g/4oz pearl barley
3 teaspoons yeast extract
salt and freshly ground black pepper

For the dumplings
110g/4oz self-raising flour
55g/2oz vegetable suet
2 tablespoons chopped fresh parsley

1. Trim the root and outer leaves from the leeks. Wash thoroughly and cut into 1cm/½in lengths. Peel the carrot, swede, turnip and parsnip and cut into chunks about the same size as the leek slices.
2. Heat the oil in a large saucepan, add the onions and fry over a low heat until soft and golden-brown. Add the leeks, carrots, swede, turnip and parsnip. Cover and cook gently until slightly softened.
3. Pour the stock into the pan and bring to the boil, scraping any sticky sediment from the base of the pan. Stir in the barley and yeast extract and season with salt and pepper. Simmer gently for 1 hour.
4. When the barley is nearly tender, make the dumplings: mix together the flour, suet and parsley. Season with salt and pepper and bind to a soft dough with cold water. Drop spoonfuls of the mixture into the bubbling stew. Cover and cook for 10 minutes, then remove the lid and cook for a further 10 minutes.

PEARL BARLEY AND SWEET POTATO TIMBALES

These can be made in advance and reheated, either in a microwave oven or in a bain-marie in a conventional oven.

butter, for greasing
2 tablespoons olive oil
1 medium onion, chopped
1 clove of garlic, crushed
1.1 litre/2 pints summer vegetable stock (see page 530)
400g/14oz sweet potatoes, peeled and cut into small dice
340g/12oz pearl barley
55g/2oz Parmesan cheese, freshly grated
1 tablespoon chopped fresh thyme
1 tablespoon chopped fresh tarragon
2 tablespoons chopped fresh chives
85ml/3fl oz double cream
salt and freshly ground black pepper

1. Preheat the oven to 170°C/325°F/gas mark 3. Grease 4 large ramekin dishes with butter.
2. Heat the oil in a large saucepan, add the onion and garlic and cook over a low heat for 10 minutes until softened.
3. Bring the stock to the boil in another large saucepan.
4. Add the sweet potatoes to the onion and cook for 2 minutes. Add the barley and cook for a further 3–4 minutes. Add about 150ml/¼ pint of the stock and stir well until the stock has nearly evaporated, then add some more. Continue to cook in this way for 30 minutes. It is not necessary to stir continuously but the mixture will stick if left for any length of time. By the time all the stock has been added the barley should be tender, although it will retain a slight chewiness. If not, add some more boiling water and continue cooking.
5. Once the barley is cooked and most of the liquid has evaporated, add the Parmesan cheese, herbs and cream. Season to taste with salt and pepper.
6. Spoon the barley mixture into the prepared ramekin dishes and press down well. Cover

each with kitchen foil, place in a bain-marie and cook in the preheated oven for 30 minutes.

7. Remove the timbales from the oven and carefully turn out on to individual serving plates. Serve with a leafy salad.

PLAIN COUSCOUS

225g/8oz couscous
425ml/¾ pint water or summer vegetable stock (see page 530)

1. Bring the water or stock up to the boil, add the coucous, cover and leave to stand for 3–5 minutes according to manufacturers instructions.
2. Fluff up with a fork before serving.

LEMON COUSCOUS SOUP

Serve this soup with warm pitta bread and hummus to make a complete meal.

2 tablespoons olive oil
1 large onion, chopped
1 bulb of fennel, trimmed and sliced
2 cloves of garlic, chopped
a pinch of ground turmeric
½ teaspoon ground cumin
1 stalk of lemongrass, outer leaves removed and chopped
grated zest and juice of 2 lemons
a pinch of dried red chilli flakes
1 litre/1¾ pints summer vegetable stock (see page 530)
salt and freshly ground black pepper
55g/2oz couscous
2 tablespoons chopped fresh coriander

1. Heat the oil in a large saucepan, add the onion and fennel and fry over a low heat until softened. Add the garlic, turmeric, cumin and lemongrass and fry for a further 2 minutes. Stir in the lemon zest and juice, chilli flakes and stock. Season with salt and simmer for 30 minutes.
2. Add the couscous and simmer for a further 10 minutes. Check the seasoning and stir in the coriander just before serving in warmed soup bowls.

CITRUS COUSCOUS WITH YELLOW PEPPER AND FENNEL

8 tablespoons olive oil
1 medium onion, sliced
1 yellow pepper, deseeded and sliced
1 bulb of fennel, trimmed and cut into wedges
1 clove of garlic, crushed
1 tablespoon lemon juice
225g/8oz couscous
290ml/½ pint hot summer vegetable stock (see
  page 530)
2 courgettes, trimmed and cut into 5cm/2in
  lengths
grated zest and juice of 1 orange
grated zest and juice of 1 lime
1 teaspoon ground cumin
1 teaspoon ground turmeric
a pinch of cayenne pepper
salt and freshly ground black pepper
85g/3oz unpeeled almonds, toasted (see page 22)
2 tablespoons parsley, freshly chopped

1. Heat 2 tablespoons of the oil in a large saucepan and add the onion, pepper, fennel, garlic and lemon juice. Cover tightly with the lid and cook over a very low heat for 20 minutes or until the vegetables are soft, stirring occasionally to ensure they do not burn. Remove the lid and boil to evaporate any liquid.
2. Mix the orange and lime zest and juice with the cumin, turmeric, cayenne and the remaining oil and season with salt and pepper. Add to the hot stock.
3. Put the couscous into a large bowl and pour over the stock. Cover with a clean tea-towel and leave to stand for 5 minutes or until the liquid is absorbed. Fork through the couscous to separate the grains.
4. Blanch the courgettes for 30 seconds in a pan of boiling water. Drain and add to the couscous.
5. Add to the couscous with the cooked vegetable mixture and the almonds. Mix well and adjust the seasoning to taste. Garnish with the parsley and serve immediately.

COUSCOUS WITH COURGETTES, FETA CHEESE, BASIL AND RED ONIONS

340g/12oz couscous
340ml/12fl oz summer vegetable stock (see
  page 530)
30g/1oz butter
1 small clove of garlic, finely chopped
340g/12oz courgettes, trimmed
1 small red onion, thinly sliced
3 tablespoons lemon juice
salt and freshly ground black pepper
30g/1oz fresh basil leaves, torn into pieces
200g/7oz feta cheese, crumbled into small
  chunks
2 tablespoons extra virgin olive oil

1. Put the couscous into a large bowl. Bring the stock to the boil, pour it over the couscous and stir well to make sure there are no lumps. Cover the bowl with a clean tea-towel and leave to soak for 5 minutes, then fork through the couscous to separate the grains.
2. Put the butter and garlic into a frying pan and melt over a medium heat. Lower the heat, add the couscous and stir it with a fork for 2–3 minutes until it is dry and fluffy. Tip it on to a large flat plate and leave to cool. Meanwhile, cut the courgettes in half lengthways, then crossways into thin slices.
3. Tip the couscous into a serving bowl and fork through the courgettes, red onion, lemon juice and plenty of salt and pepper. Add the basil and cheese and fork through very lightly. Drizzle over the oil and serve.

GINGERED COUSCOUS

2 large red onions
1 bulb of garlic
3 tablespoons olive oil
110g/4oz pinenuts
2 teaspoons cumin seeds
170g/6oz couscous
8cm/3in piece of fresh root ginger, peeled and
*   finely chopped*
110g/4oz sultanas
340ml/12fl oz boiling water
2 tablespoons chopped fresh coriander
2 tablespoons chopped fresh mint

To serve
harissa sauce (see page 510)

1. Preheat the oven to 200°C/400°F/gas mark 6.
2. Peel the onions and cut into wedges. Slice the top off the garlic to expose the cloves but leave the skin on. Put the onions and garlic into a roasting tin and toss with the oil. Roast in the preheated oven for 30–40 minutes until the onion is slightly caramelized and the garlic meltingly soft. Add the pinenuts and cumin seeds for the last 10 minutes of cooking.
3. Put the couscous, ginger and sultanas into a bowl and pour over the water. Cover with a clean tea-towel and leave to stand for 5 minutes until the water has been absorbed.
4. Spread the couscous out on a baking tray and heat in the oven for 10 minutes. Fork through to separate the grains, then stir in the onions and pinenuts. Hold the bulb of garlic in a tea-towel, turn it upside down and squeeze out the cloves into the couscous. Season well with salt and pepper and scatter with the coriander and mint before serving. Hand the harissa sauce separately.

WARM MARINATED BABY CARROTS WITH HERB BUTTERED COUSCOUS

450g/1lb baby carrots, scrubbed
4 tablespoons olive oil
3 tablespoons Marsala wine
1½ tablespoons lemon juice
salt and freshly ground black pepper

For the couscous
170g/6oz couscous
85g/3oz unsalted butter
1½ tablespoons each chopped fresh tarragon,
*   chives, chervil and flat-leaf parsley*
finely grated zest and juice of 1 lemon
55g/2oz pinenuts, toasted (see page 22)
sprigs of fresh chervil, to garnish

1. Cook the carrots in a saucepan of boiling salted water until just tender. Drain well.
2. Heat 2 tablespoons of the oil in a wok or large, heavy frying pan, add the carrots and fry over a high heat for 1–2 minutes until lightly browned. Pour in the Marsala and allow to sizzle for a few seconds, then turn off the heat.
3. Pour the remaining oil into the pan. Add the lemon juice and season with salt and pepper. Leave the carrots to cool in the pan, turning occasionally, for 20–30 minutes.
4. Put the couscous into a large sieve lined with a piece of muslin or a clean 'J'-cloth. Pour over a kettleful of boiling water and allow to drain. Transfer the couscous to a bowl and fork through to separate the grains.
5. Melt the butter in a small saucepan and add the chopped herbs. Heat gently for 1 minute, then remove from the heat and add the lemon zest and juice.
6. Pour the herb butter over the couscous, add the pinenuts and stir to mix thoroughly. Season well with salt and plenty of pepper. Spread the couscous over a flat serving dish.
7. Gently reheat the carrots for 1–2 minutes, then lift them from the marinade with a slotted spoon, discarding the liquid. Arrange the carrots on top of the couscous and serve garnished with sprigs of chervil.

BRAISED FENNEL AND TOMATO COUSCOUS

2 bulbs of fennel
85ml/3fl oz dry white wine
5 tablespoons olive oil
salt and freshly ground black pepper
1 onion, chopped
1 clove of garlic, crushed
1 tablespoon ground turmeric
2 teaspoons ground cumin
a large pinch of chilli powder
2 tablespoons lemon juice
720ml/1¼ pints summer vegetable stock (see
    page 530)
340g/12oz couscous
3 tablespoons chopped fresh mint
1 tablespoon chopped fresh fennel leaves or dill
8 tomatoes, peeled and quartered (see page 22)

1. Preheat the oven to 190°C/375°F/gas mark 5.
2. Remove the feathery fennel fronds and
reserve. Cut the fennel into wedges and put into
an ovenproof dish. Pour over the wine and 1
tablespoon of the oil. Season with salt and
pepper, cover and bake in the preheated oven
for 25 minutes or until the fennel is tender.
3. Heat 1 tablespoon of the remaining oil in a
large saucepan, add the onion and garlic and
cook over a low heat for 10 minutes until
softened but not coloured.
4. Add the turmeric, cumin and chilli powder
and cook for 2 minutes. Add the lemon juice
and stock and bring to the boil. Pour on to the
couscous in a large bowl. Stir well, cover and
leave to swell for 5 minutes.
5. Just before serving, add the mint, fennel
leaves or dill and the remaining oil to the
couscous. Season well with salt and pepper.
Gently mix in the tomatoes.
6. Pile into a warmed serving dish and arrange
the fennel on top, pouring over any juices from
the tin.

ROASTED TOMATO AND CAPER COUSCOUS

This recipe needs to be started a day ahead.

900g/2lb ripe plum tomatoes
2 teaspoons coarse sea salt
1½ tablespoons soft light brown sugar
6 bay leaves
a few sprigs of fresh thyme
3–4 tablespoons balsamic vinegar
225g/8oz couscous
8 tablespoons olive oil
85g/3oz salt-packed capers, rinsed, dried and
    roughly chopped
a large handful each of fresh flat-leaf parsley
    and basil, roughly chopped
salt and freshly ground black pepper
flat-leaf parsley, to garnish

1. Preheat the oven to 100°C/200°F/gas mark
½.
2. Cut the tomatoes in half lengthways and lay
them in a roasting tin in a single layer, cut side
up. Sprinkle over the salt and sugar and lay the
bay leaves and sprigs of thyme on top.
3. Roast the tomatoes in the centre of the
preheated oven for 3–4 hours or until wrinkled
and just beginning to brown at the edges.
Discard the bay leaves and thyme. Pour the
vinegar over the tomatoes and leave in a cool
place for several hours or overnight.
4. Put the couscous into a large colander lined
with a piece of muslin or a clean 'J'-cloth. Pour
over a kettleful of boiling water and allow to
drain well.
5. Transfer the couscous to a bowl and fork
through to separate the grains, then pour in the
oil. Stir in the capers and chopped herbs.
6. Roughly chop half the tomatoes and fold
into the couscous. Season to taste with salt and
pepper.
7. Pile the couscous on to a flat serving dish,
arrange the remaining tomatoes on top and
garnish with parsley.

NUTTY COUSCOUS SALAD

190ml/⅓ pint boiling water
110g/4oz couscous
85g/3oz no-soak dried apricots
170g/6oz mixed nuts, such as hazels, cashews,
*   almonds, walnuts, brazils*
3 tablespoons olive oil
5cm/2in piece of fresh root ginger, peeled and
*   grated*
juice and grated zest of 1 orange
salt and freshly ground black pepper
a handful of fresh flat-leaf parsley leaves, to
*   garnish*

1. Pour the boiling water over the couscous in a bowl. Cover with a clean tea-towel and leave to stand for 5 minutes.
2. Roughly chop the apricots and nuts. Mix the oil with the ginger.
3. Fork through the couscous to separate the grains. Add the fruit, nuts, oil mixture, orange juice and zest. Season with salt and pepper. Scatter with the parsley leaves before serving.

MEDJOOL DATES STUFFED WITH COUSCOUS

These dates can be served as a canapé, for dessert or as an accompaniment to a main course.

butter, for greasing
10–12 medjool dates

For the stuffing
55g/2oz couscous
150ml/¼ pint boiling water
55g/2oz unsalted butter
a pinch of ground ginger
a pinch of ground cinnamon
30g/1oz almonds, toasted and chopped (see
*   page 22)*
½ teaspoon icing sugar
sea salt and freshly ground black pepper

1. Preheat the oven to 180°C/375°F/gas mark 5. Grease a shallow roasting tin with butter.
2. Slit the dates in half lengthways and remove the stones and any stalks.
3. Soak the couscous in the boiling water in a bowl. Melt half the butter in a small pan, add the ginger and cinnamon and fry for 1 minute.
4. When the couscous has absorbed all the liquid, fork through the spicy butter. Add the almonds and icing sugar and season with a little salt and pepper. Add a little extra butter if the mixture is too dry.
5. Pile the couscous into the dates. Set in the roasting tin and dot with the remaining butter. Bake in the preheated oven for 15 minutes until the filling is piping hot all the way through.

NOTE: As an alternative, add ½ chopped red chilli and 2 teaspoons chopped fresh mint to the couscous and omit the spices, almonds and sugar.

CRACKED WHEAT PILAFF

1 tablespoon olive oil
½ large onion, chopped
2 cloves of garlic, sliced
a walnut-sized piece of fresh root ginger, peeled
    and grated
1 medium leek, trimmed and thickly sliced
1 red or yellow pepper, deseeded and sliced
110g/4oz cracked wheat
290ml/½ pint summer vegetable stock (see
    page 530)
1 × 225g/8oz can of chopped tomatoes
1 teaspoon saffron threads
salt and freshly ground black pepper
1 large courgette, trimmed
110g/4oz baby spinach leaves
110g/4oz mangetout or sugar-snap peas
6 sun-dried tomatoes, chopped

1. Heat the oil in a saucepan, add the onion
and fry until soft and transparent. Add the
garlic, ginger, leek and pepper and fry for a
further few minutes. Add the cracked wheat
and stir until well coated in the juices. Pour in
the stock and tomatoes. Add the saffron and
season with salt and pepper. Cover and simmer
for 10 minutes.
2. Meanwhile, halve the courgettes lengthways
and slice thickly. Remove any tough stalks from
the spinach and wash thoroughly. Top and tail
the mangetout or sugar-snap peas. Stir into the
pilaff with the sun-dried tomatoes and simmer
for a further 5–10 minutes.

KISSIR

140g/5oz bulghur wheat
150ml/¼ pint boiling water
450g/1lb ripe tomatoes, peeled and deseeded
    (see page 22)
1 green pepper
1 yellow pepper
1 bunch of spring onions, trimmed and finely
    chopped
1 green chilli, deseeded and chopped (see
    page 22)
3 tablespoons olive oil
1 tablespoon pomegranate syrup or 2
    tablespoons lemon juice
1 teaspoon paprika
salt and freshly ground black pepper
4 tablespoons chopped fresh flat-leaf parsley

1. Put the bulghur wheat into a large bowl and
gradually add the water. Cover with a clean tea-
towel and leave to stand for 15 minutes. Drain,
pressing out as much water as possible.
2. Chop the tomatoes. Quarter the peppers and
remove the pith and seeds. Chop the flesh into
pieces about the same size as the tomatoes.
3. Add the spring onions to the bulghur wheat
and fork through to separate the grains.
Carefully mix in the tomatoes, peppers, chilli,
oil and pomegranate syrup or lemon juice.
Season with paprika, salt and pepper. Add the
parsley and mix well.

MIXED TOMATO TABOULEH

85g/3oz bulghur wheat
juice of 1 lemon
3 tablespoons olive oil
340g/12oz assorted tomatoes, such as plum,
*   cherry, beefsteak, yellow*
1 small red onion, finely chopped
2 tablespoons chopped fresh mint
2 tablespoons chopped fresh flat-leaf parsley
12 black olives, pitted and halved
salt and freshly ground black pepper
110g/4oz feta cheese (optional)

1. Put the bulghur wheat into a bowl, cover
with cold water and leave to soak for 15
minutes. Drain well, pressing out as much
water as possible. Stir in the lemon juice and
oil.
2. Cut the plum tomatoes into sixths, halve the
cherry tomatoes, cut the beefsteak tomatoes
into thin wedges and halve the yellow tomatoes.
Stir gently into the bulghur wheat with the
onion, mint, parsley and olives. Season with salt
and pepper. Crumble in the feta cheese, if used.

CRACKED WHEAT SALAD WITH DILL PICKLES

140g/5oz cracked wheat or roasted buckwheat
290ml/½ pint summer vegetable stock (see
*   page 530)*
3–4 tablespoons mustard dressing (Courgette
*   salad, see page 260)*
½ red onion, finely chopped
1 large carrot, grated
3 dill pickles, finely chopped
2 tablespoons poppy seeds
2 tablespoons chopped fresh flat-leaf parsley
1 tablespoon pomegranate syrup or lemon juice
salt and freshly ground black pepper

1. Put the cracked wheat or buckwheat and the
stock in a saucepan and simmer for about 10–15
minutes until the stock is absorbed and the

grains are tender. Remove from the heat, stir in
enough mustard dressing to moisten and leave
to cool.
2. Add all the remaining ingredients and mix
well. Season with salt and pepper. Leave to
stand for 1–2 hours before serving, to allow the
flavours to blend.

PRUNE, PECAN AND HERB BULGHAR WHEAT SALAD

170g/6oz bulghar wheat
85g/3oz pecan nuts, roughly chopped
110g/4oz no-soak pitted prunes
½ bunch of fresh flat-leaf parsley
½ bunch of fresh chervil
1 bunch of fresh chives
3 tablespoons mango chutney, chopped

For the dressing
5 tablespoons lemon-flavoured olive oil
2 tablespoons balsamic vinegar
finely grated zest and juice of 1 lemon
salt and freshly ground black pepper

1. Line a colander with a piece of muslin or a
clean tea-towel. Put the bulghar wheat into the
colander and pour over a kettleful of boiling
water. Leave the bulghar wheat to stand for 5
minutes.
2. Meanwhile, toast the pecans lightly under
the grill or in a dry frying pan over a medium
heat. Cool and chop roughly.
3. Chop the prunes and herbs roughly.
4. Transfer the bulghar wheat to a large bowl.
Add the pecans, prunes and herbs. Stir in the
mango chutney and season with salt and
pepper.
5. Mix together all the ingredients for the
dressing, then mix thoroughly with the bulghar
wheat. Adjust the seasoning to taste.

MILLET PILAFF WITH YELLOW AND ORANGE PEPPERS

For the peppers
2 tablespoons olive oil
1 small onion, thinly sliced
1 yellow pepper, deseeded and thinly sliced
1 orange pepper, deseeded and thinly sliced
a good pinch of saffron strands
a handful of fresh basil leaves, roughly torn
salt and freshly ground black pepper

For the pilaff
2 tablespoons olive oil
1 onion, finely chopped
1 clove of garlic, crushed
1 bay leaf
¼ teaspoon ground turmeric
110–170g/4–6oz millet
425–570ml/¾–1 pint summer vegetable stock
   (see page 530)
salt and freshly ground black pepper

To finish
110–225g/4–8oz crumbly cheese, such as feta or
   Cheshire

1. Prepare the peppers: heat the oil in a saucepan and add the onion and peppers. Cook over a low heat until the vegetables are soft but not coloured. Add the saffron and most of the basil leaves and season to taste with salt and pepper. Mix thoroughly and allow to stand for at least 30 minutes to allow the flavours to develop.
2. Prepare the millet pilaff: heat the oil in a saucepan, add the onion, garlic and bay leaf and sauté until soft. Add the turmeric and continue cooking over a low heat for 1–2 minutes. Add the millet and toss for 1 minute.
3. Add the stock and bring to the boil, then lower the heat and simmer for about 20 minutes until tender. Check regularly in case more liquid needs to be added. If there is too much stock by the time the millet is cooked, remove the lid and allow the excess liquid to evaporate.

Discard the bay leaf and season to taste with salt and pepper.
4. Reheat the peppers. Spoon the millet into a warmed serving dish, pile the peppers on the top and scatter over the crumbled cheese and the reserved basil.

NOTE: The peppers can be prepared well in advance (step 1).

MILLET PATTIES

MAKES ABOUT 12

110g/4oz millet
30g/1oz butter
1 bunch of spring onions, trimmed and chopped
1 clove of garlic, crushed
30g/1oz wholemeal flour
¼ teaspoon cayenne pepper
150ml/¼ pint milk
2 teaspoons wholegrain mustard
salt and freshly ground black pepper
2 tablespoons chopped fresh chives
110g/4oz fresh wholemeal breadcrumbs
plain flour, for shaping
oil, for frying

To serve
cherry tomatoes, crisp lettuce, slices of
   cucumber or red onion
sweet lime sauce (see page 507) or cucumber
   and mint raita (see page 513)

1. Put the millet into a large saucepan of boiling water, lower the heat and simmer for 20 minutes until soft.
2. Meanwhile, melt the butter in a small saucepan, add the spring onions and fry over a low heat until soft. Add the garlic and fry for 1 further minute. Stir in the flour and cayenne and fry gently for 2 minutes. Gradually add the milk, stirring all the time until the mixture is thick and boiling. Pour the sauce into a bowl, stir in the mustard and season with salt and pepper. Leave to cool.
3. Drain the millet and add to the sauce with the chives and breadcrumbs. With floured

hands, shape the mixture into about 12 patties.
4. Heat about 4cm/1½in oil in a frying pan
and fry the patties for about 5 minutes on each
side until well browned. Drain on kitchen
paper. Serve immediately with the salad and the
sauce or raita on the side.

FRIED POLENTA

*400ml/14fl oz summer vegetable stock (see
   page 530)*
170g/6oz polenta
salt and freshly ground black pepper
30g/1oz butter
85g/3oz Parmesan cheese, freshly grated
2 tablespoons olive oil

1. Put the stock into a large saucepan and bring
to the boil. Add the polenta and cook over a
medium heat, stirring all the time, for 10
minutes or according to the manufacturer's
instructions. The mixture should be very thick.
Remove from the heat and season with salt and
pepper, add the butter and cheese and mix well.
Pour on to a wet, shallow tray and spread flat
to a thickness of about 2cm/¾in. Allow to cool
completely.
2. Once cold, cut into squares, diamonds or
circles. Heat the oil in a frying pan and fry the
polenta on both sides, ensuring that it is hot all
the way through.

NOTE: Liquid quantities and cooking times for
polenta may vary – always check the
manufacturer's instructions.

POLENTA FLORENTINE AL FORNO

SERVES 6

30g/1oz butter, plus extra for greasing
1 recipe polenta (see previous recipe)
3 tablespoons olive oil, plus extra for brushing
450g/1lb fresh spinach
1 clove of garlic, crushed
salt and freshly ground black pepper
freshly grated nutmeg
290ml/½ pint tomato sauce II (see page 527)
2 × 150g/5oz mozzarella cheeses
30g/1oz Parmesan cheese, freshly grated

1. Grease a shallow roasting tin with butter.
Spread the polenta out in the tin and leave to
cool. Preheat the oven to 190°C/375°F/gas
mark 5. Brush a wide, shallow ovenproof dish
with oil.
2. Remove any tough stalks from the spinach
and wash thoroughly. Lift the wet spinach into
a large saucepan and shake over a medium heat
until it is tender. Drain well to remove the
excess moisture. Return the spinach to the pan
and heat to evaporate any remaining liquid.
When the spinach is quite dry, add the garlic
and butter and stir over the heat for 1 minute.
Season with salt, pepper and nutmeg.
3. Cut the polenta into rounds with a 5cm/2in
pastry cutter. Save the neatest for the top and
arrange the remainder in an overlapping layer
in the bottom of the prepared dish. Spread the
tomato sauce over the top. Spread the spinach
on top of the sauce.
4. Slice the mozzarella cheeses thinly and
arrange on top of the spinach. Finally arrange
the remaining polenta on top in an overlapping
layer. Brush with oil and scatter over the
Parmesan cheese. Bake in the preheated oven
for 40–50 minutes until the polenta is golden-
brown and sizzling.

POLENTA CHIPS WITH FRIED EGGS AND ROASTED VINE TOMATOES

For the polenta
2 litres/3½ pints summer vegetable stock (see
*   page 530)*
285g/10oz polenta
salt and freshly ground black pepper
1 tablespoon olive oil, plus extra for brushing
340g/12oz vine-ripened cherry tomatoes
seasoned plain flour
2 eggs, beaten
dried white breadcrumbs
oil, for frying

To serve
4 duck's or large free-range hen's eggs, fried to
*   taste (see page 434)*

1. Put the stock into a large saucepan and bring
to the boil.
2. Remove from the heat and sprinkle over the
polenta, whisking quickly to prevent lumps
from forming. Lower the heat.
3. Return the pan to the heat and continue to
cook, stirring often, until the polenta is very
thick. Season well with salt and pepper.
4. Brush a shallow 28 × 18cm/11 × 7in tin with
oil. Spread the polenta out evenly in the tin,
allow to cool, then chill for 1 hour until very
firm.
5. Turn the polenta out of the tin and cut into
5 × 1cm/2 × ½in sticks. Chill until required.
6. Preheat the oven to 200°C/400°F/gas mark 6.
7. Put the tomatoes into a roasting tin, sprinkle
over the oil and season with salt and pepper.
Cook on the top shelf of the preheated oven for
15–20 minutes or until the tomatoes are lightly
browned and the skins are just beginning to split.
8. Meanwhile, dust the polenta chips with
seasoned flour and dip first into the beaten egg,
then into the breadcrumbs.
9. Pour enough oil into a large, deep frying pan
to come 2cm/¾in up the sides of the pan. Heat
until very hot.
10. Fry the polenta chips in small batches until
golden-brown, then remove with a slotted
spoon and drain on kitchen paper. Sprinkle
with a little salt.
11. To serve, put a pile of polenta chips on to 4
warmed individual plates. Top with a fried egg
and place the roasted tomatoes on the side.

NOTE: see note page 390

RED ONION POLENTA TATIN

SERVES 6–8

170g/6oz flour quantity polenta pastry (see
  page 524)

For the topping
55g/2oz butter
900g/2lb red onions, thinly sliced
2 tablespoons white wine
2 cloves of garlic, crushed
1 tablespoon soft light brown sugar
2 large red peppers
1 tablespoon capers, rinsed
¼ tablespoon chopped fresh rosemary

1. Preheat the oven to 190°C/375°F/gas mark 5.
2. Make the topping: melt 30g/1oz of the
butter in a heavy, ovenproof frying pan. Add
the onions and cook, covered, for 15 minutes,
until they begin to soften. Add the wine, garlic
and half the sugar and cook for 20 minutes.
Turn up the heat and reduce, by boiling rapidly,
until the liquid coats the onions.
3. Preheat the grill to its highest setting. Cut
the peppers into quarters, then remove the
stalks, membrane and seeds. Grill the peppers,
skin side uppermost, until the skin is black and
blistered. Scrape off the skin with a small knife.
4. Melt the remaining butter in the pan, stir in
the remaining sugar and remove from the heat.
Arrange the red pepper pieces in the pan in a
daisy pattern. Place the capers between the
peppers and cover with the cooked onions,
taking care not to dislodge the peppers.
5. Place the pan over a high heat until the
butter and sugar start to caramelize, which may
take 5 minutes. Remove the pan from the heat
and place it on a baking sheet.
6. Lay the polenta pastry on top of the onions
and press down lightly. Bake in the preheated
oven for 25 minutes. Allow to cool slightly,
then invert the pan over a serving plate and
serve warm.

QUICK QUINOA SALAD

Quinoa is a grain similar to tapioca. It is
available in large supermarkets and health food
shops.

110–170g/4–6oz quinoa
225–340ml/8–12fl oz summer vegetable stock
  (see page 530) or water
salt and freshly ground black pepper
½ cucumber, diced
3 tomatoes, diced
30g/1oz sultanas or raisins
2 tablespoons roughly chopped fresh mixed
  herbs, such as parsley, basil, mint
2 tablespoons sunflower seeds
1 quantity French dressing (see page 528)

1. Rinse the quinoa thoroughly. Put into a
saucepan with the stock or water and a good
pinch of salt. Bring to the boil, then lower the
heat and simmer for 15–20 minutes or until the
quinoa is soft.
2. Drain thoroughly and allow to cool for a
few minutes, then transfer to a mixing bowl.
Add the remaining ingredients, reserving some
of the herbs to garnish. Pour over the dressing
and mix well. Season to taste with salt and
pepper. Chill.
3. Pile into a serving bowl and scatter over the
reserved herbs.

QUINOA AND APRICOT SALAD WITH TOASTED PINENUTS

6 dried apricots, sliced
30g/1oz sultanas or raisins
110–170g/4–6oz quinoa
225–340ml/8–12fl oz water
salt

For the dressing
juice of 1 large orange, about 110ml/4fl oz
2 tablespoons olive oil
white wine vinegar
salt and freshly ground black pepper
1–2 tablespoons roughly chopped fresh parsley
 and coriander
pinenuts, toasted (see page 22), to garnish

1. First make the dressing: combine all the ingredients in a small bowl, reserving some of the herbs to garnish. Add the dried fruit and leave to soak for at least 10 minutes.
2. Rinse the quinoa thoroughly. Put into a saucepan with the water and a good pinch of salt. Bring to the boil, then lower the heat and simmer for about 15–20 minutes or until the quinoa is soft.
3. Drain thoroughly and allow to cool for a few minutes, then transfer to a mixing bowl. Pour over the dressing and mix well, adjusting the seasoning to taste. Allow to cool competely before serving.
4. Pile into a serving bowl and scatter over the reserved herbs and the pinenuts.

QUINOA AND LIME SALAD

SERVES 8

225g/9oz quinoa
720ml/1¼ pints water
salt

For the dressing
juice of 6 limes
125ml/4fl oz groundnut oil
salt and freshly ground black pepper
1 tablespoon caster sugar
1 tablespoon dry-roasted Sichuan peppercorns,
 ground
4 small cloves of garlic, crushed
1 tablespoon each chopped fresh flat-leaf
 parsley, basil and coriander

To serve
10 Kalamata olives, pitted and slivered
140g/5oz cooked kidney beans
1 head of radicchio
1 small bunch of fresh basil or coriander

1. Rinse and drain the quinoa well before use to remove bitterness. It can then be lightly toasted in oil to enhance the flavour, if liked.
2. Put the quinoa into a saucepan with the water and salt. Bring to the boil, then reduce the heat, cover and cook for 15–20 minutes or until the liquid has been absorbed and the quinoa looks transparent. If not all the liquid has been absorbed, drain well.
3. Remove from the heat and fluff up with a fork. Allow to cool.
4. Make the dressing: put the ingredients into a blender and process until smooth, then season well to make a strong-flavoured dressing.
5. Mix the dressing with the quinoa and mix in most of the olives and the kidney beans, reserving a few for garnish.
6. Line a serving bowl with the radicchio leaves, spoon in the quinoa, scatter over the reserved olives and kidney beans and garnish with basil or coriander leaves.

NOTE: The dressing is also very good with hot or cold pasta. It should be made on the day that it is eaten. It loses some of its brilliant green if kept overnight.

BRAZIL NUT LOAF

*1 tablespoon sunflower oil, plus extra for
  brushing*
1 large onion, chopped
2 cloves of garlic, crushed
*2.5cm/1in piece of fresh root ginger, peeled and
  grated*
30g/1oz ground almonds
½ teaspoon cayenne pepper
1 teaspoon ground cumin
1 teaspoon ground coriander
4 tablespoons cold water
170g/6oz brazil nuts, roughly chopped
75g/3oz wholemeal breadcumbs
2 eggs, beaten
salt and freshly ground black pepper

To serve
pineapple salsa (see page 514)

1. Preheat the oven to 190°C/375°F/gas mark 5.
Brush a 450g/1lb loaf tin with oil. Line the base
and sides with greaseproof paper and brush
with oil.
2. Heat the oil in a frying pan, add the onion
and fry over a low heat until soft and golden-
brown. Add the garlic and cook for 1 further
minute.
3. Meanwhile, put the ginger, ground almonds
and spices into a bowl and mix to a smooth
paste with the water. Stir into the onion and
cook for 2 minutes. Cool.
4. Put the nuts into a large mixing bowl with the
breadcrumbs. Bind with the spice paste and
beaten eggs. Season with salt and pepper. Spoon
the mixture into the prepared tin. Cover with a
sheet of oiled kitchen foil and bake in the
preheated oven for 1 hour until set. Remove the
foil and bake for a further 15 minutes to allow the
top to brown. Remove from the oven and leave
to stand for 10 minutes before slicing and serving
with the pineapple salsa handed separately.

CARBONADE OF CHESTNUTS

1 tablespoon sunflower or vegetable oil
1 onion, sliced
1 medium leek, trimmed and sliced
3 sticks of celery
1 red pepper
1 clove of garlic, crushed
170g/6oz dried chestnuts
425ml/¾ pint beer
*300ml/½ pint winter vegetable stock (see
  page 530)*
1 orange
2 juniper berries, crushed
a pinch of ground allspice
salt and freshly ground black pepper
1 courgette, trimmed
55g/2oz dried cranberries
55g/2oz raisins
2 tablespoons white wine vinegar
15g/½oz softened butter
1 tablespoon Dijon mustard
1 baguette

1. Heat the oil in a large pan, add the onions
and fry over a low heat until golden-brown.
Add the leek and fry until softened.
2. Meanwhile, remove any stringy threads
from the celery. Remove the stalk, pith and
seeds from the pepper, then quarter and slice.
Add to the onion mixture and fry for a few
minutes until softened. Stir in the garlic and
cook for 1 further minute.
3. Add the chestnuts to the pan and stir until well
covered in the juices. Pour on the beer and stock.
4. Using a potato peeler, pare 2 strips of zest
from the orange. Squeeze the juice and add both
to the carbonade. Add the juniper and allspice
and season with salt and pepper. Bring to the
boil, then lower the heat and simmer for 30
minutes.
5. Cut the courgette in half lengthways, then
crossways into 1cm/½in slices. Stir into the
carbonade with the cranberries, raisins and
vinegar. Simmer for a further 20 minutes.
Adjust the seasoning to taste and pour into a
flameproof serving dish.

6. Preheat the grill. Remove the orange zest from the carbonade. Mix the butter and mustard together. Cut the baguette into 8 × 1cm/½in slices and spread with the mustard mixture. Arrange the bread slices on top of the carbonade and grill until brown and crisp.

CHESTNUT, LEEK, APPLE AND STILTON CRUMBLE

1 tablespoon sunflower oil
30g/1oz butter
1 large onion, sliced
2 leeks
15g/½oz plain flour
290ml/½ pint summer vegetable stock (see page 530)
225g/8oz dried chestnuts, soaked overnight
1 teaspoon fresh thyme leaves
salt and freshly ground black pepper
2 green dessert apples

For the crumble
110g/4oz plain flour
55g/2oz butter
55g/2oz Stilton cheese, crumbled
¼ teaspoon cayenne pepper

1. Heat the oil and butter in a saucepan and when foaming, add the onion and fry over a low heat until soft and golden-brown.
2. Trim the roots and the outer leaves from the leeks. Cut into 2.5cm/1in pieces and wash thoroughly. Add to the pan with the onion, cover and cook for 5–10 minutes until soft. Stir in the flour and cook for 1 minute.
3. Gradually pour on the stock and stir until smooth and boiling. Drain the chestnuts and add to the pan with the thyme. Season to taste with salt and pepper and simmer for about 15 minutes until the chestnuts are tender.
4. Peel, quarter and core the apples. Cut into 2.5cm/1in pieces. Stir into the pan and tip the mixture into an ovenproof dish. Leave to cool.
5. Preheat the oven to 190°C/375°F/gas mark 5.
6. Make the crumble: sift the flour into a mixing bowl and rub in the butter. Stir in the cheese and cayenne. Spread evenly over the top of the filling and bake in the preheated oven for 30 minutes until the crumble is browned and the filling piping hot.

PEANUT DHAL

85g/3oz yellow split peas
1 litre/1¾ pints water
5cm/2in piece of fresh root ginger, peeled
3 cloves of garlic
3 tablespoons sunflower oil
1 medium onion, chopped
1 large potato
1 large carrot
¼ teaspoon chilli powder
½ teaspoon ground turmeric
1 teaspoon garam masala
110g/4oz fresh or frozen peas
110g/4oz unsalted, unskinned peanuts
2 kaffir lime leaves
4 tomatoes, peeled and chopped (see page 22)
3 tablespoons chopped fresh coriander
salt and freshly ground black pepper
2 teaspoons cumin seeds
2 teaspoons black mustard seeds

1. Put the split peas into a saucepan with the water. Take half the ginger and one clove of the garlic and whack them with a rolling pin so that they split a little. Add to the pan and simmer for about 40 minutes until the split peas are completely soft. Drain, reserving the stock and discarding the garlic and ginger.
2. Heat 2 tablespoons of the oil in a large saucepan, add the onion and fry over a low heat until soft and golden. Peel the potato and carrot and cut into 1cm/½in chunks. Add to the onion, cover and fry gently for 10–15 minutes until soft.
3. Crush the remaining garlic and finely chop the remaining ginger. Stir into the onion mixture with the chilli powder, turmeric and garam masala and fry for a further 2 minutes. Add the peas, peanuts, lime leaves, tomatoes and coriander and 290ml/½ pint of the reserved stock. Season with salt and pepper and simmer, uncovered, for about 30 minutes until the vegetables are tender.
4. Stir in the split peas and reheat. Meanwhile, heat the remaining oil in a small, heavy frying pan and fry the cumin and mustard seeds until they begin to pop. Spoon the dhal into a warmed serving dish and pour the seeds and oil over the top.

NUT KOFTAS

oil, for brushing
30g/1oz butter
1 large onion, finely chopped
2 cloves of garlic, crushed
½ teaspoon chilli powder
1 teaspoon cumin seeds, crushed
1 teaspoon coriander seeds, crushed
225g/8oz whole mixed nuts, such as unsalted
    peanuts, cashews, hazelnuts, walnuts
1 tablespoon chopped fresh mint
1 tablespoon chopped fresh coriander
55g/2oz fresh wholemeal breadcrumbs
salt and freshly ground black pepper
2 small eggs, beaten

To serve
cucumber and mint raita (see page 513) or
    yoghurty onions (see page 516)

1. Preheat the oven to 200°C/400°F/gas mark 6. brush a baking tray with oil.
2. Melt the butter in a frying pan, add the onion and fry over a low heat until soft and golden-brown. Add the garlic, chilli powder, cumin and coriander seeds and fry for a further 1–2 minutes. Remove from the heat and allow to cool.
3. Chop the nuts in a food processor or blender. Blend in the onion mixture, herbs and breadcrumbs. Season with salt and pepper and bind with the eggs. Shape into balls about the size of a walnut.
4. Heat the baking tray. Place the koftas on the hot tray and bake in the preheated oven for 10 minutes. Serve immediately with the yoghurt and mint raita or the yoghurty onions handed separately.

NOTE: The koftas can also be fried in a little oil until golden.

NUT ROAST LAYERED WITH SPINACH

2 tablespoons olive oil
1 large onion, finely chopped
110g/4oz unsalted, unskinned peanuts
110g/4oz cashew nuts
55g/2oz hazelnuts
55g/2oz walnuts
30g/1oz pinenuts
1 tablespoon chopped fresh parsley
1 tablespoon chopped fresh chives
2 eggs, beaten
salt and freshly ground black pepper
freshly grated nutmeg
110g/4oz fresh spinach leaves
30g/1oz Parmesan cheese, freshly grated

1. Brush a 450g/1lb loaf tin with a little of the oil. Preheat the oven to 190°C/375°F/gas mark 5.
2. Heat the remaining oil in a frying pan, add the onion and fry over a low heat until soft and golden-brown. Cool.
3. Mix all the nuts together. Grind half of them finely and roughly chop the remainder. Set aside a handful of the chopped nuts and mix the remainder together with the ground nuts in a mixing bowl. Stir in the parsley, chives and eggs. Season well with salt, pepper and nutmeg.
4. Remove any tough stalks from the spinach. Wash thoroughly and shred.
5. Put half the nut mixture into the prepared tin. Lay the spinach leaves on top. Spread over the remaining nut mixture. Mix together the reserved chopped nuts and the cheese and press on top of the nut roast. Bake in the preheated oven for 30 minutes. Remove and allow to cool for 5–10 minutes before slicing.

PRUNE NUT LOAF WITH GRAINS

butter, for greasing
110g/4oz walnuts
110g/4oz blanched almonds
110g/4oz cashew nuts
1 × 140g/15oz can of unsweetened prunes
30g/1oz rolled oats
140g/5oz wheatgerm
55g/2oz Parmesan cheese, freshly grated
3 eggs, beaten
1 large onion, finely chopped
1 teaspoon fresh thyme leaves
2 teaspoons chopped fresh oregano
¼ teaspoon cayenne pepper
salt and freshly ground black pepper

To serve
pitta bread
wedges of cucumber, tomato and red onion
Greek yoghurt

1. Preheat the oven to 180°C/350°F/gas mark 4. Grease a 900g/2lb loaf tin with butter.
2. Grind the walnuts, almonds and cashew nuts finely. Remove any stones from the prunes and purée with the juice.
3. Put all the remaining ingredients together with the nuts and prunes in a bowl and season with ½ teaspoon salt and plenty of pepper. Mix well and spoon into the prepared tin. Bake in the preheated oven for 45 minutes until firm. Remove from the oven and allow to cool slightly before slicing.
4. Serve the slices of nut loaf inside warm pitta bread filled with salad topped with Greek yoghurt.

NOTE: This loaf is very good cold and also reheats well.

PASTA AND NOODLES

INTRODUCTION

Pasta is available in some 600 different shapes. To confuse the issue, some shapes may be known by several different names. Although we associate pasta with Italy it is also an essential part of the classic cooking of China and Japan where many varieties of noodles, stuffed pasta and dumplings are produced. Pasta is perfect for putting a quick meal together and delicious with an infinite number of sauces and dressings. Although pasta itself is low in fat and a good source of carbohydrate, like potatoes, it is the additions that can turn it into a high-fat food.

Most pasta is made from hard durum wheat, so as to absorb the minimum amount of water when cooked. It can be made with or without egg. **Egg pasta** is more nutritious and it is more difficult to overcook. Generally when egg pasta is made into long strips, such as tagliatelle, it is coiled into nests as it is more delicate. Pasta can be flavoured and coloured, usually with spinach or tomato, but beetroot, saffron, herbs or even chocolate may be used.

Wholewheat pasta contains more fibre and will take longer to cook. It is still slightly chewy when cooked. **Buckwheat pasta** is darker and has a nutty flavour. It is sold in thin flat noodles rolled into nests and is the classic pasta for pizzocheri. Buckwheat pasta is gluten free and is very nutritious, containing protein, minerals and vitamins. It is usually available in health food shops. **Corn pasta** is also gluten free. It is a rich yellow colour and is sometimes available flavoured with spinach or tomato.

It does not especially matter which type of pasta is chosen for any particular dish. However, long thin pasta is generally served with simple sauces of tomato, butter, herbs, garlic or cheese. Richer, more complex sauces cling better to shaped pasta, such as *farfalle* (butterflies), *fiochetti* (bows), *conchiglie* (shells)

or *rigatoni*, where the sauce can be caught in the hollows, curves and ridges.

Pasta should be cooked in plenty of boiling water to prevent it sticking together. Make sure the water is at a rolling boil before adding the pasta and give an occasional stir to keep it separate. A little olive oil can be added during cooking but this is a matter of personal preference. Dried pasta will take approximately 10 minutes to cook and fresh about 3 minutes. Test for readiness by tasting a piece; when cooked, pasta should be *al dente* – tender but still retaining some bite in the centre. This way it will mix perfectly with sauces. Overcooked pasta loses its texture and becomes a sticky mass.

Oriental noodles are made with wheat flour, buckwheat flour, rice or mung bean flour. They are available in a variety of thicknesses and shapes and may be sold in bundles or in nests. The most usually found are udon noodles, somen noodles or egg noodles. Soba noodles are made from buckwheat. Rice noodles are opaque and fine. They are all precooked so only need to be soaked in boiling water before use. Cellophane noodles and vermicelli are made from mung bean flour. Fresh noodles are found in the chilling cabinets of ethnic stores. They should be stored in the refrigerator where they will only keep for a few days. Dried noodles will keep for several months stored in an airtight container in a cool, dry place.

COMMON PASTA SHAPES

Spaghetti: originally made by pulling the dough into thin strands, now usually made by machine.

Macaroni: made commercially into short tube-like pieces.

Tagliatelle (fettucine): thin ribbons of pasta, usually served with a sauce.

Ravioli: flat sheets used to form small stuffed envelopes, which are then boiled and served with or without sauce.

Tortellini: small stuffed pasta shaped like curled half moons.

Cannelloni: rectangles about the size of a side plate. They are rolled and generally stuffed (like a pancake) after boiling, then reheated.

NOTE: For all pasta recipes use strong '00' pasta flour if available.

EGG PASTA

450g/1lb strong '00' flour
4 large eggs
1 tablespoon oil

1. Sift the flour on to a wooden board. Make a well in the centre and put in the eggs and oil.
2. Using the fingers of one hand, mix together the eggs and oil and gradually draw in the flour, to make a very stiff dough.
3. Knead for about 15 minutes until smooth and elastic. Wrap in clingfilm and leave to relax in a cool place for 1 hour.
4. Roll out one small piece of dough at a time until paper-thin. Cut into the required shape.
5. Allow to dry (unless making ravioli), hanging over a chair back if long noodles, or lying on a wire rack or dry tea-towel if small ones, for at least 30 minutes before cooking. Ravioli is dried after stuffing.

NOTE: If more or less pasta is required the recipe can be altered on a pro-rata basis, for example a 340g/12oz quantity of flour calls for a pinch of salt, 3 eggs and 1 scant tablespoon of oil.

HALF-HOUR PASTA

With a food processor and a pasta machine you can be eating pasta within half an hour of thinking about it. Use the same ingredients as for the traditional egg pasta (see previous recipe). While the dough is resting, make your favourite quick pasta sauce and sit down to enjoy the best fast food there is.

450g/1lb strong '00' flour
a pinch of salt
4 eggs
1 tablespoon oil

1. Put the flour and salt into a food processor and blend well. Beat the eggs and oil together, then, with the motor running, gradually add them to the flour until the mixture resembles breadcrumbs. Remove from the food processor. Bring a small amount of the mixture together with your fingertips. It should come together easily, but not be too wet. If it does feel too wet add a little extra flour.
2. Knead the dough briefly to bring it together, wrap it in clingfilm and leave it to relax for 10 minutes. Pass it through the widest setting of the pasta machine 3–4 times, then roll it through the different settings of the machine until you can get it through the narrowest gauge. Cut the pasta into the required shape, then drop it straight into a large bowl of boiling salted water.
3. Cook until *al dente*, then drain and serve with the sauce of your choice.

MINESTRONE SOUP

To make the minestrone into a hearty main course, serve with dumplings (see page 532).

55g/2oz dried green flageolet beans, soaked
    overnight
2 tablespoons olive oil
1 medium onion, sliced
2 cloves of garlic, crushed
2 carrots
2 sticks of celery
1 courgette, trimmed
570ml/1 pint summer vegetable stock (see
    page 530)
1 × 225g/8oz can of tomatoes
1 teaspoon dried oregano
salt and freshly ground black pepper
a large handful of leafy greens, such as spinach
    or cabbage, roughly shredded
30g/1oz spaghetti, broken into small pieces

To serve
freshly grated Parmesan cheese

1. Rinse and drain the flageolet beans.
2. Heat the oil in a heavy saucepan. Add the onions and fry over a low heat until soft and transparent. Add the garlic and fry for 1 further minute.
3. Meanwhile, chop the carrot, celery and courgette into 1cm/½in chunks. Add to the pan, then cover and cook over a low heat for 5 minutes until the vegetables are soft.
4. Pour in the stock and add the beans, tomatoes and oregano and season with salt and pepper. Simmer for 45 minutes until the beans are tender.
5. Add the greens and pasta to the soup and bring back to the boil, then simmer for 10 minutes. Serve with the cheese handed separately.

FUSILLI WITH CELERY AND GARLIC CRUMBS

This recipe can also be made with 340g/12oz asparagus, trimmed and cooked until tender, instead of the celery.

6 sticks of celery with leaves
85g/3oz unsalted butter
110g/4oz fresh white breadcrumbs
2 cloves of garlic, chopped
¼ teaspoon cayenne pepper
salt and freshly ground black pepper
340g/12oz fusilli or other pasta shapes
3 tablespoons olive oil
4 sun-dried tomatoes, chopped
grated zest of 1 lemon
1 tablespoon chopped fresh flat-leaf parsley

To serve
freshly grated Parmesan or Pecorino cheese

1. Remove any stringy threads from the celery and slice. Chop the leaves.
2. Heat 55g/2oz of the butter in a sauté pan, add the breadcrumbs and fry until beginning to brown. Add the garlic and cook for a further 1–2 minutes until the crumbs are well browned and crisp. Season with the cayenne, salt and pepper and keep warm.
3. Bring a large saucepan of salted water to the boil. Add the pasta and cook for 10 minutes or until *al dente*. Drain thoroughly.
4. Heat the remaining butter and the oil, add the celery and fry for 5 minutes. Stir into the pasta with the sun-dried tomatoes, lemon zest, parsley and celery leaves. Season with salt and plenty of pepper. Toss in the garlic crumbs and serve immediately before the crumbs become soggy, with the cheese handed separately.

Lasagne of Mushrooms with Hollandaise

Savoury American Pancakes

Braised Fennel and Tomato Couscous

Fried Tofu with Sichuan Pepper and Cabbage

Vegetable Jambalaya with Roasted Chillies and Spiced Nuts

Apricot and Carrot Streusel Cake

Pink Grapefruit Cheesecake

Selection of Breads (clockwise from jar): Yoghurt Cheese, Roast Red Pepper Bread, Mint and Thyme Soda Rolls, Apricot and Orange Bread, Oatmeal Seed Bread

SPROUTS WITH CHESTNUTS AND FUSILLI

340g/12oz Brussels sprouts
salt and freshly ground black pepper
340g/12oz fusilli
85g/3oz unsalted butter
225g/8oz dried chestnuts, soaked overnight and
*   halved*
1 red chilli, deseeded and chopped (see page 22)
2 cloves of garlic, chopped

To serve
freshly grated Parmesan cheese

1. Trim the roots and outer leaves from the Brussels sprouts and shred finely.
2. Bring a large saucepan of salted water to the boil, add the fusilli and cook for 10 minutes or until *al dente.*
3. Meanwhile, melt the butter in a frying pan, add the chestnuts and fry over a low heat until they begin to take on some colour. Add the Brussels sprouts, chilli and garlic and toss over the heat for a further 2 minutes to soften. Season with salt and plenty of pepper.
4. Drain the pasta thoroughly and toss together with the sprout and chestnut mixture. Serve topped with a few twists of pepper and a generous sprinkling of cheese.

SPINACH GNOCCHI CARBONARA

140g/5oz baby spinach leaves, cooked and
*   chopped*
170g/6oz ricotta cheese
55g/2oz coarse-ground semolina
55g/2oz Parmesan cheese, firmly grated
1 egg, beaten
salt and freshly ground black pepper
freshly grated nutmeg
plain flour

For the sauce
4 egg yolks
6 tablespoons single cream
55g/2oz Parmesan cheese, freshly grated

1. Beat the spinach, ricotta, semolina and Parmesan cheese together in a bowl. Mix in the egg and add the salt, pepper and nutmeg to taste.
2. Take tablespoons of the mixture and shape into small egg shapes. Roll the gnocchi lightly in flour.
3. Bring a large saucepan of salted water to a simmer and poach the gnocchi gently, a few at a time, for about 2–3 minutes, until they rise to the surface.
4. Remove the gnocchi from the pan with a slotted spoon, allowing the excess water to drain well, and discard the cooking water. Return the gnocchi to the still hot pan.
5. Preheat the grill. Make the sauce: whisk the egg yolks and cream together. Add half the cheese, and season with salt and pepper.
6. Pour the egg mixture into the pan with the hot gnocchi. Stir quickly and gently over a very low heat for about 30 seconds until the sauce just thickens. (It may be necessary to return the pan briefly to the heat.)
7. Transfer the gnocchi to a shallow flameproof dish. Sprinkle over the remaining cheese and place under the grill to brown.

ARTICHOKE HEARTS CARBONARA

1 × 400g/14oz can of artichoke hearts
340g/12oz tagliatelle or spaghetti
salt and freshly ground black pepper
25g/1oz butter
1 small onion, chopped
2 cloves of garlic, chopped
1 egg
3 tablespoons crème fraîche
50g/2oz Parmesan cheese, freshly grated
1 tablespoon chopped fresh flat-leaf parsley

1. Drain the artichokes and pat dry on kitchen paper. Cut into quarters. Bring a large saucepan of salted water to the boil, add the pasta and cook for about 10 minutes until *al dente*.
2. Meanwhile, melt the butter in a heavy frying pan, add the onion and fry over a low heat until softened. Add the artichokes and garlic and fry for 2 further minutes.
3. Whisk together the egg, crème fraîche and half the cheese. Season to taste with salt and pepper. Add to the pan with the artichokes and stir until hot but not boiling and very slightly thickened.
4. Drain the pasta thoroughly. Return to the saucepan and stir in the artichoke sauce. Season with salt and plenty of pepper. Sprinkle with the remaining cheese and the parsley.

TAGLIATELLE WITH BROCCOLI, GOAT'S CHEESE AND TOASTED WALNUTS

110g/4oz walnuts
225g/8oz broccoli
340g/12oz tagliatelle
salt and freshly ground black pepper
2 tablespoons olive oil
2–3 cloves of garlic, crushed
4 tablespoons mascarpone cheese
55g/2oz Pecorino or Parmesan cheese, freshly grated
140g/5oz soft, mild goat's cheese
1 tablespoon chopped fresh flat-leaf parsley

1. Heat a heavy frying pan and toast the walnuts until browned, then chop roughly. Trim the broccoli and blanch in boiling water for about 3 minutes until only just tender. Drain and refresh under cold running water. Drain again.
2. Bring a large saucepan of salted water to the boil, add the tagliatelle and cook for 5–10 minutes until *al dente*, then drain thoroughly.
3. Heat the oil in the saucepan, add the garlic and fry over a low heat for 1 minute. Stir in the mascarpone and Pecorino cheese and heat gently until warm. Add the pasta and broccoli to the pan, then add the goat's cheese in chunks. Season with salt and plenty of pepper. Serve scattered with the walnuts and parsley.

TAGLIATELLE WITH BROCCOLI AND RED PEPPERS

3 large red peppers
150ml/¼ pint olive oil
2 cloves of garlic, chopped
1 red chilli, deseeded and chopped (see page 22)
salt and freshly ground black pepper
170g/6oz broccoli florets
340g/12oz tagliatelle
2 tablespoons chopped fresh flat-leaf parsley

To serve
freshly grated Parmesan cheese

1. Remove the pith and seeds from the peppers. Cut into quarters and slice finely. Heat the oil in a sauté pan with a lid. Add the peppers, garlic and chilli and season with salt and pepper. Cover over a low heat and fry for about 20 minutes until the peppers are meltingly soft and have almost made a sauce with the oil.
2. Bring a large saucepan of salted water to the boil. Trim the tough stalks from the broccoli and cook the florets in the boiling water for about 5 minutes until just tender. Lift out with a slotted spoon and add to the pan with the peppers.
3. Cook the tagliatelle in the broccoli cooking water for 5–10 minutes or until *al dente*. Drain thoroughly and toss together with the peppers and broccoli. Stir in the parsley. Serve immediately with a good twist of pepper and a sprinkling of cheese.

TAGLIATELLE WITH CHILLI, TOMATO AND GREEN BEANS

4 ripe tomatoes, peeled (see page 22)
110g/4oz French, flat or runner beans
340g/12oz tagliatelle
salt and freshly ground black pepper
4 tablespoons olive oil
2 cloves of garlic, chopped
2 green chillies, deseeded and chopped (see page 22)
a pinch of caster sugar
12 cherry tomatoes, halved
12 black olives, pitted
2 tablespoons shredded fresh basil

To serve
freshly grated Parmesan cheese

1. Cut the tomatoes into sixths. Top, tail and trim the beans and cut into 1cm/½in lengths, on the diagonal in the case of flat or runner beans.
2. Bring a large saucepan of salted water to the boil, add the tagliatelle and cook for 5–10 minutes until *al dente*.
3. Meanwhile, heat the oil in a small saucepan, add the garlic and fry for 1 minute. Add the peeled tomatoes, green beans and chillies. Season to taste with salt, pepper and sugar.
4. Cook over a medium heat for a few minutes until the tomatoes and beans begin to soften but still retain some shape and the beans are crunchy.
5. Drain the pasta thoroughly and toss together with the tomato and bean sauce, the cherry tomatoes, olives and basil. Season to taste with salt, pepper and a little sugar. Serve with the cheese handed separately.

TAGLIATELLE WITH GORGONZOLA AND RUNNER BEAN SAUCE

225g/8oz runner beans
salt and freshly ground black pepper
150ml/¼ pint double cream
110g/4oz Gorgonzola or Dolcelatte cheese
340g/12oz tagliatelle
2 tablespoons shredded fresh basil
freshly grated nutmeg

To serve
freshly grated Parmesan cheese

1. Trim the sides of the runner beans and cut into 5mm/¼in slices on the diagonal. Bring 2 large saucepans of salted water to the boil.
2. Put the cream into a saucepan and crumble in the cheese. Heat gently until the cheese has melted.
3. Meanwhile, boil the tagliatelle and the runner beans in separate pans of boiling salted water until *al dente*.
4. Drain the pasta and beans thoroughly. Toss them together with the cream and cheese mixture and half the basil. Season to taste with salt, pepper and nutmeg. Scatter with the remaining basil, a few twists of pepper and the Parmesan cheese.

CREAMY PEA AND LETTUCE TAGLIATELLE

30g/1oz butter
1 tablespoon oil
2 shallots, finely chopped
170g/6oz frozen peas, defrosted
2 Little Gem lettuce hearts, finely shredded
150ml/¼ pint summer vegetable stock (see page 530)
5 tablespoons double cream
1 teaspoon chopped fresh tarragon
lemon juice
salt and freshly ground black pepper
340g/12oz tagliatelle
55g/2oz Parmesan cheese, freshly grated

1. Heat the butter and oil in a frying pan. Add the shallots and fry over a low heat for 5–10 minutes until soft but not coloured.
2. Add the peas and cook for 1 further minute. Stir in the shredded lettuce and the stock. Bring to the boil, then lower the heat and simmer for 2–3 minutes.
3. Stir in the cream, tarragon and a dash of lemon juice and season with salt and pepper.
4. Meanwhile, bring a large saucepan of salted water to the boil, add the tagliatelle and cook for 5–10 minutes.
5. Drain the pasta thoroughly and mix it with the sauce. Adjust the seasoning to taste. Transfer the pasta to a warmed serving dish and sprinkle over the cheese.

HERB TAGLIATELLE WITH CORIANDER DRESSING

450g/1lb strong '00' flour, plus extra for rolling
4 large eggs
1 tablespoon oil
a small handful each of fresh chives, chervil and
  basil, chopped

For the dressing
170ml/6fl oz extra virgin olive oil
1 clove of garlic, crushed
110g/4oz cherry tomatoes, halved
grated zest of 1 lemon
salt and freshly ground black pepper
30g/1oz roughly chopped fresh coriander

To serve
55g/2oz Parmesan cheese, freshly grated

1. Place the flour, eggs, oil and herbs in the bowl of a food processor and process until the mixture forms a softish paste. Wrap in clingfilm and leave to relax in a cool place for 30 minutes.
2. Roll out a small piece of the dough at a time on a floured surface. Cut into long noodles and allow to dry on a floured tray.
3. Bring a large saucepan of salted water to the boil.
4. Make the dressing: heat the oil in a saucepan. Add the garlic, tomatoes, lemon zest, salt and pepper. Leave to infuse over a low heat for 2–3 minutes. Remove from the heat and stir in the coriander. Season to taste with salt and pepper.
5. Cook the tagliatelle in the boiling water for 1–2 minutes. Drain well.
6. Serve the tagliatelle with the herb dressing drizzled over. Hand the cheese separately.

LINGUINE WITH GREEN BEANS AND POTATOES

110g/4oz French, runner or flat beans
225g/8oz new potatoes
salt and freshly ground black pepper
225g/8oz linguine
1 tablespoon pesto (see page 526)

To serve
freshly grated Parmesan cheese

1. Top and tail the beans and cut into 2.5cm/ 1in lengths, on the diagonal in the case of runner or flat beans. Scrub the new potatoes and cut into quarters.
2. Bring a large saucepan of salted water to the boil, add the potatoes and cook until almost tender, then add the linguine and cook for about 5 minutes. Add the beans and cook for a further 2 minutes until the pasta is *al dente* and the beans are crunchy.
3. Reserve 2 tablespoons of the cooking liquid and drain thoroughly. Return the pasta and vegetables to the pan. Add the pesto and the reserved cooking liquid and toss. Serve with the cheese handed separately.

LINGUINE WITH SAUTÉED LEEK, CHERVIL AND MASCARPONE SAUCE

1 tablespoon olive oil
55g/2oz butter
4 large leeks, trimmed and thinly sliced
200g/7oz mascarpone
1½ tablespoons wholegrain mustard
1 large bunch of fresh chervil, chopped
salt and freshly ground black pepper
225/8oz linguine
55g/2oz Parmesan or Pecorino cheese, freshly
    grated

1. Heat the oil and butter in a large frying pan with a lid.
2. Add the leeks, cover and cook over a very low heat for about 25 minutes until completely soft but not coloured.
3. Increase the heat, stir in the mascarpone and mustard and bring to the boil, then simmer for 2 minutes. Stir in the chervil, salt and pepper.
4. Meanwhile, bring a large saucepan of water to the boil, add the linguine and cook for 5–10 minutes until *al dente*. Drain thoroughly and mix with the sauce. Check the seasoning and tip into a serving bowl. Serve sprinkled with the cheese.

LINGUINE WITH SAMPHIRE AND HERB BUTTER SAUCE

Samphire is rather like salty asparagus. It is available from specialist greengrocers or fishmongers. If not available, use asparagus or spinach instead.

340g/12oz linguine
170g/6oz samphire
2 tomatoes, peeled, deseeded and chopped (see
    page 22)

For the sauce
290ml/½ pint summer vegetable stock (see
    page 530)
110g/4oz unsalted butter
2 shallots, finely chopped
1 tablespoon each chopped fresh chives, chervil
    and tarragon
lemon juice
salt and freshly ground black pepper

To serve
shavings of Parmesan cheese

1. Bring a large saucepan of salted water to the boil.
2. Make the sauce: boil the stock until reduced by three-quarters. Melt a knob of butter in a small, heavy pan, add the shallot and fry over a low heat until softened. Pour the reduced stock on to the shallot and gradually whisk in the remaining butter. The sauce should be light and frothy. Fold in the herbs and season with lemon juice, salt and pepper.
3. Cook the linguine in the boiling water for 5–10 minutes until *al dente*. Add the samphire for the last 2 minutes. Drain thoroughly and return to the pan.
4. Add the tomatoes and pour in the herb butter sauce. Toss briefly and adjust the seasoning to taste. Serve with a few twists of pepper, scattered with the shavings of cheese.

PAPARDELLE WITH LEMON OIL AND HERB DRESSING

150ml/¼ pint extra virgin lemon oil
grated zest of 2 lemons
1 bunch of fresh chives
½ bunch of fresh flat-leaf parsley
1 bunch of fresh basil
salt and freshly ground black pepper
340g/12oz papardelle
45g/1½oz pinenuts, toasted (see page 22)
55g/2oz Parmesan cheese, freshly grated

1. Put the oil and lemon zest into a saucepan. Warm over a low heat for 2–3 minutes.
2. Chop the herbs roughly and stir into the warm oil. Turn off the heat and leave to infuse for 5 minutes.
3. Meanwhile, bring a large saucepan of salted water to the boil, add the pasta and cook for 3–4 minutes or according to packet instructions until *al dente*.
4. Drain the pasta thoroughly and return to the hot pan. Pour in the warm lemon and herb oil and add the pinenuts.
5. Divide the pasta between 4 warmed serving bowls, sprinkle with cheese and serve immediately.

PENNE WITH ASPARAGUS TIPS AND PINENUTS

450g/1lb penne
3 tablespoons olive oil
2 shallots, chopped
1 large clove of garlic, crushed
200g/7oz asparagus tips
140g/5oz cherry tomatoes, halved
2 tablespoons chopped fresh thyme
100ml/3½fl oz crème fraîche
salt and freshly ground black pepper
4 tablespoons pinenuts, toasted (see page 22)
4 tablespoons freshly grated Parmesan cheese

1. Bring a large saucepan of salted water to the boil, add the penne and cook for about 10 minutes until *al dente*.
2. Heat the oil in a saucepan and add the shallots and garlic. Cook over a low heat for 5 minutes.
3. Meanwhile, steam the asparagus tips for 5–7 minutes or until just tender.
4. Add the tomatoes to the shallots and cook for 1 minute. Carefully mix in the thyme and crème fraîche and heat through gently. Season well with salt and pepper.
5. When the pasta is cooked, drain thoroughly and return to the pan. Add the sauce, asparagus and pinenuts. Mix together very gently. Serve sprinkled with the cheese and a few twists of pepper.

PENNE WITH CREAM OF TOMATO SAUCE

2 × 400g/14oz cans of cherry tomatoes
½ tablespoon tomato purée
1½ tablespoons caster sugar
2 bay leaves
salt and freshly ground black pepper
5 tablespoons double cream
2 tablespoons crème fraîche
a handful of fresh basil leaves, finely shredded
Tabasco sauce
340g/12oz penne
3 tablespoons extra virgin olive oil

To garnish
shavings of Parmesan cheese
fresh basil leaves

1. Put the tomatoes into a large saucepan with the tomato purée, sugar, bay leaves and salt and pepper. Bring to the boil, then lower the heat and simmer, uncovered, until reduced by half.
2. Remove the bay leaves and stir in the cream, crème fraîche, basil and a few drops of Tabasco.
3. Bring a large saucepan of salted water to the boil, add the penne and cook for about 10 minutes until *al dente*. Drain thoroughly and toss with the oil. Season with salt and pepper and transfer to a warmed serving bowl.
4. Pour the tomato sauce over the pasta, toss and serve topped with the shavings of cheese and basil leaves.

PEASANT PASTA

3 tablespoons olive oil
1 medium onion, chopped
1 tablespoon chopped fresh parsley
1 clove of garlic, crushed
225g/8oz mushrooms, thinly sliced
225g/8oz tomatoes, peeled and chopped (see page 22)
salt and freshly ground black pepper
a pinch of sugar
340g/12oz linguine
55g/2oz rocket

To serve
shavings of Parmesan or Pecorino cheese

1. Heat the oil in a sauté pan, add the onion, parsley and garlic and fry over a low heat until soft and transparent. Add the mushrooms and fry until soft. Stir in the tomatoes and season with salt, pepper and the sugar. Cover and simmer gently for about 20 minutes until reduced and well flavoured.
2. Bring a large saucepan of salted water to the boil, add the linguine and cook for 5–10 minutes until *al dente*. Drain thoroughly and toss together with the sauce and rocket. Serve immediately, topped with shavings of cheese.

PASTA WITH SAUTÉED COURGETTES AND GARLIC TOMATOES

3 courgettes, trimmed
salt and freshly ground black pepper
340g/12oz short pasta shapes
4 tablespoons olive oil
2 cloves of garlic, chopped
6 tomatoes, peeled and deseeded (see page 22)
1 green chilli, chopped
a pinch of sugar
1 tablespoon shredded fresh basil leaves

To serve
freshly grated Parmesan cheese

1. Slice the courgettes on the diagonal. Bring a large saucepan of salted water to the boil, add the pasta and cook until *al dente.*
2. Heat the oil in a heavy frying pan, add the courgette slices, a few at a time, and fry until golden-brown. Set aside.
3. Add the garlic to the oil in the pan and fry for 1 minute. Add the tomatoes and chilli and cook over a fierce heat until the tomato has cooked and any watery liquid has evaporated. Return the courgettes to the pan and season with salt, pepper and the sugar.
4. Drain the pasta thoroughly and toss together with the sauce and basil. Serve with the cheese handed separately.

PASTA WITH LENTILS

110g/4oz Puy lentils
1 litre/1¾ pints summer vegetable stock (see page 530)
4 tablespoons olive oil, plus extra for serving
1 medium onion, chopped
2 cloves of garlic, chopped
4 large ripe tomatoes, peeled (see page 22)
a large pinch of dried red chilli flakes
salt and freshly ground black pepper
225g/8oz pasta spirals or similar shapes
2 tablespoons chopped fresh flat-leaf parsley
½ teaspoon chopped fresh rosemary

To serve
shavings of Parmesan or Pecorino cheese

1. Put the lentils and stock into a large saucepan and bring to the boil, then lower the heat and simmer for 20 minutes until tender.
2. Meanwhile, heat the oil in a frying pan, add the onion and cook over a low heat until softened. Stir in the garlic and cook for a further 2 minutes.
3. Halve the tomatoes, squeeze out some of the juice and chop. Add to the pan with the chilli flakes and season with salt and pepper. Simmer to evaporate some of the liquid.
4. When the lentils are tender, add the pasta to the pan and cook for a further 10 minutes or until the pasta is *al dente.* Drain, reserving the stock for soups or casseroles, and toss the pasta and lentils with the tomato sauce. Adjust the seasoning to taste and stir in the parsley and rosemary. Serve with a drizzle of oil and the cheese handed separately.

PASTA WITH TOMATOES AND AVOCADO

2 tablespoons olive oil, plus extra for brushing
225g/8oz cherry tomatoes
salt and freshly ground black pepper
½ bunch of spring onions
1 ripe avocado
340g/12oz pasta spirals or bows
1 clove of garlic, crushed
2 tablespoons mascarpone cheese
grated zest of 1 lemon
2 tablespoons freshly grated Parmesan cheese,
    plus extra to serve
1 tablespoon shredded fresh basil, to garnish

1. Preheat the grill to high. Brush a baking tray with oil. Halve the cherry tomatoes horizontally and arrange them cut side down on the tray. Brush the tops with oil, season with salt and pepper and grill until the skins begin to char.
2. Trim the spring onions and slice them on the diagonal. Halve the avocado and remove the stone. Peel and slice.
3. Bring a large saucepan of salted water to the boil. Add the pasta and cook for about 10 minutes until *al dente*. Drain thoroughly.
4. Heat the remaining oil in the saucepan, add the spring onions and garlic and fry for 2 minutes. Return the pasta to the pan and stir in the mascarpone, lemon zest and 2 tablespoons Parmesan cheese. Toss in the tomatoes and avocado slices and serve sprinkled with the basil and the remaining Parmesan cheese.

PASTA WITH SMOKED TOFU AND PEAS

4 tablespoons olive oil
225g/8oz smoked tofu, diced
1 medium onion, chopped
2 cloves of garlic, crushed
340g/12oz tagliatelle
4 tomatoes, peeled and chopped (see page 22)
110g/4oz fresh or frozen peas, mangetout or
    sugar-snap peas
salt and freshly ground black pepper
2 tablespoons chopped fresh flat-leaf parsley

To serve
freshly grated Parmesan cheese

1. Bring a large saucepan of salted water to the boil. Meanwhile, heat half the oil in a heavy frying pan, add the tofu and sauté until golden-brown. Drain on kitchen paper and set aside. Heat the remaining oil in the pan, add the onion and fry over a low heat until soft and transparent. Add the garlic and fry for 1 further minute.
2. Put the pasta into the boiling water and cook for 10 minutes until *al dente*.
3. Meanwhile, add the tomatoes and peas to the onion and season with salt and pepper. Cook briskly for a few minutes until the peas are just tender. Stir in the tofu and adjust the seasoning to taste.
4. Drain the pasta thoroughly and toss together with the tofu, the tomato and pea mixture and the parsley. Serve with the cheese handed separately.

FRESH AUBERGINE SAUCE FOR PASTA

3 tablespoons olive oil
1 large red onion, chopped
3 cloves of garlic, crushed
1 teaspoon ground cumin
1 medium aubergine, chopped
3 ripe tomatoes, peeled and chopped (see
  page 22)
salt and freshly ground black pepper
a handful of torn fresh basil leaves

1. Heat the oil in a heavy pan, add the onion and fry over a low heat until softened. Add the garlic and cumin and fry for 1 further minute. Stir in the aubergine and cook gently until soft and beginning to brown.
2. Add the tomatoes to the sauce. Season with salt and pepper and simmer over a low heat for a few minutes until bubbling all the way through. Adjust the seasoning to taste and add the basil leaves just before serving.

PEA SAUCE FOR LONG PASTA

This pea sauce can also be used as a side dish. Leave out the cream to make the sauce lighter.

30g/1oz butter
1 medium onion, finely chopped
2 cloves of garlic, crushed
340g/12oz fresh or frozen peas
150ml/¼ pint summer vegetable stock (see
  page 530)
salt and freshly ground black pepper
a pinch of sugar
150ml/¼ pint double cream
340g/8oz freshly cooked long pasta

To serve
freshly grated Parmesan cheese
torn fresh basil leaves

1. Melt the butter in a saucepan and when foaming, add the onion and fry over a low heat for about 10 minutes until very soft. Stir in the garlic and cook for a further 2 minutes
2. Add the peas and stock and season with salt, pepper and the sugar. Cover and simmer gently for about 30 minutes until the stock is reduced by about half.
3. Stir the peas to crush them slightly. Add the cream and bring just to the boil, then remove from the heat and adjust the seasoning to taste. Toss together with the drained cooked pasta. Serve topped with a few twists of pepper and the cheese and basil leaves.

CHILLED TOMATO SAUCE FOR PASTA

450g/1lb ripe tomatoes, peeled and deseeded
  (see page 22)
3 cloves of garlic
2 shallots, finely chopped
150ml/¼ pint olive oil
salt and freshly ground black pepper
1 tablespoon shredded fresh basil

1. Chop the tomato flesh finely. Peel the garlic and flatten with the back of a knife. Mix together with the tomatoes, shallots and oil and season with salt and pepper. Cover and chill for 3–4 hours or overnight.
2. Remove the garlic, stir in the basil, and serve the sauce on top of piping hot, freshly cooked pasta.

STUFFED PASTA SHELLS

SERVES 4–6

340–450g/¾–1lb large pasta shells

For the tomato sauce
2 tablespoons olive oil
1 small red onion, finely chopped
1 clove of garlic, crushed
1 stick of celery, thinly sliced
1 small bulb of fennel, cored and thinly sliced
1 small red pepper, deseeded and diced
2 sprigs of fresh thyme
salt and freshly ground black pepper
1 × 400g/14oz can of tomatoes
290ml/½ pint summer vegetable stock (see page 530)
1 heaped tablespoon tomato purée
sugar to taste
1–2 tablespoons chopped fresh mixed herbs, such as parsley and oregano

For the filling
a knob of butter
450g/1lb fresh spinach, washed and stalks removed
freshly grated nutmeg
250g/9oz mascarpone cheese
1 egg, beaten
1–2 tablespoons pinenuts, toasted (see page 22)
225g/8oz mozzarella cheese, chopped
1–2 tablespoons pesto (see page 526)

1. First make the tomato sauce: heat the oil in a saucepan and add the onion, garlic, celery and fennel. Cover and sauté for 3–4 minutes. Add the pepper and thyme, season lightly with salt and pepper and cook for a further 3–4 minutes until the onion is transparent. Add the tomatoes, stock and tomato purée and cook for a further 10 minutes. Remove the thyme and season to taste with salt, pepper and sugar. Liquidize the sauce in a food processor or blender until smooth. Add the herbs and set aside.

2. Make the spinach filling: melt the butter in a large frying pan. Add the spinach and allow to wilt over a medium heat. Season with salt, pepper and nutmeg, then chop roughly. Set aside.

3. Bring a large saucepan of salted water to the boil, add the pasta shells and cook until *al dente* (the cooking time will depend on the size of the shells). Drain thoroughly, then cool in plenty of cold water and drain again.

4. Preheat the oven to 200°C/400°F/gas mark 6.

5. Pour enough of the tomato sauce into a large ovenproof dish to cover the base of the dish.

6. Combine the spinach with the mascarpone, egg and pinenuts. Mix thoroughly and season to taste with salt and pepper. Using a teaspoon, fill the pasta shells with the mixture. Arrange the stuffed pasta shells on the tomato sauce.

7. Spoon over the remaining tomato sauce, scatter with the chopped mozzarella cheese and dot the surface with teaspoonfuls of pesto.

8. Bake near the top of the preheated oven for 20–25 minutes or until golden-brown and bubbling.

NOTE: For a smoother filling, the spinach, egg and mascarpone can be whizzed quickly in a food processor and the pinenuts can be scattered over the surface of the dish with the cheese.

BROCCOLI AND MOZZARELLA CANNELLONI

225g/8oz broccoli florets
salt and freshly ground black pepper
225g/8oz mozzarella cheese
freshly grated nutmeg
1–2 tablespoons olive oil
8 × 10 × 15cm/4 × 6in sheets of fresh lasagne
1 tablespoon shredded fresh basil
290ml/½ pint tomato sauce II (see page 527)
55g/2oz Parmesan cheese, freshly grated

1. Cook the broccoli florets in boiling salted water for 5 minutes until *al dente*. Drain and refresh under cold running water. Drain again.
2. Cut the mozzarella cheese into 1cm/½in cubes. Cut the broccoli into walnut-sized pieces and mix together with the mozzarella. Season with salt, pepper and nutmeg and mix with enough oil to moisten.
3. Preheat the oven to 200°C/400°F/gas mark 6. Brush a shallow ovenproof dish with oil.
4. Bring a large saucepan of salted water to the boil, add the lasagne sheets and cook for 2–3 minutes until *al dente*. Drain and pat dry with a clean tea-towel. Divide the broccoli mixture between the lasagne sheets and roll up to form cannelloni. Place them seam side down in the prepared dish.
5. Stir the basil into the tomato sauce and pour over the cannelloni. Sprinkle with the Parmesan cheese and bake in the preheated oven for 20–30 minutes until piping hot and browned.

RED ONION AND RED PEPPER CANNELLONI

1 tablespoon olive oil
1 medium red onion, chopped
1 red pepper, sliced
1 clove of garlic, crushed
1 courgette, trimmed and diced
55g/2oz cream cheese
30g/1oz almonds, toasted (see page 22)
30g/1oz pistachio nuts, toasted (see page 22)
1 tablespoon fresh thyme leaves
salt and freshly ground black pepper
8 sheets of fresh lasagne, or 8 sheets of dried lasagne, cooked and drained
1 tablespoon shredded fresh basil
1 tablespoon chopped fresh parsley
425ml/¾ pint tomato sauce II (see page 527)
150ml/¼ pint Greek yoghurt
45g/1½oz Cheddar cheese, grated
15g/½oz Parmesan cheese, freshly grated
1 tablespoon fresh white breadcrumbs

1. Preheat the oven to 180°C/350°F/gas mark 4.
2. Heat the oil in a medium saucepan. Add the onion, pepper and garlic and cook over a low heat for 10–15 minutes until softened. Add the courgette and cook for 1 further minute. Remove from the heat and add the cream cheese, almonds, pistachio nuts, thyme, salt and pepper.
3. Lay the sheets of lasagne on a worktop. Divide the filling between them and roll up. Place them seam side down in a shallow ovenproof dish.
4. Add the basil and parsley to the tomato sauce and pour over the cannelloni.
5. Mix together the yoghurt, 30g/1oz of the Cheddar cheese, the Parmesan cheese, salt and pepper. Spread carefully over the tomato sauce.
6. Mix the remaining Parmesan cheese with the breadcrumbs and sprinkle over the top. Place on a baking sheet and bake in the centre of the preheated oven for 35–45 minutes until piping hot and brown and bubbling on top.

RICOTTA, BROAD BEAN AND ROCKET CANNELLONI

225g/8oz flour quantity egg pasta (see page 403)
1 × 570ml/1 pint béchamel sauce (see page 525)
30g/1oz Parmesan cheese, freshly grated

For the filling
45g/1½oz unsalted butter
1 bunch of spring onions, trimmed and sliced
*   on the diagonal*
340g/12oz fresh broad beans, tough outer skins
*   removed*
225g/8oz ricotta cheese
30g/1oz Pecorino cheese, freshly grated
30g/1oz rocket, roughly chopped
salt and freshly ground black pepper
butter, for greasing

1. Cut the rolled pasta into 10 × 6cm/4 × 2½in strips. Allow to dry for 30 minutes.
2. Make the filling: heat the butter in a small saucepan, add the spring onions and cook over a low heat until soft but not coloured. Transfer to a large bowl and allow to cool.
3. Cook the broad beans in boiling salted water until tender. Drain and add to the spring onions.
4. Add the ricotta, Pecorino cheese and rocket to the bowl and stir in half of the béchamel sauce. Season to taste with salt and pepper and mix thoroughly.
5. Bring a large saucepan of salted water to the boil, add the pasta and cook for 3–4 minutes. Drain thoroughly and pat dry with a clean tea-towel.
6. Preheat the oven to 200°C/400°F/gas mark 6. Preheat the grill to its highest setting. Grease an ovenproof dish with butter.
7. Divide the broad bean mixture between the strips of pasta and roll them up to form cannelloni. Place them seam side down in the prepared dish. Pour over the remaining béchamel sauce and sprinkle with the Parmesan cheese.
8. Bake in the preheated oven for 15 minutes until hot and bubbling, then place under the hot grill until nicely browned.

FRESH SPINACH CANNELLONI

225g/8oz flour quantity egg pasta (see page 403)
olive oil, for brushing

For the sauce
2 tablespoons olive oil
110g/4oz shallots, finely diced
900g/2lb tomatoes, peeled, deseeded and diced
*   (see page 22)*
1 teaspoon tomato purée
a pinch of sugar
2 tablespoons dry white vermouth
salt and freshly ground black pepper

For the filling
900g/2lb spinach, cooked
250g/9oz mascarpone
30g/1oz Parmesan cheese, freshly grated
salt and freshly ground black pepper
freshly grated nutmeg
olive oil for brushing
225g/8oz French beans, cooked
4 tomatoes, peeled, deseeded and quartered (see
*   page 22)*
1 tablespoon shredded fresh basil

To garnish
fresh thyme leaves
olive oil
2 tomatoes, peeled, deseeded and finely diced
*   (see page 22)*

1. Leave the pasta to relax in a cool place for 30 minutes.
2. Make the sauce: heat the oil in a medium saucepan. Add the shallots and cook over a low heat for 10 minutes until soft and transparent. Add all the remaining sauce ingredients and leave to simmer for a further 10 minutes.
3. Make the filling: put the spinach, mascarpone and Parmesan cheese into a bowl and mix together. Season to taste with salt, pepper and nutmeg.
4. Preheat the oven to 190°C/375°F/gas mark 5.
5. Roll out the pasta thinly and cut into 8 × 12 × 13.5cm/4 × 5½in strips. Bring a large

saucepan of salted water to the boil. Add the pasta and cook in batches for 3 minutes. Drain and put into a bowl of cold water until ready to use.

6. Drain the pasta thoroughly and pat dry with kitchen paper. Brush both sides with oil.

7. Lay the strips out on a flat surface. Divide the spinach mixture between them, keeping it to one end. Cover with the French beans, reserving a few for the garnish, tomato quarters, basil and plenty of salt and pepper. Roll up the pasta to make cannelloni.

8. Put the cannelloni into an ovenproof dish, seam side down. Spoon over two-thirds of the tomato sauce. Cover with a lid or wet greaseproof paper and bake in the preheated oven for 20–30 minutes or until piping hot all the way through.

9. Gently reheat the remaining tomato sauce.

10. To serve: place 2 cannelloni on each warmed individual plate and spoon around the tomato sauce. Sprinkle with thyme leaves, drizzle with oil and garnish with the reserved French beans and diced tomato. Serve immediately.

BOCCONCINI DI PARMA

SERVES 8

900g/2lb ricotta cheese
4 egg yolks
1 egg
170g/6oz Parmesan cheese, freshly grated
55g/2oz butter, softened
freshly grated nutmeg
salt and freshly ground black pepper
16 French pancakes (see page 532), made with a
    pinch of freshly grated nutmeg added to the
    batter
butter, for greasing

1. Drain the ricotta and put into a bowl. Using a wooden spoon, start to break it up, adding the egg yolks, whole egg, Parmesan cheese and butter. Mix well and season to taste with nutmeg, salt and pepper. Chill for 30 minutes.

2. Place a pancake on a board and spread 3

heaped tablespoons of the filling along one side. Roll up. Place the rolled pancake, seam side down, on a baking sheet. Repeat until all the pancakes are filled. Chill for 30 minutes.

3. Preheat the oven to 190°C/375°F/gas mark 5.

4. Grease a 33 × 22cm/13 ½ × 8in baking dish with butter. Using a very sharp knife, cut each pancake into thirds. Arrange them standing up in the baking dish, side by side. Bake in the preheated oven for 20 minutes and serve hot.

LASAGNE OF MUSHROOMS WITH HOLLANDAISE

Serve with crusty bread and a crisp green salad to offset the richness of the dish.

450g/1lb assorted mushrooms
1 tablespoon olive oil
55g/2oz butter
1–2 cloves of garlic, crushed
2 tablespoons chopped fresh flat-leaf parsley
salt and freshly ground black pepper
lemon juice
8 sheets of plain or spinach lasagne

For the Hollandaise sauce
3 egg yolks
170g/6oz unsalted butter, softened
2 tablespoons white wine vinegar
salt and cayenne pepper

1. Cut the mushrooms into even-sized pieces about the size of a walnut. Heat the oil in a sauté pan, add the butter and when foaming, add the mushrooms and fry briskly until tender. Stir in the garlic and fry for 1 further minute. Add the parsley and season with salt, pepper and a dash of lemon juice. Set aside.

2. Bring a large saucepan of salted water to the boil, add the lasagne sheets and cook for 5–10 minutes until al dente.

3 Meanwhile, make the hollandaise sauce: put the egg yolks into a small heatproof bowl. Beat together with a knob of the butter and a pinch of salt. Bring the vinegar to the boil and pour on to the egg yolks. Set the bowl over, not in, a pan of simmering water and beat in the remaining softened butter a little at a time, allowing the sauce to thicken after each addition. Season with a little salt and cayenne. Remove the pan from the heat and leave the bowl of sauce over the water to keep warm.

4. Preheat the grill. Drain the lasagne sheets thoroughly and arrange them, slightly crumpled, in a single layer in a warmed ovenproof dish. Put spoonfuls of the mushroom mixture on top of each sheet of lasagne and top with a spoonful of the hollandaise sauce. Flash under the grill to brown the top of the hollandaise.

NOTE: Alternatively, the lasagne can be served on individual plates and the hollandaise sauce browned with a blowtorch.

FRESH HERB RAVIOLI WITH WALNUT SAUCE

Serve with a leafy green salad to offset the richness of the sauce.

For the ravioli
340g/12oz flour quantity fresh pasta (see page 403)
250g/9oz ricotta cheese
55g/2oz Parmesan cheese, freshly grated
2 tablespoons chopped fresh flat-leaf parsley
2 tablespoons chopped fresh chives
2 tablespoons shredded fresh basil
1 egg, beaten
salt and freshly ground black pepper
freshly grated nutmeg

For the sauce
45g/1½oz white bread, crusts removed
170g/6oz walnuts, lightly toasted (see page 22)
1 clove of garlic, sliced
4 tablespoons freshly grated Parmesan cheese
4 tablespoons olive oil
85ml/3fl oz double cream
salt

1. Leave the pasta in a cool place to rest for 30 minutes.

2. Meanwhile, make the filling: mix the ricotta, Parmesan cheese and herbs together in a large bowl. Add the egg and season with salt, pepper and nutmeg.

3. Roll the pasta out on a highly floured worktop into a very thin rectangle and cut it in half. Take one sheet of pasta (keep the other well covered to prevent it from drying out) and place teaspoons of filling about 3cm/1½in apart in even rows all over it. Brush around the mounds of filling with a little water. Cover loosely with the other sheet of pasta and press firmly round each mound of filling; check carefully that there are no pockets of air.

4. Cut between the rows with a sharp knife or pasta wheel, making sure that all the edges are sealed. Allow to dry on a wire rack for 30 minutes.

5. Meanwhile, make the sauce: soak the bread in warm water for 5 minutes. Lightly squeeze out the excess water and put the bread into a food processor. Add the toasted walnuts and garlic and process until smooth. Add the Parmesan cheese, oil, cream and salt to taste and process again.

6. Cook the ravioli in a large saucepan of simmering, salted water for 4–5 minutes or until tender. Drain very thoroughly.

7. Put the pasta back into the pan and mix carefully with the walnut sauce.

NOTE: To make round ravioli, stamp out circles of pasta with a biscuit cuttter, place a teaspoon of filling in the centre, brush round the edge with water, cover with another circle of pasta and press the edges to seal.

RAVIOLI OF ROASTED SQUASH, CARAMELIZED ONIONS AND RICOTTA WITH CORIANDER PESTO

3 tablespoons olive oil
a small knob of butter, about 7g/¼oz
1 medium onion, thinly sliced
a pinch of granulated sugar
450g/1lb butternut squash
salt and freshly ground black pepper
250g/9oz ricotta cheese

For the pasta
225g/8oz strong plain flour, plus extra for
*   rolling*
¼ teaspoon salt
2 medium eggs
2 medium egg yolks
½ teaspoon olive oil

For the coriander pesto
45g/1½oz fresh coriander leaves
30g/1oz macadamia nuts
1 large clove of garlic, crushed
110ml/4fl oz olive oil
30g/1oz Parmesan cheese, freshly grated

1. Heat 1 tablespoon of oil and the butter in a large frying pan. Add the onion and sugar and cook over a medium to high heat, stirring from time to time, for about 20 minutes until the onion is soft and richly caramelized.

2. Meanwhile, preheat the oven to 200°C/ 400°F/gas mark 6. Cut the squash into 6–8 wedges and scoop out the seeds and fibres with a teaspoon. Rub each wedge with the remaining oil and season well with salt and pepper. Lay the wedges flesh side up in a roasting tin and roast in the preheated oven for 40 minutes or until tender. Remove from the oven and leave to cool.

3. Make the pasta dough: sift the flour and salt into the bowl of a food processor. Add the eggs, egg yolks and olive oil and process briefly until the mixture starts to come together into a ball.

Turn out on to a lightly floured worktop and knead for 10 minutes until very smooth. Wrap in clingfilm and leave to rest for 15 minutes.

4. While the pasta dough is resting, cut the flesh away from the skin of the squash, put it into a bowl and crush to a coarse purée with a fork. Stir in the caramelized onion, ricotta and plenty of salt and pepper.

5. Divide the pasta dough in half; keep one piece wrapped in clingfilm while you work with the other. Roll out very thinly on a lightly floured worktop into a 37.5cm/15in square. You should be able to see your hand quite clearly through the dough. Over one half of the square, make small indentations with the tip of your finger at 7.5cm/3in intervals, 3cm/1½in from the outside edges.

6. Put a teaspoon of the filling into each indentation. Brush water between the mounds of filling and all around the edges of the pasta. Fold over the other half of the square so that the edges meet and working from the centre outwards, press firmly around each pile of mixture so as to push out any trapped air and seal in the filling. Trim away the rough edges of the dough, then cut between the rows with a sharp knife or pasta wheel. Repeat with the other piece of pasta dough.

7. Bring a very large saucepan of well-salted boiling salted water (1 teaspoon of salt per 575ml/1 pint water) to the boil. Meanwhile, make the coriander pesto: put the coriander, macadamia nuts, garlic and olive oil into a food processor and blend to a coarse paste. Transfer to a bowl and stir in the Parmesan cheese and salt to taste.

8. Cook the ravioli in batches in the boiling water for 4–5 minutes until *al dente*. Drain thoroughly and return to the pan, add the coriander pesto and toss together gently.

ROASTED VEGETABLE RAVIOLI

225g/8oz flour quantity egg pasta (see page 403)
plain flour, for rolling

For the filling
1 red onion, finely diced
1 clove of garlic, crushed
1 small aubergine, trimmed and finely diced
1 courgette, trimmed and finely diced
2 tablespoons olive oil
salt and freshly ground black pepper
1–2 tablespoons chopped fresh mixed herbs,
*   such as parsley, thyme, basil*

For the sauce
150ml/¼ pint olive oil
1 red pepper, deseeded and thinly sliced
1 clove of garlic, thinly sliced
roughly torn fresh basil leaves

1. Preheat the oven to 200°C/400°F/gas mark 6.
2. Leave the pasta in a cool place to relax for 30 minutes.
3. Put the onion, garlic, aubergine and courgette on to a baking sheet, drizzle over the oil and season with salt and pepper. Bake on the top shelf of the preheated oven for 15–20 minutes, turning the vegetables occasionally until they are soft and evenly browned. Add the herbs and allow to cool.
4. Roll the pasta out on a lightly floured worktop into a very thin rectangle and cut in half. Take one sheet of pasta (keep the other well covered to prevent it from drying out) and place half teaspoons of the roasted vegetable filling about 3cm/1½in apart in even rows all over it. Cover loosely with the other sheet of pasta and press together firmly all around each mound of filling. Cut between the rows with a sharp knife or pasta wheel, making sure that the edges are sealed. Leave the ravioli on a wire rack to dry for 30 minutes.
5. Simmer the ravioli in near-boiling salted water for 5–8 minutes or until the pasta is tender and the filling is hot. Drain thoroughly.
6. Meanwhile, heat the oil in a small frying pan, add the pepper and garlic and cook over a low heat until the pepper is softened. Season with salt and pepper and add the basil leaves just before pouring the sauce over the cooked ravioli. Serve immediately.

MACARONI BAKE

For the lentil layer
1 tablespoon olive oil
1 onion, finely chopped
1 clove of garlic, crushed
2 carrots, finely diced
110g/4oz red lentils
1 × 400g/14oz can of chopped tomatoes
1 tablespoon tomato purée
a pinch of sugar
salt and freshly ground black pepper
1 bay leaf
a few drops of Tabasco sauce
2–3 tablespoons mango chutney

For the topping
110g/4oz macaroni
20g/¾oz butter
20g/¾oz plain flour
a pinch of cayenne pepper
425ml/¾ pint milk
salt and freshly ground black pepper
wholegrain mustard
85g/3oz Cheddar cheese, grated
85g/3oz Parmesan cheese, freshly grated
1 teaspoon dried breadcrumbs
1 teaspoon mustard seeds (optional)
1 teaspoon sesame seeds (optional)

1. Preheat the oven to 200°C/400°F/gas mark 6.
2. First make the lentil layer: heat the oil in a saucepan and add the onion, garlic and carrots. Cover and cook over a low heat for about 5 minutes or until the onion is softened and transparent.
3. Add the lentils, tomatoes, tomato purée, sugar, salt, pepper, bay leaf, Tabasco and chutney to the pan. Bring to the boil, then lower the heat and simmer for 15–20 minutes until the lentils are cooked and the excess liquid has evaporated, leaving a thick but not dry mixture.

Discard the bay leaf and transfer the lentil mixture to a deep ovenproof dish.

4. Make the macaroni topping: bring a large saucepan of salted water to the boil, add the macaroni and cook, uncovered, until *al dente*. The water must boil steadily to keep the macaroni moving freely and prevent it from sticking to the pan. Drain thoroughly and rinse under boiling water.

5. Melt the butter in another saucepan and add the flour and cayenne. Cook, stirring, for 1 minute. Remove from the heat, pour in the milk and mix well. Return to the heat and stir until boiling, then lower the heat and simmer, stirring constantly, for 2 minutes.

6. Add the cooked macaroni to the sauce and season to taste with salt, pepper and mustard. Stir in all but 1 tablespoon of the grated cheeses and spoon the macaroni mixture on top of the lentil layer. Mix the reserved cheese with the breadcrumbs and the mustard and sesame seeds, if used, and sprinkle evenly over the surface. Place on a baking tray and bake in the preheated oven for 15–20 minutes or until the cheese has melted and the topping is golden-brown.

PASTICCIO OF VEGETABLES

225g/8oz tagliatelle
salt and freshly ground black pepper

For the vegetable sauce
1 small aubergine
1 courgette
½ red pepper, deseeded
½ green pepper, deseeded
2 tablespoons olive oil
1 medium onion, chopped
1 clove of garlic, crushed
1 × 225g/8oz can of tomatoes
1 tablespoon shredded fresh basil

For the cream sauce
30g/1oz butter
30g/1oz plain flour
1 bay leaf
285ml/½ pint milk
150ml/¼ pint double cream
2 eggs, beaten
freshly grated nutmeg
85g/3oz Parmesan cheese, freshly grated

1. Bring a large saucepan of salted water to the boil, add the tagliatelle and cook for 5–10 minutes until *al dente*. Drain the tagliatelle thoroughly, then press it into an ovenproof dish about 20cm/8in square.

2. Make the vegetable sauce: peel the aubergine and chop with the courgette and peppers into 1cm/½in cubes. Heat the oil in a large frying pan, add the onion and fry over a low heat until softened. Add the garlic and fry for 1 further minute. Stir in the aubergine, courgette and peppers. Cover and fry gently for 10 minutes. Pour in the tomatoes and season with salt and pepper. Cover and simmer gently for 30–40 minutes until the vegetables are very soft and have reduced to a thick, rich sauce. Stir in the basil and allow to cool.

3. Preheat the oven to 190°C/375°F/gas mark 5.

4. Make the cream sauce: melt the butter in a saucepan, stir in the flour and bay leaf and cook over a low heat for 2 minutes. Gradually add the milk, stirring all the time until the sauce is smooth, thick and boiling. Remove the bay leaf. Remove from the heat and whisk in the cream. Cool slightly, then gradually whisk in the eggs. Add 55g/2oz of the cheese and season with salt, pepper and nutmeg.

5. Spoon the vegetable sauce on top of the tagliatelle, pushing it right down into the pasta. Pour the cream sauce over the top and sprinkle with the remaining cheese. Bake in the preheated oven for about 30 minutes until piping hot and golden-brown.

PIZZOCHERI

Traditionally pizzocheri is made with buckwheat pasta but any other type can be substituted. Gruyère cheese can be used if Fontina is not available.

170g/6oz savoy or pointed cabbage
110g/4oz French beans
225g/8oz new potatoes
salt and freshly ground black pepper
225g/8oz buckwheat pasta
110g/4oz unsalted butter
2 cloves of garlic, crushed
12 fresh sage leaves, finely chopped
freshly grated nutmeg
4 sun-dried tomatoes, finely chopped
170g/6oz Fontina cheese, grated
75g/3oz Parmesan cheese, freshly grated

1. Wash the cabbage, trim away any woody stalks and shred. Top and tail the beans and cut them into 2.5cm/1in lengths. Thickly slice the potatoes and simmer gently in salted water until just tender. Steam the cabbage and beans over the potatoes until tender but still a little crunchy.
2. Bring a large saucepan of salted water to the boil. Add the pasta and cook for 5–10 minutes until *al dente*.
3. Preheat the oven to 190°C/375°F/gas mark 5.
4. Melt the butter in a saucepan, add the garlic and fry for 1 minute, then stir in the sage, sun-dried tomatoes and cooked vegetables. Season with salt, pepper and nutmeg. Mix the Fontina and Parmesan cheeses together.
5. Drain the pasta thoroughly and spread half in a layer in a warmed serving dish. Top with half the vegetable mixture and sprinkle with half the cheese. Repeat these layers. Top with a few twists of pepper and bake in the preheated oven for about 20 minutes until the cheese has melted and the pizzocheri is piping hot all the way through.

QUICK PASTA CAKE

1 tablespoon olive oil
1 leek, trimmed and thinly sliced
2 cloves of garlic, crushed
½ bulb of fennel, cored and finely chopped
½ red onion, finely chopped
1 carrot, finely chopped
1 red pepper, deseeded and diced
1 bay leaf
salt and freshly ground black pepper
1 × 400g/14oz can of chopped tomatoes
290ml/½ pint summer vegetable stock (see
  page 530)
2 tablespoons tomato purée
a pinch of caster sugar
255g/9oz fettuccine
55–85g/2–3oz Cheddar cheese, grated

1. Preheat the oven to 180°C/350°F/gas mark 4.
2. Heat the oil in a large ovenproof saucepan. Add the leek, garlic, fennel, onion, carrot, pepper and bay leaf and season with salt and pepper. Cover and cook over a low heat for about 10 minutes until the vegetables are soft.
3. Add the tomatoes, stock, tomato purée and sugar. Cook for a further 2–3 minutes. (The sauce needs to be runny in order to cook the pasta. More liquid can be added or the sauce reduced further once the pasta is added if required.) Season to taste with salt and pepper.
4. Add the fettuccine and submerge it in the sauce to ensure even cooking. Scatter the cheese over the surface and bake in the centre of the oven for about 20 minutes or until the pasta is cooked and the cheese is bubbling and brown.

NOTES: This is an excellent recipe for making a few ingredients go a long way. Any combination of vegetables can be used in the sauce with oddments of cheese on the top. The only crucial element is to make sure the pasta you are using is the same thickness to ensure an even cooking time.

If an ovenproof saucepan is not available, the sauce can be made in a saucepan then, once the pasta is added, the ingredients can be transferred to an ovenproof dish to continue the cooking.

PASTA ROULADE PROVENÇAL

110g/4oz flour quantity egg pasta (see page 403)
plain flour, for rolling

For the filling
1 tablespoon olive oil
½ red onion, finely chopped
1 clove of garlic, crushed
4–5 sun-dried tomatoes, chopped
1 sun-dried pepper, chopped
1 sun-dried aubergine, chopped
150ml/¼ pint summer vegetable stock (see
*   page 530)*
1–2 tablespoons chopped mixed fresh thyme
*   and basil*
1 teaspoon capers, rinsed and chopped
6 black olives, pitted and chopped
450g/1lb ricotta cheese
salt and freshly ground black pepper

1 quantity tomato sauce II (see page 527)
freshly grated Parmesan cheese

1. Leave the pasta in a cool place for 30 minutes to relax.
2. Make the filling: heat the oil in a saucepan, add the onion and garlic, cover and cook over a low heat for 5 minutes or until the onion is soft. Add the sun-dried vegetables, pour in the stock and simmer until all the vegetables are soft and the liquid has evaporated. Add the herbs, capers, olives and ricotta cheese. Season to taste with salt and pepper. Set aside.
3. Roll the pasta out thinly on a lightly floured worktop. Cut into a 50 × 25cm/20 × 10in rectangle.
4. Spread the filling over the surface of the pasta, then roll up like a Swiss roll. Brush off excess flour with a pastry brush as you roll. Wrap the roulade in a clean 'J'-cloth or piece of muslin and tie the ends with string, like a Christmas cracker.
5. Cook the roulade in a large saucepan of simmering, salted water for about 20 minutes.
6. Preheat the oven to 200°C/400°F/gas mark 6.
7. Unwrap the roulade. Slice thickly and

arrange the slices in an ovenproof dish. Pour over half the tomato sauce, sprinkle with the Parmesan cheese and reheat in the oven for 20 minutes. Warm the remaining tomato sauce and hand separately.

NOTE: It can be easier to roll the roulade if the pasta is rolled out on a well-floured tea-towel.

PASTA ROULADE WITH TOMATO SAUCE

SERVES 4–6

225g/8oz flour quantity egg pasta (see page 403)
plain flour, for rolling
tomato sauce (see page 527)
freshly grated Parmesan cheese

For the filling
30g/1oz butter
1kg/2¼lb spinach, cooked and chopped
225g/8oz ricotta cheese
85g/3oz pinenuts, toasted (see page 22)
freshly grated nutmeg
salt and freshly ground black pepper
1 tablespoon roughly chopped fresh basil

1. First make the filling: melt the butter in a saucepan, add the spinach and cook for 1 minute, stirring continuously to prevent sticking. Add the ricotta, pinenuts, nutmeg, salt, pepper and basil. Remove from the heat and leave to cool.
2. Roll out the pasta on a lightly floured worktop into a large thin circle. Spread the spinach filling evenly over the surface, then roll up like a Swiss roll. Wrap the roll in a clean 'J'-cloth or piece of muslin and tie the ends with string, like a Christmas cracker.
3. Cook in a large saucepan or fish kettle of salted simmering water for about 20 minutes.
4. Preheat the oven to 200°C/400°F/gas mark 6.
5. Unwrap the roulade. Slice thickly and arrange in an ovenproof dish. Pour over the tomato sauce, sprinkle with cheese and reheat in the oven for 20 minutes.

TRICOLOUR PASTA SALAD

225g/8oz pasta twists
1 red pepper, cored, deseeded and quartered
450g/1lb broccoli
6 tablespoons French dressing (see page 528)
2 tablespoons chopped fresh parsley

1. Bring a large saucepan of salted water to the boil, add the pasta and cook until *al dente*. Rinse under cold running water until completely cold, then drain thoroughly.
2. Grill the pepper until the skin is well charred, scrape off the skin and cut the flesh into 5mm/¼ in strips.
3. Cut the broccoli into small florets and cook in boiling water for 1 minute. Rinse under cold running water and drain well.
4. Toss the pasta, peppers and broccoli in the French dressing and parsley. Serve chilled.

IONIAN PASTA SALAD

225g/8oz pasta shapes such as bows, spirals or
    shells
salt and freshly ground black pepper
3 tablespoons olive oil
1 tablespoon white wine vinegar
1 clove of garlic, crushed
1 teaspoon Dijon mustard
225g/8oz cherry tomatoes, halved
110g/4oz feta cheese, crumbled
1 small red onion, sliced
55g/2oz pinenuts, toasted (see page 22)
55g/2oz Kalamata olives, halved and pitted
55g/2oz rocket, shredded
2 tablespoons roughly chopped fresh flat-leaf
    parsley

1. Bring a saucepan of salted water to the boil, add the pasta and cook for about 10 minutes until *al dente*. Meanwhile, whisk together the oil, vinegar, garlic and mustard and season with salt and pepper.
2. When the pasta is cooked, drain thoroughly, rinse with cold water, drain again and put into a large mixing bowl. Toss in the dressing and set aside.
3. Mix the tomatoes and cheese into the pasta together with the onion, pinenuts, olives, rocket and parsley. Season with salt and pepper.

VERMICELLI NESTS WITH SUN-DRIED VEGETABLE SAUCE

4 vermicelli nests, about 170g/6oz

For the sauce
2 tablespoons olive oil
½ red onion, roughly chopped
1 red pepper, deseeded and roughly chopped
2 cloves of garlic, crushed
1 bay leaf
salt and freshly ground black pepper
3 slices of sun-dried aubergine
1 sun-dried red pepper
3 sun-dried tomatoes
8 cherry tomatoes
150ml/¼ pint summer vegetable stock (see page 530)
1 tablespoon tomato purée
capers, rinsed
black olives
2 tablespoons roughly chopped fresh mixed herbs, such as basil, parsley, thyme

1. Heat the oil in a saucepan and add the onion, pepper, garlic and bay leaf. Season with salt and pepper, cover and cook over a low heat for 5 minutes until softened.
2. Roughly chop the sun-dried vegetables. Add them to the pan together with the cherry tomatoes, stock and tomato purée. Cover and continue to cook over a low heat until all the vegetables are soft and the liquid has reduced to the consistency of a thick sauce. Remove the bay leaf. Add capers and olives to taste and stir in the herbs. Season to taste with salt and pepper.
3. Bring a large saucepan of salted water to the boil. Add the pasta nests and cook for 2 minutes or until *al dente*. Drain thoroughly.
4. To serve, twist the pasta back into nests and place on individual plates. Spoon over the sun-dried vegetable sauce and serve immediately.

NOTE: The sauce can be made in advance and reheated.

SPINACH SPATZLE

55g/2oz butter
1 large onion, chopped
salt and freshly ground black pepper
310g/11oz plain flour
freshly grated nutmeg
3 eggs, beaten
250ml/9fl oz water
250g/9oz spinach, cooked, drained and roughly chopped
butter, for greasing
110g/4oz mature Cheddar cheese, grated

1. Melt the butter in a medium saucepan, add the onion and fry over a low heat for 15–20 minutes until softened but not coloured.
2. Bring a large saucepan of salted water to the boil. Preheat the oven to 180°C/350°F/gas mark 4.
3. Sift the flour and add 1 teaspoon salt, nutmeg and pepper. Make a well in the centre and add the eggs. Mix carefully, adding the water to make a thick batter.
4. Pass the batter through a coarse sieve into the rapidly boiling water. Take care not to let the sieve get too close to the water or the batter will cook and block the holes. Cook until the spatzle noodles rise to the surface.
5. Drain and rinse with hot water.
6. Add the cooked spinach to the onion and season with salt, pepper and nutmeg. Mix with the spatzle.
7. Grease a large, shallow, ovenproof dish with butter. Put in half the spatzle, scatter over half the cheese, cover with the remaining spatzle and finish with the remaining cheese. Bake in the preheated oven for 15 minutes.

STIR-FRIED EGG NOODLES WITH STRAW VEGETABLES

225g/8oz Chinese egg noodles
1 carrot
110g/4oz mooli or radish
1 courgette
55g/2oz mangetout
110g/4oz shiitake mushrooms
2 tablespoons sesame oil
110g/4oz cashew nuts
1 onion, sliced
2 teaspoons sweet chilli sauce
juice of ½ lemon or lime
salt and freshly ground black pepper

1. Soak the noodles in boiling salted water for 6 minutes. Drain and set aside.
2. Peel the carrot and mooli or radish and trim the courgette. Cut the carrot, mooli or radish and the courgette into fine matchsticks, keeping them in separate piles. Top and tail and shred the mangetout. Slice the mushrooms.
3. Heat half the oil in a large wok or heavy frying pan. Add the cashew nuts and fry briefly until golden-brown. Remove from the pan and drain on kitchen paper. Set aside.
4. Heat the remaining oil, add the onion and stir-fry for 2 minutes. Add the carrot and cook for 1 further minute. Add the mooli or radish and courgette and cook for 1 minute, and finally add the mushrooms and mangetout and cook for 1 minute.
5. Toss in the noodles, chilli sauce and lemon or lime juice. Season to taste with salt and pepper. Heat through for 2 minutes. Toss in the cashew nuts and serve immediately.

NOODLES WITH ORIENTAL LEEKS

340g/12oz leeks
225g/8oz egg noodles
30g/1oz sesame seeds
2 tablespoons sesame oil
2 cloves of garlic, crushed
2.5cm/1in piece of fresh root ginger, peeled and
    chopped
1 red chilli, deseeded and chopped (see page 22)
1 tablespoon chopped fresh coriander
salt and freshly ground black pepper

To serve
soy sauce

1. Trim the dark green leaves from the leeks. Cut the leeks in half lengthways and wash thoroughly, then shred into thin matchsticks about 5cm/2in long.
2. Put the noodles into a deep bowl and cover with boiling water. Stir well to separate and leave to stand for about 6 minutes. Drain.
3. Meanwhile, heat a wok or heavy frying pan and toss the sesame seeds over the heat until light brown and toasted. Set aside.
4. Heat the sesame oil in the pan, add the garlic, ginger and chilli and fry briefly. Add the leeks and fry for a further 2 minutes. Toss the noodles into the pan and add the sesame seeds and coriander. Season with salt and pepper and mix well before serving with soy sauce.

NOODLES WITH PEANUT SAUCE AND RAW VEGETABLES

¼ cucumber
½ bunch of spring onions
Chinese leaves
225g/8oz mooli or radish, peeled and grated
salt and freshly ground black pepper
225g/8oz egg noodles
1 quantity sweet lime sauce (see page 507)

For the peanut sauce
1 tablespoon smooth or crunchy peanut butter
30g/1oz creamed coconut, crumbled
150ml/¼ pint boiling water
2.5cm/1in piece of lemongrass, finely chopped
1 clove of garlic, crushed
a small pinch of dried red chilli flakes
a walnut-sized piece of fresh root ginger, grated
a pinch of sugar

1. Chop the cucumber into 5mm/¼in cubes. Trim the spring onions and cut them into fine shreds. Wash the Chinese leaves and shred. Mix all the vegetables together with the mooli or radish.
2. Make the peanut sauce: combine all the ingredients in a saucepan and bring slowly to the boil. Add a little extra boiling water if the sauce is too thick. It should coat the back of a wooden spoon.
3. Bring a large saucepan of salted water to the boil, add the noodles and cook for 5 minutes, then drain thoroughly. Toss the noodles in the peanut sauce. Toss the raw vegetables in the sweet lime sauce. Season with salt and pepper.
4. Make a bed of noodles on 4 warmed individual plates and pile the vegetables on top. Serve immediately.

SINGAPORE STIR-FRIED NOODLES

170g/6oz Chinese egg noodles
3 tablespoons sesame oil, plus extra for serving
a walnut-sized piece of fresh root ginger, peeled and finely chopped
1 clove of garlic, crushed
1 red chilli, finely chopped
1 bunch of spring onions, trimmed and chopped
1 yellow pepper, deseeded and sliced
1 red pepper, deseeded and sliced
170g/6oz beansprouts
salt and freshly ground black pepper

For the sauce
1 teaspoon cornflour
150ml/¼ pint water
1 tablespoon soft light brown sugar
2 tablespoons wine vinegar
2 tablespoons soy sauce
2 tablespoons tomato ketchup

To garnish
¼ cucumber, diced
110g/4oz roasted peanuts

1. Put the noodles into a bowl, cover with boiling water and leave to stand for about 10 minutes until tender. Drain.
2. Make the sauce: mix the cornflour to a smooth paste with a little of the water and then combine with the remaining ingredients in a saucepan. Bring to the boil, then lower the heat and simmer until reduced by half.
3. Heat the sesame oil in a wok or heavy frying pan, add the ginger, garlic and chilli and fry for 2 minutes. Add the spring onions, peppers and beansprouts and stir-fry briskly for a few minutes. Add the noodles and toss over the heat.
4. Pour in the sauce, mix well and season with salt and pepper. Spoon into 4 warmed individual dishes and scatter the cucumber and nuts on top. Drizzle with a little sesame oil before serving.

TERYAKI TOFU WITH STEAMED BOK CHOI AND SESAME SOBA NOODLES

340g/12oz firm tofu
4 heads of bok choi
225g/8oz soba noodles
3 tablespoons sesame oil
55g/2oz sesame seeds, toasted (see page 22)

For the teryaki marinade
3 tablespoons sweet soy sauce
2 teaspoons caster sugar
3 tablespoons sake or rice wine vinegar
2 tablespoons mirin (Japanese rice wine)
a walnut-sized piece of fresh root ginger, peeled
    and grated

1. Cut the tofu into slices about 5mm/¼in thick.
2. Make the marinade: warm the soy sauce in a small saucepan, add the sugar and heat until dissolved. Stir in the remaining ingredients. Pour over the tofu, cover and leave to marinate for at least 1 hour.
3. Trim any tough stalks from the bok choi. Bring a large saucepan of salted water to the boil. Add the noodles and place the bok choi in a colander covered with a lid set over the noodles. Cook for a few minutes until both the bok choi and noodles are just tender.
4. Heat the sesame oil in a wok or heavy frying pan. Add the tofu with the marinade and fry briskly, then remove from the pan and set aside. Add the noodles to the pan and toss over the heat with the sesame seeds. Pile a bed of noodles on to 4 warmed individual plates, top with some bok choi and then the teryaki tofu. Serve immediately.

CRISP ANGEL HAIR PASTA WITH SAUTÉED GARLIC MUSHROOMS

85g/3oz unsalted butter
2 tablespoons olive oil, plus extra for brushing
3 large cloves of garlic, crushed
170g/6oz angel hair pasta
salt and freshly ground black pepper
2 teaspoons fresh thyme leaves
340g/12oz button mushrooms, wiped and
    halved if large

1. Melt the butter and 1 tablespoon of the oil in a large frying pan. Add the garlic, turn off the heat and leave to infuse for 20 minutes.
2. Bring a large saucepan of salted water to the boil. Add the pasta and cook for a few minutes until *al dente*. Drain thoroughly and toss with the thyme, salt, pepper and the remaining oil.
3. Preheat the oven to 200°C/400°F/gas mark 6. Brush a baking sheet lightly with oil.
4. Divide the pasta into 4 portions and, using a large serving fork, twist each portion into a 'nest'. Make a small dip in the middle of each nest, then transfer them to the baking sheet. Bake in the preheated oven for 10–12 minutes until crisp and brown.
5. Meanwhile, reheat the garlic butter. Add the mushrooms and fry briskly until well browned. Season with salt and pepper.
6. Put the pasta nests on to warmed individual plates and fill with the garlic mushrooms. Pour over the buttery juices and serve.

EGGS

INTRODUCTION

Eggs have invaluable properties for use in cooking and are very nutritious. Alone, they make a complete meal, but they are also a vital component of quiches, soufflés, cakes, mousses, ice cream and more. Eggs are a valuable source of protein and contain minerals and vitamins A, C and B_1. It is the yolk that contains the fat. Yolks are used to thicken and enrich sauces and soups. They are emulsified with oil or butter to make mayonnaise or hollandaise sauce. Egg whites are high in protein and contain no fat. The protein contains tiny filaments which expand on whisking and incorporate air in tiny bubbles. The puffed-up structure formed can be up to 8 times the original volume.

There are many different types of egg for sale. All have the same nutritional value. The best sort to buy are organic, free-range eggs. If possible, buy them from a local producer to be sure of freshness and the conditions under which the hens are kept. Organic eggs are laid by hens free to roam on land approved by the Soil Association. They are reputed to have a better life than other free-range hens. Barn eggs come from hens that are kept indoors but are still free to roam. Four-grain eggs are produced by hens who enjoy the same living conditions as barn hens but are fed on a diet based on barley, oats, wheat and rye. Battery eggs are the cheapest. However, the hens have a poor life, living in cages with little space, and are usually debeaked to prevent them from pecking other hens. Check the labels on egg boxes carefully Some use phrases such as 'farm fresh' or 'country fresh' which have no meaning.

Eggs require gentle cooking. When the protein coagulates it squeezes the liquid out and the eggs become rubbery and unpleasant to eat. It is best to store eggs in the refrigerator for health and safety reasons but for cooking they should be at room temperature, so remove from the refrigerator 30 minutes before they are required. This is especially important when whisking egg whites as they bulk better if warm.

BASIC EGG RECIPES

It is a good idea to set aside a frying pan for cooking eggs. A 20cm/8in pan is ideal. Choose a non-stick frying pan with a solid base or a heavy cast-iron pan which should be well seasoned (see page 22). Then take an oath to use the pan only for omelettes, fried or scrambled eggs.

Fried Eggs

Heat 1 tablespoon oil or 15g/½oz butter in the pan. Carefully break 1–2 eggs into the hot butter. Fry over a medium to low heat, basting the yolk with some of the butter until the white is set and the yolk is covered with a film of white and is cooked to your liking.

Scrambled Eggs

2 eggs per person
1 tablespoon cream or milk
salt and freshly ground black pepper
15g/½oz butter

Beat the eggs together with the cream or milk. Season with salt and pepper. Melt the butter in a small non-stick pan and swirl it around so that it coats the bottom. Pour in the eggs and stir over the heat for 3 minutes. Remove from the heat and stir until just set but still soft and creamy.

VARIATIONS: Just before removing the eggs from the heat, stir in 15g/½oz Boursin or freshly grated Parmesan cheese, or 1 tablespoon chopped fresh chives, dill or chervil.

French Omelette

2 eggs per person
1 teaspoon cold water
salt and freshly ground black pepper
15g/½oz butter

Beat the eggs together with the water. Season with salt and pepper. Melt the butter in the pan. When foaming, pour in the eggs. As the eggs set around the edge of the pan, hold the pan handle and use a palette knife to draw the cooked egg to the middle while tipping the runny mixture

to the edge of the pan. Repeat this once or twice until the omelette is set at the edge and underneath but is still slightly runny on top. Use the knife to fold the sides of the omelette to the centre, then flip the omelette over on to a serving plate.

Poached Eggs

Bring a pan of salted water to the boil and add a dash of lemon juice or ½ teaspoon vinegar. Break the egg into a cup. Stir the water vigorously, then carefully slide the egg into the centre of the whirl that has been created. Turn down the heat so that the water is barely moving. Poach for about 3 minutes until just set. Lift out with a slotted spoon and blot any excess water away with kitchen paper.

Boiled Eggs

Pierce the blunt end of the egg with a pin, to release the air that is held in the sac at this end. Carefully lower the egg into a pan of simmering water and keep the water barely simmering. Time the cooking from the moment the egg is immersed in the water. The following times are for medium-sized eggs:

- 4 minutes for soft-boiled eggs.
- 6 minutes for 'mollet' eggs with yolk that is set on the rim but thick and wet inside.
- 10 minutes for a hard-boiled egg. Cool hard-boiled eggs immediately in cold running water.

TOMATO BROTH WITH POACHED EGGS AND HALLOUMI CHEESE

2 tablespoons olive oil
1 medium onion, finely chopped
2 cloves of garlic, chopped
225g/8oz fresh tomatoes, peeled and chopped
  (see page 22), or canned chopped tomatoes
570ml/1 pint summer vegetable stock (see
  page 530)
1 heaped teaspoon red pesto
salt and freshly ground black pepper
1 teaspoon fresh basil or oregano leaves

To serve
110g/4oz halloumi cheese
4 poached eggs (see page 434)
a few torn fresh basil leaves

1. Heat the oil in a large saucepan, add the onion and fry over a low heat until softened. Add the garlic and fry for 1 further minute. Add the tomatoes, stock and pesto. Season with salt and pepper and bring to the boil, then lower the heat and simmer for 30 minutes. Stir in the herbs.
2. Meanwhile, warm 4 soup plates. Slice the halloumi cheese thinly. Check the broth for seasoning and when nearly cooked, poach the eggs.
3. Divide the cheese between the soup plates and set a poached egg on top. Carefully spoon over the broth and add a few basil leaves. Serve immediately.

NOTE: Instead of the poached eggs, poach ½ quantity spinach gnocchi (see page 405) in the soup.

CIABATTA WITH POACHED EGGS AND GRILLED VEGETABLES

1 large aubergine
2 courgettes
2 red peppers
1 red onion
110g/4oz cherry tomatoes
150ml/¼ pint olive oil
4 eggs
4 ciabatta rolls or other crusty bread rolls or
  chunks of foccacia bread
pesto (see page 526) or balsamic hollandaise
  (see Globe artichokes, page 267)
freshly ground black pepper

1. Cut the aubergine in half lengthways and then into 5mm/¼in thick slices. Trim the courgettes and slice lengthways. Core, deseed and quarter the red pepper. Cut the onion into thick slices.
2. Preheat the grill to high. Brush the vegetables liberally with the oil. Grill the peppers skin side up until black and charred. Grill the other vegetables, turning from time to time and brushing with more oil, until well cooked and browned.
3. When the vegetables are nearly ready, poach the eggs (see page 434).
4. Cut the bread rolls in half and toast the cut side under the grill. Put the rolls cut side up on 4 warmed individual plates. Pile a selection of vegetables on top of each roll and top with a poached egg. Drizzle with pesto or balsamic hollandaise and season with plenty of pepper. Serve immediately.

SPINACH MASH WITH POACHED DUCK'S EGGS AND HOLLANDAISE SAUCE

340g/12oz floury potatoes, such as Maris Piper,
  cut into chunks
salt and freshly ground black pepper
55g/2oz unsalted butter
170g/6oz baby spinach leaves, washed and well
  drained
2 tablespoons crème fraîche
freshly grated nutmeg
4 duck's eggs
1 quantity hollandaise sauce (see page 526)

1. Cook the potatoes in a large saucepan of boiling salted water until tender. Drain thoroughly and push through a sieve or vegetable mill.
2. Meanwhile, melt the butter in a large saucepan and when foaming, add the spinach. Cook for 1 minute or until just wilted, then stir in the crème fraîche and season well with salt, pepper and nutmeg.
3. Stir the hot spinach and buttery juices into the hot potatoes and mix together well. Divide between 4 warmed bowls and keep warm.
4. Meanwhile, poach the eggs (see page 434).
5. Place a poached egg on top of each bowl of spinach mash and spoon over the warm hollandaise sauce. Serve immediately.

OEUFS FLORENTINE

450g/1lb fresh spinach, cooked and chopped
15g/½oz butter, melted
salt and freshly ground black pepper
a good pinch of freshly grated nutmeg
4 eggs, chilled
290ml/½ pint cheese sauce (see page 525)
a little grated cheese
browned breadcrumbs

1. Turn the spinach in the melted butter. Season with salt, pepper and nutmeg. Place in the bottom of an ovenproof dish.
2. Preheat the oven to 150°C/300°F/gas mark 2. Preheat the grill.
3 Poach the eggs (see page 434).
4. Arrange the poached eggs on top of the spinach and coat with the cheese sauce. Sprinkle over the cheese and crumbs.
5. Brown the top under the hot grill.

BOILED EGGS WITH SPINACH SALAD AND PARMESAN CROÛTES

The girolles add colour and rich flavour to this salad but any type of mushroom can be used if girolles are not available.

450g/1lb baby spinach leaves
1 baguette
olive oil, for frying
salt and freshly ground black pepper
30g/1oz Parmesan cheese, freshly grated
6 medium eggs
2 tablespoons walnut or hazelnut oil
110g/4oz girolles, roughly sliced
2 cloves of garlic, chopped
2 tablespoons balsamic vinegar

1. Wash the spinach and remove any tough stalks.
2. Make the croûtes: cut the baguette into 12 thin slices. Heat the oil in a heavy frying pan until a crumb sizzles vigorously. Fry the croûtes on both sides until golden. Drain on kitchen paper. While still warm, sprinkle with salt and the cheese.
3. Boil the eggs for 10 minutes (see page 434). Cool slightly, then peel carefully.
4. Meanwhile, add the nut oil to the pan. Add the girolles and fry briskly until tender. Add the garlic, turn down the heat slightly and cook for 2 minutes.
5. Toss the mushrooms, all the pan juices and the vinegar together with the spinach. Season with salt and pepper. Halve the boiled eggs and spoon carefully through the salad. Scatter the croûtes on top. Serve immediately.

WHIZZED EGGS WITH MUSHROOMS AND ASPARAGUS

This is a good recipe to serve for brunch. To make a more substantial meal, serve with a jacket potato (see page 97).

8 large eggs
salt and freshly ground black pepper
225g/8oz slender asparagus spears
2 tablespoons olive oil
170g/6oz assorted mushrooms, roughly sliced
1 clove of garlic, chopped

1. Beat the eggs well in a bowl and season with salt and pepper. Trim the tough stalks from the asparagus and cut the spears into 5cm/2in lengths.
2. Heat the oil in a large, heavy or non-stick frying pan, add the asparagus and mushrooms and sauté briskly until tender. Add the garlic and fry for 1 further minute.
3. Pour the eggs into the pan and, keeping the heat high, stir the mixture until it begins to set. Serve immediately.

PIPÉRADE WITH GRIDDLED FRENCH BREAD

This dish, from the Basque region in south-west France, is a cross between an omelette and scrambled eggs. Many other vegetables can be added, such as peppers, chopped chillies, potatoes or mushrooms. Serve as a brunch dish or as a main course with a crisp green salad.

2 tablespoons olive oil
55g/2oz butter
1 medium onion, thinly sliced
1 red pepper, deseeded and sliced
6 eggs
salt and freshly ground black pepper
2 cloves of garlic, chopped
3 tomatoes, peeled, deseeded and sliced (see
* page 22)*
fresh basil leaves

For the griddled bread
2 baguettes
1 tablespoon olive oil

1. Heat the oil and half the butter in a small pan. Add the onion and pepper and cook over a low heat until soft and golden.
2. Make the griddled bread: cut the baguettes in half lengthways then crossways to make 8 pieces. Heat a heavy griddle pan. Brush the cut sides of the bread with oil and cook, cut side down, until golden-brown and slightly charred at the edges. Keep warm.
3. Beat the eggs in a bowl and season with salt and pepper to taste. Melt half the remaining butter in a heavy or non-stick frying pan. Add the eggs and cook over a medium heat, stirring all the time, until half set. Remove from the heat, add the remaining butter and continue stirring, returning to the heat briefly if necessary, until soft and creamy.
4. Add the garlic and tomato to the onion and pepper mixture and cook for 1 minute. Tear the basil leaves into small pieces. Stir the vegetables and basil into the scrambled eggs and serve with the griddled bread.

ASPARAGUS FRITTATA WITH GOAT'S CHEESE AND MINT

450g/1lb fresh asparagus
salt and freshly ground black pepper
3 tablespoons olive oil
2 cloves of garlic, chopped
4 eggs
140g/5oz mild soft goat's cheese
1 teaspoon chopped fresh mint
a few green or black olives, pitted

1. Trim the tough stalks from the asparagus. Cut the spears into 2.5cm/1in lengths. Blanch in boiling salted water for 2 minutes, then drain.
2. Heat the oil in a heavy 17.5cm/7in frying pan. Add the garlic and fry over a low heat for 1 minute. Add the asparagus and turn in the garlicky oil.
3. Beat the eggs in a bowl and season with salt and pepper. Pour into the frying pan and cook over a medium heat until set underneath and around the edges.
4. Invert a plate over the pan and hold both firmly. Turn over so that the frittata is now on the plate. Slide the frittata, runny side down, back into the pan and continue to cook until set underneath.
5. Turn the frittata on to a warmed serving plate and spread the cheese over the top. Scatter with the mint and arrange the olives at the side.

BROAD BEAN AND PESTO FRITTATA

225g/8oz shelled fresh or frozen broad beans
6 medium eggs
salt and freshly ground black pepper
3 tablespoons olive oil
2 cloves of garlic, peeled and chopped
85g/3oz fresh Pecorino or Parmesan cheese
2 teaspoons pesto (see page 526)

1. Cook fresh broad beans in boiling salted water for about 5 minutes until just tender. If using frozen beans, cook for about 2 minutes. Refresh under cold running water and when cool, slip off the tough outer skins.
2. Beat the eggs in a bowl and season with salt and pepper.
3. Heat the oil in a heavy 17.5cm/7in frying pan. Add the garlic and fry over a low heat for 1 minute. Add the broad beans and turn in the garlicky oil.
4. Pour the eggs into the pan and stir briefly, then cook over a medium heat until set underneath and around the edges. Crumble the cheese and swirl the pesto into the liquid egg and continue to cook over a very low heat until the egg is set and only slightly runny in the middle.
5. Invert a plate over the frying pan and hold both together firmly, then turn over so that the frittata is on the plate. Slide the frittata, runny side down, back into the pan and continue to cook gently until set underneath. Serve warm or cold.

FETA AND RED ONION FRITTATA

3 tablespoons olive oil
1 red onion, sliced
6 medium eggs
salt and freshly ground black pepper
1 teaspoon chopped fresh oregano or marjoram
110g/4oz feta cheese, crumbled
6 green olives, pitted and halved (optional)

1. Heat 1 tablespoon of the oil in a frying pan, add the onion and fry over a low heat until very soft and caramelized.
2. Beat the eggs in a bowl and season with salt and pepper. Add the herbs.
3. Heat the remaining oil in a heavy or non-stick 17.5cm/7in frying pan. Pour in the egg mixture and cook gently until it is set underneath and at the edges. Spoon the onion, cheese and the olives, if used, into the runny centre and continue to cook gently until the base and sides are firm.
4. Loosen the sides of the frittata with a palette knife. Invert a plate over the pan and hold both together firmly. Turn over so that the frittata is on the plate. Slide the frittata, runny side down, back into the pan and continue to cook until set underneath.

PASTA AND SPINACH FRITTATA

This is a good way of using up leftover pasta. The frittata can be eaten hot or at room temperature.

30g/1oz butter, melted
340g/12oz spinach
170g/6oz cooked pasta, any shape
6 eggs
200ml/7fl oz milk
110g/4oz Parmesan cheese, freshly grated
*½ bunch of spring onions, trimmed and
    chopped*
salt and freshly ground black pepper
freshly grated nutmeg

1. Preheat the oven to 200°C/400°F/gas mark 6. Brush a 20cm/8in flan dish or baking tin with the melted butter.
2. Remove any tough stalks from the spinach and wash thoroughly. Put the spinach into a saucepan, cover and shake over a medium heat for a few minutes until wilted. Drain, squeeze out all the water and chop roughly. If using long pasta, chop roughly.
3. Beat the eggs with the milk in a bowl. Stir in the Parmesan cheese, spring onions, pasta and spinach. Season well with salt, pepper and nutmeg. Pour into the prepared dish or tin and bake in the preheated oven for about 40 minutes until set and golden-brown. Cool slightly before cutting into wedges.

SWISS CHARD OMELETTE

SERVES 1

3 eggs
1 tablespoon milk or water
salt and freshly ground black pepper
110g/4oz Swiss chard
30g/1oz butter
freshly grated nutmeg
15g/½oz Parmesan cheese, freshly grated

1. Beat the eggs with the milk or water in a bowl and season with salt and pepper.
2. Trim the bottom 1cm/½in of the stalks from the chard. Roll the leaves into a tight bundle and shred. Melt half the butter in a small frying pan, add the chard and sauté until tender. Season with salt, pepper and nutmeg and keep warm.
3. Melt the remaining butter in a small, heavy or non-stick frying pan and when foaming, pour in the eggs. As the eggs set around the edge of the pan, hold the pan handle and use a knife to draw the cooked egg to the middle while tipping the runny mixture to the edge of the pan. Repeat once or twice until the omelette is set at the edge and underneath but is still slightly runny on top.
4. Spoon the warm chard over half the omelette. Sprinkle with the Parmesan cheese. Tilt the pan and use a palette knife to fold one half of the omelette over the other, then flip on to a warmed serving plate.

THAI VEGETABLE OMELETTE

SERVES 2

4 eggs
1 red chilli, deseeded and finely chopped (see
  page 22)
1 tablespoon water
salt and freshly ground black pepper
110g/4oz French beans
1 tablespoon sesame oil
3 spring onions, trimmed and chopped
1 small carrot, very finely shredded
55g/2oz beansprouts
1 stalk of lemongrass, outer leaves removed and
  finely chopped
1 teaspoon peeled and grated fresh root ginger
1 small clove of garlic, chopped
1 teaspoon soft light brown sugar
2 teaspoons dark soy sauce
1 teaspoon rice or white wine vinegar
15g/½oz butter
a few sprigs of fresh coriander, to garnish

1. Beat the eggs with the chilli and water in a
bowl. Season with salt and pepper. Top and tail
the beans and cut them in half.
2. Heat the oil in a wok or heavy frying pan,
add the spring onions, carrot, beansprouts and
beans and stir-fry for a few minutes. Add the
lemongrass, ginger and garlic and fry for 1
further minute, then stir in the sugar, soy sauce
and vinegar. Season to taste with salt and
pepper.
3. Melt the butter in a large omelette pan or
non-stick frying pan. When foaming, pour in
the eggs. As the egg sets around the edge of the
pan, hold the pan handle and use a palette knife
to draw the cooked egg to the middle, while
tipping the runny egg to the edge of the pan.
Repeat once or twice until the omelette is set at
the sides and underneath but is still a little
runny on top. Pile the vegetables over half of
the omelette. Fold the other half on top. Slice in
half crossways and serve scattered with
coriander.

HERB OMELETTE SALAD

For the omelette
5 eggs
3 tablespoons olive oil
1 tablespoon chopped fresh parsley
salt and freshly ground black pepper

For the salad
2 red peppers, quartered and deseeded
2 large tomatoes, peeled and cut into strips (see
  page 22)
1 cucumber, peeled, deseeded and cut into
  strips
1 head of lettuce
1 bunch of fresh chives, roughly chopped
12 fresh basil leaves, chopped

For the dressing
1 clove of garlic, crushed
1 teaspoon Dijon mustard
2 tablespoons wine vinegar
8 tablespoons olive oil
salt and freshly ground black pepper

To garnish
10 small black olives, pitted

1. Make the omelette: in a bowl, mix together
the eggs, 2 tablespoons of the oil, the parsley,
salt and pepper.
2. Use the remaining oil to fry the omelette.
Lightly grease the base of an omelette pan.
When hot, add enough of the omelette mixture
to cover the base of the pan. The omelette
mixure should be the thickness of a pancake.
Cook the omelette for about 1 minute. Slide on
to a plate and leave to cool. Continue to cook
the remaining omelette mixture in the same
way.
3. When cool, cut the omelettes into thin strips.
4. Meanwhile, prepare the salad: place the
peppers under a hot grill. When charred, hold
under cold running water and scrape off the
skin, then cut the flesh into 1cm/½in strips.
5. Prepare the dressing: mix together all the
ingredients, and whizz in a blender. Season with
salt and pepper.

6. Mix together all the salad ingredients, the omelette strips and the herbs. Add the dressing and toss well.

7. Pile on to a serving dish and scatter over the olives.

HERB EGG ROLLS FILLED WITH ROASTED VEGETABLES

For the egg rolls
6 eggs
3 tablespoons olive oil
1 tablespoon chopped fresh parsley
1 tablespoon chopped fresh chives

For the filling
2 red or yellow peppers
1 large aubergine
1 courgette
12 cherry tomatoes
olive oil
about 6 fresh basil leaves
10 black olives, pitted and quartered
salt and freshly ground black pepper

1. Beat the eggs with 2 tablespoons of the oil and the herbs in a bowl. Season with salt and pepper. Set aside.

2. Preheat the grill to high. Core, deseed and quarter the pepper. Cut the aubergine in half lengthways, then into 5mm/¼in slices crossways. Trim the courgette and slice on the diagonal. Cut the cherry tomatoes in half.

3. Brush the vegetables liberally with oil. Grill the peppers skin side up until black and charred. Grill the other vegetables, turning from time to time and brushing with more oil, until well cooked and browned.

4. Meanwhile, cook the eggs: use the remaining oil to grease the base of an omelette pan. When the pan is hot, add about a quarter of the egg mixture. This should be enough just to cover the bottom of the pan. Cook until set and golden on one side, then flip over and cook briefly to set the other side. Continue in the

same way until 4 thin omelettes have been made.

5. Mix the grilled vegetables together with the basil leaves and olives. Season with salt and pepper. Spoon the vegetables down the centre of the omelettes and roll up.

EGG FU YUNG

6 medium eggs
3 tablespoons vegetable oil
a walnut-sized piece of fresh root ginger, peeled and grated
½–1 red chilli, deseeded and chopped (see page 22)
1 clove of garlic, crushed
6 spring onions, trimmed and sliced
110g/4oz beansprouts
55g/2oz sugar-snap peas, roughly sliced
salt and freshly ground black pepper
1 teaspoon sesame oil

To serve
sweet soy sauce

1. Beat the eggs in a large mixing bowl. Set aside.

2. Heat 2 tablespoons of the oil in a wok or heavy frying pan. Add the ginger, chilli and garlic and fry for 1 minute. Stir in the spring onions, beansprouts and sugar-snap peas and toss over the heat for 1 further minute. Season with salt and pepper and the sesame oil. Spoon the vegetables into the beaten eggs.

3. Heat the remaining oil in a heavy frying pan and fry the egg mixture in small omelettes about 10cm/4in in diameter. Cook each one for about 30 seconds on each side and keep warm while cooking the remainder. Serve with soy sauce.

TORTILLA

Spanish tortillas have no connection with the Mexican variety, apart from sharing the name, which means a round cake. The classic Spanish recipe given here is a thick omelette made with potato and served as a snack or tapa. It also makes a speedy supper served hot or cold with crusty bread.

340g/12oz waxy potatoes
3 tablespoons olive oil
3 eggs
salt and freshly ground black pepper

1. Peel the potatoes and cut into 1cm/½in cubes. Heat 2 tablespoons of the oil in a heavy, 15–20cm/6–8in frying pan with a lid. Add the potatoes, then cover tightly and cook over a low heat for about 15 minutes until they are tender. Shake the pan from time to time to make sure that they do not stick.
2. Meanwhile, beat the eggs in a bowl and season with salt and pepper.
3. When the potatoes are cooked, tip them into the egg mixture. Wipe out the pan with kitchen paper and heat the remaining oil. Pour the egg and potato mixture into the pan and cook over a low heat until golden-brown underneath, set around the edges and still runny in the middle.
4. Invert a plate over the frying pan and hold both together firmly, then turn over so that the tortilla is inverted on to the plate. Slide the tortilla, runny side down, back into the pan and continue to cook and turn 2–3 times until the tortilla is set all the way through.

POTATO AND ONION TORTILLA

SERVES 6–8

85ml/3fl oz olive oil
1 large onion, thinly sliced
450g/1lb potatoes
8 medium eggs
salt and freshly ground black pepper
3 tablespoons chopped flat-leaf parsley

1. Heat the oil in a deep, 23cm/9in non-stick frying pan. Add the onion and cook over a high heat for 3–4 minutes, stirring now and then, until soft and lightly browned.
2. Peel the potatoes and cut lengthways into chunky chips 1cm/½in thick. Add them to the onions and cook over a medium heat for 15 minutes, stirring from time to time, until the potatoes are tender but not browned. Remove the pan from the heat and turn down the heat to low.
3. Beat the eggs in a bowl, season with salt and pepper and then stir in the parsley. Pour the egg mixture into the pan and give it a little shake to distribute it evenly among the potatoes and onions. Return the pan to the heat and leave to cook, undisturbed, for 15 minutes until almost completely set. Meanwhile, preheat the grill to high.
4. Slide the pan under the hot grill for 2–3 minutes until the tortilla is puffed up and lightly browned on top. Serve cut into wedges.

VARIATIONS:
Potato, Pea and Mint Tortilla
Add 110g/4oz peas to the onion and potato mixture 3 minutes before the potatoes are cooked. Whisk 30g/1oz freshly grated Parmesan cheese into the eggs and substitute chopped mint for the parsley.

Tortilla Paisana (Country-style Omelette)
Use only 225g/8oz potatoes. Add 1 chopped clove of garlic, 55g/2oz peas, 110g/4oz topped, tailed and blanched French beans, 1 peeled and deseeded roasted red pepper, cut into strips, and 110g/4oz blanched asparagus tips to the pan once the potatoes are cooked.

Manchego Cheese Tortilla
Add 110g/4oz diced Manchego cheese to the pan once the potatoes are cooked.

FRIED EGGS ON SPICED BROCCOLI

450g/1lb purple sprouting broccoli
salt and freshly ground black pepper
1 tablespoon vegetable or groundnut oil
1 teaspoon black mustard seeds
55g/2oz butter
a walnut-sized piece of fresh root ginger, peeled
  and chopped
2 cloves of garlic, chopped
1–2 red chillies, deseeded and chopped (see
  page 22)
1 teaspoon ground coriander
1 tablespoon lemon juice
4 large eggs
paprika

1. Trim the tough stalks from the broccoli. Cook in a saucepan of boiling salted water for about 5 minutes until *al dente*. Drain and set aside.
2. Heat the oil in a frying pan, add the mustard seeds and fry until they begin to pop. Turn down the heat and add half the butter. When the butter has melted, add the ginger, garlic, chilli, coriander and lemon juice and fry over a low heat for 2 minutes. Stir in the broccoli and toss gently over the heat for about 5 minutes until hot and well coated in the spicy mixture.
3. Meanwhile, melt the remaining butter in another frying pan and fry the eggs (see page 434). Divide the broccoli between 4 warmed individual plates. Top each serving with a fried egg and sprinkle with a little paprika.

HUEVOS RANCHEROS

Literally 'ranch-style eggs', this Tex Mex snack can be eaten at any time of day but in Mexico is traditionally eaten for breakfast with refried beans (see page 339). The tortillas used in this recipe are the thin Mexican variety, usually sold as flour tortillas in most major supermarkets.

30g/1oz butter
4 large eggs
4 flour tortillas
110g/4oz Cheddar cheese, grated
2 small avocados, peeled, stones removed and
  sliced

For the tomato sauce
1 tablespoon sunflower oil
1 small onion, finely chopped
1 green pepper, deseeded and finely chopped
1 clove of garlic, crushed
1 teaspoon finely chopped red chilli (see
  page 22)
1 × 225g/8oz can of chopped tomatoes
1 teaspoon chopped fresh oregano
salt and freshly ground black pepper

To serve
refried beans (see page 339)

1. First make the tomato sauce: heat the oil in a small pan. Add the onion and pepper and cook over a low heat for 5 minutes. Add the garlic and chilli and fry for 2 minutes. Add the tomatoes and oregano, season to taste with salt and pepper and simmer for 10 minutes or until thickened. Keep hot over a low heat.
2. Meanwhile, melt the butter in a frying pan and fry the eggs until just set (see page 434). Heat a dry frying pan and cook the tortillas for 1 minute each until puffed up and lightly browned.
3. To serve, slide the tortillas on to 4 individual plates and top each one with a spoonful of tomato sauce and a fried egg. Scatter with grated cheese and some slices of avocado. Serve with a helping of refried beans on the side.

CHILLI-BAKED EGGS

1 small red pepper
1 small green pepper
2 tablespoons sunflower oil
1 medium onion, finely chopped
2 cloves of garlic, crushed
2 jalapeño chillies, deseeded and finely chopped
  (see page 22)
½ teaspoon ground cumin
½ teaspoon chilli powder
1 × 400g/14oz can of chopped tomatoes
1 × 225g/8oz can of chopped tomatoes
½ teaspoon Tabasco sauce
½ teaspoon dried oregano
salt and freshly ground black pepper
8 medium eggs
110g/4oz Cheddar cheese, thinly sliced

To serve
crusty French bread

1. Cut the red and green peppers in half and
remove the stalks, pith and seeds. Cut the flesh
into small dice.
2. Heat the oil in a large, deep, non-stick frying
pan with a lid. Add the peppers and onion and
fry over a low heat for 4–5 minutes until soft
but not browned. Add the garlic, chillies, cumin
and chilli powder and fry for 1 minute. Add the
chopped tomatoes, Tabasco and oregano and
simmer for 15 minutes until the sauce has
reduced and thickened. Season to taste with salt
and pepper.
3. Make 8 hollows in the sauce with the back
of a wooden spoon and carefully break an egg
into each one. Crumble over the cheese, cover
and simmer for 10–12 minutes until the eggs are
set to your liking and the cheese has melted.
Meanwhile, preheat the grill to high.
4. Slide the frying pan under the grill and cook
for 1 minute until the cheese is golden and
bubbling. Serve with crusty French bread.

EGG AND AUBERGINE LASAGNE

You can use fresh or dried lasagne for this
recipe. You do not need to cook it first.

2 large aubergines
salt and freshly ground black pepper
5 tablespoons olive oil
2 red onions, sliced
1 large clove of garlic, crushed
55ml/2fl oz red wine
2 × 400g/14oz cans of chopped tomatoes
1 tablespoon tomato purée
150ml/¼ pint water
2 tablespoons shredded fresh basil
2 tablespoons chopped fresh oregano
250g/9oz button mushrooms, sliced
8 sheets of lasagne
570ml/1 pint cheese sauce (see page 525), using
  85g/3oz cheese
4 hard-boiled eggs, sliced
1 tablespoon grated Cheddar cheese

1. Cut the aubergines into slices lengthways.
Lightly salt them and leave on a wire rack set
over a tray to degorge for 30 minutes.
2. Heat 1 tablespoon of the oil in a saucepan,
add the onions and garlic and cook over a low
heat for 10–15 minutes until softened. Add the
wine and bring to the boil, then lower the heat
and simmer for 2 minutes. Add the tomatoes,
tomato purée, water, basil and oregano. Season
to taste with salt and pepper. Simmer for 15
minutes.
3. Preheat the oven to 180°C/350°F/gas mark 4.
Preheat the grill to high.
4. Heat 1 tablespoon of the remaining oil in a
frying pan, add the mushrooms and cook until
all the liquid has evaporated.
5. Rinse the aubergines and lay them on the
grill rack. Brush with oil and grill until
browned. Turn them over, brush again with oil
and grill until browned and cooked through.
6. Assemble the lasagne: put half the
aubergines in the bottom of a large, shallow,
ovenproof dish. Cover with half the mushrooms
and half the tomato sauce. Put 4 sheets of

lasagne on top and coat carefully with half the cheese sauce. Put the slices of egg on top of the cheese sauce. Layer with the remaining aubergines, mushrooms, tomato sauce and lasagne and finally pour over the remaining cheese sauce. Sprinkle with the grated cheese.

7. Bake in the preheated oven for 40 minutes or until the pasta is cooked and the top is browned and bubbling.

EGG AND COCONUT DHANSAK

2 tablespoons sunflower oil
1 medium onion, thinly sliced
2 cloves of garlic, crushed
2.5cm/1in piece of fresh root ginger, peeled and finely grated
30g/1oz ground almonds
½ teaspoon cayenne pepper
½ teaspoon ground turmeric
½ teaspoon ground coriander
1 teaspoon ground cumin
1 teaspoon finely chopped red chilli (see page 22)
1 × 225g/8oz can of chopped tomatoes
150ml/¼ pint spicy vegetable stock (see page 531)
1 bay leaf or 2 curry leaves
30g/1oz creamed coconut
55ml/2fl oz boiling water
salt
8 eggs, hard-boiled

To garnish
150ml/¼ pint Greek yoghurt
chopped fresh coriander

To serve
naan bread or basmati rice (see page 352)

1. Heat the oil in a saucepan. Add the onion and fry over a low heat until soft and golden-brown. Add the garlic and fry for 1 further minute.
2. Mix together the ginger, ground almonds, cayenne, turmeric, coriander and cumin and add enough water to make a smooth paste.

3. Lower the heat under the onions and add the chilli. Cook for 30 seconds. Add the spice paste and fry gently for about 2 minutes.
4. Add the tomatoes, stock and bay or curry leaves. Dissolve the creamed coconut in the boiling water. Add to the pan, season to taste with salt and simmer for 15 minutes. Remove the bay leaf or curry leaves.
5. Peel and halve the eggs. Add them to the pan and spoon a little sauce over each egg. Simmer for a few minutes until hot. Swirl over the yoghurt and sprinkle with coriander. Serve with warm naan bread or basmati rice.

EGG AND SPINACH KOULIBIAC IN A BRIOCHE CRUST

Brioche dough makes a good pastry to contain this pie. The secret of successfully rolling it into shape is not to knock it back after its initial rising: take it straight from the bowl to roll it out.

450g/1lb flour quantity brioche dough (see page 503), using only 2 teaspoons sugar
2 tablespoons olive oil
340g/12oz leeks, trimmed and sliced into rings
1 clove of garlic, crushed
110g/4oz long-grain rice
75ml/2½fl oz dry white wine
290ml/½ pint summer vegetable stock (see page 530)
1 tablespoon fresh thyme leaves
1 bay leaf
salt and freshly ground black pepper
225g/8oz fresh spinach
4 hard-boiled eggs, chopped
30g/1oz almonds, toasted (see page 22)
150ml/¼ pint crème fraîche
1 egg, beaten

1. Make up the brioche dough and leave in a warm place, covered, to rise for 45 minutes.
2. Heat the oil in a large saucepan, add the leeks and cook over a low heat for 10 minutes until soft but not coloured. Add the garlic and cook for a further 2 minutes.

3. Add the rice and stir over a low heat until it is opaque and glossy. Add the wine and bring to the boil. Boil for 2 minutes, then add the stock, thyme, bay leaf, salt and pepper. Bring back to the boil, then cover, lower the heat and cook for 15 minutes or until the liquid has been absorbed and the rice is cooked. Add more water if necessary.

4. Meanwhile, cook the spinach. Wash it well and remove the tough stalks. Put it into a saucepan, cover and cook over a medium heat until just wilted. Remove the spinach from the pan, squeeze out the excess moisture and chop finely.

5. Once the rice is cooked, remove the bay leaf and add the spinach, eggs, almonds and crème fraîche. Season well with salt and pepper.

6. Preheat the oven to 190°C/375°F/gas mark 5.

7. Roll out one-third of the brioche dough to a 20 × 25cm/8 × 10in rectangle. Place on a greased lipless baking sheet. (If your baking sheet has a lip, turn it over.) Brush the surface of the dough with a little beaten egg.

8. Place the rice mixture on the dough, leaving a 2.5cm/1in border all the way round. Brush the border again with beaten egg.

9. Roll out the remaining brioche dough to a 30 × 37.5cm/12 × 15in rectangle. Lift it carefully with a rolling pin and lay it over the filling. Press down gently to remove any air bubbles and seal the edges. Trim off the excess dough. Crimp the edges with a thumb and forefinger. Brush with beaten egg and score the top in a lattice pattern, using the back of a knife.

10. Bake in the preheated oven for 25–30 minutes until the brioche is golden-brown. Serve immediately.

CHEAT'S CHEESE SOUFFLÉ

This quick soufflé is rather like a light and puffy bread pudding. It makes a delicious supper served with a selection of fresh vegetables.

45g/1½oz butter
110g/4oz fresh white breadcrumbs
4 eggs
1 teaspoon dry English mustard
425ml/¾ pint milk
140g/5oz mature Cheddar cheese, grated
a pinch of cayenne pepper
salt and freshly ground black pepper

1. Preheat the oven to 190°C/375°F/gas mark 5. Grease a 1 litre/1¾ pint soufflé dish with some of the butter, then sprinkle with 1 tablespoon of the breadcrumbs so that the inside of the dish is coated.

2. Separate the eggs into 2 bowls. Add the mustard to the yolks and mix together with a fork.

3. Put the milk and the remaining butter into a small saucepan and heat gently until the butter has melted. Pour on to the egg yolks, stirring all the time, then stir in the remaining breadcrumbs and the cheese, cayenne salt and pepper. Leave to stand for 5 minutes to allow the breadcrumbs to swell.

4. Whisk the egg whites until they form soft peaks. Fold into the cheese mixture, using a large metal spoon. Pour into the prepared soufflé dish and bake in the preheated oven for 20 minutes. Lower the oven temperature to 180°C/350°F/gas mark 4 and bake for a further 25 minutes until risen and golden-brown.

VARIATIONS:

Spinach soufflé: stir in 170g/6oz well-drained and roughly chopped spinach before adding the egg whites.

Stilton soufflé: use finely grated Stilton cheese instead of Cheddar and stir in with 1 tablespoon chopped fresh parsley before adding the egg whites.

Mediterranean soufflé: use 85g/3oz freshly grated Parmesan cheese instead of Cheddar. Before adding the egg whites, stir in 2 teaspoons pesto instead of the mustard, 6 chopped spring onions and 55g/2oz chopped sun-dried tomatoes.

DESSERTS

INTRODUCTION

Whatever style of diet we choose, most of us enjoy a little sweet indulgence from time to time. This does not necessarily mean dishes laden with fat and sugar. Many of the recipes in this section are healthy and wholesome. There is a selection of quick desserts that can be put together in minutes alongside recipes for those occasions when something more elaborate is required.

Homemade ice creams and frozen yoghurts are a real treat and are a good way to use up excess soft fruit from the garden. They can be made with cream, milk or soya milk. The more fat there is in the ice cream mixture, the softer and creamier the texture will be when frozen.

Ice crystals form in the mixture during freezing and regular beating is required in order to break down the crystals and incorporate air. This can be done by hand: the ice cream is frozen in a shallow tray, tipped into a bowl and beaten with an electric whisk several times during freezing. For regular ice-cream makers a small electric ice-cream machine might be a good investment. Ice cream that has not been beaten enough will be difficult to scoop and eat. It is a good idea to remove homemade ice cream from the freezer 20 minutes before serving to allow it to soften. Once frozen, ice cream can be stored for several months. The texture deteriorates over time, so rewhisk before serving.

APPLE AND APRICOT PIE

For the filling
110g/4oz no-soak dried apricots
grated zest and juice of 1 orange
3 dessert apples
1 tablespoon soft light brown sugar
beaten egg or milk, to glaze
caster sugar

For the dough
85g/3oz butter
140g/5oz plain flour, plus extra for rolling
1 teaspoon caster sugar
4 tablespoons cold water

To serve
vanilla ice cream, Greek yoghurt or crème
*   fraîche*

1. Cut the apricots into quarters and place in a
bowl with the orange zest and juice. Set aside.
2. Make the dough: cut the butter into small
cubes and stir into the flour with the sugar.
Bind to a rough dough with the water, taking
care not to overmix. Cover and chill.
3. Peel, core and thickly slice the apples. Mix
together with the apricots and the brown sugar.
4. Preheat the oven to 200°C/400°F/gas mark 6.
5. Roll out the dough on a floured surface into
a 40cm/14in circle. Fold in half and lift into a
20cm/8in spring-release tin. Press the dough
over the base and into the sides, leaving the
excess pastry hanging over the sides.
6. Pile the fruit mixture into the centre. Fold
the excess pastry over the edge. Brush with
beaten egg or milk. Sprinkle the top of the pie
generously with caster sugar. Bake in the
preheated oven for 20–30 minutes until well
browned. Serve with vanilla ice cream, Greek
yoghurt or crème fraîche.

APPLE AND PEAR CHARLOTTE

450g/1lb prepared weight Bramley apples,
*   peeled, cored and sliced*
450g/1lb prepared weight Conference pears,
*   peeled, cored and sliced*
85g/3oz Muscovado sugar
juice of ½ lemon

For the topping
55g/2oz butter, melted
85g/3oz fresh white breadcrumbs
85g/3oz pecan nuts, chopped
zest of ½ lemon
1 tablespoon caster sugar

To serve
custard, cream or ice cream

1. Put the prepared fruit into a large saucepan
with the sugar and lemon juice. Cover and cook
over a low heat for 10–15 minutes until
softened. Transfer to an ovenproof dish.
2. Preheat the oven to 200°C/400°F/gas mark 6.
3. Make the topping: combine all the
ingredients and mix well. Sprinkle evenly over
the surface of the fruit. Bake near the top of the
preheated oven for 20 minutes or until golden-
brown. Serve warm with custard, cream or ice
cream.

HOT APRICOT SOUFFLÉ

110g/4oz no-soak dried apricots
290ml/½ pint water
2 tablespoons orange juice
1 tablespoon lemon juice
melted butter, for greasing
30g/1oz cornflour
150ml/¼ pint milk
3 eggs, separated
1 tablespoon caster sugar
icing sugar, for dusting

1. Put the apricots and water into a saucepan. Bring to the boil, then lower the heat and cook gently for 5–10 minutes. Purée in a food processor or blender. Add extra water if necessary to make at least 150ml/¼ pint purée. Add the orange and lemon juice.
2. Preheat the oven to 200°C/400°F/gas mark 6. Put a baking sheet in the oven to heat. Grease 4 large ramekin dishes with melted butter.
3. Mix the cornflour to a smooth paste with 3 tablespoons of milk. Add the remaining milk to the apricot purée and bring to the boil. Pour it on to the slaked cornflour, return the mixture to the pan and cook for 30 seconds. Remove from the heat and allow to cool slightly.
4. Add the egg yolks to the apricot mixture. Whisk the egg whites until stiff but not dry. Fold in the caster sugar and continue whisking until stiff and shiny.
5. Stir 1 tablespoon of the egg whites into the sauce to loosen the mixture, then fold in the remainder carefully and quickly, using a large metal spoon.
6. Pour into the prepared ramekin dishes. Place on the hot baking sheet and bake for 10–12 minutes. Serve immediately, dusted with icing sugar.

MANGO AND PAPAYA TART WITH PASSION-FRUIT SAUCE

170g/6oz digestive biscuits, crushed
70g/2½oz butter, melted
1 ripe medium mango
1 ripe papaya
2–3 tablespoons lime juice
2–3 tablespoons caster sugar
290ml/½ pint double cream

For the sauce
4 ripe passion-fruit
1 tablespoon caster sugar
30ml/1fl oz orange juice

1. Preheat the oven to 150°C/300°F/gas mark 2.
2. Mix together the crushed biscuits and melted butter. Line the base and sides of a 20cm/8in flan tin with the mixture. Bake in the preheated oven for 10 minutes. Allow to cool completely.
3. Peel the mango and cut the flesh away from the stone. Cut half the flesh into small dice and put the other half, roughly chopped, into a food processor.
4. Peel the papaya, cut in half and scoop out and discard the seeds. Cut one half of the flesh into small dice and put the other half, roughly chopped, into the food processor.
5. Process the fruit until smooth and add 2 tablespoons of lime juice and sugar.
6. Whip the cream until it holds its shape. Add the mango and papaya purée and mix with the cream. The mixture should be thick enough to hold its shape. Fold in the diced mango and papaya. Taste and add more lime juice or sugar as necessary. Pile into the cooled flan case.
7. Make the sauce: cut the passion-fruit in half and scoop the seeds into a bowl. Add the sugar and orange juice.
8. Serve the tart cut into slices, with the passion-fruit sauce drizzled over them.

STEAMED MAPLE AND PECAN SPONGE

110g/4oz butter, softened, plus extra for
    greasing
3 tablespoons maple syrup
30g/1oz pecan nuts, roughly chopped
110g/4oz soft light brown sugar
2 eggs, beaten
110g/4oz self-raising flour

To serve
custard or cream

1. Grease a 860ml/1½ pint pudding basin with butter.
2. Put the maple syrup into the bottom of the bowl and sprinkle the nuts into the syrup.
3. In a mixing bowl, cream the butter until very soft, then add the sugar. Beat until light and fluffy.
4. Gradually add the eggs, beating very well after each addition.
5. Sift the flour, then fold it into the mixture. Turn into the pudding basin. Cover with a sheet of pleated greased greaseproof paper, then with a sheet of pleated kitchen foil. Secure with string.
6. Steam the pudding in a covered saucepan containing about 2.5cm/1in simmering water for 1½ hours. Check that the pan does not boil dry, topping up if necessary with more boiling water.
7. Loosen the pudding at the edges with a knife and turn out on to a plate. Serve warm with custard or cream.

OAT AND DATE PUDDING

170g/6oz butter, plus extra for greasing
150ml/¼ pint water
110g/4oz stoned dates
170g/6oz soft light brown sugar
170g/6oz plain flour
½ teaspoon bicarbonate of soda
110g/4oz rolled oats

To serve
ice cream, whipped cream or nutmeg custard
    (see page 469)

1. Grease a 20cm/8in square shallow tin with butter and line the base with greased greaseproof paper. Preheat the oven to 190°C/375°F/gas mark 5.
2. Put the water, dates and 55g/2oz of the sugar into a saucepan and simmer for about 5 minutes until thick and smooth. Set aside.
3. Sift the flour and bicarbonate of soda into a mixing bowl. Rub the butter into the flour until the mixture resembles fine breadcrumbs. Add the oats and the remaining sugar and mix well.
4. Put half the oat mixture into the bottom of the prepared tin. Spread over the cooked dates. Cover with the remaining oat mixture and press down lightly.
5. Bake in the preheated oven for 40 minutes. Allow to cool slightly in the tin before cutting into wedges. Serve hot with ice cream, whipped cream or nutmeg custard.

BLUEBERRY GRUNT

55g/2oz butter, plus extra for greasing
450g/1lb blueberries
110g/4oz sugar
grated zest and juice of ½ lemon
3 tablespoons water
225g/8oz self-raising flour
1 teaspoon baking powder
1 teaspoon ground cinnamon
55g/2oz soft light brown sugar
400ml/14fl oz milk

To serve
nutmeg custard (see page 469)

1. Grease a 1 litre/1¾ pint pudding basin with butter. Put the blueberries into a pan with the sugar, lemon juice and water. Simmer gently for 5 minutes. Remove from the heat and leave to cool, then spoon into the prepared basin.
2. Sift the flour, baking powder and cinnamon into a mixing bowl. Add the lemon zest and sugar. Rub in the butter until the mixture resembles fine breadcrumbs. Gradually add the milk and beat to a smooth batter. Spoon over the blueberries.
3. Cover the pudding with a sheet of pleated greased greaseproof paper, then with a sheet of pleated kitchen foil. Secure with string. Set the basin in a saucepan containing about 2.5cm/1in simmering water. Cover and simmer for 1½ hours, checking that the pan does not boil dry, topping up with more boiling water if necessary.
4. Loosen the pudding at the edges with a knife and turn out on to a plate. Hand the nutmeg sauce separately.

PASSION-FRUIT TART

For the pastry case
55g/2oz butter
110g/4oz plain flour
1 tablespoon icing sugar
1 egg, separated

For the filling
10 passion-fruits
4 eggs
110g/4oz caster sugar
grated zest and juice of ½ lemon
225/8fl oz double cream
200g/7oz crème fraîche

1. Preheat the oven to 190°C/375°F/gas mark 5.
2. Make the pastry: rub the butter into the flour until the mixture resembles fine breadcrumbs. Add the icing sugar and bind to a stiff dough with the egg yolk and a little cold water if necessary.
3. Use the pastry to line a 17.5cm/7in flan dish, pressing the pastry well into the corners and trimming the edges. Chill for at least 30 minutes. Loosen the egg white with a fork and brush over the pastry case. Bake blind in the preheated oven (see page 22). Remove the paper and beans from the pastry case halfway through cooking and brush again with egg white. Bake for a further 10 minutes. Lower the oven temperature to 180°C/300°F/gas mark 4.
4. Meanwhile, make the filling: set one passion-fruit aside. Halve the remainder and scoop out the seeds and flesh into a sieve. Use a wooden spoon to push the pulp through, and discard the seeds.
5. Whisk the eggs and sugar together and add the passion-fruit pulp, lemon zest and juice and the cream. Pour into the flan case and bake in the hot oven for 20–30 minutes until the filling is set.
   6. Leave the tart to cool, then spread the crème fraîche over the top. Halve the remaining passion-fruit and scoop the pulp and seeds over the top.

BRÛLÉED PINEAPPLE WITH COCONUT SABLÉS

For the sablés
110g/4oz plain flour, plus extra for rolling
a pinch of salt
45g/1½oz desiccated coconut
45g/1½oz caster sugar
1 egg yolk
1 teaspoon coconut liqueur
85g/3oz unsalted butter, softened
icing sugar, to dust

For the pineapple
1 medium pineapple
2 tablespoons coconut liqueur
caster sugar, for dredging
fresh sprigs of mint, to decorate

1. First make the sablés: sift the flour with a pinch of salt on to a worktop. Scatter over the coconut. Make a large well in the centre and put in the sugar, egg yolk and coconut liqueur.
2. Using the fingertips of one hand, 'peck' the egg and sugar together until creamy. Add the softened butter and continue gradually to draw in the flour and coconut.
3. Knead gently to a paste. Wrap in clingfilm and chill for 10 minutes.
4. Preheat the oven to 180°C/350°F/gas mark 4.
5. On a floured worktop, roll out the pastry to the thickness of a £1 coin and trim the edges. Using a large knife, cut the pastry into 7.5 × 2.5cm/3 × 1in rectangles.
6. Bake the sablé biscuits on the top shelf of the preheated oven for 5–7 minutes or until dry to the touch and a pale biscuit colour. Remove from the oven and allow to cool, then dust with icing sugar.
7. Meanwhile, peel and slice the pineapple into 1cm/½in slices. Remove the core and sprinkle over the coconut liqueur. Dredge the slices heavily with sugar.
8. Put the pineapple on to a baking sheet and using a blowtorch, brûlée until caramelized. Allow to cool and serve with the coconut sablés.

PLUM STREUSEL TARTLETS

For the pastry
170g/6oz plain flour, plus extra for rolling
a pinch of salt
85g/3oz butter
2 tablespoons very cold water

For the filling
340g/12oz ripe plums, stoned and cut into 1cm/ ½in chunks
4 teaspoons soft light brown sugar

For the topping
110g/4oz plain flour
55g/2oz butter
45g/1½oz soft light brown sugar
15g/½oz porridge oats
1 teaspoon ground cinnamon

To serve
cream, crème fraîche or custard

1. Preheat the oven to 200°C/400°F/gas mark 6.
2. Make the pastry: sift the flour into a bowl with the salt. Rub the butter into the flour until it resembles breadcrumbs. Add the water to bind together to a dough.
3. Cut the pastry into 4 equal pieces. Roll each piece out on a lightly floured surface into a circle large enough to line an individual 10cm/ 4in tartlet tin. Chill for 15 minutes.
4. Meanwhile, prepare the topping: sift the flour into a bowl and rub in the butter until it resembles breadcrumbs. Add the sugar, oats and cinnamon.
5. Put the chopped plums into the pastry cases and sprinkle a teaspoon of sugar over each tartlet. Spoon the topping on top and press down very lightly. Use a fork to roughen the top.
6. Place on a baking tray and bake in the preheated oven for 10 minutes. Lower the oven temperature to 180.C/350°F/gas mark 4 and bake for a further 20 minutes or until the topping has browned and the plums are cooked.
7. Serve with cream, crème fraîche or custard.

RHUBARB COMPOTE WITH SUGAR-FRIED NOODLES AND CLOTTED CREAM

450g/1lb rhubarb
2 tablespoons rose-water
2 tablespoons golden caster sugar
2 vanilla pods
110g/4oz caster sugar
oil, for deep-frying
4 large wonton wrappers

To serve
clotted cream

1. Cut the rhubarb into 2.5cm/1in pieces on the diagonal.
2. Put the rhubarb, rose-water and golden caster sugar into a large saucepan.
3. Split one of the vanilla pods in half lengthways and add to the pan. Cook the rhubarb over a very low heat for 10–15 minutes, stirring occasionally, until tender but still holding its shape. Remove from the heat and allow to cool slightly.
4. Scrape the seeds from the remaining vanilla pod and using your fingertips, mix well with the caster sugar. Set aside.
5. Heat 10cm/4in oil in a large, heavy saucepan until a cube of bread sizzles and browns in 30 seconds.
6. Place the wonton wrappers on top of each other, roll up to form a cylinder and cut across into 5mm/¼in pieces.
7. Unravel the noodles and fry in small batches in the hot oil for 30–45 seconds or until crisp and brown. Remove from the pan with a slotted spoon. Drain briefly on kitchen paper and toss thoroughly in the vanilla sugar.
8. Divide the warm rhubarb between 4 individual dishes, top each with a generous spoonful of clotted cream and finish with a pile of sugar-fried noodles.

NOTE: A used vanilla pod can be washed and dried and left in a jar of caster sugar indefinitely. Top up with more sugar as required.

RHUBARB CRÊPES

600g/1lb 5oz fresh rhubarb, trimmed and cut into 2.5cm/1in lengths
finely grated zest and juice of 1 orange
4 tablespoons caster sugar
250g/9oz mascarpone
8 pancakes (see page 532)
1 tablespoon demerara sugar

To serve
Greek yoghurt

1. Put the rhubarb into a saucepan with the orange juice and half the caster sugar. Bring to the boil, then lower the heat, cover and cook very gently until the rhubarb is soft but still retains its shape. Be careful as it disintegrates very easily.
2. When the rhubarb is cooked, drain it through a sieve and return the juice to the pan. Bring to the boil and reduce to about 4 tablespoons. Remove from the heat and allow to cool.
3. Preheat the oven to 180°C/350°F/gas mark 4.
4. Beat the mascarpone with the orange zest and the remaining caster sugar. Add 2 tablespoons of the cooled reserved rhubarb juice then carefully fold in the rhubarb. Taste and add more sugar if necessary.
5. Divide the filling equally between the pancakes and fold up into parcels. Place them seam side down in a shallow ovenproof dish, pour over the remaining rhubarb juice and sprinkle with the demerara sugar. Bake in the preheated oven for 15 minutes. Serve hot with Greek yoghurt.

RICOTTA AND ORANGE FILO PIES

butter, for greasing
grated zest of 1 orange
juice of ½ orange
55g/2oz pistachio nuts, finely chopped
225g/8oz ricotta cheese
1–2 tablespoons caster sugar
4 sheets of strudel pastry (see page 523) or
*   bought filo pastry*
85g/3oz butter, melted
icing sugar, for dusting

1. Preheat the oven to 200°C/400°F/gas mark 6. Grease a baking tray with butter.
2. Beat the orange zest and juice and the pistachio nuts into the ricotta. Sweeten to taste with the sugar.
3. Brush the sheets of pastry with melted butter and fold in half lengthways. Divide the ricotta mixture into four equal portions and spoon along the narrow top edge of each sheet of pastry, leaving a 5cm/2½in gap at each side. Fold the sides in over the filling and roll up like a spring roll.
4. Arrange the parcels seam side down on the prepared baking tray and brush the tops with melted butter. Bake in the preheated oven for 20 minutes until golden-brown. Dust with icing sugar before serving.

SUMMER FRUIT CLAFOUTIS

55g/2oz plain flour
55g/2oz caster sugar
3 eggs
200ml/7fl oz milk
100ml/3½oz double cream
1 teaspoon vanilla extract
butter, for greasing
140g/5oz raspberries
140g/5oz blueberries
170g/6oz small strawberries
icing sugar, for dusting

1. Preheat the oven to 180°C/350°F/gas mark 4.
2. Sift the flour into a large bowl and add the sugar. Make a well in the centre and break the eggs into it.
3. Beat the eggs with a wooden spoon, gradually drawing in the flour. Beat in the milk gradually until the batter is smooth. Mix in the cream and vanilla extract. Chill for 30 minutes.
4. Grease a shallow ovenproof dish with butter and spoon in the fruit. Pour over the batter, ensuring it covers all the fruit.
5. Bake in the preheated oven for 40 minutes, then lower the temperature to 150°C/300°F/gas mark 2 and bake for a further 30–40 minutes until a sharp knife inserted into the centre comes out clean.
6. Serve warm, lightly dusted with icing sugar.

MARBLED CHOCOLATE AND GRAND MARNIER CHEESECAKE

85g/3oz butter
10 plain chocolate digestive biscuits, crushed
200g/7oz cream cheese
100ml/3½fl oz double cream
2 eggs
1 egg yolk
2 tablespoons caster sugar
85g/3oz plain chocolate, chopped
2 tablespoons Grand Marnier
150ml/¼ pint soured cream
1 tablespoon cocoa powder

1. Preheat the oven to 150°C/300°F/gas mark 2.
2. Melt the butter and remove from the heat, add the crushed biscuits and mix well.
3. Press into the bottom of a 20cm/8in loose-based cake tin. Bake in the preheated oven for 10 minutes. Remove and allow to cool.
4. Beat the cream cheese in a bowl, gradually add the cream and then the eggs, egg yolk and sugar and beat until smooth.
5. Carefully melt the chocolate in a medium heatproof bowl set over, not in, a pan of simmering water. Add two-thirds of the cream cheese mixture and mix well.
6. Add the Grand Marnier to the remaining cream cheese mixture.
7. Pour the chocolate mixture, which will be quite thick, on to the biscuit base. Pour over the Grand Marnier mixture and using a fork, stir gently to give a marbled effect. Place on a baking sheet and bake in the centre of the preheated oven for 30 minutes or until set. Remove from the oven and allow to cool.
8. Remove the cheesecake from the tin, spread over the soured cream and just before serving sift the cocoa powder over the surface.

LIME MOUSSECAKE

This recipe works equally well with 3 large lemons instead of the limes.

110g/4oz gingernuts
45g/1½oz butter
5 limes
290ml/½ pint double cream
1 × 400g/14oz can of condensed milk

1. Crush the biscuits with a rolling pin or in a food processor. Melt the butter and mix with the biscuit crumbs. Spread over the base of a 17.5cm/7in or 20cm/8in spring-release cake tin, pressing down well.
2. Pare strips of lime zest from one of the limes and cut into fine shreds. Douse in boiling water, drain and pat dry on kitchen paper. Set aside. Grate the remaining zest from the limes and squeeze the juice.
3. Lightly whip the cream. Fold in half the condensed milk and the grated lime zest and juice. Sweeten to taste with extra condensed milk.
4. Pour the mixture on top of the biscuit base. Cover and chill for at least 2 hours or overnight until set. Remove the moussecake from the cake tin and scatter the lime shreds around the edge before serving.

PINK GRAPEFRUIT CHEESECAKE

For the crust
85g/3oz butter, melted
200g/7oz digestive biscuits, crushed

For the filling
200g/7oz cream cheese
100ml/3½fl oz double cream
grated zest of 1 pink grapefruit
1 egg
1 egg yolk
1½ tablespoons caster sugar

To decorate
3 pink grapefruit

1. Preheat the oven to 150°C/300°F/gas mark 2.
2. Make the crust: mix together the melted butter and biscuit crumbs and press into the base and up the sides of a shallow 20cm/8in loose-based sandwich tin or flan tin.
3. Bake in the preheated oven for 10 minutes.
4. Make the filling: beat the cream cheese in a bowl, then add the remaining filling ingredients. Beat well until smooth and pour into the crust.
5. Place on a baking sheet and bake in the centre of the oven for about 25 minutes until the filling has set.
6. Remove from the oven and allow to cool completely.
7. Peel the grapefruit with a serrated knife, removing all the pith. Cut out the grapefruit segments, leaving behind the membranes and pips.
8. Arrange the segments on top of the cheesecake.

CITRUS SYLLABUB TRIFLE

4 trifle sponges
1 teaspoon raspberry jam
45g/1½oz amaretti or ratafia biscuits
2 tablespoons Grand Marnier, brandy or sherry
225g/8oz fresh raspberries

For the custard
290ml/½ pint milk
4 egg yolks
2 tablespoons caster sugar
½ teaspoon vanilla essence

For the syllabub
grated zest of 1 lemon
3 tablespoons lemon juice
grated zest of 1 lime
2 tablespoons lime juice
4 tablespoons caster sugar
55ml/2fl oz white wine
290ml/½ pint double cream

1. Split the sponges in half horizontally and spread thinly with jam. Put into a glass serving bowl. Add the amaretti or ratafia biscuits, pour over the alcohol and scatter over the raspberries.
2. Make the custard: bring the milk to scalding point. Mix the egg yolks and sugar together in a bowl. Pour the hot milk over and mix well. Return to the rinsed-out pan and cook over a low heat until the mixture thickens. Do not allow it to boil or it will curdle. Add the vanilla essence and strain over the sponges through a sieve. Allow to get completely cold.
3. Make the syllabub: mix the lemon zest and juice, lime zest and juice, sugar and wine together in a bowl. Pour on the cream and using an electric beater, whip until the mixture holds its shape. Pour over the custard. Cover and chill for at least 1 hour before serving.

RASPBERRY AND RATAFIA TRIFLE

340g/12oz raspberries
55g/2oz icing sugar
2 tablespoons Framboise liqueur
250g/9oz mascarpone
2–3 tablespoons double cream
icing sugar
1 teaspoon vanilla extract
about 32 ratafia biscuits
fresh mint leaves, to decorate

1. Reserve 12 raspberries for decoration. Purée the remainder with the icing sugar and Framboise in a food processor or blender. Sieve to remove the pips, cover and chill.
2. Soften the mascarpone with the cream, taking care not to overmix. It should be a reluctant dropping consistency. Sweeten to taste with icing sugar and flavour with vanilla extract. Cover and chill.
3. Put a spoonful of the raspberry purée in the bottom of 4 ramekins or individual glass dishes. Divide the ratafia biscuits between the dishes, reserving 4 for decoration. Divide the remaining raspberry purée between the dishes. Spoon the mascarpone mixture on top of the purée (do not level the surface). Cover loosely and chill until required.
4. Put 3 of the reserved raspberries in the centre of each trifle, together with a ratafia biscuit. Just before serving, dust with icing sugar and decorate each trifle with a mint leaf.

APRICOT AND ALMOND CREAM

225g/8oz no-soak dried apricots
juice of 1 orange
150ml/¼ pint water
caster sugar
55g/2oz blanched almonds, toasted (see page 22)
    and chopped
200ml/7fl oz double cream
2 tablespoons orange-flower water

1. Put the apricots and orange juice into a saucepan with the water. Bring to the boil, then lower the heat, cover and cook gently for 10 minutes. Purée in a food processor or blender. Taste and add sugar if necessary.
2. Allow the purée to cool. Pour into a glass dish or 4 glasses. Sprinkle over the chopped nuts.
3. Whip the cream until it is just holding its shape. Add 1 tablespoon sugar and the orange-flower water. Spoon over the apricot purée and serve.

COFFEE AND AMARETTI CUSTARDS

150ml/¼ pint milk
150ml/¼ pint double cream
2 teaspoons instant coffee
1 egg
1 egg yolk
1½ tablespoons caster sugar
4 amaretti biscuits

To serve
85ml/3fl oz double cream

1. Preheat the oven to 150°C/300°F/gas mark 2.
2. Put the milk, cream and coffee into a saucepan and bring just to scalding point.
3. Beat the egg, egg yolk and sugar together in a bowl. Pour over the hot coffee cream mixture. Stir well and strain into a jug.
4. Put an amaretti biscuit into each of 4 ramekin dishes. Pour over the coffee custard and leave to stand for 5 minutes.
5. Push each biscuit down into the custard, so that it is still just visible.
6. Put the custards into a bain-marie and cook in the preheated oven for 20 minutes or until set. Remove from the bain-marie and allow to cool.
7. Whip the cream until it just holds its shape and spread on top of the custards.

GRAPE AND MOSCATEL CREAMS

SERVES 5

sunflower oil, for brushing
200ml/7fl oz milk
425ml/¾ pint double cream
1 vanilla pod, split
5 egg yolks
85g/3oz caster sugar
3 tablespoons Moscatel de Valencia dessert
  wine

For the sauce
150ml/¼ pint white grape juice
4 tablespoons Moscatel de Valencia dessert
  wine
225g/8oz seedless grapes
lemon juice

1. Preheat the oven to 150°C/300°F/gas mark 2. Lightly brush 6 ramekin dishes with oil and line the bases with discs of oiled greaseproof paper.
2. Put the milk, cream and vanilla pod into a saucepan and bring just to scalding point.
3. Beat the egg yolks in a bowl with the sugar. Pour on the warm cream mixture, mix well and strain through a sieve. Discard the vanilla pod and stir in the wine.
4. Pour the cream mixture into the prepared ramekins and stand them in a bain-marie. Bake in the preheated oven for 15–20 minutes or until just set. Remove from the bain-marie and allow to cool, then chill for 3–4 hours or overnight.
5. Make the sauce: put the grape juice and wine into a saucepan and bring to the boil. Cook over a high heat for 1–2 minutes or until reduced by one third. Stir in the grapes and allow to cool.
6. Turn the Moscatel creams out of the ramekins, remove the greaseproof paper discs and place on individual serving plates. Spoon the grapes around the creams and pour over the sauce.

BROWN BREAD ICE CREAM

SERVES 4

110g/4oz wholemeal breadcrumbs
110g/4oz dark brown sugar
2 eggs
290ml/½ pint double cream
150ml/¼ pint single cream
2 drops of vanilla essence

1. Preheat the oven to 200°C/400°F/gas mark 6.
2. Place the breadcrumbs in the oven for 15 minutes or until dry.
3. Mix the sugar and breadcrumbs and return to the oven for a further 15 minutes or until the sugar caramelizes. Remove, allow to cool and crush lightly.
4. Separate the eggs. Beat the yolks, add the creams and fold in the caramelized crumbs. Add the vanilla essence.
5. Whisk the egg whites to soft peaks and folk into the mixture. Freeze until required.

BLACKCURRANT ICE CREAM

450g/1lb fresh or frozen blackcurrants
150ml/¼ pint water, plus 2 tablespoons
170g/6oz granulated sugar
290ml/½ pint double cream

1. Remove the blackcurrants from their stalks, wash them and put into a saucepan with 2 tablespoons water. Bring to the boil, then lower the heat, cover and simmer gently for 5 minutes. Push through a sieve to form a purée.
2. Dissolve the sugar in the remaining water. Bring to the boil and boil for about 4 minutes or until the syrup forms short threads when pulled between a wet thumb and forefinger.
3. Add the sugar syrup to the blackcurrant purée and mix well. Allow to cool.
4. Lightly whip the cream and fold into the sweetened purée. Put into a freezer container and freeze.
5. When frozen, remove from the freezer, allow to soften a little, cut into cubes and process in a food processor or blender until smooth. Alternatively, break up with a hand-held electric whisk or a fork. Freeze again.

GOOSEBERRY AND ELDERFLOWER ICE CREAM

450g/1lb gooseberries
2 tablespoons water
110g/4oz caster sugar
70ml/2½fl oz elderflower cordial
290ml/½ pint double cream

1. Top and tail the gooseberries, wash them and put them into a saucepan with the water and the sugar. Cover and bring slowly to the boil. Stir and mix to a pulp. Lower the heat and simmer, uncovered, for 5 minutes. Put into a food processor or blender and process until smooth, then push through a sieve to make a smooth purée and allow to cool.
2. When the purée is cold, add the elderflower cordial and the cream. Mix well and check for sweetness, adding more sugar if necessary. Put into a plastic container and freeze.
3. When the ice cream is nearly frozen, remove from the container, cut into cubes and put into a food processor or blender. Process until smooth. Alternatively, use a hand-held electric whisk. Return the ice cream to its container and freeze agan.
4. Allow the ice cream to soften for 10 minutes before serving.

LEMON AND LIME AMARETTI CRUMBLE ICE CREAM

sunflower oil, for brushing
1 × 400g/14oz can of condensed milk
grated zest and juice of 1 lime
grated zest and juice of 2 lemons
290ml/½ pint double cream, lightly whipped
85g/3oz amaretti biscuits, crushed

To serve
raspberry coulis (see page 517)
strawberries or other soft berries

1. Brush a 450g/1lb loaf tin lightly with oil and line the base with a piece of oiled greaseproof paper.
3. Put the condensed milk in a large bowl. Add the lime and lemon zest and juice and mix well.
3. Fold in the lightly whipped cream and the crushed amaretti biscuits.
4. Pour the mixture into the prepared loaf tin and freeze for 6 hours.
5. Remove the ice cream from the freezer, dip the tin into boiling water and turn out on to a board. Allow to soften slightly for a few minutes, then, using a knife dipped into hot water, cut into slices. Arrange on individual serving plates with a little raspberry coulis, decorated with strawberries.

MANGO AND PASSION-FRUIT ICE CREAM

This is delicious served with slices of fresh ripe mango or papaya.

1 large ripe mango
4 ripe passion-fruit
juice of ½ lime
70g/2½oz caster sugar
150ml/¼ pint boiling water
3 egg yolks
290ml/½ pint double cream

1. Peel the mango and cut the flesh away from the stone. Place the flesh in a food processor or blender and process until smooth. Add the pulp from the passion-fruit and process briefly, making sure the seeds do not break up. Sieve into a bowl and discard the seeds. Add the lime juice to the sieved mango and passion-fruit purée.
2. Put the sugar into a small, heavy saucepan. Pour on the boiling water and allow to stand for a couple of minutes. Stir very gently to dissolve the sugar. Set over a medium heat and bring to the boil, ensuring the sugar is completely dissolved before allowing to boil. Boil to the short thread stage (108°C/225°–6°F): when a little syrup is put between a wet finger and thumb and the fingers opened, it should form a sticky thread about 2.5cm/1in long.
3. Remove from the heat and allow to cool for 30 seconds.
4. Using a hand-held electric whisk, whisk the egg yolks in a bowl and pour on the sugar syrup taking care not to let the syrup touch the whisk. Continue to whisk for 3–5 minutes until the mixture is thick and mousse-like.
5. Add the mango purée and the cream and mix thoroughly. Check for sweetness and add more sugar if necessary.
6. Pour into a plastic container and freeze. When nearly frozen, remove from the freezer, cut into cubes and place in a food processor. Process for a couple of minutes to remove any large ice crystals. Put back into the plastic container and freeze again immediately.

RASPBERRY YOGHURT ICE

225g/8oz fresh raspberries
150ml/¼ pint double cream, lightly whipped
570ml/1 pint Greek yoghurt
2–3 tablespoons clear honey

1. Purée the raspberries in a food processor or blender. Push the purée through a nylon or stainless-steel sieve to remove all the pips.
2. Fold the cream into the yoghurt. Stir in the raspberry purée and sweeten to taste with honey.
3. Pour the mixture into a plastic container and freeze, beating several times with a hand-held whisk, until firm. Alternatively, freeze in an ice-cream machine. Remove the yoghurt ice from the freezer 20 minutes before serving.

STRAWBERRY TEQUILA SORBET

This recipe needs to be started a day ahead.

225g/8oz ripe strawberries
55g/2oz caster sugar
85ml/3fl oz tequila
juice of 1 lime

To serve
wedges of fresh fruit

1. Hull and slice the strawberries. Scatter with the sugar and sprinkle over the tequila and lime juice. Cover and chill overnight.
2. Purée the strawberry mixture in a food processor or blender. Pour into a plastic container and freeze, beating every hour with a hand-held electric whisk until the sorbet becomes firm. Alternatively, freeze in an ice-cream machine.
3. Scoop the mixture into glasses. Add a handful of fresh fruit and top with a dash of tequila.

NOTE: White rum may be used instead of tequila.

TOFFEE APRICOTS

450g/1lb apricots
110g/4oz soft light brown sugar
85ml/3fl oz boiling water
150ml/¼ pint double cream
30g/1oz unsalted butter

To serve
Greek yoghurt

1. Halve the apricots and remove the stones.
2. Put the sugar into a saucepan. Add the water and bring slowly to the boil, ensuring that the sugar has dissolved before the syrup boils. Boil rapidly for 4 minutes or until the mixture caramelizes and darkens slightly in colour.
3. Immediately add the cream, taking care as the mixture will hiss and splutter. Simmer to allow any lumps of caramel to dissolve. Add the butter.
4. Put the apricots into the butterscotch sauce and cook gently for 5 minutes, stirring occasionally. The skins should wrinkle a little and the apricots should be soft but still holding their shape. Be careful as the sauce will be very hot; do not be tempted to taste it at this point. Remove from the heat and allow to cool slightly.
5. Serve the apricots with Greek yoghurt.

BAKED FIGS WITH PINK CREAM

290ml/½ pint red wine
45g/1½oz soft light brown sugar
2 strips of thinly pared lemon zest
½ teaspoon ground cinnamon
a pinch of freshly grated nutmeg
4 large or 8 small figs
290ml/½ pint double cream

1. Preheat the oven to 170°C/325°F/gas mark 3.
2. Put the wine, sugar, lemon zest, cinnamon and nutmeg into a saucepan. Bring to the boil and reduce by half.
3. Meanwhile, wash the figs and cut off the stalks. Cut the figs in half and place, cut side up, in a single layer in a shallow ovenproof dish.
4. Pour over the spiced wine and cover with kitchen foil. Bake in the centre of the preheated oven for 15–20 minutes or until the figs have softened.
5. Remove 2 tablespoons of the spiced wine from the dish and allow to cool.
6. Whip the cream to soft peaks and fold in the reserved cooled, spiced wine.
7. Serve the figs warm with the pink cream.

SPICED STUFFED NECTARINES

4 ripe nectarines
45g/1½oz amaretti biscuits
15g/½oz almonds, chopped
15g/½oz dried apricots, chopped
30g/1oz caster sugar
½ teaspoon ground cinnamon
150ml/¼ pint Muscat wine
15g/½oz unsalted butter
15g/½oz caster sugar mixed with ¼ teaspoon ground cinnamon, to finish

To serve
crème fraîche

1. Preheat the oven to 200°C/400°F/gas mark 6.
2. Cut the nectarines in half and remove the stones.
3. Scoop out some of the flesh and chop finely.
4. Crush the amaretti biscuits and add the almonds, apricots, sugar, cinnamon and reserved nectarine flesh. Moisten with a little wine.
5. Stuff the nectarines witth the amaretti mixture. Place in a single layer in a shallow ovenproof dish. Dot the nectarines with butter and pour the remaining wine around them. Sprinkle the sugar and cinnamon mixture over the top.
6. Bake in the preheated oven for 35–40 minutes until the nectarines are soft and toasted on the top. Serve with crème fraîche.

REDCURRANT-SOAKED STRAWBERRIES

110g/4oz redcurrants
30g/1oz caster sugar
1 tablespoon water
675g/1½lb strawberries, hulled

To serve
cracked black pepper biscuits (see page 485)

1. Remove the redcurrants from their stalks, wash them and place in a saucepan with the sugar and water. Bring to the boil, then lower the heat and cook gently for 3–5 minutes. Remove from the heat and push through a sieve. Taste and add more sugar if required. Allow the purée to cool completely.
2. Pour the cooled redcurrant purée over the strawberries and leave them to macerate for at least 2 hours before serving. Serve with the cracked black pepper biscuits.

NOTE: Do not allow the strawberries to soak in the redcurrant purée for more than 4 hours before serving or they will begin to go soggy.

STRAWBERRY TOFU FOOL WITH RASPBERRY SAUCE

170g/6oz silken tofu
340g/12oz strawberries, hulled
290ml/ ½ pint double cream, whipped
icing sugar
lemon juice
110g/4oz fresh raspberries or frozen, defrosted

1. Put the tofu into a food processor or blender and process until smooth. Slice 225g/8oz of the strawberries, add to the tofu and blend to a purée.
2. Gently fold the strawberry mixture into the cream. Sweeten to taste with icing sugar and a dash of lemon juice. Spoon the fool into 4 individual serving dishes, cover and chill.
3. Meanwhile, make the raspberry sauce: push the raspberries through a nylon or stainless-steel sieve to remove all the pips. Sweeten the purée to taste with icing sugar.
4. Halve the remaining strawberries and pile on top of the fools. Drizzle the raspberry sauce over just before serving.

WINTER FRUIT AND NUT COMPOTE

110g/4oz no-soak dried apricots
110g/4oz no-soak prunes
55g/2oz large raisins
290ml/ ½ pint water
55g/2oz dried pineapple
2 oranges
55g/2oz blanched almonds, toasted (see page 22)
1 tablespoon pistachio nuts, toasted
(see page 22)
1 tablespoon pinenuts, toasted (see page 22)
2 tablespoons orange-flower water

1. Put the apricots, prunes and raisins into a saucepan with the water. Bring to the boil, then lower the heat and cook very gently for 10 minutes. Remove from the heat, add the pineapple and allow to cool.
2. Finely grate the zest of the oranges and add to the fruit. Peel the oranges with a serrated knife, removing the skin and pith. Cut the oranges into segments and add to the fruit salad.
3. Sprinkle with the toasted nuts and orange-flower water and serve.

BAKED AND PEPPERED FRUIT SALAD

675g/1½lb summer stone fruits, such as apricots, nectarines, plums (any mixture will do)
85g/3oz caster sugar
2 teaspoons Sichuan peppercorns, crushed
1 teaspoon coriander seeds, crushed
juice of 1 lemon
225g/8oz strawberries or raspberries

To serve
Greek yoghurt or crème fraîche

1. Preheat the oven to 180°C/350°F/gas mark 4. Cut the fruit in half and remove the stones. If using larger fruit such as nectarines, cut them in half again.
2. Arrange in an ovenproof dish and sprinkle over the sugar, peppercorns, coriander and lemon juice. Cover the dish with kitchen foil and bake in the preheated oven for about 30 minutes until the fruit is tender. Remove the foil, cool and then chill.
3. If using strawberries, hull and slice them. Mix the strawerries or raspberries with the baked fruit and serve with yoghurt or cream.

GREEK YOGHURT WITH HONEY AND PASSION-FRUIT

570ml/1 pint Greek yoghurt, well chilled
4–8 tablespoons clear honey
4 passion-fruit
1 tablespoon extra-thick double cream

1. Divide the yoghurt between 4 glass dessert dishes. Top each with 1–2 tablespoons honey according to taste.
2. Cut the passion-fruit in half and scoop out the pulp of 1 fruit over each dish. Top each with a teaspoonful of cream.

MANGO YOGHURT WITH CARDAMOM

12 cardamom pods
1 ripe mango
30g/1oz pistachio nuts, chopped
570ml/1 pint Greek yoghurt
clear honey

1. Crush the cardamom pods and remove the seeds. Toast the seeds in a dry, heavy frying pan and crush in a mortar.
2. Peel the mango and slice the flesh from the stone. Chop finely. Chop the pistachio nuts.
3. Fold the mango and cardamom into the yoghurt and sweeten to taste with the honey. Spoon into 4 individual dishes. Decorate with the pistachios.

HOMEMADE YOGHURT

570ml/1 pint milk
2 tablespoons live yoghurt

1. Heat the milk to boiling point. Remove from the heat and cool to 45°C/113°F. This will feel slightly too hot for comfort to the fingertips.
2. Put the yoghurt into a bowl and gradually whisk in the milk. Pour the yoghurt into a vacuum flask and leave for 10–12 hours until set. Store in the refrigerator.

NUTMEG CUSTARD

2 egg yolks
30g/1oz caster sugar
2 teaspoons cornflour
290ml/½ pint creamy milk
1 teaspoon freshly grated nutmeg

1. Beat together the egg yolks, sugar and cornflour.
2. Put the milk and nutmeg together in a saucepan and heat gently, to allow the nutmeg to infuse, until steaming. Slowly pour on to the egg mixture, stirring all the time.
3. Pour the custard back into the pan and stir over a low heat until the mixture thickens sufficiently to coat the back of a wooden spoon.

NOTE: For an extra-rich custard, stir in 2 tablespoons double cream with the nutmeg.

STRAWBERRY AND BANANA BREAKFAST SMOOTHIE

Most fruits can be used to make a smoothie. Peel the fruit, remove any core and cut into thick chunks before blending. Other cereals or seeds can also be included. For a richer smoothie add 1–2 scoops of ice cream.

1 large banana
225g/8oz strawberries
2 tablespoons muesli
150ml/¼ pint Greek yoghurt
290ml/½ pint milk
6 ice cubes
clear honey or caster sugar

1. Peel and thickly slice the banana. Hull and halve the strawberries.
2. Place the fruit in a food processor or blender with the muesli, yoghurt, milk and ice cubes. Process until smooth and creamy. Sweeten to taste with honey or sugar and serve immediately for maximum nutritional benefit.

PECAN NUT AND ALMOND GRANOLA

This granola is best served with ice-cold milk. It can also be scattered on yoghurt to give a crunchy topping. It will keep in an airtight container for 3 weeks.

225g/8oz rolled oats
85g/3oz sunflower seeds
55g/2oz wheat bran
110g/4oz oat bran
110g/4oz pecan nuts, chopped
55g/2oz almonds, chopped
30g/1oz sesame seeds
1 tablespoon ground cinnamon
55ml/2fl oz maple syrup
55ml/2fl oz clear honey
110ml/4fl oz sunflower oil
½ teaspoon vanilla extract
110g/4oz raisins
110g/4oz dried apricots, chopped

1. Preheat the oven to 100°C/200°F/gas mark ½. Line 2 baking trays with kitchen foil.
2. Mix the oats, sunflower seeds, wheat bran, oat bran, pecan nuts, almonds, sesame seeds and cinnamon together in a large bowl.
3. Mix the maple syrup with the honey, oil and vanilla extract. Add to the dry ingredients and mix very well.
4. Spread over the baking trays and place in the preheated oven for 2 hours. Stir the mixture with a wooden spoon or spatula every 20 minutes and spread out again on the trays.
5. Remove from the oven, place the trays on wire racks and leave to cool completely. Once cold, mix in the raisins and apricots and store in a sealed container.

CAMEMBERT TOAST WITH WARM GRAPE SAUCE

The combination of fruit and cheese is classic. This unusual way of serving it works well instead of a pudding or with a salad for lunch.

170g/6oz black or red seedless grapes
2 tablespoons red grape juice
½ tablespoon caster sugar
4 thick slices of brioche
225g/8oz Camembert cheese
salt and freshly ground black pepper

1. Preheat the grill.
2. Wash and halve the grapes. Place them in a saucepan with the grape juice and sugar and bring to the boil. Lower the heat and simmer for 2–3 minutes, stirring occasionally.
3. Meanwhile, toast the brioche on both sides and spread with the Camembert cheese. Return to the grill for 1 minute or until the cheese is beginning to soften.
4. Remove the grapes from the pan with a slotted spoon and keep warm. Bring the juices to the boil and reduce by half or until syrupy. Season with a little salt and pepper.
5. Put a piece of brioche on to each of the warmed serving plates, top with the grapes and pour over the syrupy juices. Serve immediately.

CAKES, BISCUITS AND BREADS

INTRODUCTION

Homemade cakes and cookies are delicious and need not be time-consuming to make. Apart from the incomparable taste of home baking, it is good to have control over the ingredients included. The addition of wholemeal flour, oats, nuts, seeds or dried fruit will improve the nutritional value and fibre content.

A good homemade loaf can make a meal of a snack, side dish or soup. In addition, bread provides carbohydrate, vitamins and minerals, especially when made with wholemeal flour. Strong wheat flour is most commonly used for breadmaking. This is ground from hard wheat with a high gluten content. Gluten is a protein that produces the sticky strands that make bread dough stretchy. Bread made with wholemeal flour is undoubtedly healthier but is also heavier than bread made with white flour. Maize and millet all lack gluten and are usually mixed with strong flour for breadmaking. Wholewheat and wholemeal flour are the same.

Traditionally bread is made with fresh baker's yeast. This is a single-cell organism which needs moisture, warmth and food to reproduce. The yeast produces carbon dioxide, which aerates the mixture. When the bread is cooked, the gas leaks out and is replaced by air. Dried yeast is granular and requires sponging to reconstitute it before use. If using dried yeast, only half the weight of fresh is needed. Easy-blend yeast looks the same as dried but can be mixed straight into the flour. 7g/¼oz easy-blend yeast is equivalent to 15g/½oz dried and 30g/1oz fresh. Bread made with this yeast needs only one rising.

Baked bread should be golden-brown and sound hollow when tapped on the underside. It should be cooled on a wire rack. It is delicious but slightly indigestible when still warm. After 2 hours the bread will slice easily. Make sure it is absolutely cold before storing in an airtight container or plastic bag.

APPLE AND PEAR CAKE

This cake does not contain eggs and is therefore fairly close textured. It is moist and keeps very well. It also freezes well.

oil, for brushing
225g/8oz cooking apples
110g/4oz pears
2 tablespoons water
110g/4oz butter
225g/8oz Caster Sugar
225g/8oz plain flour, sifted
1 teaspoon ground cinnamon
1 teaspoon bicarbonate of soda
170g/6oz dried fruit such as pears, peaches,
    apricots, raisins

1. Preheat the oven to 180°C/350°F/gas mark 4. Brush a 15cm/7in cake tin with oil and line the base with greased greaseproof paper.
2. Peel and core the apples and pears and cut into chunks. Put into a saucepan with the water. Cover and cook over a low heat, stirring occasionally, until pulpy. Beat with a wooden spoon to get rid of any lumps and set aside to cool.
3. Meanwhile, cream the butter in a mixing bowl and add the sugar. Beat together until light and fluffy.
4. Add the cooled fruit purée, flour, cinnamon, bicarbonate of soda and dried fruit. Mix well and turn into the prepared tin.
5. Bake in the centre of the oven for 1–1½ hours or until a skewer inserted into the middle of the cake comes out clean.
6. Remove the cake from the oven and allow to cool in the tin for 10 minutes before turning out on to a wire rack to cool completely.

NOTE: This cake can also be baked in a 900g/2lb loaf tin.

APRICOT AND CARROT STREUSEL CAKE

225g/8oz butter, plus extra for greasing
225g/8oz caster sugar
3 eggs, beaten
225g/8oz plain flour
1 teaspoon bicarbonate of soda
1 teaspoon baking powder
170ml/6fl oz milk
110g/4oz carrots, grated
140g/5oz dried apricots, chopped

For the streusel topping
110g/4oz soft light brown sugar
110g/4oz pecan nuts, chopped
55g/2oz plain flour
1½ tablespoons ground cinnamon
55g/2oz butter, melted

1. Preheat the oven to 180°C/350°F/gas mark 4. Grease a 20cm/8in loose-based cake tin with butter and line the base with greased greaseproof paper.
2. Cream the butter and sugar together until light and fluffy. Add the eggs a little at a time, beating well between each addition.
3. Sift the flour, bicarbonate of soda and baking powder together and fold carefully into the mixture, using a large metal spoon.
4. Add the milk and grated carrot. Put the mixture into the prepared tin, spreading it flat.
5. Put the dried apricots on top of the cake mixture.
6. Make the streusel topping: put the sugar, pecan nuts, flour and cinnamon into a bowl. Add the melted butter and mix well.
7. Bake in the centre of the preheated oven for 1–1½ hours or until a skewer inserted into the middle of the cake comes out clean. If the cake is not cooked, but the top is looking dark, lower the oven temperature slightly and cover with a piece of greased greaseproof paper. When the cake is cooked, remove from the oven and allow to cool for 10 minutes before removing from the tin and turning out on to a wire rack to cool completely.

BRÛLÉED LEMON RISOTTO CAKE

butter, for greasing
4–5 lemon verbena leaves (optional)
2 tablespoons semolina

For the cake
140g/5oz risotto rice
1.1 litre/2 pints full-cream milk
6 large eggs
110g/4oz Caster Sugar
4 tablespoons double cream
4 tablespoons Limoncello lemon liqueur or
    sweet dessert wine
finely grated zest of 2 lemons

For the topping
caster sugar

1. Preheat the oven to 150°C/300°F/gas mark 2. Grease a 25cm/10in cake tin generously with butter and lay the lemon verbena leaves, if used, in the base of the tin. Butter the leaves. Sprinkle over the semolina and carefully tap out the excess.
2. Put the rice and two-thirds of the milk into a large saucepan and bring to the boil, then drain.
3. Put the eggs and sugar into a large bowl and beat with an electric hand-held whisk until thick, light and fluffy.
4. Stir the rice into the egg mixture with the remaining milk, the cream, Limoncello liqueur or wine and the lemon zest. Pour into the prepared tin.
5. Bake in the centre of the oven for 45–50 minutes or until the cake is set and lightly browned and a skewer inserted into the middle comes out clean. Loosen the cake around the edges and leave to cool in the tin, then chill for at least 1 hour.
6. When cold, turn the cake out on to a baking sheet. Sprinkle the top with a layer of caster sugar.
7. Preheat the grill to its highest setting. Put the cake as close as possible to the heat until the sugar melts and caramelizes. Watch carefully, turning the cake if the sugar is browning unevenly. Alternatively this can be done using a blow torch.
8. Allow to cool completely before serving. The top should be hard and crackly.

BEST CARROT CAKE

butter, for greasing
200g/7oz plain flour
1 heaped teaspoon salt
1 teaspoon bicarbonate of soda
1½ teaspoons baking powder
1½ teaspoons ground cinnamon
225ml/8fl oz vegetable oil
225g/8oz soft light brown sugar
3 eggs
200g/7oz carrots, grated
85g/3oz walnuts, roughly chopped

For the icing
125g/4½oz cream cheese
110g/4oz icing sugar, sifted
1 teaspoon almond essence

1. Preheat the oven to 170°C/325°F/gas mark 3. Grease a 20cm/8in deep cake tin and line the base with greased greaseproof paper.
2. Sift together the flour, salt, bicarbonate of soda, baking powder and cinnamon. Whisk the oil and sugar together in a large bowl. Beat in the eggs one at a time until the mixture resembles mayonnaise. Fold in the flour mixture and then the carrots and walnuts.
3. Pour the mixture into the prepared tin and bake in the centre of the oven for 1–1½ hours until the cake is well risen and feels firm when pressed with the fingertips and a skewer inserted into the middle comes out clean. Remove the cake from the tin and cool on a wire rack.
4. Beat the cream cheese with a wooden spoon and add the icing sugar and almond essence. Spread over the top of the cake.

RICH CHOCOLATE AND PEACH CAKE

This is very rich and can be served either as a cake for a special occasion or as a pudding. It can be made in advance and frozen, then iced once it has defrosted.

55g/2oz dried peaches, chopped
3 tablespoons orange juice
2 tablespoons Grand Marnier
110g/4oz butter, plus extra for greasing
3 eggs, separated
110g/4oz caster sugar, plus 2 teaspoons
200g/7oz plain chocolate, chopped
55g/2oz self-raising flour
85g/3oz ground almonds

For the icing
110g/4oz plain chocolate, cut into pieces
100ml/3½fl oz double cream
2 tablespoons peach conserve
2 tablespoons Grand Marnier

1. Soak the peaches in the orange juice and Grand Marnier for at least 4 hours or overnight.
2. Preheat the oven to 180°C/350°F/gas mark 4. Grease a 20cm/8in deep cake tin with butter and line the base with greased greaseproof paper.
3. Beat the egg yolks with the 4oz sugar until pale and mousse-like.
4. Melt the chocolate in a heatproof bowl set over, not in, a pan of simmering water. Remove from the heat and stir in the butter piece by piece. Mix until smooth.
5. Sift the flour and mix with the ground almonds.
6. Whisk the egg whites until stiff but not dry, add the 2 teaspoons caster sugar and whisk again until shiny.
7. Fold the chocolate into the egg yolk mixture, add the flour and almonds and carefully fold in the egg whites, using a large metal spoon. Pour into the prepared tin and bake in the preheated oven for 30–40 minutes until the cake is still moist in the middle (do not overcook it).

Remove from the oven and allow to cool completely in the tin. When cold, remove from the tin and place upside down on a serving plate. Peel off the lining paper.
8. Meanwhile, make the icing: put the chocolate and cream into a small saucepan and heat carefully together until melted. Remove immediately from the heat and stir well. Allow to cool completely.
9. To finish the cake: mix together the peach conserve and Grand Marnier. Spread over the top and sides of the cake. Leave for about 1 hour.
10. Spread the chocolate icing very carefully over the top and sides of the cake. Finish by swirling the icing with a palette knife.

CRANBERRY AND CHERRY CAKE

oil, for brushing
140g/5oz self-raising flour
55g/2oz plain flour
85g/3oz ground almonds
75g/2½oz dried cranberries
75g/2½oz dried cherries
170g/6oz butter
170g/6oz caster sugar
3 eggs, beaten

1. Brush a 20cm/8in deep cake tin with oil and line the base with greased greaseproof paper. Preheat the oven to 170°C/325°F/gas mark 3.
2. Sift the flours together into a bowl and add the ground almonds, cranberries and cherries.
3. Cream the butter in a bowl, add the sugar and beat until light and fluffy. Add the eggs little by little, beating well between each addition.
4. Fold in the flour and fruit mixture and pour into the prepared tin. Spread flat.
5. Bake in the centre of the preheated oven for 45–60 minutes until the cake is risen and firm to the touch and a skewer inserted into the middle comes out clean. Turn out on to a wire rack and leave to cool.

NOTE: Take care if using a fan oven as this cake can easily dry out.

DATE AND ORANGE LOAF

85g/3oz butter, plus extra for greasing
285g/10oz dates, stoned
150ml/¼ pint orange juice
grated zest of 1 orange
55g/2oz muscovado sugar
a pinch of salt
110g/4oz self-raising flour
a pinch of bicarbonate of soda
55g/2oz walnuts or pecan nuts, roughly
  chopped (optional)

1. Preheat the oven to 150°C/300°F/gas mark 2. Grease a 450g/1lb loaf tin with butter and line the base with greased greaseproof paper.
2. Put the dates, orange juice and zest, butter, sugar and salt into a saucepan and cook over a low heat until the dates are softened, taking care not to let the mixture boil. Remove from the heat when the dates have formed a paste and allow to cool.
3. Sift the flour with the bicarbonate of soda into the cooled mixture and stir thoroughly. Add the nuts, if used. Turn into the prepared tin and level the surface. Bake in the centre of the preheated oven for 45–60 minutes or until a sharp knife inserted into the middle comes out clean.
4. Allow the loaf to cool completely in the tin before turning out.

NOTE: Stored in an airtight container, the loaf will keep moist for a week. It also freezes well.

FIG CRUMBLE CAKE

This cake is also delicious served hot with ice cream.

110g/4oz butter, plus extra for greasing
225g/8oz no-soak dried figs
3 tablespoons apple or orange juice
225g/8oz self-raising flour
½ teaspoon baking powder
½ teaspoon ground cinnamon
½ teaspoon ground ginger
grated zest of 1 lemon
140g/5oz soft light brown sugar

1. Preheat the oven to 190°C/375°F/gas mark 5. Grease a 17.5cm/7in spring-release cake tin with butter and line the base with greased greaseproof paper.
2. Slice the figs and put into a bowl with the fruit juice. Set aside.
3. Sift the flour into a large mixing bowl with the baking powder, cinnamon and ginger.
4. Add the lemon zest. Cut the butter into small pieces and rub into the flour until the mixture resembles fine breadcrumbs. Stir in 110g/4oz of the sugar, the fruit and juice and stir a couple of times so that the ingredients are loosely mixed together.
5. Spoon the mixture into the prepared tin. Sprinkle the top with the remaining brown sugar and bake in the centre of the preheated oven for 1–1¼ hours until the cake is golden-brown and a skewer inserted into the middle comes out clean. Cool slightly in the tin before turning out on to a wire rack. Leave to cool completely.

GINGER AND LEMON CAKE

This cake is made with grated raw potato. It is lovely and moist, with a slightly chewy crust.

melted lard or oil, for greasing
170g/6oz butter
170g/6oz soft dark brown sugar
3 eggs, beaten
170g/6oz self-raising flour
2 teaspoons ground ginger
2 teaspoons ground cinnamon
110g/4oz potato, grated

For the icing
170g/6oz icing sugar, sifted
2 tablespoons lemon juice
1 teaspoon finely grated lemon zest

1. Preheat the oven to 180°C/350°F/gas mark 4. Grease a 450g/1lb loaf tin and line the base with greased greaseproof paper.
2. Cream the butter and sugar together in a mixing bowl until light and fluffy. Add the eggs gradually, beating well between each addition. Add a little of the flour if necessary to prevent the mixture from curdling.
3. Sift the flour and spices together on to the mixture and fold in, using a large metal spoon. Fold in the grated potato. Turn into the prepared tin.
4. Bake in the centre of the oven for 50–60 minutes or until the top of the cake springs back when pressed lightly with a fingertip. Leave to cool in the tin for 10 minutes, then turn out on to a wire rack and leave to cool completely.
5. When the cake is cold, make the icing: mix the icing sugar with the lemon juice and zest. Spread on top of the cake and leave to set.

NOTE: The cake will keep well for 4–5 days in a tin or it can be frozen.

LEMON AND POPPY-SEED LOAF CAKE

140g/5oz butter, softened, plus extra for
   greasing
140g/5oz caster sugar
grated zest of 1 lemon
2 eggs
140g/5oz self-raising flour
30g/1oz poppy seeds
110ml/4fl oz milk

For the topping
2 tablespoons icing sugar
juice of 1 lemon

1. Preheat the oven to 180°C/350°F/gas mark 4.
Grease a 900g/2lb loaf tin with butter and line
the base with greased greaseproof paper.
2. Put the butter, sugar and lemon zest into a
mixing bowl and beat until light and fluffy.
3. Break the eggs into a bowl and whisk
together with a fork. Gradually beat into the
creamed mixture a little at a time. Sift in the
flour and add the poppy seeds. Carefully fold
into the mixture, adding enough milk to give a
soft dropping consistency. Spoon the mixture
into the prepared tin and spread flat. Bake in
the centre of the preheated oven for 40 minutes
until golden-brown and firm to the touch.
4. Mix the icing sugar with the lemon juice.
Prick the top of the cake with a fork and pour
the juice mixture over the cake while still warm.
Leave to cool for 15 minutes, then turn out and
leave to cool completely on a wire rack.

PARSNIP AND PECAN NUT CAKE

This is an all-in-one recipe and is quick to
make. The cake does not rise very much. If a
deep cake is required, double the quantities and
bake in 2 tins. Sandwich the cakes together with
the icing and dust with icing sugar before
serving.

For the cake
oil, for brushing
140g/5oz plain flour
2 teaspoons baking powder
140g/5oz parsnips, grated
55g/2oz pecan nuts, chopped
1 teaspoon peeled and grated fresh root ginger
1 egg, lightly beaten
a pinch of salt
150ml/¼ pint sunflower oil
140g/5oz caster sugar

For the icing
85g/3oz unsalted butter, softened
110g/4oz cream cheese
55g/2oz icing sugar, sieved
2 tablespoons orange juice
110ml/4fl oz water
2 tablespoons caster sugar
pared zest of 1 orange, cut into thin strips

1. Preheat the oven to 180°C/350°F/gas mark 4.
Brush a 20cm/8in moule manqué or sandwich
tin with oil. Line the base with oiled
greaseproof paper.
2. Put all the cake ingredients into a large
mixing bowl and mix together thoroughly.
Turn into the prepared tin.
3. Bake in the centre of the preheated oven for
about 30 minutes or until a skewer inserted into
the middle of the cake comes out clean.
4. Remove the cake from the oven and leave to
cool completely in the tin.
5. Meanwhile, make the icing: put the butter
into a bowl and beat until smooth. Gradually
add the cream cheese, beating all the time. Add
the icing sugar and orange juice and continue
beating until light and fluffy. Chill.

6. Put the water and sugar into a small saucepan and heat slowly until all the sugar has dissolved. Add the orange zest and bring to the boil, then boil for 5 minutes. Using a slotted spoon, remove the zest and leave on kitchen paper to drain and cool.

7. When the cake is cold, remove from the tin, spread with the icing and decorate with the orange zest.

RASPBERRY AND COCONUT POLENTA CAKE

55g/2oz unsalted butter, softened, plus extra for
  greasing
plain flour, for dusting
30g/1oz desiccated coconut
grated zest and juice of 1 lime
110g/4oz caster sugar
2 eggs, separated
85g/3oz quick-cook polenta

For the topping
110g/4oz mascarpone
icing sugar
225g/8oz raspberries

1. Preheat the oven to 180°C/350°F/gas mark 4. Grease a 17.5cm/7in sandwich tin with butter, line the base with greased greaseproof paper and dust the base and sides with flour. Tap out the excess.

2. Put the coconut and lime zest into a bowl and mix with the lime juice.

3. Beat the butter with 85g/3oz of the sugar until light and fluffy. Beat in the egg yolks one at a time, adding a teaspoonful of polenta wih each yolk. Fold in the remaining polenta and the coconut and lime mixture.

4. Whisk the egg whites to soft peaks. Gradually whisk in the remaining sugar until the mixture is very stiff. Loosen the polenta mixture with 1 tablespoon of the whisked egg white then fold in the remainder, using a large metal spoon. Turn the mixture into the prepared tin and bake in the centre of the preheated oven for 1 hour until the cake feels

firm when pressed with the fingertips. Remove from the oven and leave in the tin for 10 minutes before turning on to a wire rack to cool.

5. When the cake is completely cold, sweeten the mascarpone with icing sugar to taste. Spread over the top of the cake and decorate with the raspberries.

APPLE FLAPJACKS

170g/6oz butter, plus extra for greasing
1 medium cooking apple
30g/1oz sultanas
140g/5oz soft light brown sugar
55g//2oz wholemeal self-raising flour
170g/6oz rolled oats

1. Preheat the oven to 180°C/350°F/gas mark 4. Grease a 20cm/8in square tin with butter and line the base with greased greaseproof paper.

2. Peel, core, quarter and grate the apple. Put it into a saucepan with the sultanas and 30g/1oz of the sugar. Heat the mixture and simmer gently for 5 minutes until the apple begins to thicken slightly.

3. Melt the butter in a separate pan. Stir in the flour, oats and the remaining sugar. Spread half of this mixture over the base of the prepared tin. Spread the apple mixture on top. Top with the remaining oat mixture and spread evenly. Bake in the preheated oven for 30–40 minutes until golden-brown. Cool before cutting into fingers.

DATE, FIG AND MACADAMIA NUT CRUMBLE SHORTCAKES

For the shortcake base
110g/4oz unsalted butter
55g/2oz caster sugar
grated zest of 2 lemons
170g/6oz plain flour
a pinch of salt

For the fruit layer
85g/3oz dried dates, stoned
85g/3oz no-soak dried figs
85g/3oz no-soak dried prunes, pitted

For the crumble
85g/3oz plain flour
a pinch of salt
55g/2oz butter, diced
30g/1oz caster sugar
85g/3oz macadamia nuts, roughly chopped
icing sugar, for dusting

1. Preheat the oven to 190°C/375°F/gas mark 5.
2. Make the shortcake base: beat the butter, sugar and lemon zest together until light and fluffy.
3. Work in the flour and salt with a wooden spoon and bring together to form a dough. Knead lightly, then roll into a square 1cm/½in thick on a baking sheet. Chill for 10 minutes.
4. Bake the shortcake base in the preheated oven for 15 minutes or until dry to the touch and a pale biscuit colour.
5. Prepare the fruit layer: process the diced fruit in a food processor until it forms a thick paste, or chop finely by hand. Set aside.
6. Make the crumble topping: sift the flour and salt into a bowl. Rub in the butter until the mixture resembles coarse breadcrumbs. Stir in the sugar and chopped nuts.
7. Spread the fruit purée over the shortcake base. Top with the crumble mixture and bake in the centre of the hot oven for 15–20 minutes or until the topping is crisp and brown. Transfer to a wire rack and allow to cool. Dust with icing sugar and cut into squares.

DATE AND ORANGE SLICES

oil, for greasing
285g/10oz dates, stoned
4 tablespoons lemon juice
4 tablespoons orange juice
grated zest of 1 orange
225g/8oz plain flour
110g/4oz porridge oats
½ teaspoon ground mixed spice
140g/5oz butter, melted
1 tablespoon sesame seeds

1. Preheat the oven to 200°C/400°F/gas mark 6. Brush a 22.5cm/9in square cake tin very lightly with oil.
2. Put the dates and the lemon and orange juices into a saucepan together with the orange zest. Cook over a very low heat until the dates form a paste.
3. Meanwhile, combine the flour, porridge oats and spice together in a bowl with the melted butter. Mix thoroughly.
4. Put half the oat mixture in the bottom of the prepared tin and press down firmly with the back of a spoon. Spoon over the date paste and level. Cover with the remaining oat mixture and level gently. Sprinkle with the sesame seeds.
5. Bake in the centre of the preheated oven for 20–25 minutes. Mark into 9 squares and leave to cool completely in the tin. Cut into squares and store in an airtight container.

PUMPKIN MUFFINS

These muffins make a delicious dessert served warm with ice cream.

MAKES 12

100ml/4fl oz sunflower or vegetable oil
110g/4oz soft light brown sugar
2 eggs
110g/4oz self-raising flour
½ teaspoon baking powder
½ teaspoon bicarbonate of soda
1 teaspoon ground cinnamon
½ teaspoon salt
30g/1oz chopped dates
140g/5oz pumpkin or butternut squash, peeled, deseeded and grated

1. Preheat the oven to 190°C/375°F/gas mark 5. Line a tray of 12 muffin tins with paper cases.
2. Whisk the oil and sugar together and beat in the eggs one at a time until the mixture resembles mayonnaise.
3. Sift the flour with the baking powder, bicarbonate of soda, cinnamon and salt. Fold into the mixture together with the dates and pumpkin or squash. Spoon into the muffin cases and bake in the centre of the preheated oven for 20–30 minutes until risen and firm when pressed lightly in the centre.

SWEET POTATO AND APPLE MUFFINS

MAKES 12

340g/12oz sweet potatoes
110ml/4fl oz water
225g/8oz cooking apples
225g/8oz plain flour
1 teaspoon bicarbonate of soda
1 teaspoon ground cinnamon
½ teaspoon freshly grated nutmeg
140g/5oz caster sugar
110g/4oz butter
1 egg
110ml/4fl oz milk
85g/3oz dried apricots, chopped

1. Preheat the oven to 180°C/350°F/gas mark 4. Line a tray of 12 large muffin tins with paper cases.
2. Peel the sweet potato and cut into small dice. Put into a saucepan with the water. Bring to the boil, cover and cook over a very low heat for 5–10 minutes, stirring occasionally. Do not let the mixture dry out and add more water if necessary.
3. Peel and core the apples and cut into small dice. Add to the softened sweet potato. Cook over a low heat until the apple is soft. Ensure the mixture does not dry out and add more water if necessary. Mash with a fork or potato masher to remove any lumps. Allow to cool.
4. Sift the flour with the bicarbonate of soda, cinnamon and nutmeg into a large bowl. Add the sugar.
5. Melt the butter and allow to cool.
6. Mix the egg and milk together and add to the sweet potato mixture. Add the cooled butter and apricots.
7. Make a well in the centre of the flour mixture and pour in the sweet potato mixture. Mix quickly and thoroughly, using a hand whisk or a fork.
8. Spoon the mixture into the muffin cases. Bake in the centre of the preheated oven for 30 minutes or until the muffins are risen and firm and spring back when pressed lightly.

CHOCOLATE AND PEANUT BUTTER BROWNIES

140g/5oz plain chocolate, chopped
110g/4oz butter
225g/8oz caster sugar
170g/6oz plain flour
½ teaspoon baking powder
170g/6oz crunchy peanut butter
3 eggs, beaten

1. Preheat the oven to 170°C/325°F/gas mark 3. Line a 20cm/8in square tin with non-stick baking paper.
2. Melt the chocolate, butter and sugar together in a heatproof bowl set over, not in, a pan of simmering water. Allow to cool.
3. Sift the flour and baking powder together into a large bowl.
4. Mix the peanut butter into the chocolate mixture.
5. Make a well in the centre of the flour. Add the eggs and chocolate mixture and gradually draw in the flour, using a hand whisk to beat out any lumps. Pour the mixture into the prepared tin and level out.
6. Bake in the centre of the preheated oven for 20 minutes until the crust has set on the top and a sharp knife inserted into the centre comes out slightly wet. Remove from the oven and allow to cool in the tin before cutting into squares.

NOTE: If these brownies are cooked for too long they become very dry.

CRACKED BLACK PEPPER BISCUITS

110g/4oz butter
55g/2oz caster sugar
110g/4oz plain flour
55g/2oz cornflour
1 teaspoon peppercorns, crushed in a mortar
caster sugar, for dusting

1. Preheat the oven to 170°C/325°F/gas mark 3.
2. Beat the butter in a bowl until soft, add the sugar and beat until light and fluffy.
3. Sift in the flours, add the peppercorns and work to a smooth paste.
4. Roll out the dough to the thickness of a £1 coin and stamp into rounds with a pastry cutter. Place on an ungreased baking sheet and chill for 10 minutes.
5. Bake in the preheated oven for 15–20 minutes. Remove from the oven, transfer to a wire rack to cool and dust with caster sugar while still hot.

NOTE: If you do not have a pestle and mortar, the peppercorns can be crushed in a saucepan using the end of a rolling pin.

PESTO BISCUITS

225g/8oz flour quantity shortcrust pastry (see page 521)
plain flour, for rolling
3 tablespoons red pesto
10–12 large fresh basil leaves, roughly torn
110g/4oz Parmesan cheese, freshly grated
freshly ground black pepper
1 egg beaten, to glaze

1. Preheat the oven to 200°C/400°F/gas mark 6.
2. Roll the pastry out thinly on a lightly floured worktop.
3. Spread the pesto over the pastry, almost to the edges, and scatter over the basil leaves. Sprinkle with 85g/3oz of the cheese and season with pepper.
4. Fold the pastry in half and with a lightly floured rolling pin, carefully roll the pastry back to its original size or until the pesto just begins to show through.
5. Brush the pastry with beaten egg and sprinkle over the remaining cheese. Cut the pastry into triangles or, using a pastry cutter, stamp into rounds. Place on a baking sheet and chill for 15 minutes.
6. Bake at the top of the preheated oven for 5–7 minutes or until the biscuits are browned and the cheese is bubbling. Transfer to a wire rack and allow to cool completely.

CHEESE AND DOUBLE ONION CREAM CRACKERS

1 tablespoon vegetable oil
2 onions, very thinly sliced
45g/1½oz butter, diced, plus extra for greasing
225g/8oz plain flour, plus extra for rolling
¼ teaspoon salt
1 teaspoon baking powder
45g/1½oz Gruyère cheese, grated
½ teaspoon black onion seeds
5 tablespoons soured cream
1 egg, beaten, to glaze

1. Heat the oil in a pan and add the onions. Cover and cook over a low heat for 30–45 minutes or until very soft but not coloured. Drain in a sieve and allow to cool completely.
2. Preheat the oven to 200°C/400°F/gas mark 6. Grease 2 baking sheets with butter.
3. Sift the flour, salt and baking powder into a large bowl. Rub in the butter until the mixture resembles coarse breadcrumbs. Stir in the cheese and onion seeds.
4. Using a knife, mix in the soured cream and cooled onions and bring together to form a dough.
5. Roll the dough out thinly on a lightly floured worktop. Using a sharp knife, cut the dough into 7.5 × 3.5cm/3 × 1½in strips. Brush with beaten egg and transfer to the prepared baking sheets.
6. Bake the crackers on the top shelf of the preheated oven for 10–12 minutes or until crisp and golden-brown. Transfer to a wire rack to cool.

PARMESAN AND TOMATO SABLÉS

110g/4oz wholemeal flour
1 level teaspoon baking powder
a good pinch of cayenne pepper
110g/4oz butter, chilled and diced
6 sun-dried tomatoes in oil, drained and
  chopped
55g/2oz Parmesan cheese, freshly grated
55g/2oz Cheddar cheese, grated
½ teaspoon dried oregano
2 egg yolks
plain flour, for rolling

1. Preheat the oven to 220°C/425°F/gas mark 7.
2. Sift the flour, baking powder and cayenne into a mixing bowl. Rub in the butter until the mixture resembles breadcrumbs.
3. Add the sun-dried tomatoes with the cheeses and oregano. Stir in the egg yolks to bind to a stiff dough. Wrap in clingfilm and chill for at least 1 hour.
4. Knead the dough to a smooth ball on a well-floured worktop and roll out about 1cm/½in thick. Stamp out 5cm/2in rounds with a pastry cutter and put on to an ungreased baking sheet. Bake in the preheated oven for 10 minutes until golden-brown. Leave to cool for 2 minutes before lifting on to a wire rack to cool completely.

BLUE CHEESE AND APPLE FILO PARCELS

Any hard blue cheese can be used in this recipe.

55g/2oz butter
2 shallots, finely chopped
1 clove of garlic, crushed
225g/8oz cooking apples
140g/5oz hard blue cheese, such as Stilton
1 tablespoon chopped fresh sage
salt and freshly ground black pepper
4 large sheets of filo pastry
1 egg, beaten

1. Preheat the oven to 200°C/400°F/gas mark 6.
2. Melt 15g/½oz of the butter in a saucepan, add the shallots and garlic and sweat over a low heat for 5 minutes until softened but not coloured.
3. Peel, quarter and core the apples. Cut into very small dice. Chop the cheese into small pieces and combine with the apple. Add the sage, salt, pepper and the shallots.
4. Melt the remaining butter and brush it over a sheet of filo pastry. Cut the pastry in half lengthways. Put a spoonful of the filling at one end of each strip. Form a triangle by folding the right-hand corner over to the opposite side and then fold across from the left-hand corner to the right-hand edge. Continue folding until the pastry is used up. Place on a baking sheet and brush well with beaten egg. Continue in the same way to make 8 parcels in all.
5. Bake the parcels in the preheated oven for 10–15 minutes until golden-brown and crisp.

CHEESE CHOUX PUFFS WITH CAPER SAUCE

2-egg quantity choux pastry (see page 524)
2 tablespoons freshly grated Parmesan cheese

For the filling
140g/5oz Cheddar cheese, grated
1 tablespoon chopped fresh thyme
1 egg, beaten
a pinch of cayenne pepper
salt and freshly ground black pepper

For the sauce
150ml/¼ pint double cream
½ tablespoon Dijon mustard
1 tablespoon small capers, rinsed

1. Preheat the oven to 200°C/400°F/gas mark 6.
2. Make the choux pastry and add the
Parmesan cheese to the mixture after all the egg
has been beaten in. Place teaspoonfuls of the
mixture on baking sheets, about 5cm/2in apart.
3. Bake in the preheated oven for 20–30
minutes until the buns are puffed up and
browned. (If they are removed from the oven
too soon they will be soggy when cool.)
4. Using a skewer, make a hole the size of a pea
in the base of each bun and return to the oven
for 5 minutes to allow the insides to dry out.
Leave to cool on a wire rack.
5. Meanwhile, make the filling: mix the
Cheddar cheese, thyme, egg and cayenne
together in a bowl. Season with salt and pepper.
6. Once the buns are cold, make a large hole in
the base and stuff with the cheese filling. Place
in a shallow ovenproof dish.
7. Mix the cream, mustard and capers together
and season carefully with salt and pepper.
8. Pour the caper sauce round the buns and
bake in the hot oven for 10 minutes. Serve
immediately.

HOT BUTTERED RADISHES WITH BRIE AND SOUR APPLE SCONES

For the scones
225g/8oz self-raising flour, plus extra for rolling
  and dusting
85g/3oz Brie
a pinch of salt
55g/2oz butter, diced
1 small cooking apple, unpeeled and grated
3 tablespoons buttermilk

For the topping
55g/2oz unsalted butter
1 large bunch of radishes, washed and trimmed
salt and freshly ground black pepper
1 tablespoon lemon juice
55g/2oz rocket, roughly chopped

1. Preheat the oven to 190°C/375°F/gas mark 5.
Dust a baking sheet with flour.
2. Freeze the Brie for 10 minutes, then grate
coarsely and set aside.
3. Make the scones: sift the flour and salt into a
bowl and rub in the butter until the mixture
resembles coarse breadcrumbs. Stir in the
grated apple and Brie.
4. Using a knife, mix in the buttermilk to form
a softish dough. Turn the mixture on to a
floured worktop and flatten slightly with the
palm of your hand.
5. Lightly flour a large pastry cutter and stamp
out 4 rounds. Dust with flour and transfer to
the prepared baking sheet. Bake on the top shelf
of the preheated oven for 10–12 minutes or until
well risen and golden-brown. Allow to cool
slightly.
6. Meanwhile, make the topping: melt the
butter in a frying pan and when foaming, add
the radishes, season with salt and pepper and
fry briskly for 1–2 minutes or until just
beginning to brown, then stir in the lemon juice.
7. Split the scones and put 2 halves on to each
of 4 individual plates. Divide the rocket
between the scones and top with the hot
radishes. Pour over the buttery juices and serve
immediately.

BUTTERMILK AND ONION SEED SCONES WITH CHIVE BUTTER

For the scones
225g/8oz self-raising flour, plus extra for rolling and dusting
½ teaspoon salt
30g/1oz butter
2 teaspoons black onion seeds
85g/3oz Parmesan cheese, freshly grated
150ml/¼ pint buttermilk

For the chive butter
110g/4oz unsalted butter, softened
1 bunch of fresh chives, finely chopped
freshly ground black pepper
lemon juice

1. Preheat the oven to 220°C/425°F/gas mark 7. Dust a baking sheet with flour.
2. Make the scones: sift the flour and salt into a large bowl.
3. Rub in the butter until the mixture resembles coarse breadcrumbs. Stir in the onion seeds and cheese.
4. Make a deep well in the centre of the flour, pour in the buttermilk and mix to a soft, spongy dough with a knife.
5. Knead the dough very lightly on a floured worktop until just smooth. Roll out about 2.5cm/1 in thick and using a pastry cutter, stamp into small rounds.
6. Dust the scones with flour and bake at the top of the preheated oven for 7 minutes or until well risen and brown.
7. Make the chive butter: mix together the softened butter and chives. Season to taste with pepper and a dash of lemon juice.
8. Serve the scones warm, spread with the chive butter.

WATERCRESS SCONE ROUND WITH LIME BUTTER

225g/8oz self-raising flour, plus extra for rolling and dusting
½ teaspoon salt
55g/2oz butter
85g/3oz watercress, washed and stalks removed
150ml/¼ pint buttermilk
1 egg, beaten to glaze

For the lime butter
85g/3oz unsalted butter
finely grated zest and juice of 1 lime
freshly ground black pepper

1. Preheat the oven to 220°C/425°F/gas mark 7. Dust a baking sheet with flour.
2. Sift the flour and salt into a large mixing bowl. Rub in the butter until the mixture resembles coarse breadcrumbs.
3. Finely chop the watercress and stir into the mixture.
4. Make a deep well in the centre, stir in the buttermilk and mix to a soft, spongy dough with a knife.
5. Knead the dough very lightly on a floured worktop until just smooth. Shape the dough into a large round with floured hands and with a large knife, mark into 6 wedges. Brush the scone round with beaten egg.
6. Put the scone on to the prepared baking sheet and bake at the top of the preheated oven for about 15–20 minutes until well risen and brown. Remove from the oven and cool on a wire rack.
7. Make the lime butter: beat the butter, lime zest and juice together and season with pepper. Break the scone into wedges, split and spread with the lime butter.

PIROSHKI WITH SAGE AND ONION FILLING

MAKES 16

For the dough
285g/10oz unbleached strong white flour, plus
    extra for kneading and dusting
140g/5oz wholemeal flour
55g/2oz cornmeal
1 teaspoon salt
225ml/8fl oz water
15g/½oz fresh yeast
1 teaspoon caster sugar
3 tablespoons olive oil

For the filling
15g/½oz butter
1 large onion, finely chopped
salt and freshly ground black pepper
2 teaspoons roughly chopped fresh sage
30g/1oz Cheddar cheese, grated

1. Make the dough: sift the flours and cornmeal with the salt into a warmed mixing bowl. Make a well in the centre.
2. Heat the water to blood temperature. Cream the yeast and sugar together in a jug. Mix with the water, add the oil and pour into the well. Mix thoroughly.
3. Knead the dough on a floured worktop for 10–15 minutes or until smooth and elastic. Put into a clean bowl and cover with lightly oiled clingfilm. Leave to prove in a warm place for about 1 hour until doubled in bulk.
4. Make the filling: melt the butter in a small saucepan and add the onion. Season with salt and pepper, cover and cook over a very low heat until the onion is transparent. Add the sage and allow to cool slightly before adding the cheese. Cool completely.
5. Preheat the oven to 200°C/400°F/gas mark 6.
6. Knock back the dough on a lightly floured worktop. Divide into 16 equal pieces and knead into smooth balls. With the palm of the hand press each ball flat, put a small amount of the filling into the centre and gather the dough around the filling making sure it is thoroughly sealed. Repeat with each dough ball. Place on a floured baking sheet, smooth side uppermost, and leave to prove for 5 minutes. Dust lightly with white flour and bake in the preheated oven for 10–15 minutes. Remove from the oven and allow to cool for at least 10 minutes before serving.

SAVOURY AMERICAN PANCAKES

These are ideal for brunch or a quick teatime snack.

For the batter
225g/8oz self-raising flour
½ teaspoon baking powder
a pinch of salt
2 eggs, beaten
290ml/½ pint milk
30g/1oz butter, melted
oil, for frying

For the spiced butter
85g/3oz butter, softened
1 teaspoon cumin seeds, toasted and ground
    (see page 22)
1 tablespoon chopped fresh coriander
salt and freshly ground black pepper
lemon juice

1. First make the spiced butter: beat the butter until soft. Stir in the cumin seeds and coriander and season with salt, pepper and a dash of lemon juice. Spoon the butter on to a sheet of greaseproof paper or kitchen foil. Roll up in a cylinder and twist the ends. Chill.
2. Make the batter: sift the flour, baking powder and salt into a large mixing bowl. Make a well in the centre and put the eggs and a little of the milk into it. Mix with a wooden spoon, gradually drawing in the flour. Keep adding the milk, stirring slowly, until the batter is smooth and the consistency of double cream. Stir in the melted butter.
3. Heat a heavy frying pan. Brush a thin film of oil over the base of the pan. When you see a

heat haze begin to rise from the pan, drop in 2 tablespoons of batter. The batter should sizzle slightly and spread out to about 10cm/4in in diameter. When holes appear on top, turn the pancakes over and cook for a further minute. Continue in the same way until all the batter is used up, brushing the pan with more oil from time to time. Cut the spiced butter into slices. Top each pancake with a slice of butter just before serving.

ALTERNATIVE FLAVOURINGS:

Sweetcorn and Roasted Red Pepper Core, deseed and quarter ½ a red pepper. Cook skin side up under a hot grill until the skin is black and charred. Cool, remove the skin and chop the flesh finely. Fold into the pancake batter with 2 tablespoons sweetcorn kernels. Cook as described above.

Goat's Cheese and Herbs Fold 1 tablespoon chopped fresh chives, 1 tablespoon chopped fresh basil and 4 black olives, pitted and chopped, into the pancake batter. Cook the pancakes on one side as described above. Crumble on 110g/4oz mild goat's cheese, dividing it between the pancakes. Turn over and cook the other side.

Red Onion and Pinenut Thinly slice 1 medium red onion and fry in 1 tablespoon oil until soft. Cool, stir into the pancake batter with 1 tablespoon chopped fresh parsley or chives and 55g/2oz toasted pinenuts and cook as described above.

COCONUT PANCAKES WITH PINEAPPLE AND CORIANDER SALSA

SERVES 6

For the pancakes
110g/4oz plain flour
110g/4oz cornflour
1 × 400ml/14fl oz can of coconut milk
5 tablespoons water
2 eggs
a pinch of ground cumin
salt and freshly ground black pepper
oil, for frying

For the salsa
*2 × 140g/5oz cans of pineapple chunks in
  natural juice, drained and chopped*
*½ small bulb of fennel, cored and very finely
  chopped*
1 small red onion, very finely chopped
*4 large tomatoes, peeled, deseeded and diced
  (see page 22)*
110g/4oz fresh coriander, roughly chopped
finely grated zest of 1 lime
4 tablespoons extra virgin olive oil

To garnish
lime wedges
fresh coriander leaves

1. First make the pancakes: put all the ingredients except for the oil into a blender and process for 30 seconds. Taste for seasoning, cover and chill.
2. Make the salsa: mix together all the ingredients in a medium bowl, season with salt and pepper, cover and chill.
3. Heat a little oil in a large frying pan and pour in a ladleful of the batter. Cook for 30–45 seconds, then turn and repeat on the other side until lightly browned. Remove from the pan and keep warm. Repeat with the remaining batter.
4. Put a spoonful of the salsa on each pancake, roll up or fold into triangles, and garnish with a wedge of lime and a sprig of coriander.

GARLIC AND SESAME PITTA BREAD

MAKES 6

55g/2oz butter
2 cloves of garlic, crushed
salt and freshly ground black pepper
6 pitta breads
1 tablespoon sesame seeds, lightly toasted (see page 22)

1. Put the butter, garlic, salt and pepper into a small saucepan and leave over a very low heat for 5 minutes.
2. Preheat the grill to high. Lightly toast the pitta bread on both sides. Remove and brush with some of the garlic butter. Sprinkle with a few sesame seeds and slide back under the grill for a few seconds until the butter is sizzling. Remove and cut into chunky fingers. Serve warm.

POPPY-SEED PIZZA WITH FETA CHEESE, PEARS AND PARMESAN

1 × 450g/1lb packet pizza mix
2 teaspoons salt
2 tablespoons poppy seeds
3 firm, ripe pears
3 tablespoons apple juice
170g/6oz mascarpone
85g/3oz feta cheese
85g/3oz Parmesan cheese, freshly grated
freshly ground black pepper
55g/2oz shavings of Parmesan cheese

1. Preheat the oven to 200°C/400°F/gas mark 6.
2. Make up the pizza mix with the salt and poppy seeds according to the packet instructions. Leave to rise in a warm place for 40–50 minutes.
3. Peel and core the pears. Cut them into quarters and cut each quarter into 3 slices. Put the pear slices into a bowl with the apple juice and toss together.
4. Roll the pizza dough into 2 × 22.5cm/9in circles and place on a baking sheet. Spread the mascarpone over the surface of the pizza bases, leaving a 2.5cm/1in border round the edges.
5. Arrange the pear slices overlapping on the mascarpone, crumble over the feta cheese and sprinkle with the Parmesan cheese. Season with pepper.
5. Bake the pizzas on the top shelf of the preheated oven for 30 minutes. Remove from the oven and sprinkle the Parmesan shavings on top. Bake for a further 15 minutes or until the crust is brown and the cheese bubbling. Serve hot.

MINT AND THYME SODA ROLLS

The secret of good soda bread is to make the dough soft and to handle it as little as possible once it is mixed.

30g/1oz butter, plus extra for greasing
340g/12oz wholemeal flour
110g/4oz plain flour
1 teaspoon salt
1 teaspoon bicarbonate of soda
2 teaspoons cream of tartar
1 teaspoon sugar
2 tablespoons chopped fresh mint
1 tablespoon chopped fresh thyme
290ml/½ pint buttermilk or yoghurt

1. Preheat the oven to 190°C/375°F/gas mark 5. Grease a baking tray with butter.
2. Sift all the dry ingredients together into a large bowl and rub in the butter until the mixture resembles breadcrumbs.
3. Add the mint and thyme and make a well in the centre of the flour.
4. Pour in the milk and mix together with a knife and then with one hand to form a soft dough. Add more milk if necessary.
5. Divide the dough into 8 equal pieces and shape each piece very quickly into a roll. Place on the prepared baking tray.
6. Using the floured handle of a wooden spoon, mark a deep cross in each roll.
7. Bake in the preheated oven for 15 minutes. Remove from the oven and cool on a wire rack. Serve warm with yoghurt and herb cheeses (see page 516) or soup.

MEDITERRANEAN 'CHELSEA BUNS'

MAKES 8

450g/1lb flour quantity Italian bread dough (see page 531)
flour, for kneading
oil for greasing

For the filling
1 red pepper, halved and deseeded
1 yellow pepper, halved and deseeded
1 large courgette
3 tablespoons extra virgin olive oil
2 plum tomatoes, peeled, quartered and deseeded (see page 22)
a handful of fresh basil leaves, shredded
1½ tablespoons balsamic vinegar
salt and freshly ground black pepper
1 clove of garlic, crushed

1. Lightly oil a 20cm/8in round cake tin. Preheat the grill to its highest setting.
2. Grill the peppers skin side up until they are black and blistered. Place in a bowl and cover with a plate. Leave to cool, then skin and cut the flesh into strips.
3. Top and tail the courgette, then, using a vegetable peeler, shred into long ribbons.
4. Heat 1 tablespoon of the oil in a griddle pan and cook the courgettes for 30–45 seconds on each side or until browned.
5. Put the peppers and courgettes into a bowl and add the tomatoes and basil. Pour over the vinegar and season with salt and pepper.
6. On a floured worktop, roll the dough into a 25cm/10in square. Mix the garlic with the remaining oil and brush over the surface of the dough.
7. Preheat the oven to 200°C/400°F/gas mark 6.
8. Spread the vegetables over the dough and roll up like a Swiss roll. Cut into 3.5cm/½in slices. Arrange cut side up in the cake tin.
9. Bake in the preheated oven for 20–25 minutes. Transfer to a wire rack and leave to cool before separating the buns.

NOTE: These savoury buns are particularly good served with a soft, creamy goat's cheese.

HOT PLUM AND CAMBOZOLA CIABATTA ROLLS

55g/2oz unsalted butter
340g/12oz red plums, stones removed and
  quartered
1 tablespoon soft dark brown sugar
1 tablespoon water
1 tablespoon balsamic vinegar
salt and freshly ground black pepper
2 ciabatta rolls, split horizontally
170g/6oz Cambozola cheese, cut into 4 wedges

1. Preheat the grill to its highest setting.
2. Melt the butter in a large frying pan and when foaming, add the plums and sugar. Cook over a low heat for 2–3 minutes or until beginning to brown.
3. Pour in the water and vinegar and season with salt and pepper. Lower the heat and cook for a further 5–10 minutes or until the plums are tender and the juices syrupy.
4. Meanwhile, toast the rolls on both sides. Put a slice of cheese on to the cut side of each of the rolls and return to the grill until the cheese is just beginning to melt. Place the rolls on warmed serving plates and top with the plums. Pour over the syrupy juices and serve immediately.

QUICK SESAME ROLLS

butter, for greasing
340g/12oz strong white or granary flour, plus
  extra for kneading
a large pinch of salt
5g/about ½ sachet of easy-blend dried yeast
2 teaspoons olive or vegetable oil
190ml/⅓ pint warm water
beaten egg, to glaze
30g/1oz sesame seeds

1. Preheat the oven to 230°C/450°F/gas mark 8. Grease a baking tray with butter.
2. Sift the flour into a mixing bowl with the salt. Make a well in the centre and add the yeast and oil. Add enough water to mix to a soft but not sticky dough.
3. Knead the dough on a floured worktop for 5–10 minutes until very smooth and elastic. Shape into 6 rolls and place on the prepared baking tray. Leave in a warm place to rise until doubled in bulk.
4. Brush the rolls with beaten egg and scatter with sesame seeds. Bake for 10–15 minutes until they are golden-brown and sound hollow when tapped on the underside.

APPLE AND CIDER BREAD

225g/8oz dried apples, finely chopped
325ml/11½fl oz dry cider
55g/2oz butter
15g/½oz fresh yeast
225g/8oz strong plain flour, plus extra for
* kneading*
225g/8oz malted brown flour
1 teaspoon salt
1 egg, beaten

1. Put the apple pieces, cider and butter into a small saucepan. Bring to the boil, then remove from the heat and leave to cool.
2. Mix 2 tablespoons of the cooled liquid with the yeast until creamy.
3. Sift the flours and salt into a large mixing bowl and make a well in the centre.
4. Put the yeast into the well and strain on the juice from the saucepan (reserve the apples). Mix to a soft, pliable dough with a round-bladed knife.
5. When the dough leaves the sides of the bowl, press it into a ball and tip it out on to a lightly floured worktop. Knead for about 10 minutes until smooth, elastic and shiny.
6. Put the dough back into the clean bowl and cover with a piece of lightly oiled clingfilm. Leave in a warm place to prove for about 1 hour until doubled in bulk.
7. Preheat the oven to 200°C/400°F/gas mark 6.
8. Knock back the dough, knead in the apple pieces and shape into 1 round loaf or 12 rolls. Place on a baking sheet.
9. Cover the loaf or rolls with lightly greased clingfilm and leave in a warm place to prove until 1½ times the original size. Brush with beaten egg.
10. Bake the loaf in the oven for 30–40 minutes or the rolls for 12–15 minutes until they sound hollow when tapped on the underside. Transfer to a wire rack and leave to cool.

APRICOT AND ORANGE BREAD

225g/8oz strong white flour, plus extra for
* kneading and dusting*
225g/8oz wholemeal flour
1 teaspoon salt
15g/½oz fresh yeast
290ml/½ pint lukewarm milk
1 tablespoon olive oil
grated zest of 1 orange
110g/4oz dried apricots, chopped

1. Sift the flours into a large mixing bowl with the salt and make a well in the centre.
2. Mix the yeast with 1 tablespoon of the milk. Pour into the well with the remaining milk and the oil.
3. Mix with a round-bladed knife, then draw together with the fingers of one hand to make a soft but not sticky dough.
4. Knead on a floured worktop for about 10 minutes until smooth and elastic, using more flour if necessary.
5. Put the dough into a large, clean bowl and cover with a piece of lightly greased clingfilm. Leave to prove in a warm place for about 1 hour until doubled in bulk.
6. Preheat the oven to 190°C/375°F/gas mark 5.
7. Knock back the dough and knead the orange zest and apricots into it. Shape into a round loaf and place on a baking tray. Score a lattice pattern on the top with a sharp knife.
8. Cover the loaf with lightly greased clingfilm and leave in a warm place until 1½ times its original size. Dust the top with a little flour.
9. Bake the loaf in the preheated oven for 30 minutes or until it sounds hollow when tapped on the underside.
10. Turn the loaf out on to a wire rack and leave to cool.

AUSTRIAN RYE BREAD

If you like a heavier and darker rye bread, change the proportions of white and rye flour. The more white flour, the lighter the loaf will be and the more rye flour, the denser and darker the loaf.

150ml/¼ pint lager
110ml/4fl oz cold water
30g/1oz fresh yeast
1 teaspoon soft light brown sugar
225g/8oz strong white flour, plus extra for
    kneading and dusting
1 teaspoon salt
225g/8oz rye flour
1 tablespoon pumpkin seeds
1 tablespoon sunflower seeds
1 teaspoon caraway seeds
butter, for greasing
1 egg, beaten

1. Bring the lager to the boil in a saucepan and add the water. Remove from the heat and leave to cool until lukewarm.
2. Mix the yeast and sugar together and add a little of the lukewarm liquid.
3. Sift the white flour into a large bowl with the salt and add the rye flour and seeds. Make a well in the centre and add the egg, yeast and lager and water. Mix together first with a round-bladed knife, then with the fingers of one hand, to make a soft but not wet dough. If necessary, add more water. Place on a lightly floured worktop and knead for 10 minutes.
4. Put into a large, clean bowl and cover with oiled clingfilm. Leave in a warm place to prove until doubled in bulk. This will take 30 minutes–1 hour, depending on the temperature of the room.
5. Preheat the oven to 200°C/400°F/gas mark 6. Grease a baking tray.
6. Remove the dough from the bowl and knock back to remove any large air pockets. Shape into a large, oval loaf, place on the prepared baking tray and make a slash down the length of the loaf with a serrated knife. Cover with oiled clingfilm and leave in a warm place to prove for 15–20 minutes or until the loaf is 1½ times the original size.
7. Dust the loaf with white flour and bake in the top of the preheated oven for 25 minutes or until it sounds hollow when tapped on the underside. Transfer to a wire rack and leave to cool.

CARROT AND PARSNIP LOAF

225g/8oz butter, melted and cooled, plus extra
    for greasing
285g/10oz plain flour
2 teaspoons bicarbonate of soda
a pinch of salt
2 teaspoons ground cinnamon
1 teaspoon ground ginger
225g/8oz caster sugar
3 eggs, beaten
2 teaspoons vanilla essence
140g/5oz carrots, grated
140g/5oz parsnips, grated

1. Preheat the oven to 170°C/325°F/gas mark 3. Grease a 900g/2lb loaf tin with butter and line the base with greased greaseproof paper.
2. Sift the flour into a large bowl with the bicarbonate of soda, salt, cinnamon and ginger. Add the sugar.
3. Make a well in the centre of the flour mixture and add the eggs, butter and vanilla essence. Mix together and add the carrots and parsnips. Mix well and put into the prepared tin.
4. Bake in the oven for 1¼–1½ hours until a skewer inserted into the middle of the loaf comes out clean. Remove from the oven and allow to cool in the tin for 10 minutes before turning out on to a wire rack to cool completely.

CHEESE CORNBREAD

55g/2oz butter, melted, plus extra for greasing
110g/4oz plain flour
1 tablespoon baking powder
½ teaspoon salt
a good pinch of cayenne pepper
110g/4oz polenta or coarse cornmeal
55g/2oz Cheddar cheese, grated
55g/2oz Gruyère cheese, grated
2 eggs, beaten
290ml/½ pint milk

1. Preheat the oven to 200°C/400°F/gas mark 6.
Grease a 675g/1½lb loaf tin with butter.
2. Sift the flour into a large bowl with the
baking powder, salt and cayenne and add the
polenta and cheeses. Mix well together.
3. Make a well in the centre and add the eggs,
milk and butter. Mix well and pour into the
prepared tin.
4. Bake the loaf in the preheated oven for 40–
45 minutes or until it sounds hollow when
tapped on the underside. Turn out on to a wire
rack and leave to cool. Serve warm.

CHILLI CORNBREAD

1 tablespoon olive oil, plus extra for brushing
30g/1oz butter
1 green chilli, deseeded and finely chopped (see
  page 22)
70g/2½oz plain flour
2 teaspoons baking powder
1 teaspoon bicarbonate of soda
225g/8oz cornmeal
55g/2oz caster sugar
225ml/8fl oz plain yoghurt
1 egg, beaten

1. Preheat the oven to 180°C/350°F/gas mark 4.
Brush a 22.5cm/9in square cake tin very lightly
with oil.
2. Heat the oil and butter in a small frying pan.
Add the chilli and soften for a few minutes.
Remove from the heat and set aside to cool.
3. Sift the flour with the baking powder and
bicarbonate of soda into a bowl, add the
cornmeal and sugar and mix thoroughly. Add
the yoghurt, egg and the contents of the frying
pan. Mix quickly but thoroughly. Turn into the
prepared tin and level the surface. Bake in the
centre of the preheated oven until the bread has
risen and is golden-brown and firm to the
touch. While still warm, divide into squares.
Allow to cool completely in the tin. Use or
freeze on the day of baking.

NOTE: This basic recipe is very versatile as any
combination of extra ingredients can be added,
such as chopped fresh herbs, grated cheese or
different sautéed vegetables.

CINNAMON AND ORANGE SWEET BREAD

30g/1oz fresh yeast
55g/2oz caster sugar
200ml/7fl oz lukewarm milk
85ml/3fl oz orange juice
30g/1oz unsalted butter, melted
1 egg, beaten
550g/1¼lb strong white flour, plus extra for
    kneading and dusting
grated zest of 1 orange
½ teaspoon salt

For the filling
85g/3oz demerara sugar
1 tablespoon ground cinnamon
30g/1oz unsalted butter, melted, plus extra for
    greasing

1. Mix the yeast with a teaspoon of the caster sugar and 2 tablespoons of the milk. Mix the remaining milk with the orange juice, butter and egg.
2. Sift the flour into a large bowl and add the remaining caster sugar, orange zest and salt. Make a well in the centre and add the yeast and the milk mixture. Mix first with a round-bladed knife and then with one hand to form a soft but not sticky dough. Add more flour if necessary.
3. Knead on a floured worktop for about 10 minutes or until the dough is smooth and elastic. Put into a clean bowl, cover with greased clingfilm and leave to prove in a warm place for 45–60 minutes or until doubled in bulk.
4. Meanwhile, mix together the demerara sugar, cinnamon and melted butter.
5. Preheat the oven to 190°C/375°F/gas mark 5. Grease a baking tray with butter.
6. Remove the dough from the bowl and roll out to a 30 × 20cm/12 × 8in rectangle. Spread over the cinnamon and sugar mixture, taking it right to the edges. Roll up as tightly as possible and place seam side down on the prepared baking tray. Cover with greased clingfilm and leave in a warm place to prove for 15–20 minutes or until 1½ times the original size.

7. Dust the loaf with flour and bake in the oven for 30–40 minutes until it sounds hollow when tapped on the underside. Transfer to a wire rack and leave to cool.

COURGETTE AND CHEESE PICNIC BREAD

This bread is ideal for slicing and taking on picnics as it is very easy to transport and fairly substantial when served with salads, tomatoes, etc. It is equally good served slightly warm with soup.

85g/3oz butter, melted and cooled, plus extra
    for greasing
225g/8oz self-raising flour
½ teaspoon salt
a pinch of cayenne pepper
110g/4oz Cheddar cheese, grated
3 eggs, beaten
55ml/2fl oz milk
225g/8oz courgettes, trimmed and grated

1. Preheat the oven to 180°C/350°F/gas mark 4. Grease a 900g/2lb loaf tin with butter and line the base with greased greaseproof paper.
2. Sift the flour with the salt and cayenne into a large bowl. Stir in the cheese.
3. Make a well in the centre and add the eggs, butter and milk. Mix with the flour, using a wooden spoon.
4. Mix in the courgettes to make a thick batter. Spoon into the prepared tin and level the surface. Bake in the preheated oven for 45–50 minutes or until a skewer inserted into the middle of the loaf comes out clean. Transfer to a wine rack and leave to cool.

OATMEAL SEED BREAD

30g/1oz butter, plus extra for greasing
450g/1lb strong white flour, plus extra for
    kneading and dusting
225g/8oz oatmeal
1 teaspoon salt
290ml/½ pint lukewarm milk
20g/¾oz fresh yeast
1 teaspoon caster sugar
1 egg, beaten
30g/1oz pumpkin seeds
30g/1oz sesame seeds
30g/1oz sunflower seeds
30g/1oz pinenuts

1. Preheat the oven to 200°C/400°F/gas mark 6.
Grease a baking tray with butter.
2. Sift the flour into a large bowl and add the
oatmeal and salt. Melt the butter, cool and add
to the milk. Cream the yeast with the sugar
until liquid.
3. Make a well in the centre of the flour
mixture and pour in the milk, yeast liquid and
beaten egg. Mix first with a round-bladed knife,
then with the fingers to a soft but not sloppy
dough, adding more flour or milk as necessary.
4. Put the dough on to a floured worktop and
knead well for about 10 minutes until very
smooth and elastic.
5. Put the dough into a large, clean bowl.
Cover with oiled clingfilm and leave in a warm
place until doubled in bulk.
6. Take the dough out of the bowl and place on
a floured worktop. Scatter over the seeds and
knead them into the dough.
7. Shape the dough into an oval loaf and place
on the prepared baking tray. Cover with oiled
clingfilm and leave in a warm place until it is
about 1½ times the original size.
8. Dust the loaf with a little flour and bake in
the preheated oven for about 40 minutes until it
sounds hollow when tapped on the underside.
Transfer to a wire rack and leave to cool.

NOTE: This loaf can be baked in a lightly
greased terracota flowerpot for an interesting
shape as photographed.

ROASTED PEPPER BREAD

butter, for greasing
2 red or yellow peppers
450g/1lb strong white flour, plus extra for
    kneading
1 teaspoon salt
1 teaspoon caster sugar
30g/1oz fresh yeast
3 tablespoons olive oil
290ml/½ pint lukewarm water
2 tablespoons shredded fresh basil
2 tablespoons freshly grated Parmesan cheese

1. Preheat the oven to 200°C/400°F/gas mark 6.
Grease a 22.5cm/9in square tin with butter and
line the base with non-stick baking paper.
2. Cut the peppers into quarters and remove the
pith and seeds. Grease a baking tray with butter
and place the peppers on it, skin side up. Roast
in the preheated oven for 20 minutes or until the
skins are blistered and beginning to blacken.
Remove from the baking tray and put into a
bowl, cover with a plate and leave to cool.
3. Sift the flour and salt into a large bowl. Cream
the sugar and yeast together until it becomes
liquid. Mix 2 tablespoons of the oil with the
water. Add the water and yeast liquid to the flour
and using a knife and then the fingers of one
hand, mix to a soft but not sticky dough.
4. Knead the dough on a floured worktop for
about 10 minutes until smooth and elastic. Put
into a clean bowl, cover with oiled clingfilm
and leave in a warm place to prove for about 1
hour until doubled in bulk.
5. Meanwhile, peel the peppers and cut into
fine dice. Mix with the basil and Parmesan
cheese.
6. Take the dough out of the bowl and roll into
a 30cm/12in square. Spread over the peppers
and Parmesan cheese, making sure they go right
up to the edges.
7. Roll up as tightly as possible and place seam
side down on a board. Cut into 12 slices and lay
them side by side, cut side up, in the prepared
tin. Cover with oiled clingfilm and leave in a
warm place to prove for about 20 minutes or
until the loaf is about 1½ times the original
size.

8. Bake the loaf in the preheated oven for 10 minutes. Lower the oven temperature to 190°C/375°F/gas mark 5 and bake for a further 20 minutes, or until the centre of the bread is cooked.
9. Turn the loaf on to a wire rack and leave to cool. Brush the top with the remaining oil.

NOTE: This bread is batch-baked in rolls that look like Chelsea buns. Try to ensure that most of the red pepper is tucked into the rolls so that it does not burn. Alternatively, the red pepper filling can be kneaded into the bread at step 6 and then baked as a loaf.

POTATO, CHEESE AND GARLIC BREAD

This delicious bread is perfect to accompany a light meal. Serve with soups, salads or a selection of mezze-style dishes and dips.

butter, for greasing
2 cloves of garlic
2 teaspoons salt
340g/12oz self-raising flour
2 teaspoons dry English mustard
a large pinch of cayenne pepper
110g/4oz Cheddar cheese, grated
340g/12oz potatoes, grated
1 egg
freshly ground black pepper
5 tablespoons milk or plain yoghurt

1. Preheat the oven to 200°C/400°F/gas mark 6. Grease a baking tray with butter.
2. Peel the garlic and place on a chopping board with the salt. Using a round-bladed knife, mash to a smooth paste.
3. Sift the flour, mustard and cayenne into a mixing bowl. Add the cheese, potato, egg and garlic paste and season with pepper. Stir in the milk or yoghurt and mix to a smooth dough. Shape into a round, dome-shaped loaf and place on the prepared baking tray. Use a sharp knife to mark into 8 wedge-shaped portions.
4. Bake in the preheated oven for 30–40 minutes until golden-brown. Transfer to a wire rack and leave to cool.

PUMPKIN CORNBREAD

45g/1½oz butter, plus extra for greasing
450g/1lb pumpkin flesh, peeled, deseeded and chopped
1 medium onion, finely chopped
225g/8oz plain flour
225g/8oz polenta or coarse cornmeal
1 teaspoon cumin
a large pinch of chilli powder
2 teaspoons salt
2 teaspoons baking powder
1 teaspoon bicarbonate of soda
2 tablespoons caster sugar
3 eggs, beaten
150ml/¾ pint plain yoghurt
2 tablespoons mustard seeds, toasted (see page 22)

1. Preheat the oven to 180°C/350°F/gas mark 4. Grease 2 × 450g/1lb loaf tins with butter.
2. Melt the butter in a medium saucepan. Add the pumpkin and onion, cover and cook over a low heat for 20 minutes or until the pumpkin is very soft. Mash to a pulp and allow to cool.
3. Sift the flour, polenta or cornmeal, cumin, chilli powder, salt, baking powder, bicarbonate of soda and sugar together into a large bowl.
4. Add the eggs and yoghurt to the pumpkin purée. Mix well. Stir in the mustard seeds.
5. Make a well in the flour mixture and add the pumpkin and onion mixture, stirring well to form a batter. Pour into the prepared loaf tins and bake in the centre of the preheated oven for 40–45 minutes or until the bread springs back when pressed.
6. Remove from the tins and allow to cool on a wire rack.

SUN-DRIED PEPPER AND TOMATO BREAD

1 quantity Italian bread dough (see page 531)
1 tablespoon olive oil
½ red onion, thinly sliced
2 cloves of garlic, sliced
salt and freshly ground black pepper
1 sun-dried pepper, thinly sliced
4 sun-dried tomatoes, thinly sliced
flour, for dusting
1 tablespoon roughly chopped fresh thyme

To finish
olive oil
rock salt

1. Make the dough and leave to rise until it doubles in bulk.
2. Heat the oil in a small frying pan and add the onion and garlic. Season with salt and pepper and cook over a low heat until the onion is transparent. Add the pepper and tomatoes and cook for a further 1–2 minutes. Remove from the heat and set aside to cool.
3. Preheat the oven to 230°C/450°F/gas mark 8. Dust a 17.5 × 27.5cm/7 × 11in shallow baking tin with flour.
4. Knock back the bread dough on a lightly floured surface and gradually knead in the pepper and tomato mixture and the thyme. Press the dough firmly into the prepared tin and mark the surface all over with the fingertips to make pockets. Cover the dough again with oiled clingfilm and leave to prove for about 10 minutes or until puffy.
5. Drizzle some oil over the surface of the bread and sprinkle with rock salt. Bake as for Italian bread (see page 531).

SUN-DRIED TOMATO, OLIVE AND PESTO SPOONBREAD

425ml/¾ pint milk
150ml/¼ pint double cream
1 bay leaf
125g/4½oz fine white or yellow cornmeal
70g/2½oz butter, melted
55g/2oz Parmesan cheese, freshly grated
6 large sun-dried tomatoes, roughly chopped
8 green or black olives, pitted and chopped
4 eggs, separated
salt and freshly ground black pepper
freshly grated nutmeg
1–2 tablespoons roughly chopped fresh basil
2–3 tablespoons pesto (see page 526)

For coating
melted butter
dried white breadcrumbs

1. Put the milk, cream and bay leaf into a large saucepan and bring slowly to the boil. Lower the heat and remove the bay leaf. Gradually add the cornmeal, stirring constantly for 3–5 minutes until thick. Remove from the heat and set aside.
2. Preheat the oven to 180°C/350°F/gas mark 4.
3. Stir the butter, cheese, sun-dried tomatoes, olives and egg yolks into the cornmeal mixture. Season well with salt, pepper and nutmeg and add the basil.
4. Grease a 1.7 litre/3 pint ovenproof dish generously with butter. Coat lightly with breadcrumbs.
5. Whisk the egg whites until stiff but not dry and fold them into the cornmeal mixture, using a large metal spoon. Pour the mixture gently into the prepared dish. Spoon teaspoonfuls of pesto over the surface of the spoonbread. Bake in the preheated oven for 25–30 minutes until the top is crusty and the centre is cooked but still soft. Serve immediately.

NOTE: This works very well using a ring mould. Unmould the spoonbread on to a platter and drizzle the pesto over the surface. Garnish with extra basil.

ROLLED ITALIAN BREAD

For the bread dough
450g/1lb strong or plain white flour, plus extra
for kneading
1 teaspoon salt
1 teaspoon sugar
1 × 10g/1 sachet easy-blend dried yeast
290ml/½ pint hand-hot water
oil, for brushing

For the filling
200g/7oz canned artichoke hearts, drained
140g/5oz mozzarella cheese
4 sun-dried tomatoes, chopped
2 teaspoons chopped fresh rosemary
1 clove of garlic, crushed
olive oil
salt and freshly ground black pepper

1. Sift the flour into a mixing bowl with the salt, sugar and yeast. Make a well in the centre and gradually mix with enough water to make a soft but not sticky dough. Knead on a floured worktop for 5–10 minutes until elastic. Put back into a clean oiled bowl, cover with oiled clingfilm and leave to prove in a warm place until doubled in bulk.
2. Preheat the oven to 200°C/400°F/gas mark 6. Brush a baking tray with oil.
3. Make the filling: roughly chop the artichoke hearts. Leave to dry on kitchen paper. Slice the cheese. Mix the artichokes, cheese and sun-dried tomatoes together with the rosemary and garlic. Add a drizzle of oil and season with salt and pepper.
4. When the bread has risen, knock back and knead again for 2 minutes, then roll out to a rectangle about 5mm/¼in thick. Scatter the filling over the dough and roll up like a Swiss roll. Carefully cut the roll into 2.5cm/1in slices. Arrange the slices on the prepared baking tray, cut side uppermost, leaving small gaps in between. Bake in the preheated oven for 20 minutes until golden-brown. Pull the rolls apart to separate them and serve immediately.

QUICK WALNUT BREAD

310g/11oz wholemeal flour, plus extra for
kneading
1 teaspoon easy-blend yeast
1½ teaspoons soft light brown sugar
salt
225ml/8fl oz warm water
15g/½oz butter, melted, plus extra for greasing
30g/1oz walnut pieces
a little beaten egg, to glaze
1 tablespoon bulghar wheat (optional)

1. Sift the flour, yeast, sugar and 1 teaspoon salt into a warmed mixing bowl. Make a well in the centre and add the water and melted butter. Gradually mix the flour into the liquid to make a soft, sticky dough.
2. Turn the dough out on to a lightly floured worktop and knead for 3 minutes. Knead in the walnut pieces.
3. Grease a 450g/1lb loaf tin with butter. Shape the dough into a short, stumpy sausage and place it in the prepared tin. Slide the tin into a large plastic bag, seal in some air and leave to prove in a warm place for 45–60 minutes or until doubled in bulk. Preheat the oven to 230°C/450°F/gas mark 8.
4. Remove the tin from the bag and gently brush the surface of the loaf with beaten egg. Sprinkle over the bulghar wheat, if used, and bake in the centre of the preheated oven for 25–30 minutes.
5. Remove the loaf from the tin and return it to the oven for a further 5 minutes to crisp up the outside. Leave to cool on a wire rack.

BRIOCHE

15g/½oz fresh yeast
4 teaspoons caster sugar
2 tablespoons water
285g/10oz plain flour, plus extra for kneading
½ teaspoon salt
2 eggs, beaten
110g/4oz unsalted butter, melted and cooled
1 egg, beaten with a pinch of sugar, to glaze

1. Put the yeast into a small bowl and add 1 teaspoon of the sugar and the water. Mix until creamy.

2. Sift the flour into a large bowl and add the remaining sugar and the salt. Make a well in the centre and add the beaten eggs, yeast mixture and melted butter. Bring together to form a dough. At first it will seem very sticky but keep working it and it will soon leave the sides of the bowl. Knead on a lightly floured worktop for 10 minutes, adding extra flour if necessary.

3. Put into a clean bowl, cover with oiled clingfilm and leave in a warm place to prove for 1 hour or until doubled in bulk.

4. Preheat the oven to 190°C/375°F/gas mark 5. Grease a 450g/1lb loaf tin with butter.

5. Remove the dough from the bowl and knock back, kneading to remove all the large air bubbles. Shape into a loaf and put into the prepared tin. Cover with oiled clingfilm and leave to prove in a warm place for 15 minutes or until 1½ times the original size.

6. When the loaf is ready to bake, carefully brush it with the egg and sugar glaze. Bake in the oven for about 25 minutes until it sounds hollow when tapped on the underside. Remove from the tin and place on a wire rack to cool.

ACCOMPANIMENTS

CRANBERRY SAUCE

2 oranges
1 lemon
110g/4oz cranberries
110g/4oz redcurrant jelly
1 shallot, thinly sliced
caster sugar to taste

1. Thinly pare the zest of 1 orange with a vegetable peeler. Cut the zest into fine shreds. Squeeze the juice from both oranges and the lemon.
2. Combine all the ingredients together in a small pan, adding sugar to taste, and simmer for 10 minutes. Serve as required. The sauce is delicious hot or cold.

NOTE: If fresh cranberries are not available, the same quantity of cranberry jelly can be substituted, in which case sugar may not be needed.

TOMATO AND ORANGE SAUCE WITH CORIANDER

1 × 400g/14oz can of tomatoes
grated zest and juice of 1 orange
1 clove of garlic, crushed
1 teaspoon clear honey or black treacle
salt and freshly ground black pepper
1 tablespoon chopped fresh coriander

1. Put the tomatoes, orange juice and garlic into a food processor or blender and process until smooth.
2. Pour the mixture into a saucepan, add the honey or treacle and season to taste with salt and pepper. Simmer gently for 20 minutes, adding a little water if the sauce becomes too thick. Stir in the orange zest and coriander before serving.

TOMATO, GARLIC AND BASIL SAUCE

6 tablespoons olive oil
1 clove of garlic, thinly sliced
3 tomatoes, peeled, deseeded and finely diced (see page 22)
1 tablespoon finely shredded fresh basil
1 tablespoon fresh thyme leaves
1 tablespoon lemon juice
salt and freshly ground black pepper

1. Gently heat the oil in a saucepan with the garlic. Do not allow the garlic to brown and let the oil infuse for 5 minutes. Strain into a bowl and discard the garlic. Allow the oil to cool.
2. Add the tomatoes, herbs, lemon juice, salt and pepper. Mix well and allow to stand for 20–30 minutes before serving.

SWEET LIME SAUCE

grated zest and juice of 2 limes
1 tablespoon soft light brown sugar
1 red chilli, deseeded and finely chopped (see page 22)
2 teaspoons chopped fresh coriander
2 tablespoons water

1. Mix all the ingredients together thoroughly.
2. Cover and chill until required.

CHILLI JAM

Adjust the heat of the jam to taste. Use 2 chillies for mild heat. Add some of the seeds or an extra chilli for a more fiery flavour.

2 tablespoons olive oil
1 large onion, chopped
2–3 red chillies, finely chopped (see page 22)
150ml/¼ pint water
2 tablespoons white wine vinegar
30g/1oz soft dark brown sugar
a pinch of dried red chilli flakes
salt and freshly ground black pepper

1. Heat the oil in a saucepan, add the onion and chilli and fry over a low heat for 20–30 minutes until very soft and golden. Stir in the water, vinegar, sugar and chilli flakes. Season with salt and pepper and simmer for about 10–15 minutes, stirring occasionally, until the mixture is reduced and thickened.
2. Purée in a food processor or blender. The jam will be thick but still slightly lumpy. Adjust the seasoning to taste and reheat before serving.

FRESH LIME PICKLE

225g/8oz limes, washed
150ml/¼ pint water
1 tablespoon salt
1½ tablespoons white wine vinegar
2 tablespoons demerara sugar
½ teaspoon ground turmeric
1 teaspoon chilli powder
1 teaspoon garam masala
1 teaspoon mustard seeds
1 tablespoon olive oil

1. Cut the limes into very small pieces, remove any pips and reserve the juice. Put the lime flesh and juice into a saucepan, add the water and bring to the boil. Cover and simmer gently for 25–30 minutes or until the lime skins have softened.
2. Add the salt, vinegar and sugar and bring back to the boil. Lower the heat and simmer for 3 minutes, then add the spices and oil.

3. Put into a sterilized jar with a non-metallic lid. Leave for 2 weeks to mature. Once opened, keep in the refrigerator and use within 3 months.

NOTE: This pickle can be used as an accompaniment to curries. A small amount can also be added to dishes to spice them up.

FRESH CORIANDER AND CHILLI RELISH

85g/3oz fresh coriander leaves
1 jalapeño chilli, roughly chopped (see page 22)
1 tablespoon sunflower oil
1½ tablespoons lemon juice
½ teaspoon ground cumin
½ teaspoon salt
freshly ground black pepper

1. Put all the ingredients into a food processor and process to a coarse paste.

MANGO AND LIME CHILLI RELISH

1 large ripe mango
1 red chilli, finely chopped (see page 22)
juice of 1 lime
salt and freshly ground black pepper

1. Peel the mango and cut the flesh into dice.
2. Mix the mango with the chilli and lime juice and season to taste with salt and pepper.
3. Allow to stand for 2 hours to let the flavours develop. Use within 24 hours.

BAKED TOMATO RELISH

450g/1lb ripe tomatoes
3 tablespoons olive oil
3 tablespoons balsamic vinegar
½ teaspoon dried red chilli flakes
2 tablespoons light muscovado sugar
a walnut-sized piece of fresh root ginger, peeled
and finely chopped
salt and freshly ground black pepper

1. Preheat the oven to 220°C/425°F/gas mark 7.
2. Quarter the tomatoes and put into a shallow
ovenproof dish. Mix together the oil, vinegar
and chilli and pour over the tomatoes.
3. Sprinkle with the sugar and ginger. Season
with salt and pepper and bake in the preheated
oven for 30–40 minutes until the tomatoes are
well reduced and slightly charred. Stir to give a
relish-like consistency and adjust the seasoning
to taste. Serve hot, warm or cold as an
accompaniment or side dish.

CRANBERRY RELISH

225g/8oz cranberries
110g/4oz granulated sugar
grated zest and juice of 1 orange
a walnut-sized piece of fresh root ginger, peeled
and grated
2 tablespoons port or red wine

1. Put all the ingredients together in a saucepan
and heat gently until the sugar has dissolved.
Simmer until the cranberries pop and the sauce
thickens. Add more sugar if required.

DATE AND GINGER RELISH

This is delicious served with cheese or as a
accompaniment to hot spicy casseroles or
curries.

110g/4oz fresh dates
2 spring onions
a walnut-sized piece of fresh root ginger, peeled
and chopped
1 tablespoon chopped fresh coriander
1 tablespoon balsamic vinegar
salt and freshly ground black pepper
a pinch of soft dark brown sugar

1. Stone and chop the dates. Trim the spring
onions, cut them in half lengthways and chop.
2. Mix the dates and spring onions with the
ginger, coriander and vinegar. Season with salt,
pepper and sugar. Leave to stand at room
temperature for 1 hour before serving.

BEETROOT RELISH

about 225–340g/8–12oz cooking apples
2 large onions
5cm/2in piece of fresh root ginger
290ml/½ pint white wine vinegar
1 teaspoon salt
340g/12oz granulated sugar
450/1lb freshly cooked beetroot

1. Peel and grate the apples and onions or chop
finely in a food processor. Peel and grate the
ginger. Put the ginger and apples into a large
stainless-steel pan with the vinegar, salt and
sugar. Simmer gently for about 15–20 minutes
until soft.
2. Meanwhile, peel and grate or process the
beetroot. Add to the pan with the cooked
vegetables and simmer for 5 minutes. Spoon
into clean jars and seal when cool. Store in a
cool cupboard for up to 4 months and
refrigerate once opened.

PRESERVED LEMONS

These are delicious served as a garnish or as an integral part of the dish. They are traditionally served in this way in Morocco.

TO FILL A 75ML/1 PINT KILNER JAR

6 lemons
5 tablespoons coarse sea salt
1 teaspoon paprika
1 teaspoon cayenne pepper
12 cloves
1 cinnamon stick
570ml/1 pint olive oil

1. Sterilize the kilner jar by washing and heating in a warm oven for 15 minutes.
2. Cut each lemon into either 1cm/½in slices or 6 wedges. Remove the membrane and any pips.
3. Put a layer of the lemons in the bottom of the jar, sprinkle with a generous amount of salt and a little paprika, cayenne and cloves, followed by more lemon slices. Continue to layer the lemons and seasonings until the jar is full.
4. Lay the cinnamon stick on top of the last layer to help wedge them in and pour the oil over the top, making sure that the lemons are completely submerged.
5. Seal the jar tightly and store in a cool, dark place for at least 3–4 weeks before using.

HARISSA

1 roasted red pepper peeled (see page 214)
1 teaspoon tomato purée
1 teaspoon ground coriander
a pinch of saffron strands
2 medium-hot red Dutch chillies, stalks removed
    and roughly chopped (see page 22)
¼ teaspoon cayenne pepper
¼ teaspoon salt

1. Put the roasted red pepper, tomato purée, coriander, saffron, chillies, cayenne and salt into a food processor.
2. Process to a smooth paste. Cover and chill until required.

TAPENADE

110g/4oz black olives, pitted
45g/1½oz capers in brine, drained and rinsed
4 cloves of garlic, roughly chopped
110ml/4fl oz olive oil
salt and freshly ground black pepper

1. Put the olives, capers and garlic into a food processor and process until smooth.
2. With the machine still running, gradually add the oil through the hole in the lid to make a smooth paste. Season to taste with salt and pepper. Cover and chill until required.

GREEN OLIVE PASTE

Use as a spread for canapés on bread or crackers or as a dip with grissini or vegetable sticks.

20 green olives, pitted
1 teaspoon capers in brine, rinsed
grated zest of ½ lemon
1 teaspoon ground almonds
2 cloves of garlic, crushed
4 tablespoons olive oil
½ teaspoon ground cumin
½ teaspoon paprika
freshly ground black pepper

1. Put all the ingredients into a food processor or blender and process until smooth.

TOASTED PUMPKIN SEED SPREAD

This spread can be eaten on toast, with French bread or crackers. It also makes a good filling for jacket potatoes or a topping to spoon over steamed greens or Brussels sprouts.

170g/6oz pumpkin seeds
3 ripe fresh tomatoes, peeled (see page 22)
1 teaspoon cumin seeds
½ green chilli, deseeded and chopped (see page 22)
2 cloves of garlic, chopped
½ red onion, sliced
juice of 1 lime
salt and freshly ground black pepper

1. Preheat the grill and toast the pumpkin seeds in the bottom of the grill pan for 8–10 minutes until golden-brown. Leave until completely cool. Cut the tomatoes into quarters.
2. Roughly grind the seeds in a food processor or blender. Add all the remaining ingredients and whizz to a paste. Season with salt and pepper. Stir in a little water or tomato juice if very stiff.

RED WINE GRAVY

30g/1oz butter
1 carrot, diced
1 small leek, trimmed and sliced
1 stick of celery, trimmed and chopped
1 clove of garlic, chopped
15g/½oz plain flour
150ml/¼ pint red wine
570ml/1 pint winter vegetable stock (see page 530)
2 sprigs of fresh parsley
2 sprigs of fresh thyme
salt and freshly ground black pepper
1 teaspoon redcurrant jelly (optional)
grated zest of 1 orange (optional)

1. Melt the butter in a saucepan and when foaming, add the carrot, leek and celery. Fry over a low heat for 15 minutes until the vegetables are soft and golden-brown. Stir in the garlic and flour. Fry very gently until the flour turns golden-brown.
2. Gradually add the wine and stock, stirring all the time. Season with salt and pepper and add the parsley and thyme. Simmer for 30–40 minutes until reduced by half. Adjust the seasoning to taste and stir in the redcurrant jelly and orange zest if used.

MUSTARD GRAVY

15g/½oz butter
½ onion, sliced
15g/½oz plain flour
290ml/½ pint winter vegetable stock (see page 530)
salt and freshly ground black pepper
1 bay leaf
1–2 teaspoons wholegrain mustard

1. Melt the butter in a saucepan and when foaming, add the onion and fry over a low heat until well browned and meltingly soft. Stir in the flour and cook for 1 further minute. Gradually pour in the stock, stirring all the time. Season to taste with salt and pepper, add the bay leaf and simmer for 20 minutes.
2. Remove the gravy from the heat and strain. Reheat, whisk in the mustard and adjust the seasoning to taste.

ROASTED GARLIC MAYONNAISE

MAKES ABOUT 290ml/ ½ pint

4 large cloves of garlic
150ml/ ¼ pint sunflower oil
salt and freshly ground black pepper
150ml/ ¼ pint olive oil
2 egg yolks or 1 yolk and 1 whole egg
a pinch of dry English mustard
juice of ½ lemon

1. Put the garlic into a small, heavy saucepan with 2 tablespoons of the sunflower oil. Cover, place over a low heat and sweat for about 20 minutes until the garlic is soft and golden. Alternatively, the garlic can be roasted in the oven at 190°C/375°F/gas mark 5. Put the cloves into a small roasting tin with 2 tablespoons of the sunflower oil and roast for 40 minutes or until soft and golden. Leave to cool in the oil.
2. Squeeze the garlic out of its skin. Sprinkle with a good pinch of salt and mash to a paste with a small palette knife.
3. Mix the two oils together. Use an electric hand-held whisk or food processor to beat together the egg yolks or the egg yolk and the egg. Add a good pinch of salt and mustard. Gradually beat in half the oil, drop by drop. Add 1 tablespoon lemon juice.
4. Now add the remaining oil in a little trickle. Fold in the garlic paste with all the oil and season to taste with salt, pepper and lemon juice.

LEMON MAYONNAISE

MAKES ABOUT 290ml/ ½ pint

1 medium egg
finely grated zest of 1 small lemon
1 tablespoon lemon juice
½ teaspoon salt
150ml/ ¼ pint olive oil
150ml/ ¼ pint sunflower oil

1. Put the egg, lemon zest and juice and the salt into a food processor or blender and process for a few seconds.
2. With the machine still running, gradually add the oil through the hole in the lid. Scrape into a bowl, cover and chill until required.

ROUILLE

MAKES ABOUT 290ml/ ½ pint

30g/1oz day-old white bread, crusts removed
2 tablespoons harissa (see page 510)
3 large cloves of garlic, roasted (see page 340)
1 egg yolk
¼ teaspoon salt
225ml/8fl oz olive oil

1. Cover the bread with cold water and leave to soak for 5 minutes. Squeeze the excess liquid from the bread and put it into a food processor with the harissa, garlic, egg yolk and salt. Process until smooth.
2. With the machine still running, gradually add the oil through the hole in the lid to make a smooth, mayonnaise-like mixture. Scrape into a bowl, cover and chill until required.

CUCUMBER AND MINT RAITA

290ml/½ pint Greek yoghurt
¼ cucumber, finely chopped
1 tablespoon finely chopped fresh mint
½ teaspoon cumin seeds, toasted and ground
*   (see page 22)*
a pinch of cayenne pepper
salt and freshly ground black pepper

1. Mix all the ingredients together and season with salt and pepper.
2. Cover and chill before serving.

VARIATIONS: Substitute ½ ripe mango, finely chopped, or 1 small banana, chopped, for the cucumber.

AUBERGINE AND CUMIN RAITA

This dish can be served as a salad or as an accompaniment to a main course such as millet patties (see page 389) or a curry.

1 small aubergine
3–4 tablespoons olive oil
1 teaspoon cumin seeds
1 teaspoon mustard seeds
2 cloves of garlic, chopped
1 teaspoon caster sugar
225ml/8fl oz Greek yoghurt
1 tablespoon chopped fresh mint
salt and freshly ground black pepper
a pinch of cayenne pepper

1. Cut the aubergine into 1cm/½in cubes. Heat the oil in a frying pan and add the cumin and mustard seeds. When the seeds begin to pop, add the aubergine, lower the heat and fry gently until the aubergine is very soft and beginning to brown. Stir in the garlic and sugar and fry for a further few minutes. Remove from the heat and leave until cold.
2. Put the yoghurt into a bowl. Stir in the mint and season with salt, pepper and cayenne.
3. Stir in the cooked aubergine with all the oil and the pan juices. Leave to stand for 30 minutes before serving.

SALSAS

These are fresh sauces from Central and Latin America. Their tantalizing flavours are quite addictive. They can transform a humble grilled wedge of aubergine into a gourmet feast or be served as a dip with tortilla chips. The combinations of ingredients in salsas are infinite, but all should be based on fresh chilli, chopped onion and the juice of citrus fruit. After this anything goes. The recipes below are quite mild but you can add as many chillies as you like (see chilli chart, page 194, for heat).

CLASSIC TOMATO SALSA

1 ripe beefsteak tomato, chopped
1 fresh green chilli, deseeded and finely chopped
(see page 22)
1 teaspoon finely chopped onion
juice of ½ lime
salt and freshly ground black pepper
a pinch of ground cumin
1 tablespoon chopped fresh coriander

1. Mix the tomato and chilli with the onion and lime juice.
2. Season with plenty of salt, a little pepper and the cumin. Stir in the coriander. Leave to stand for 10 minutes before serving.

VARIATIONS: Substitute chopped fresh mint for the coriander. Add 1 small ripe avocado, stoned, peeled and chopped.

ORANGE SALSA

1 orange
1 fresh red chilli, deseeded and finely chopped
(see page 22)
½ red onion, finely chopped
lime juice
1 tablespoon chopped fresh coriander
salt and freshly ground black pepper

1. Peel the orange as you would an apple. Cut into segments, removing all the pith and seeds.

Squeeze the pithy remains over a mixing bowl to extract the juice. Chop the segments and add the juice.
2. Mix the chilli with the orange segments and stir in the onion, a dash of lime juice and the coriander. Season with plenty of salt and a little pepper. Allow to stand for 10 minutes before serving.

VARIATIONS: Substitute 1 tablespoon orange juice and 1 small banana, peeled and finely chopped, for the orange.

PINEAPPLE SALSA

Fresh pineapple is best for this recipe but if canned has to be used, add extra lime juice to sharpen the flavour.

225g/8oz fresh pineapple
1–2 red chillies, deseeded and finely chopped
1 teaspoon peeled and grated fresh root ginger
¼ red onion, finely chopped
1 tablespoon chopped fresh coriander
a pinch of ground cumin
juice of ½–1 lime
salt and freshly ground black pepper
soft light brown sugar (optional)

1. Remove the woody core from the pineapple and chop the flesh. Mix together with all the remaining ingredients and season with salt and pepper. If the pineapple is very sharp, season with a little sugar as well. Leave to stand for about 1 hour for the flavours to mingle.

VARIATION: Fresh mint may be substituted for the coriander.

SPICY TOMATO KETCHUP

MAKES 1 LITRE/1¾ PINTS

900g/2lb plum tomatoes, roughly chopped
225g/8oz shallots, roughly chopped
30g/1oz fresh root ginger, peeled and roughly
    chopped
3 cloves of garlic
½ medium-hot red Dutch chilli, deseeded and
    roughly chopped (see page 22)
2 sticks of celery, trimmed and halved
1 tablespoon coriander seeds
½ teaspoon cloves
blade of mace
1 × 700ml/1¼ pints bottle of tomato passata
225ml/8fl oz cider vinegar
70g/2½oz caster sugar
2 teaspoons salt
4 teaspoons sweet paprika

1. Put the tomatoes, shallots, ginger, garlic and
chilli into a food processor and process to a
coarse paste. Put the celery, coriander seeds,
cloves and mace into the centre of a square of
muslin and tie into a pouch.
2. Put the chopped tomato mixture, the muslin
pouch and the tomato passata into a large
saucepan. Bring to the boil, then lower the heat and
simmer, stirring from time to time, for 25 minutes.
3. Remove the muslin pouch and leave the
mixture to cool. Bring back to the boil and cook
rapidly until reduced by half to a loose purée
(about 1.1 litres/2 pints). As soon as the muslin
pouch is cool enough to handle, squeeze the
juices back into the pan, to extract all the
flavour.
4. Add the vinegar, sugar, salt and paprika to
the pan and bring back to the boil. Lower the
heat slightly and simmer vigorously, stirring
from time to time, for 30 minutes until reduced
to a good sauce consistency (it will thicken a
little more as it cools).
5. Preheat the oven to 160°C/325°F/gas mark 3.
Prepare 4 × 450g/1lb glass jars with non-
metallic lids. Wash them in hot soapy water,
rinse well and put them into the oven until you
are ready to use them.
6. Liquidize the sauce in batches to a smoother
sauce if preferred. Remove the jars from the
oven, pour in the hot sauce and seal the lids
tightly. Heat-seal the jars by placing a flat trivet
in a large saucepan. Put the jars into the pan
and cover with water by at least 2.5cm/1in.
Bring the water to the boil and boil for 20
minutes. Remove the jars, tighten the lids if
necessary and leave to cool. The sauce will keep
for up to 2 years in a cool, dark place.

READ AND BUTTER PICKLE

MAKES 4 × 450g/1lb jars

675g/1½lb small cucumbers, thinly sliced
450g/1lb onions, halved and thinly sliced
1 green pepper, deseeded and thinly sliced
55g/2oz salt
340g/12oz soft light brown sugar
½ teaspoon ground turmeric
¼ teaspoon ground cloves
1 tablespoon yellow mustard seeds
½ teaspoon celery seed
425ml/¾ pint cider vinegar

1. Mix the cucumbers, onions, pepper and salt
together in a bowl. Cover and set aside for 3
hours.
2. Put the remaining ingredients into a pan and
bring slowly to the boil, stirring to dissolve the
sugar. Boil for 5 minutes, then set aside.
3. Meanwhile, preheat the oven to 160°C/
325°F/gas mark 3 and prepare 4 × 450g/1lb jars
with non-metallic lids. Wash them in hot soapy
water, rinse well and place in the oven until you
are ready to use them.
4. Drain the vegetables and rinse them
thoroughly under running cold water. Leave
them to drain well in a colander. Add them to
the hot syrup and heat slowly to just below
boiling point, stirring from time to time.
5. Remove the jars from the oven and leave
them to cool slightly. Spoon the pickle into the
jars, seal and leave to cool. This pickle is ready
to eat immediately and will also keep for up to
1 year in a cool, dark place.

SPICED ONION AND BITTERSWEET DAMSON CHUTNEY

MAKES ABOUT 1.8kg/4lb

2 tablespoons oil
675g/1½lb onions, thinly sliced
1kg/2¼lb damsons, halved and stoned
900g/2lb cooking apples, peeled, cored and
  chopped
570ml/1 pint cider vinegar
2 teaspoons salt
5cm/2in piece of fresh root ginger, peeled and
  grated
1 cinnamon stick
1½ teaspoons cloves
1½ teaspoons allspice berries
1 teaspoon whole black peppercorns
450g/1lb soft light brown sugar

1. Heat the oil in a very large stainless-steel saucepan and add the onions. Cover and cook over a low heat until soft but not coloured.
2. Add the damsons and apples to the pan. Stir in the vinegar, salt, ginger and cinnamon.
3. Tie the whole spices in a piece of muslin and add the spice bag to the pan.
4. Bring to the boil, add the sugar and stir until dissolved. Lower the heat and simmer for 2–2½ hours or until the chutney is fairly thick. Remove the cinnamon stick and spice bag. Pour or ladle the chutney into warm, sterilized jars and cover with non-metallic lids.

YOGHURTY ONIONS

2 tablespoons sunflower or vegetable oil
½ teaspoon cumin seeds
½ teaspoon mustard seeds
1 large onion, quartered and sliced
290ml/½ pint Greek yoghurt
salt and freshly ground black pepper

1. Heat the oil in a heavy frying pan. Add the seeds and fry until they begin to pop. Add the onion and fry briskly until golden-brown.
2. Stir in the yoghurt and season with salt and pepper. Serve immediately.

YOGHURT AND HERB CHEESES

570ml/1 pint Greek yoghurt
1 clove of garlic, crushed
3 tablespoons chopped fresh herbs, such as
  parsley, mint, thyme
1 teaspoon salt
about 570ml/1 pint olive oil
sprigs of fresh thyme

1. Boil a 'J'-cloth in water for 3–5 minutes. Squeeze dry and use to line a sieve.
2. Mix the yoghurt, garlic, herbs and salt together.
3. Pour into the sieve suspended over a bowl. Chill for 24 hours.
4. Sterilize a 750ml/1¼ pint preserving jar.
5. Pour in some of the oil until the jar is about half full. Shape the cheese mixture in the sieve into balls using oiled hands the size of a ping-pong ball. Drop them into the oil one by one, ensuring that each one is coated with oil before adding the next. Pour in more oil as necessary.
6. Make sure all the cheeses are coated with oil and push in some sprigs of thyme. Seal the jar and leave in a cool place. Use within 2 weeks. Serve with mint and thyme soda rolls (see page 493) or any of the savoury breads.

NOTE: If this is kept in the refrigerator the oil will become cloudy and will start to solidify, but it will clear again after about 20 minutes at room temperature. The oil can be used for dressings or stir-frying.

LEMON CURD

grated zest and juice of 2 lemons
85g/3oz butter
225g/8oz caster sugar
3 eggs, beaten

1. Mix all the ingredients together in a bowl and set over a pan of simmering water. Stir gently and continuously until the mixture is thick. Alternatively, cook in a microwave on full power for 4–5 minutes, stirring every minute.

RASPBERRY COULIS

225g/8oz frozen raspberries, defrosted if frozen
about 55g/2oz icing sugar, sifted
lemon juice
1 tablespoon kirsch (optional)

1. Purée the raspberries in a food processor or blender. Push through a nylon sieve to remove the pips.
2. Sweeten the raspberry purée to taste with the icing sugar. Add a dash of lemon juice and the kirsch, if used. The sauce should be of a pouring consistency. Add a little water if it is too thick.

BASICS

SHORTCRUST PASTRY

170g/6oz plain flour
a pinch of salt
30g/1oz solid vegetable fat
55g/2oz butter
very cold water, to mix

1. Sift the flour with the salt into a large bowl.
2. Rub in the fats until the mixture resembles coarse breadcrumbs.
3. Add 2 tablespoons water to the mixture. Mix to a firm dough, first with a round-bladed knife, and then with one hand. It may be necessary to add more water, but the pastry should not be too damp. (Though crumbly pastry is more difficult to handle, it produces a shorter, lighter result.)
4. Chill, wrapped, for 30 minutes before using. Or allow to relax after rolling out but before baking.

RICH SHORTCRUST PASTRY

170g/6oz plain flour
a pinch of salt
100g/3½oz butter
1 egg yolk
very cold water, to mix

1. Sift the flour with the salt into a large bowl.
2. Rub in the butter until the mixture resembles breadcrumbs.
3. Mix the egg yolk with 2 tablespoons water and add to the mixture.
4. Mix to a firm dough, first with a round-bladed knife, then with one hand. It may be necessary to add more water, but the pastry should not be too damp. (Though crumbly pastry is more difficult to handle, it produces a shorter, lighter result.)
5. Chill, wrapped, for 30 minutes before using. Or allow to relax after rolling out but before baking.

NOTE: To make sweet rich shortcrust pastry, mix in 1 tablespoon caster sugar once the fat has been rubbed into the flour.

WHOLEMEAL PASTRY

110g/4oz wholemeal flour
110g/4oz plain flour
a pinch of salt
140g/5oz butter
very cold water, to mix

1. Sift the flours with the salt into a large bowl and add the bran from the sieve. Rub in the butter until the mixture resembles coarse breadcrumbs.
2. Add 2 tablespoons water and mix to a firm dough, first with a round-bladed knife, then with one hand. It may be necessary to add more water, but the pastry should not be too damp. (Although crumbly pastry is more difficult to handle, it produces a shorter, lighter result.)
3. Chill, wrapped, for at least 30 minutes before using, or allow the rolled-out pastry to relax before baking.

NOTES: To make sweet wholemeal pastry, mix in 2 tablespoons sugar once the fat has been rubbed into the flour.

All wholemeal flour may be used if preferred.

HERB WHOLEMEAL PASTRY

110g/4oz plain flour
110g/4oz wholemeal flour
a pinch of salt
110g/4oz butter, chopped
1 tablespoon chopped fresh thyme
very cold water, to mix

1. Sift the flours with the salt into a large bowl and add the bran from the sieve.
2. Rub in the butter until the mixture resembles coarse breadcrumbs. Add the thyme.
3. Add enough water to the mixture to mix first with a round-bladed knife, then with one hand, to a firm dough. Chill, wrapped, for 10 minutes and use as required.

OATMEAL PASTRY

170g/6oz plain flour
a pinch of salt
110g/4oz butter
55g/2oz oatmeal
2 tablespoons cold water

1. Sift the flour and salt into a large bowl.
2. Add the butter and rub in until the mixture resembles coarse breadcrumbs.
3. Add the oatmeal and mix in.
4. Add the water and mix to a firm dough, first with a knife and then with one hand. It may be necessary to add more water but the pastry should not be too wet.
5. Chill, wrapped in clingfilm, for 30 minutes before using.

PUFF PASTRY

225g/8oz plain flour, plus extra for rolling
a pinch of salt
30g/1oz solid vegetable fat
120–150ml/4–5fl oz iced water
140–200g/5–7oz butter

1. If you have never made puff pastry before, use the smaller amount of butter: this will give a normal pastry. If you have some experience, more butter will produce a lighter, very rich pastry.
2. Sift the flour with the salt into a large bowl. Rub in the vegetable fat. Add enough water to mix with a round-bladed knife to a doughy consistency. Turn on to a floured board and knead quickly until just smooth. Chill, wrapped, for 30 minutes.
3. Lightly flour the board and roll the dough into a rectangle about 30 × 10cm/12 × 4in.
4. Tap the butter lightly with a floured rolling pin to shape it into a flattened block about 9 × 8cm/3½ × 3in. Put the butter on the rectangle of pastry and fold both ends over to enclose it. Fold the third closest to you over first and then bring the top third down. Press the sides together to prevent the butter escaping.

Give it a 90-degree anti-clockwise turn so that the folded, closed edge is on your left.

5. Now tap the pastry parcel with the rolling pin to flatten the butter a little; then roll out, quickly and lightly, until the pastry is 3 times as long as it is wide. Fold it very evenly in 3, first folding the third closest to you over, then bringing the top third down. Give it a 90-degree anti-clockwise turn so that the folded, closed edge is on your left. Again press the edges firmly with the rolling pin. Then roll out again to form a rectangle as before.

6. Now the pastry has had 2 rolls and folds, or 'turns' as they are called. It should be put to rest in a cool place for 30 minutes or so. The rolling and folding must be repeated twice more, the pastry again rested, and then again given 2 more turns. This makes a total of 6 turns. If the butter is still very streaky, roll and fold it once more.

ROUGH PUFF PASTRY

225g/8oz plain flour, plus extra for rolling
a pinch of salt
140g/5oz butter
120–150ml/4–5fl oz very cold water, to mix

1. Sift the flour with the salt into a chilled bowl. Cut the butter into knobs about the size of a sugar lump and add to the flour. Do not rub in but add enough water to just bind the paste together. Mix first with a knife, then with one hand. Knead very lightly.

2. Chill, wrapped, for 10 minutes.

3. On a floured board, roll the pastry into a strip about 30 × 10cm/12 × 4in long. This must be done carefully: with a heavy rolling pin, press firmly on the pastry and give short, sharp rolls until the pastry has reached the required size. Take care not to over-stretch and break the surface of the pastry.

4. Fold the strip into 3 and turn so that the folded edge is to your left, like a closed book.

5. Again roll out into a strip 1cm/½in thick. Fold in 3 again and chill, wrapped, for 15 minutes.

6. Roll and fold the pastry as before, then chill again for 15 minutes.

7. Roll and fold again, by which time the pastry should be ready for use, with no signs of streakiness. If it is still streaky, roll and fold once more.

8. Roll into the required shape.

9. Chill again before baking.

FILO OR STRUDEL PASTRY

285g/10oz plain flour, plus extra for rolling
a pinch of salt
1 egg
150ml/¼ pint water
1 teaspoon oil

1. Sift the flour with the salt into a large bowl.

2. Beat the egg and add the water and oil. First with a round-bladed knife, then with one hand, mix the water and egg into the flour, adding more water if necessary to make a soft dough.

3. The dough has now to be beaten: lift the whole mixture up in one hand and then, with a flick of the wrist, slap it on to a lightly floured board. Continue doing this until the dough no longer sticks to your fingers, and the whole mixture is smooth and very elastic. Put it into a clean floured bowl. Cover and leave in a warm place for 15 minutes.

4. The pastry is now ready for rolling and pulling. To do this, flour a tea-towel or large cloth on a worktop and roll out the pastry as thinly as possible. Now put your hand (well floured) under the pastry and, keeping your hand fairly flat, gently stretch and pull the pastry, gradually and carefully working your way round until the paste is paper-thin. (You should be able to see through it easily.) Trim off the thick edges.

5. Use immediately, as strudel pastry dries out or cracks very quickly. Brushing with melted butter or oil helps to prevent this. Or the pastry sheet may be kept covered with a damp cloth.

NOTE: If this pastry is being used to make individual samosas or rolls, cut into sheets measuring about 25–30cm/10–12in.

CHOUX PASTRY

85g/3oz butter
220ml/7½fl oz water
105g/3¾oz plain flour, well sifted
a pinch of salt
3 eggs

1. Put the butter and water into a heavy saucepan. Bring slowly to the boil so that by the time the water boils the butter is completely melted.
2. Immediately the mixture is boiling really fast, tip in all the flour with the salt and remove the pan from the heat.
3. Working as fast as you can, beat the mixture hard with the wooden spoon: it will soon become thick and smooth and leave the sides of the pan.
4. Stand the bottom of the saucepan in a bowl or sink of cold water to speed up the cooling process.
5. When the mixture is cool, beat in the eggs, a little at a time, until it is soft, shiny and smooth. If the eggs are large, it may not be necessary to add all of them. The mixture should be of a dropping consistency – not too runny. ('Dropping consistency' means that the mixture will fall off a spoon rather reluctantly and all in a blob; if it runs off, it is too wet, and if it will not fall even when the spoon is jerked slightly, it is too thick.)
6. Use as required.

CREAM CHEESE PASTRY

This pastry is very rich and can be a little tricky to handle. Do not allow it to get too warm while working with it and always chill both before and after rolling.

85g/3oz butter
85g/3oz cream cheese
250g/9oz plain flour, sifted
a pinch of salt

1. Cream the butter and cream cheese together in a mixing bowl.
2. Add the flour and salt and work together to a dough.
3. Wrap in clingfilm like a flat parcel and chill for 30 minutes before using.
4. Allow the pastry to soften slightly before rolling out to prevent it from cracking. Chill again before baking.

POLENTA PASTRY

This can be made in a food processor, but be careful not to overwork it once you have added the flour and water.

110g/4oz butter
2 egg yolks
140g/5oz plain flour, sifted
55g/2oz polenta
a pinch of salt
2 tablespoonfuls chopped fresh chives
2 tablespoons cold water

1 Cream the butter and egg yolks together in a mixing bowl.
2. Add the flour, polenta, salt and chives. Mix together and add the water. Mix to a firm dough.
3. Shape into a flattened circle, wrap in clingfilm and chill for 10–15 minutes before rolling.

BÉCHAMEL SAUCE

290ml/ ½ pint creamy milk
1 slice of onion
1 blade of mace
a few fresh parsley stalks
4 white peppercorns
1 bay leaf
30g/1oz butter
20g/¾oz plain flour
salt and freshly ground white pepper

1. Place the milk with the onion, mace, parsley, peppercorns and bay leaf in a saucepan and slowly bring to simmering point.
2. Remove from the heat and leave for the flavour to infuse for 8–10 minutes.
3. Melt 20g/¾ oz of the butter in a heavy saucepan, stir in the flour and stir over heat for 1 minute.
4. Remove from the heat. Strain in the infused milk and mix well.
5. Return the sauce to the heat and stir or whisk continuously until boiling. Add the remaining butter and beat very well (this will help to make the sauce shiny).
6. Simmer, stirring well, for 3 minutes.
7. Season to taste with salt and pepper.

NOTE: To make a professionally shiny béchamel sauce, pass through a tammy strainer before use or whizz in a blender.

WHITE SAUCE

This is a quick and easy basic white sauce.

20g/¾oz butter
20g/¾oz plain flour
a pinch of dry English mustard
290ml/ ½ pint creamy milk
salt and freshly ground black pepper

1. Melt the butter in a heavy saucepan.
2. Add the flour and mustard and stir over the heat for 1 minute. Remove the pan from the heat, pour in the milk and mix well.
3. Return the pan to the heat and stir continuously until boiling.
4. Simmer well for 2–3 minutes. Season to taste with salt and pepper.

CHEESE SAUCE

(MORNAY SAUCE)

20g/¾oz butter
20g/¾oz plain flour
a pinch of dry English mustard
a pinch of cayenne pepper
290ml/ ½ pint milk
55g/2oz Gruyère or strong Cheddar cheese,
* grated*
15g/ ½oz Parmesan cheese, freshly grated
* (optional)*
salt and freshly grated black pepper

1. Melt the butter in a heavy saucepan and stir in the flour, mustard and cayenne. Cook, stirring, for 1 minute. Remove the pan from the heat. Pour in the milk and mix well.
2. Return the pan to the heat and stir until boiling. Simmer well for 2 minutes.
3. Add all the cheese and mix well, but do not re-boil.
4. Season to taste with salt and pepper.

HOLLANDAISE SAUCE

3 tablespoons wine vinegar
6 black peppercorns
1 bay leaf
1 blade of mace
2 egg yolks
salt
110g/4oz unsalted butter, softened
lemon juice

1. Place the vinegar, peppercorns, bay leaf and mace in a small, heavy saucepan and reduce by simmering to 1 tablespoon.
2. Cream the egg yolks with a pinch of salt and a nut of the butter in a small heatproof bowl. Set over, not in, a saucepan of gently simmering water. Using a wooden spoon, beat the mixture until slightly thickened, taking care that the water immediately around the bowl does not boil. Mix well.
3. Strain on the reduced vinegar. Mix well. Stir over the heat until slightly thickened. Beat in the softened butter bit by bit, increasing the temperature as the sauce thickens and you add more butter, but take care that the water does not boil.
4. When the sauce has become light and thick, remove from the heat and beat or whisk for 1 minute. Check the seasoning and add lemon juice, and salt if necessary. Keep warm by standing the bowl in hot water. Serve warm.

NOTE: Hollandaise sauce will set too firmly if allowed to get cold and it will curdle if overheated. It can be made in larger quantities in a blender or a food processor: simply put the eggs and salt into the blender and blend lightly. Add the hot reduction and allow to thicken slightly. Set aside when ready to serve, pour in warm melted butter, slowly allowing the sauce to thicken as you pour.

PESTO

2 cloves of garlic
2 large cups of fresh basil leaves, about 85g/3oz
55g/2oz pinenuts
55g/2oz Parmesan cheese, freshly grated
150ml/¼ pint olive oil
salt

1. In a blender or mortar, grind the garlic and basil together to a paste. Add the nuts, cheese, oil and plenty of salt. Keep in a covered jar in a cool place.

NOTE: Pesto is sometimes made with walnuts instead of pinenuts, and the nuts may be pounded with the other ingredients to give a smooth paste.

ROCKET PESTO

55g/2oz rocket
55g/2oz blanched almonds
85ml/3fl oz olive oil
55g/2oz Parmesan cheese, freshly grated
salt and freshly ground black pepper

1. Put all the ingredients into a blender and process until smooth. Season to taste with salt and pepper. If the paste begins to look oily and too thick, add 1 tablespoon water.

RED PESTO

2 cloves of garlic
1 small bunch of fresh basil
55g/2oz pinenuts
55g/2oz sun-dried tomatoes, chopped
150ml/¼ pint olive oil
55g/2oz Pecorino cheese, freshly grated
salt and freshly ground black pepper

1. In a food processor or blender, whizz the garlic and basil together to a paste.
2. Add the nuts and sun-dried tomatoes and whizz again, then add the oil slowly with the motor still running. Add the cheese and whizz quickly.
3. Season to taste with salt and pepper. Keep in a covered jar in a cool place.

TOMATO SAUCE I

1 large onion, finely chopped
3 tablespoons oil
10 tomatoes, roughly chopped
salt and freshly ground black pepper
a pinch of caster sugar
150ml/¼ pint stock (see page 530)
1 teaspoon fresh thyme leaves

1. Sweat the onions in the oil in a saucepan. Add the tomatoes, salt, pepper and sugar, and cook for a further 25 minutes. Add the stock and cook for 5 minutes.
2. Purée the sauce in a food processor or blender and push through a sieve. If it is too thin, reduce, by boiling rapidly, to the desired consistency. Take care: it will spit and has a tendency to catch.
3. Add the thyme. Check the seasoning, adding more salt or sugar if necessary.

TOMATO SAUCE II

1 × 400g/14oz can of tomatoes
1 small onion, chopped
1 small carrot, chopped
1 stick of celery, chopped
½ clove of garlic, crushed
1 bay leaf
parsley stalks
salt and freshly ground black pepper
juice of ½ lemon
a dash of Worcestershire sauce
1 teaspoon caster sugar
1 teaspoon chopped fresh basil or thyme

1. Put all the ingredients together in a heavy saucepan, cover and simmer over a medium heat for 30 minutes.
2. Purée the sauce in a food processor or blender and push through a sieve. Return it to the pan.
3. If it is too thin, reduce by boiling rapidly. Check the seasoning, adding more salt or sugar if necessary.

MAYONNAISE

2 egg yolks
salt and freshly ground white pepper
1 teaspoon dry English mustard
290ml/½ pint olive oil, or 150ml/¼ pint each
olive and sunflower oil
a squeeze of lemon juice
1 tablespoon white wine vinegar

1. Put the yolks into a bowl with a pinch of salt and the mustard and beat well with a wooden spoon.
2. Add the oil, literally drop by drop, beating all the time. The mixture should be very thick by the time half the oil is added.
3. Beat in the lemon juice.
4. Resume pouring in the oil, going more quickly now, but alternating the dribbles of oil with small quantities of vinegar.
5. Season to taste with salt and pepper.

NOTE: If the mixture curdles, another egg yolk should be beaten in a separate bowl, and the curdled mixture beaten into it drop by drop.

FRENCH DRESSING

(VINAIGRETTE)

3 tablespoons sunflower oil
1 tablespoon wine vinegar
salt and freshly ground black pepper

1. Put all the ingredients into a screw-top jar. Before using, shake until well emulsified.

NOTES: This dressing can be flavoured with crushed garlic, mustard, a pinch of sugar, chopped fresh herbs, etc., as desired.
If kept refrigerated, the dressing will more easily form an emulsion when whisked or shaken, and has a slightly thicker consistency.

CURRY POWDER

This mixture is quite hot: to increase or lessen the heat, adjust the quantity of chillies accordingly. The art of good curry powders is in the toasting; when the seeds are split by the heat, their full flavour comes through. Take care not to burn the seeds or the powder will taste bitter.

To keep the curry powder fresh it is best stored in the freezer or a cool, dark place. Use within 3 months: any longer and the spices lose their flavour.

This quantity makes enough powder for several curries; halve the amount of seeds to make a smaller quantity.

6 tablespoons coriander seeds
4 tablespoons cumin seeds
6 dried red chillies
1 tablespoon black peppercorns
1 tablespoon mustard seeds, preferably black
3 tablespoons ground turmeric
3 teaspoons ground fenugreek

1. Heat a large frying pan. Add the coriander seeds and toss and toast over a medium heat until they begin to pop and colour. Transfer to a plate to cool.
2. Add the cumin seeds and chillies and toast in the same way until the cumin pops and the chillies turn dark reddish-brown in colour. Add them to the coriander and allow to cool.
3. Toast the peppercorns and mustard seeds individually in the same way and allow to cool.
4. When all the seeds are cold, put into a spice/ coffee grinder or mortar. Pound together until a fine powder is formed. Stir the turmeric and fenugreek into the powder. Transfer to an airtight container and store until required.

THAI RED CURRY PASTE

3 red chillies, deseeded and chopped
2 dried red chillies, deseeded
1 canned pimiento, drained and sliced
1 tablespoon caraway seeds
1 tablespoon ground coriander
2 stalks of lemon grass, chopped
*2.5cm/1in piece of galangal, peeled and
 chopped*
2 shallots, chopped
2 teaspoons light soy sauce

1. Put all the ingredients into a liquidizer and
whizz to a smooth paste.
2. Store the paste in a sealed jar in the
refrigerator. It will keep for 2–3 days.

NOTE: This paste is quite hot. For a milder
version, decrease the amount of chilli used.

CAJUN SPICE

1 tablespoon black peppercorns
1 tablespoon rock salt
1 tablespoon paprika
1 teaspoon cayenne pepper
1 teaspoon cumin seeds
1 teaspoon dried thyme

1. Grind all the ingredients together in a
mortar or coffee grinder.
2. Transfer to an airtight container and store
until required.

CLARIFIED BUTTER

Put the butter into a small saucepan and leave
over a low heat until it has melted. Skim off any
scum from the surface and pour the clear butter
into a bowl, leaving behind the milky white
solids that will have settled on the base of the
pan.

STOCKS

A homemade, full-bodied stock is the best base for a soup, stew or risotto. The secret of making a good stock is not to over-boil the ingredients which would cause the flavour to become tired and sometimes bitter. Cut the vegetables into small pieces to maximize the flavour released. Vegetables should always be thoroughly washed but there is no need for peeling. Simmer the stock for about 1 hour, strain to remove the vegetables and then boil to reduce the liquid and strengthen the flavour. To darken the colour of the stock, slowly brown an assortment of onion, leek and carrot in a little oil before adding the remaining vegetables and liquid.

Commercially made stock can be used for speed or to strengthen a weak stock but the flavour often lacks subtlety and can be over-salty. Chilled stocks or powdered vegetable bouillon are the best. Always look for one that has no monosodium glutamate content.

There follows a selection of stock recipes to suit the season or to enhance the flavour of a particular dish. The recipes in this book specify which stock to use but any stock can of course be used in any of the recipes.

WINTER VEGETABLE STOCK

This is a strong brown stock for hearty, robust dishes.

3 tablespoons vegetable or sunflower oil
2 large onions, sliced
2 leeks, sliced
2 large carrots, sliced
½ head of garlic, broken into cloves
8 sticks of celery from the outside of the head, sliced
a few outside cabbage leaves or chard stalks, shredded
55g/2oz brown lentils
2 bay leaves

a handful of fresh parsley
1 teaspoon sea salt
2 litres/3½ pints water
½ teaspoon black peppercorns

1. Heat the oil in a large saucepan. Add the onions, leeks, carrots and cloves of garlic. Cook over a low heat for 30–40 minutes until the vegetables are browned and caramelized. Add all the remaining ingredients. Bring to the boil, then lower the heat, partially cover and simmer for 1 hour. Strain and discard the vegetables. Return the liquid to the pan and reduce to the desired strength.

SUMMER VEGETABLE STOCK

3 leeks, sliced
3 carrots, sliced
outside cabbage leaves, shredded
chard, shredded
4 sticks of celery, sliced
a few mushroom stalks
a large handful of assorted herbs, such as basil, marjoram, lovage, borage
a handful of fresh parsley
½ teaspoon black peppercorns
1 teaspoon sea salt
1 bay leaf
pea pods, if available
2 litres/3½ pints water

1. Put all the ingredients together in a large saucepan. Bring to the boil, then lower the heat, partially cover and simmer for 1 hour. Strain and discard the vegetables. Return the liquid to the pan and reduce to the desired strength.

SPICY STOCK

This is a very spicy stock; adjust the heat by removing the chilli.

olive oil
2 onions
3 leeks
½ head of garlic, broken into cloves
a few cumin and coriander seeds
1 red chilli, deseeded if liked, and sliced
1 courgette or ½ butternut squash
1 red pepper, deseeded and sliced
2–3 over-ripe tomatoes, chopped
1 teaspoon sea salt
½ teaspoon black peppercorns
2 litres/3½ pints water

1. Heat the oil in a large saucepan and add the onions, leeks and garlic. Stir in the spices, then cover and cook over a low heat for 10 minutes until the vegetables are softened. Add all the remaining ingredients. Bring to the boil, partially cover and simmer for 1 hour. Strain and discard the vegetables. Return the liquid to the pan and reduce to the desired strength.

MUSHROOM STOCK

2 tablespoons olive oil
1 onion, sliced
2 carrots, sliced
2 leeks, sliced
30g/1oz dried mushrooms
170g/6oz chestnut or cup mushrooms, roughly chopped
2 cloves of garlic, chopped
a handful of fresh parsley
1 bay leaf
4 sprigs of fresh thyme
1 teaspoon sea salt
½ teaspoon black peppercorns
2 litres/3½ pints water

1. Heat the oil in a large saucepan. Add all the vegetables, garlic and parsley, then cover and cook over a low heat for 10 minutes until the vegetables are softened. Add the bay leaf, thyme, salt, peppercorns and water. Bring to the boil, then lower the heat, partially cover and simer for 1 hour. Strain and discard the vegetables. Return the liquid to the pan and reduce to the desired strength.

ITALIAN BREAD

This is a basic olive oil bread which can be easily adapted by adding a variety of herbs, such as finely chopped rosemary or sage, or grated cheese.

30g/1oz fresh yeast
225ml/8fl oz warm water
450g/1lb strong plain flour
2 teaspoons salt
2 tablespoons olive oil

1. Dissolve the yeast in the water.
2. Sift the flour with the salt into a large bowl and make a well in the centre. Pour in the dissolved yeast and the oil. Gradually draw in the flour and, when all ingredients are well mixed, knead the dough for 8 minutes.
3. Put the dough into a lightly greased bowl. Cover with oiled clingfilm and leave to prove in a warm place for about 1 hour.
4. Shape as required. Cover again with oiled clingfilm and leave to prove until 1½ times the original size.
5. Preheat the oven to 230°C/450°F/gas mark 8.
6. Place the loaf on a baking sheet and bake in the preheated oven for 10 minutes. Lower the oven temperature to 190°C/375°F/gas mark 5 and bake for a further 45 minutes. Transfer to a wire rack and leave to cool completely.

FRENCH PANCAKES

(CRÊPES)

MAKES ABOUT 12

110g/4oz plain flour
a pinch of salt
1 egg
1 egg yolk
290ml/½ pint milk, or milk and water mixed
1 tablespoon oil, plus extra for cooking

1. Sift the flour with the salt into a bowl and make a well in the centre.
2. Put the egg and egg yolk with a little of the milk into the well.
3. Using a wooden spoon or whisk, mix the egg and milk together, then gradually draw in the flour from the sides of the bowl as you mix.
4. When the mixture reaches the consistency of thick cream, beat well and stir in the oil.
5. Add the remaining milk; the consistency should now be that of thin cream. (Batter can also be made by processing all the ingredients together in a blender for a few seconds, but take care not to over-whizz or the mixture will be bubbly.)
6. Cover the bowl and chill for about 30 minutes to allow the starch cells to swell, giving a lighter result.
7. Prepare a pancake pan or frying pan by heating well and wiping with oil. Pancakes are not fried in fat – the purpose of the oil is simply to prevent sticking.
8. When the pan is ready, pour in about 1 tablespoon batter and swirl about the pan until evenly spread across the bottom.
9. Place over heat and, after 1 minute, using a palette knife and your fingers, turn the pancake over and cook again until brown. (Pancakes should be extremely thin, so if the first one is too thick, add a little extra milk to the batter. The first pancake is unlikely to be perfect, and is often discarded.)
10. Make up all the pancakes, turning them out on to a tea-towel or plate.

NOTES: Pancakes can be kept warm in a folded tea-towel on a plate over a saucepan of simmering water, in the oven, or in a warmer. If allowed to cool, they may be reheated by being returned to the frying pan or by warming in the oven.

Pancakes freeze well, but should be separated by pieces of greaseproof paper. They may also be refrigerated for a day or two.

BRUSCHETTA

2 baguettes
1 tablespoon olive oil
1 clove of garlic

1. Preheat the grill to high. Cut the bread in half lengthways and toast on the cut side only.
2. Brush the bread with the oil. Peel the garlic and crush it slightly, then rub over the bread. Toast again until browned and charred.

NOTE: Green or red pesto, goat's cheese, tomatoes, peeled, deseeded and chopped, with fresh basil all make delicious toppings.

DUMPLINGS

110g/4oz self-raising flour
55g/2oz shredded vegetable suet
150ml/¼ pint water
salt and freshly ground black pepper

1. Mix all the ingredients together and bind to a stiffish dough with the water. It should be of a consistency that will fall reluctantly from a wooden spoon. Season with salt and pepper.
2. Form the dough into 8 small or 4 large dumplings and drop into a simmering soup or vegetable casserole. Cook for 10 minutes, covered, then for a further 10 minutes, uncovered.

PARMESAN SCONES

butter, for greasing
225g/8oz self-raising flour, plus extra for rolling
¼ teaspoon baking powder
¼ teaspoon English mustard powder
¼ teaspoon cayenne pepper
3 tablespoons extra virgin olive oil
50g/2oz sun-dried tomatoes or about 12 green
*   or black olives, pitted (optional)*
50g/2oz Parmesan cheese, freshly grated
salt and freshly ground black pepper
1 egg
2 tablespoons milk, plus extra for glazing

1. Preheat the oven to 220°C/425°F/gas mark 7. Grease a baking tray with butter.
2. Sift the flour, baking powder, mustard and cayenne into a large mixing bowl. Add the oil and mix together with a knife until the mixture resembles coarse breadcrumbs.
3. Roughly chop the sun-dried tomatoes or olives, if used, and add them to the mixture with the cheese. Season with salt and pepper.
4. Beat together the egg and 2 tablespoons milk. Use to bind the mixture to a spongy dough.
5. Tip the dough on to a floured worktop and knead gently until smooth. The dough should be handled as little as possible.
6. Roll or pat the dough out to a 2.5cm/1in thickness and stamp into rounds with a small plain scone cutter. Re-roll the trimmings and stamp out more rounds.
7. Place the scones on the prepared baking tray, brush the tops with a little milk and bake in the preheated oven for 7–8 minutes until golden-brown. Cool on a wire rack.

PIZZA DOUGH

170g/6oz strong white flour, plus extra for
*   rolling*
a large pinch of salt
1 heaped teaspoon fast-action dried yeast
1 tablespoon olive oil
110ml/4fl oz warm water

1. Put the flour into a warm mixing bowl and make a well in the centre. Put the salt, yeast and oil into the well. Mix with enough water to make a soft dough.
2. Knead the dough for 5–10 minutes on a floured worktop until very smooth and elastic. Roll the dough into a 30cm/12in circle. Use as required.

BIBLIOGRAPHY

Clare Connery, *The Hamlyn Book of Vegetables* (Hamlyn, 1998)

Nicola Graimes, *The Practical Encyclopaedia of Wholefoods* (Lorenz Books, 1999)

Jane Grigson, *Jane Grigson's Vegetable Book* (Michael Joseph, 1978)

Madhur Jaffrey, *World Vegetarian* (Ebury, 1998)

Christine McFadden and Michael Michaud, *Cool Green Leaves and Red Hot Peppers* (Frances Lincoln, 1998)

Marlena Spieler, *The Flavour of California* (Thorsons, 1992)

A NOTE ON THE CONTRIBUTORS

Fiona Burrell is the former co-Principal of Leiths School of Food and Wine. She is the author of *Leiths Book of Cakes*, the co-author of *Leiths Complete Christmas* and a contributing writer to the *Leiths Cookery Bible*.

Max Clark worked at Leiths School of Food and Wine for twelve years as a senior teacher and is currently the buyer for the school.

Alison Cavaliero is the Vice-Principal of Leiths School of Food and Wine and runs the Leiths List, our successful employment agency.

Debbie Major is a self-taught cook who later trained at Leiths School of Food and Wine. She now works as a freelance food-stylist and writer.

INDEX